Milton Alexander

Operations Research
An Introduction

Hamdy A. Taha

Department of Industrial Engineering, University of Arkansas

OPERATIONS RESEARCH
An Introduction

THE MACMILLAN COMPANY · New York

Collier-Macmillan Limited · London

The Macmillan Company
866 Third Avenue, New York, New York 10022

Collier-Macmillan Canada, Ltd., Toronto, Ontario

Library of Congress catalog card number: 75-121680

First Printing

To Karen

Preface

THIS book is the result of five years of teaching experience in the field of operations research both at the undergraduate and graduate levels. During this period it has been continually felt that there is a persisting need for a textbook suitable for a comprehensive introductory course in operations research. This book is intended to satisfy such a need.

The author believes that operations research techniques should not be taught without an adequate understanding of their development. A practitioner who is familiar only with the mechanics of the solution procedure will always be handicapped when dealing with nonroutine problems. In keeping with this philosophy, no technique is presented here without first investigating the necessary background which will enable the reader fully to understand the material and to make intelligent inferences about possible extensions of the problem.

This book is designed for two courses of one semester each. The first course introduces the beginning reader to the development, application, and computation of the basic operations research techniques. These include linear programming, game theory, dynamic programming, PERT/CPM, inventory models, queueing theory, and simulation. The prerequisite for this course is strictly college algebra except for the last two sections on inventory and queueing where a knowledge of basic calculus and elementary probability theory is assumed. Although the presentation at this level is rather elementary and relies occasionally on intuitive proofs, it is by no means superficial. While in most of the introductory books, the results of queueing models are presented at the "cookbook" level, hence depriving the reader of the opportunity to check their validity, this book gives a complete background which, at the option of the reader, may be skipped without loss of continuity. It is expected that the reader completing this course will be able to communicate intelligently about operations research and its applications.

The second course, a continuation of the first, is designed for those who wish to go beyond the introductory-level material. It provides the theoretical foundation of the basic operations research techniques including linear programming in matrix form, parametric programming, integer programming, queueing theory and imbedded Markov chains, and nonlinear programming. Although this course requires a higher level of mathematical maturity, a dedicated effort has been made to avoid complex mathematical notations. The basic prerequisites for this course are also included either as part of the text or in separate appendixes. The reader completing this course is expected to follow adequately the literature published in the technical journals of operations research.

The accompanying diagram divides the various chapters (and appendixes) of the book between the first (I) and the second (II) courses proposed above. The precedence relationships between the different chapters are indicated in solid lines. Dotted lines indicate preferable but not mandatory prerequisites.

A basic feature of the book is that every new idea is illustrated by complete numerical examples. There are approximately ten complete numerical examples in each chapter. These examples were developed through teaching experience and hence are designed to answer the specific questions that usually come to the student's mind. There are also over 400 exercises in the book. Almost every problem presents a new idea to help the reader build a solid background. A complete solutions manual is also available for all the exercises.

The book is oriented toward practical applications. Thus, while in most books some of the important practical tools are presented at an advanced mathematical level, this book treats these topics at a rather elementary, yet not superficial, level. For example, sensitivity analysis in linear programming, which represents an important practical aspect that is often neglected in the study of the simplex algorithm, is presented fully as part of the first course. Another important practical topic is project scheduling by PERT/CPM. Because of its practical importance, this technique is covered completely in a full chapter. Case studies and practical examples are also introduced whenever appropriate so as to give the reader an appreciation of the uses of the various tools of operations research.

Following the introductory chapter, the book is organized in three main parts: (1) "Linear Programming and Related Topics" (Chapters 2 through 11); (2) "Probability, Inventory, and Queueing Theory" (Chapters 12 through 15); and (3) "Nonlinear Programming" (Chapters 16 and 17). Chapter 2 introduces the general definition of the linear programming problem together with different types of its application. Chapter 3 develops the simplex method procedure for solving linear programming problems. Although no theory is presented in this chapter, a comprehensive analysis of the screening process in the simplex method is introduced. The special cases of degeneracy, alternative solutions, unbounded solutions, and nonexisting feasible solutions are completely covered.

Chapter 4 presents the dual problem and its application to the sensitivity

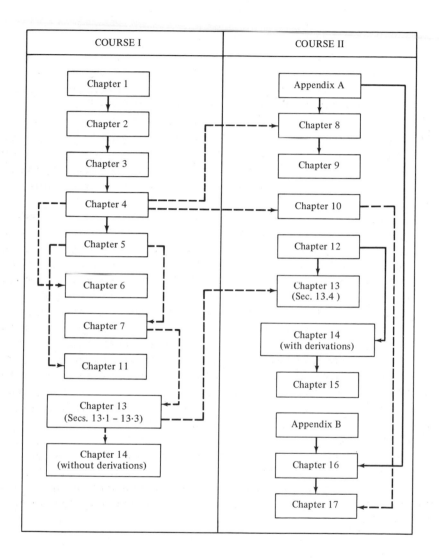

ORGANIZATION OF THE BOOK

analysis problem. Chapter 5 presents the transportation problem and its variants which include the transportation model, the transshipment model, the least-time transportation model, the assignment model, and the generalized transportation model. The transportation technique is fully interpreted in terms of duality theory. Network representation of transportation systems is also presented in this chapter. Chapter 6 presents the elements of the two-person zero-sum game and its relationship to linear programming. Dynamic programming is covered in Chapter 7. The forward and backward recursive formulations are discussed and the computational problem is investigated.

Chapter 8 presents the mathematical theory of linear programming. Additional techniques including the revised simplex method, the decomposition algorithm, and the bounded variables technique are covered in detail. Parametric linear programming is investigated in Chapter 9. Integer linear programming algorithms including Gomory's cutting plane techniques, the branch and bound algorithm, and Balas' zero-one algorithm are covered in Chapter 10. Several applications of integer programming are also presented.

Chapter 11 introduces a topic which is seldom presented in operations research textbooks. This is project scheduling by PERT-CPM. The theoretical relationship between CPM-PERT and linear programming is also discussed.

Chapter 12 reviews basic probability theory including ample discussion of stochastic processes and Markov chains. Chapter 13 presents a variety of deterministic and probabilistic inventory models. Some of these models are solved by linear and dynamic programming. Chapter 14 presents queueing theory. The procedure followed in this chapter is first to give the model together with a summary of its results; a detailed derivation of these results is then given as an appendix to each model. These derivations may be skipped without loss of continuity. Simulation techniques are also discussed in the chapter. The chapter closes with a case study which summarizes the main features of queueing theory applications. The advanced topic of queueing theory and imbedded Markov chains is then given in Chapter 15.

Chapter 16 presents a complete summary of the classical optimization techniques for both the constrained and the unconstrained nonlinear programming problems. Chapter 17 then summarizes a number of nonlinear programming algorithms including separable programming, quadratic programming, geometric programming, stochastic programming, and gradient methods.

ACKNOWLEDGMENTS

I should like to thank all the individuals at Cairo University, The University of Oklahoma, and The University of Arkansas who have helped generously during the writing of this book. Special thanks are due to my friends and colleagues, C. Ray Asfahl, Bob L. Foote, and Hillel J. Kumin.

This acknowledgment is not complete without an honorable mention of my students who suffered through the early drafts of this book. I am grateful to the hundreds of students at Cairo University, The University of Oklahoma, and The University of Arkansas who discovered many errors and suggested several significant changes that made the book more readable. I am especially grateful to my graduate student Shrikant S. Panwalker for editing the first draft and for his assistance in preparing the solutions manual. I should like also to acknowledge my appreciation for the help I received from Guy Curry, Gene Payne, and Al Schuermann.

Finally, I wish to express my deep appreciation to Mrs. Pat Hubbell, who, in spite of the cruel deadline, did an excellent typing job.

H. A. T.

Contents

Contents

PART 2:
Probability, Inventory, and Queueing Theory

CHAPTER 1

Introduction

§ 1·1
The Development of Operations Research

During World War II, the military management in England called upon a team of scientists to study the strategic and tactical problems associated with air and land defense of the country. Their objective was to decide upon the most effective utilization of limited military resources. The applications included, among others, studies of the way to use the newly invented radar and of the effectiveness of new types of bombers. The establishment of this scientific team marked the first formal operations research activity.

The name "operations research" (sometimes abbreviated OR) was apparently coined because the team was dealing with research on (military) operations. Since its birth, this new decision-making field has been characterized by the use of scientific knowledge through interdisciplinary team effort for the purpose of deciding upon the best utilization of limited resources.

The encouraging results achieved by the British operations research teams motivated the United States military management to start on similar activities. Successful applications of the U.S. teams included the study of complex logistical problems, invention of new flight patterns, planning sea mining, and effective utilization of electronic equipment.

Following the end of the war, the success of the military teams attracted the attention of industrial managers who were seeking solutions to their complex executive-type problems. Such problems were becoming more acute because of the introduction of functional specialization into business organizations. Despite the fact that specialized functions are established primarily to serve the over-all objective of the organization, the individual objectives of these functions may not be always consistent with the goals of the organization. This has resulted in complex decision problems which ultimately have forced business organizations to seek the utilization of the effective tools of operations research.

Although Great Britain is credited for the initiation of operations research

1

as a new discipline, leadership in the rapidly growing field was soon taken over by the United States. The first mathematical technique in the field, called the simplex method of linear programming, was developed in 1947 by the American mathematician, George B. Dantzig. Since then, new techniques and applications have been developed through the efforts and cooperation of interested individuals in both academic institutions and industry.

The impressive progress in the field of operations research is due in a large part to the parallel development of the modern digital computer with its tremendous capabilities in computational speed and information storage and retrieval. In fact, had it not been for the digital computer, operations research with its large-scale computational problems would not have acquired the present promising status in all kinds of operational environments.

Today, the impact of operations research can be felt in many areas. This is indicated by the number of academic institutions that are offering this field at all degree levels. A large number of management consulting firms are currently engaged in operations research activities. These activities have gone beyond military and business applications to include hospitals, financial institutions, libraries, city planning, transportation systems, and even crime investigation studies, to mention only a few.

§ 1-2
Modeling in Operations Research

A model in the sense used in operations research is defined as an idealized representation of a real-life system. This system may be already in existence or it may still be a conceived idea awaiting execution. In the first case, the objective of the model is to provide means for analyzing the behavior of the system for the purpose of improving its performance. In the second case, the objective is to define the ideal structure of the future system which includes the functional relationships among its components.

The reliability of the solution obtained from the model depends on the validity of this model in representing the *real* system. This means that the resulting solution actually applies to the *assumed-real* system represented by the model. The discrepancies between the real and the assumed-real solutions depends directly on the accuracy of the model in describing the behavior of the original system.

Models may be classified generally as (1) iconic, (2) analog, or (3) symbolic. *Iconic* models represent the system as it is by scaling it up or down. For example, a toy airplane is an iconic model of a real one.

Analog models basically require the substitution of one property for another for the ultimate purpose of achieving convenience in manipulating the model. After the problem is solved, the solution is reinterpreted in terms of the original system. For example, graphs are simple analog models which may be used to study the relationship between two or more properties. In this case, each property is represented by one axis and its value is measured by the distance on this axis.

Finally, *symbolic* or *mathematical* models employ a set of mathematical symbols to represent the decision variables of the system. These variables are related together using the appropriate mathematical functions to describe the behavior of the system. The solution of the problem is then obtained by applying well-developed mathematical techniques to the model.

Of the above three types, iconic models are the least abstract, and hence the most trivial from the viewpoint of operations research. Mathematical models, on the other hand, are the most abstract and by far the most important type in operations research applications. In fact, to most practitioners, the name operations research is identified primarily with the use of mathematical models. This follows because such models are amenable to mathematical analysis, which usually makes it possible to find the best solution through the use of convenient mathematical tools. It is not surprising then that most of the attention in operations research has been given to the development of mathematical models.

The development of the digital computer has led to the introduction of two other types of modeling in operations research. These are the simulation and heuristic models. *Simulation* models are digital representations which "imitate" the behavior of a system using the digital computer. The statistics describing the different measures of performance of the system are accumulated as the simulator advances on the computer.

Simulation modeling has the advantage of being more flexible than mathematical modeling, and hence may be used to represent complex systems which otherwise cannot be formulated mathematically. On the other hand, simulation has the disadvantage of not yielding general solutions like those obtained from successful mathematical models. In fact, simulation results are generally imprecise (due to the inherent experimental error) and there is no reliable way for measuring such imprecision. Moreover, the use of this technique may, in general, be uneconomical.

While mathematical and simulation models are used to represent systems having well-defined strategies (or courses of action), *heuristic* models are mainly used to explore alternative strategies which have been overlooked previously. Heuristic models, thus, do not claim to find the best solution to the problem. Rather, by applying some intuitive rules or guidelines, new strategies can be generated which will yield improved solutions to the model.

§ 1·3
The Structure of Mathematical Models

Unlike simulation or heuristic models for which no fixed structures can be suggested, a mathematical model includes mainly three basic sets of elements:

(1) *Decision Variables and Parameters.* The decision variables are the

unknowns which are to be determined from the solution of the model. For example, in the simple inventory model, the purchase lot size represents the decision variable. Examples of the parameters in this case include the per unit purchase price and the consumption rate of the stocked item. In general, the parameters of the model may be deterministic or probabilistic.

(2) *Constraints or Restrictions.* In order to account for the physical limitations of the system, the model must include constraints which limit the decision variables to their *feasible* (or permissible) values. This is usually expressed in the form of constraining mathematical functions. For example, let x_1 and x_2 be the number of units to be produced of two products (decision variables) and let a_1 and a_2 be their respective per unit requirements of raw material (parameters). If the total amount available of this raw material is A, then the corresponding constraint function is given by $a_1 x_1 + a_2 x_2 \leq A$.

Another common contraint is the so-called *nonnegativity* constraint which requires all the decision variables to be either zero or positive. This reflects the fact that operations research models deal mainly with real-life systems, and consequently to allow negative values, in most cases, would be non-sensical.

(3) *Objective Function.* This defines the measure of effectiveness of the system as a mathematical function of its decision variables. For example, if the objective of the system is to maximize the total profit, then the objective function must specify the profit in terms of the decision variables. In general, it is said that the *optimum* solution to the model has been obtained if the corresponding values of the decision variables would yield the *best* value of the objective function, while satisfying all the constraints. This means that the objective function acts as an indicator for the achievement of the optimum solution. Consequently, a poor formulation of the objective function can only lead to a poor solution to the problem.

A common case of poor formulation of the objective function occurs when some aspects of the system are neglected. For example, in determining the optimal inventory level of a certain commodity, the objective function may reflect the goals of the sales and finance departments only while neglecting that of the production department. In such cases, the model will yield what is called a *suboptimal* solution with the disadvantage that it may not serve the best interest of the entire operation.

To summarize the above discussion, mathematical models in operations research may be viewed generally as determining the values of the decision variables x_j, $j = 1, 2, \ldots, n$, which will

$$\text{optimize} \quad x_0 = f(x_1, \ldots, x_n),$$

subject to

$$g_i(x_1, \ldots, x_n) \leq b_i, \quad i = 1, 2, \ldots, m,$$

$$x_j \geq 0, \quad j = 1, 2, \ldots, n.$$

The function f is the objective function while $g_i \leq b_i$ represents the ith constraint, where b_i is constant. The constraints $x_j \geq 0$ are the nonnegativity constraints.

In general, *optimization* of the objective function signifies either a *maximization* or a *minimization* of this function. For example, in an industrial plant the objective may be viewed as maximizing profit or productive time, or minimizing cost or idle time. Optimization in this sense has received wide acceptance among researchers and practitioners because it reflects the common goal of obtaining the *best* solution to the model. Moreover, the tremendous advances in the mathematics of optimization have offered unifying approaches for tackling such problems.

§ 1·4
Mathematical Techniques of Operations Research

The discussion in the above section shows that the types of the objective and constraint functions of a mathematical model depend directly on the systems which they represent. Thus, these functions may be linear or nonlinear. Also the decision variables may be continuous or discrete and the parameters of the system may be deterministic or probabilistic.

The result of this diversity in system representation is the development of a corresponding number of optimization techniques suitable for solving these models. These mainly include linear programming, integer programming, dynamic programming, stochastic programming, and nonlinear programming. *Linear* programming is used to analyze models with strictly linear objective and constraint functions, while *integer* programming applies to models having integer (or discrete) variables. *Dynamic* programming deals with models where the complete problem can be decomposed into smaller (and hence simpler) subproblems. *Stochastic* programming applies to a special class of programming models in which the system's parameters are described by probability distributions. Finally, *nonlinear* programming treats models containing nonlinear functions.

A characteristic that dominates almost all of the above mathematical programming techniques is that the optimal solution to the problem cannot be obtained in a single step. Rather the technique is started by selecting an initial solution (which generally is not the optimal solution); a set of computational rules are then specified to select a new solution which is usually superior to its predecessor.[1] The indicated techniques are thus iterative in nature with each new iteration yielding an improved solution. The final iteration should eventually lead to the optimal solution (provided it exists).

The above mathematical programming techniques are general in the sense that they can be applied to models representing systems from different

---

[1] These sets of computational rules are usually referred to as *algorithms*.

operational environments. There are three application areas in operations research, however, which are characterized generally by special model formulation. These are the inventory problem, the queueing (or waiting line) problem and the competitive (or game) problem.

Inventory problems are concerned with the determination of the optimal stock level of a commodity having an economic value. The common objective is to minimize the sum of three conflicting costs: the cost of holding extra inventory, the cost of ordering, and the cost of running out of stock when the commodity is needed.

Queueing problems are concerned with the study of congestive systems. Customers arrive according to known probability distributions to be serviced at a service installation. Their service time may be fixed or may follow a known probability distribution. Because of the presence of the randomness element in the system, it may not be possible to schedule the operation of the installation efficiently. Thus, an arriving customer may have to wait too long before commencing service. On the other hand, a service facility may remain excessively idle. Such a conflicting situation creates what is known as a queueing problem. The usual objective in this case is to improve the performance of the congestive system by balancing the customer's waiting time against the level of service. In effect, the final result is to determine the "optimum" levels of performance for the system.

Queueing theory was thus developed to determine the measures of performance of queueing systems such as the expected waiting time per customer, the expected number waiting in the system, and the average idle time of the service facility. These measures, which are determined based completely on probability theory, constitute the basis for analyzing queueing problems.

It should be noted that queueing theory, unlike most techniques of operations research, does not yield the optimum solution directly. Rather, it is a tool for analysis. The ultimate goal is to use the resulting measures of performance in some cost model to determine an optimal procedure for the operation of the system. For example, the cost model may be designed to balance the "cost" of offering faster service against the "cost" of causing excessive delay for the customer.

Competitive problems exist in situations where two or more opponents are competing for the achievement of conflicting goals. In general, losses from one opponent signify gains to the others. Gains and losses (called payoffs) are known functions of the specific strategies which each opponent chooses. It is assumed that each opponent has a complete knowledge of all the different strategies of his opponents, but that he is completely ignorant of their specific selections or choices. This type of situation is normally referred to as decision under *uncertainty* (as opposed to decisions under *certainty* where a complete knowledge of the system is assumed, and decision under *risk*, where the system is not known with certainty but can be described by known probability distributions). Because of the lack of information in this case, the decision is based on a rather conservative criterion where each opponent selects the strategies which will yield him the *best* of the *worst* outcomes. The underlying theory for this type of problem is known as *game* theory.

§ 1·5
Phases of the Operations Research Study

The procedure for an operations research study generally involves the following five major phases:

1. Definition of the problem.
2. Construction of the model.
3. Solution of the model.
4. Validation of the model.
5. Implementation of the final results.

Although the above sequence is by no means standard, it seems generally acceptable to most practitioners in the field.

Except for the "model solution" phase, which is based generally on well-developed model-solving techniques, the analysis of the remaining phases does not seem to follow fixed sets of rules. This stems from the fact that the procedures for these phases are dependent upon the type of problem under investigation, as well as the operating environment in which it exists. In this respect, an operations research team would be guided in the study principally by the different professional experiences of its members rather than by fixed sets of rules.

In spite of the apparent difficulties in setting fixed rules for the execution of these phases, it seems desirable to present some discussion which may be used as a general guide in these areas. The remainder of this section is thus devoted to providing an orientation of the main points involved in an operations research study.

The first phase of the study requires a clear definition of the problem. From the viewpoint of operations research, this indicates three major aspects; (1) an exact description of the goal or the objective of the study, (2) an identification of the decision alternative of the system, and (3) a clear recognition of the limitations, restrictions, and requirements of the system.

A description of the objective of the study must reflect an accurate representation of the overall interest of the system. A common pitfall in this respect is to identify some goal which can represent only a portion of the entire system. Under such conditions, what is considered best for this portion of the system may actually prove harmful for the entire operation. In a similar manner a study that does not account for all the decision alternatives and limitations of the system is liable to yield an inadequate solution.

The second phase of the study is concerned with the model construction. Depending upon the definition of the problem, the operations research team should decide on the most suitable model for representing the system. Such a model should formally specify quantitative expressions for the objective and the constraints of the problem all in terms of its decision variables. If the resulting model fits into one of the well-known mathematical models (for example, linear programming), then a convenient solution may be obtained by using these techniques. On the other hand, if the mathematical relationships of the model are too complex to allow analytic solutions, then a simulation model may be more appropriate. In some cases, this may even require the use of a combination of mathematical, simulation and heuristic models. This, of course, is largely dependent on the nature and the complexity of the system under investigation.

The third phase of the study deals with the derivation of the solution to the model. In mathematical models, this is achieved by using well-defined optimization techniques. In this case, the model is said to yield an "optimum" solution. On the other hand, if simulation or heuristic models are used, then the concept of optimality is not as well-defined and the solution in these cases is used to obtain approximate evaluations of the measures of the system.

In addition to the (optimum) solution of the model, one must also secure, whenever possible, additional information concerning the behavior of the solution due to changes in the system's parameters. This is usually referred to as "sensitivity analysis." Such an analysis is specially needed when the parameters of the system cannot be estimated accurately. In this case, it is important to study the behavior of the optimal solution in the neighborhood of these estimates.

The fourth phase calls for checking the validity of the model. A model is valid if, despite its inexactness in representing the system, it can give a reliable prediction of the system's performance. A common method for testing the validity of a model is to compare its performance with some past data which are available for the actual system. The model will be valid if under similar conditions of inputs, it can reproduce the past performance of the system. The problem here is that there is no assurance that the future performance of the system will continue to duplicate its past history. Also, since the model is based on careful examination of past data, this comparison should always reveal favorable results. In some instances this problem may be overcome by using data from trial runs of the system.

It must be noted that such a validation method is not appropriate for nonexisting systems since there will be no available data for comparison. In some cases, if the original system is investigated by a mathematical model, it may be feasible to construct a simulation model from which data are obtained to carry out the indicated comparison.

The final phase of the study deals with the implementation of the tested results of the model. The burden of executing these results lies primarily on the shoulders of the operations researchers. This would basically involve the translation of these results into detailed operating instructions. Such instructions must be issued in an understandable form to the individuals who will administer and operate the system after its execution. The interaction between the operations research team and the operating personnel will reach its maximum in this phase. Communication between the two groups can be improved by seeking the participation of the operating personnel in developing the implementation plan. In fact, this participation should be sought through all the phases of the study. In this way no practical consideration, that otherwise may lead to system failure, will be overlooked. Meanwhile, possible modifications or adjustments in the system may be checked by the operating personnel for practical feasibility. In other words, it is imperative that the implementation phase be executed through the cooperation of both the operations research team and those who will be responsible for managing and operating the system.

SELECTED REFERENCES

1. CHURCHMAN, C. W., R. ACKOFF, and E. L. ARNOFF, *Introduction to Operations Research*, New York: Wiley, 1957.
2. ELMAGHRABY, S. E., "The Role of Modeling in IE Design," *The Journal of Industrial Engineering*, Vol. XIX, No. 6, 292–305 (1968).
3. MCCLOSKEY, J. F., and F. N. TREFETHEN, (eds.), *Operations Research for Management*, Baltimore: The Johns Hopkins University Press, 1954.

Part 1

Linear Programming and Related Topics

CHAPTER 2

The General Linear Programming Problem

§ 2-1
Definition and Properties of the Linear Programming Problem

The general linear programming problem calls for optimizing (maximizing or minimizing) a linear function of variables, called the "objective function," subject to a set of linear equalities and/or inequalities called "constraints" or "restrictions." This definition is best illustrated by an example.

Consider the situation of deciding on the number of units to be manufactured of two different products. Let the profits per unit of product 1 and product 2 be 2 and 5, respectively. Each unit of product 1 requires 3 machine-hours and 9 units of raw material while each unit of product 2 requires 4 machine-hours and 7 units of raw material. The maximum available machine-hours and raw material units are 200 and 300, respectively. A minimum of 20 units is required for product 1.

This problem can be formulated "mathematically" by recognizing that the decision variables are the number of units produced of each product. Let x_1, x_2 be the decision variables corresponding to product 1 and product 2, respectively. The above information can thus be summarized as:

		Product 1	Product 2
Number of units produced (variables):		x_1	x_2
Profit	:	$2x_1$	$5x_2$
Number of machine hours	:	$3x_1$	$4x_2$
Units of raw material	:	$9x_1$	$7x_2$
Minimum requirements	:	20	0

The objective of the problem is to maximize the total profit, $2x_1 + 5x_2$, for the two products. This maximization is subject to the machine-hours constraint, the raw material constraint, and the minimum requirements constraint.

The machine-hours constraint specifies that the total number of machine-hours used by the two products should not exceed the maximum number of hours available; that is, $3x_1 + 4x_2 \leq 200$. Similarly, for the raw material constraint, $9x_1 + 7x_2 \leq 300$, and for the minimum requirements constraint, $x_1 \geq 20$ and $x_2 \geq 0$. This problem is usually put in the format:

$$\text{maximize} \quad x_0 = 2x_1 + 5x_2,$$

subject to

$$3x_1 + 4x_2 \leq 200,$$
$$9x_1 + 7x_2 \leq 300,$$
$$x_1 \geq 20,$$
$$x_2 \geq 0,$$

where x_0 is the value of the objective function.

The above example illustrates three main properties of the general linear programming problem:

1. The objective function and the constraints are linear expressions of the decision variables. In terms of the objective function, this means that the contribution of each activity (in the above example, each product represents an activity) is directly proportional to the level of the activity. A similar explanation can be applied to the constraints. This property also indicates that the contributions of the different activities in both the objective function and the constraints are additive.

2. Each constraint may be one of three types: "less than or equal" ($\leq$), "greater than or equal" ($\geq$), or "equal" ($=$). The last type is not illustrated in the above example. However, if a market restriction requiring that the ratio of product 1 to product 2 be equal to 6, then an additional constraint

$$\frac{x_1}{x_2} = 6, \quad \text{or} \quad x_1 - 6x_2 = 0$$

should be added to the above problem. This last restriction serves as a constraint of the type ($=$). It should be noted that in a linear programming problem, constraints of the strong inequality type[1] are not allowed since, from the mathematical viewpoint, the problem *may* not have a solution. Experience with linear programming application, however, has shown that, for all practical purposes, inequality-type constraints can always be taken in the weak sense.

3. All the variables of the linear programming problem are nonnegative. This property reflects the fact that linear programming deals mainly with

---

[1] Strong inequalities are inequalities in the strict sense; that is, $>$ or $<$. Weak inequalities are of the types $\geq$ or $\leq$.

real-life problems for which negative quantities are generally illogical. It is shown in Section 2·3, however, that if any of the variables is unrestricted in sign (i.e., positive, negative, or zero), a "trick" can be employed which will enforce the nonnegativity constraint without changing the original information of the problem.

The general linear programming problem can now be defined as follows:

maximize (or minimize)

$$x_0 = c_1 x_1 + c_2 x_2 + \cdots + c_n x_n,$$

subject to

$$a_{11} x_1 + a_{12} x_2 + \cdots + a_{1n} x_n \ (\leq, =, \text{ or } \geq) \ b_1,$$
$$a_{21} x_1 + a_{22} x_2 + \cdots + a_{2n} x_n \ (\leq, =, \text{ or } \geq) \ b_2,$$
$$\vdots$$
$$a_{m1} x_1 + a_{m2} x_2 + \cdots + a_{mn} x_n \ (\leq, =, \text{ or } \geq) \ b_m,$$
$$x_1 \geq 0, \quad x_2 \geq 0, \ldots, x_n \geq 0,$$

where c_j, b_i, and a_{ij} $(i = 1, 2, \ldots, m; j = 1, 2, \ldots, n)$ are constants which are determined depending on the technology of the problem, and x_j are the decision variables. It is noted that for each constraint, only one of the signs $(\leq, =, \geq)$ holds.

The above formulation may be put in the following compact form by using the summation sign.

$$\text{Maximize (or minimize)} \quad x_0 = \sum_{j=1}^{n} c_j x_j,$$

subject to

$$\sum_{j=1}^{n} a_{ij} x_j (\leq, =, \geq) b_i, \quad i = 1, 2, \ldots, m,$$

$$x_j \geq 0, \quad j = 1, 2, \ldots, n.$$

§ 2·2
Examples of the Applications of Linear Programming

This section presents examples illustrating the application of linear programming to different situations. The objective here is to familiarize the reader with some of the areas where this technique may be applicable. These examples will stress mainly the formulation aspect of the problem rather than its solution aspect. Chapter 3 will then present the general method (called the simplex method) for solving any linear programming problem.

▶ **Example 2·2–1** (Production Allocation Problem)

A factory manufactures three products. These products are processed through three different production stages. The time required to manufacture one unit of each of the three products and the daily capacity of the stages are given by the following data:

Stage	Time per unit (minutes)			Stage capacity min./day
	Product 1	Product 2	Product 3	
1	1	2	1	430
2	3	–	2	460
3	1	4	–	420

It is required to determine the daily number of units to be manufactured of each product given that the profit per unit for product 1, product 2, and product 3 are 3, 2, and 5, respectively. Assume that all the amounts produced are absorbed by the market.

Let x_1, x_2, and x_3 be the amounts manufactured of products 1, 2, and 3, respectively. Since all the amounts produced are sold, the total profit becomes $3x_1 + 2x_2 + 5x_3$. The only restrictions in this problem are the stage capacity constraints and the nonnegativity constraints. Thus, for *each* of the three stages, the total time consumed by all three products should not exceed the capacity of the stage. This means that, for stage 1

$$1x_1 + 2x_2 + 1x_3 \leq 430,$$

for stage 2

$$3x_1 + 0x_2 + 2x_3 \leq 460,$$

and for stage 3

$$x_1 + 4x_2 + 0x_3 \leq 420.$$

The complete linear programming problem is then given by:

$$\text{maximize} \quad x_0 = 3x_1 + 2x_2 + 5x_3,$$

subject to

$$x_1 + 2x_2 + x_3 \leq 430,$$
$$3x_1 \qquad + 2x_3 \leq 460,$$
$$x_1 + 4x_2 \qquad \leq 420,$$
$$x_1 \geq 0, \quad x_2 \geq 0, \quad x_3 \geq 0. \quad \blacktriangleleft$$

▶ **Example 2·2–2** (Production Planning Problem)

A factory manufactures a product with each complete unit consisting of four units of component *A* and three units of component *B*. The two components

(*A* and *B*) are manufactured from two different raw materials of which 100 units and 200 units, respectively, are available. Three departments are engaged in the production process with each department using a different method for manufacturing the components. The following table gives the raw material requirements per production run and the resulting units of each component.

	Input per run (Units)		Output per run (Units)	
Department	Raw material 1	Raw material 2	Component *A*	Component *B*
1	8	6	7	5
2	5	9	6	9
3	3	8	8	4

The objective is to determine the number of production runs for each department which will maximize the total number of complete units of the final product.

Let x_1, x_2, and x_3 be the number of production runs for departments 1, 2, and 3, respectively. The total number of units of component A produced by the three departments is $7x_1 + 6x_2 + 8x_3$. Similarly, the total number of units of component B is $5x_1 + 9x_2 + 4x_3$. The corresponding constraints on the raw materials are given by $8x_1 + 5x_2 + 3x_3 \le 100$ for raw material 1 and $6x_1 + 9x_2 + 8x_3 \le 200$ for raw material 2.

Since the objective is to maximize the total number of units of the final product and since each such unit requires four (4) units of component *A* and three (3) units of component *B*, it follows that the maximum number of units of the final product cannot exceed the smaller value of

$$\frac{7x_1 + 6x_2 + 8x_3}{4}, \quad \text{and} \quad \frac{5x_1 + 9x_2 + 4x_3}{3}.$$

Thus the problem becomes:

$$\text{maximize} \quad x_0 = \min\left\{\frac{7x_1 + 6x_2 + 8x_3}{4}, \frac{5x_1 + 9x_2 + 4x_3}{3}\right\},$$

subject to

$$8x_1 + 5x_2 + 3x_3 \le 100,$$
$$6x_1 + 9x_2 + 8x_3 \le 200,$$
$$x_1 \ge 0, \quad x_2 \ge 0, \quad x_3 \ge 0.$$

The above formulation violates the linear programming properties since the objective function is nonlinear. A trick can be used, however, which will reduce the above model to the acceptable linear programming format. Let

$$y = \min\left\{\frac{7x_1 + 6x_2 + 8x_3}{4}, \frac{5x_1 + 9x_2 + 4x_3}{3}\right\}.$$

This means that

$$\frac{7x_1 + 6x_2 + 8x_3}{4} \geq y$$

and

$$\frac{5x_1 + 9x_2 + 4x_3}{3} \geq y.$$

These two inequalities are equivalent to

$$7x_1 + 6x_2 + 8x_3 - 4y \geq 0$$

and

$$5x_1 + 9x_2 + 4x_3 - 3y \geq 0.$$

It immediately follows that the above problem reduces to the following linear programming problem:

$$\text{maximize} \quad x_0 = y,$$

subject to

$$7x_1 + 6x_2 + 8x_3 - 4y \geq 0,$$
$$5x_1 + 9x_2 + 4x_3 - 3y \geq 0,$$
$$8x_1 + 5x_2 + 3x_3 \qquad \leq 100,$$
$$6x_1 + 9x_2 + 8x_3 \qquad \leq 200,$$

$$x_1 \geq 0, \quad x_2 \geq 0, \quad x_3 \geq 0, \quad y \geq 0. \quad \blacktriangleleft$$

▶ **Example 2·2–3** (Caterer Problem)

A caterer, who is in charge of serving meals for the next five days, is faced with the problem of deciding on the daily supply of fresh napkins. His requirements for the five days are known to be 110, 210, 190, 120 and 100, respectively. His alternatives are:

1. Buy new napkins at the price of 10 cents a piece.
2. Send soiled napkins to the laundry where they can receive either 48-hour service at the cost of 3 cents a piece, or 24-hour service at the cost of 5 cents a piece.

Let x_i be the number of napkins bought on the ith day and let y_i and z_i be the number of soiled napkins sent on the ith day for the 24-hour and 48-hour services, respectively. Denote by v_i the number of soiled napkins used on the ith day but which were not sent to the laundry on the same day.

Since on the first and the second days the caterer has to buy napkins, it follows that for the first two days $x_1 = 110$ and $x_2 = 210$. At the *end* of the first day, he will send y_1 and z_1 for the 24-hour and the 48-hour services, respectively while v_1 will be kept in the inventory of soiled napkins. Thus y_1 and z_1 will be received from the laundry for use at the *beginning* of the third and the fourth days, respectively. Similarly, y_2 and z_2 for the second day will be received for use at the beginning of the fourth and the fifth days while y_3 will be received at the beginning of the fifth day. The amount z_3, however, if sent will be received on the sixth day which is past the planning period and hence should be equal to zero. Thus the supply of clean napkins for the five days is summarized by.

Source \ Day	1	2	3	4	5
New	x_1	x_2	x_3	x_4	x_5
24-hour	0	0	y_1	y_2	y_3
48-hour	0	0	0	z_1	z_2
Total required	110	210	190	120	100

which yields the following constraints

$$x_1 = 100,$$
$$x_2 = 210,$$
$$x_3 + y_1 = 190,$$
$$x_4 + y_2 + z_1 = 120,$$
$$x_5 + y_3 + z_2 = 100.$$

The first two constraints give the solution for the first two days and hence can be eliminated from the general formulation of the problem.

Another set of constraints is still required to ensure that $y_i + z_i + v_i$ does not exceed the number of soiled napkins on the ith day. Notice that the number of soiled napkins on the ith day is equal to the number used on ith day plus the number left from the $(i - 1)$st day. These constraints are thus given by

$$y_1 + z_1 + v_1 = 110,$$
$$y_2 + z_2 + v_2 = 210 + v_1,$$
$$y_3 + z_3 + v_3 = 190 + v_2$$
$$y_4 + z_4 + v_4 = 120 + v_3,$$
$$y_5 + z_5 + v_5 = 100 + v_4.$$

The last two constraints are trivial since y_4, z_4, y_5, and z_5, if sent to the laundry, will be received after the five-day planning period. Consequently, the decision for the fourth and fifth days is to not send any soiled napkins; that is, $y_4 = z_4 = y_5 = z_5 = 0$. The same argument applies to z_3, hence $z_3 = 0$.

The complete formulation of the problem thus becomes:

$$\text{minimize} \quad x_0 = 10(x_3 + x_4 + x_5) + 5(y_1 + y_2 + y_3) + 3(z_1 + z_2),$$

subject to

$$x_3 + y_1 = 190,$$
$$x_4 + y_2 + z_1 = 120,$$
$$x_5 + y_3 + z_2 = 100,$$
$$y_1 + z_1 + v_1 = 110,$$
$$y_2 + z_2 + v_2 = 210 + v_1,$$
$$y_3 + v_3 = 190 + v_2,$$

with all the variables being nonnegative. This formulation implies, as discussed above, that $x_1 = 110$, $x_2 = 210$, $z_3 = y_4 = z_4 = y_5 = z_5 = 0$, $v_4 = 120 + v_3$, and $v_5 = 100 + v_4$. ◄

▶   **Example 2·2–4**   (Trim Loss Problem)

A paper mill received three orders for paper rolls with the widths and lengths indicated in the following table.

Order number	Width in feet	Length in feet
1	5	100
2	7	300
3	9	200

Rolls are produced in the mill in two standard widths; 10 and 20 feet. These standard rolls will be cut to the sizes specified by the orders. It can be assumed that there is no limit on the lengths of the standard rolls since, for practical purpose, limited-length rolls can be connected together to yield the required lengths. The objective is to determine the production schedule (cutting patterns) which minimizes the trim losses while satisfying the given demand.

The formulation of the linear programming model for this problem is not straightforward. The immediate question is how will the width of the standard rolls be cut. This is answered by considering all the possible combinations of cutting the 10′ and 20′ widths to the required widths of 5′, 7′ and 9′. For example, the 10′ roll may be cut according to the plan

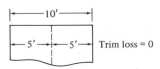

while the 20′ roll may be cut according to the plan

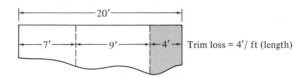

Trim loss = 4′/ ft (length)

This plan requires 50 feet of the 10′ roll and 300 feet of the 20′ roll to satisfy the three orders. The resulting trim loss is zero for the 10′ roll since it satisfies exactly the requirements of the 5′-width order. For the 20′ roll, trim loss is given by $4 \times 300 + 9 \times 100 = 2100$ ft^2 where (9×100) is the extra 100′ $(= 300 - 200)$ of width 9′ that were produced needlessly.

The above illustration is just an example of a possible cutting pattern. Notice that for the purpose of minimizing the trim losses, the entire order need not be satisfied by a single cutting pattern. Rather, by using different cutting patterns, the optimum solution must specify the length of the standard roll which must be cut according to each pattern.

Let x_{ij} be the length of the ith reel ($i = 1$, for 10′ and $i = 2$, for 20′) which is cut according to the jth pattern. The table below shows the possible patterns for both standard rolls. For example, the patterns specified by x_{11} and x_{25} were illustrated above. Notice that none of the patterns yields a trim loss (per foot length) which exceeds the smallest width required ($= 5′$ in this case). Consideration of such patterns is obviously nonoptimal and hence must be discarded.

Width	$i = 1$, (10′)			$i = 2$, (20′)						Requirements
	x_{11}	x_{12}	x_{13}	x_{21}	x_{22}	x_{23}	x_{24}	x_{25}	x_{26}	
5′	2	0	0	4	2	2	1	0	0	100
7′	0	1	0	0	1	0	2	1	0	300
9′	0	0	1	0	0	1	0	1	2	200
Trim loss	0	3	1	0	3	1	1	4	2	——

Let S_1, S_2, and S_3 be the surplus lengths produced of the rolls with widths 5′, 7′, and 9′, respectively. Then the complete problem is given as follows.

Minimize

$$x_0 = 3x_{12} + x_{13} + 3x_{22} + x_{23} + x_{24} + 4x_{25} + 2x_{26} + 5S_1 + 7S_2 + 9S_3,$$

subject to

$$2x_{11} + 4x_{21} + 2x_{22} + 2x_{23} + x_{24} - S_1 \qquad = 100,$$
$$x_{12} + \ x_{22} + 2x_{24} + \ x_{25} \qquad - S_2 \qquad = 300,$$
$$x_{13} + \ x_{23} + \ x_{25} + 2x_{26} \qquad -S_3 = 200,$$

and $x_{ij} \geq 0$, $S_i \geq 0$, for all i and all j. ◄

▶ **Example 2·2–5**   (Blending Problem)

The manager of an oil refinery must decide on the optimal mix of two possible blending processes, of which the inputs and outputs per production run are as follows:

	Input		Output	
Process	Crude A	Crude B	Gasoline X	Gasoline Y
1	5	3	5	8
2	4	5	4	4

The maximum amounts available of crudes A and B are 200 units and 150 units, respectively. Market requirements show that at least 100 units of gasoline X and 80 units of gasoline Y must be produced. The profits per production run from process 1 and process 2 are 3 and 4, respectively.

Let x_1 and x_2 be the number of production runs of process 1 and process 2, respectively. Thus the constraints on crude oils A and B are

$$5x_1 + 4x_2 \leq 200,$$
$$3x_1 + 5x_2 \leq 150.$$

The constraints reflecting sales commitments of gasolines X and Y are

$$5x_1 + 4x_2 \geq 100,$$
$$8x_1 + 4x_2 \geq \ 80,$$

where x_1 and x_2 are ≥ 0. The objective function is $3x_1 + 4x_2$ and the complete problem is given by:

$$\text{maximize} \quad x_0 = 3x_1 + 4x_2,$$

subject to

$$5x_1 + 4x_2 \leq 200,$$
$$3x_1 + 5x_2 \leq 150,$$
$$5x_1 + 4x_2 \geq 100,$$
$$8x_1 + 4x_2 \geq \ 80,$$
$$x_1 \geq 0, \quad x_2 \geq 0. \quad ◄$$

▶   **Example 2·2–6**   (Diet Problem)

An individual wants to decide on the constituents of a diet which will satisfy his daily needs of proteins, fats, and carbohydrates at the minimum cost. Choices from five different types of foods can be made. The yields per unit of these foods are given by:

Food type	Yields per unit			Cost per unit
	Proteins	Fats	Carbohydrates	
1	p_1	f_1	c_1	d_1
2	p_2	f_2	c_2	d_2
3	p_3	f_3	c_3	d_3
4	p_4	f_4	c_4	d_4
5	p_5	f_5	c_5	d_5
Minimum daily requirement	P	F	C	—

Let x_1, x_2, x_3, x_4, and x_5 be the number of units used of the first, second, third, fourth, and fifth type of food, respectively. Thus the minimum daily requirements of the individual are satisfied if

$$p_1 x_1 + p_2 x_2 + p_3 x_3 + p_4 x_4 + p_5 x_5 \geq P,$$
$$f_1 x_1 + f_2 x_2 + f_3 x_3 + f_4 x_4 + f_5 x_5 \geq F,$$
$$c_1 x_1 + c_2 x_2 + c_3 x_3 + c_4 x_4 + c_5 x_5 \geq C,$$

where $x_1 \geq 0$, $x_2 \geq 0$, $x_3 \geq 0$, $x_4 \geq 0$, and $x_5 \geq 0$. The objective function is

$$\text{minimize} \quad x_0 = d_1 x_1 + d_2 x_2 + d_3 x_3 + d_4 x_4 + d_5 x_5. \quad ◀$$

▶   **Example 2·2–7**   (Transportation Problem)

A commodity is transported from two factories to three retail stores. The individual requirements at the three stores are b_1, b_2, and b_3 while the supply at the two factories are a_1 and a_2. It is assumed that $a_1 + a_2 = b_1 + b_2 + b_3$. It is required to determine the number of units to be transported from each factory to the different stores so as to minimize transportation costs while satisfying the supply and demand restrictions. Transportation cost is c_{ij} per unit transported from factory i ($i = 1, 2$) to store j ($j = 1, 2, 3$). The total transportation cost is assumed to be directly proportional to the number of units transported.

Let x_{ij} be the amount transported from source (factory) i to destination (store) j. The objective is minimize $\quad x_0 = \sum\limits_{i=1}^{2} \sum\limits_{j=1}^{3} c_{ij} x_{ij} = c_{11}x_{11} + c_{12}x_{12} + c_{13}x_{13}$

$$+ c_{21}x_{21} + c_{22}x_{22} + c_{23}x_{23}.$$

The constraints, on the other hand, should reflect two points:

1. The total number of units taken from each factory i should be equal to a_i.
2. The total number of units transported to each store j should be equal to b_j.

This means that

$$x_{11} + x_{12} + x_{13} = a_1,$$
$$x_{21} + x_{22} + x_{23} = a_2,$$
$$x_{11} + x_{21} = b_1,$$
$$x_{12} + x_{22} = b_2,$$
$$x_{13} + x_{23} = b_3,$$
$$x_{ij} \geq 0, \quad i = 1, 2, \quad j = 1, 2, 3,$$

(Notice that $a_1 + a_2 = b_1 + b_2 + b_3$.)

The transportation problem presents an important class of linear programming problems. There exist many practical situations which can be formulated as a transportation-type model. This point is discussed in more detail in Chapter 5. ◄

§ 2·3
Canonical and Standard Forms of the Linear Programming Problem

In the last section some examples were presented of the formulation of the linear programming problem. The next step after formulating the problem is to consider the method of obtaining the solution. This point is dealt with in Chapter 3. However, before this method can be used, the problem must be available in a particular form. It was shown by the examples of Section 2·2 that the linear programming problem can be presented in a variety of forms (maximization or minimization for the objective function, ($\leq$), ($=$), and/or ($\geq$) for the constraints). Consequently, it is necessary to show how these different forms can be modified to fit the solution procedure which will be presented in the following chapters. Two forms will be introduced for this purpose, the *canonical* form and the *standard* form. The canonical form will be especially useful in considering the *duality theory* which will be presented in

Chapter 4. The standard form, on the other hand, will be used to develop the general procedure for solving any linear programming problem.

§ 2·3·1
The Canonical Form

The general linear programming problem defined in Section 2·1 can be put always in the following form which will be referred to as the *canonical* form.

$$\text{Maximize} \quad x_0 = \sum_{j=1}^{n} c_j x_j$$

subject to

$$\sum_{j=1}^{n} a_{ij} x_j \leq b_i, \qquad i = 1, 2, \ldots, m,$$

$$x_j \geq 0, \qquad j = 1, 2, \ldots, n.$$

The characteristics of this form are

1. All decision variables are nonnegative.
2. All constraints are of the ($\leq$) type.
3. The objective function is of the maximization type.

It is now shown that any linear programming problem can be put in the canonical form by the use of five elementary transformations.

1. The *minimization* of a function, $f(x)$, is equivalent to the *maximization* of the negative expression of this function, $-f(x)$. For example, the linear objective function,

$$\text{minimize} \quad x_0 = c_1 x_1 + c_2 x_2 + \cdots + c_n x_n,$$

is equivalent to

$$\text{maximize} \quad g_0 = -x_0 = -c_1 x_1 - c_2 x_2 - \cdots - c_n x_n,$$

with $x_0 = -g_0$. Consequently, in any linear programming problem, the objective function can be put in the maximization form.

2. An inequality in one direction ($\leq$, or $\geq$) may be changed to an inequality in the opposite direction ($\geq$, or $\leq$) by multiplying both sides of the inequality by -1. For example, the linear constraint

$$a_1 x_1 + a_2 x_2 \geq b,$$

is equivalent to

$$-a_1 x_1 - a_2 x_2 \leq -b.$$

Also,

$$p_1 x_1 + p_2 x_2 \le q,$$

is equivalent to

$$-p_1 x_1 - p_2 x_2 \ge -q.$$

3. An equation may be replaced by two weak inequalities in opposite directions. For example,

$$a_1 x_1 + a_2 x_2 = b$$

is equivalent to the two simultaneous constraints,

$$a_1 x_1 + a_2 x_2 \le b \quad \text{and} \quad a_1 x_1 + a_2 x_2 \ge b,$$

or

$$a_1 x_1 + a_2 x_2 \le b \quad \text{and} \quad -a_1 x_1 - a_2 x_2 \le -b.$$

4. An inequality constraint with its left-hand side in the absolute form can be changed into two regular inequalities. Thus, for $b \ge 0$,

$$|a_1 x_1 + a_2 x_2| \le b$$

is equivalent to

$$a_1 x_1 + a_2 x_2 \ge -b \quad \text{and} \quad a_1 x_1 + a_2 x_2 \le b.$$

Similarly, for $q \ge 0$,

$$|p_1 x_1 + p_2 x_2| \ge q$$

is equivalent to either

$$p_1 x_1 + p_2 x_2 \ge q \quad \text{or} \quad p_1 x_1 + p_2 x_2 \le -q.[2]$$

5. A variable which is unconstrained in sign (that is, positive, negative or zero) is equivalent to the difference between two nonnegative variables. Thus, if x is unconstrained in sign, it can be replaced by $(x^+ - x^-)$ where x^+ and x^- are both nonnegative; that is, $x^+ \ge 0$, and $x^- \ge 0$.

▶   **Example 2·3–1**
Consider the linear programming problem:

$$\text{minimize} \quad x_0 = 3x_1 - 3x_2 + 7x_3,$$

---

[2] The "either-or" constraints require a special modification before they can be used in a linear programming model. This point will be investigated in Section 10·5·2 as an application of mixed integer programming.

subject to

$$
\begin{aligned}
x_1 + x_2 + 3x_3 &\leq 40, \\
x_1 + 9x_2 - 7x_3 &\geq 50, \\
5x_1 + 3x_2 &= 20, \\
|5x_2 + 8x_3| &\leq 100, \\
x_1 \geq 0, \, x_2 &\geq 0,
\end{aligned}
$$

x_3 is unconstrained in sign.

This problem can be put in the canonical form as follows. By the fourth transformation,

$$
|5x_2 + 8x_3| \leq 100
$$

is equivalent to

$$
5x_2 + 8x_3 \leq 100
$$

and

$$
5x_2 + 8x_3 \geq -100.
$$

By the fifth transformation,

$$
x_3 = x_3^+ - x_3^-,
$$

where $x_3^+ \geq 0$ and $x_3^- \geq 0$. Thus, the canonical form is given by:

$$
\text{maximize} \quad g_0 = (-x_0) = -3x_1 + 3x_2 - 7(x_3^+ - x_3^-),
$$

subject to

$$
\begin{aligned}
x_1 + x_2 + 3(x_3^+ - x_3^-) &\leq 40, \\
-x_1 - 9x_2 + 7(x_3^+ - x_3^-) &\leq -50, \\
5x_1 + 3x_2 &\leq 20, \\
-5x_1 - 3x_2 &\leq -20, \\
5x_2 + 8(x_3^+ - x_3^-) &\leq 100, \\
-5x_2 - 8(x_3^+ - x_3^-) &\leq 100, \\
x_1 \geq 0, \quad x_2 \geq 0, \quad x_3^+ \geq 0, \quad x_3^- &\geq 0. \quad \blacktriangleleft
\end{aligned}
$$

It is noted in this case that the only difference between the original and the canonical forms occurs in the objective function where x_0 in the original problem becomes equal to $(-g_0)$ in the canonical form. The values of the variables are the same in both cases, however, since the constraints are essentially the same.

§ 2·3·2
The Standard Form

The characteristics of the *standard form* are

    1. All the constraints are equations except for the nonnegativity constraints which remain inequalities (≥ 0).
    2. The right-hand side element of each constraint equation is nonnegative.
    3. All the variables are nonnegative.
    4. The objective function is of the maximization or the minimization type.

    Constraints of the inequality type can be changed to equations by augmenting (adding or subtracting) the left-hand side of each such constraint by a nonnegative variable. These new variables are called *slack variables* and are added if the constraint is ($\leq$) or subtracted if the constraint is ($\geq$).[3] The right-hand side can be made always positive by multiplying both sides of the resulting equation by (-1) whenever necessary. The remaining characteristics can be realized using, when necessary, the elementary transformations introduced with the canonical form.
    To illustrate the concept of the slack variables, the constraint

$$a_1 x_1 + a_2 x_2 \geq b, \quad b \geq 0$$

is changed in the standard form to

$$a_1 x_1 + a_2 x_2 - S_1 = b,$$

where $S_1 \geq 0$. Also, the constraint

$$p_1 x_1 + p_2 x_2 \leq q, \quad q \geq 0$$

is changed to

$$p_1 x_1 + p_2 x_2 + S_2 = q,$$

where $S_2 \geq 0$.

    The standard form plays an important role in the solution of the linear programming problem. A useful way of presenting the information of the standard form in preparation for the solution is the so-called "tableau form." For example, consider the problem with all ($\leq$) constraints:

$$\text{maximize} \quad x_0 = \sum_{j=1}^{n} c_j x_j,$$

---

   [3] Since in the case of ($\geq$) constraints, the subtracted variable represents the surplus of the left-hand side over the right-hand side, it is common to refer to it as *surplus* variable. For convenience, however, the name "slack" variable will be used also to represent this type. In this respect, a surplus is regarded as a negative slack.

subject to

$$\sum_{j=1}^{n} a_{ij} x_j \le b_i, \quad (b_i \ge 0), \qquad i = 1, 2, \ldots, m,$$

$$x_j \ge 0, \qquad\qquad j = 1, 2, \ldots, n.$$

This is expressed in the standard form as:

$$\text{maximize} \quad x_0 = \sum_{j=1}^{n} c_j x_j,$$

subject to

$$\sum_{j=1}^{n} a_{ij} x_j + S_i = b_i, \qquad i = 1, 2, \ldots, m,$$

$$x_j \ge 0, \qquad j = 1, 2, \ldots, n,$$

$$S_i \ge 0, \qquad i = 1, 2, \ldots, m.$$

The above standard form may be presented in its equivalent tableau form as follows:

Objective value	Decision variables				Slack variables				R.H.S. constants	
x_0	x_1	x_2	$\cdots$	x_n	S_1	S_2	$\cdots$	S_m	0	
1	$-c_1$	$-c_2$	$\cdots$	$-c_n$	0	0	$\cdots$	0	0	$\Big\}x_0$-equation
0	a_{11}	a_{12}	$\cdots$	a_{1n}	1	0	$\cdots$	0	b_1	
0	a_{21}	a_{22}	$\cdots$	a_{2n}	0	1	$\cdots$	0	b_2	Constraint equations
$\vdots$	$\vdots$	$\vdots$		$\vdots$	$\vdots$	$\vdots$		$\vdots$	$\vdots$	
0	a_{m1}	a_{m2}	$\cdots$	a_{mn}	0	0	$\cdots$	1	b_m	

where the x_0-equation is obtained by considering

$$x_0 - \sum_{j=1}^{n} c_j x_j = 0.$$

The tableau form assumes that all x_j and S_i are nonnegative.

It is observed that the standard linear programming problem has reduced (in the tableau form) to a system of $(m + 1)$ equations (objective $+ m$ constraints) in $(m + n + 1)$ unknowns (objective value, x_0, $+ n$ decision variables, x_j, $+ m$ slack variables, S_i). The variable x_0 is a dependent variable, however, and is readily determined as soon as the remaining $(m + n)$ variables are known. This means that the system is, in effect, equivalent to m equations in $(m + n)$ unknowns.

It is noted that in general the number of slack variables may not be equal to m since this depends on the type of the constraints. It can still be assumed, however, that the number of variables in the *standard form* is equal to $m + n$ where n becomes equal to the total number of variables minus the number of constraints.

The idea of obtaining the solution can now be expressed in terms of the new tableau form. The main issue is to determine the set of nonnegative values of the variables x_j and S_i which will yield the largest value of x_0 while satisfying all the constraint equations. The concept is simple, but the problem here is that a set of m equations in $(m + n)$ unknowns yields an infinite number of solutions. One thus immediately realizes that it is computationally infeasible to use trial and error in finding the required solution. Consequently, there is a definite need for an efficient and systematic procedure which will yield the desired solution in a finite number of trials. In the next chapter, an *iterative* procedure, called the "Simplex Method," is presented. This procedure was developed by George B. Dantzig (1947) and is proved to reach the optimum solution (if one exists) in a finite number of iterations.

§ 2·4
Graphical Solution of Two-Variable Linear Programming Problems

A linear programming problem with only two variables presents a simple case for which the solution can be obtained using a rather elementary graphical method. This method is best illustrated by an example.

▶ **Example 2·4–1**
Consider the blending problem given by Example 2·2–5.

$$\text{Maximize} \quad x_0 = 3x_1 + 4x_2,$$

subject to

$$5x_1 + 4x_2 \leq 200,$$
$$3x_1 + 5x_2 \leq 150,$$
$$5x_1 + 4x_2 \geq 100,$$
$$8x_1 + 4x_2 \geq 80,$$
$$x_1 \geq 0, \quad x_2 \geq 0.$$

It is noted that the nonnegativity constraints $x_1 \geq 0$ and $x_2 \geq 0$ imply that the values of the two variables x_1 and x_2 are restricted only to the points lying in the first quadrant (shaded area in Figure 2-1) of the two-dimensional space. The effect of the remaining constraints can now be added to Figure 2-1. This is achieved by plotting all the constraints with the inequality changed into an equality sign. The direction in which each constraint holds is then determined

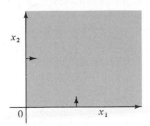

Figure 2–1

by observing the direction of the inequality. For example, in Figure 2-2, it is shown that the constraint $5x_1 + 4x_2 \leq 200$ holds only in the direction toward the origin.

The area which is satisfied by all the constraints (including all the boundaries) is called the *solution space*. This is shown in Figure 2-2 by the shaded area ABCDE.

Notice that the last constraint $8x_1 + 4x_2 \geq 80$ does not affect the solution space since it is dominated by the third constraint $5x_1 + 4x_2 \geq 100$. The constraint $8x_1 + 4x_2 \geq 80$ is thus called a *redundant* constraint.

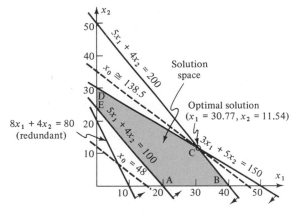

Figure 2–2

Any point (x_1, x_2) within, or on the boundaries of, the solution space should satisfy all four constraints simultaneously. Obviously, there is an *infinite* number of such points; however, one is interested in determining the point (or points) in this solution space which yields the maximum value of x_0. An investigation of the objective function, $x_0 = 3x_1 + 4x_2$, reveals that by increasing the value of x_0, the straight line $x_0 = 3x_1 + 4x_2$ will move parallel to itself and away from the origin. The only limitation on this increase is that the straight line $x_0 = 3x_1 + 4x_2$ should satisfy at least one point in the solution space. This clearly occurs in Figure 2-2 when $x_0 = 3x_1 + 4x_2$ touches the solution space at point C. The coordinates of point C represent the best solution to the problem. This is given by $x_1 = 30.77$ and $x_2 = 11.54$ and is usually referred to as the *optimal* solution. The corresponding optimum value of x_0 is obtained by direct substitution in the objective function and is given by $x_0 \doteq 138.5$. ◄

The applicability of the graphical method presented here is feasible only for two-dimensional problems. Problems involving three or more variables will have their constraints in the form of planes and hence it becomes difficult (if not impossible) to visualize the solution space.

SELECTED REFERENCES

1. SIMMONARD, M., *Linear Programming*, translated by W. Jewell, Englewood Cliffs, New Jersey: Prentice-Hall, 1966.
2. VAJDA, S., *Readings in Linear Programming*, New York: Wiley, 1958.
3. ZUKHOVITSKIY, S., and L. AVDEYEVA, *Linear and Convex Programming*, translated by Scripta Technica, Inc., Philadelphia, Pennsylvania: W. B. Saunders Company, 1966.

PROBLEMS

□ **2-1** Consider the problem of assigning three different types (sizes) of aircrafts to four routes. The following table gives the maximum capacity (in number of passengers) and the number of aircrafts available for each type, the number of daily trips that each aircraft can make on a given route, and the daily number of customers expected for each route.

Aircraft type	Capacity (passengers)	Number of aircrafts	Number of daily trips on route,			
			1	2	3	4
1	50	5	3	2	2	1
2	30	8	4	3	3	2
3	20	10	5	5	4	2
Daily number of customers			100	200	90	120

The associated operating costs per trip on the different routes together with the penalty cost (lost profit) for not servicing a customer are summarized below.

Aircraft type	Operating cost per trip on given route($)			
	1	2	3	4
1	1000	1100	1200	1500
2	800	900	1000	1000
3	600	800	800	900
Penalty cost per customer	40	50	45	70

Formulate the problem as a linear programming model so as to determine the assignment of aircrafts to routes which will minimize the total costs of the system.

□ **2-2** A manufacturer is producing three models (I, II, and III) of a certain product. He uses two types of raw material (A and B) of which 2000 and 3000 units are available, respectively. The raw material requirements per unit of the three models are given below.

Raw material	Requirements per unit of given model		
	I	II	III
A	2	3	5
B	4	2	7

The labor requirement per unit of Model I is twice that of Model II and three times that of Model III. The maximum number of units of Model I that can be produced by the available labor hours is 700 units. A market survey has shown that the minimum requirement of the three models are 200, 200, and 150 respectively. However, the ratios of the number of units produced must be equal to 3 : 2 : 5. Assume that the profit per unit of Models I, II, and III are 30, 20, and 50 dollars respectively. Formulate the problem as a linear programming model in order to determine the number of units of each product which will maximize profit.

□ **2-3** A businessman has the option of investing his money in two plans. Plan A guarantees that each dollar invested will earn 70 cents a year hence, while Plan B guarantees that each dollar invested will earn $2.00 two years hence. In Plan B, only investments for periods that are multiples of two years are allowed. Suppose that the businessman has a total of $100,000. How should he allocate this sum in order to maximize his earnings at the end of three years? Formulate the problem as a linear programming model.

☐ **2-4** For a 24-hour cafeteria the following number of waitresses are required:

Time of day	Minimum number of waitresses
2–6	4
6–10	8
10–14	10
14–18	7
18–22	12
22–2	4

Each waitress works eight consecutive hours per day. The objective is to find the smallest number required to comply with the above requirements. Formulate the problem as a linear programming model.

☐ **2-5**   A certain final product consists of three parts. The three parts can be produced in four different departments with each department having a limited number of production hours. The table below gives the production rates for the three parts. The objective is determine the number of hours of each department to be assigned to each part so as to maximize the number of completed units of the final product.

Department	Capacity (hours)	Production rate/hour		
		Part 1	Part 2	Part 3
1	100	10	15	5
2	150	15	10	5
3	80	20	5	10
4	200	10	15	20

Formulate the problem as a linear programming model. (Hint: use the idea of Example 2·2-2.)

☐ **2-6** Two alloys A and B are made from four different metals I, II, III, and IV according to the following specification:

Alloy	Specifications
A	At most 80% of I At most 30% of II At least 50% of IV
B	Between 40% and 60% of II At least 30% of III At most 70% of IV

The four metals are extracted from three different ores whose constituents percentage of these metals, maximum available quantity, and cost per ton are tabulated as follows:

Ore	Maximum quantity	Constituents (%)					Price/ton
		I	II	III	IV	Others	
1	1000 (Tons)	20	10	30	30	10	$30
2	2000	10	20	30	30	10	$40
3	3000	5	5	70	20	0	$50

Assuming that the selling prices of alloys A and B are $200 and $300 per ton, formulate the problem as a linear programming model selecting the appropriate objective function which will make the best use of the given information. (Hint: Let X_{ijk} be the amount (tons)of the ith metal ($i =$ I, II, III, IV) obtained from the jth ore ($j = 1, 2, 3$) and allocated to the kth alloy ($k =$ A, B))

☐ **2-7** Reformulate the caterer problem of Example 2·2-3 for a seven-day planning period assuming that the demands are 100, 150, 140, 130, 200, 300, and 220 for the respective seven days.

☐ **2-8** Reformulate the trim problem of Example 2·2-4 assuming the availability of one standard 15′-width roll only.

☐ **2-9** In the trim loss problem of Example 2·2-4 show that the expression for the objective function can be put in the more simplified form,
minimize $x_0 = 10(x_{11} + x_{12} + x_{13}) + 20(x_{21} + \cdots + x_{26})$.

☐ **2-10** A gambler plays a game which requires dividing his money among four different choices. The game has three outcomes. The following table gives the corresponding gain (or loss) per dollar deposited in each of the four choices for the three outcomes.

Outcome	Gain (or loss) per dollar deposited in given choice			
	1	2	3	4
1	-3	4	-7	15
2	5	-3	9	4
3	3	-9	10	-8

Assume that the gambler has a total of $500 with which he may play only once. The exact outcome of the game is not known *a priori* and in face of this uncertainty the gambler decided to make the allocation which would maximize his *minimum* return. Formulate the problem as a linear programming model. (Hint: The gambler's return may be negative, zero, or positive.)

□ **2-11**   Consider the linear programming problem:

$$\text{minimize} \quad x_0 = 2x_1 + 3x_2 + 5x_3,$$

subject to

$$x_1 + x_2 - x_3 \geq -5,$$
$$-6x_1 + 7x_2 - 9x_3 = 15,$$
$$|19x_1 - 7x_2 + 5x_3| \leq 13,$$
$$x_1 \geq 0, \quad x_2 \geq 0,$$

x_3, unrestricted in sign.

Put this problem in, (a) the canonical form, and, (b) the standard form.

□ **2-12**   Consider the following linear programming problem.

$$\text{Maximize} \quad x_0 = 5x_1 + 2x_2,$$

subject to

$$x_1 + x_2 \leq 10,$$
$$x_1 = 5,$$
$$x_1 \geq 0, \quad x_2 \geq 0.$$

Solve this problem graphically and define its solution space.

□ **2-13**   Show graphically that the maximum and minimum values of the objective function for the following problem are the same.

$$\text{Maximize (or minimize)} \quad x_0 = 5x_1 + 3x_2,$$

subject to

$$x_1 + x_2 \le 6,$$
$$x_1 \ge 3,$$
$$x_2 \ge 3,$$
$$2x_1 + 3x_3 \ge 3,$$
$$x_1 \ge 0, \quad x_2 \ge 0.$$

Define the solution space in this case. What is the solution space if the right-hand side of the first constraint is changed to 5 instead of 6?

☐ **2-14** Solve the following problem graphically.

$$\text{Maximize} \quad x_0 = \text{Min}\ \{3x_1 - 10, -5x_1 + 5\},$$

subject to

$$x_1 \le 5,$$
$$x_1 \ge 0.$$

☐ **2-15** Consider the following problem.

$$\text{Maximize} \quad x_0 = 6x_1 - 2x_2,$$

subject to

$$x_1 - x_2 \le 1,$$
$$3x_1 - x_2 \le 6,$$
$$x_1 \ge 0, \quad x_2 \ge 0.$$

Show graphically that at the optimal solution the variables x_1 and x_2 can be increased indefinitely while the value of the objective function will remain constant.

☐ **2-16** Consider the following linear programming problem.

$$\text{Maximize} \quad x_0 = 4x_1 + 4x_2,$$

subject to

$$2x_1 + 7x_2 \le 21,$$
$$7x_1 + 2x_2 \le 49,$$
$$x_1 \ge 0, \quad x_2 \ge 0.$$

Find the optimal solution (x_1^*, x_2^*) graphically. What are the ranges of variation of the coefficients of the objective function which will keep (x_1^*, x_2^*) as the optimal solution?

☐ **2-17**   Solve the following problem graphically.

$$\text{Maximize} \quad x_0 = 5x_1 + 6x_2,$$

subject to

$$x_1 - 2x_2 \geq 2,$$
$$-2x_1 + 3x_2 \geq 2,$$

where x_1 and x_2 are unrestricted in sign.

CHAPTER 3

The Simplex Method

§ 3·1
Introduction

In Chapter 2 it was shown that the general linear programming problem in any form can be reduced to the standard form consisting of a set of m equations in $(m + n)$ unknowns (where n is equal to the *total* number of variables *minus* the number of equations m). It was also indicated that such a system of equations yields an infinite number of solutions and consequently there is a need for a "selective" iterative procedure which will yield the optimum solution in a finite number of iterations. This chapter presents the "simplex method" procedure for solving linear programming problems. The main concern here is to develop the computational aspect of the procedure. Questions regarding the validity of the procedure will be treated mathematically in Chapter 8.

§ 3·2
Development of the Simplex Method

The simplex method procedure (as developed by G. Dantzig) recognizes the following three points for effecting a systematic reduction from an infinite number of solutions to a finite number of promising solutions:

1. A candidate for the optimal solution is obtained by setting any n unknowns (out of $m + n$ unknowns) equal to zero and then solving for the remaining m unknowns, provided that the solution exists and is unique.[1] In

---

[1] For example, for the system

$$2x_1 + 3x_2 + 8x_3 = 9$$
$$4x_1 + 6x_2 + 7x_3 = 8$$

by setting $x_3 = 0$, the resulting two equations obviously yield no solution. Similarly, if the right-hand side of the second equation is 18 instead of 8, then for $x_3 = 0$, the resulting two equations become identical thus yielding an infinite number of solutions.

this case the n zero-variables are called *nonbasic* variables. The remaining m variables are called *basic* variables and are said to constitute a basic solution. It is noticed that by using such a condition, the number of candidates for the optimum solution is reduced from an infinite to a finite number of which the maximum limit is

$$\binom{m + n}{m} = \frac{(m + n)!}{m! \, n!}.$$

Although this is a promising step toward reducing the number of trials for the optimal solution, the resulting number of candidate solutions may be too large to be computationally feasible. Consequently, there is still a need for another criterion which will allow a second selection of the most promising candidates from among all possible basic solutions.

2. As stated in the definition of the linear programming problem, all the variables must be nonnegative. Since the basic solutions selected by (1) above are not necessarily nonnegative, further reduction in the number of candidates for the optimum solution is still possible by eliminating all *infeasible basic* solutions (that is, solutions having variables less than zero). This is achieved in the simplex method by selecting a *starting* basic solution which is non-negative (≥ 0). A condition is then provided (called the *feasibility condition*) which guarantees that the next basic solution to be selected from among all possible basic solutions is always feasible (≥ 0). The solution generated in this way is called *basic feasible* solution, or a feasible solution of the variables associated with a *basis*. If all the basic variables are strictly positive (> 0), the solution is called *nondegenerate*; otherwise, if some of the basic variables are zero, the solution is called *degenerate*. It will be shown in Section 3·3 that a new basic feasible solution can be generated from a previous basis by setting *one* of the m basic variables equal to zero and replacing it by a new nonbasic variable. The basic variable set equal to zero is called a "leaving variable" while the new one is called an "entering variable." (Notice that at all times, a basic solution must include m variables.)

3. Since, as stated in (2) above, a new basic solution can be generated from a previous one by selecting an entering and a leaving variable, it is possible to select the entering variable such that it causes improvement in the value of the objective function and hence guarantees that the new solution is better (in terms of the value of the objective function) than the previous one.[2] This is achieved in the simplex method by the use of another condition (called the *optimality condition*) which selects the nonbasic variable with the largest *per-unit* gain in the objective function as the entering variable. This is repeated successively until no further improvements in the value of the objective function is possible. In this case it is said that an *optimal basic feasible* solution

---

[2] This statement is true provided that the entering variable is not zero (degenerate case). It will be assumed throughout this section that the solutions are nondegenerate. Section 3·6 will deal with the degeneracy case.

(henceforth called *optimal* solution) has been reached. This, of course, is true provided that the objective function has a finite value.

The above procedure shows that the simplex method procedure is based on a screening process which eliminates the solutions that are not promising candidates for the optimum solution. Figure 3-1 summarizes the screening

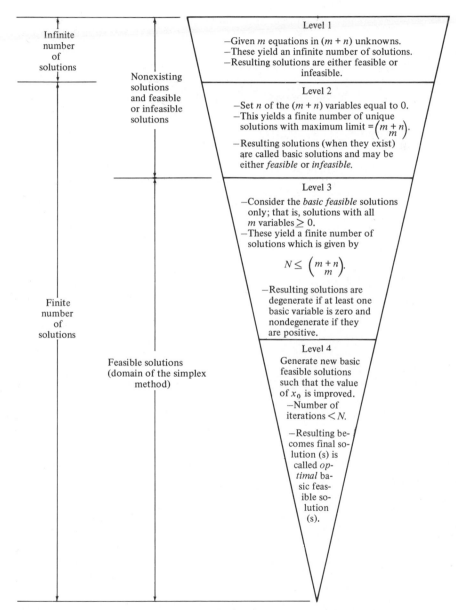

Infinite number of solutions

Nonexisting solutions and feasible or infeasible solutions

Finite number of solutions

Feasible solutions (domain of the simplex method)

Level 1
—Given m equations in $(m + n)$ unknowns.
—These yield an infinite number of solutions.
—Resulting solutions are either feasible or infeasible.

Level 2
—Set n of the $(m + n)$ variables equal to 0.
—This yields a finite number of unique solutions with maximum limit $= \binom{m + n}{m}$.
—Resulting solutions (when they exist) are called basic solutions and may be either *feasible* or *infeasible*.

Level 3
—Consider the *basic feasible* solutions only; that is, solutions with all m variables ≥ 0.
—These yield a finite number of solutions which is given by

$$N \leq \binom{m + n}{m}.$$

—Resulting solutions are degenerate if at least one basic variable is zero and nondegenerate if they are positive.

Level 4
Generate new basic feasible solutions such that the value of x_0 is improved.
—Number of iterations $< N$.

—Resulting becomes final solution (s) is called *optimal* basic feasible solution (s).

Figure 3–1. The Screening Process in the Simplex Method

process associated with this procedure. An *inverted* pyramid-shape is used with its "top" representing the infinite number of solutions and its "bottom" representing the selected optimal solution(s). The figure shows the different levels of screening in the simplex method. Notice that the important question arises at Level 2 of the screening process where the selection of promising solution is effected by setting n of the $(n + m)$ variables equal to zero. This is a key point in the development of the simplex method and is accepted for the time being without proof (see Chapter 8). It should be noted that the simplex method procedure operates within the feasible solutions range only. This includes Levels 3 and 4 where the feasibility and optimality conditions are used.

An example is now introduced to clarify the above concepts.

▶ **Example 3·2-1**

Consider the linear programming problem:

$$\text{maximize} \quad x_0 = 3x_1 + 5x_2 - 2x_3,$$

subject to

$$x_1 + 2x_2 + 2x_3 \leq 10,$$
$$2x_1 + 4x_2 + 3x_3 \leq 15,$$
$$x_1 \geq 0, \quad x_2 \geq 0, \quad x_3 \geq 0.$$

After adding the slack variables S_1 and S_2, the above problem can be put in the tableau form as follows:

x_0	x_1	x_2	x_3	S_1	S_2	
1	-3	-5	2	0	0	0
0	1	2	2	1	0	10
0	2	4	3	0	1	15

Using the condition that a candidate for the optimal solution is obtained by setting $n(= 3)$ variables equal to zero and then solving for the remaining variables (provided the solution exists), Table 3-1 summarizes all possible basic solutions $\left(\binom{m + n}{m} = \binom{5}{2} = 10 \right)$ together with the properties of the solution and the corresponding value of x_0. This gives the optimal value of $x_0 = 22.5$ and the optimal basic feasible solution $x_1 = 7.5$ and $S_1 = 2.5$ while all other variables are equal to zero.

It is noted from Table 3–1 that only seven of the ten candidate solutions are feasible. The remaining three are either infeasible or do not yield a solution.

Table 3–1

Possible basis	Solution	Property*	x_0	Possible basis	Solution	Property*	x_0
(x_1, x_2)	No solution exists	—	—	(x_2, x_3)	(0, 5)	B, F, D	-10
(x_1, x_3)	(0, 5)	B, F, D	-10	(x_2, S_1)	(3.75, 2.5)	B, F, ND	18.75
(x_1, S_1)	(7.5, 2.5)	B, F, ND	22.5	(x_2, S_2)	(5, -5)	B, IF	—
(x_1, S_2)	(10, -5)	B, IF	—	(x_3, S_1)	(5, 0)	B, F, D	-10
(S_1, S_2)	(10, 15)	B, F, ND	0	(x_3, S_2)	(5, 0)	B, F, D	-10

* B = Basic	D = Degenerate
F = Feasible	ND = Nondegenerate
IF = Infeasible	

It is also noted that there is no way of predicting which basic solution yields the optimum until *all* basic solutions have been considered. These false trials are one of the main disadvantages of this enumeration method and it will be seen later that the simplex method does not allow such false trials. In fact, for this example, the simplex method yields the optimal solution in exactly two iterations (see next section). ◄

§ 3·3
Optimality and Feasibility Conditions of the Simplex Method

It is indicated in the preceding section that in order to avoid the false trials associated with the enumeration method of Example 3·2–1, two criteria must be developed. These are the *optimality* and the *feasibility* conditions which respectively determine the entering and the leaving variables in a new basic solution. Given a starting basic feasible solution, the two conditions generate new basic feasible solutions which lead much faster to the optimal solution. The idea of the two conditions is best illustrated by an example. Specifically, Example 3·2-1 will be used to allow comparison between the previous enumeration method and the simplex method. It should be noted that there is a slight difference between the optimality conditions of the maximization and the minimization problems. This section first develops the criterion for the maximization case. This is generalized later to cover the minimization problem.

A starting basic solution for Example 3·2-1 can be obtained directly by using the slack variables.[3] This gives $S_1 = 10$ and $S_2 = 15$ since all the nonbasic variables x_1, x_2, and x_3 are equal to zero. The corresponding value of the

---

[3] For the case where all the constraints are ($\leq$), the slack variables always provide an obvious starting solution. For the other cases involving ($=$) or ($\geq$) constraints, a special trick is needed to find a starting solution. This is explained in Section 3·5.

objective function is equal to zero reflecting the fact that all the "resources" are allocated to the slack variables. This information can be expressed directly in the tableau form as follows:

Basic	x_0	x_1	x_2	x_3	S_1	S_2	Solution
x_0	①	-3	-5	2	0	0	0
S_1	0	1	2	2	①	0	10
S_2	0	2	4	3	0	①	15

Notice that the column under x_0 contains a one-element (circled) in the first row and zero-elements otherwise. The columns under S_1 and S_2 similarly contain one-elements in the second and the third rows, respectively. Because of this arrangement, the right-hand side of the tableau yields the values of the starting solution directly.

It is important to observe the special structure of the starting tableau which will be used throughout this book. The last m columns ($m = 2$ in the given example) on the left-hand side of the tableau must correspond to the starting basic solution. In addition, the coefficients of the starting basic variables in the x_0-equation must be equal to zero. This will always be the case when all the constraints are of the type ($\leq$). In general, these coefficients may not be readily equal to zero. In this case, direct substitution from the constraints using simple row operations (which will be introduced later in this section) is used to effect this result. Finally, it will be required that all the *constraint* coefficients under the starting basic variables appear in an identity-matrix form; that is, all the elements are equal to zero except for the *diagonal* elements which are equal to one (this is shown by circles in the above tableau). This arrangement will allow the tableau to possess certain useful properties which will be used in later chapters.

Given the above conditions, the optimality criterion selects the entering variable by observing the coefficients of the *non*basic variables in the x_0-equation. Since this is a maximization problem, a nonbasic variable having a positive x_0-coefficient in the tableau can only worsen the value of x_0. Similarly, a zero coefficient will leave the value of x_0 unchanged. Consequently, the entering variable is selected as the nonbasic variable having the most negative coefficient in the x_0-equation. If there is a tie, it can be broken arbitrarily. Thus, for the given example, x_2 is the entering variable.

The above optimality condition is actually equivalent to selecting the nonbasic variable having the largest (positive) *per unit* gain in the *original* objective function. Although this may not be generally the best way to improve the value of x_0, experience has shown that other methods may involve more computational effort.

Since x_2 will enter the solution, one of the current basic variables (S_1 or S_2) must leave the solution and become nonbasic at zero level. (Recall that a candidate for the optimum solution can include m variables only.) The determination of the specific leaving variable is achieved by using the feasibility condition. This is derived directly from the constraint equations. Thus, in the given example, since x_2 is the entering variable, the constraint equations may be written as,

$$x_2 = \tfrac{1}{2}(10 - S_1 - x_1 - 2x_3)$$
$$x_2 = \tfrac{1}{4}(15 - S_2 - 2x_1 - 3x_3).$$

The objective here is to select the largest value of x_2 such that when S_1 is set equal to zero, S_2 will not become infeasible, and *vice versa*. Since $x_1 = x_3 = 0$, investigation will show that if $S_1 = 0$, then $x_2 = 5$. From the second equation this yields $S_2 = -5$; that is, S_2 is infeasible. However, if $S_2 = 0$, then $x_2 = 3.75$ which, from the first equation, yield $S_1 = 2.5$; that is, S_1 is feasible. Consequently S_2 becomes the leaving variable.

The leaving variable can actually be determined directly by taking the ratios of the values of the current basic variables (excluding x_0) to the corresponding constraint coefficients of the entering variable. As indicated above, the leaving variable will correspond to the smallest ratio. Thus applying this to the example, one gets,

Current basic solution	Ratios to coefficients of x_2
$S_1 = 10$	$10/2 = 5$
$S_2 = 15$	$15/4 = 3.75, \quad \leftarrow S_2 = 0, \quad x_2 = 3.75$

Hence S_2 leaves and x_2 enters the solution. This gives the new solution $S_1 = 2.5$, $x_2 = 3.75$ and $x_0 = 18.75$ (cf. with Table 3–1).

It is important to observe that if any of the constraints coefficients for the entering variable are either *zero* or *negative* then the corresponding ratios must be disregarded when deciding on the leaving variable. To illustrate this point, suppose that the coefficients of x_2 in the second constraint of the above example is changed to 0 instead of 4. Then the constraint equations become,

$$S_1 = 10 - x_1 - 2x_2 - 2x_3,$$
$$S_2 = 15 - 2x_1 - 0x_2 - 3x_3.$$

The second equation (where the coefficient of $x_2 = 0$) is independent of x_2 and hence its value can be increased indefinitely without causing S_2 to become negative. The only limit on the value of x_2 in this case is dictated by the first equation and is given by $\tfrac{10}{2} = 5$.

Similarly, if the coefficient of x_2 in the second equation is changed to -9 instead of 4, then,

$$S_2 = 15 - 2x_1 + 9x_2 - 3x_3.$$

This equation shows again that x_2 can assume any positive value without causing S_2 to be negative.

The next step after determining the entering variable, x_2, and the leaving variable, S_2, is to modify the last tableau form to give directly the solution of the new basic variables. This is achieved by substituting out x_2 (entering variable) in terms of the nonbasic variables in the objective and the constraint equations *except* in the constraint equation where S_2 (leaving variable) appears. This will also cause the objective equation to be expressed in terms of the new nonbasic variables (x_1, x_3 and S_2). In this case, the new tableau form becomes ready for a new iteration where the optimality and feasibility conditions can be applied directly.

The process of eliminating the entering variable from all but one equation can be effected by simple row operations. This is illustrated as follows. (The last tableau is repeated here for convenience.)

Basic	x_0	x_1	x_2	x_3	S_1	S_2	Solution
x_0	①	-3	-5	2	0	0	0
S_1	0	1	2	2	①	0	10
S_2	0	2	☐4	3	0	①	15

The coefficient "4" of the entering variable x_2 (designated by ☐) corresponding to the minimum ratio is called the *pivot* element. The variable x_2 is thus eliminated from all equations except the one where the pivot element appears. This includes for this example the objective and the first constraint equations. In order for the right-hand side of the second constraint equation to yield the value of x_2 directly, the whole equation must be divided by the pivot element ($= 4$). This row, which will be referred to as the pivot equation, appears in the new tableau as:

Basic	x_0	x_1	x_2	x_3	S_1	S_2	Solution
x_2	0	2/4	①	3/4	0	1/4	$15/4 = 3.75$

The elimination of x_2 from the x_0-equation and the first constraint equation is equivalent to creating zero coefficients for x_2 in these two equations. This is done using the following row operations:

1. Multiply the *new* pivot equation by 5 and add the result to the x_0-equation.
2. Multiply the new pivot equation by -2 and add the result to the first constraint equation.

This yields the following new tableau which now represents the start of a new *iteration*.

Basic	x_0	x_1	x_2	x_3	S_1	S_2	Solution
x_0	①	$-1/2$	0	$23/4$	0	$5/4$	$18\frac{3}{4}$
S_1	0	0	0	$1/2$	①	$-1/2$	$2\frac{1}{2}$
x_2	0	$1/2$	①	$3/4$	0	$1/4$	$3\frac{3}{4}$

Notice that by using the row operations, the elements of the new column under x_2 (entering variable) become identical with the elements of the old column under S_2 (leaving variable). The row operations process does not affect the information content of the problem since it only causes the addition or subtraction of simultaneous equations.

Investigation of the last tableau reveals that the current solution is non-optimal since the coefficient of x_1 in the x_0-equation is negative.[4] Hence applying the same conditions, x_1 should enter the solution. The leaving variable is determined as follows,

Current basic solution	Ratios to coefficients of x_1
$S_1 = 2.5$	2.5/0, (Ignore, since the denominator is zero.)
$x_2 = 3.75$	$3.75/\frac{1}{2} = 7.5$, $\leftarrow x_2 = 0$, $x_1 = 7.5$

---

[4] A common error is to neglect the *slack* variables when checking the optimality condition. This is based on the assumption that these variables do not usually appear in the original objective function and hence they cannot influence its value. This is erroneous since it is obvious from the constraints that changes in the values of the slacks have direct effect on the values of the decision variables which in turn will affect the value of the objective function. Consequently, the slacks must be treated in exactly the same way as the decision variables. This remark is justified mathematically in Section 8·5.

indicating that x_2 is the leaving variable. The new tableau is then given by:

Basic	x_0	x_1	x_2	x_3	S_1	S_2	Solution
x_0	①	0	1	13/2	0	3/2	$22\frac{1}{2}$
S_1	0	0	0	1/2	①	$-1/2$	$2\frac{1}{2}$
x_1	0	①	2	3/2	0	1/2	$7\frac{1}{2}$

This yields the optimal solution $x_1 = 7.5$, $x_2 = 0$ and $x_0 = 22.5$ since all the coefficients in the x_0-equation are ≥ 0.

It is now possible to summarize the optimality and feasibility conditions.

Optimality Condition (maximization problem). Given the x_0-equation in terms of the nonbasic variables, the entering variable is selected as the nonbasic variable having the most negative coefficient in the x_0-equation. If more than one variable appears with the same most negative coefficient, any one of these variables can be selected arbitrarily. If all the coefficients are nonnegative (zero or positive), the optimal solution is reached and the process ends.

Feasibility Condition. The leaving variable is selected as the basic variable corresponding to the smallest ratio of the values of the current solution (excluding x_0) to the *positive* constraint coefficients of the entering variable. For the case where two or more variables have the same minimum ratio, any one such variable is selected arbitrarily.

It is noted that the above optimality condition is applicable to the maximization problem only. Although it has been shown in Section 2·3 that a minimization problem can be converted to the maximization form, the above optimality condition can be easily modified to handle minimization problems directly. This is done by selecting the nonbasic variable having the largest *positive* coefficient in the x_0-equation. When all the coefficients of the x_0-equation are nonpositive, the optimal solution is reached. (See Example 3·5-1 for an illustration of this case.) The above feasibility condition, on the other hand, is applicable to both the minimization and the maximization problems.

§ 3·4
Summary of the Computational Procedure of the Simplex Method

The optimal solution of a general linear programming problem (when it exists) is obtained in the following steps:

Step 1: Express the problem in tableau form. This step was explained in Section 2·3·2.

Step 2: Select a starting basic feasible solution. This step involves two cases.

1. If all the constraints in the original problem are ($\leq$), the slack variables are used for a starting solution.
2. If *any* of the constraints in the original problem is ($\geq$) or ($=$), a technique called the "artificial variables technique" is used to give a starting basis. This is given in Section 3·5.

Step 3: Generate new basic feasible solutions using both the optimality and the feasibility conditions until the optimal solution is attained. This step assumes that the optimal solution exists and is bounded. The cases where no solution exists or where the solution is unbounded are discussed in Section 3·6.

The following example is now introduced to sum up the basic features of the simplex method.

▶ **Example 3·4-1**

Consider the production allocation problem given by Example 2·2-1. The corresponding linear programming problem was given by:

$$\text{maximize} \quad x_0 = 3x_1 + 2x_2 + 5x_3,$$

subject to

$$x_1 + 2x_2 + x_3 \leq 430,$$
$$3x_1 \quad\quad + 2x_3 \leq 460,$$
$$x_1 + 4x_2 \quad\quad \leq 420,$$
$$x_1 \geq 0, \quad x_2 \geq 0, \quad x_3 \geq 0.$$

This is expressed in tableau form as follows:

Starting Tableau:

Basic	x_0	x_1	x_2	x_3	S_1	S_2	S_3	Solution
x_0	①	-3	-2	-5	0	0	0	0
S_1	0	1	2	1	①	0	0	430
S_2	0	3	0	2	0	①	0	460
S_3	0	1	4	0	0	0	①	420

First Iteration.　x_3 is the entering variable. Taking ratios,

Current basic solution	Ratios to coefficients of x_3
$S_1 = 430$	$430/1 = 430$
$S_2 = 460$	$460/2 = 230, \leftarrow S_2 = 0, x_3 = 230$
$S_3 = 420$	$420/0 = -$

S_2 becomes the leaving variable. The new tableau is thus given by,

Basic	x_0	x_1	x_2	x_3	S_1	S_2	S_3	Solution
x_0	①	$9/2$	-2	0	0	$5/2$	0	1150
S_1	0	$-1/2$	2	0	①	$-1/2$	0	200
x_3	0	$3/2$	0	①	0	$1/2$	0	230
S_3	0	1	4	0	0	0	①	420

Second Iteration.　x_2 is the entering variable. Taking ratios,

Current basic solution	Ratios to coefficients of x_2
$S_1 = 200$	$200/2 = 100, \leftarrow S_1 = 0, \quad x_2 = 100$
$x_3 = 230$	$230/0 = -$
$S_3 = 420$	$420/4 = 105$

S_1 leaves the solution. The new tableau is

Basic	x_0	x_1	x_2	x_3	S_1	S_2	S_3	Solution
x_0	①	4	0	0	1	2	0	1350
x_2	0	$-1/4$	①	0	$1/2$	$-1/4$	0	100
x_3	0	$3/2$	0	①	0	$1/2$	0	230
S_3	0	2	0	0	-2	1	①	20

This is the optimal solution since *all* the coefficients in the x_0-equation are nonnegative. The optimal solution is thus given by $x_1 = 0$, $x_2 = 100$, $x_3 = 230$, $S_1 = 0$, $S_2 = 0$, $S_3 = 20$, and $x_0 = 1350$.　◄

The above simplex procedure can be presented in a more compact form by computing the minimum ratio directly from the tableau. There are also other procedures which, although based on the same conditions, are easier to manipulate. The above procedure, however, will be especially useful in considering the sensitivity analyses of the optimal solution. The tableau form given previously offers an exceptionally lucid way for presenting this material (see Chapter 4). Consequently, this procedure will be used throughout the text. The reader, after learning the basic concepts, may then wish to employ a computationally more compact procedure.

§ 3·5
Artificial Variables Techniques

It was indicated in Section 3·4 that for problems with ($\geq$) or ($=$) constraints, the slack variables cannot provide a starting (feasible) solution. In this section a method, called the " M-technique " or the " method of penalty " will be presented for finding such a starting solution. Another method, called the " two-phase method," can also be used to obtain the same result. The discussion of the latter method is deferred until Section 3·6·5·1. The reason for classifying these two methods as artificial variables methods will be made clear later.

The idea of the M-technique is summarized as follows:

1. Express the problem in the standard form given in Section 2·3·2.
2. Add nonnegative variables to the left-hand side of each of the equations corresponding to constraints of the types ($\geq$) and ($=$). These variables are called " artificial variables " and their addition causes violation of the corresponding constraints. This difficulty is overcome by introducing a condition which ensures that the artificial variables will be zero ($= 0$) in the final solution (provided the solution of the problem exists).[5] This is achieved by assigning a very large per-unit penalty to these variables in the objective function. Such a penalty will be designated by $- M$ for maximization problems and $+ M$ for minimization problems, $M > 0$.
3. Use the artificial variable for the starting solution and then proceed with the simplex procedure until the optimal solution is obtained.

This technique has acquired the name " artificial variables " since these variables are fictitious and cannot have any physical meaning. In fact, these variables can be eliminated from the simplex tableau as soon as they become nonbasic.

To illustrate the above technique, consider the general linear programming problem with m_1 constraints of the type ($\leq$), m_2 constraints of the type ($=$),

---

[5] If the problem does not have a solution, at least one of the artificial variables will appear in the final solution at a positive level. See Section 3·6·5.

and m_3 ($= m - m_1 - m_2$) constraints of the type ($\geq$). Augmenting the problem with slack variables, this gives the standard form:

$$\text{maximize} \quad x_0 = \sum_{j=1}^{n} c_j x_j,$$

subject to

$$\sum_{j=1}^{n} a_{ij} x_j + S_i = b_i, \qquad i = 1, 2, \ldots, m_1,$$

$$\sum_{j=1}^{n} a_{ij} x_j \quad\;\; = b_i, \qquad i = m_1 + 1, \ldots, m_1 + m_2,$$

$$\sum_{j=1}^{n} a_{ij} x_j - S_i = b_i, \qquad i = m_1 + m_2 + 1, \ldots, m,$$

$$x_j \geq 0, \quad S_i \geq 0, \quad b_i \geq 0, \qquad \text{for all } i \text{ and } j.$$

Now, let R_i represent the artificial variables for the ith constraint, $i = m_1 + 1, \ldots, m$, the new problem becomes:

$$\text{maximize} \quad x_0 = \sum_{j=1}^{n} c_j x_j - \sum_{i=m_1+1}^{m} M R_i,$$

subject to

$$\sum_{j=1}^{n} a_{ij} x_j + S_i \quad\;\; = b_i, \qquad i = 1, 2, \ldots, m_1,$$

$$\sum_{j=1}^{n} a_{ij} x_j + R_i \quad\;\; = b_i, \qquad i = m_1 + 1, \ldots, m_1 + m_2,$$

$$\sum_{j=1}^{n} a_{ij} x_j - S_i + R_i = b_i, \qquad i = m_1 + m_2 + 1, \ldots, m,$$

$$R_i \geq 0, \quad S_i \geq 0, \quad x_j \geq 0, \qquad \text{for all } i \text{ and } j,$$

where M is a very large positive number, (10^6, say).

The starting basic feasible solution is thus given by,

$$S_i = b_i, \qquad i = 1, 2, \ldots, m_1,$$

$$R_i = b_i, \qquad i = m_1 + 1, m_1 + 2, \ldots, m.$$

▶ **Example 3·5-1**

Consider the problem:

$$\text{minimize} \quad x_0 = 2x_1 + x_2,$$

subject to

$$3x_1 + x_2 = 3,$$

$$4x_1 + 3x_2 \geq 6,$$

$$x_1 + 2x_2 \leq 3,$$

$$x_1 \geq 0, \quad x_2 \geq 0.$$

This problem, in addition to being an example of the application of artificial variables, will also illustrate the direct application of the optimality condition to a minimization case.

Adding the slack and artificial variables, the problem becomes:

Basic	x_0	x_1	x_2	S_2	R_1	R_2	S_3	R.H.S.
x_0	①	-2	-1	0	$-M$	$-M$	0	0
R_1	0	3	1	0	①	0	0	3
R_2	0	4	3	-1	0	①	0	6
S_3	0	1	2	0	0	0	①	3

with (R_1, R_2, S_3) as the starting solution. Notice that this tableau does not give the value of x_0 directly since the two basic variables R_1 and R_2 have nonzero coefficients in the objective equation. Notice also that the coefficients of the artificials in the *original* objective function is $+M$ since this is a minimization problem.

In order to apply the optimality condition, it is first necessary to express the x_0-equation in terms of the nonbasic variables only. Since R_1 and R_2 are in the starting basic solution, they are eliminated from the x_0-equation using the appropriate row operations. Thus the starting tableau becomes,

Basic	x_0	x_1	x_2	S_2	R_1	R_2	S_3	Solution
x_0	①	$-2+7M$	$-1+4M$	$-M$	0	0	0	$9M$
R_1	0	3	1	0	①	0	0	3
R_2	0	4	3	-1	0	①	0	6
S_3	0	1	2	0	0	0	①	3

Noting that this is a minimization problem, the entering variable is selected as the one having the largest positive coefficient in the x_0-equation (see the last paragraph of Section 3·3). Thus,

First Iteration: Introduce x_1 and drop R_1.

Basic	x_0	x_1	x_2	S_2	R_1	R_2	S_3	Solution
x_0	①	0	$\dfrac{-1+5M}{3}$	$-M$	$\dfrac{2-7M}{3}$	0	0	$2+2M$
x_1	0	①	$1/3$	0	$1/3$	0	0	1
R_2	0	0	$5/3$	-1	$-4/3$	①	0	2
S_3	0	0	$5/3$	0	$-1/3$	0	①	2

Second Iteration: Introduce x_2 and drop R_2.

Basic	x_0	x_1	x_2	S_2	R_1	R_2	S_3	Solution
x_0	①	0	0	$-1/5$	$2/5 - M$	$1/5 - M$	0	$12/5$
x_1	0	①	0	$1/5$	$3/5$	$-1/5$	0	$3/5$
x_2	0	0	①	$-3/5$	$-4/5$	$3/5$	0	$6/5$
S_3	0	0	0	1	1	-1	①	0

This gives the optimal solution, $x_1 = \frac{3}{5}$, $x_2 = \frac{6}{5}$ and $x_0 = \frac{12}{5}$. ◀

§ 3·6
Variants of the Simplex Method Applications

This section introduces some important cases which are often encountered in the simplex method applications. The vehicles of explanation here are numerical examples illustrating the different cases. These examples are depicted graphically to allow the reader to visualize the properties of the different cases.

The cases discussed here include:

1. degeneracy.
2. unbounded solutions.
3. alternative optimal solutions.
4. nonexisting feasible solutions.

§ 3·6·1
Degeneracy

It was indicated in discussing the feasibility condition of the simplex method (Section 3·3) that a tie may occur between two or more leaving variables, in which case any of these variables may be selected arbitrarily to leave the solution. The problem, however, occurs in the next iteration where the values of one or more basic variables become equal to zero. At this point, there is no assurance that the value of the objective function will improve (since the new solutions may remain degenerate). It is then possible, theoretically, that the simplex iterations may enter a loop which will repeat the same sequence of iterations without ever reaching the optimal solution. The problem is called "cycling" or "circling." Fortunately, this problem is seldom encountered in practice. Procedures exist, however, which will handle such cases,[6] but

---

[6] See the procedure introduced by A. Charnes, "Optimality and Degeneracy in Linear Programming," *Econometrica*, Vol. 20, 160–170, (1952).

because of the rare occurrence of the problem, such procedures will not be discussed here.

Aside from the cycling problem, a degeneracy case raises another question concerning the termination of the simplex iterations as soon as a degenerate solution appears (since the value of the objective function may not improve). The following two examples illustrate that it is essential to carry out the simplex iterations until the optimality condition is completely satisfied.

▶ **Example 3·6-1** (Degenerate Optimal Solution)

$$\text{Maximize} \quad x_0 = 3x_1 + 9x_2,$$

subject to

$$x_1 + 4x_2 \le 8,$$
$$x_1 + 2x_2 \le 4,$$
$$x_1 \ge 0, \quad x_2 \ge 0.$$

Starting Tableau:

Basic	x_0	x_1	x_2	S_1	S_2	Solution
x_0	①	-3	-9	0	0	0
S_1	0	1	4	①	0	8
S_2	0	1	2	0	①	4

First Iteration: Introduce x_2 and drop S_1.

Basic	x_0	x_1	x_2	S_1	S_2	Solution
x_0	①	$-3/4$	0	$9/4$	0	18
x_2	0	$1/4$	①	$1/4$	0	2
S_2	0	$1/2$	0	$-1/2$	①	0

Second Iteration: Introduce x_1 and drop S_2.

Basic	x_0	x_1	x_2	S_1	S_2	Solution
x_0	①	0	0	$3/2$	$3/2$	18
x_2	0	0	①	$1/2$	$-1/2$	2
x_1	0	①	0	-1	2	0

The optimal solution is $x_1 = 0$, $x_2 = 2$, and $x_0 = 18$.

Notice that the values of the variables in the first and second iterations are exactly the same. These are degenerate solutions since at both iterations one of the basic variables is zero. The question now is: if this is the case, why can't one stop at the iteration where the degenerate solution first appears? (This question is *partially* justified since the entering variables may be introduced at zero level and hence the value of x_0 may not improve). The answer here is that one cannot be sure that such degenerate solution when it first appears will coincide with the optimal solution. In other words, the problem may be *temporarily* degenerate at one of the intermediate iterations before it becomes nondegenerate again. This point will be illustrated by the next example.

The solution of the current example is shown graphically in Figure 3-2

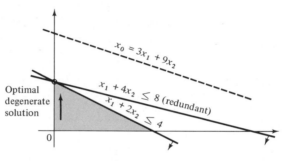

Figure 3–2

where the arrows indicate the changes in the basic solution at the different iterations of the simplex method. It is noted that a degenerate solution occurs when *more* than m ($= 2$, in this case) constraints pass through the same solution point. In this example, the constraints $x_1 \geq 0$, $x_1 + 4x_2 \leq 8$, and $x_1 + 2x \leq 4$ pass through the optimal (degenerate) solution point. ◄

▶ **Example 3·6-2**   (Temporary Degenerate Solution)

$$\text{Maximize} \quad x_0 = 2x_1 + x_2,$$

subject to

$$4x_1 + 3x_2 \leq 12,$$
$$4x_1 + x_2 \leq 8,$$
$$4x_1 - x_2 \leq 8,$$
$$x_1 \geq 0, \quad x_2 \geq 0.$$

Starting Tableau:

Basic	x_0	x_1	x_2	S_1	S_2	S_3	Solution
x_0	①	-2	-1	0	0	0	0
S_1	0	4	3	①	0	0	12
S_2	0	4	1	0	①	0	8
S_3	0	4	-1	0	0	①	8

First Iteration: Introduce x_1 and drop S_2.

Basic	x_0	x_1	x_2	S_1	S_2	S_3	Solution
x_0	①	0	$-1/2$	0	$1/2$	0	4
S_1	0	0	2	①	-1	0	4
x_1	0	①	$1/4$	0	$1/4$	0	2
S_3	0	0	-2	0	-1	①	0

Second Iteration: Introduce x_2 and drop S_1.

Basic	x_0	x_1	x_2	S_1	S_2	S_3	Solution
x_0	①	0	0	$1/4$	$1/4$	0	5
x_2	0	0	①	$1/2$	$-1/2$	0	2
x_1	0	①	0	$-1/8$	$3/8$	0	3/2
S_3	0	0	0	1	-2	①	4

The optimal solution is $x_1 = \frac{3}{2}$, $x_2 = 2$ and $x_0 = 5$.

Notice that the solution at the first iteration is degenerate while the optimal solution given by the second iteration is nondegenerate. The problem is thus temporarily degenerate. Observe that it is possible to get out of the degeneracy situation in this case because as x_2 is introduced in the second iteration its constraint coefficient corresponding to the zero basic value is negative ($= -2$). According to the feasibility condition, the corresponding ratio must be excluded from the comparison.

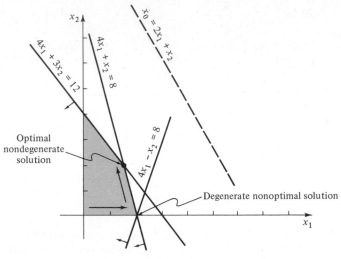

Figure 3–3

The graphical solution of this example is shown in Figure 3–3. A comparison with the simplex solution shows that the first iteration occurs at a degenerate point ($x_1 = 2$, $x_2 = 0$) while the second iteration moves the solution to the optimal nondegenerate point ($x_1 = \frac{3}{2}$, $x_2 = 2$). Notice that the slope of the objective function is a critical factor in deciding which solution is selected for the optimum. ◄

Examples 3·6-1,2 reveal the important result that in a degenerate situation, one should continue with the iterations until the objective equation satisfies the optimality condition.

§ 3·6·2
Unbounded Solutions

This case occurs when the solution space is unbounded such that the value of the objective function can be increased indefinitely. It is not necessary, however, that an unbounded solution space should yield an unbounded value for the objective function. The following two examples are designed to illustrate these points.

► **Example 3·6-3**   (Unbounded Optimal Solution)

$$\text{Maximize} \quad x_0 = 2x_1 + x_2,$$

subject to

$$x_1 - x_2 \leq 10,$$
$$2x_1 - x_2 \leq 40,$$
$$x_1 \geq 0, \quad x_2 \geq 0.$$

Starting Tableau:

Basic	x_0	x_1	x_2	S_1	S_2	Solution
x_0	①	-2	-1	0	0	0
S_1	0	1	-1	①	0	10
S_2	0	2	-1	0	①	40

It can be seen from the starting tableau that x_1 and x_2 are candidates for the entering variable. Since x_1 has the most negative coefficient, it should be selected as the entering variable. It is noticed, however, that if x_2 is selected as the entering variable its value (and hence the value of x_0) can be increased indefinitely without affecting the feasibility of the problem (since it has all negative coefficients in the constraints). It is thus concluded that the problem has no bounded solution. This also can be seen from the graphical solution of the problem which is given by Figure 3–4. In general, an unbounded solution

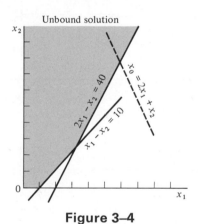

Figure 3–4

can be detected if, at any iteration, *any* of the candidates for the entering variable has all negative or zero coefficients in the constraints. ◄

▶ **Example 3·6-4** (Unbounded Solution Space but Bounded Optimal Solution)

$$\text{Maximize} \quad x_0 = 6x_1 - 2x_2,$$

subject to

$$2x_1 - x_2 \le 2,$$
$$x_1 \le 4,$$
$$x_1 \ge 0, \quad x_2 \ge 0.$$

Starting Tableau:

Basic	x_0	x_1	x_2	S_1	S_2	Solution
x_0	①	-6	2	0	0	0
S_1	0	2	-1	①	0	2
S_2	0	1	0	0	①	4

First Iteration: Introduce x_1 and drop S_1.

Basic	x_0	x_1	x_2	S_1	S_2	Solution
x_0	①	0	-1	3	0	6
x_1	0	①	$-1/2$	$1/2$	0	1
S_2	0	0	$1/2$	$-1/2$	①	3

Second Iteration: Introduce x_2 and drop S_2.

Basic	x_0	x_1	x_2	S_1	S_2	Solution
x_0	①	0	0	2	2	12
x_1	0	①	0	0	1	4
x_2	0	0	①	-1	2	6

The optimal solution is $x_1 = 4$, $x_2 = 6$, and $x_0 = 12$.

It is noticed from the starting tableau that the constraint coefficients of x_2 are negative or zero (-1 and 0). This is an immediate indication that the solution space is not bounded (see also the graphical presentation, Figure 3–5). The optimal solution is bounded, however, ($x_0 = 12$). Consequently, a problem may have unbounded solution space but still the optimal solution is bounded. ◄

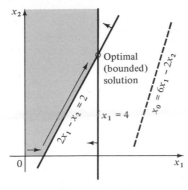

Figure 3–5

§ 3·6·4
Alternative Optimal Solutions

This case occurs when the objective function is parallel to a *binding* constraint (that is, a constraint which is satisfied in equality sense by the optimal solution). In such cases, the objective function may assume the same optimal value at more than one basic (feasible) solution. Such solutions are called *alternative basic* solutions. On the other hand, any weighted average of these optimal *basic* solutions should also yield an *alternative nonbasic* solution. This implies that the problem has an infinite number of solutions with each solution yielding the same value of the objective function. This situation is best illustrated by an example.

► **Example 3·6-5**   (Infinite Number of Solutions)

$$\text{Maximize} \quad x_0 = 4x_1 + 14x_2,$$

subject to

$$2x_1 + 7x_2 \le 21,$$
$$7x_1 + 2x_2 \le 21,$$
$$x_1 \ge 0, \quad x_2 \ge 0.$$

Figure 3–6 shows the graphical solution of the problem. It is seen that x_0 is parallel to the constraint $2x_1 + 7x_2 \le 21$ (which is a binding constraint) and hence the optimal (basic) solution is given by either of the two points indicated in the figure. Notice that any point on the line joining these two basic solutions will give an alternative nonbasic solution yielding the same value x_0. The question now is: how can one detect such situations from the simplex procedure? The answer is shown using the simplex solution of the same example.

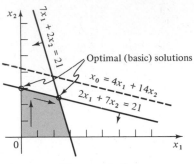

Figure 3–6

Starting Tableau:

Basic	x_0	x_1	x_2	S_1	S_2	Solution
x_0	①	-4	-14	0	0	0
S_1	0	2	7	①	0	21
S_2	0	7	2	0	①	21

First Iteration: Introduce x_2 and drop S_1.

Basic	x_0	x_1	x_2	S_1	S_2	Solution
x_0	①	0	0	2	0	42
x_2	0	2/7	①	1/7	0	3
S_2	0	45/7	0	$-2/7$	①	15

This is the optimal solution and is given by $x_1 = 0$, $x_2 = 3$ and $x_0 = 42$. However, inspection of the above tableau (first iteration) shows that the *nonbasic* variable x_1 has a zero coefficient in the x_0-equation. This is an indication that an alternative solution exists. The alternative solution is basic since x_1 can be made basic. Thus,

Second Iteration: Introduce x_1 and drop S_2.

Basic	x_0	x_1	x_2	S_1	S_2	Solution
x_0	①	0	0	2	0	42
x_2	0	0	①	7/45	−2/45	7/3
x_1	0	①	0	−2/45	7/45	7/3

The new optimal solution gives $x_1 = \frac{7}{3}$, $x_2 = \frac{7}{3}$ and $x_0 = 42$. Obviously the value of x_0 has not changed ($= 42$) since x_1 has zero coefficient in the x_0-equation of the first iteration.

Now, given the two alternative basic solutions, $x_1 = 0$, $x_2 = 3$, and $x_1 = x_2 = \frac{1}{3}$, the infinite number of *nonbasic* solutions can be obtained by realizing that any weighted average of these two basic solutions is also an alternative solution. Mathematically, the family of alternative (optimal) solutions is given by

$$\tilde{x}_1 = \lambda(0) + (1 - \lambda)(7/3) \quad \text{and} \quad \tilde{x}_2 = \lambda(3) + (1 - \lambda)(7/3),$$

or

$$\tilde{x}_1 = \tfrac{7}{3}(1 - \lambda) \quad \text{and} \quad \tilde{x}_2 = \tfrac{1}{3}(7 + 2\lambda),$$

where $0 \le \lambda \le 1$. It can be verified that the solution $(\tilde{x}_1, \tilde{x}_2)$ will always yield the same value of x_0 for $0 \le \lambda \le 1$.

In general, suppose that the problem has p alternative (optimal) *basic* solutions $(x_1^{(i)}, x_2^{(i)}, \ldots, x_m^{(i)})$, $i = 1, 2, \ldots, p$; then the family of alternative *nonbasic* solutions is given by $(\tilde{x}_1, \tilde{x}_2, \ldots, \tilde{x}_m)$, where

$$\tilde{x}_1 = \sum_{i=1}^{p} \lambda_i x_1^{(i)},$$

$$\tilde{x}_2 = \sum_{i=1}^{p} \lambda_i x_2^{(i)},$$

$$\vdots$$

$$\tilde{x}_m = \sum_{i=1}^{p} \lambda_i x_m^{(i)},$$

where

$$1 > \lambda_i \ge 0,$$

and

$$\sum_{i=1}^{p} \lambda_i = 1. \quad \blacktriangleleft$$

§ 3·6·5
Nonexisting Feasible Solutions

This case occurs when the problem is such that no one point can be satisfied by *all* the constraints. In this case it is said that the solution space is empty and that the problem does not have a feasible solution. The following example shows how such a situation can be detected by the simplex method.

▶ **Example 3·6-6**   (Problems with No Feasible Solution)

$$\text{Maximize} \quad x_0 = 3x_1 + 2x_2$$

subject to

$$2x_1 + x_2 \leq 2,$$
$$3x_1 + 4x_2 \geq 12,$$
$$x_1 \geq 0, \quad x_2 \geq 0.$$

Starting Tableau:

Basic	x_0	x_1	x_2	S_2	S_1	R_1	Solution
x_0	(1)	$-3 - 3M$	$-2 - 4M$	M	0	0	$-12M$
S_1	0	2	1	0	(1)	0	2
R_1	0	3	4	-1	0	(1)	12

First Iteration: Introduce x_2 and drop S_1.

Basic	x_0	x_1	x_2	S_2	S_1	R_1	Solution
x_0	(1)	$1 + 5M$	0	M	$2 + 4M$	0	$4 - 4M$
x_2	0	2	(1)	0	1	0	2
R_1	0	-5	0	-1	-4	(1)	4

According to the optimality condition, this solution is optimal. Notice, however, that the optimal (basic) solution includes the artificial variable R_1 at a *positive* level ($= 4$). This immediately indicates that the problem has no feasible solution. Notice also that a positive value of R_1 means that the second constraint is not satisfied and hence the above solution actually represents a different problem. It must be stated that when an artificial variable appears in the optimal basis at *zero* level, this would mean that the corresponding constraint is not violated and hence the problem has a feasible solution.

The graphical solution of the above example is illustrated in Figure 3–7.

This shows that the problem has no feasible solution space. Comparison with the algebraic procedure of the simplex method reveals that, even in such cases, there is nothing that would stop the simplex method from obtaining a solution. This solution may be called "pseudo-optimal" since, as clear from Figure 3–7, it does not satisfy all the constraints but it satisfies the optimality condition of the simplex method. ◄

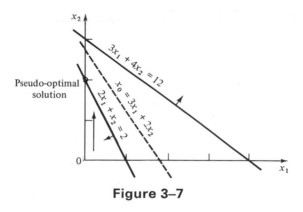

Figure 3–7

§ 3·6·5·1
The Two-phase Method

Although the M-technique can always be used to check for the existence of a feasible solution, it may be computationally inconvenient because of the manipulation of the constant, M. Another method is thus developed which, although based on the use of artificial variables, eliminates the constant M from the calculations. This method consists of two phases:

Phase I.   Formulate a new problem by replacing the original objective function by the sum of the artificial variables while keeping the same constraints as in the original problem. The new objective function is then minimized subject to the indicated constraints. If the problem has a feasible space, the minimum value of the *new* objective function will be zero (which indicates that all artificial variables are equal to zero). Otherwise, if the minimum value is greater than zero, the problem is terminated with the information that no feasible solution exists.

Phase II.   If the solution of Phase I indicates that the problem has a feasible space, use the last basic feasible solution obtained from Phase I as a starting solution for the original problem. In this case the original objective function must be expressed in terms of the nonbasic variables using the usual row operations procedure. It should be noted that in Phase II, the artificial variables are removed from the problem except when they appear at *zero level* in the optimal *basic* solution to Phase I. In this case, the corresponding artificial variables must be carried out into the starting solution of Phase II.

▶ **Example 3·6-7**

Consider the same problem in Example 3·6-6.

Phase I. Since there is only one artificial variable, R_1, the new objective function is given by $x_0 = R_1$. Thus, in Phase I the problem is:

$$\text{minimize} \quad r_0 = R_1,$$

subject to

$$2x_1 + x_2 + S_1 = 2,$$
$$3x_1 + 4x_2 - S_2 + R_1 = 12,$$
$$x_1 \geq 0, \quad x_2 \geq 0, \quad S_1 \geq 0, \quad S_2 \geq 0, \quad R_1 \geq 0.$$

The problem is written in tabular form as,

Basic	r_0	x_1	x_2	S_2	S_1	R_1	R.H.S.
r_0	①	0	0	0	0	−1	0
S_1	0	2	1	0	①	0	2
R_1	0	3	4	−1	0	①	12

and the starting tableau is given by

Basic	r_0	x_1	x_2	S_2	S_1	R_1	Solution
r_0	①	3	4	−1	0	0	12
S_1	0	2	1	0	①	0	2
R_1	0	3	4	−1	0	①	12

Thus, the first iteration is

Basic	r_0	x_1	x_2	S_2	S_1	R_1	Solution
r_0	①	−5	0	−1	−4	0	4
x_2	0	2	①	0	1	0	2
R_1	0	−5	0	−1	−4	①	4

which is optimal (minimization). Since the value of r_0 is 4 (> 0), it follows that the problem has no feasible solution. Notice that the value of r_0 is equal to the value of R_1. This is the same result as in Example 3·6-6. It then follows that Phase II cannot be carried out. ◄

▶ **Example 3·6-8**

In Example 3·6-7, the problem has no feasible space and hence Phase II is not used. This example is constructed to show how Phase II may be carried out in case the problem has a feasible space.

Consider the problem:

$$\text{maximize} \quad x_0 = x_1 + 2x_2 + x_3 + 3x_4,$$

subject to

$$x_1 + 2x_2 + x_3 + 3x_4 \geq 400,$$
$$x_1 + x_2 + x_3 + x_4 \leq 200,$$
$$x_1 + 2x_2 \leq 100,$$
$$x_3 + 2x_4 \leq 200,$$
$$x_1 \geq 0, \quad x_2 \geq 0, \quad x_3 \geq 0, \quad x_4 \geq 0.$$

First consider Phase I. The initial tableau may be written as

Basic	r_0	x_1	x_2	x_3	x_4	S_1	R_1	S_2	S_3	S_4	R.H.S.
r_0	①	0	0	0	0	0	-1	0	0	0	0
R_1	0	1	2	1	3	-1	①	0	0	0	400
S_2	0	1	1	1	1	0	0	①	0	0	200
S_3	0	1	2	0	0	0	0	0	①	0	100
S_4	0	0	0	1	2	0	0	0	0	①	200

After four iterations the optimal solution to this phase is given by

Basic	r_0	x_1	x_2	x_3	x_4	S_1	R_1	S_2	S_3	S_4	Solution
r_0	①	0	0	$-1/2$	0	0	0	0	-1	$-3/2$	0
x_2	0	1/2	①	0	0	0	0	0	1/2	0	50
S_2	0	1/2	0	1/2	0	0	0	①	$-1/2$	$-1/2$	50
S_1	0	0	0	1/2	0	①	-1	0	1	3/2	0
x_4	0	0	0	1/2	①	0	0	0	0	1/2	100

Since optimal $r_0 = 0$. this means that the problem has a feasible space. The last tableau can now be used to start Phase II. The artificial variable R_1 is eliminated since it is nonbasic. The initial tableau for Phase II is obtained by replacing the r_0-equation by the original x_0-equation. This yields,

Basic	x_0	x_1	x_2	x_3	x_4	S_1	S_2	S_3	S_4	R.H.S.
x_0	①	-1	-2	-1	-3	0	0	0	0	0
x_2										
S_2										
S_1										
x_4										

with all the remaining elements of the tableau being the same as in the optimal tableau of Phase I.

Since x_2 and x_4 are in the starting solution of Phase II, zero-coefficients must be created for them in the starting tableau of Phase II. This yields:

Basic	x_0	x_1	x_2	x_3	x_4	S_1	S_2	S_3	S_4	Solution
x_0	①	0	0	1/2	0	0	0	1	3/2	400
x_2	0	1/2	①	0	0	0	0	1/2	0	50
S_2	0	1/2	0	1/2	0	0	①	$-1/2$	$-1/2$	50
S_1	0	0	0	1/2	0	①	0	1	3/2	0
x_4	0	0	0	1/2	①	0	0	0	1/2	100

The starting tableau happens to coincide with the optimal tableau of Phase II since all the coefficients in the x_0-equation are nonnegative. Naturally, if any of these coefficients were negative, then the regular simplex iterations must be carried out until the optimum is achieved. ◄

It should be noted that, in general, the application of Phase II is straightforward. Complications can arise only if the optimal solution to Phase I includes any artificial variables (which naturally must be equal to zero if Phase II is to be carried out). In this case, the system includes redundant constraints and the artificial variables must be carried out through Phase II computations.

Thus, provisions must be made so that these variables never appear at positive levels at any iteration of Phase II. The complete procedure for this case is somewhat involved and the reader is referred to Dantzig ([1], Section 5·2) for the details.

SELECTED REFERENCES

1. DANTZIG, G. B., *Linear Programming and Extensions*, Princeton, N.J.: Princeton University Press, 1963.
2. GASS, S., *Linear Programming*, New York: McGraw-Hill, (Second Edition), 1964.
3. VAJDA, S., *Mathematical Programming*, Reading, Massachusetts: Addison-Wesley, 1961.

PROBLEMS

□ **3-1** Consider the following linear programming problem.

$$\text{Maximize} \quad x_0 = 3x_1 + 9x_2 + 5x_3 + 4x_4,$$

subject to

$$x_1 + 4x_2 + 5x_3 + 8x_4 \le 8,$$
$$x_1 + 2x_2 + 6x_3 + 4x_4 \le 4,$$
$$x_1 \ge 0, \quad x_2 \ge 0, \quad x_3 \ge 0, \quad x_4 \ge 0.$$

(a) What is the maximum number of possible basic solutions?
(b) Identify all the basic feasible solutions.
(c) Identify all the nondegenerate basic feasible solutions.
(d) Identify all the degenerate basic feasible solutions.
(e) Find the optimal basic feasible solution of the problem by direct substitution of the basic feasible solutions in the objective function.

□ **3-2** Solve Problem 3-1 using the simplex method. Compare this method with the enumeration procedure followed in that problem.

□ **3-3** Solve the following problem by the simplex method.

$$\text{Maximize} \quad x_0 = 2x_1 + x_2 - 3x_3 + 5x_4,$$

subject to

$$x_1 + 7x_2 + 3x_3 + 7x_4 \le 46,$$
$$3x_1 - x_2 + x_3 + 2x_4 \le 8,$$
$$2x_1 + 3x_2 - x_3 + x_4 \le 10,$$
$$x_1 \ge 0, \quad x_2 \ge 0, \quad x_3 \ge 0, \quad x_4 \ge 0.$$

□ **3-4** In Example 3·2-1, any of the basic feasible solutions listed in Table 3–1 may be used as a starting solution. Solve the same problem using the starting solution (x_2, x_3).

□ **3-5** Solve the following minimization problem.

$$\text{Minimize} \quad x_0 = x_1 - 3x_2 - 2x_3,$$

subject to

$$3x_1 - x_2 + 2x_3 \le 7,$$
$$-2x_1 + 4x_2 \quad\quad \le 12,$$
$$-4x_1 + 3x_2 + 8x_3 \le 10,$$
$$x_1 \ge 0, \quad x_2 \ge 0, \quad x_3 \ge 0.$$

What are the changes in the iterations if the objective function is first converted into the maximization form and the maximization optimality condition is used in solving the problem?

□ **3-6** Solve the following using the M-technique.

$$\text{(a) Maximize} \quad x_0 = 2x_1 + 3x_2 - 5x_3,$$

subject to

$$x_1 + x_2 + x_3 = 7,$$
$$2x_1 - 5x_2 + x_3 \ge 10,$$
$$x_1 \ge 0, \quad x_2 \ge 0, \quad x_3 \ge 0.$$

$$\text{(b) Minimize} \quad x_0 = 5x_1 - 6x_2 - 7x_3,$$

subject to

$$x_1 + 5x_2 - 3x_3 \ge 15,$$
$$5x_1 - 6x_2 + 10x_3 \le 20,$$
$$x_1 + x_2 + x_3 = 5,$$
$$x_1 \ge 0, \quad x_2 \ge 0, \quad x_3 \ge 0.$$

□ **3-7** Consider the problem:

$$\text{maximize} \quad x_0 = x_1 + 5x_2 + 3x_3,$$

subject to

$$x_1 + 2x_2 + x_3 = 3,$$
$$2x_1 - x_2 \quad\quad = 4,$$

with all x_j being nonnegative. Using x_3 *and* an artificial variable for the starting solution, find the optimum solution.

☐ **3-8** Consider the problem:

$$\text{maximize} \quad x_0 = 2x_1 + 4x_2 + 4x_3 - 3x_4,$$

subject to

$$x_1 + x_2 + x_3 \quad = 4,$$
$$x_1 + 4x_2 \quad + x_4 = 8,$$

with all x_j being nonnegative. Using (x_3, x_4) as the starting basic solution, find the optimum solution.

☐ **3-9** Solve the trim-loss problem of Example 2·2-4 using the M-technique. Resolve the same problem using the objective function defined in Problem 2-9.

☐ **3-10** Solve the caterer problem of Example 2·2-3 using the M-technique.

☐ **3-11** Consider the problem:

$$\text{maximize} \quad x_0 = 6x_1 + 5x_2,$$

subject to

$$x_1 + x_2 \le 4,$$
$$-x_1 \ge 2,$$
$$x_1 \le 0,$$
$$x_2 \ge 0,$$

(Notice that x_1 is nonpositive.) Devise two procedures using the simplex method to solve this problem. Check the solution by solving the problem graphically.

☐ **3-12** The following is the initial simplex tableau for a maximization problem with all ($\le$) constraints.

Basic	x_0	x_1	x_2	x_3	x_4	x_5	S_1	S_2	S_3	Solution
x_0	①	-1	3	7	-5	8	0	0	0	0
S_1	0	0	0	1	-4	1	①	0	0	10
S_2	0	-5	1	0	4	5	0	①	0	5
S_3	0	-3	0	6	1	9	0	0	①	5

Find the optimal solution.

☐ **3-13** Show that the alternative nonbasic solutions $(\tilde{x}_1, \tilde{x}_2)$ for Example 3·6-5 yield the same value of x_0 ($= 42$). Generalize the result to the case where there are m alternative basic solutions.

☐ **3-14** Consider the problem:

$$\text{maximize} \quad x_0 = x_1 + 2x_2 + 3x_3,$$

subject to

$$x_1 + 2x_2 + 3x_3 \leq 10,$$
$$x_1 + x_2 \leq 5,$$
$$x_1 \leq 1,$$
$$x_1 \geq 0, \quad x_2 \geq 0, \quad x_3 \geq 0.$$

Find all the alternative optimal basic solutions of the problem then write a general expression for all the *non*basic optimal solutions.

☐ **3-15** Consider the following linear programming problem:

$$\text{maximize} \quad x_0 = 2x_1 - x_2 + 3x_3,$$

subject to

$$x_1 - x_2 + 5x_3 \leq 10,$$
$$2x_1 - x_2 + 3x_3 \leq 40,$$
$$x_1 \geq 0, \quad x_2 \geq 0, \quad x_3 \geq 0.$$

Show that the problem has alternative solutions which are all *non*basic. What could one conclude concerning the solution space and the objective function? Show that for the alternative solutions, the values of the optimal basic variables can be increased indefinitely while the value of x_0 remains constant.

☐ **3-16** Construct a graphical example in the two dimensional space which will illustrate the ideas introduced in Problem 3-15 and then verify the given results.

☐ **3-17** Give the optimal solution of the following problem by inspection and justify your method of solution in terms of the simplex method procedure.

$$\text{Maximize} \quad x_0 = 5x_1 - 6x_2 + 3x_3 - 5x_4 + 12x_5,$$

subject to

$$x_1 + 3x_2 + 5x_3 + 6x_4 + 3x_5 \leq 90,$$
$$x_1 \geq 0, \quad x_2 \geq 0, \quad x_3 \geq 0, \quad x_4 \geq 0, \quad x_5 \geq 0.$$

☐ **3-18** Consider the problem:

$$\text{maximize} \quad x_0 = 3x_1 + x_2,$$

subject to

$$x_1 + 2x_2 \leq 5,$$
$$x_1 + x_2 - x_3 \leq 2,$$
$$7x_1 + 3x_2 - 5x_3 \leq 20,$$

with all $x_i \geq 0$. Show that the optimal solution is degenerate and that there exist alternative solutions that are all nonbasic.

☐ **3-19** In which direction is the solution space of the following problem unbounded?

$$\text{Maximize} \quad x_0 = 20x_1 + 10x_2 + x_3,$$

subject to

$$3x_1 - 3x_2 + 5x_3 \leq 50,$$
$$x_1 \qquad + \; x_3 \leq 10,$$
$$x_1 - \; x_2 + 4x_3 \leq 20,$$
$$x_1 \geq 0, \quad x_2 \geq 0, \quad x_3 \geq 0.$$

Without any further computations, what could one conclude concerning the optimal solution to the problem?

☐ **3-20** Consider the problem:

$$\text{maximize} \quad x_0 = 3x_1 + 2x_2 + 3x_3,$$

subject to

$$2x_1 + \; x_2 + \; x_3 \leq 2,$$
$$3x_1 + 4x_2 + 2x_3 \geq 8,$$

with all $x_j \geq 0$. Using the M-technique, show that the optimal solution includes an artificial basic variable at *zero* level. Hence conclude that a feasible optimal solution exists.

☐ **3-21** In the two-phase method, what is the significance of the optimal solution for Phase I? Why is it necessary to have a zero value for the new objective function of Phase I in order for the problem to have a feasible solution space? What is the interpretation when the value of this objective is positive?

☐ **3-22** Solve Problem 3-6 using the two-phase method.

CHAPTER 4

The Dual Problem and Postoptimality Analysis

§ 4·1
Introduction

Every linear programming problem has a twin problem associated with it. One problem is called "primal" while the other is called "dual." The two problems possess very closely related properties so that the *optimal* solution of one problem can yield complete information about the *optimal* solution of the other problem.

In this chapter, illustrative examples are used to point out the relationships between the two problems. In certain cases these relationships may prove useful in reducing the computational effort associated with solving linear programming problems. More important will be the use of these relationships to obtain additional information about the variations in the optimal solution due to certain changes in the coefficients and the formulation of the problem. This is usually referred to as *postoptimality* or *sensitivity* analysis.

§ 4·2
Definition of the Dual Problem

This section defines the dual problem when its primal is given in one of two forms:

1. canonical form.
2. standard form.

These two forms were defined in Section 2·3. The dual problem for each case will be considered separately.

74

§ 4·2·1
Dual Problem When Primal is in Canonical Form

Consider the following linear programming problem in canonical form.

$$\text{Maximize} \quad x_0 = \sum_{j=1}^{n} c_j x_j,$$

subject to

$$\sum_{j=1}^{n} a_{ij} x_j \le b_i, \qquad i = 1, 2, \ldots, m,$$

$$x_j \ge 0, \qquad j = 1, 2, \ldots, n.$$

It was shown in Section 2·3 that any linear programming problem can be put in this form. If this problem is referred to as primal, its associated dual will then be given by:

$$\text{minimize} \quad y_0 = \sum_{i=1}^{m} b_i y_i,$$

subject to

$$\sum_{i=1}^{m} a_{ij} y_i \ge c_j, \qquad j = 1, 2, \ldots, n,$$

$$y_i \ge 0, \qquad i = 1, 2, \ldots, m,$$

where $y_1, y_2, \ldots, y_m$ are the dual variables.

The dual problem (in canonical form) is constructed from the primal problem (and *vice versa*) as follows:

    1. Each constraint in one problem corresponds to a variable in the other problem.

    2. The elements of the right-hand side of the constraints in one problem are equal to the respective coefficients of the objective function in the other problem.

    3. One problem seeks maximization and the other seeks minimization.

    4. The maximization problem has ($\le$) constraints and the minimization problem has ($\ge$) constraints.

    5. The variables in both problems are nonnegative.

The construction of the primal-dual problems can be summarized in the following form due to A. Tucker.

a_{11}	a_{12}	$\cdots$	a_{1n}	$\leq$	b_1	y_1	≥ 0
a_{21}	a_{22}	$\cdots$	a_{2n}	$\leq$	b_2	y_2	≥ 0
$\vdots$	$\vdots$		$\vdots$	$\vdots$	$\vdots$	$\vdots$	$\vdots$
a_{ml}	a_{m2}	$\cdots$	a_{mn}	$\leq$	b_m	y_m	≥ 0
$\geq$	$\geq$	$\cdots$	$\geq$				Minimize
c_1	c_2	$\cdots$	c_n				y_0
				Maximize			
x_1	x_2	$\cdots$	x_n	x_0			

$$\geq 0 \qquad \geq 0 \qquad \cdots \qquad \geq 0$$

It is clear from the symmetry of the two problems that the dual of the dual is the primal.

▶ **Example 4·2-1**

Consider the problem:

$$\text{maximize} \quad x_0 = 5x_1 + 6x_2,$$

subject to

$$x_1 + 9x_2 \leq 60,$$
$$2x_1 + 3x_2 \leq 45,$$
$$5x_1 - 2x_2 \leq 20,$$
$$x_2 \leq 30,$$
$$x_1 \geq 0, \quad x_2 \geq 0.$$

Let y_1, y_2, y_3, and y_4 be the corresponding dual variables, then the dual problem is given by:

$$\text{minimize} \quad y_0 = 60y_1 + 45y_2 + 20y_3 + 30y_4,$$

subject to

$$y_1 + 2y_2 + 5y_3 \qquad \geq 5,$$
$$9y_1 + 3y_2 - 2y_3 + y_4 \geq 6,$$
$$y_1 \geq 0, \quad y_2 \geq 0, \quad y_3 \geq 0, \quad y_4 \geq 0.$$

Notice that the dual problem has a fewer number of constraints in this case. Since as proposed in the introduction (Section 4·1), the optimal solution of one problem can be obtained from the optimal solution of the other (see Section 4·3), it is evident that it is computationally more efficient to solve the dual in this case. This follows from the fact that the computational difficulty in the linear programming problem is mainly associated with the number of constraints rather than the number of variables. This point indicates one of the advantages of the dual problem. ◀

§ 4·2·2
Dual Problem When Primal is in Standard Form

In the standard form, all constraints are equations ($=$). It is now shown that an equality constraint in the primal (dual) corresponds to an unconstrained variable in the dual (primal). Consider the problem:

$$\text{maximize} \quad x_0 = c_1 x_1 + c_2 x_2,$$

subject to

$$a_{11} x_1 + a_{12} x_2 = b_1,$$
$$a_{21} x_1 + a_{22} x_2 \leq b_2,$$
$$x_1 \geq 0, \quad x_2 \geq 0.$$

In the canonical form, the first constraint is replaced by

$$a_{11} x_1 + a_{12} x_2 \leq b_1,$$

and

$$-a_{11} x_1 - a_{12} x_2 \leq -b_1.$$

Let y_1^+, y_1^-, and y_2 be the dual variables corresponding to the canonical form. Thus the dual problem is:

$$\text{minimize} \quad y_0 = b_1(y_1^+ - y_1^-) + b_2 y_2,$$

subject to

$$a_{11}(y_1^+ - y_1^-) + a_{21} y_2 \geq c_1,$$
$$a_{12}(y_1^+ - y_1^-) + a_{22} y_2 \geq c_2,$$
$$y_1^+ \geq 0, \quad y_1^- \geq 0, \quad y_2 \geq 0.$$

It is noted that the term $(y_1^+ - y_1^-)$ is repeated in the objective function and all the constraints. This will always be the case whenever there is an equality constraint in the primal. Thus letting $y_1 = y_1^+ - y_1^-$, the new variable, y_1, which is the difference between two nonnegative variables, becomes unrestricted in sign and the dual problem reduces to:

$$\text{minimize} \quad y_0 = b_1 y_1 + b_2 y_2,$$

subject to

$$a_{11} y_1 + a_{21} y_2 \geq c_1,$$
$$a_{12} y_1 + a_{22} y_2 \geq c_2,$$
$$y_1 \text{ unrestricted in sign,}$$
$$y_2 \geq 0.$$

The new dual form has as many variables as the number of constraints in the primal. It clearly can be obtained directly from the original form using the same procedure as in the canonical form. The only difference is that the dual variable corresponding to an equality constraint must be unrestricted in sign. Conversely, when a primal variable is unrestricted in sign, its dual constraint must be in equation form.

It follows from the above discussion that the dual variables corresponding to a primal in the standard form must all be unrestricted in sign. This condition, however, will be satisfied only for the primal constraints that were *initially* in equation form since the dual problem should be the same for both the canonical and standard forms (see Example 4·2-2).

In general, given the primal problem in the standard form:

$$\text{maximize} \quad x_0 = \sum_{j=1}^{n} c_j x_j,$$

subject to

$$\sum_{j=1}^{n} a_{ij} x_j = b_i, \qquad i = 1, 2, \ldots, m,$$
$$x_j \geq 0, \qquad j = 1, 2, \ldots, n.$$

The dual becomes,

$$\text{minimize} \quad y_0 = \sum_{i=1}^{m} b_i y_i,$$

subject to

$$\sum_{i=1}^{m} a_{ij} y_i \geq c_j, \qquad j = 1, 2, \ldots, n,$$
$$y_i \text{ are unrestricted in signs for all } i.$$

On the other hand, consider the primal problem:

$$\text{maximize} \quad x_0 = \sum_{j=1}^{n} c_j x_j,$$

subject to

$$\sum_{j=1}^{n} a_{ij} x_j \le b_i, \qquad i = 1, 2, \ldots, m,$$

where all x_j are unrestricted in sign. The dual problem is given by:

$$\text{minimize} \quad y_0 = \sum_{i=1}^{m} b_i y_i,$$

subject to

$$\sum_{i=1}^{m} a_{ij} y_i = c_j, \qquad j = 1, 2, \ldots, n,$$

$$y_i \ge 0, \qquad i = 1, 2, \ldots, m.$$

Notice that the dual problem is in the standard form in this case.

▶ **Example 4·2-2**

Consider the problem:

$$\text{maximize} \quad x_0 = 5x_1 + 12x_2 + 4x_3,$$

subject to

$$x_1 + 2x_2 + x_3 \le 5,$$
$$2x_1 - x_2 + 3x_3 = 2,$$
$$x_1 \ge 0, \quad x_2 \ge 0, \quad x_3 \ge 0,$$

The standard form of this problem is:

$$\text{maximize} \quad x_0 = 5x_1 + 12x_2 + 4x_3 + 0S_1,$$

subject to

$$x_1 + 2x_2 + x_3 + S_1 = 5,$$
$$2x_1 - x_2 + 3x_3 + 0S_1 = 2,$$
$$x_1 \ge 0, \quad x_2 \ge 0, \quad x_3 \ge 0, \quad S_1 \ge 0.$$

The dual is then given by:

$$\text{minimize} \quad y_0 = 5y_1 + 2y_2,$$

subject to

$$y_1 + 2y_2 \ge 5,$$
$$2y_1 - y_2 \ge 12,$$
$$y_1 + 3y_2 \ge 4,$$
$$y_1 \ge 0,$$

y_2 unrestricted in sign.

Notice that the last constraint, $y_1 \geq 0$, corresponds to S_1 in the primal. This same result could have been obtained from the original form of the problem where y_1 corresponds to ($\leq$) constraint and y_2 corresponds to ($=$) constraint. ◀

Although, as mentioned above, the canonical and standard forms of a primal problem always yield equivalent duals, the standard form is more convenient to handle, particularly when the primal problem involves all three types of constraints. The standard form will be especially useful in dealing with the postoptimality problem. (See Section 4·6.) It also offers a direct contribution to the development of an efficient computational approach for the transportation problem which will be discussed in Chapter 5.

§ 4·3
The Optimal Dual Solution in the Simplex Tableau

In this section it is shown that the *optimal* dual solution can be obtained directly from the *optimal* primal (simplex) tableau. Also, an important economic interpretation of the dual variables is given in terms of the contribution of the scarce resources to the objective function.

§ 4·3·1
Relationship Between the Objective Values of the Primal and Dual

Property.   Assume the primal-dual problems are in either the canonical or standard forms and the two problems have finite optimal solutions. Let x_0 and y_0 be the values of the objective function in the maximization and minimization problems as defined in Section 4·2. Then for any two *feasible* (not necessarily basic) solutions of the primal and the dual, $x_0 \leq y_0$. Moreover, at the optimal solutions of both problems, min $y_0 =$ max x_0.

This property indicates that for any two feasible solutions, the value of y_0 (in the minimization problem) acts as an upper bound on the value of x_0 (in the maximization problem). When the *optimal* solution of both problems is reached, the corresponding values of x_0 and y_0 become equal.

The proof of the first part is straightforward. From the constraints of the primal (maximization) problem defined in Section 4·2, one has

$$\sum_{j=1}^{n} a_{ij} x_j \leq b_i, \qquad i = 1, 2, \ldots, m.$$

Multiplying both sides by y_i (≥ 0) and then summing over i, thus,

$$\sum_{i=1}^{m} y_i \left(\sum_{j=1}^{n} a_{ij} x_j \right) \leq \sum_{i=1}^{m} b_i y_i = y_0 \qquad\qquad \text{(i)}$$

Notice that the right-hand side of (i) defines y_0. Now consider the constraints of the dual (minimization) problem. These are given by

$$\sum_{i=1}^{m} a_{ij} y_i \geq c_j, \qquad j = 1, 2, \ldots, n.$$

Multiplying both sides by x_j (≥ 0) and then summing over j, thus

$$\sum_{j=1}^{n} x_j \left(\sum_{i=1}^{m} a_{ij} y_i \right) \geq \sum_{j=1}^{n} c_j x_j = x_0 \tag{ii}$$

Again notice that the right-hand side of (ii) defines x_0.

From (i) and (ii) above, since the left-hand sides are identical, it follows that $x_0 \leq y_0$. The same result can be verified if either the dual or the primal is in standard form.

To illustrate the given property, consider the primal and dual problems of Example 4·2-2. It is easily seen that ($x_1 = 1$, $x_2 = 1$, $x_3 = 1/3$, and $y_1 = 7$, $y_2 = 2$) are feasible solutions of the primal and dual problems, respectively. This yields $x_0 = 18\frac{1}{3}$ and $y_0 = 39$ which shows that $x_0 < y_0$. This result reveals the immediate information that the *optimal* value of the objective function lies between $18\frac{1}{3}$ and 39.

The second point of the property is now illustrated by applying the regular simplex method to the primal and dual problems of Example 4·2-2. This example is solved in detail since its results will be used throughout the remainder of this chapter.

Thus for the primal problem, the starting tableau is obtained from the standard form and after expressing the x_0-equation in terms of the nonbasic variables this gives:

Basic	x_0	x_1	x_2	x_3	S_1	R_1	Solution
x_0	①	$-5 - 2M$	$-12 + M$	$-4 - 3M$	0	0	$-2M$
S_1	0	1	2	1	①	0	5
R_1	0	2	-1	3	0	①	2

where R_1 is an artificial variable (see Section 3·5).

First Iteration: Introduce x_3 and drop R_1.

Basic	x_0	x_1	x_2	x_3	S_1	R_1	Solution
x_0	①	$-7/3$	$-40/3$	0	0	$4/3 + M$	$8/3$
S_1	0	$1/3$	$7/3$	0	①	$-1/3$	$13/3$
x_3	0	$2/3$	$-1/3$	①	0	$1/3$	$2/3$

Second Iteration: Introduce x_2 and drop S_1.

Basic	x_0	x_1	x_2	x_3	S_1	R_1	Solution
x_0	①	$-3/7$	0	0	$40/7$	$-4/7 + M$	$192/7$
x_2	0	$1/7$	①	0	$3/7$	$-1/7$	$13/7$
x_3	0	$5/7$	0	①	$1/7$	$2/7$	$9/7$

Third Iteration: Introduce x_1 and drop x_3.

Basic	x_0	x_1	x_2	x_3	S_1	R_1	Solution
x_0	①	0	0	$3/5$	$29/5$	$-2/5 + M$	$28\frac{1}{5}$
x_2	0	0	①	$-1/5$	$2/5$	$-1/5$	$8/5$
x_1	0	①	0	$7/5$	$1/5$	$2/5$	$9/5$

which is the optimal solution with $x_1 = 9/5$, $x_2 = 8/5$, $x_3 = 0$, and $x_0 = 28\frac{1}{5}$.

The dual problem will now be solved. Since y_2 is unrestricted in sign, it is replaced by $y_2^+ - y_2^-$ in the simplex tableau where $y_2^+ \geq 0$ and $y_2^- \geq 0$. Thus adding the artificial variables R_1, R_2, and R_3 and expressing the y_0-equation in terms of the nonbasic variables, the starting tableau becomes:

Basic	y_0	y_1	y_2^+	y_2^-	S_1	S_2	S_3	R_1	R_2	R_3	Solution
y_0	①	$-5 + 4M$	$-2 + 4M$	$2 - 4M$	$-M$	$-M$	$-M$	0	0	0	$21M$
R_1	0	1	2	-2	-1	0	0	①	0	0	5
R_2	0	2	-1	1	0	-1	0	0	①	0	12
R_3	0	1	3	-3	0	0	-1	0	0	①	4

Noting that this is a minimization problem, the optimal solution is obtained in five iterations and its simplex tableau is given by:

Basic	y_0	y_1	y_2^+	y_2^-	S_1	S_2	S_3	R_1	R_2	R_3	Solution
y_0	①	0	0	0	$-9/5$	$-8/5$	0	$9/5 - M$	$8/5 - M$	$-M$	$28\frac{1}{5}$
S_3	0	0	0	0	$-7/5$	$1/5$	①	$7/5$	$-1/5$	-1	$3/5$
y_2^-	0	0	-1	①	$2/5$	$-1/5$	0	$-2/5$	$1/5$	0	$2/5$
y_1	0	①	0	0	$-1/5$	$-2/5$	0	$1/5$	$2/5$	0	$29/5$

This yields $y_1 = \frac{29}{5}$, $y_2^+ = 0$, $y_2^- = \frac{2}{5}$ and $y_0 = 28\frac{1}{5}$. Thus, $y_2 = y_2^+ - y_2^- = 0 - \frac{2}{5} = -\frac{2}{5}$. (Notice that y_2 is unrestricted in sign.)

A comparison of the primal and dual solutions show that

$$\max x_0 = 28\frac{1}{5} = \min y_0,$$

which agrees with the above mentioned property. Notice that the value of the objective function ($= 28\frac{1}{5}$) lies between the previously estimated values, $18\frac{1}{5}$ and 39.

§ 4·3·2
Relationship Between the Optimal Values of the Primal and Dual Variables

An investigation of the optimal tableaus of the primal and the dual reveal the following interesting results. Consider the variables of the *starting* solution in the primal of the above example. These are S_1 and R_1. The dual variables y_1 and y_2 correspond to the primal constraint equations containing S_1 and R_1, respectively. Now consider the coefficient of S_1 and R_1 in the x_0-equation of the *optimal* primal tableau. These are given by

Starting solution variables (primal)	S_1	R_1
x_0-equation coefficients	29/5	$(-2/5) + M$
Corresponding dual variables	y_1	y_2

Ignoring the constant M, it is noticed that the resulting coefficients, $\frac{29}{5}$ and $-\frac{2}{5}$, directly give the optimal solution of the dual problem. This means that optimal y_1 equals $\frac{29}{5}$ and optimal y_2 equals $-\frac{2}{5}$ which is the same as obtained by solving the dual problem independently.

The above result is not accidental since a similar investigation of the coefficients of R_1, R_2, and R_3 in the y_0-equation of the optimal dual tableau gives:

Starting solution variables (dual)	R_1	R_2	R_3
y_0-equation coefficients	$9/5 - M$	$8/5 - M$	$0 - M$
Corresponding primal variables	x_1	x_2	x_3

Again ignoring the constant M, these coefficients give directly the optimal primal solution, $x_1 = \frac{9}{5}$, $x_2 = \frac{8}{5}$, and $x_3 = 0$. This result is the same as obtained from the direct solution of the primal.

The above discussion leads to the important conclusion that the optimal solution of the primal (dual) gives directly the optimal solution of the dual (primal). The following general rules for determining the optimal solution of one problem from the optimal solution of the other problems are now in order:

> *Rule 1:* If the dual variable corresponds to a slack *starting* variable in the primal problem, its *optimal* value is given directly by the coefficient of this slack variable in the *optimal* x_0-equation.
>
> *Rule 2:* If the dual variable corresponds to an artificial *starting* variable in the primal problem, its *optimal* value is given by the coefficient of this artificial variable in the optimal x_0-equation after deleting the constant M.

Investigation of Rule 2 shows that by deleting the constant M, this is actually equivalent to adding the *original* cost coefficient of the artificial variable to the corresponding coefficient of the x_0-equation. This cost coefficient is given by $-M$ for the maximization problem and $+M$ for the minimization problem. For example, in the above primal problem, the cost coefficient of R_1 in the original problem can be obtained from

$$x_0 = 5x_1 + 12x_2 + 4x_3 - MR_1$$

which is equal to $-M$. Thus adding this to the corresponding x_0-equation coefficient, this gives $(-\frac{2}{5} + M) + (-M) = -\frac{2}{5}$ which is the optimal value of y_2. This leads to the point that if *any* variable in the problem is used as a starting variable and if its coefficient in the original objective function is c_j, then the optimal value of the corresponding dual variables is obtained by *adding* c_j to the appropriate coefficient of the x_0-equation. This again explains why the coefficients of the slack variable give the optimal values of the dual directly since their coefficients in the objective function are zero.

The results given above were shown only by illustrative examples. Chapter 8 will give general mathematical proofs of these relationships.

§ 4·3·3
An Interpretation of the Dual Variables

An important interpretation of the dual variables can be recognized from the definition of the dual objective function. This was given in Section 4·2 by

$$y_0 = \sum_{i=1}^{m} b_i y_i,$$

where y_i ($i = 1, 2, \ldots, m$) are the dual variables and b_i represent the availability of ith scarce resource. Since at the optimal solution, $x_0 = y_0$, the dual variables, y_i, may be interpreted as the *per-unit* contribution of the ith resource to the value of the objective function.

To illustrate this point, consider the solution of Example 4·2-2 given in Section 4·3·1. The objective function of the dual problem is given by

$$y_0 = 5y_1 + 2y_2,$$

and the optimal dual values are $y_1 = \frac{29}{5}$ and $y_2 = -\frac{2}{5}$. It is noticed that each unit of the first resource ($b_1 = 5$) contributes $\frac{29}{5}$ in the objective function while each unit of the second resource ($b_2 = 2$) contributes $-\frac{2}{5}$. This shows that it does not pay to increase the second resource since each additional unit will decrease y_0 (and hence x_0) by $\frac{2}{5}$. An increase in the first resource is promising since each unit increases the value of the objective function by $\frac{29}{5}$. This conclusion is, of course, true as long as the current primal (dual) solution is optimal and feasible. Otherwise, the values of y_1 and y_2 will change and the above interpretation becomes invalid. This point is discussed further in Section 4·6.

§ 4·4
Important Primal-Dual Properties

This section presents some important primal-dual properties which are needed for carrying out the postoptimality analyses. For the purpose of presenting these properties, it will be convenient to introduce first the elementary definitions of (vector by matrix) and (matrix by vector) multiplications.[1] (The reader familiar with these definitions may skip directly to the properties.)

Definition.   An $(m \times n)$ matrix is a rectangular array of numbers with m rows and n columns. A row-vector of size n is a $(1 \times n)$ matrix and a column-vector of size m is an $(m \times 1)$ matrix. Thus a matrix of size $(m \times n)$ consists of m row-vectors of size n each and n column-vectors of size m each. For example, the matrix,

$$A = \begin{bmatrix} 3 & 2 \\ 4 & -1 \\ 1 & 0 \end{bmatrix},$$

is of size (3×2). It has the two column-vectors

$$\begin{bmatrix} 3 \\ 4 \\ 1 \end{bmatrix} \quad \text{and} \quad \begin{bmatrix} 2 \\ -1 \\ 0 \end{bmatrix},$$

each of size 3 and the three row-vectors $(3, 2)$, $(4, -1)$, and $(1, 0)$, each of size 2.

---

[1] Appendix A gives a more complete summary of vectors and matrices.

Row-Vector × Matrix Multiplication

Given the row-vector $\mathbf{V}$ and the matrix $\mathbf{A}$, the product $\mathbf{V} \cdot \mathbf{A}$ is defined if, and only if, the size of $\mathbf{V}$ is equal to the number of rows of $\mathbf{A}$. Thus, if

$$\mathbf{V} = (v_1, v_2, \ldots, v_m)$$

and

$$\mathbf{A} = \begin{bmatrix} a_{11} & a_{12} & \cdots & a_{1n} \\ a_{21} & a_{22} & \cdots & a_{2n} \\ \vdots & \vdots & & \vdots \\ a_{m1} & a_{m2} & \cdots & a_{mn} \end{bmatrix},$$

then

$$\mathbf{V} \cdot \mathbf{A} = (v_1, v_2, \ldots, v_m) \begin{bmatrix} a_{11} & a_{12} & \cdots & a_{1n} \\ a_{21} & a_{22} & \cdots & a_{2n} \\ \vdots & \vdots & & \vdots \\ a_{m1} & a_{m2} & \cdots & a_{mn} \end{bmatrix}$$

$$= \left[\sum_{i=1}^{m} v_i a_{i1}, \quad \sum_{i=1}^{m} v_i a_{i2}, \ldots, \quad \sum_{i=1}^{m} v_i a_{in} \right].$$

Notice that the result is a row-vector of size n.

To illustrate this numerically, consider

$$(1, 0, 2) \begin{bmatrix} 3 & -1 \\ 4 & 8 \\ 6 & 9 \end{bmatrix} = (3 \times 1 + 4 \times 0 + 6 \times 2, \, -1 \times 1 + 8 \times 0 + 9 \times 2)$$

$$= (15, 17).$$

Matrix × Column-Vector Multiplication

The product $\mathbf{A} \cdot \mathbf{P}$ of the matrix $\mathbf{A}$ and a column-vector $\mathbf{P}$ is defined if, and only if, the number of columns of $\mathbf{A}$ is equal to the size of $\mathbf{P}$. Thus, if

$$\mathbf{P} = \begin{bmatrix} p_1 \\ p_2 \\ \vdots \\ p_n \end{bmatrix},$$

then for the matrix $\mathbf{A}$ defined above,

$$\mathbf{A} \cdot \mathbf{P} = \begin{bmatrix} a_{11} & a_{12} & \cdots & a_{1n} \\ a_{21} & a_{22} & \cdots & a_{2n} \\ \vdots & \vdots & & \vdots \\ a_{m1} & a_{m2} & \cdots & a_{mn} \end{bmatrix} \begin{bmatrix} p_1 \\ p_2 \\ \vdots \\ p_n \end{bmatrix} = \begin{bmatrix} \sum_{j=1}^{n} a_{1j} p_j \\ \sum_{j=1}^{n} a_{2j} p_j \\ \vdots \\ \sum_{j=1}^{n} a_{mj} p_j \end{bmatrix},$$

which is a column-vector of size m.

Numerically, this can be illustrated by

$$\begin{bmatrix} 1 & 5 & 7 \\ 2 & 0 & 8 \\ 3 & 6 & 9 \\ -1 & 4 & -2 \end{bmatrix} \begin{bmatrix} 11 \\ 22 \\ 33 \end{bmatrix} = \begin{bmatrix} 11 \times 1 + 22 \times 5 + 33 \times 7 \\ 11 \times 2 + 22 \times 0 + 33 \times 8 \\ 11 \times 3 + 22 \times 6 + 33 \times 9 \\ 11 \times -1 + 22 \times 4 + 33 \times -2 \end{bmatrix} = \begin{bmatrix} 352 \\ 286 \\ 462 \\ 11 \end{bmatrix}.$$

The primal-dual properties will now be presented. *These properties are based on the assumption that the dual problem is obtained from the standard form of the primal.* This restriction allows simpler and more general presentation of the properties since it determines directly the signs of the dual variable especially when the primal problem includes all three types of constraints. There is no loss of generality here, however, since any problem can be put in the standard form. Example 4·2-2 will be used to illustrate these properties. This example is repeated here for convenience.

Primal problem:

$$\text{Maximize} \quad x_0 = 5x_1 + 12x_2 + 4x_3,$$

subject to

$$x_1 + 2x_2 + x_3 \leq 5,$$
$$2x_1 - x_2 + 3x_3 = 2,$$
$$x_1 \geq 0, \quad x_2 \geq 0, \quad x_3 \geq 0.$$

Dual problem:

$$\text{Minimize} \quad y_0 = 5y_1 + 2y_2,$$

subject to

$$y_1 + 2y_2 \geq 5,$$
$$2y_1 - y_2 \geq 12,$$
$$y_1 + 3y_2 \geq 4,$$
$$y_1 \geq 0,$$
$$y_2 \text{ unrestricted in sign.}$$

The iterative solutions of these two problems were given previously in Section 4·3·1.

Property I. At *any* iteration of the simplex solution of either the primal or the dual, the matrix under the variables of the *starting* solution (not including the objective-equation row) can be used to generate the objective-equation coefficients corresponding to the starting solution. This is achieved as follows:

Step 1. Identify the *original* coefficients of the objective function corresponding to the basic variables of the current iteration and arrange them in a *row*-vector in *the same order* of their respective rows in the simplex tableau.

For example, consider the *second* iteration of the above primal problem (Section 4·3·1). The basic variables in the order of their rows (which can be read directly under the " Basic " column of the tableau) are x_2 and x_3. Thus, the row-vector of their original coefficients in the objective function is given by (12, 4). Similarly for the last (optimal) iteration of the dual, the basic variables are S_3, y_2^-, and y_1 and their corresponding vector is (0, −2, 5).

Step 2.   Multiply the resulting vector by the matrix defined above. For example, for the second iteration of the primal,

$$(12, 4)\begin{bmatrix} 3/7 & -1/7 \\ 1/7 & 2/7 \end{bmatrix} = (40/7, -4/7),$$

and for the optimal iteration of the dual

$$(0, -2, 5)\begin{bmatrix} 7/5 & -1/5 & -1 \\ -2/5 & 1/5 & 0 \\ 1/5 & 2/5 & 0 \end{bmatrix} = (9/5, 8/5, 0).$$

Step 3.   Subtract the original coefficients of the objective function corresponding to the variables of the starting solution from the respective coefficients obtained in Step 2. This will directly give the result indicated by the property.

For example, for the second iteration of the primal,

$$\text{Coefficient of } S_1 = 40/7 - (0) = 40/7,$$
$$\text{Coefficient of } R_1 = -4/7 - (-M) = -4/7 + M,$$

which checks with the results of the second iteration of the primal. Similarly, for the optimal iteration of the dual;

$$\text{Coefficient of } R_1 = 9/5 - (M) = 9/5 - M,$$
$$\text{Coefficient of } R_2 = 8/5 - (M) = 8/5 - M,$$
$$\text{Coefficient of } R_3 = \ 0\ - (M) = -M.$$

The results obtained in Step 2 above are of special interest since if they correspond to the optimal iteration they will give the optimal values of the other problem directly (cf. Sec. 4·3·2). Equivalent results at intermediate iterations are also important as will be shown by Property II. In general, the values obtained at Step 2 are referred to as the "simplex multipliers."[2] At the optimal iteration, these simplex multipliers will obviously give the optimal solution to the other problem.

Property II.   At *any* iteration of the simplex solution, by substituting the corresponding simplex multipliers for the respective variables in the dual

---

[2] The name "simplex multipliers" was pioneered by George B. Dantzig. Other names include "shadow costs," "implicit costs," and "opportunity costs."

constraints, the coefficients of the x_0-equation in the primal are given by the differences between the left-hand side and the right-hand side of the corresponding dual constraints. This property is equally applicable to generating the coefficients of the y_0-equation from the primal constraints.

To illustrate this property, consider the second iteration of the primal. The corresponding simplex multipliers are $\frac{40}{7}$ and $-\frac{4}{7}$. Thus, the dual constraint corresponding to x_1 is $y_1 + 2y_2 \geq 5$. Substituting the values of the simplex multipliers for y_1 and y_2, and taking the difference between the left- and the right-hand sides of the constraint, then $\frac{40}{7} + 2(-\frac{4}{7}) - 5 = -\frac{3}{7}$ which is the same as the coefficients of x_1 in the x_0-equation. For x_2, the corresponding dual constraint is $2y_1 - y_2 \geq 12$. Substituting and taking the difference one gets $2(\frac{40}{7}) - (-\frac{4}{7}) - 12 = 0$, which again checks with the coefficient of x_2 in the x_0-equation. The same result applies to x_3.

This property reveals a very important result. Notice that a negative coefficient in the x_0-equation of the primal implies that the solution is not optimal. Since this coefficient represents the difference between the left and the right sides of the dual constraints, it is seen from the direction of the inequality that such a negative coefficient indicates that the corresponding dual constraint is not satisfied. This leads to the conclusion that when the primal is non-optimal the dual is infeasible and *vice versa*. Another remark can also be made here. For every basic variable in the primal, the corresponding dual constraint must be satisfied in equality sense (why?) and *vice versa*.

The above discussion gives the following result. While the primal problem starts feasible but nonoptimal and it continues to be feasible until the optimal solution is reached, the dual problem starts infeasible but better-than-optimal and it continues to be infeasible until the "true" optimal solution is reached. In other words, while the primal problem is seeking optimality the dual problem is automatically seeking feasibility. This result suggests that it is possible to construct a simplex-like procedure for solving the dual-type problems. The solution will start optimal (or actually better-than-optimal) and infeasible and it will remain infeasible until the "true" optimal is reached at which point the solution becomes feasible. Such a procedure is called the "dual simplex method" and is discussed in Section 4·5.

Property II gives an important interpretation of the dual variables. Consider the *j*th dual constraint for a maximization primal problem. This is given by

$$a_{1j}y_1 + a_{2j}y_2 + \cdots + a_{mj}y_m \geq c_j,$$

where a_{ij} is the per unit requirement of the *j*th primal variable, x_j, from the *i*th scarce resource and c_j is the coefficient of x_j in the objective function. Let z_j designate the left-hand side of the above dual constraint. Thus, by Property II, $z_j - c_j$ gives the coefficient of x_j in the x_0-equation. Now, according to the optimality condition, x_j is a promising variable if $z_j - c_j < 0$. Since in this case the primal is a maximization problem, then c_j may be regarded as a "profit" value while z_j (with an opposite sign) may be taken as a "cost" value. It follows that the smaller the value of z_j, the more attractive x_j will be. From the economic point of view, z_j is regarded as the "imputed price" per unit of x_j. The dual variables, y_i, thus define the cost per unit of the requirement a_{ij}.

The above discussion indicates that a nonbasic variable x_j is considered a promising candidate for the optimum solution as long as its per unit "profit" value, c_j, exceeds its per unit "imputed price," z_j; that is, $c_j > z_j$, or $z_j - c_j < 0$. When $z_j = c_j$, the corresponding variable cannot change the present value of the objective function. Finally, when z_j exceeds c_j; that is, $z_j - c_j > 0$, then the variable x_j becomes nonpromising and hence should remain nonbasic (at zero level). This remark also implies that for a *basic* variable, z_j must be equal to c_j indicating that the corresponding variable has been used to the fullest extent and as such it cannot improve the solution any further.[3]

Property III. At *any* iteration of the primal or the dual, the corresponding values of the basic variables can be obtained by multiplying the matrix defined in Property I by the column-vector comprising the *original* elements of the right-hand side of the constraints.

For example, at the optimal iteration of the dual problem,

$$\text{original right-hand side of the constraints} = \begin{pmatrix} 5 \\ 12 \\ 4 \end{pmatrix}.$$

Thus, the *corresponding* solution is

$$\begin{pmatrix} S_3 \\ y_2^- \\ y_1 \end{pmatrix} = \begin{pmatrix} 7/5 & -1/5 & -1 \\ -2/5 & 1/5 & 0 \\ 1/5 & 2/5 & 0 \end{pmatrix} \begin{pmatrix} 5 \\ 12 \\ 4 \end{pmatrix} = \begin{pmatrix} 3/5 \\ 2/5 \\ 29/5 \end{pmatrix},$$

which checks with the optimal solution of the dual.

Property IV. At *any* iteration of the primal or the dual, the constraint coefficients under any variable (including those of the starting solution) can be obtained by multiplying the matrix defined in Property I by the column-vector comprising the *original* elements of the constraints coefficients under the designated variable.

---

[3] The above discussion implies the so-called "complementary slackness theorem." Let $w_j = z_j - c_j$ then w_j defines the slack variable of the jth dual constraint. Thus, at the optimal solution of the primal if $w_j > 0$, then $x_j = 0$. A similar result can be established if S_i defines the slack variable of the ith primal constraint and y_i defines its corresponding dual variable. Then at the optimal solution, $S_i = 0$ whenever $y_i > 0$ and $y_i = 0$ whenever $S_i > 0$. This result may also be written in a compact form as $w_j x_j = y_i S_i = 0$.

For example, in the primal problem, the column-vectors corresponding to the *original* coefficients of the constraints are

$$\underset{x_1}{\underline{\binom{1}{2}}} \quad \underset{x_2}{\underline{\binom{2}{-1}}} \quad \underset{x_3}{\underline{\binom{1}{3}}}.$$

Hence the corresponding coefficients of x_1 in the third iteration are

$$\begin{pmatrix} 2/5 & -1/5 \\ 1/5 & 2/5 \end{pmatrix}\begin{pmatrix} 1 \\ 2 \end{pmatrix} = \begin{pmatrix} 0 \\ 1 \end{pmatrix},$$

and for x_2

$$\begin{pmatrix} 2/5 & -1/5 \\ 1/5 & 2/5 \end{pmatrix}\begin{pmatrix} 2 \\ -1 \end{pmatrix} = \begin{pmatrix} 1 \\ 0 \end{pmatrix},$$

and finally for x_3

$$\begin{pmatrix} 2/5 & -1/5 \\ 1/5 & 2/5 \end{pmatrix}\begin{pmatrix} 1 \\ 3 \end{pmatrix} = \begin{pmatrix} -1/5 \\ 7/5 \end{pmatrix}.$$

The above properties indicate that, at any iteration, given the original information about the problem, all the elements of the simplex tableau can be generated from the knowledge of the matrix under the starting solution. This makes it possible to check the computations at any iteration. More important will be the use of these properties in the sensitivity analysis problem (see Section 4·6).

§ 4·5
Dual Simplex Method

As mentioned in Property II, the dual simplex applies to problems which start optimal but infeasible. Such a situation is recognized by first expressing the constraints in the form ($\leq$) as in the canonical case, Section 2·3·1. The objective function may be in either the maximization or the minimization form. After adding the slack variables and putting the problem in the tableau form, if any of the right-hand side elements is negative and if the optimality condition is satisfied, then the problem can be solved by the dual simplex method. Notice that by the above arrangement, a negative element in the right-hand side signifies that the corresponding slack variable is negative. This means that the problem starts optimal but infeasible as required by the dual simplex procedure. At the iteration where the basic solution becomes feasible, this will be the optimal basic feasible solution. This procedure is similar to the regular simplex method except that, in the latter, the solution starts feasible but nonoptimal.

The dual simplex method is best illustrated by an example. Consider the problem:

$$\text{minimize} \quad x_0 = 2x_1 + x_2,$$

subject to

$$3x_1 + x_2 \geq 3,$$
$$4x_1 + 3x_2 \geq 6,$$
$$x_1 + 2x_2 \geq 3,$$
$$x_1 \geq 0, \quad x_2 \geq 0.$$

Putting the constraints in the form ($\leq$) and adding the slack variables, the corresponding tableau form is given by,

Basic	x_0	x_1	x_2	S_1	S_2	S_3	Solution
x_0	①	-2	-1	0	0	0	0
S_1	0	-3	-1	①	0	0	-3
S_2	0	-4	-3	0	①	0	-6
S_3	0	-1	-2	0	0	①	-3

The first basic solution is infeasible since $S_1 = -3$, $S_2 = -6$, and $S_3 = -3$. In the meantime, the x_0-equation is optimal since all its coefficients are non-positive (minimization problem). This problem is typical of the type that can be handled by the dual simplex method.

Like the regular simplex method, the method of solution requires two conditions, the optimality condition and the feasibility condition. The optimality condition ascertains that the solution remains optimal all the time while the feasibility condition forces the basic solutions toward the feasible space. These conditions are given as:

Feasibility Condition.   The leaving variable is selected as the basic variable having the most negative value. If all the basic variables are nonnegative the process ends and the feasible (optimal) solution is reached.

Optimality Condition.   The entering variable is selected from among the nonbasic variables as follows. Take the ratios of the x_0-equation coefficients to the coefficients in the equation associated with the leaving variable. Ignore positive or zero denominators. Select the entering variable as the one associated with the smallest ratio if the problem is minimization, or the smallest *absolute value* of the ratios if the problem is maximization. If all the denominators are zero or positive, the problem has no feasible solution.

After selecting the entering and the leaving variables, row operations are applied as usual to obtain the next iteration of the solution.

Thus, from the above tableau, S_2 ($= -6$) is the leaving variable since it has the most negative value. For the entering variable, the ratios are given by:

	x_1	x_2	S_1	S_2	S_3
x_0-equation	-2	-1	0	0	0
S_2-equation	-4	-3	0	1	0
Ratios	$1/2$	$1/3$	—	—	—

Since this is a minimization problem, the entering variable corresponds to the smallest ratio $\frac{1}{3}$. Thus x_2 enters the solution.

Applying row operations as usual, the new tableau becomes

Basic	x_0	x_1	x_2	S_1	S_2	S_3	Solution
x_0	①	$-2/3$	0	0	$-1/3$	0	2
S_1	0	$-5/3$	0	①	$-1/3$	0	1
x_2	0	$4/3$	①	0	$-1/3$	0	2
S_3	0	$5/3$	0	0	$-2/3$	①	1

The new solution is still optimal but infeasible. Thus, S_1 ($= -1$) leaves the solution and x_1 enters the solution. This yields,

Basic	x_0	x_1	x_2	S_1	S_2	S_3	Solution
x_0	①	0	0	$-2/5$	$-1/5$	0	$12/5$
x_1	0	①	0	$-3/5$	$1/5$	0	$3/5$
x_2	0	0	①	$4/5$	$-3/5$	0	$6/5$
S_3	0	0	0	1	-1	①	0

which is now optimal and feasible.

The application of the dual simplex method is especially useful in the sensitivity analysis problem. This occurs, for example, when a new constraint is added to the problem after the optimal solution is obtained. If this constraint is not satisfied by the optimal solution, the problem remains optimal but it becomes infeasible. The dual simplex method is then invoked to clear the new infeasibility in the problem.

§ 4-6
Postoptimality or Sensitivity Analyses

Following the attainment of the optimal solution to a linear programming problem, it is often desirable to study the effect of discrete changes in the different parameters of the problem on the *current* optimal solution. One way to accomplish this is to solve the problem anew. This, however, may be computationally inefficient; since if one makes use of the properties of the simplex solution, it is possible to reduce the additional computational effort considerably. This will be the objective of the postoptimality analyses.

The changes in the linear programming problem which are usually studied by postoptimality analyses include,

1. Tightness of the constraints, that is, changes in the right-hand side of the constraints.
   2. Coefficients of the objectives function (profit or cost). These include:
   (a) Coefficients of the basic variables.
   (b) Coefficients of the nonbasic variables.
   3. Technological coefficients of decision variables. These include:
   (a) Coefficients of the basic variables.
   (b) Coefficients of the nonbasic variables.
   4. Addition of new variables to the problem.
   5. Addition of new (or secondary) constraint(s).

These cases are depicted schematically in Figure 4–1.

In general, these changes may result in one of three cases:

1. The optimal solution remains unchanged; that is, the basic variables and their values remain essentially unchanged.
   2. The *basic* variables remain the same but their values are changed.
   3. The basic solution changes completely.

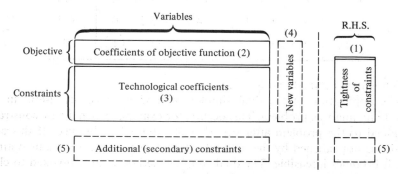

Figure 4–1

The detection of these cases using sensitivity analyses is based mainly on the primal-dual properties presented in Section 4·4, These properties especially reveal the following important remarks:

1. Changes in the tightness of the constraints in the primal (dual) can only affect the feasibility of the primal (dual), or equivalently the optimality of the dual (primal). (Property III.)

2. Changes in the coefficients of the objective function in the primal (dual) can only affect the optimality of the primal (dual), or equivalently the feasibility of the dual (primal). (Properties I and II.)

3. Changes in the technological coefficients of *non*basic variables of the primal (dual) can only affect the optimality of the primal (dual), or equivalently the feasibility of the dual (primal). (Property II.)

The above remarks provide the key ideas in the postoptimality analyses. The techniques for treating the different changes in the linear programming problem will now be introduced. Example 4·2-2 will again be used to illustrate these techniques.

§ 4·6·1
Changes in the Tightness of the Constraints

Suppose in Example 4·2-2 that the right-hand side of the primal constraints is changed from

$$\begin{bmatrix} 5 \\ 2 \end{bmatrix} \text{ to } \begin{bmatrix} 7 \\ 2 \end{bmatrix}.$$

How would this affect the current optimal solution which is given by $x_0 = \frac{141}{5}$, $x_1 = \frac{9}{5}$, $x_2 = \frac{8}{5}$, and $x_3 = 0$? According to the above remarks, such a change can only affect the feasibility of the problem. Thus by Property III, Section 4·4, the new values of the current basic variables are given by

$$\begin{bmatrix} x_2 \\ x_1 \end{bmatrix} = \begin{bmatrix} 2/5 & -1/5 \\ 1/5 & 2/5 \end{bmatrix}\begin{bmatrix} 7 \\ 2 \end{bmatrix} = \begin{bmatrix} 12/5 \\ 11/5 \end{bmatrix},$$

since both x_1 and $x_2 > 0$, the current basic solution (consisting of x_1 and x_2) remains feasible and optimal *at the new values*, $x_1 = \frac{11}{5}$, $x_2 = \frac{12}{5}$, while x_3 remains zero. The new value of x_0 is $5(\frac{11}{5}) + 12(\frac{12}{5}) + 4(0) = \frac{199}{5}$.

Consider another case where the new right-hand side of the primal constraints is given by

$$\begin{bmatrix} 3 \\ 10 \end{bmatrix} \text{ instead of } \begin{bmatrix} 5 \\ 2 \end{bmatrix},$$

then

$$\begin{bmatrix} x_2 \\ x_1 \end{bmatrix} = \begin{bmatrix} 2/5 & -1/5 \\ 1/5 & 2/5 \end{bmatrix}\begin{bmatrix} 3 \\ 10 \end{bmatrix} = \begin{bmatrix} -4/5 \\ 23/5 \end{bmatrix}.$$

Notice that x_2 becomes infeasible (< 0). This means that the first constraint is not satisfied and it follows that this change leaves the current optimal solution infeasible. Therefore, a new basis must be determined and the variable x_2 must be dropped from the solution. Here, the dual simplex method becomes useful in restoring the feasibility of the problem. This is done by first changing the right-hand side of the (primal) optimal tableau to show the new values of x_0 and the current basic variables. Since, new $x_0 = 5(\frac{23}{5})$ $+ 12(-\frac{4}{5}) + 4(0) = \frac{67}{5}$, the *changes* in the (primal) optimal tableau appear as follows:

Basic	x_0	x_1	x_2	x_3	S_1	R_1	Solution
x_0							67/5
x_2							$-4/5$
x_1							23/5

with all the other elements of the tableau remaining unchanged. Since the x_0-equation is optimal (all nonnegative coefficients, maximization) and the basic solution is infeasible ($x_2 = -\frac{4}{5}$), the dual simplex method is used to clear the infeasibility with x_2 as the leaving variable.

It is interesting to note that if one wants to increase one of the resources, the immediate question is, "which resource should be increased in order to achieve the best marginal increase in the value of the objective function?" The answer to this question was discussed in Section 4·3·2 and it calls for considering the dual objective function given by

$$y_0 = 5y_1 + 2y_2$$

where $y_1 = \frac{29}{5}$ and $y_2 = -\frac{2}{5}$ are the dual optimal values. Obviously, the first resource should be increased since each additional unit increases the value of the objective function by $\frac{29}{5}$ while each additional unit of the second resource decreases it by $\frac{2}{5}$. The next question then is, "how far can one go about increasing the first resource while maintaining the property that each additional unit will contribute $\frac{29}{5}$ to the value of the objective function?" Clearly the value $\frac{29}{5}$ will remain correct as long as the primal problem remains feasible. This gives the clue that if Δ represents the increase in the first resource, then the maximum value of Δ can be determined using the same procedure given above. Thus,

$$\begin{pmatrix} x_2 \\ x_1 \end{pmatrix} = \begin{pmatrix} 2/5 & -1/5 \\ 1/5 & 2/5 \end{pmatrix} \begin{pmatrix} 5 + \Delta \\ 2 \end{pmatrix} = \begin{pmatrix} \dfrac{8 + 2\Delta}{5} \\ \dfrac{9 + \Delta}{5} \end{pmatrix} \geq \begin{pmatrix} 0 \\ 0 \end{pmatrix}.$$

Clearly, x_1 and x_2 will remain feasible (≥ 0) for any $\Delta > 0$. This means that the first resource can be increased indefinitely while maintaining the property that each additional unit will contribute $\frac{29}{5}$ in the objective function.

To illustrate the case where there is an upper limit on the value of Δ, consider the case where Δ represents the decrease in the value of the second resource. Then the current solution remains basic and feasible as long as

$$\begin{pmatrix} x_2 \\ \\ x_1 \end{pmatrix} = \begin{pmatrix} 2/5 & -1/5 \\ \\ 1/5 & 2/5 \end{pmatrix} \begin{pmatrix} 5 \\ \\ 2 - \Delta \end{pmatrix} = \begin{pmatrix} \dfrac{(8 + \Delta)}{5} \\ \\ \dfrac{(9 - 2\Delta)}{5} \end{pmatrix} \geq \begin{pmatrix} 0 \\ \\ 0 \end{pmatrix}.$$

This shows that the given solution will remain feasible at the new values as long as $\Delta \leq \frac{9}{2}$. For $\Delta > \frac{9}{2}$, x_2 must leave the solution.

§ 4·6·2
Changes in the Coefficients of the Objective Function

It was indicated previously that changes in the coefficients of the objective function can only affect the optimality of the problem (or the feasibility of its dual). Differentiation, however is made between the cases where these changes occur in the basic or nonbasic coefficients. In the case of basic coefficients, the simplex multipliers (dual values) will change (Property I), and hence must be recomputed before the optimality of the problem (or the feasibility of its dual) is checked. In the other case, the simplex multipliers will remain unchanged and hence the problem can be checked directly. Each of these two cases will be considered separately.

Basic Coefficients
According to Property I, the simplex multipliers are dependent on the coefficients of the basic variables in the objective function. In order for the current solution to remain optimal, the *new* simplex multipliers must yield a new objective equation with *all* its coefficients satisfying the optimality condition.

To illustrated this point, suppose that in the primal of Example 4·2-2 the coefficients of the objective function corresponding to x_1 and x_2 were changed from 5 and 12 to 4 and 10. Thus by Property I, the new simplex multipliers are (notice the order of coefficients in the row-vector; x_2, x_1),

$$(10, 4) \begin{bmatrix} 2/5 & -1/5 \\ 1/5 & 2/5 \end{bmatrix} = (24/5, -2/5),$$

and the new coefficients of S_1 and R_1 in the objective equation are as follows:

Coefficient of $S_1 = 24/5 - (0) = 24/5 > 0,$

Coefficient of $R_1 = -2/5 - (-M) = -2/5 + M > 0,$

which both satisfy the optimality condition. (It is not necessary actually to check for R_1. Why?)

Now, the remaining coefficients of the objective equation will be checked using Property II by checking the feasibility of the corresponding *new* dual constraints.[4] Thus,

$$\text{Coefficient of } x_1 = 1(24/5) + 2(-2/5) - 4 = 0,$$
$$\text{Coefficient of } x_2 = 2(24/5) - 1(-2/5) - 10 = 0,$$
$$\text{Coefficient of } x_3 = 1(24/5) + 3(-2/5) - 4 = -2/5, (<0).$$

Since one of the coefficients is negative the current optimal solution is no longer optimal and must be changed. This is done by applying the regular simplex to the current optimal tableau after changing its x_0-equation coefficients to show the new changes. These changes should appear as follows:

Basic	x_0	x_1	x_2	x_3	S_1	R_1	Solution
x_0		0	0	$-2/5$	24/5	$-2/5 + M$	116/5
x_2							
x_1							

where the new value of $x_0 = 4(\frac{9}{5}) + 10(\frac{8}{5}) + 4(0) = \frac{116}{5}$ and all the other elements in the tableau remain unchanged. According to the regular simplex method the variable x_3 should enter the solution. The feasibility condition can be used then to determine the leaving variable. This is repeated until the optimal solution is obtained.

Nonbasic Coefficients:

This type of change does not affect the simplex multipliers. Consequently, the available multipliers can be used directly in order to check the objective-equation coefficients. This is done by checking the feasibility of the corresponding new dual constraints with their right-hand sides changed to the *new* values. For example, suppose in the same primal problem of Example 4·2-2 the coefficient of x_3 is changed from 4 to 8, then its corresponding dual constraint is changed from $y_1 + 3y_2 \geq 4$ to $y_1 + 3y_2 \geq 8$. Using the same simplex multipliers, $y_1 = \frac{29}{5}$ and $y_2 = -\frac{2}{5}$, it follows that this constraint is not satisfied. Thus the new coefficient of x_3 in the x_0-equation is $1(\frac{29}{5}) + 3(-\frac{2}{5}) - 8 = -\frac{17}{5}$. This will be the only change in the optimal tableau and the variable x_3 thus becomes the entering variable.

---

[4] Notice that the right-hand sides of the *new* dual constraints are given by the corresponding *new* coefficients 4 and 10, instead of 5 and 12, for the first and second dual constraints, respectively. Notice also that it is not necessary to check the basic variables for nonoptimality since they are already basic.

It should be noted that *simultaneous* changes in basic and nonbasic coefficients can be dealt with by combining the above two procedures. First, the new simplex multipliers (using the new basic coefficients) are determined and the coefficients of the starting solution in the objective equation are checked for nonoptimality. Second, the *new* dual constraints (using the new coefficients) are checked for the feasibility of the dual (or the optimality of the primal).

§ 4·6·3
Changes in the Technological Coefficients

It is shown by Property II that changes in the technological coefficients of the problem can affect the left-hand side of its dual constraints and hence the feasibility of the dual (or equivalently the optimality of the primal). The important point here is that changes in the technological coefficients of a *basic* variable will directly affect the elements of the matrix under the starting solution.[5] Since this matrix plays the important role in all sensitivity analyses computations, the new changes may cause the current solution to be infeasible or nonoptimal or it may even cease to be basic at all. Except in very special cases, such problems make it difficult to consider systematically the effect of changes in the technological coefficients of the basic variables on the optimal solution. Even in the special cases that can be dealt with, the analysis, unlike the other cases, does not yield immediate information concerning the optimality or the feasibility of the new problem. For these reasons this type of change is not investigated here. Instead, changes in the technological coefficients of nonbasic variables only will be studied.

Suppose that the technological coefficients of x_3 in the primal of Example 4·2-2 were changed from

$$\begin{bmatrix} 1 \\ 3 \end{bmatrix} \quad \text{to} \quad \begin{bmatrix} -5 \\ 2 \end{bmatrix}.$$

The new dual constraint corresponding to x_3 becomes

$$-5y_1 + 2y_2 \geq 4.$$

The values of the simplex multipliers will remain unchanged and by Property II the new coefficient of x_3 in the x_0-equation is $-5(\frac{29}{5}) + 2(-\frac{2}{5}) - 4 = -\frac{169}{5}$. This shows that the current solution is no longer optimal. Thus the new changes in the coefficients under x_3 must be introduced in the optimal tableau and the regular simplex method is then applied to obtain a new optimal

---

[5] This statement will be qualified in Chapter 8 when adequate theory has been presented.

solution. The changes in the optimal tableau are given by

Basic	x_0	x_1	x_2	x_3	S_1	R_1	Solution
x_0				$-169/5$			
x_2				$-12/5$			
x_1				$-1/5$			

with all other elements remaining unchanged. Notice that the *new* technological coefficient of x_3 are obtained by using Property IV. That is,

$$\begin{bmatrix} 2/5 & -1/5 \\ 1/5 & 2/5 \end{bmatrix}\begin{bmatrix} -5 \\ 2 \end{bmatrix} = \begin{bmatrix} -12/5 \\ -1/5 \end{bmatrix}.$$

(The new problem has no bounded solution since all the constraint coefficients
are negative.)

§ 4·6·4
Addition of a New Variable

This case is essentially the same as considering *simultaneous* changes in the
objective-function coefficients and the technological coefficients of a corresponding nonbasic variable. Consequently, the addition of a new variable can
only affect the optimality of the problem. This means that the new variable
will enter the solution if, and only if, it improves the value of the objective
function. Otherwise, the new variable becomes like a nonbasic variable ($= 0$).

To illustrate this point, consider the addition of a new variable x_4 to the
original primal problem of Example 4·2-2. Let the coefficient of x_4 in the
objective function be 6 and its technological coefficients in the first and second
constraints be 5 and 7, respectively. The corresponding dual constraint is
$5y_1 + 7y_2 \geq 6$. The optimal dual values $y_1 = \frac{29}{5}$ and $y_2 = -\frac{2}{5}$ satisfy this
constraint and hence x_4 cannot improve the current optimal solution. If,
instead, the corresponding dual constraint was $5y_1 + 7y_2 \geq 30$, the constraint
becomes unsatisfied and x_4 must enter the solution. Using Property II and IV,
the changes in the optimal tableau are:

Basic	x_0	x_1	x_2	x_3	x_4	S_1	R_1	Solution
x_0					$-19/5$			
x_2					$3/5$			
x_1					$19/5$			

with all other elements remaining unchanged. The regular simplex method is
then used to restore the optimal solution.

§ 4·6·5
Addition of a New Constraint

A new constraint can affect the feasibility of the current optimal solution only if it is active. Consequently, the first step would be to check whether the new constraint is satisfied by the current optimal solution. If it is satisfied, the new constraint is redundant and the optimal solution remains unchanged. Otherwise, the new constraint must be added to the system as will be shown below.

Consider the addition of the constraint $5x_1 + 5x_2 + 3x_3 \leq 20$ to the primal of Example 4·2-2. Since the optimal solution is $x_1 = \frac{9}{5}$, $x_2 = \frac{8}{5}$ and $x_3 = 0$, this constraint is satisfied and hence it is redundant. Suppose, instead, that the constraint was $5x_1 + 5x_2 + 3x_3 \leq 10$, then it is not satisfied and the current solution becomes infeasible. In order to clear the infeasibility, the new constraint must be added to the optimal tableau. Thus, adding the slack variable S_3, the constraint appears in the (modified) optimal tableau as

Basic	x_0	x_1	x_2	x_3	S_1	R_1	S_3	Solution
x_0	①	0	0	3/5	29/5	$-2/5 + M$	0	141/5
x_2	0	0	①	$-1/5$	2/5	$-1/5$	0	8/5
x_1	0	①	0	7/5	1/5	2/5	0	9/5
S_3	0	5	5	3	0	0	①	10

Since x_1 and x_2 are in the basic solution, their corresponding coefficients in the additional constraint must be zero. This is done using the appropriate row operations thus yielding

Basic	x_0	x_1	x_2	x_3	S_1	R_1	S_3	Solution
x_0	①	0	0	3/5	29/5	$-2/5 + M$	0	141/5
x_2	0	0	①	$-1/5$	2/5	$-1/5$	0	8/5
x_1	0	①	0	7/5	1/5	2/5	0	9/5
S_3	0	0	0	-3	-3	-1	①	-7

The x_0-equation is optimal but the current basic solution is infeasible. Consequently the dual simplex method is used to clear the infeasibility in the problem.

The idea of treating additional constraints can sometimes be used to reduce the computational effort in solving a problem. Since the computational difficulty depends on the number of constraints, it may be possible first to delete the constraints which one suspects are not binding. The new problem is then solved with a fewer number of constraints. After the optimal solution of the new problem is obtained, the deleted constraints are checked for feasibility using the above procedure. It is common to refer to these constraints as "secondary constraints."

§ 4·6·6
Concluding Remarks

Section 4·6 has presented the techniques for dealing with separate changes in the parameters of the linear programming problem. It is possible, however, to consider all these changes in one problem. For example, one may be interested in studying the effect of *simultaneous* changes which otherwise may be meaningless if treated independently. Specific examples of this type include the case of changing the technological coefficients and the objective-function coefficients of a nonbasic variable, or changing the objective-function coefficients of basic and nonbasic variables. Such cases can be treated in the same manner presented above and following the basic properties given in Section 4.4.

Another problem occurs when changes in the parameters of the problem take place systematically (rather than in a discrete manner) according to predetermined linear functions. This is called "parametric linear programming" and its treatment is basically the same as in the sensitivity analyses. Chapter 9 is devoted to the analysis of this type of problem.

SELECTED REFERENCES

1. DANTZIG, G. B., *Linear Programming and Extensions*, Princeton, N.J.: Princeton University Press, 1963.
2. SIMMONARD, MICHEL, *Linear Programming*, translated by W. Jewell, Englewood Cliffs, New Jersey: Prentice-Hall, 1966.

PROBLEMS

☐ **4-1** Write the dual problem for the canonical and standard forms of the following primal problem.

$$\text{Maximize} \quad x_0 = x_1 + 2x_2 - 3x_3 + 4x_4,$$

subject to

$$-x_1 + x_2 + x_3 - 3x_4 = 5,$$
$$6x_1 + 7x_2 - 3x_3 - 5x_4 \geq 8,$$
$$12x_1 - 9x_2 + 9x_3 + 9x_4 \leq 20,$$
$$x_1 \geq 0, \quad x_2 \geq 0, \quad x_3 \geq 0,$$

$$x_4 \text{ is unrestricted in sign.}$$

Show that the dual problem is unique regardless of the form of the primal problem.

□ **4-2** Consider the primal problem

$$\text{maximize} \quad x_0 = 3x_1 + 2x_2 + 5x_3,$$

subject to

$$x_1 + 2x_2 + x_3 \leq 500,$$
$$3x_1 \quad\quad + 2x_3 \leq 460,$$
$$x_1 + 4x_2 \quad\quad \leq 420,$$
$$x_1, x_2, x_3 \geq 0.$$

Write the dual problem for the above primal. Without carrying out the simplex method computations on either the primal or the dual problems, estimate an approximate range for the optimum value of the objective function.

□ **4-3** Consider Problem 2-4 (Chapter 2). The equivalent linear programming formulation is given by:

$$\text{minimize} \quad x_0 = x_1 + x_2 + x_3 + x_4 + x_5 + x_6,$$

subject to

$$
\begin{aligned}
x_1 \quad\quad\quad\quad\quad\quad + x_6 &\geq 4, \\
x_1 + x_2 \quad\quad\quad\quad &\geq 8, \\
x_2 + x_3 \quad\quad\quad &\geq 10, \\
x_3 + x_4 \quad\quad &\geq 7, \\
x_4 + x_5 \quad &\geq 12, \\
x_5 + x_6 &\geq 4, \\
x_j \geq 0, \quad \text{for all } j,
\end{aligned}
$$

where x_j is the number of waitresses starting at the beginning of the jth period. Write the dual problem to the above primal then find the optimal solution to the primal by solving the dual.

□ **4-4** Solve the following problem by considering its dual.

$$\text{Minimize} \quad x_0 = 5x_1 + 6x_2 + 3x_3,$$

subject to

$$5x_1 + 5x_2 + 3x_3 \geq 50,$$
$$x_1 + x_2 - x_3 \geq 20,$$
$$7x_1 + 6x_2 - 9x_3 \geq 30,$$
$$5x_1 + 5x_2 + 5x_3 \geq 35,$$
$$2x_1 + 4x_2 - 15x_3 \geq 10,$$
$$12x_1 + 10x_2 \qquad \geq 90,$$
$$x_2 - 10x_3 \geq 20,$$
$$x_1 \geq 0, \quad x_2 \geq 0, \quad x_3 \geq 0.$$

Compare the number of constraints in the two problems.

☐ **4-5** Solve the following problem using the artificial variables technique, then find the dual solution from the optimal tableau.

$$\text{Maximize} \quad x_0 = 5x_1 + 2x_2 + 3x_3,$$

subject to

$$x_1 + 5x_2 + 2x_3 = 30,$$
$$x_1 - 5x_2 - 6x_3 \geq 40,$$
$$x_1 \geq 0, \quad x_2 \geq 0, \quad x_3 \geq 0.$$

Check the dual solution by solving the dual problem graphically. (Save the solution of this problem for later use with Problem 4-23.)

☐ **4-6** Consider Problem 3-7 (Chapter 3). Write its dual problem and then find its solution directly from the optimal primal tableau. Verify this result by showing that these optimal dual values yield the same optimal value of the objective function obtained in the primal.

☐ **4-7** Repeat the same question in Problem 4-6 for Problem 3-8 (Chapter 3).

☐ **4-8** Consider the problem:

$$\text{maximize} \quad x_0 = 8x_3 + 6x_2,$$

subject to

$$x_1 - x_2 \leq \tfrac{3}{5},$$
$$x_1 - x_2 \geq 2,$$
$$x_1, \quad x_2 \geq 0.$$

Show that both the primal and the dual problems have no feasible space. Hence it is not always true that when one problem is infeasible, its dual is unbounded.

☐ **4-9** Given that a linear programming problem has an unbounded solution, why is it that its dual must necessarily be infeasible? (Notice the important difference between the argument in this problem and the one in Problem 4-8.)

☐ **4-10** Consider the following problem.

$$\text{Minimize} \quad y_0 = y_1 - 5y_2 + 6y_3,$$

subject to

$$2y_1 \quad\quad + 4y_3 \geq 50,$$
$$y_1 + 2y_2 \quad\quad \geq 30,$$
$$y_3 \geq 10,$$
$$y_1, y_2, y_3 \text{ unrestricted in sign.}$$

Show that the solution to this problem is unbounded by showing that the only solution to its dual is infeasible and that the primal has a feasible space. Suppose the above problem is not checked for a feasible space, would it be possible to make this conclusion? Why?

☐ **4-11** Consider the solution of Example 3·6-1. It was shown that the solution of the first iteration yields the optimal value of x_0 but that the given tableau does not correspond to the optimal solution because the latter is degenerate. Ascertain this result by showing that the dual solution corresponding to the first iteration is infeasible while that corresponding to the second (optimal) iteration is feasible.

☐ **4-12** Consider the linear programming problem:

$$\text{minimize} \quad x_0 = 2x_1 + 3x_2,$$

subject to

$$2x_1 + 3x_2 \leq 30,$$
$$x_1 + 2x_2 \geq 10,$$
$$x_1 - x_2 \geq 0,$$
$$x_1 \geq 5,$$
$$x_2 \geq 0.$$

(a) Solve the above problem graphically.
(b) Write its dual problem.
(c) Indicate the dual variables which will definitely appear in the optimal basic solution for the dual problem.

☐ **4-13** The final optimal tableau of a maximization linear programming problem with three constraints of type ($\leq$) and two unknowns (x_1, x_2) is given by,

Basic	x_0	x_1	x_2	S_1	S_2	S_3	Solution
x_0	①	0	0	0	3	2	?
S_1	0	0	0	①	1	-1	2
x_2	0	0	①	0	1	0	6
x_1	0	①	0	0	-1	1	2

where S_1, S_2, and S_3 are slack variables. Find the value of the objective function, x_0, in *two* different ways using the primal-dual relationships introduced in Section 4·4.

☐ **4-14** Consider the problem:

$$\text{maximize} \quad x_0 = 2x_1 + x_2 + 5x_3 + 6x_4,$$

subject to

$$2x_1 \qquad + x_3 + \ x_4 \leq 8,$$
$$2x_1 + 2x_2 + x_3 + 2x_4 \leq 12,$$
$$x_1, \quad x_2, \quad x_3, \quad x_4 \ \geq 0.$$

Using the primal-dual relationship for the objective functions, show that x_3 and x_4 constitute the optimal basic solution. What is the optimal dual solution?

☐ **4-15** Solve Problem 4-3 using the dual simplex method.

☐ **4-16** Solve Problem 4-12 using the dual simplex method.

☐ **4-17** Consider the following problem.

$$\text{Minimize} \quad y_0 = 6y_1 + 7y_2 + 3y_3 + 5y_4,$$

subject to

$$5y_1 + 6y_2 - 3y_3 + 4y_4 \geq 12,$$
$$y_2 - 5y_3 - 6y_4 \geq 10,$$
$$2y_1 + 5y_2 + y_3 + y_4 \geq 8,$$
$$y_1 \geq 0, \quad y_2 \geq 0, \quad y_3 \geq 0, \quad y_4 \geq 0.$$

It is required to solve this problem for the optimal values of y_1, y_2, y_3, and y_4.

(a) Indicate *three* different methods for solving this problem and give the complete starting tableau in each case.
(b) Compute the maximum number of possible iterations in each of the three cases.
(c) Which of the above methods would you use and why?

☐ **4-18** The optimum simplex tableau for a maximization problem with all ($\leq$) constraints is given by,

Basic	x_0	x_1	x_2	S_1	S_2	S_3	Solution
x_0	①	0	0	1/4	1/4	0	5
x_2	0	0	①	1/2	$-1/2$	0	2
x_1	0	①	0	$-1/8$	3/8	0	3/2
S_3	0	0	0	1	-2	①	4

where x_1 and x_2 are the decision variables and S_1, S_2, and S_3 are the slack variables. Suppose it is decided to increase the right-hand side of one of the constraints, which one do you recommend for expansion and why? What is the maximum amount of increase in this case? Find the corresponding new value of the objective function.

☐ **4-19** In Problem 4-18 above, let c_1 and c_2 be the coefficients of x_1 and x_2 in the objective function, respectively. Using the information of the optimum tableau in the mentioned problem, find the range of the ratio c_1/c_2 which will always keep the given basic solution optimal.

☐ **4-20** Consider the production planning problem of Example 2·2-1. The complete solution of this problem was given in Example 3·4-1. In view of the given solution, answer the following questions using postoptimality analysis whenever possible.

(a) What are the efficiencies of the three production stages as compared with their respective maximum capacities?

(b) Suppose it is necessary to add a *fourth* processing stage to all three products. The maximum capacity of this stage based on 480 minutes per day is 120 units of product 1, 480 units of product 2, *or* 240 units of product 3. Assuming that the capacity of this stage is 548 minutes per day, find the new optimal solution.

(c) Let y_0, y_1, y_2, and y_3 be the objective and the dual variables, respectively, which are associated with the original problem. Write the complete dual problem and give its solution.

(d) Suppose a *fourth* product is scheduled through the same stages as given in the original problem with the following data:

Stage:	1	2	3	
Product:	3	2	4	minutes/unit

The profit per unit of the new product is $9. How much of each product should be produced? What is the new value of the objective function?

(e) Consider the original problem as given in Example 3·4-1. Suppose it is possible to increase the capacities of the three stages *one at a time*. What is the maximum increase in the capacities of each stage which will leave the variables of the present basic solution unchanged. What are the corresponding values of x_1, x_2, and x_3?

(f) In part (e) above, which stage would you recommend for expansion? Why?

☐ **4-21** Consider the optimal solution of Example 3·4-1. This solution indicates that $x_1 = 0$ while $x_2 = 100$ even though product 1 contributes higher per unit profit ($= 3$) than product 2 ($= 2$). The management has decided to study the reason for the nonprofitability of this product. Their main attention is directed to the time each unit of product 1 consumes at the three production stages. Which stage, if any, should be the first to be considered for adjustment? What is the minimum percentage decrease in the production time of the selected stage beyond which any decrease should cause x_1 to be profitable?

☐ **4-22** Consider the optimal solution to the problem of Example 3·4-1 again. Suppose that the times per unit of product 1 on the three stages (technological coefficients) were changed to $(1, 1, 6)$ instead of $(1, 3, 1)$. Assume further that the profits per unit of products 2 and 3 were changed to $(1, 3)$ instead of $(2, 5)$. What is the new optimal solution to the problem?

☐ **4-23** Consider Problem 4-5. Suppose that the technological coefficients of x_2 were $(5 - \theta, -5 + \theta)$ instead of $(5, -5)$, where θ is a nonnegative parameter. Find the values of θ for which the solution to Problem 4-5 remains optimal.

☐ **4-24** In Problem 4-5, suppose that the right-hand side of the constraints becomes $(30 + \theta, 40 - \theta)$, where θ is a nonnegative parameter. Assume further that the coefficients of the objective function are changed to $(5 - \theta, 2 + \theta, 3 + \theta)$. Find the values of θ for which the solution to Problem 4-5 remains basic, feasible, and optimal.

☐ **4-25** Consider the problem:

$$\text{maximize} \quad x_0 = 2x_2 - 5x_3,$$

subject to

$$x_1 \qquad + x_3 \geq 2,$$
$$2x_1 + x_2 + 6x_3 \leq 6,$$
$$x_1 - x_2 + 3x_3 = 0,$$
$$x_1, \quad x_2, \quad x_3 \geq 0.$$

(a) Write the complete dual problem from the standard form of the above primal.

(b) Solve the primal problem and then find the solution to the dual.

(c) Suppose that the right-hand side of the primal is changed to (2, 10, 5) instead of (2, 6, 0), find the new optimal solution.

(d) Suppose that the coefficients of x_2 and x_3 in the objective function are changed to (1, 1) instead of (2, −5), find the new solution.

☐ **4-26** In Problem 4-6, suppose the objective function is changed to read:

$$\text{maximize} \quad x_0 = 2x_1 + 5x_2 + 2x_3.$$

Find the new optimal solution.

CHAPTER 5

The Transportation Problem and Network Models

§ 5·1
Introduction

This chapter deals with an important class of the linear programming problem called the transportation model. In its obvious sense, this model seeks the minimization of the cost of transporting a certain commodity from a number of sources to a number of destinations. A typical illustration was given by Example 2·2-7 where the factories represent sources and the retail stores represent destinations. There exists a variety of problems, however, which can be formulated indirectly as a transportation model. For example, the caterer problem given by Example 2·2-3 can be formulated as a transportation model. (See Problem 5-4.)

Although the transportation model can be solved using the regular simplex method, its special properties offer a more convenient procedure for solving this type of problem. This procedure, as will be shown later, is based on the same theory of the simplex method. It makes use, however, of some short cuts which yield a less cumbersome computational scheme.

This chapter is organized in three major sections. Section 5·2 introduces the basic transportation technique. The development is based completely on the duality theory introduced in Chapter 4. Section 5·3 presents some applications of the transportation technique. These include the transshipment model, the least-time transportation model, and the generalized transportation model. Such models are especially useful when dealing with special classes of the linear programming problem. Finally, Section 5·4 deals with the network representation of the transportation problem. This section also presents two types of problems which are not readily reducible to the ordinary transportation model but which are of special value in designing transportation systems. These are the problems dealing with the maximization and minimization of networks.

§ 5·2
The Transportation Model

§ 5·2·1
Definition of the Model

Suppose there are m sources and n destinations. Let a_i be the number of supply units available at source i, ($i = 1, 2, \ldots, m$) and let b_j be the number of demand units required at destination j, ($j = 1, 2, \ldots, n$). Let c_{ij} be the *per unit* transportation cost on route (i,j) joining source i and destination j. The objective is to determine the number of units transported from source i to destination j such that the total transportation costs are minimized. In the meantime, the supply limits at the sources and the demand requirements at the destinations must be satisfied exactly. Let x_{ij} (≥ 0) be the number of units shipped from source i to destination j, then the equivalent linear programming model is given as follows.

$$\text{Minimize} \quad x_0 = \sum_{i=1}^{m} \sum_{j=1}^{n} c_{ij} x_{ij},$$

subject to

$$\sum_{j=1}^{n} x_{ij} = a_i, \quad i = 1, 2, \ldots, m,$$

$$\sum_{i=1}^{m} x_{ij} = b_j, \quad j = 1, 2, \ldots, n,$$

$$x_{ij} \geq 0.$$

It is noted that the two sets of constraints are consistent if

$$\sum_{i=1}^{m} a_i = \sum_{j=1}^{n} b_j.$$

This is easily seen since

$$\sum_{j=1}^{n} b_j = \sum_{j=1}^{n} \left(\sum_{i=1}^{m} x_{ij} \right) = \sum_{i=1}^{m} \left(\sum_{j=1}^{n} x_{ij} \right) = \sum_{i=1}^{m} a_i.$$

Such a restriction represents no special difficulty in the formulation of a transportation model since it can always be satisfied by adding a dummy source or a dummy destination. This point is discussed further in Section

5·2·5. It is seen, however, that this restriction causes one of the constraints to be redundant. This means that the problem reduces to $(m + n - 1)$ constraints in $(m \times n)$ unknowns.

Suppose, for simplicity, that $m = 2$ and $n = 3$. Then the above linear programming problem appears in the tableau form as shown in Table 5–1 with all the missing elements being equal to zero.

Table 5–1

		Source 1 variables			Source 2 variables			R.H.S.
	x_0	x_{11}	x_{12}	x_{13}	x_{21}	x_{22}	x_{23}	R.H.S.
Objective equation	1	$-c_{11}$	$-c_{12}$	$-c_{13}$	$-c_{21}$	$-c_{22}$	$-c_{23}$	0
Sources constraints	0	1	1	1				a_1
	0				1	1	1	a_2
Destinations constraints	0	1			1			b_1
	0		1			1		b_2
	0			1			1	b_3

Notice that all the nonzero technological coefficients are equal to $+1$. Notice also the triangular arrangement of the technological coefficients corresponding to the variables of each source. These are the special properties of the transportation model which allow the development of the so-called transportation technique.

The tableau form in Table 5–1 shows that the problem does not offer an obvious starting solution. This difficulty, as will be shown in the next section, is overcome by reformulating the problem in a more convenient form. Table 5–2 illustrates the new representation for the problem in Table 5–1.

Table 5–2

From \ To	Destination j			
	1	2	3	a_i
Source i — 1	c_{11} / x_{11}	c_{12} / x_{12}	c_{13} / x_{13}	a_1
2	c_{21} / x_{21}	c_{22} / x_{22}	c_{23} / x_{23}	a_2
b_j	b_1	b_2	b_3	

This array also will be useful in presenting the transportation technique. Notice that the rows of the array represent the source constraints while its columns represent the destination constraints.

§ 5·2·2
The Transportation Technique

The basic steps of the transportation technique are

Step 1: Determine a starting basic feasible solution.

Step 2: Determine an entering variable from among the nonbasic variables. If all such variables satisfy the optimality condition (of the simplex method), stop; otherwise, pass to step 3.

Step 3: Determine a leaving variable (using the feasibility condition) from among the variables of the current basic solution; then find the new basic solution. Return to Step 2.

These steps will now be considered in detail. The vehicle of explanation is the problem in Table 5–3. The reader should notice that the procedure is

Table 5–3

From \ To	j 1	2	3	4	a_i
1	$\boxed{10}$ x_{11}	$\boxed{0}$ x_{12}	$\boxed{20}$ x_{13}	$\boxed{11}$ x_{14}	15
2	$\boxed{12}$ x_{21}	$\boxed{7}$ x_{22}	$\boxed{9}$ x_{23}	$\boxed{20}$ x_{24}	25
3	$\boxed{0}$ x_{31}	$\boxed{14}$ x_{32}	$\boxed{16}$ x_{33}	$\boxed{18}$ x_{34}	5
b_j	5	15	15	10	

the same as the simplex method. The only difference occurs in the special way of checking the optimality and feasibility conditions. This stems mainly from the special structure of the transportation model.

Step 1. As in the simplex method, the first step is to find a starting basic feasible solution to the problem. Since the problem has $m + n - 1$ independent constraint equations, the starting solution must consist of $m + n - 1$ basic variables. The method used to obtain such a solution employs the so-called "northwest corner rule." The rule calls for allocating the maximum amount to the variable x_{11} (the variable in the northwest corner of the array) such that the constraints of the first source and the first destination are not violated. The satisfied column (row) is then crossed out indicating that the remaining variables in the crossed column (row) are zero. (If both the column and the row are satisfied simultaneously, either one may be crossed out.) The first uncrossed element in the next column (row) is then selected and the maximum feasible amount is allocated to it. Again the satisfied column (row) is crossed out. This is continued until all the columns and rows are crossed out.

To illustrate the application of the northwest corner rule, consider the above example. The maximum amount that can be allocated to x_{11} is 5 in which case the first column is crossed out. (See Table 5–4.) The remaining supply for the first source then becomes equal to 10. These changes are designated in Table 5–4 by the symbol (a).

Table 5–4

From \ To	j 1	2	3	4	(a)	(b)	(c)	(d)	(e)	(f)
i 1	(5) (a)	(10) (b)			15	10				
2		(5) (c)	(15) (d)	(5) (e)			25	20	5	
3				(5) (f)						5
(a)	5									
(b)		15								
(c)		5								
(d)			15							
(e)				10						
(f)				5						

Since the first column is crossed out, the next element to be considered is x_{12}. The changes corresponding to x_{12} are indicated by the symbol (b) and the maximum amount allocated to x_{12} is 10. The first row is thus crossed out and x_{22} is selected as the next element with a maximum allocation of 5 (symbol c). The process continues in the same way until the third (last) row and the fourth (last) column are crossed out. This yields the complete starting solution shown in Table 5–4.

The indicated starting solution includes $m + n - 1 = 3 + 4 - 1 = 6$ positive basic variables. The northwest corner rule always yields such a solution with the exception of the degenerate cases which are discussed in Section 5·2·3.

There are other methods which are also used to find a starting basic feasible solution to the transportation problem. These will be discussed in Section 5·2·4.

Step 2. Following the determination of the starting solution, the next step is to check the solution for optimality. This is done in the usual manner using the same optimality condition of the simplex method. The only difference occurs in the method of computing the coefficients of the objective equation. The reader will recall from Property II of the primal-dual relationships (Section 4·4) that, given the simplex multipliers of the current iteration, the coefficients of the objective equation are obtained by taking the difference between the left and the right sides of the dual constraints. This property will be used in the transportation technique to identify the entering variable. To do this, it is necessary first to identify the dual of the transportation problem.

To show how the general dual problem is obtained for the transportation model, consider first the special case of $m = 2$ and $n = 3$ given in Table 5–1. Let u_1 and u_2 be the dual variables corresponding to the sources constraints and let v_1, v_2, and v_3 be the dual variables corresponding to the destination constraints. Thus, the dual problem becomes (see Section 4·2·2):

$$\text{maximize } y_0 = (a_1 u_1 + a_2 u_2) + (b_1 v_1 + b_2 v_2 + b_3 v_3),$$

subject to

$$
\begin{aligned}
u_1 \quad\;\; + v_1 \quad\quad\quad\;\; &\le c_{11}, \\
u_1 \quad\quad\;\; + v_2 \quad\quad\; &\le c_{12}, \\
u_1 \quad\quad\quad\quad\; + v_3 &\le c_{13}, \\
u_2 + v_1 \quad\quad\quad\;\; &\le c_{21}, \\
u_2 \quad\;\; + v_2 \quad\quad\; &\le c_{22}, \\
u_2 \quad\quad\quad\; + v_3 &\le c_{23}.
\end{aligned}
$$

The variables u_1, u_2, v_1, v_2, and v_3 are unrestricted in sign since the primal problem is in the standard form.

Notice the special structure of the dual constraints resulting from the special arrangement of the " $+1$ " (and " 0 ") elements in the primal problem. Notice also that each constraint includes one u-variable and one v-variable only. Finally, observe that for each dual constraint, the single subscripts of the u and v variables are consistent with the double subscripts of the c-element on the right-hand side of the constraint. Thus, in general, if u_i and v_j are the dual variables corresponding to the constraints of the ith source and the jth destination, respectively, $(i = 1, 2, \ldots, m; \; j = 1, 2, \ldots, n)$, then the corresponding dual problem is given by:

$$\text{maximize} \quad y_0 = \sum_{i=1}^{m} a_i u_i + \sum_{j=1}^{n} b_j v_j,$$

subject to

$$u_i + v_j \le c_{ij}, \quad \text{for all } i \text{ and } j,$$

where u_i and v_j are unrestricted in sign.

Having identified the dual constraints, the problem now is to determine the values of the simplex multipliers. Since by Property II, Section 4·4, the dual constraints corresponding to the basic feasible variables must be satisfied in equality sense, then

$$u_i + v_j = c_{ij}$$

for all *basic* x_{ij}. Except for the degeneracy case, there are $m + n - 1$ such dual equations in $m + n$ dual unknowns (u_i and v_j). The corresponding simplex multipliers can thus be determined by assuming an arbitrary value (usually zero) for any of the dual variables and then solving for the remaining $m + n - 1$ unknowns. The coefficients of the objective equation for the nonbasic variables are then obtained from the corresponding dual constraints using the above mentioned property.

Applying this to the above example, since $x_{11}, x_{12}, x_{22}, x_{23}, x_{24}$, and x_{34} are the current basic variables, their corresponding dual equations are given by

$$
\begin{aligned}
x_{11}: \quad & u_1 + v_1 = c_{11} = 10, \\
x_{12}: \quad & u_1 + v_2 = c_{12} = 0, \\
x_{22}: \quad & u_2 + v_2 = c_{22} = 7, \\
x_{23}: \quad & u_2 + v_3 = c_{23} = 9, \\
x_{24}: \quad & u_2 + v_4 = c_{24} = 20, \\
x_{34}: \quad & u_3 + v_4 = c_{34} = 18.
\end{aligned}
$$

Thus, letting $u_1 = 0$, then $v_1 = 10$, $v_2 = 0$, $u_2 = 7$, $v_3 = 2$, $v_4 = 13$, and $u_3 = 5$.

The objective equation coefficients corresponding to the nonbasic variable are now determined.

$$
\begin{aligned}
x_{13}: \quad & u_1 + v_3 - c_{13} = 0 + 2 - 20 = -18 \\
x_{14}: \quad & u_1 + v_4 - c_{14} = 0 + 13 - 11 = 2 \\
x_{21}: \quad & u_2 + v_1 - c_{21} = 7 + 10 - 12 = 5 \\
x_{31}: \quad & u_3 + v_1 - c_{31} = 5 + 10 - 0 = 15 \leftarrow \\
x_{32}: \quad & u_3 + v_2 - c_{32} = 5 + 0 - 14 = -9 \\
x_{33}: \quad & u_3 + v_3 - c_{33} = 5 + 2 - 16 = -9.
\end{aligned}
$$

This indicates that the variable x_{31} must enter the solution (minimization problem).

Before explaining how x_{31} is introduced, it is convenient to present a more compact form for computing the simplex multipliers and evaluating the coefficients of the nonbasic variables in the objective equation. First arrange the dual variables as indicated in Table 5–5 and let $u_1 = 0$ (or any arbitrary value). Since $u_i + v_j = c_{ij}$ for each *basic* variable, x_{ij} (indicated by ●), then

Table 5–5

u_i \\ v_j	$v_1 = 10$	$v_2 = 0$	$v_3 = 2$	$v_4 = 13$	a_i
$u_1 = 0$	10 ●	0 ●	20 -18	11 2	15
$u_2 = 7$	12 5	7 ●	9 ●	20 ●	25
$u_3 = 5$	0 15	14 -9	16 -9	18 ●	5
b_j	5	15	15	10	

Key

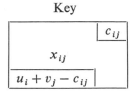

$$\begin{array}{|c|} \hline c_{ij} \\ x_{ij} \\ \hline u_i + v_j - c_{ij} \\ \hline \end{array}$$

knowing u_1, (and c_{11} and c_{12}), v_1 and v_2 can be determined. Next, knowing v_2, u_2 is determined which in turn determines v_3 and v_4. Finally, u_3 is determined from v_4. The nonbasic variables are then evaluated by computing $u_i + v_j - c_{ij}$ and the corresponding result is entered in the bottom left corner of each nonbasic square.

Step 3. The next step after determining the entering variable is to obtain a new basic solution by determining the leaving variable. This is done in the transportation technique using the same feasibility condition of the simplex method. However, the special properties of the transportation model allows the following simple method for determining the leaving variable.

For each nonbasic variable in the transportation array, define a closed path which starts and ends at the square containing this nonbasic variable. The segments of this path are either *horizontal* or *vertical* lines which connect squares containing basic variables only. These closed paths exist and are unique for each nonbasic variable provided the current basic solution is nondegenerate (see next section for treatment of the degeneracy case). Define as "corner elements" the squares where the closed path changes directions (i.e., corners). Thus by interchangeably subtracting and adding the amount allocated to the entering variable from and to the successive *corner elements* of the closed path, the supply and demand constraints can always be satisfied. However, the amount allocated to the entering variable must be limited by the maximum quantity which will render nonnegative values for all the variables in the new solution. This automatically determines the leaving variable as illustrated below.

Consider the same example. The entering variable, x_{31}, has the closed path indicated in Table 5–6. The corner elements for this path are given by the

Table 5–6

squares (1, 1), (1, 2), (2, 2), (2, 4), and (3, 4). Thus by assigning the sign $(-)$ and $(+)$ to the successive corner elements to indicate the interchangeable process of subtraction and addition mentioned above, it is obvious that the maximum amount allocated to x_{31} must be equal to the minimum of the values corresponding to corner elements with $(-)$ signs. (This is equivalent to the selection of minimum ratio in the feasibility condition of the simplex method.) Table 5–7 shows that the negative corner elements are x_{11}, x_{22}, and x_{34}. Since they all are equal to 5, the entering variable x_{31} is also equal to 5 and any one of the variables x_{11}, x_{22}, and x_{34} becomes a leaving variable. (Notice that these three variables reach zero value simultaneously.) The new basic solution is then given by Table 5–8.

Table 5–7

From \ To	1	2	3	4	a_i
1	5 $(-)$	10 $(+)$			15
2		5 $(-)$	15	5 $(+)$	25
3	$(+)$			5 $(-)$	5
b_j	5	15	15	10	

Table 5–8

From \ To	j 1	2	3	4	a_i
1		15			15
i 2			15	10	25
3	5				5
b_j	5	15	15	10	

The corresponding value of the objective function is equal to 15×0 $+ 15 \times 9 + 10 \times 20 + 5 \times 0 = 335$ as compared with $5 \times 10 + 10 \times 0 + 5$ $\times 7 + 15 \times 9 + 5 \times 20 + 5 \times 18 = 410$ in the previous iteration. The difference $410 - 335 = 75$ is equal to the product of the amount allocated to the entering variable, x_{31} ($= 5$) and its corresponding $u_i + v_j - c_{ij}$ ($= 15$); that is, $5 \times 15 = 75$. This shows that the optimality indicator $(u_i + v_j - c_{ij})$ of any nonbasic variable gives directly the per unit improvement in the value of the objective function (compare with the optimality condition in the simplex method).

The new basic solution is degenerate since the number of *positive* basic variables ($= 4$) is less than $m + n - 1$ ($= 6$). It is noted that the determination of the simplex multipliers for the new solution is impossible in this case since the "apparent" number of dual equations ($= 4$) will not be sufficient. This leads to the consideration of the degeneracy problem.

§ 5·2·3
Solution of the Degeneracy Problem

The degeneracy problem can be solved by augmenting the current positive basic variables by as many zero-valued variables as is necessary to complete the required $m + n - 1$ basic variables. These zero-valued variables are selected such that the resulting $m + n - 1$ variables constitute a basic solution. Although these variables may be selected in a number of ways, a straightforward method is to select them from among the basic variables that simultaneously were driven to zero in the immediately preceding iteration. In general, however, any variables can be selected provided they allow the determination of the simplex multipliers.

It is conventional to designate the selected zero-variables by assigning a very small positive value ε to each one of them. These ε's are then treated like any other positive basic variable and are kept in the transportation array until temporary degeneracy is removed or until the optimal solution is reached, whichever occurs first. At that point, all the ε's are discarded.

The above example can now be handled. Since the current basic solution includes four positive variables, two zero-variables should be selected to complete the basis. Let these two variables be x_{11} and x_{22} so that the transportation array appears as in Table 5–9.

Table 5–9

To From	1	2	j 3	4	a_i
1	ε	15			$15 + \varepsilon$
i 2		ε	15	10	$25 + \varepsilon$
3	5				5
b_j	$5 + \varepsilon$	$15 + \varepsilon$	15	10	

The simplex multipliers can now be evaluated and the nonbasic variables are tested for optimality. The corresponding results are given by Table 5–10.

Table 5–10

u_i \ v_j	$v_1 = 10$	$v_2 = 0$	$v_3 = 2$	$v_4 = 13$	a_i
$u_1 = 0$	10 ●	0 ●	20 -18	11 2	$15 + \varepsilon$
$u_2 = 7$	12 5	7 ●	9 ●	20 ●	$25 + \varepsilon$
$u_3 = -10$	0 ●	14 -24	16 -24	18 -15	5
b_j	$5 + \varepsilon$	$15 + \varepsilon$	15	10	

Since x_{21} has the largest positive $u_i + v_j - c_{ij}$ ($= 5$), it is admitted as the entering variable. The corner elements of the closed path for x_{21} are x_{11}, x_{12}, and x_{22}. This yields the new solution in Table 5–11 which has only caused a change in the location of ε. The new solution is again degenerate. (Notice that ε is infinitesimally small and hence its effect can be neglected when it is added or subtracted to or from a positive value.)

Table 5–11

From \ To (j)	1	2	3	4	a_i
1		$15 + \varepsilon$			$15 + \varepsilon$
2	ε		15	10	$25 + \varepsilon$
3	5				5
b_j	$5 + \varepsilon$	$15 + \varepsilon$	15	10	

The next iteration is formulated by adding the zero-variable x_{22} to the basis and the new basic solution becomes as given in Table 5–12. This solution when tested for optimality will yield the results in Table 5–13.

Table 5–12

From \ To (j)	1	2	3	4	a_i
1		15			15
2	ε	ε	15	10	$25 + 2\varepsilon$
3	5				5
b_j	$5 + \varepsilon$	$15 + \varepsilon$	15	10	

Table 5–13

u_i \ v_j	$v_1 = 5$	$v_2 = 0$	$v_3 = 2$	$v_4 = 13$	a_i
$u_1 = 0$	10 — -5	0 ●	20 — -18	11 — 2	15
$u_2 = 7$	12 ●	7 ●	9 ●	20 ●	$25 + 2\varepsilon$
$u_3 = -5$	0 ●	14 — -19	16 — -19	18 — -10	5
b_j	$5 + \varepsilon$	$15 + \varepsilon$	15	10	

This shows that x_{14} must enter the solution. The corner elements of the closed path for x_{14} are x_{12}, x_{22}, and x_{24}. Making the necessary changes, the new solution is given in Table 5–14. Again, the nonbasic variables for this solution are tested for optimality. This gives the results in Table 5–15.

Table 5–14

From \ To	1	2	3	4	a_i
1		5		10	15
2	ε	10	15		$25 + \varepsilon$
3	5				5
	$5 + \varepsilon$	15	15	10	

Table 5–15

u_i \ v_j	$v_1 = 5$	$v_2 = 0$	$v_3 = 2$	$v_4 = 11$	a_i
$u_1 = 0$	[10] -5	[0] ●	[20] -18	[11] ●	15
$u_2 = 7$	[12] ●	[7] ●	[9] ●	[20] -2	$25 + \varepsilon$
$u_3 = -5$	[0] ●	[14] -19	[16] -19	[18] -12	5
b_j	$5 + \varepsilon$	15	15	10	

This shows that the last solution is optimal and the value of the objective function is $5 \times 0 + 10 \times 11 + 10 \times 7 + 15 \times 9 + 5 \times 0 = 315$.

Notice the above simplex multipliers correspond to the optimal dual values. Consequently, the value of the objective function can also be obtained from the dual objective function; that is

$$\sum_{i=1}^{3} a_i u_i + \sum_{j=1}^{4} b_j v_j = (15 \times 0 + 25 \times 7 + 5 \times -5)$$

$$+ (5 \times 5 + 15 \times 0 + 15 \times 2 + 10 \times 11) = 315.$$

§ 5·2·4
Improved Starting Solution

In the northwest corner rule the starting solution is determined without any consideration of the transportation costs. Two other methods thus have been developed which usually yield better (less costly) starting solutions than the one developed by the northwest corner rule. These are known as the least-cost method and the (Vogel) approximation method. The first method is straight-forward while the second method requires additional computations. The approximation method, however, usually yields a starting solution which is very close, if not equal, to the optimal solution.

The least-cost method is now illustrated by an example. Consider the problem introduced in Table 5–3. Select the smallest cost element in the matrix and allocate to it the maximum feasible amount, then cross out the satisfied column or row. Since (0), the smallest cost element, occurs at x_{12} and x_{31}, the maximum units allocated to these two variables are 15 and 5 respectively. This exhausts the supply of the first and third sources and satisfies the demand of the first and second destinations. Consequently, the corresponding rows and columns are crossed out. The next (uncrossed) smallest element is (9) which occurs at x_{23}. The maximum amount that can be allocated to it is 15. This crosses out the third column. The remaining 10 units are then assigned to x_{24} and this yields the starting solution given in Table 5–16.

Table 5–16

From \ To	1	2	3	4	a_i
1		15			15
2			15	10	25
3	5				5
b_j	5	15	15	10	

This starting solution costs $5 \times 0 + 15 \times 0 + 15 \times 9 + 10 \times 20 = 335$ as compared with a cost of 410 which is given by the starting solution of the northwest corner rule.

Consider next the Vogel approximation method (VAM). The steps of this method are given by

Step 1.   From the cost matrix of the transportation problem determine the penalty for each row and each column which is incurred as a result of not assigning a positive value to the square having the smallest cost. These penalties are evaluated for each row (column) by subtracting the *smallest* cost element in the row (column) from the *next smallest* cost element in the same row (column).

Step 2. Identify the row or column with the largest penalty among all the rows and columns. If a tie exists, it may be broken arbitrarily. Allocate as much amount as possible to the variable having the smallest cost element in the selected row or column. The corresponding supply and demand quantities (a_i and b_j) are then adjusted accordingly and the satisfied row or column is excluded from further consideration. When all the columns and rows have been excluded the process ends; otherwise, pass to Step 3.

Step 3. Recompute the column and row penalties for the reduced cost matrix then go to Step 2.

Although it is indicated in Step 2 that a tie between equal penalties may be broken arbitrarily, the complete VAM provides more detailed steps for selecting the one row or column which will yield the best results. These details are not discussed here, however.[1]

To illustrate the application of this method consider the same problem used with the least-cost method. The steps of the solution are given below, starting with Table 5–17.

Table 5–17

From \ To	*j* 1	2	3	4	a_i	Row penalties
i 1	10	0	20	11	15	10
2	12	7	9	20	25	2
3	0 5	14	16	18	~~5~~	14
b_j	~~5~~	15	15	10		
Column penalties	10	7	7	7		

---

[1] For a complete presentation of VAM see, S. Zukhovitskiy and L. Avdeyeva, *Linear and Convex Programming*, Philadelphia, Pa., B. W. Saunders Company, 1966, pp. 147–155.

Since Row 3 has a penalty of 14, the least-cost square is (3, 1) to which the quantity 5 is allocated. This exhausts a_3 and satisfies b_1 simultaneously and hence Row 3 and Column 1 are excluded from the process. The next tableau with the new penalties appears as in Table 5–18. This eliminates Column 3.

Table 5–18

From \ To	1	2	3	4	a_i	Row penalties
1		[0]	[20]	[11]	15	11
2		[7]	[9] 15	[20]	25	2
3	5				~~5~~	—
b_j	~~5~~	15	~~15~~	10		
Column penalties	—	7	(11)	9		

Continuing in the same manner, this successively gives $x_{22} = 10$, $x_{12} = 5$, and $x_{14} = 10$. This finally yields the starting solution given in Table 5-19 which happens to be the optimal solution.

Table 5–19

From \ To	1	2	3	4	a_i
1		5		10	15
2		10	15		25
3	5				5
b_j	5	15	15	10	

§ 5·2·5
Unbalanced Transportation Problems

It was stated in Section 5·2·1 that the constraints of the transportation model are consistent provided the problem is balanced; that is, the total supply, $\sum_{i=1}^{m} a_i$, and the total demand, $\sum_{j=1}^{n} b_j$, are equal. In real problems this may not be true always. In this case the problem is said to be *unbalanced* Consequently, the problem should be modified to fit into the transportation model.

The idea here is simple and it calls for determining a fictitious source or destination which will provide the surplus supply or demand, respectively. The per unit transportation costs from the fictitious source to all destinations are obviously zero. Similarly, the per unit transportation costs from all sources to a fictitious destination are also zero.

§ 5·3
Contributions of The Transportation Model

§ 5·3·1
The Transshipment Model

Situations arise where it may not be economical to ship directly from sources to destinations. Rather, the commodity may pass through one or more of the other sources and destinations before eventually reaching its ultimate destination. This case is referred to as the *transshipment* problem. The transportation model given above cannot be used directly to handle this problem. A slight modification, however, would allow the use of the same technique. This is best illustrated by an example.

Consider the following transportation problem with two sources and three destinations. The data for *direct* shipment are summarized in Table 5–20.

Table 5–20

From \ To	j 1	2	3	a_i
i 1	10	20	30	100
2	20	50	40	200
b_j	100	100	100	

The idea of the transshipment model is based on the fact that each source (destination) represents a potential point of supply and demand. This means that, at any stage of transshipping, the total supply ($\sum_i a_i$) may be concentrated at any of these locations (sources or destinations). Each location will then act as a supply point to all other locations. The above transportation array can thus be extended so that each location will act as a potential supply and demand point.

Following this argument, the extended problem for the above example should thus include five "supply" and five "demand" points. Since *all* the demand may be concentrated at any one location, fictitious supply and demand quantities may be assumed for each of these locations. These quantities may be regarded as "buffer stocks." Each of these buffer stocks (of size B, say) should at least be equal to the total supply (demand) in the original problem. This means that $B \geq \sum_i a_i (= \sum_j b_j)$. Thus, letting $B = 300$, the modified transshipment problem for the given example is shown in Table 5–21.

Table 5–21

From	To	i 1	2	j 1	2	3	Supply
i	1			10	20	30	$100 + B$
	2			20	50	40	$200 + B$
j	1						B
	2						B
	3						B
	Demand	B	B	$100 + B$	$100 + B$	$100 + B$	

The model is not complete until the unit costs for the remaining entries of the new array are identified. Notice that all the diagonal elements (1, 1), (2, 2), ..., etc. have zero unit costs. The other unit-shipping costs between sources or destinations are secured from the technology of the problem. Finally, unit-shipping costs from destination to source points may or may not be the same as the unit costs from sources to destination points which were given by the original problem.

Assuming that all unit costs have been estimated, the complete transshipment model is given by Table 5–22.

The extended problem is then solved using the regular transportation technique which yields the optimal solution given in Table 5–23. (This problem has an alternative optimal solution.)

The diagonal elements are ignored in the above solution since they do not

Table 5–22

From \ To		i 1	i 2	j 1	j 2	j 3	Supply
i	1	0	80	10	20	30	400
i	2	10	0	20	50	40	500
j	1	20	30	0	40	10	300
j	2	40	20	10	0	20	300
j	3	60	70	80	20	0	300
Demand		300	300	400	400	400	

Table 5–23

From \ To		i 1	i 2	j 1	j 2	j 3	Supply
i	1	300			100		400
i	2		300	200			500
j	1			200		100	300
j	2				300		300
j	3					300	300
Demand		300	300	400	400	400	

have any physical meaning. The remaining entries can be interpreted graphically as shown in Figure 5–1. Notice that the second source ($i = 2$) sends all its supply to the first destination ($j = 1$) where 100 units are kept to fulfill the demand at that destination. The remaining 100 units are then shipped to the third destination ($j = 3$) to fill its demand. The demand for the second destination ($j = 2$) is received directly from the first source ($i = 1$).

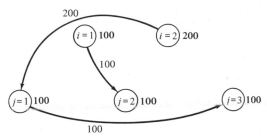

Figure 5–1

§ 5·3·2
The Least-Time Transportation Model

Transportation problems exist where the objective is to minimize the time, rather than the transportation costs, required to fill *all* the demand at the destinations. A typical example occurs in transporting military supplies where the speed of delivery is more important than the transportation costs.

The structure of this type of problem is the same as in the regular transportation problem except that for each route the cost per unit is replaced by the *total* time required to effect a complete shipment. (Notice that the transportation time is assumed independent of the size of shipment.) Thus, if t_{ij} is the time required to ship the quantity x_{ij} from source i to destination j ($i = 1, 2, \ldots, m$; $j = 1, 2, \ldots, n$), the corresponding transportation array is given as in Table 5–24.

Table 5–24

From \ To		1	2	$\cdots$	n	a_i
		t_{11}	t_{12}		t_{1n}	
	1					a_1
		t_{21}	t_{22}		t_{2n}	
i	2					a_2
	$\vdots$					$\vdots$
		t_{m1}	t_{m2}		t_{mn}	
	m					a_m
b_j		b_1	b_2	$\cdots$	b_n	$\sum_i a_i = \sum_j b_j$

It is noted that the shipment of a feasible plan is completed when the shipment with the largest time is completed. Let T_k be the largest time associated with the kth feasible plan, the objective then is to select the plan which yields

$$\min_k \{T_k\}, \quad \text{for all } k.$$

This is achieved using the following iterative procedure:

Step 1.   Construct a starting basic feasible solution using the same methods of the regular transportation technique.

Step 2.   Find T_k corresponding to the current solution and cross out all the nonbasic squares having $t_{ij} \geq T_k$.

Step 3.   Construct a closed path (as in the regular transportation technique) for the basic variable corresponding to T_k such that when the values at the corner elements are shifted around, this basic variable is driven toward zero and no variable becomes negative. If no such closed path can be constructed, the process ends; otherwise, go to Step 2.

To illustrate this procedure, consider the problem in Table 5–25 with the

Table 5–25

To From	1	2	3	4	a_i
1	10 12	0 3	20	11	15
2	1	7 5	9 15	20 5	25
3	12	14	16	18 5	5
b_j	12	8	15	10	

indicated starting feasible plan. This plan is obtained by using the northwest corner rule and is given by $x_{11} = 12$, $x_{12} = 3$, $x_{22} = 5$, $x_{23} = 15$, $x_{24} = 5$, and $x_{34} = 5$ with all other variables equal to zero. The corresponding shipping times are $t_{11} = 10$, $t_{12} = 0$, $t_{22} = 7$, $t_{23} = 9$, $t_{24} = 20$, and $t_{34} = 18$. Consequently all the shipments for this plan are completed after

$$T_1 = \max \{t_{11}, t_{12}, t_{22}, t_{23}, t_{24}, t_{34}\} = t_{24} = 20$$

time units. Thus, square (1, 3) is eliminated since it has $t_{13} = 20$ ($= T_1$). The closed path for x_{24} is as shown in Table 5–26.

This indicates that x_{24} can be decreased by a maximum of three units only. Otherwise, x_{12} will become negative. The variable x_{14} thus will enter the solution at level 3. This yields the solution given in Table 5–27.

Table 5–26

From \ To	1	2	3	4	a_i
1	●	● (−)	✕	(+)	15
2		● (+)	●	● (−)	25
3				●	5
b_j	12	8	15	10	

Table 5–27

From \ To	1	2	3	4	a_i
1	12 (−)		✕	3 (+)	15
2	(+)	8	15	2 (−)	25
3				5	5
b_j	12	8	15	10	

Table 5–27 shows that T_2 equals 20, which still corresponds to x_{24}. Using the closed path (2, 4), (1, 4), (1, 1), and (2, 1), the variable x_{24} is dropped from the solution (at zero level) as shown in Table 5–28.

The solution in Table 5–28 has $T_3 = t_{34} = 18$ corresponding to x_{34}. Hence x_{24} is eliminated ($t_{24} = 20 > 18$). The closed path for x_{34} is given by (3, 4), (1, 4), (1, 1), and (3, 1). Thus, $T_4 = 12$ and the new solution is shown in Table 5–29.

Table 5–28

From \ To	1	2	3	4	a_i
1	10 $\ominus$		$\times$	5 $\oplus$	15
2	2	8	15	$\times$	25
3	$\oplus$			5 $\ominus$	5
b_j	12	8	15	10	

Table 5–29

From \ To	1	2	3	4	a_i
1	10 | 5	0 |	$\times$	11 | 10	15
2	1 | 2	7 | 8	9 | 15	$\times$	25
3	12 | 5	$\times$	$\times$	$\times$	5
b_j	12	8	15	10	

From the solution in Table 5–29, it follows that no closed path can be constructed for x_{31} without increasing the present minimum time. The above plan is thus optimal and the total shipment time is 12. Details of the plan are:

$$x_{11} = 5 \quad \text{with} \quad t_{11} = 10,$$
$$x_{14} = 10 \quad \text{with} \quad t_{14} = 11,$$
$$x_{21} = 2 \quad \text{with} \quad t_{21} = 1,$$
$$x_{22} = 8 \quad \text{with} \quad t_{22} = 7,$$
$$x_{23} = 15 \quad \text{with} \quad t_{23} = 9,$$
$$x_{31} = 5 \quad \text{with} \quad t_{31} = 12.$$

§ 5·3·3
The Assignment Model

Consider the situation of assigning m jobs (or workers) to n machines. A job i ($= 1, 2, \ldots, m$) when assigned to machine j ($= 1, 2, \ldots, n$) is assumed to incur a cost c_{ij}. The objective is to assign the jobs to the machines (one job per machine) at the least total cost. Such a situation is known as the assignment problem.

The formulation of this problem may be regarded as a special case of the transportation model. Here the jobs represent "sources" while the machines represent "destinations." The supply available at each source is 1; that is, $a_i = 1$ for all i. Similarly, the demand required at each destination is 1; that is $b_j = 1$, for all j. The cost of "transporting" (assigning) job i to machine j is equivalent to c_{ij}. If a job cannot be assigned to a certain machine, this may be indicated by putting the corresponding $c_{ij} = M$, a very high cost. The resulting transportation model can thus be represented as shown in Table 5–30.

Table 5–30

i \ j		1	2	$\cdots$	n	a_i
			Machine			
	1	c_{11}	c_{12}		c_{1n}	1
	2	c_{21}	c_{22}		c_{2n}	1
Job	$\vdots$					$\vdots$
	m	c_{m1}	c_{m2}	$\cdots$	c_{mn}	1
b_j		1	1	$\cdots$	1	

Before this model can be solved by the transportation technique, it is necessary first to balance the problem by adding fictitious jobs or machines depending on whether $m < n$ or $m > n$, respectively. In these cases, the corresponding c_{ij} equals zero. It will thus be assumed that $m = n$ without loss of generality.

The above model can be expressed mathematically as follows. Let,

$$x_{ij} = \begin{cases} 0, \text{ if the } j\text{th job is } not \text{ assigned to the } i\text{th machine} \\ 1, \text{ if the } j\text{th job is assigned to the } i\text{th machine.} \end{cases}$$

The model is thus given by:

$$\text{minimize} \quad x_0 = \sum_{i=1}^{n} \sum_{j=1}^{n} c_{ij} x_{ij},$$

subject to

$$\sum_{j=1}^{n} x_{ij} = 1, \qquad i = 1, 2, \ldots, n,$$

$$\sum_{i=1}^{n} x_{ij} = 1, \qquad j = 1, 2, \ldots, n,$$

$$x_{ij} = 0, \quad \text{or } 1.$$

To illustrate the development of the assignment model, consider the problem in Table 5–31 with three jobs and three machines. The initial

Table 5–31

i \ j	Machine 1	Machine 2	Machine 3	a_i
1	1 ⌐5	⌐7	⌐9	1
2	⌐14	1 ⌐10	⌐12	1
3	⌐15	⌐13	1 ⌐16	1
b_j	1	1	1	

solution (using the northwest corner rule) is obviously degenerate. This will always be the case in the assignment model regardless of the method used to obtain the starting basis. In fact, the solution will continue to be degenerate at every iteration. The degeneracy technique (Section 5·2·3) should thus be used as necessary with the transportation technique until the optimal solution is obtained.

The special structure of the assignment model allows a different, and perhaps more convenient, method of solution. This method will be illustrated using the above example.

The basic idea of the method is that the optimal solution remains the same if a constant is added or subtracted to any row or column of the cost matrix. Thus if p_i and q_j are subtracted from the ith row and the jth column, respectively, the new cost elements will become $c'_{ij} = c_{ij} - p_i - q_j$. This yields the new objective function

$$x'_0 = \sum_i \sum_j c'_{ij} x_{ij}$$

$$= \sum_i \sum_j (c_{ij} - p_i - q_j) x_{ij}$$

$$= \sum_i \sum_j c_{ij} x_{ij} - \sum_i p_i \sum_j x_{ij} - \sum_j q_j \sum_i x_{ij}.$$

Since from the constraints of the problem $\sum_j x_{ij} = \sum_i x_{ij} = 1$, then one gets

$$x_0' = x_0 - \text{constant}.$$

This shows that the minimization of the original objective function x_0 yields the same solution as the minimization of x_0'.

The above idea indicates that if one can create a new c_{ij}'-matrix with zero entries, and if these zero elements, or a subset thereof, constitute a feasible solution, then this feasible solution is the *optimal* solution (since the cost cannot go negative).

Applying this idea to the above example, the zero elements are created by subtracting the smallest element in each row (column) from the corresponding row (column). Considering the rows first, the new c_{ij}'-matrix is shown in Table 5–32.

Table 5–32

	1	2	3	
1	0	2	4	$p_1 = 5$
$\|c_{ij}'\| = 2$	4	0	2	$p_2 = 10$
3	2	0	3	$p_3 = 13$

The last matrix can be made to include more zeros by subtracting $q_3 = 2$ from its third column. This yields Table 5–33.

Table 5–33

	1	2	3
1	[0]	2	2
$\|c_{ij}'\| = 2$	4	0	[0]
3	2	[0]	1

The squares in Table 5–33 indicate a feasible (and hence optimal) assignment to the zero-elements. Thus the optimal assignment is (1, 1), (2, 3), and (3, 2) with a total cost of $5 + 12 + 13 = 30$. Notice that this cost is equal to $p_1 + p_2 + p_3 + q_3$.

Unfortunately, it is not always possible to obtain a feasible assignment as in the above example. In this case, further rules are required to find the optimal solution. These rules will be illustrated by the example shown in Table 5–34.

Table 5–34

	1	2	3	4
1	1	4	6	3
2	8	7	10	9
3	4	5	11	7
4	6	7	8	5

Now, carrying out the same initial steps as in the previous example one gets Table 5–35.

Table 5–35

	1	2	3	4
1	0	3	2	2
2	1	0	0	2
3	0	1	4	3
4	1	2	0	0

Clearly, a feasible assignment to the zero elements is not possible in this case. The procedure then is to draw a *minimum* number of lines through some of the rows and columns such that all the zeros are crossed out. Table 5–36 shows the application of this rule.

Table 5–36

	1	2	3	4
1	0	3	2	2
2	1	0	0	2
3	0	1	4	3
4	1	2	0	0

The next step is to select the *smallest* uncrossed element ($= 1$ in Table 5–36). This element is subtracted from every *un*crossed element and is then added to every element that lies at the intersection of two lines. This yields Table 5–37 which gives the optimal assignment (1, 1), (2, 3), (3, 2) and (4, 4). The corresponding total cost is $1 + 10 + 5 + 5 = 21$.

Table 5–37

	1	2	3	4
1	0	2	1	1
2	2	0	0	2
3	0	0	3	2
4	2	2	0	0

It should be noted that if the optimal solution had not been obtained in the above step, then the given procedure of drawing lines should be repeated until a feasible assignment is achieved.

§ 5·3·4
The Generalized Transportation Model

Consider the following linear programming model.

$$\text{Minimize} \quad x_0 = \sum_{i=1}^{m} \sum_{j=1}^{n} c_{ij} x_{ij}$$

subject to

$$\sum_{j=1}^{n} p_{ij} x_{ij} \le a_i, \qquad i = 1, 2, \ldots, m$$

$$\sum_{i=1}^{m} x_{ij} = b_j, \qquad j = 1, 2, \ldots, n$$

$$x_{ij} \ge 0, \qquad \text{for all } i \text{ and } j.$$

After adding the necessary (nonnegative) slack variables, S_i, to the first m constraints; that is,

$$\sum_{j=1}^{n} p_{ij} x_{ij} + S_i = a_i, \qquad i = 1, 2, \ldots, m,$$

the resulting model defines the so-called *generalized transportation* problem. Although this model can be handled by the regular simplex method, its special properties allow a much simpler solution similar to the one developed for the regular transportation model.

To illustrate the application of the generalized transportation model, consider the situation of assigning n jobs to m different work centers. Each of these centers is capable of handling any of the given jobs but with varying degrees of efficiency. The number of production hours available at the ith work center is limited to a_i, $(i = 1, 2, \ldots, m)$ while the exact number of units required of the jth job is equal to b_j, $(j = 1, 2, \ldots, n)$. Each unit of the jth job consumes p_{ij} hours in the ith work center and its corresponding per unit production cost is c_{ij}. The objective is to determine the number of units x_{ij} of job j to be processed at center i so as to minimize the total cost of completing all the jobs. This problem obviously has the same formulation as the generalized transportation model given above.

For the purpose of solving the generalized transportation problem, a tabular representation is used which is similar to that of the regular transportation model. The new table should include the parameters p_{ij}, however. This is accomplished as shown in Table 5–38.

Table 5–38

i	\multicolumn{2}{c}{1}	\multicolumn{2}{c}{2}	$\cdots$	\multicolumn{2}{c}{n}	\multicolumn{2}{c}{Slacks}	a_i
1	p_{11} \ c_{11}		p_{12} \ c_{12}		$\cdots$	p_{1n} \ c_{1n}		1 \ 0		a_1
	x_{11}		x_{12}			x_{1n}		S_1		
2	p_{21} \ c_{21}		p_{22} \ c_{22}		$\cdots$	p_{2n} \ c_{2n}		1 \ 0		a_2
	x_{21}		x_{22}			x_{2n}		S_2		
$\vdots$	$\vdots$		$\vdots$			$\vdots$		$\vdots$		$\vdots$
m	p_{m1} \ c_{m1}		p_{m2} \ c_{m2}		$\cdots$	p_{mn} \ c_{mn}		1 \ 0		a_m
	x_{m1}		x_{m2}			x_{mn}		S_m		
b_j	b_1		b_2		$\cdots$	b_n		—		

Notice that for each slack variable, $p_{ij} = 1$ and $c_{ij} = 0$. Notice also that the slacks column does not correspond to a constraint in the original problem.

The method of solution for the generalized transportation problem is based on the same idea of the simplex multipliers used in the regular transportation technique. It is thus important to define the dual problem corresponding to the generalized transportation model. Let u_i $(i = 1, 2, \ldots, m)$ be the dual variables corresponding to the first set of m constraints given by

$$\sum_{j=1}^{n} p_{ij} x_{ij} + S_i = a_i, \qquad i = 1, 2, \ldots, m,$$

respectively and let v_j $(j = 1, 2, \ldots, n)$ be the dual variable corresponding to the remaining n constraints given by

$$\sum_{i=1}^{m} x_{ij} = b_j, \qquad j = 1, 2, \ldots, n,$$

respectively. Then, following a similar argument as in the regular transportation model, the dual problem for the generalized model is given by:

$$\text{maximize} \quad w_0 = \sum_{i=1}^{m} a_i u_i + \sum_{j=1}^{n} b_j v_j,$$

subject to

$$p_{ij} u_i + v_j < c_{ij} \qquad i = 1, 2, \ldots, m,$$
$$u_i \leq 0 \qquad j = 1, 2, \ldots, n,$$

where v_j is unrestricted in sign. The constraints $u_i \leq 0$ correspond to the slack variables, S_i, in the first m constraints of the primal.

Now, by Property II, Section 4·4, every *basic* variable x_{rs} must have its corresponding dual constraint satisfied in equality sense; that is

$$p_{rs} u_r + v_s = c_{rs}.$$

Similarly, for every *basic* slack variable S_r,

$$u_r = 0.$$

Since all $(m + n)$ constraints of the primal problem in the generalized model are independent equations (compare with the regular transportation model where there are $m + n - 1$ independent constraint equations only), any basic solution must include $m + n$ basic variables. This yields $m + n$ dual equations in $m + n$ unknowns (simplex multipliers). Unlike the regular transportation model where any one unknown can be assigned an arbitrary value, these equations are solved uniquely for the corresponding $m + n$ simplex multipliers u_r and v_s. Once the simplex multipliers are determined, the remaining *nonbasic* variables are checked for optimality by computing

$$q_{ij} = p_{ij} u_i + v_j - c_{ij}, \qquad \text{for } x_{ij},$$

and

$$q_i = u_i - 0 = u_i, \qquad \text{for } S_i.$$

If any q_{ij} or q_i is greater than zero, the nonbasic variable having the largest positive value is introduced into the solution (minimization problem). The necessary changes should then be made to determine the new basic solution. On the other hand, if all q_{ij} and q_i are less than or equal to zero, the optimal solution is reached and the process ends.

The generalized transportation technique will now be illustrated by the following numerical example.

$$\text{Minimize} \quad x_0 = 4x_{11} + 2x_{12} + x_{21} + 5x_{22} + 0S_1 + 0S_2,$$

subject to

$$
\begin{aligned}
.5x_{11} + .1x_{12} \qquad\qquad\quad + S_1 \qquad &= 10, \\
x_{21} + 2x_{22} \qquad + S_2 &= 25, \\
x_{11} \qquad\quad + x_{21} \qquad\qquad\quad &= 15, \\
x_{12} \qquad\quad + x_{22} \qquad\qquad &= 30,
\end{aligned}
$$

$$
x_{11} \geq 0, \quad x_{12} \geq 0, \quad x_{21} \geq 0, \quad x_{22} \geq 0, \quad S_1 \geq 0, \quad S_2 \geq 0.
$$

The first step is to obtain a starting solution for the problem. This is done by applying the northwest corner method or the least-cost element method to the equivalent tabular form of the problem. The two methods were introduced in previous sections of this chapter. Thus applying the northwest corner method, the initial tableau is given by Table 5–39.

Table 5–39

		1		2		Slacks		a_i
	.5	4	.1	2	1	0		
1		15		25				~~10~~ 2.5
	1	1	2	5	1	0		
2				5		15		~~25~~ ~~15~~
b_j		~~15~~		~~30~~ 5		—		

This solution is obtained as follows:

$$
x_{11} = \min\left(\frac{a_1}{p_{11}}, b_1\right) = \min\left(\frac{10}{.5}, 15\right) = 15,
$$

which satisfies the constraint for Column 1. This leaves $15 - 15 \times .5 = 2.5$ for Row 1. Thus

$$
x_{12} = \min\left(\frac{2.5}{.1}, 30\right) = 25,
$$

which satisfies the constraint for Row 1 leaving $30 - 25 = 5$ for Column 2. Next

$$
x_{22} = \min\left(\frac{25}{2}, 5\right) = 5.
$$

This satisfies Column 2 and leaves $25 - 5 \times 2 = 15$ for Row 2. Since the slacks have no column constraint, the amount 15 is allocated to S_2 to satisfy Row 2 constraint.

This process results in four $(m + n = 2 + 2 = 4)$ basic variables. The corresponding dual equations are then given by

$$x_{11} : \quad .5u_1 + v_1 = 4,$$
$$x_{12} : \quad .1u_1 + v_2 = 2,$$
$$x_{22} : \quad 2u_2 + v_2 = 5,$$
$$S_2 : \quad u_2 = 0.$$

Solving these four equations gives the following simplex multipliers,

$$u_1 = -30, \quad u_2 = 0, \quad v_1 = 19, \quad \text{and} \quad v_2 = 5.$$

Now checking the nonbasic variables for nonoptimality gives

$$S_1 : \quad q_1 = u_1 - 0 = -30$$
$$x_{21} : \quad q_{21} = u_2 + v_1 - c_{21} = 0 + 19 - 1 = 18.$$

Since $q_{21} = 18 > 0$, x_{21} becomes the entering variable.

The change in basis can now be made by determining the leaving variable. Let the value of x_{21}, the entering variable, be given by $\theta (\geq 0)$ in the new solution. Suppose the revised values of the *current basic* solution are given by $x_{ij} + \Delta x_{ij}$ and $S_i + \Delta S_i$ where Δx_{ij} and ΔS_i represent the changes in the corresponding basic variables. Noting that all the nonbasic variables other than the entering variable will remain zero, the constraints of the problem can be written in terms of θ and the basic variables as

$$.5(x_{11} + \Delta x_{11}) + .1(x_{12} + \Delta x_{12}) = 10$$
$$\theta + 2(x_{22} + \Delta x_{22}) + S_2 + \Delta S_2 = 25$$
$$x_{11} + \Delta x_{11} + \theta = 15$$
$$x_{12} + \Delta x_{12} + x_{22} + \Delta x_{22} = 30.$$

Thus, the original constraints are satisfied if all the additional changes will net to zero; that is, if

$$(1) \quad .5\Delta x_{11} + .1\Delta x_{12} = 0$$
$$(2) \quad \theta + 2\Delta x_{22} + \Delta S_2 = 0$$
$$(3) \quad \Delta x_{11} + \theta = 0$$
$$(4) \quad \Delta x_{12} + \Delta x_{22} = 0.$$

Now solving for all the Δ's in terms of θ, one gets from (3),

$$\Delta x_{11} = -\theta,$$

from (1),

$$\Delta x_{12} = 5\theta,$$

from (4),

$$\Delta x_{22} = -5\theta,$$

and from (2),

$$\Delta S_2 = 9\theta.$$

This gives the increments (or decrements) in the basic variables as a function of θ which will keep all the constraint equations satisfied.

The following step is to determine the largest value of θ (≥ 0) which will keep the new solution feasible (≥ 0). Thus given the current solution $x_{11} = 15$, $x_{12} = 25$, $x_{22} = 5$, and $S_2 = 15$, the new solution is feasible if

$$x_{11} + \Delta x_{11} = 15 - \theta \geq 0, \quad \text{or} \quad \theta \leq 15,$$
$$x_{12} + \Delta x_{12} = 25 + 5\theta \geq 0, \quad \text{or} \quad \theta \geq 0,$$
$$x_{22} + \Delta x_{22} = 5 - 5\theta \geq 0, \quad \text{or} \quad \theta \leq 1,$$
$$S_2 + \Delta S_2 = 15 + 9\theta \geq 0, \quad \text{or} \quad \theta \geq 0.$$

This indicates that the largest value of θ is 1 corresponding to x_{22}. Thus, x_{22} becomes the leaving variable. (Investigation would show that this procedure is exactly the same as the feasibility condition of the simplex method.) The new basic solution is thus given by

$$x_{11} = 15 - 1 = 14,$$
$$x_{12} = 25 + 5 = 30,$$
$$x_{21} = \theta = 1,$$
$$S_2 = 15 + 9 = 24,$$

with an improved total cost of 117 as compared with 135 in the previous iteration. In the tableau form, the new solution is shown in Table 5–40.

Table 5–40

	1		2		Slack		a_i
	.5	4	.1	2	1	0	
1	14		30				10
	1	1	2	5	1	0	
2	1					24	25
b_j	15		30		—		

The second iteration is initiated by computing the new simplex multipliers. The corresponding dual equations are given by

$$x_{11}: \quad .5u_1 + v_1 = 4$$
$$x_{12}: \quad .1u_1 + v_2 = 2$$
$$x_{21}: \quad u_2 + v_1 = 1$$
$$S_2: \quad u_2 = 0.$$

Thus, $u_1 = 6$, $u_2 = 0$, $v_1 = 1$, $v_2 = 1.4$. The evaluation of the nonbasic variables for optimality is given as

$$S_1: \quad q_1 = u_1 - 0 = 6$$
$$x_{22}: \quad q_{22} = 2u_2 + v_2 - c_{22} = 0 + 1.4 - 5 = -3.6.$$

Thus S_1 becomes the entering variable.

Again, letting $\Delta S_1 = \theta$, the following equations are obtained.

$$.5\Delta x_{11} + .1\Delta x_{12} + \theta = 0$$
$$\Delta x_{21} + \Delta S_2 = 0$$
$$\Delta x_{11} + \Delta x_{21} = 0$$
$$\Delta x_{12} = 0.$$

(Notice that these equations can be constructed directly by observing the basic variables in the given tableau.) This gives,

$$\Delta x_{11} = -2\theta$$
$$\Delta x_{12} = 0$$
$$\Delta x_{21} = 2\theta$$
$$\Delta S_2 = -2\theta.$$

Checking the feasibility of the problem to determine θ, one gets,

$$x_{11} + \Delta x_{11} = 14 - 2\theta \geq 0, \quad \text{or} \quad \theta \leq 7,$$
$$x_{21} + \Delta x_{21} = 1 + 2\theta \geq 0, \quad \text{or} \quad \theta \geq 0,$$
$$S_2 + \Delta S_2 = 24 - 2\theta \geq 0, \quad \text{or} \quad \theta \leq 12.$$

This gives $\theta = 7$ and x_{11} leaves the solution.

The new tableau is shown in Table 5–41. The corresponding solution costs 75 as compared with 117 in the last iteration.

Computing the new simplex multipliers, one gets $u_1 = 0$, $u_2 = 0$, $v_1 = 1$, $v_2 = 2$ and hence $q_{11} = -3$ and $q_{22} = -3$. This shows that the last solution is optimal. (Notice that the last simplex multipliers give the optimal dual values. By substituting in the dual objective function one gets

$$w_0 = 10u_1 + 25u_2 + 15v_1 + 30v_2 = 75,$$

which is the same as the optimal objective value in the primal.)

Table 5–41

	1		2		Slacks		a_i
	.5	4	.1	2	1	0	
1			30		7		10
	1	1	2	5	1	0	
2	15				10		25
b_j	15		30		—		

§ 5·4
Network Representation of Transportation Systems

§ 5·4·1
Definitions

A network consists of two or more distinct points, called *nodes*, with lines joining pairs of these points, called *arcs*. Associated with each arc is a flow of some kind. For example, in a transportation network, cities represent nodes while highways represent arcs. The flow in such a network is characterized by vehicles driven on highways. To illustrate, a typical network representation of five nodes and eight arcs is shown in Figure 5–2. Note that there is no direct arc between nodes 1 and 5 or nodes 2 and 5.

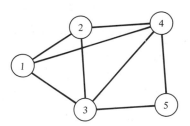

Figure 5–2

The maximum allowable rate of flow in a network is usually determined either by the capacity of the arc or by the input rates at the nodes. For example, in a network of pipelines transporting oil products between different refineries, the rate of flow in the arcs is determined either by input rates at the refineries (nodes) or by the maximum capacity of the pipes (arcs).

In this section four network models will be investigated. These include determination of the shortest route between two nodes in a network, determination of the arcs interconnecting a number of nodes such that the sum of the lengths of these arcs is minimal, determination of the maximum flow in a network, and finally, solution of a special type of the transportation problem as a network model.

Before carrying out this analysis, it is necessary to introduce some new definitions.

1. An arc is said to be *directed* or *oriented* if the flow is positive in one direction and zero in the opposite direction. A directed network is thus a network with all directed arcs.

2. A *chain* or a *path* joining nodes i and j is a sequence of arcs (i, i_1), $(i_1, i_2), \ldots, (i_n, j)$, connecting i and j regardless of the orientation of these arcs. For example, in Figure 5–2 the arcs $(1, 3)$, $(3, 2)$, $(2, 4)$ represent a chain (path) connecting nodes 1 and 4.

3. A *loop* is a chain that connects a node to itself. For example, in Figure 5–2, the arcs $(1, 2)$, $(2, 4)$, $(4, 5)$, $(5, 3)$, $(3, 1)$ form a loop.

4. A *connected network* is a network in which there is a chain connecting every two distinct nodes. Thus, the network in Figure 5–2 is connected.

5. A *tree* is a connected network containing no loops. This means that the network is Figure 5–2 is not a tree. Figure 5–3, however, gives a representation of a tree.

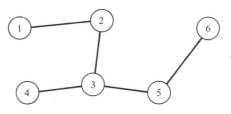

Figure 5–3

§ 5·4·2
Shortest Route Problem

Consider an n-node connected network. Let d_{ij} be the length of the arc joining nodes i, j. The problem is to determine the chains yielding the shortest distances between a *fixed* node and any other node in the network. For any two fixed nodes, this problem can be formulated as a linear programming model. In fact, it is indicated in Problem 5-11 at the end of this chapter that this problem can be formulated as a transshipment model.

Rather than using the simplex method, a more efficient, and comparatively elementary, procedure will be utilized. Assume that it is required to find the shortest distance between node 1 and any node j, $j = 2, 3, \ldots, n$. Table 5–42 summarizes all d_{ij} of the network. If any arc is not defined, its corresponding square in the d_{ij}-table is left empty.

Table 5–42

i \ j	1	2	$\cdots$	$n-1$	n	u_i
1	d_{11}	d_{12}		$d_{1,\,n-1}$	d_{1n}	u_1
2	d_{21}	d_{22}		$d_{2,\,n-1}$	d_{2n}	u_2
$\vdots$			$\cdots$			$\vdots$
n	d_{n1}	d_{n2}		$d_{n,\,n-1}$	d_{nn}	u_n
v_j	v_1	v_2	$\cdots$	v_{n-1}	v_n	

Step 1.   Let v_j be the minimum sum of the lengths of the arcs comprising a chain from node 1 to node j. By definition, $v_1 = 0$. Let u_i be defined such that $u_i = v_j$ when $i = j$. Thus $u_1 = v_1 = 0$. Now, provided that the arc between nodes i and j is defined, the different v_j's are determined from the formula

$$v_j = \min_i \{u_i + d_{ij}\}$$

which can be initiated starting with $i = 1$.

     The significance of u_i must be clear now since it summarizes the distance up to node i which is then used to find the closest node j. By virtue of this arrangement, it will be necessary to enter the value $u_i = v_j$ for $i = j$, right after v_j is generated and before any new v_j is computed.

Step 2.   Consider the first row $i = 1$ of Table 5–42.

     (a) Compute $v_j - u_i$ for all j.

     (b) If $d_{ij} \geq v_j - u_i$, for all j, this implies that no shorter route can be found between nodes i and j. If this is the last row, go to (d) below; if not, consider the next row $i + 1$ and go back to (a) above.

     (c) If $d_{ij} < v_j - u_i$, compute a new value of v_j, v_j', which is given by

$$v_j' = u_i + d_{ij}$$

The new v_j' is then entered in place of v_j and u_i for $i = j$. If this is the last row, go to (d) below; otherwise using the updated values of u_i and v_j so far obtained, consider the next row $i + 1$ and go back to (a) above.

(d) If any of the values of u_i and v_j has been revised in (c) above, repeat Step 2 on the revised values; otherwise, go to Step 3.

Step 3. The v_j's resulting from Step 2 now define the shortest distances between nodes 1 and j, $j = 2, 3, \ldots, n$. In order to determine the corresponding chains, it is noted that the last arc (i_1, j) of the chain (i, j) must satisfy the condition

$$u_{i_1} = v_j - d_{i_1 j}.$$

Thus, given v_j, by searching under column j of the d_{ij}-table, one can determine i_1 which satisfies the given equation. The node i_1 is then used to determine the penultimate node i_2 using the equation

$$u_{i_2} = v_{i_1} - d_{i_2 i_1}.$$

This process is repeated until node 1 is reached. It should be noted that by virtue of the method of computing v_j, it is always guaranteed that a new node will be found which will satisfy the given equation.

▶ **Example 5·4-1**

Consider the network in Figure 5–4.

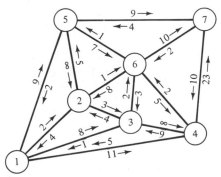

Figure 5–4

The numbers on each arc define the two-way distances between the indicated nodes. If the arc is directed (for example, one way traffic), the distance in the other direction is set equal to ∞.

The d_{ij}-table corresponding to the above network together with its preliminary values of u_i and v_i is given in Table 5–43 (the significance of the numbers in parentheses will be made clear later).

Table 5–43

i \ j	1	2	3	4	5	6	7	u_i
1		2	8	11	9			0
2	4		3		5	1		2
3	1	4		∞		2		5
4	5		9			2	23	11 (8)
5	2	∞				7	9	7 (4)
6		8	3	5	1		10	3
7				10	4	2		13
v_j	0	2	5	11 (8)	7 (4)	3	13	

The values of v_j (and u_i) are determined as follows. First set $u_1 = v_1 = 0$ for the first row, $(i = 1)$. Then using the formula

$$v_j = \min_i \{u_i + d_{ij}\},$$

since so far u_i is defined for $i = 1$ only, it follows that

$$v_2 = 0 + 2 = 2 \ (= u_2).$$

Now, entering the value of u_2 and v_2 in the table, one proceeds to compute v_3. This is given by

$$v_3 = \min_{i=1,\,2} \{u_i + d_{i3}\},$$
$$= \min_{i=1,\,2} \{0 + 8, 2 + 3\} = 5.$$

Thus $u_3 = v_3 = 5$ are entered in row 3 and column 3.

Proceeding in the same manner, then

$$v_4 = \min_{i=1,\,3} \{0 + 11, 5 + \infty\} = 11 = u_4,$$
$$v_5 = \min_{i=1,\,2} \{0 + 9, 2 + 5\} = 7 = u_5,$$
$$v_6 = \min_{i=2,\,3,\,4,\,5} \{2 + 1, 5 + 2, 11 + 2, 7 + 7\} = 3 = u_6,$$
$$v_7 = \min_{i=4,\,5,\,6} \{11 + 23, 7 + 9, 3 + 10\} = 13 = u_7.$$

Moving to Step 2, optimality is checked by comparing $(v_j - u_i)$ with d_{ij}. Thus

$i = 1$:

j	1	2	3	4	5	6	7
$v_j - u_1$	—	2	5	11	7	—	—
d_{1j}	—	2	8	11	9	—	—

which satisfies the condition $v_j - u_1 \le d_{1j}$. Notice that d_{1j} is not defined for $j = 1, 6, 7$ and consequently the corresponding values are not compared in the table. Proceeding with the successive values of i, it is shown below that the optimality condition is violated for the first time at $i = 6$. Thus,

$i = 2$:

j	1	2	3	4	5	6	7
$v_j - u_2$	-2	—	3	—	5	1	—
d_{2j}	4	—	3	—	5	1	—

$i = 3$:

j	1	2	3	4	5	6	7
$v_j - u_3$	-5	-3	—	6	—	-2	—
d_{3j}	1	4	—	∞	—	2	—

$i = 4$:

j	1	2	3	4	5	6	7
$v_j - u_4$	-11	—	-6	—	—	-8	2
d_{4j}	5	—	9	—	—	2	23

$i = 5$:

j	1	2	3	4	5	6	7
$v_j - u_5$	-7	-5	—	—	—	-4	6
d_{5j}	2	∞	—	—	—	7	9

$i = 6$:

j	1	2	3	4	5	6	7
$v_j - u_6$	—	-1	2	8	4	—	10
d_{6j}	—	8	3	5	1	—	10
				↑	↑		

The optimality condition is violated for both $j = 4$ and $j = 5$. Thus the new values of v_4 and v_5 are given by,

$$v_4' = u_6 + d_{64} = 3 + 5 = 8,$$

$$v_5' = u_6 + d_{65} = 3 + 1 = 4.$$

These values will now replace v_4 (and u_4) and v_5 (and u_5) as indicated by parentheses in the Table 5–43.

$i = 7$: (Notice that the new values of v_4 and v_5 are used now.)

j	1	2	3	4	5	6	7
$v_j - u_7$	—	—	—	-5	-9	-10	—
d_{7j}	—	—	—	10	4	2	—

The *revised* values of u_i and v_j are now used to check the optimality condition by repeating the same procedure above starting with $i = 1$. The results can be summarized as shown in Table 5–44.

This shows that the optimality condition is satisfied. Since no new revised values of u_i and v_j are generated, the last solution is optimal. The values of v_j give the length of the shortest route between node 1 and node j.

Suppose it is necessary now to determine the shortest chain between nodes 1 and 7. In Table 5–43, under column $j = 7$, the equation,

$$v_7 = u_i + d_{i7},$$

is satisfied for $i = 5$ and $i = 6$. This indicates an alternative solution. Considering $i = 5$ first, then under column $j = 5$,

$$v_5 = u_i + d_{i5}$$

is satisfied for $i = 6$. Again under column $j = 6$,

$$v_6 = u_i + d_{i6}$$

Table 5–44

i		j 1	2	3	4	5	6	7	u_i
1	$v_j - u_1$	—	2	5	8	4	—	—	0
	d_{1j}	—	2	8	11	9	—	—	
2	$v_j - u_2$	-2	—	3	—	2	1	—	2
	d_{2j}	4	—	3	—	5	1	—	
3	$v_j - u_3$	-5	-3	—	4	—	-2	—	5
	d_{3j}	1	4	—	∞	—	2	—	
4	$v_j - u_4$	-9	—	-4	—	—	-6	4	8
	d_{4j}	5	—	9	—	—	2	23	
5	$v_j - u_5$	-4	-2	—	—	—	-1	9	4
	d_{5j}	2	∞	—	—	—	7	9	
6	$v_j - u_6$	—	1	2	5	1	—	10	3
	d_{6j}	—	8	3	5	1	—	10	
7	$v_j - u_7$	—	—	—	-5	-9	-10	—	13
	d_{7j}	—	—	—	10	4	2	—	
	v_j	0	2	5	8	4	3	13	

is satisfied for $i = 2$. Finally for column $j = 2$,

$$v_2 = u_i + d_{i2}$$

is satisfied for $i = 1$. The corresponding chain includes the arcs $(1, 2)$, $(2, 6)$; $(6, 5)$, $(5, 7)$ with the length $v_7 = 13$.

The alternative solution indicated above can be determined similarly and it is given by the arcs $(1, 2)$ $(2, 6)$, $(6, 7)$ yielding the same length $v_7 = 13$.

A similar procedure is followed to obtain the other chains. These are summarized in the following table.

Nodes (i, j)	Chain	Shortest distance v_j
$(1, 2)$	$1 \to 2$	2
$(1, 3)$	$1 \to 2 \to 3$	5
$(1, 4)$	$1 \to 2 \to 6 \to 4$	8
$(1, 5)$	$1 \to 2 \to 6 \to 5$	4
$(1, 6)$	$1 \to 2 \to 6$	3
$(1, 7)$	$\begin{cases} 1 \to 2 \to 6 \to 5 \to 7 \\ 1 \to 2 \to 6 \to 7 \end{cases}$	13

◄

§ 5·4·3
Network Minimization Problem

Given n nodes of a network and the lengths, d_{ij}, of the arcs joining each pair of nodes i and j, the objective is to connect all the nodes of the network by arcs so that the sum of the lengths of the resulting arcs is minimum. This is actually equivalent to determining the minimal *tree* which encloses all the nodes of the network (recall that a tree is a connected network with no loops).

The idea of this algorithm is based mainly on the condition that every *unconnected* node must be joined to the *closest* node in the set of *connected* nodes. At the start of the algorithm any one of the nodes is selected arbitrarily to form the *initial set* of "connected nodes." It must be noted that the determination of the minimal tree is independent of the specific choice of the node which defines the indicated initial set (see Problem 5-21).

The procedure will now be illustrated by an example.

▶   **Example 5·4-2**
Consider a 6-node network with the following symmetric d_{ij}-table.

i \ j	1	2	3	4	5	6
1	*	1	5	7	9	11
2	1	*	5	4	3	∞
3	5	5	*	5	∞	6
4	7	4	5	*	6	3
5	9	3	∞	6	*	∞
6	11	∞	6	3	∞	*

Suppose that node 1 is selected as the initial set of connected notes. Then column 1 is eliminated from the d_{ij}-table to ensure that no loops will be formulated in later steps of the algorithm. The closest node to node 1 is found by considering the first row of the d_{ij}-table.

j	1	2	3	4	5	6	$\min_j \{d_{1j}\}$
d_{1j}	*	①	5	7	9	11	$d_{12} = 1$

Thus, node 2 is the closest to node 1 with $d_{12} = 1$. The new set of connected nodes now consists of nodes 1 and 2.

Next, for the same reason of eliminating column 1, column 2 is eliminated from the d_{ij}-table. Consider the determination of the new node that is closest to the set $\{1, 2\}$. This is accomplished by comparing the elements of rows 1 and 2 in the d_{ij}-table. Thus,

i \ j	1	2	3	4	5	6	
1	*	*	5	7	9	11	
2	*	*	5	4	③	∞	$\min_{i,j} \{d_{ij}\}$
$\min_i \{d_{ij}\}$			5	4	③	11	$d_{25} = 3$

so that node 5 is connected to node 2 with nodes $(1, 2, 5)$ forming the new set of connected nodes. Column 5 should thus be eliminated from the table. Consider now the addition of the fifth row to the d_{ij}-table.

i \ j	1	2	3	4	5	6	
1	*	*	5	7	*	11	
2	*	*	5	④	*	∞	
5	*	*	∞	6	*	∞	$\min_{i,j} \{d_{ij}\}$
$\min_i \{d_{ij}\}$			5	④		11	$d_{24} = 4$

Node 4 is connected to node 2 thus forming the new set of connected nodes (1, 2, 4, 5). Column 4 is eliminated now from the d_{ij}-table.

Again, adding the fourth row of the d_{ij}-table,

i \ j	1	2	3	4	5	6	
1	*	*	5	*	*	11	
2	*	*	5	*	*	∞	
5	*	*	∞	*	*	∞	
4	*	*	5	*	*	③	$\min_{i,j} \{d_{ij}\}$
$\min_{i} \{d_{ij}\}$			5			③	$d_{46} = 3$

which shows that node 6 should be connected to node 4 and column 6 should be eliminated.

Finally, adding the sixth row of the d_{ij}-table, this gives,

i \ j	1	2	3	4	5	6	
1	*	*	⑤	*	*	*	
2	*	*	⑤	*	*	*	
5	*	*	∞	*	*	*	
4	*	*	⑤	*	*	*	
6	*	*	6	*	*	*	$\min_{i,j} \{d_{ij}\}$
$\min_{i} \{d_{ij}\}$			⑤				$d_{43} = d_{23} = d_{13} = 5$

This means that node 3 can be connected to any of the nodes 1, 2, or 4.

This completes the problem and the resulting tree is shown in Figure 5–5. It is understood that any *one* of the dotted arcs can be used in which case all *other* dotted arcs must be eliminated. The sum of the lengths of the arcs in the minimal tree is thus equal to 16. ◄

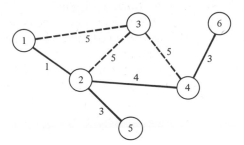

Figure 5–5

§ 5·4·4
Maximal Flow Problem

In this section, the problem of determining the maximum flow between
terminal nodes of a connected network is considered. The arcs of the network
may be either directed or undirected. Associated with each arc are two-way
capacities which specify the maximum allowable flow in either direction of
the arc. Let c_{ij} be the capacity of arc (i, j) in the direction $i \rightarrow j$. The notation
c_{ji} will then be used to represent the capacity of the same arc in the opposite
direction $j \rightarrow i$. If the arc is directed, then the capacity in the opposite direction
is equal to zero. That is, either $c_{ij} = 0$ or $c_{ji} = 0$.

Let the capacities c_{ij} (and c_{ji}) of the arcs be arranged in a matrix form.
Let S and T represent the "master" source and "master" terminal nodes of
the connected network between which the flow is to be maximized. Assume
further that the network has exactly n *other* nodes. The following steps are
then used to determine the maximal flow between S and T.

Step 1. Determine a chain which connects S and T such that the net flow
in this chain is positive in the direction $S \rightarrow T$. If no such chain
exists, go to Step 3. Otherwise, go to Step 2.

Step 2. Let c_{ij} be the capacities of the arcs (i, j) of the selected (S, T)-
chain. Let c_{ij}^- be the capacities of the arcs of the same chain in
direction $(S \rightarrow T)$ while c_{ij}^+ be the capacities of the arcs in the
opposite direction $(T \rightarrow S)$. Define

$$\theta = \min\{c_{ij}^-\} > 0.$$

Then the c_{ij}-matrix is modified as follows
(a) subtract θ from all c_{ij}^-; and,
(b) add θ to all c_{ij}^+, then using the new c_{ij}-matrix to replace the
immediately preceding one, go to Step 1.

Part (a) indicates that an amount θ can be transferred from S
to T over the given chain and hence the respective capacities must
be reduced by θ. Part (b), on the other hand, is introduced to

allow for preservation of the original flow capacities in the network. It indicates that a decrease in the capacity of an arc in one direction is equivalent to an increase in the capacity of the same arc in the opposite direction.

Step 3. This step determines the maximum flow in the network as follows. Let $\mathbf{C} = \|c_{ij}\|$ be the original capacity matrix of the network and assume that $\mathbf{C}^* = \|c_{ij}^*\|$ is the last modified capacity matrix beyond which no feasible chain between nodes S and T can be constructed. Thus, the optimal flow $\mathbf{X} = \|x_{ij}\|$ in the different arcs is given by

$$x_{ij} = \begin{cases} c_{ij} - c_{ij}^*, & c_{ij} > c_{ij}^* \\ 0, & c_{ij} \leq c_{ij}^*. \end{cases}$$

The maximum flow between S and T is thus given by

$$x_0 = \sum_i x_{Si} = \sum_j x_{jT}.$$

It is noted that x_0 is also equal to the sum of positive θ's determined in the different iterations (Step 2) of the solution. This should explain directly why only the positive elements of $\mathbf{C} - \mathbf{C}^*$ contribute to the net flow in the direction $S \to T$.

▶ **Example 5·4-3**

Consider the network in Figure 5–6 with the indicated capacities. The corresponding **C**-matrix is given by

$$\mathbf{C} =$$

i $\diagdown$ j	S	1	2	3	4	T	
S		10^-	3	14	4		
1	5^+		5	9	5^-		
2	5	6		15		10	Chain $\{S \to 1 \to 4 \to T\}$
3	12	7	10		7	2	$\theta = \min\{10, 5, 13\} = 5$
4	3	9^+		8		13^-	
T			3	4	5^+		

Let the first selected (S, T)-chain be given by $S \to 1 \to 4 \to T$. Thus c_{S1}, c_{14}, and c_{4T} are labeled with negative signs (see the above matrix) while c_{1S}, c_{41}, and c_{T4} are labeled with positive signs. Notice that a chain can be selected

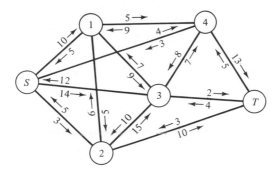

Figure 5–6

directly from the current **C**-matrix without reference to the network itself. This is achieved by starting from the first row of the matrix (corresponding to S), then selecting another node which is connected to S by a positive capacity element. The row of the new node is now considered and a second distinct node yielding a positive connecting arc is selected. This is repeated until node T is reached. Such procedure is suitable for solving the problem on the digital computer.

Now

$$\theta = \min\{c_{S1}, c_{14}, c_{4T}\}$$

$$= \min\{10, 5, 13\} = 5$$

and the new matrix is obtained by subtracting θ from the negative-labeled elements and adding it to the positive-labeled ones. This yields;

i \ j	S	1	2	3	4	T	
S		5	3	14^-	4		
1	10		5	9	0		
2	5	6		15^+		10^-	Chain $\{S \to 3 \to 2 \to T\}$
3	12^+	7	10^-		7	2	$\theta = \min\{14, 10, 10\} = 10$
4	3	14		8		8	
T			3^+	4	10		

The new (S, T)-chain together with its corresponding θ are shown above. Continuing in the same manner, the remaining matrices are successively given by,

i \ j	S	1	2	3	4	T
S		5	3^-	4	4	
1	10		5^+	9^-	0	
2	5^+	6^-		25		0
3	22	7^+	0		7	2^-
4	3	14		8		8
T			13	4^+	10	

Chain $\{S \to 2 \to 1 \to 3 \to T\}$

$\theta = \min\{3, 6, 9, 2\} = 2$

i \ j	S	1	2	3	4	T
S		5	1	4	4^-	
1	10		7	7	0	
2	7	4		25		0
3	22	9	0		7	0
4	3^+	14		8		8^-
T			13	6	10^+	

Chain $\{S \to 4 \to T\}$

$\theta = \min\{4, 8\} = 4$

i \ j	S	1	2	3	4	T
S		5	1	4^-	0	
1	10		7	7	0	
2	7	4		25		0
3	22^+	9	0		7^-	0
4	7	14		8^+		4^-
T			13	6	14^+	

Chain $\{S \to 3 \to 4 \to T\}$

$\theta = \min\{4, 7, 4\} = 4$

$$\mathbf{C}^* =$$

i \ j	S	1	2	3	4	T
S		5	1	0	0	
1	10		7	7	0	
2	7	4		25		0
3	26	9	0		3	0
4	7	14		12		0
T			13	6	18	

No chains possible between S and T

It is noted that no (S, T)-chain can be constructed from the last matrix since all the arcs leading to node T now have zero capacities. Consequently, this matrix gives $\mathbf{C}^*$. The flow in the different arcs is thus given by

$$\mathbf{X} = \mathbf{C} - \mathbf{C}^*, \quad x_{ij} > 0.$$

Thus,

$$\mathbf{X} =$$

i \ j	S	1	2	3	4	T
S		5	2	14	4	
1				2	5	
2		2				10
3			10		4	2
4						13
T						

This shows that

$$x_0 = \sum_i x_{Si} = 5 + 2 + 14 + 4 = 25$$

$$= \sum_j x_{jT} = 10 + 2 + 13 = 25.$$

Notice also that the sum of the θ's obtained at the different iterations is $5 + 10 + 2 + 4 + 4 = 25$ as should be expected.

The **X**-matrix can be interpreted on the network as shown in Figure 5–7. ◄

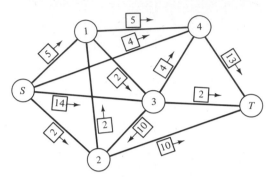

Figure 5–7

At this point, it is worth introducing the concept of a minimal cut. A *cut* in a connected network is the set of arcs which are selected such that if their capacities are set equal to zero, no flow can be effected between *S* and *T*. The capacity of a cut is defined as the sum of the *maximum* capacities of its respective arcs. Thus in Figure 5–6, some cuts can be identified as:

Cut set	Capacity
1. $(S, 1)$, $(S, 2)$, $(S, 3)$, $(S, 4)$	$10 + 3 + 14 + 4 = 31$
2. $(4, T)$, $(3, T)$, $(2, T)$	$13 + 2 + 10 = 25$
3. $(1, 4)$, $(S, 4)$, $(3, 4)$, $(3, T)$, $(2, T)$	$5 + 4 + 7 + 2 + 10 = 28$

Notice that a cut capacity is obtained by summing up the maximum capacities of its respective arcs; that is, by summing up the capacities specified by the original **C**-matrix.

Intuitively, if one can enumerate *all* the cuts in the network then the cut with minimal capacity will give the maximum flow in the network. This intuitive result has actually been proved using the important *maximal-flow minimal-cut theorem* which states that the maximal flow in a network is equal to the capacity of its minimal cut. It should be noted, however, that such procedure may not be practical for large networks.

§ 5·4·5
Network Representation of a Transportation Problem

In this section it will be shown how a special type of the well-known transportation problem can be handled as a maximal flow model. Let it be required to transport a certain commodity from *m* sources, $s_1, s_2, s_3, \ldots, s_m$ to *n* destinations, $d_1, d_2, \ldots, d_n$. Let the amount available at s_i be given by a_i and let the amount required at d_j be equal to b_j. It is assumed that the routes (i, j) are of limited capacities with $c_{ij} > 0$ and $c_{ji} = 0$, that is, directed arcs. The problem is to satisfy demand as much as possible with the given restrictions of the problem.

This problem can be formulated as a linear programming model as follows. Let x_{ij} be the number of units transported from i to j. Then the problem becomes:

$$\text{maximize} \quad x_0 = \sum_i \sum_j x_{ij},$$

subject to

$$\sum_j x_{ij} \le a_i, \qquad i = 1, 2, \ldots, m$$

$$\sum_i x_{ij} \le b_j, \qquad j = 1, 2, \ldots, n$$

$$0 \le x_{ij} \le c_{ij}, \quad \text{for all } i \text{ and } j.$$

It is noticed that this problem reduces to the regular transportation problem with upper bounded variables. The special procedure developed in Section 8·7·3 can be applied to this problem without explicitly including the capacity restrictions.

It will be shown now, that this problem can be solved using the maximal flow algorithm. First, a fictitious master source, S, and a fictitious master destination, D, are added to the system. The capacity of the arc from S to s_i is equal to a_i while from s_i to S the capacity is zero. Similarly, directed arcs are imposed between d_j and D with a corresponding capacity of b_j. The equivalent network thus appears as shown in Figure 5–8. Using the maximal flow procedure presented in Section 5·4·4, this network should directly give the required solution.

The network analysis discussed in this section has also been extended to solve the regular transportation problem where the objective is to minimize the total transportation costs rather than maximizing the number of units

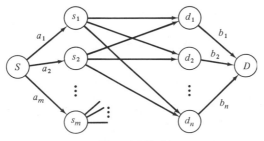

Figure 5–8

transported. In fact, this network analysis procedure is the basis for the so-called primal-dual algorithm which was developed by Ford and Fulkerson for efficiently solving the indicated transportation problem. A similar procedure has also been developed for handling the transshipment problem. These algorithms will not be discussed here, however, and the reader is referred to Dantzig [1], Chapter 20 for detailed discussion on these topics.

SELECTED REFERENCES

1. DANTZIG, G., *Linear Programming and Extensions*, Princeton, N.J.: Princeton University Press, 1963.
2. ELMAGHRABY, S., *The Design of Production Systems*, New York: Reinhold, 1966, Chapter 4.
3. FORD, L., and D. FULKERSON,, *Flows in Networks*, Princeton, N.J.: Princeton University Press, 1962.
4. HADLEY, G., *Linear Programming*, Reading, Massachusetts: Addison-Wesley, 1962.
5. SIMMONARD, M., *Linear Programming*, translated by W. Jewell, Englewood Cliffs, New Jersey: Prentice-Hall, 1966.
6. VAJDA, S., *Mathematical Programming*, Reading, Massachusetts: Addison-Wesley, 1961.
7. ZUKHOVITSKIY, S., and L. AVDEYEVA, *Linear and Convex Programming*, translated by Scripta Technica, Inc., Philadelphia, Pennsylvania: W. B. Saunders Company, 1966.

PROBLEMS

☐ **5-1** Consider the problem of assigning machines to jobs. There are four different categories of machines and five types of tasks. The number of machines available in the four categories are 25, 30, 20, and 30, respectively. The number of jobs in the five tasks are 20, 20, 30, 10, and 25, respectively. The costs of assigning machines from the different categories per job of the different tasks are summarized below.

		Task Type				
		1	2	3	4	5
	1	10	2	3	15	9
Machine	2	5	10	15	2	4
Category	3	15	5	14	7	15
	4	20	15	13	—	8

Find the optimal assignment of the machines by formulating the problem as a transportation model. Notice that Machine Category 4 cannot be assigned to Task Type 4.

□ **5-2** Consider the following transportation problem:

	From \ To j	1	2	3	4	a_i
	1	10	20	5	7	10
	2	13	9	12	8	20
i	3	4	15	7	9	30
	4	14	7	1	0	40
	5	3	12	5	19	50
	b_j	60	60	20	10	

Find the starting solution using (a) northwest corner method, (b) least-cost method, and (c) Vogel's approximation method, then obtain the optimal solution using the best starting solution.

□ **5-3** Show that the solution of Problem 5-2 remains unchanged if a constant K is added to all the cost elements of a row or a column of the cost matrix. How will this addition affect the value of the objective function?

□ **5-4** The caterer problem introduced in Example 2·2-3 can be formulated as a transportation model. Let there be N days to consider. The "sources" of the model can be represented by the sources of new napkins and the soiled napkins accumulated at the end of each of the N days. Its "destinations" include the requirements for the N days and a sink for disposing unused and soiled napkins. The "transportation costs" from the new napkin source to the different destinations can be represented by the cost of buying a new napkin except for the disposal sink where it is equal to zero. The cost of "converting" soiled napkins into clean ones depends on whether one uses fast or slow service. Thus the "transportation cost" from day i to days $i+f, \ldots, i+s-1$ is equal to the fast service cost where f and s are the number of days required for fast and slow services, respectively. Similarly the "transportation costs" from day i to days $i+s, \ldots, i+N$ is equal to the slow service cost. The "transportation" from day i to days $1, 2, \ldots, i-1$ is obviously impossible and hence the corresponding cost is taken equal to infinity. Finally, the amount available at the new napkin source can be assumed equal to the total requirements of the N days since this accounts for the remote possibility of buying all the requirements. Formulate the caterer problem as a transportation model. Using the data of Example 2·2-3, solve the resulting model and interpret the solution.

☐ **5-5** Consider the following (3 × 3) transportation problem. Let x_{ij} be the amount shipped from source i to destination j and let c_{ij} be the corresponding per unit transportation costs.

To From	1	j 2	3	a_i
1				15
i 2				30
3				85
b_j	20	30	80	

Assume that the starting solution obtained by the northwest corner method gives the *optimal* basic solution to the problem. Let the values of the *optimal* dual variables corresponding to the constraints of sources 1, 2, and 3 be given by -2, 3, and 5, respectively, while those for destination 1, 2, and 3 be given by 2, -5, and 10, respectively.

(a) Find the total transportation costs corresponding to the optimal solution.

(b) What are the smallest values of c_{ij} for the nonbasic variables which will keep the above solution optimal?

☐ **5-6** Given the following transportation problem with the indicated *degenerate* basic solution where it is required to minimize the transportation costs.

To From	1	j 2	3	a_i
1	10			10
i 2		20	20	40
b_j	10	20	20	

Let the dual variables corresponding to this basic solution be given by $(1, -1)$ for sources 1 and 2 and by $(-1, 2, -5)$ for destinations 1, 2, and 3, respectively. Let $c_{ij} = i + j\theta$, $(-\infty < \theta < \infty)$, for *all* the *zero* variables in the above solution, where c_{ij} is the cost *per unit* shipped from source i to destination j.

(a) If the above solution is the optimal solution, what is the corresponding value of the objective function? (Answer this part in two different ways.)
(b) Under the same conditions in (a), find the single value of θ for which the solution is basic and optimal.

☐ **5-7** Consider the following (3×3) transportation problem.

To From	j 1	2	3	a_i
1	1	0	2	4
i 2	3	5	4	6
3	1	2	3	10
b_j	3	5	12	

(a) Using the northwest corner method to obtain a starting solution, solve the problem using the transportation technique and the regular simplex method and show that there is a one-to-one correspondence between the iterations of the two methods.
(b) Show that the starting solution obtained by the least-cost method and the VAM will yield the optimum solution directly.

☐ **5-8** Solve the following unbalanced transportation problem using the VAM to find the starting solution.

To From	j 1	2	3	a_i
1	5	1	0	20
2	3	2	4	10
i 3	7	5	2	15
4	9	6	0	15
b_j	5	10	15	

☐ **5-9** Consider the following unbalanced transportation problem.

From \ To	j 1	2	3	a_i
i 1	5	1	7	10
2	6	4	6	80
3	3	2	5	15
b_j	75	20	50	

Since there is not enough supply, some of the demands at the three destinations may not be satisfied. Suppose that there are penalty costs for every unsatisfied demand unit which are given by 5, 3, and 2 for destinations 1, 2, and 3, respectively. Find the optimal solution.

☐ **5-10** In Problem 5-9 above, suppose there is no penalty cost in the problem. Suppose further that the demand at destination 3 must be satisfied exactly. Reformulate the problem and find the optimal solution.

☐ **5-11** Find the shortest route between nodes 1 and 7 of the following network by formulating the problem as a transshipment model. The distances between the different nodes are indicated on the network.

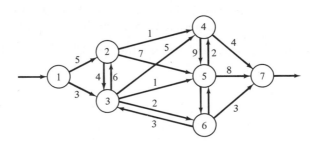

☐ **5-12** Consider the following transportation problem where two factories are supplying three retail stores with their demands of a certain commodity. The amounts available at factories 1 and 2 are 200 units and 300 units, respectively; while the amounts demanded at the three stores are 100, 200 and 50, respectively. Rather than shipping directly from sources to destinations it was decided to investigate the possibility of transshipment. The transportation costs per unit for the different routes are given by the following table.

		Factory		Store		
		1	2	1	2	3
Factory	1	0	6	7	8	9
	2	6	0	5	4	3
Store	1	7	2	0	5	1
	2	1	5	1	0	4
	3	8	9	7	6	0

Find the optimal shipping schedule.

☐ **5-13** Given the following matrix which represents the time, t_{ij}, required to go from source i to destination j. The supply a_i and demand b_j are also indicated in the table.

From \ To j	1	2	3	4	a_i
1	6	7	3	4	5
2	7	9	1	2	7
3	6	5	16	7	8
4	18	9	10	2	10
b_j	10	5	10	5	

Find the minimum time for completing the entire assignment.

☐ **5-14** Consider the problem of transporting a perishable product from three sources to four destinations. The minimum distances between the sources and destinations as well as the supply and demand quantities are given by the following table.

From \ To j	1	2	3	4	a_i
1	5	10	15	9	15
2	5	15	7	8	30
3	10	7	6	4	30
b_j	10	10	15	30	

Because the product is perishable, excessive transportation costs can be justified by reduction in spoilage. Assuming that spoilage is an increasing function of time and that the distances between sources and destinations are directly proportional to time, find the optimum schedule in terms of the objective indicated above.

☐ **5-15** Write the dual problem to the assignment problem presented in Section 5·3·3. Then using the dual, show that the solution in Table 5–37 is optimal.

☐ **5-16** Consider the problem of assigning five operators to five machines. The assignment costs are given by

		Machine				
		1	2	3	4	5
	1	5	5	—	2	6
	2	7	4	2	3	4
Operator	3	9	3	5	—	3
	4	7	2	6	7	2
	5	6	5	7	9	1

Operator 1 cannot be assigned to machine 3. Also operator 3 cannot be assigned to machine 4. Find the optimal assignment schedule.

☐ **5-17** Three machines are used to manufacture four products. The number of units required of each product are given by:

Product	1	2	3	4
Number of units required	180	150	200	130

The production capacities and the production rates of the three machines together with their hourly costs are given by:

Machine	Production rates (units/hr) for product				Capacity (hrs)	Operating cost per hour
	1	2	3	4		
1	5	10	5	2	50	50
2	2	—	2	5	50	30
3	2	5	5	2	100	60

Note that machine 2 cannot be assigned to product 2. Formulate the problem as a generalized transportation model and find the optimal solution.

□ **5-18** Consider the problem of assigning three types of aircrafts to three routes. The objective is to satisfy the passengers demand at the least operating cost. The following table summarizes the data of the problem.

Aircraft type	Aircraft capacity (No. of passengers) on route			Number of aircrafts available	Operating cost on route		
	1	2	3		1	2	3
1	20	20	20	10	800	1000	600
2	50	50	40	5	900	1200	800
3	50	100	100	4	1000	1500	1500
Number of passengers on given route					100	150	300

Find the optimal solution to the problem.

□ **5-19** In Example 5·4-1, find the shortest distance between Node 5 and all the remaining nodes of the network.

□ **5-20** Consider the network below.

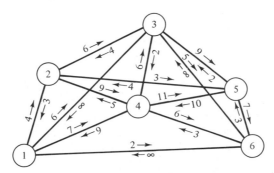

Find the shortest distance between Node 3 and the remaining nodes.

□ **5-21** Solve Example 5·4-2 starting with *each* of Nodes 2, 3, 4, 5, and 6 as the initial set of connected nodes. Show that the resulting trees are exactly the same as in the example. Hence conclude that the given algorithm yields the optimum (minimal) tree.

☐ **5-22** In Problem 5-20 suppose that the lengths of the arcs are the same in the two directions and that each is given by the minimum of the two values indicated on each arc. Find the corresponding minimal tree.

☐ **5-23** Suppose in Problem 5-20, the numbers on each arc represent capacities rather than distances. Find the maximum flow from Node 2 to Node 6.

☐ **5-24** Repeat Problem 5-23 by finding the maximum flow from Node 1 to Node 5.

☐ **5-25** In the network of Problem 5-23 identify four different cuts.

☐ **5-26** The following table identifies the supply a_i and demand b_j for source i and destination j, respectively. The maximum capacity c_{ij} of the route from source i to destination j is also given by the elements (i, j) of the table. The empty squares indicate that the corresponding routes do not exist.

i \ j	1	2	3	4	a_i
1	30	5		40	20
2			5	90	20
3	20	40	10	10	200
b_j	200	10	60	20	

Find the schedule which maximizes the amount transported from the sources to the destinations. Compute the amount of unsatisfied demand at each destination.

☐ **5-27** Repeat Problems 5-26 assuming that transshipment is allowed between sources 1, 2, and 3 with a maximum two-way capacity of 50 units each and between destinations 1, 2, 3, and 4 with a maximum two-way capacity of 50 units each. What effect does transshipping have on the amount of unsatisfied demand at the different destinations?

CHAPTER **6**

Linear Programming and Game Theory

§ 6·1
Introduction

A game represents a competitive or conflicting situation between two or more opponents. These opponents usually are referred to as *players*. Each player has a number of choices, finite or infinite, called *strategies*. A player is supposed to select his strategies without any knowledge of the strategies chosen by the other players. The simultaneous choices of all the players, however, affect the respective *outcomes* or *payoffs* of the game. For each player these outcomes may represent a loss, a gain, or a draw.

Games with *two* players, where the gain of one player signifies an *equal* loss to the other, are called *two-person zero-sum* games. In such games, it suffices to express the outcomes in terms of the payoff to one player. It will be assumed here that the number of strategies for each player is finite. The payoffs may thus be summarized in an $(m \times n)$ *matrix* where m and n represent the (finite) number of strategies for the two players, respectively. For convenience, the two players will be referred to as Player A and Player B. It is conventional in the case of a two-person zero-sum game to express the outcomes of the game in terms of the payoffs to Player A.

To illustrate these concepts, consider the coin-matching game involving two players only. Each player selects either a head (H) or a tail (T). If the outcomes match (that is, H, H or T, T), A wins \$1.00 from B, otherwise B wins \$1.00 from A. This game is a two-person zero-sum game since the winnings of one player are taken as losses for the other. Each player has his choices between two *pure* strategies (H or T). This yields the following (2×2) game matrix (in terms of the payoffs to A).

$$
\begin{array}{cc}
 & \begin{array}{cc} & B \\ H & \quad T \end{array} \\
\begin{array}{c} \\ A \\ \\ \end{array}
\begin{array}{c} H \\ \\ T \end{array}
&
\begin{array}{|c|c|}
\hline
+1 & -1 \\
\hline
-1 & +1 \\
\hline
\end{array}
\end{array}
$$

It will be shown later that the "optimal" solution to such games requires each player to play one pure strategy or a mixture of pure strategies. The latter case is known as the *mixed* strategy selection.

In general, games may involve n persons instead of two persons, the number of pure strategies may be infinite rather than finite, and the non-zero sum payoff matrix may replace the zero-sum outcome table. Unfortunately, present theory does not offer as complete an answer for these types as it does for the two-person zero-sum finite games. This chapter will thus be restricted to the two-person zero-sum type only. The reader interested in exploring the other areas may consult references [2] and [3] at the end of this chapter.

Game theory is a mathematical embodiment dealing with the determination of the "optimal" strategies for each player. In view of the conflicting nature of the problem and because of the lack of information about the specific strategies selected by each player, optimality here is based on a rather pessimistic or conservative criterion. Each player selects his strategy (mixed or pure) which guarantees a payoff that can never be worsened by the selections of his opponent. This criterion is known as the "minimax criterion" and will be considered in detail in the next section.

Game theory bears a strong relationship to linear programming since every finite two-person zero-sum game can be expressed in a linear programming form and, conversely, every linear programming problem can be represented as a game. In fact, G. Dantzig states ([1], p. 24) that, J. von Neumann, father of game theory, when he was first introduced to the simplex method of linear programming (1947) immediately recognized this relationship and further pinpointed and stressed the concept of *duality* in linear programming. Section 6·5 is thus devoted to illustrating the solution of game problems by linear programming. This is especially useful for games with large matrices where elementary methods do not offer efficient procedures for solving the problem.

§ 6·2
Minimax (Maximin) Criterion

Consider the following (two-person zero-sum) game matrix which represents the payoff to A.

$$B$$

		1	2	3	4	Row minimum
	1	8	2	9	5	2
A	2	6	⑤	7	8	⑤ Maximin value
	3	7	3	−4	7	−4

Column maximum: 8   ⑤   9   8

Minimax
value

Player *A*, when he plays his first strategy, may gain 8, 2, 9, or 5 depending on player *B*'s selected strategy. He can guarantee, however, a gain of at least min{8, 2, 9, 5} = 2 regardless of *B*'s selected strategy. Similarly, if *A* plays his second strategy, he guarantees an income of at least min{6, 5, 7, 8} = 5 and if he plays his third strategy he guarantees an income of at least min{7, 3, −4, 7} = −4. Thus, the minimum value in each row represents the minimum gain guaranteed *A* if he plays his pure strategies. These are indicated in the above matrix by "Row minimum." It is obvious that Player *A*, by selecting his second strategy, is maximizing his minimum gain. This gain is given by max{2, 5, −4} = 5. Player *A*'s selection is called the *maximin strategy* and his corresponding gain is called the *maximin* (or *lower*) *value* of the game.

Player *B*, on the other hand, wants to minimize his losses. He realizes that if he plays his first pure strategy, he can lose no more than max{8, 6, 7} = 8 regardless of *A*'s selections. A similar argument can also be applied to the three remaining strategies. The corresponding results are thus indicated in the above matrix by "Column maximum." Player *B* will then select the strategy that minimizes his maximum losses. This is given by the second strategy and his corresponding loss is given by min{8, 5, 9, 8} = 5. Player *B*'s selection is called the *minimax strategy* and his corresponding loss is called the *minimax* (or *upper*) *value* of the game.

The selections made by *A* and *B* (maximin and minimax, respectively) are based on the so-called *minimax* (*maximin*) *criterion*. The criterion expresses a conservative attitude which guarantees the best of the worst results. Such an attitude is inevitable since each player is making his decision in complete ignorance of the strategies selected by the other player.

It is seen from the conditions governing the minimax criterion that for any two-person zero-sum game, the minimax (upper) value is *greater than* or *equal to* the maximin (lower) value (see Problem 6-3). In the case where the equality holds; that is, minimax value = maximin value, the corresponding pure strategies are called " optimal " strategies and the game is said to have a *saddle point*. This saddle point is given by the common entry of the " optimal " pure strategies. The payoff in this common entry is called the " optimal " *value of the game* and is obviously equal to the maximin and the minimax values. " Optimality " here signifies that neither player is tempted to change his strategy since his opponent can counteract by selecting another strategy which will yield a worse payoff than the one given him by the minimax (maximin) strategies. In general, the value of the game must satisfy the inequality,

maximin (lower) value ≤ value of the game ≤ minimax (upper) value.

In the above example, maximin value = minimax value = 5. This implies that the game has a saddle point which is given by the entry (2, 2) of the matrix. The value of the game is thus equal to 5 and each player selects his second strategy as the optimal strategy. Notice that neither player can improve his position by selecting any other strategy.

§ 6·3
Mixed Strategies

It was shown in Section 6·2 that the existence of a saddle point immediately yields the optimal pure strategies for the game. There are cases, however, where such a saddle point does not exist. For example, consider the following zero-sum game.

		B			
	1	2	3	4	*Row minimum*
1	5	−10	9	0	−10
2	6	7	8	1	1
A 3	8	7	15	2	② Maximin value
4	3	4	−1	4	−1
Column maximum:	8	7	15	④	

Minimax value

The minimax value (= 4) is greater than the maximin value (= 2). Hence, the game does not have a saddle point and the two players cannot use the maximin-minimax strategies as their optimal strategies. This is true since each player can improve his outcomes by selecting a different strategy. In this case, the game is said to be *unstable*.

The failure of the minimax-maximin (pure) strategies, in general, to give an optimal solution to the game has lead to the idea of using mixed strategies. Each player, instead of selecting pure strategies only, may play all his strategies according to a predetermined set of ratios. Let $x_1, x_2, \ldots, x_m$ and $y_1, y_2, \ldots, y_n$ be the (nonnegative) row and column ratios representing the relative frequencies by which A and B, respectively, select their pure strategies. Then,

$$\sum_{i=1}^{m} x_i = \sum_{j=1}^{n} y_j = 1,$$

where $x_i \geq 0$ and $y_j \geq 0$ for all i and j. Thus if a_{ij} represents the (i, j)th entry of the game matrix, the ratios x_i and y_j will appear as in the following matrix.

$$B$$

	y_1	y_2	$\cdots$	y_n
x_1	a_{11}	a_{12}	$\cdots$	a_{1n}
A $\vdots$	$\vdots$	$\vdots$	$\vdots$	$\vdots$
x_m	a_{m1}	a_{m2}	$\cdots$	a_{mn}

Actually x_i and y_j may be regarded as the probabilities by which A and B select their ith and jth pure strategies, respectively.

The solution of the mixed strategy problem is based also on the minimax criterion given in Section 6·2. The only difference is that A selects the ratios x_i which maximize the smallest "average" payoff in a column, while B selects the ratios y_j which minimize the largest "average" payoff in a row. (In statistical theory, these averages are known as *expected* values.) Mathematically, the minimax criterion for a mixed strategy case is given as follows. Player A selects x_i ($x_i \geq 0$, $\sum_{i=1}^{m} x_i = 1$) which will yield,

$$\max_{x_i}\left\{\min\left(\sum_{i=1}^{m} a_{i1}x_i, \sum_{i=1}^{m} a_{i2}x_i, \ldots, \sum_{i=1}^{m} a_{in}x_i\right)\right\}$$

and Player B selects y_j ($y_j \geq 0$, $\sum_{j=1}^{n} y_j = 1$) which will yield,

$$\min_{y_j}\left\{\max\left(\sum_{j=1}^{n} a_{1j}y_j, \sum_{j=1}^{n} a_{2j}y_j, \ldots, \sum_{j=1}^{n} a_{mj}y_j\right)\right\}.$$

These values are referred to as the maximin and the minimax average (expected) payoffs, respectively.

As in the pure strategies case, the relationship,

minimax average payoff $\geq$ maximin average payoff,

holds in general. When x_i and y_j correspond to the optimal solution, the above relation holds in "equality" sense and the resulting "average" values become equal to the (optimal) expected value of the game. This result follows from the *minimax theorem* and is stated here without proof (see Problem 6-10). Now, if x_i^* and y_j^* are the optimal solutions for both players, then each payoff element a_{ij} will be associated with the probability $(x_i^* y_j^*)$. Thus, if v^* is the optimal expected value of the game, then

$$v^* = \sum_{i=1}^m \sum_{j=1}^n a_{ij} x_i^* y_j^*.$$

There are several methods for solving two-person zero-sum games for the optimal values of x_i and y_j. This chapter presents two methods only. The graphical method for solving $(2 \times n)$ or $(m \times 2)$ game is presented in Section 6·4 and the general linear programming method for solving any $(m \times n)$ game is presented in Section 6·5.

§ 6·4
Graphical Solution of $(2 \times n)$ and $(m \times 2)$ Games

Consider the following $(2 \times n)$ and $(m \times 2)$ game

$$B$$

		y_1	y_2	$\cdots$	y_n
	x_1	a_{11}	a_{12}	$\cdots$	a_{1n}
A					
	$x_2 = 1 - x_1$	a_{21}	a_{22}	$\cdots$	a_{2n}

It is assumed that the game does not have a saddle point.

Since A has two strategies, it follows that $x_2 = 1 - x_1$; $x_1 \geq 0$, $x_2 \geq 0$. His "average" payoffs corresponding to the *pure* strategies of B are given by

B's Pure strategy	A's Average payoff
1	$(a_{11} - a_{21})x_1 + a_{21}$
2	$(a_{12} - a_{22})x_1 + a_{22}$
.	.
.	.
.	.
n	$(a_{1n} - a_{2n})x_1 + a_{2n}$

This shows that A's average payoff varies linearly with x_1.

According to the minimax criterion for mixed-strategy games, Player A should select the value of x_1 so as to maximize his minimum average payoffs. This may be done by plotting the above straight lines as functions of x_1. A typical example is illustrated in Figure 6–1. Each line is numbered according

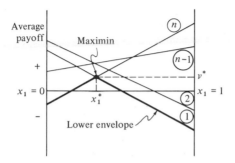

Figure 6–1

to its corresponding B's pure strategy. The lower envelope of these lines (indicated by double line segments) should give the minimum average payoff as a function of x_1. The *highest* point in this lower envelope (indicated by a dot) would then give the maximin average payoff and hence the optimum value of $x_1(= x_1^*)$.

The optimal y_j for B can be obtained by observing the definition of the average value of the game. This is given for the above ($2 \times n$) game by

$$v^* = y_1^*\{(a_{11} - a_{21})x_1^* + a_{21}\} + y_2^*\{(a_{12} - a_{22})x_1^* + a_{22}\}$$

$$+ \cdots + y_n^*\{(a_{1n} - a_{2n})x_1^* + a_{2n}\}.$$

Now, all the lines $\{(a_{1j} - a_{2j}) x_1^* + a_{2j}\}$ that do not pass through the maximin point must have their corresponding $y_j^* = 0$. This follows from the fact that at x^* any of these lines (for example, Line ② in Figure 6–1) will yield an average payoff greater than the maximin average payoff. Since $\sum_{j=1}^{n} y_j^* = 1$, $y_j^* \geq 0$, it follows that the average value of the game, v^*, will not be equal to the maximin average payoff, a result which violates the minimax theorem.

Because the maximin point is determined by the intersection of two straight lines, it follows that, except for the y_j corresponding to these two straight lines, all other y_j may be taken equal to zero. If, however, there are more than two lines passing through the maximin point, any two lines having opposite slopes may be selected to determine the *optimal* values of y_j. Each resulting solution is called an alternative solution. Consequently, any weighted average of these solutions should also yield a new optimal solution. It must be noted that any two straight lines having the same sign for their slopes will not yield an optimum solution. (See Example 6·4-1.)

The above discussion reveals the important result that any $(2 \times n)$ game is basically equivalent to a (2×2) game. Let y_{j_1} and y_{j_2} be the ratios corresponding to the two effective strategies of B. Since all other $y_j = 0$, $y_{j_2} = 1 - y_{j_1}$, $y_{j_1} \geq 0$ and $y_{j_2} \geq 0$, then B's average payoffs corresponding to A's strategy are given by

A's Pure strategy	B's Average payoff
1	$(a_{1j_1} - a_{1j_2})y_{j_1} + a_{1j_2}$
2	$(a_{2j_1} - a_{2j_2})y_{j_1} + a_{2j_2}$

These two lines are thus plotted as a function of y_{j_1} (see Figure 6–2 for a typical illustration). Since B wishes to minimize his maximum average payoff, the minimum point of the upper envelope of these two lines identifies $y_{j_1}^*$. Actually, $y_{j_1}^*$ can be obtained directly by solving for the point of intersection of the resulting two straight lines.

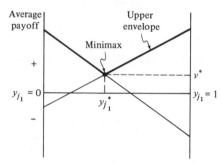

Figure 6–2

The $(m \times 2)$ games are treated similarly as in the $(2 \times n)$ games except that B's optimal strategies, y_j^*, are first determined using the minimax criterion. This automatically determines the two effective mixed strategies, x_{i_1} and x_{i_2} for A (all other $x_i = 0$) and the maximin criterion is then used to determine the optimal values $x_{i_1}^*$ and $x_{i_2}^*$.

The above two cases will now be illustrated by two numerical examples.

▶ **Example 6·4-1**

Consider the following (2×4) game.

		|	| 1	2	3	4

B

		1	2	3	4
A	1	2	2	3	−1
	2	4	3	2	6

This game does not have a saddle point. Thus, as shown above, A's average payoffs corresponding to B's pure strategies are given as follows.

B's Pure strategies	A's Average payoff
1	$-2x_1 + 4$
2	$-x_1 + 3$
3	$x_1 + 2$
4	$-7x_1 + 6$

These four straight lines are then plotted as functions of x_1 as shown in Figure 6–3.

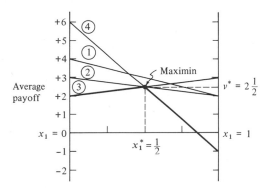

Figure 6–3

It follows from Figure 6–3 that the maximin occurs at $x_1^* = \frac{1}{2}$. This is the point of intersection of *any* two of the lines 2, 3, and 4. Consequently A's optimal strategy is $(x_1^* = \frac{1}{2}, \quad x_2^* = \frac{1}{2})$ and the value of the game is obtained by substituting for x_1 in the equation of any of the lines passing through the maximin point; that is, lines 2, 3, or 4. Thus

$$v^* = \begin{cases} -\frac{1}{2} + 3 = 2\frac{1}{2} \\ \frac{1}{2} + 2 = 2\frac{1}{2} \\ -7(\frac{1}{2}) + 6 = 2\frac{1}{2}. \end{cases}$$

In order to determine B's optimal strategies, it should be noticed that there are three lines passing through the maximin point. This is an indication that B can mix all three strategies. As mentioned before, any two lines having opposite signs for their slopes will define an alternative optimum solution. This means that of the three combinations (2, 3), (2, 4) and (3, 4), the combination (2, 4) must be excluded as nonoptimal.

The first combination (2, 3) implies that $y_1^* = y_4^* = 0$. Consequently

$y_3 = 1 - y_2$ and B's average payoffs corresponding to A's pure strategies are given as follows.

A's Pure strategy	B's Average payoff
1	$-y_2 + 3$
2	$y_2 + 2$

As stated above, by equating these two average payoffs, y_2^* (corresponding to minimax point) can be determined. Thus

$$- y_2^* + 3 = y_2^* + 2$$

or $y_2^* = \frac{1}{2}$. Notice that by substituting $y_2^* = \frac{1}{2}$ in B's average payoffs given above, the minimax value becomes equal to $2\frac{1}{2}$ which is equal to the values of the game, v^*, as should be expected.

The remaining combination $(3, 4)$ can be treated similarly to obtain an alternative optimal solution. Consequently, any weighted average of the combinations $(2, 3)$ and $(3, 4)$ will also yield a new optimal solution which mixes all the three strategies, 2, 3, and 4. The additional treatment of this case is left as an exercise for the reader. (See Problem 6-6.) ◄

▶ **Example 6·4-2**
Consider the following (4×2) game.

$$B$$

		1	2
	1	2	4
	2	2	3
A	3	3	2
	4	-2	6

The game does not have a saddle point. Let y_1 and y_2 $(= 1 - y_1)$ be B's mixed strategies. Thus

A's Pure strategy	B's Average payoff
1	$-2y_1 + 4$
2	$-y_1 + 3$
3	$y_1 + 2$
4	$-8y_1 + 6$

These four lines are plotted in Figure 6–4. In this case, the minimax point is determined as the lowest point of the upper envelope. The solution y_1^* is obtained as the point of intersection of lines 1 and 3. This yields $y_1^* = \frac{2}{3}$ and $v^* = 2\frac{2}{3}$.

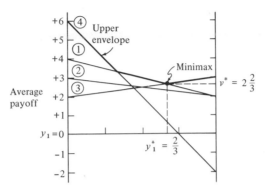

Figure 6–4

The lines intersecting at the minimax point correspond to A's pure strategies 1 and 3. This indicates that $x_2^* = x_4^* = 0$. Consequently, $x_1 = 1 - x_3$ and A's average payoffs corresponding to B's pure strategies are

B's Pure strategy	A's Average payoff
1	$- x_1 + 3$
2	$2x_1 + 2$

Equating these two payoffs to determine x_1^* at the maximin point; that is,

$$-x_1^* + 3 = 2x_1^* + 2,$$

gives $x_1^* = \frac{1}{3}$. Thus A's optimal strategies are $x_1^* = \frac{1}{3}$, $x_2^* = 0$, $x_3^* = \frac{2}{3}$, $x_4^* = 0$. This yields $v^* = 2\frac{2}{3}$ as before. ◄

§ 6·4·1
Dominance

The above discussion indicates the simplicity of solving $(2 \times n)$ and $(m \times 2)$ games. This procedure fails, however, for the general $(m \times n)$ games $(m > 2$ and $n > 2)$. It is possible sometimes to reduce the size of the game matrix by using the so-called "dominance property." This occurs when one or more of the pure strategies of either players can be deleted because they are inferior to *at least one* of the remaining strategies and hence it is never used. In this case, it is said that the deleted strategies are *dominated* by superior ones.

To illustrate this point, consider the following (3 × 3) game.

$$B$$

	1	2	3
1	1	8	3
A 2	6	4	5
3	0	1	2

It is clear that the entries for *A*'s third strategy are inferior to the entries of both the first and the second strategies. In this case, the third strategy can be deleted since *A* can do better using his first or second strategies. This means that the third strategy is dominated by the first and the second strategies. The new matrix thus becomes,

$$B$$

	1	2	3
1	1	8	3
A 2	6	4	5

which can then be solved by the graphical method.

Dominance need not be based on the superiority of *pure* strategies only. A given strategy can be dominated if it is inferior to a weighted average of two or more other pure strategies. For example, consider the following game.

$$B$$

	1	2	3
1	5	0	2
A 2	−1	8	6
3	1	2	3

None of the *pure* strategies of *A* is inferior to any of his other *pure* strategies.

However, using equal weights, a weighted average of A's first and second pure strategies gives,

$$\{(\tfrac{1}{2})\,(5-1),\quad (\tfrac{1}{2})\,(0+8),\quad (\tfrac{1}{2})\,(2+6)\},$$

or $(2, 4, 4)$. This is superior to A's third pure strategy. In this case, the third strategy may be deleted from the matrix.

Opportunities such as those provided by the dominance property should, in general, reduce the size of the game and hence the computational effort associated with its solution.

§ 6·5
Solution of $(m \times n)$ Games by Linear Programming

In Section 6·4 it was shown that A selects his optimum mixed strategies which yield

$$\max_{x_i}\left\{\min\left(\sum_{i=1}^{m} a_{i1}x_i,\ \sum_{i=1}^{m} a_{i2}x_i,\ \ldots,\ \sum_{i=1}^{m} a_{in}x_i\right)\right\},$$

subject to the constraints

$$x_1 + x_2 + \cdots + x_m = 1$$

$$x_i \geq 0, \qquad i = 1, 2, \ldots, m.$$

This problem can be put in the linear programming form as follows. Let

$$v = \min\left(\sum_{i=1}^{m} a_{i1}x_i,\ \sum_{i=1}^{m} a_{i2}x_i,\ \ldots,\ \sum_{i=1}^{m} a_{in}x_i\right),$$

then the above problem becomes: (cf. Example 2·2-2)

$$\text{maximize}\quad z_0 = v$$

subject to

$$\sum_{i=1}^{m} a_{i1}x_i \geq v$$

$$\sum_{i=1}^{m} a_{i2}x_i \geq v$$

$$\vdots$$

$$\sum_{i=1}^{m} a_{in}x_i \geq v$$

$$\sum_{i=1}^{m} x_i = 1$$

$$x_i \geq 0, \quad \text{all } i.$$

Clearly, v represents the value of the game in this case.

The above linear programming formulation can be simplified by dividing all $(n + 1)$ constraints by v. This division is correct as long as $v > 0$. Otherwise, if $v < 0$, the direction of the inequality constraints must be reversed; and if $v = 0$, division would be illegitimate. This point presents no special problem since a constant K can be added to all the entries of the matrix thus guaranteeing that the value of the game for the "modified" matrix is greater than zero. After the optimal solution is obtained, the true value of the game is obtained by subtracting K. In general, if the maximin value of the game is nonnegative then the value of the game is greater than zero (provided the game does not have a saddle point).

Thus, assuming that $v > 0$, the above constraints become

$$a_{11} \frac{x_1}{v} + a_{21} \frac{x_2}{v} + \cdots + a_{m1} \frac{x_m}{v} \geq 1,$$

$$a_{12} \frac{x_1}{v} + a_{22} \frac{x_2}{v} + \cdots + a_{m2} \frac{x_m}{v} \geq 1,$$

$$\vdots \qquad\qquad \vdots$$

$$a_{1n} \frac{x_1}{v} + a_{2n} \frac{x_2}{v} + \cdots + a_{mn} \frac{x_m}{v} \geq 1,$$

$$\frac{x_1}{v} + \frac{x_2}{v} + \cdots + \frac{x_m}{v} = \frac{1}{v}.$$

Let $X_i = x_i/v$, $i = 1, 2, \ldots, m$. Since

$$\max v \equiv \min \frac{1}{v} = \min\{X_1 + \cdots + X_m\}$$

(which is justified by the last constraint), the problem becomes:

$$\text{minimize} \quad x_0 = X_1 + X_2 + \cdots + X_m,$$

subject to

$$a_{11} X_1 + a_{21} X_2 + \cdots + a_{m1} X_m \geq 1,$$

$$a_{12} X_1 + a_{22} X_2 + \cdots + a_{m2} X_m \geq 1,$$

$$\vdots \qquad\qquad \vdots$$

$$a_{1n} X_1 + a_{2n} X_2 + \cdots + a_{mn} X_m \geq 1,$$

$$X_1 \geq 0, \quad X_2 \geq 0, \quad \ldots, \quad X_m \geq 0.$$

After the optimal solution is obtained using the simplex method, the original optimal values can be determined from the given transformation formulas.

Player B's problem, on the other hand, is given by:

$$\min_{y_j}\left\{\max\left(\sum_{j=1}^{n} a_{1j} y_j, \sum_{j=1}^{n} a_{2j} y_j, \ldots, \sum_{j=1}^{n} a_{mj} y_m\right)\right\},$$

subject to

$$y_1 + y_2 + \cdots + y_n = 1,$$

$$y_j \geq 0, \quad j = 1, 2, \ldots, n.$$

This can also be put in a linear programming form as follows.

$$\text{Maximize} \quad y_0 = Y_1 + Y_2 + \cdots + Y_n,$$

subject to

$$a_{11} Y_1 + a_{12} Y_2 + \cdots + a_{1n} Y_n \leq 1,$$

$$a_{21} Y_1 + a_{22} Y_2 + \cdots + a_{2n} Y_n \leq 1,$$

$$\vdots \qquad\qquad\qquad \vdots$$

$$a_{m1} Y_1 + a_{m2} Y_2 + \cdots + a_{mn} Y_n \leq 1,$$

$$Y_1 \geq 0, \quad Y_2 \geq 0, \quad \ldots, \quad Y_n \geq 0,$$

where

$$y_0 = \frac{1}{v}, \; Y_j = \frac{y_j}{v}, \quad j = 1, 2, \ldots, n.$$

Notice that B's problem is actually the dual of A's problem. Thus the optimal solution of one problem will automatically yield the optimal solution to the other one. Player B's problem can be solved using the regular simplex method while Player A's problem is solved by the dual simplex method. The choice of either method will depend on which problem has a smaller number of constraints. This in turn depends on the number of pure strategies for each player.

▶ **Example 6·5-1**
Consider the following (3×3) game

			B		
		1	2	3	*Row minimum*
	1	3	-1	-3	-3
A	2	-3	3	-1	-3
	3	-4	-3	3	-4
Column maximum:		3	3	3	

Since the maximin value is -3, it is possible that the value of the game may be negative or zero. Thus, a constant K is added to all the elements of the matrix which is *at least* equal to the negative of the maximin value; that is $K \geq 3$. Let $K = 5$, the above matrix becomes

$$
\begin{array}{c}
 & & B \\
 & & 1 \quad\;\; 2 \quad\;\; 3 \\
A \quad
\begin{array}{c}
1 \\
2 \\
3
\end{array}
&
\begin{array}{|c|c|c|}
\hline
8 & 4 & 2 \\
\hline
2 & 8 & 4 \\
\hline
1 & 2 & 8 \\
\hline
\end{array}
\end{array}
$$

Following the above reasoning, B's linear programming problem is:

$$\text{maximize} \quad y_0 = Y_1 + Y_2 + Y_3,$$

subject to

$$8Y_1 + 4Y_2 + 2Y_3 \leq 1$$

$$2Y_1 + 8Y_2 + 4Y_3 \leq 1$$

$$1Y_1 + 2Y_2 + 8Y_3 \leq 1$$

$$Y_1 \geq 0, \quad Y_2 \geq 0, \quad Y_3 \geq 0.$$

The final optimal tableau for this problem is given by

Basic	y_0	Y_1	Y_2	Y_3	S_1	S_2	S_3	Solution
y_0	①	0	0	0	5/49	11/196	1/14	45/196
Y_1	0	①	0	0	1/7	$-1/14$	0	1/14
Y_2	0	0	①	0	$-3/98$	31/196	$-1/14$	11/196
Y_3	0	0	0	①	$-1/98$	$-3/98$	1/7	5/49

Thus, for the original problem

$$v^* = 1/y_0 - K = 196/45 - 5 = -29/45,$$

$$y_1^* = Y_1/y_0 = \frac{1/14}{45/196} = 14/45,$$

$$y_2^* = Y_2/y_0 = \frac{11/196}{45/196} = 11/45,$$

$$y_3^* = Y_3/y_0 = \frac{5/49}{45/196} = 20/45.$$

The optimal strategies for A are obtained from the dual solution to the above problem. This is given by

$$x_0 = y_0 = 45/196, \quad X_1 = 5/49, \quad X_2 = 11/196, \quad X_3 = 1/14.$$

Hence

$$x_1^* = X_1/x_0 = 20/45,$$

$$x_2^* = X_2/x_0 = 11/45,$$

$$x_3^* = X_3/x_0 = 14/45.$$

The reader can verify that these optimal strategies satisfy the minimax theorem. ◄

SELECTED REFERENCES

1. DANTZIG, G. B., *Linear Programming and Extensions*, Princeton, N.J.: Princeton University Press, 1963, Chapters 2 and 13.
2. DRESHER, M., *Games of Strategy: Theory and Applications*, Englewood Cliffs, New Jersey: Prentice-Hall, 1961.
3. LUCE, R., and H. RAIFFA, *Games and Decisions*, New York: Wiley, 1957.
4. WILLIAMS, J., *The Compleat Strategyst*, New York: McGraw-Hill (revised edition), 1966.

PROBLEMS

☐ **6-1(a)** Find the saddle point and the value of the game for each of the following two games. The payoff is for Player A.

B

8	6	2	8
8	9	4	5
7	5	3	5

A is at left.

(i)

B

4	−4	−5	6
−3	−4	−9	−2
6	7	−8	−9
7	3	−9	5

A is at left.

(ii)

(b)   Find the range of values for "p" and "q" which will render the entry (2, 2) a saddle point in the following games.

		B	
	1	q	3
A	p	5	10
	6	2	3

(i)

		B	
	2	4	5
A	10	7	q
	4	p	6

(ii)

☐ **6-2**   Indicate whether the values of the following games are greater than, less than, or equal to zero.

		B		
	1	9	6	0
	2	3	8	4
A	−5	−2	10	−3
	7	4	−2	−5

(i)

		B		
	3	7	−1	3
A	4	8	0	−6
	6	−9	−2	4

(ii)

		B		
	−1	9	6	8
	−2	10	4	6
A	5	3	0	7
	7	−2	8	4

(iii)

		B	
	3	6	1
A	5	2	3
	4	2	−5

(iv)

☐ **6-3**   Let a_{ij} be the (i, j)th element of the payoff matrix with m and n strategies, respectively. Prove that

$$\max_{i} \min_{j} a_{ij} \leq \min_{j} \max_{i} a_{ij}.$$

☐ **6-4**   Two companies A and B are promoting two competing products. Each product currently controls 50 per cent of the market. Because of recent modifications in the two products, the two companies are now preparing for launching new advertisement campaign. If no advertisement is made by either of the two companies, the present status of the market shares will remain unchanged. However, if either company launches a stronger campaign, the other company will certainly lose a proportional percentage of its customers. A survey of the market indicated that 50 per cent of the potential customers can be reached through television, 30 per cent through newspapers, and the remaining 20 per cent through radio. The objective of each company is to select the appropriate advertisement media.

Formulate the problem as a two-person zero-sum game. Does the problem have a saddle point?

□ **6-5** Consider the game

	1	2	3
1	5	50	50
2	1	1	0.1
3	10	1	10

Verify that the strategies $(\frac{1}{6}, 0, \frac{5}{6})$ for Player A and $(\frac{49}{54}, \frac{5}{54}, 0)$ for Player B are optimal and find the value of the game.

□ **6-6** In Example 6·4-1, show that combination $(2, 4)$ for Player B does not yield optimal values for y_j while combination $(3, 4)$ yields the optimal solution. Develop a general expression which will identify all the alternative solutions to the problem.

□ **6-7** Solve the following games graphically.

$$
A \begin{array}{c|cccc} & \multicolumn{4}{c}{B} \\ \hline 1 & 3 & -3 & 7 \\ 2 & 5 & 4 & -6 \end{array}
$$
(i)

$$
A \begin{array}{c|cc} & \multicolumn{2}{c}{B} \\ & 1 & 2 \\ \hline & 5 & 6 \\ & -7 & 9 \\ & -4 & -3 \\ & 2 & 1 \end{array}
$$
(ii)

$$
A \begin{array}{c|ccc} & \multicolumn{3}{c}{B} \\ & 1 & 2 & 5 \\ \hline & 8 & 4 & 7 \\ & -1 & 5 & -6 \end{array}
$$
(iii)

$$
A \begin{array}{c|ccc} & \multicolumn{3}{c}{B} \\ \hline & 8 & 5 & 8 \\ & 9 & 6 & 5 \\ & 7 & 3 & 4 \\ & 7 & 5 & 7 \end{array}
$$
(iv)

□ **6-8** Consider the well-known Colonel Blotto game where Colonel Blotto and his enemy are trying to take over two strategic locations. The regiments available for Blotto and his enemy are 2 and 3, respectively. Both sides will distribute their regiments among the two locations. Let n_1 and n_2 be the number of regiments allocated by Colonel Blotto to locations 1 and 2, respectively. Also, let m_1 and m_2 be his enemy's allocations to the respective locations. The payoff of Blotto is computed as follows. If $n_1 > m_1$, he receives $m_1 + 1$ and if $n_2 > m_2$ he receives $m_2 + 1$. On the other hand if $n_1 < m_1$, he loses $n_1 + 1$ and if $n_2 < m_2$, he loses $n_2 + 1$. Finally, if the number of regiments from both sides are the same, each side gets zero.

Formulate the problem as a two-person zero-sum game and then solve by linear programming.

☐ **6-9** Verify that B's problem is defined by the linear programming problem given in Section 6·5.

☐ **6-10** Prove the minimax theorem using the relationship between the values of the objective function in the primal and the dual problems of the linear programming problem.

☐ **6-11** Verify that the linear programming solution to Example 6·5-1 satisfies the minimax theorem.

☐ **6-12** Consider the two-finger "Morra" game. Each player shows one or two fingers and simultaneously makes a guess of the number of fingers his opponent has. The player making the correct guess wins an amount equal to the total number of fingers shown by the two players. In all other cases, the game is a draw.

Formulate the problem as a two-person zero-sum game and then solve by linear programming.

☐ **6-13** Solve the following game by linear programming

$$B$$

$$A \quad \begin{array}{|ccc|} \hline -1 & 1 & 1 \\ 2 & -2 & 2 \\ 3 & 3 & -3 \\ \hline \end{array}$$

CHAPTER 7

Dynamic Programming

§ 7·1
The Concept of Dynamic Programming

Dynamic programming is a mathematical technique dealing with the optimization of multistage decision processes. The technique was developed in the early 1950's by Richard Bellman who also coined its name. In this technique, decisions regarding a certain problem are typically optimized in *stages* rather than simultaneously. This generally signifies that the original decision problem is divided into small subproblems (stages) which can then be handled more efficiently from the computational viewpoint.

Before discussing the dynamic programming approach to problem solving, it seems appropriate to indicate the need for such an approach by illustrating a typical situation where it can be used. Consider a simplified capital budgeting problem where there are three existing factories, each being considered for possible expansion. The total amount of capital allocated to the entire project is C. Factories 1, 2, and 3 have three, four, and two alternative plans for expansion, respectively. The expected additional costs and the corresponding revenues for the jth plan of the ith factory are given by c_{ij} and r_{ij}, respectively. The first plan ($j = 1$) for each factory, i, will be assumed to signify the possibility of no expansion so that $c_{i1} = r_{i1} = 0$ for $i = 1, 2, 3$. The objective of the decision problem is to select a plan j for each factory i which will maximize the total revenue. The cost of the selected set of plans should not exceed the total available capital, C.

A straightforward method for solving this problem is to consider it in the form of a decision tree as shown in Figure 7–1. The circles indicate the alternative plans at each stage and the arrows represent the decisions. The problem can thus be solved by first listing all the different combinations of alternatives plans (24 in this case). One can then select the best combination as the one giving the largest $\sum_{i,j} r_{ij}$, while satisfying $\sum_{i,j} c_{ij} \leq C$.

Notice the features of the above exhaustive enumeration scheme. First, *all*

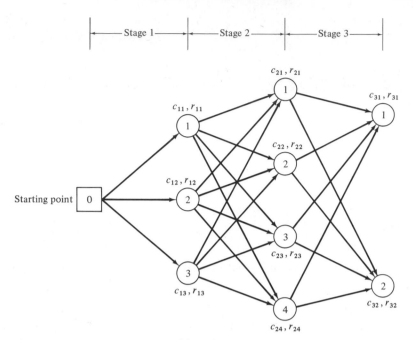

Figure 7-1

the decisions of any combination (policy) must be specified before a combination can be evaluated. Second, an optimum policy cannot be determined until all combinations have been evaluated. This method is inefficient since some of these combinations may not satisfy the capital limitation; that is, they may be infeasible. In other cases, the number of combinations may be too large (if not infinite) to allow exhaustive listing. Again, the fact that each combination encompasses the *entire* decision problem may prove computationally infeasible in large problems.

The dynamic programming approach avoids the above mentioned difficulties by first breaking (decomposing) the problem into smaller subproblems. In the terminology of dynamic programming, each subproblem is referred to as a *stage*. A stage here signifies a portion of the decision problem for which a "separate" decision can be made. The resulting decision must also be meaningful in the sense that if it is optimal for the stage it represents, then it can be used directly as part of the optimal solution to the entire problem. For example, in the above capital budgeting problem, each factory may be regarded as a stage for which an expansion plan (from among all those of the stage) may be selected. On the other hand, it will be meaningless to define a "stage" which involves alternative plans from two or three factories at the same time. In general, the number of stages in a problem may be finite or infinite.

The decision-making process at each stage involves the selection of one of the alternatives of the stage. This is usually referred to as a *stage decision.* Associated with each stage decision is a *return function* which evaluates the alternative made by this decision in terms of its contribution to the returns of the entire problem. For example, in the capital budgeting problem, the revenue r_{ij} represents the return function of the *j*th plan at the *i*th stage (factory). By selecting an *optimal* feasible alternative for each stage, the selected set of alternatives is then said to comprise an *optimal policy* for the entire decision problem.

The computational efficiency of dynamic programming stems from the fact that the optimum solution can be obtained by decomposing the problem into stages and then considering them one stage at a time. The solution is obtained in an orderly manner by going from one stage to the next and is completed after the final stage is reached. The important point here is: how can the successive stages be treated separately even though, by the very nature of the problem, these stages are dependent? For example, in the above capital budgeting problem, this dependency is dictated by the fact that all the factories are competing for a limited capital.

Separation between successive stages is achieved in dynamic programming using the concept of the *state.* Thus, at any stage, a state summarizes the current "status" of the system (regarding the limitations that bind all the stages) which will permit making a *feasible* decision for the current stage without having to "look back" and study the effect of this decision on the previously-considered stages. For example, in the capital budgeting problem (where the capital requirements represent the main binding constraint), a state may be defined as the amount of capital allocated to the current stage *and* the preceding stages.

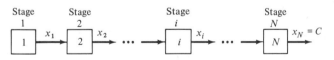

Figure 7–2

To show how the above definition of the state can allow considering one stage at a time while ensuring the feasibility of the decisions made at every stage, consider the capital budgeting problem with N stages (factories). The problem may be viewed schematically as shown in Figure 7–2, where stage i represents the *i*th factory. (Notice that it is immaterial here as to which specific factory is assigned to stage *i*.) Let x_i be the state of the system at stage i as defined above. Thus, x_1 represents the capital available for stage 1, x_2 represents the capital available for stages 1 and 2, and, in general, x_i represents the capital available for stages 1, 2, ..., and *i*. It is important to notice that, *a priori*, only the value of x_N is known exactly. That is, $x_N = C$, where C is the total capital available for the entire project. However, it is feasible to assume that $0 \leq x_i \leq C$ for all i. Thus, at any stage i, when $x_i = 0$, this is interpreted as allocating no capital to the first i stages (or allocating C to the last $N - i$ stages). On the other hand, when $x_i = C$, this means that all the capital is allocated to the first i stages. These are the two extreme cases. For the case where $0 < x_i < C$, this is interpreted similarly as allocating x_i to the first i stages and $(C - x_i)$ to the remaining ones.

Assume now that the solution starts by considering stage 1. Since the value of x_1 is not known exactly, it is logical to compute the optimal solutions at stage 1 for all feasible values of x_1. Thus, if, for simplicity, the amount of capital required for each alternative j at stage 1 (that is, c_{1j}) occurs in discrete values, then *feasible* values of x_1 can be assumed to occur in discrete values only; that is, $x_1 = 0, 1, 2, \ldots, C$. Now, for each of these values, the optimum alternative is selected from among all those alternatives of stage 1 that satisfy x_1 as the one yielding the largest revenue; that is, $\max_j\{r_{1j}\}$, where $c_{1j} \leq x_1$. This actually says that the *optimal* solution at stage 1 is a function of x_1 only. For ease of later references, let $f_1(x_1)$ represent the *optimum* revenue for stage 1 given x_1.

Now consider stage 2. By the same assumption as in stage 1, x_2 takes on the discrete values $0, 1, 2, \ldots, C$. In order for an alternative j at stage 2 to be feasible, its cost c_{2j} must not exceed x_2. If $c_{2j} = x_2$, this means that $x_1 = x_2 - c_{2j} = 0$; that is, no capital is allocated to stage 1. If $c_{2j} < x_2$, then $x_1 = x_2 - c_{2j} > 0$ will be the capital allocated to stage 1. Since the optimal solution at stage 1 is a function of x_1 only, then for a given value of x_2, the optimal alternative at stage 2 is selected from among all alternatives j satisfying $c_{2j} \leq x_2$ as the one which maximizes the *sum* of (1) the revenue r_{2j} of alternative j at stage 2, and (2) the *optimal* revenue from stage 1 given $x_1 = x_2 - c_{2j}$. In other words, it is the alternative corresponding to $\max_j\{r_{2j} + f_1(x_2 - c_{2j})\}$. Notice that the new revenue is cumulative for stages 1 and 2. Notice also that the cumulative optimal revenue is a function of x_2 only so that it is appropriate to represent it by the new function $f_2(x_2)$.

It is important to observe that in reaching an optimal decision at stage 2, given x_2, one only needs to know the cumulative optimal return from the preceding stage(s), $f_1(x_1)$, where $x_1 = x_2 - c_{2j}$. This means that no question is asked as to *how* $f_1(x_1)$ was obtained. In essence, this signifies that one does not have to "look back" to see the effect of the present decision on previous ones. Notice also that the question of feasibility is automatically settled since at no stage can an alternative costing more than the value of the state be selected. This discussion already reveals that the given definition of the states does in fact result in the required separation between the stages.

The generalization of the above procedure is now in order. Given $f_{i-1}(x_{i-1})$, the cumulative optimal returns for stages $1, 2, \ldots,$ and $i - 1$, and the current state x_i, the optimum alternative at stage i is selected from among all alternatives j at stage i as the one which maximizes $r_{ij} + f_{i-1}(x_i - c_{ij})$, where

$c_{ij} \le x_i$. This shows that future decisions (for the remaining stages) will constitute an optimal policy regardless of the policy adopted in previous stages. This is a basic property in dynamic programming which is referred to as the "principle of optimality." By virtue of this principle, it is not necessary to trace back the effect of a current decision upon any of the decisions of the previous stages. In other words, a problem which does not satisfy the principle of optimality cannot be solved by dynamic programming.

Upon reaching stage N, the above procedure will complete the essential computations of the dynamic programming approach. In order to determine the optimal policy for the entire problem one would have to start from stage N and proceed backward as follows. At stage N, given $x_N = C$, the optimal decision for this stage is automatically given. Let c_{Nk} be the cost of the optimal alternative k at stage N. Hence, $x_{N-1} = x_N - c_{Nk} = C - c_{Nk}$. Now, from computations at stage $N - 1$, the optimal alternative for this stage is the one corresponding to x_{N-1}. Knowing this alternative (and hence its cost) one can automatically determine x_{N-2}. The procedure is thus repeated until x_1 is reached at which point its optimal decision can be obtained from the corresponding computations at stage 1.

Notice that at any stage i, given its state x_i and its *optimal* decision, one can determine x_{i-1}. In other words, x_{i-1} is a function of x_i and the optimal decision at stage i. This is usually referred to as *stage inversion* or *state transformation*. This transformation could be as simple as illustrated by the above capital budgeting problem. There are some cases, however, where such a transformation could be quite complex with the result that the corresponding computations at each stage will also be complex.

In the above capital budgeting problem, the state x_i is defined as the capital allocated to stages $1, 2, \ldots,$ and i. Another definition can also be made for the same problem. This is to define the state x_i as the amount of capital allocated to stages $i, i + 1, \ldots,$ and N. The two definitions are basically equivalent and should yield the same optimal solution. The only difference may be encountered in the computational aspect of the problem since the two definitions involve different state transformation (or stage inversion). This usually leads to what is known as the *forward and backward computational schemes*. This point will be developed further in Section 7·4.

The previous discussion illustrates the case where the state of the system is described by a single element only, namely x_i. In general, the number of elements describing a state may exceed one. For example, in the capital budgeting problem, if in addition to the capital limitation, there is also a manpower constraint, then the state of the system at any stage may be described by two elements reflecting both the capital and manpower limitations. It must be noted that the number of feasible values for each state-element may be finite or infinite. The first case was illustrated above. The latter case occurs when the decision variables are continuous. (See Example 7·3-4.)

Having defined the concepts of *state, stage* and *return function* in dynamic programming, the immediate task now is to consider the aspect of formulating the problem in a mathematical model. This mathematical model basically relates the states, stages, and their associated return function in a general mathematical equation which is then used to obtain the optimal solution. Unlike linear programming, for example, the formulation of a dynamic programming model does not follow a fixed format. Dynamic programming theory, however, develops the so-called "recursive (or functional) equation approach" which offers a unifying, but not fixed, format for expressing the decision problem mathematically. The idea of the approach was introduced informally in the above discussion; that is, computing f_i from f_{i-1}. The basic properties of this approach will be introduced in Section 7·2. It must be borne in mind, however, that, in general, the development of a recursive equation depends largely on the ability and skill of the user to define the states and the stages of the system properly. This usually can be developed through frequent exposure to this type of problem. To assist in this respect, several dynamic programming examples, each with a different idea, will be presented in this chapter. Further examples can be found in Chapter 13 as applications of dynamic programming to inventory problems. This will also provide illustrations of the applications of dynamic programming to *probabilistic* situations since none of these will be given in this chapter.

The development of the recursive equation for a dynamic programming problem represents the first step in the solution. The next step is to consider the determination of the optimal policy. This requires the development of a systematic computational scheme. Sections 7·3 and 7·4 will be devoted to this problem. It will be shown that the power of dynamic programming theory may be obscured by the incapability of the most modern digital computers to handle some problems in a reasonable amount of time. This difficulty is especially pronounced by the "problem of dimensionality" which results from the increase in the number of the states, as will be discussed in Section 7·5.

Dynamic programming theory can in principle be used to solve any linear programming problem. The procedure, as compared with the simplex method, is computationally inefficient especially when the number of constraints is large. This problem will be discussed in Section 7·6.

§ 7·2
The Recursive Equation Approach

The development of the recursive equation in dynamic programming is best illustrated by an example. Consider the capital budgeting problem given in Section 7·1. Let the state x_i be defined as the capital allocated to stages 1, 2, ..., and i. Since the revenue r_{ij} is a function of the cost c_{ij}, it is convenient, for the purpose of the recursive equation, to write $r_{ij} = R_{ij}(c_{ij})$.

Consider the first stage by itself. As indicated in Section 7·1, x_1 must satisfy $0 \le x_1 \le C$, where C is the total capital available. Thus, if $f_1(x_1)$ is the revenue of an *optimal* policy at the first stage given the capital available is x_1, then

$$f_1(x_1) = \max_{\substack{j=1,2,3 \\ 0 \le c_{1j} \le x_1}} \{R_{1j}(c_{1j})\}.$$

The optimization in this case is made over the alternative plans ($j = 1, 2, 3$) at stage 1 subject to the state limitation, x_1.

Now, consider stage 2. By definition, x_2 represents the capital available for stages 1 and 2. Again, $0 \le x_2 \le C$. From the principle of optimality, given the current state, the optimum alternative for the current stage is obtained by optimizing the *sum* of (1) the returns from the current stage, and (2) the *optimum* returns from all previously-considered stages. Thus, since for stage 2, the return from the jth plan is $R_{2j}(c_{2j})$ and the optimum return from stage 1 is

$$\max_{\substack{j=1,2,3 \\ 0 \le x_1 + c_{2j} \le x_2}} \{R_{1j}(x_1)\},$$

the optimum alternative at stage 2 corresponds to,

$$f_2(x_2) = \max_{\substack{j=1,2,3,4 \\ 0 \le c_{2j} \le x_2}} \left\{ R_{2j}(c_{2j}) + \max_{\substack{k=1,2,3 \\ 0 \le x_1 + c_{2j} \le x_2}} \{R_{1k}(x_1)\} \right\}.$$

From the definition of f_1, it follows that,

$$\max_{\substack{k=1,2,3 \\ 0 \le x_1 + c_{2j} \le x_2}} \{R_{1k}(x_1)\} = \max_{\substack{k=1,2,3 \\ 0 \le x_1 \le x_2 - c_{2j}}} \{R_{1k}(x_1)\} = f_1(x_2 - c_{2j}).$$

Thus

$$f_2(x_2) = \max_{\substack{j=1,2,3,4 \\ 0 \le c_{2j} \le x_2}} \{R_{2j}(C_{2j}) + f_1(x_2 - c_{2j})\}.$$

The new equation can be interpreted as follows. Given x_2, the amount of capital available for stages 1 and 2, if c_{2j} is allocated to the jth plan at the second stage, the result will be a revenue of $R_{2j}(c_{2j})$. The remaining amount, $x_2 - c_{2j}$, should be allocated to the first stage in the best possible way which yields a revenue of $f_1(x_2 - c_{2j})$.

By a similar argument, the recursive equation for the third stage is given by

$$f_3(x_3) = \max_{\substack{j=1,2 \\ 0 \le c_{3j} \le x_3}} \{R_{3j}(c_{3j}) + f_2(x_3 - c_{3j})\}.$$

where x_3 is defined as the capital allocated to *all* the three stages. This means that $x_3 = C$.

In the general case of the budgeting problem, where there are N factories, let the ith factory have M_i alternative plans and let $R_{im_i}(c_{im_i})$ be the revenue from the (m_i)th alternative of the ith factory given its cost is c_{im_i}.[1] Thus, using the same notation above, the corresponding general recursive equation becomes

$$f_1(x_1) = \max_{\substack{m_1 \\ 0 \le c_{1m_1} \le x_1}} \{R_{1m_1}(c_{1m_1})\},$$

$$f_i(x_i) = \max_{\substack{m_i \\ 0 \le c_{im_i} \le x_i}} \{R_{im_i}(c_{im_i}) + f_{i-1}(x_i - c_{im_i})\}, \qquad i = 2, 3, \ldots, N$$

where $x_N = C$.

It is conventional to show how the recursive equation can be solved by indicating the starting function. In the above case the starting function is given by $f_1(x_1)$. Thus, the problem is solved by successively finding

$$f_1 \to f_2 \to \ldots \to f_N,$$

and given $x_N = C$, the optimal policy m_i^* is obtained in the order

$$m_N^* \to m_{N-1}^* \to \cdots \to m_1^*.$$

The recursive equation actually indicates how the entire problem can be decomposed into subproblems. In the above problem, the objective function consists of the *sum* of the revenues at the subsequent stages and consequently, it is decomposed *additively*. Another important case occurs when the revenues at the different stages are multiplied by each other. In this case the recursive equation would indicate *multiplicative* decomposition (see Example 7·3-3). A combination of multiplicative and additive functions may also, under special conditions, be decomposed in the form of a recursive equation (see Problem 7-5). Other cases which are neither additive not multiplicative can also occur. A typical illustration is given in Problem 7-10.

§ 7·3
Computational Procedure in Dynamic Programming

In this section, it will be shown how a typical recursive equation (such as the one presented in Section 7·2) is solved for the purpose of determining the optimal policy. In general, a recursive equation may involve two types of

---

[1] In the above discussion, the symbol j was used indiscriminately to represent the decision variables for all stages. Such a representation is no longer suitable for future discussion. Consequently, the subscripted symbol m_i will be used for the unique identification of the decision variable at stage i.

computations depending on whether the states of the system are discrete or continuous. In the first case, a tabular computational scheme is followed at each stage which gives the return function and the optimal decision corresponding to each state. The number of rows in each table is thus equal to the number of the corresponding feasible state values while the number of columns is equal to the number of possible decisions. In the second case the optimal decisions at each stage are obtained in "closed forms" usually by employing the classical methods of optimization (see Example 7·3-4). The two procedures will now be illustrated by examples.

▶ **Example 7·3-1** (Budgeting Problem)

Consider the capital budgeting problem presented in Section 7·1. The data of the problem is tabulated below. (For convenience, all the cost and revenue figures are scaled by 10^{-3}.)

m_i	$i = 1$		$i = 2$		$i = 3$	
	c_{1m_1}	R_{1m_1}	c_{2m_2}	R_{2m_2}	c_{3m_3}	R_{3m_3}
1	0	0	0	0	0	0
2	2	5	5	8	1	3
3	4	6	6	9	—	—
4	—	—	8	12	—	—

Assume the total capital availabe is $C = 10$.

Defining $f_0 \equiv 0$, the general recursive equation for this type of problem is given above as,

$$f_i(x_i) = \max_{\substack{m_i \\ 0 \leq c_{im_i} \leq x_i}} \{R_{im_i}(c_{im_i}) + f_{i-1}(x_i - c_{im_i})\}, \qquad i = 1, 2, \ldots, N.$$

As indicated previously the solution of this equation is obtained by first finding f_1. Since the cost, c_{im_i}, and the revenue, R_{im_i}, are given in discrete values, the tabular computation procedure will be used. In general, a table is constructed for each stage such that, given the state of the system, all the feasible alternatives of this state are evaluated accordingly and the corresponding best alternative is selected. The entries for each state value will thus be indicated by the corresponding columns in the table as shown below.

State x_i	Evaluation of feasible alternatives, m_i, of stage i given x_i $f_i(m_i\|x_i)$				Optimum solution	
	$m_i = 1$	$m_i = 2$	$\cdots$	$m_i = M_i$	Return function $f_i(x_i)$	Decision m_i^*
— ⋮ —	— ⋮ —	— ⋮ —	$\cdots$	— ⋮ —	— ⋮ —	— ⋮ —

The entries of the table should thus be computed on a row-by-row basis with each row yielding the optimal solution for the given state value. After the computational procedure has been understood, however, the reader will find that the mechanics of computation can be carried out more conveniently on a column-by-column basis; that is, by evaluating each alternative for all possible values of the state.

Applying this procedure to the first stage of the given problem, the resulting table is given by

Stage 1:

x_1	$f_1(m_1\|x_1) = R_{1m_1}(c_{1m_1})$						Optimum solution	
	$m_1 = 1$		$m_1 = 2$		$m_1 = 3$		$f_1(x_1)$	m_1^*
	$R_{11} = 0$	$c_{11} = 0$	$R_{12} = 5$	$c_{12} = 2$	$R_{13} = 6$	$c_{13} = 4$		
0	0		—		—		0	1
1	0		—		—		0	1
2	0		5		—		5	2
3	0		5		—		5	2
4	0		5		6		6	3
5	0		5		6		6	3
6	0		5		6		6	3
7	0		5		6		6	3
8	0		5		6		6	3
9	0		5		6		6	3
10	0		5		6		6	3

Since the costs c_{1m_1} are in integer values, the selection of the state x_1 (stage 1 above) in discrete values between 0 and 10 should account for all possible states of the system. Thus for $x_1 = 0$, only the first alternative $m_1 = 1$ can be considered since it has $c_{11} = 0$. The second and third alternatives require more capital than can be provided by this state. Thus $f_1(0) = 0$ and $m_1^* = 1$. The evaluation of the other rows can be reasoned in a similar way. Notice that $x_1 = 5, 6, 7, 8, 9,$ or 10 provides more capital than is required by any of the alternatives yet the corresponding return cannot exceed the revenue provided by these alternatives. This means that overexpenditures are not profitable.

The second stage will now be considered. By definition the state x_2 will vary between 0 and $C (= 10)$. Also, from the recursive equation

$$f_2(m_2 \mid x_2) = R_{2m_2}(c_{2m_2}) + f_1(x_2 - c_{2m_2})$$

The values of $f_1(x_2 - c_{2m_2})$ could be obtained directly from the table for stage 1. For example, given $x_2 = 8, c_{22} = 5$, then $f_1(x_2 - c_{22}) = f_1(3)$. From stage 1, $f_1(3) = 5$. The complete table for stage 2 is thus given by

Stage 2:

x_2	$f_2(m_2\mid x_2) = R_{2m_2}(c_{2m_2}) + f_1(x_2 - c_{2m_2})$								Optimum solution	
	$m_2 = 1$		$m_2 = 2$		$m_2 = 3$		$m_2 = 4$			
	$R_{21} = 0$	$c_{21} = 0$	$R_{22} = 8$	$c_{22} = 5$	$R_{23} = 9$	$c_{23} = 6$	$R_{24} = 12$	$c_{24} = 8$	$f_2(x_2)$	m_2^*
0	$0+0=0$		—		—		—		0	1
1	$0+0=0$		—		—		—		0	1
2	$0+5=5$		—		—		—		5	1
3	$0+5=5$		—		—		—		5	1
4	$0+6=6$		—		—		—		6	1
5	$0+6=6$		$8+0=8$		—		—		8	2
6	$0+6=6$		$8+0=8$		$9+0=9$		—		9	3
7	$0+6=6$		$8+5=13$		$9+0=9$		—		13	2
8	$0+6=6$		$8+5=13$		$9+5=14$		$12+0=12$		14	3
9	$0+6=6$		$8+6=14$		$9+5=14$		$12+0=12$		14	2, 3
10	$0+6=6$		$8+6=14$		$9+6=15$		$12+5=17$		17	4

Finally, the third stage is considered. Here $x_3 = C = 10$ since there are no further stages to be considered. The same results would be obtained if the table is computed for $x_3 = 0, 1, \ldots, 10$. The availability of the complete table at the last stage is always beneficial in studying the behavior of the optimal solution due to variations in the total resources. This is usually called *sensitivity analysis* and is carried out in dynamic programming on a rather restricted basis because of the nature of the computational procedure. Thus

Stage 3:

| x_3 | $f_3(m_3\|x_3) = R_{3m_3}(c_{3m_3}) + f_2(x_3 - c_{3m_3})$ | | | | Optimum solution | |
| | $m_3 = 1$ | | $m_3 = 2$ | | | |
	$R_{31} = 0$	$c_{31} = 0$	$R_{32} = 3$	$c_{32} = 1$	$f_3(x_3)$	m_3^*
0	$0 + 0 = 0$		—		0	1
1	$0 + 0 = 0$		$3 + 0 = 3$		3	2
2	$0 + 5 = 5$		$3 + 0 = 3$		5	1
3	$0 + 5 = 5$		$3 + 5 = 8$		8	2
4	$0 + 6 = 6$		$3 + 5 = 8$		8	2
5	$0 + 8 = 8$		$3 + 6 = 9$		9	2
6	$0 + 9 = 9$		$3 + 8 = 11$		11	2
7	$0 + 13 = 13$		$3 + 9 = 12$		13	1
8	$0 + 14 = 14$		$3 + 13 = 16$		16	2
9	$0 + 14 = 14$		$3 + 14 = 17$		17	2
10	$0 + 17 = 17$		$3 + 14 = 17$		17	1, 2

The above table shows that if $x_3 = C = 10$, the optimum selection for stage 3 (factory 3) is either $m_3^* = 1$ or $m_3^* = 2$. If $m_3^* = 1$ is selected, then $c_{31} = 0$ which means that no capital is allocated to stage 3 and $x_2 = 10 - 0 = 10$ becomes the amount of capital to be allocated to stages 1 and 2. From stage 2, given $x_2 = 10$, $m_2^* = 4$ indicating that the fourth alternative should be selected. Since $c_{24} = 8$, the remaining capital for stage 1 is $x_1 = 10 - 8 = 2$ which from stage 1 shows that $m_1^* = 2$. Thus, one optimal policy of the problem is given by $m_1^* = 2$, $m_2^* = 4$, and $m_3^* = 1$. This yields a total revenue of 17.

The alternative optimal solutions of the problem can be obtained in a similar way. It is always convenient to use a decision tree-like procedure for determining all the alternative solutions. This is especially useful where the number of solutions is large. Thus for this problem, the solutions are given by,

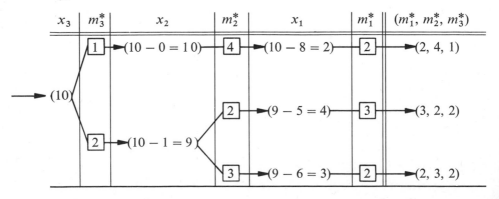

Notice the simplicity of the state transformation in this case. Given x_i and m_i^*, the value of the state at stage $i-1$ is given by $x_{i-1} = x_i - c_{im_i}^*$.

The three alternatives obviously give the same total revenue ($= 17$). Notice, however, that the solution $(2, 3, 2)$ costs 9 instead of 10 for the other two solutions. This means that, cost-wise, the solution $(2, 3, 2)$ is more attractive. This result can be secured directly from the table for stage 3 since for $x_3 = 9$, the total revenue is still equal to 17.

The sensitivity of the optimal solution to a decrease in C can be seen directly from the third table. If C is 9 instead of 10, the total revenue is still equal to 17 which indicates that $C = 10$ represents an over-expenditure. If C is decreased to 8, the total revenue is decreased by one unit while an additional decrease of one unit ($C = 7$) causes the total revenue to drop by 3 units. Such a marginal analysis should prove useful in reaching a final decision. ◄

▶ **Example 7·3-2** (Cargo-Loading Problem)[2]
Consider the well-known problem of loading a vessel with stocks of N items. Each unit of item i has a weight w_i and a value v_i, $i = 1, 2, \ldots, N$. The maximum cargo weight is W. It is required to determine the most valuable cargo load which will not exceed the maximum weight of the vessel. Specifically, consider the following special case of three items,

i	w_i	v_i
1	5	4
2	8	10
3	3	6

and let $W = 10$.

Consider the general problem of N items first. Let k_i be the number of units of item i, then the problem becomes:

$$\text{maximize} \quad v_1 k_1 + v_2 k_2 + \cdots + v_N k_N,$$

subject to

$$w_1 k_1 + w_2 k_2 + \cdots + w_N k_N \leq W,$$

$$k_i \text{ is a nonnegative integer}$$

Now, if k_i were not restricted to integer values, the solution is easily determined by the simplex method. In fact, since there is only one constraint, then by linear programming theory, only one variable will be in the solution and the problem reduces to selecting the item i for which $v_i W / w_i$ is maximum. Thus, since linear programming is not applicable here, the problem will be attempted using dynamic programming. It must be noted that this problem is also typical of the type that can be solved by integer programming techniques (see Chapter 10).

---

[2] This problem is known also as the "knapsack" or the "flyaway kit" problem.

The dynamic programming formulation of the problem is as follows. Let each item represent a stage. The states, x_i, of the system at stage i can be defined as the weight capacity available for stages $1, 2, \ldots$, and i. Define $f_i(x_i)$ as the value of the optimal allocation for stages (items) 1 through i, inclusive. Thus, for the first stage ($i = 1$),

$$f_1(x_1) = \max_{k_1 = 0, 1, \ldots, [x_1/w_1]} \{k_1 v_1\},$$

where $[x_1/w_1]$ is the *largest* integral amount included in (x_1/w_1). This means that the alternatives for stage 1 are

$$k_1 = 0, 1, \ldots, \left[\frac{x_1}{w_1}\right]$$

and the corresponding return function is given by $k_1 v_1$.

The reader can see the similarity between this problem and the budgeting problem since both problems are of the resource allocation type. The major difference is that for the cargo-loading problem, the alternatives of each stage are not readily defined as in the budgeting problem. However, from the definition of the states, these alternatives are easily determined. The general recursive equation for this problem is thus given by

$$f_1(x_1) = \max_{k_1 = 0, 1, \ldots, [x_1/w_1]} \{k_1 v_1\},$$

$$f_i(x_i) = \max_{k_i = 0, 1, \ldots, [x_i/w_i]} \{k_i v_i + f_{i-1}(x_i - k_i w_i)\}, \qquad i = 2, \ldots, N,$$

where x_i is limited by the maximum available weight, $W = 10$; that is $0 \le x_i \le W$, for all i. The solution of the problem starts with f_1 and is completed when f_N is obtained.

For the given special case, the following three tables can be computed.

Stage 1:

x_1	$f_1(k_1\|x_1) = 4k_1$			Optimum solution	
	$k_1 = 0$	$k_1 = 1$	$k_1 = 2$	$f_1(x_1)$	k_1^*
	$k_1 w_1 = 0$	$k_1 w_1 = 5$	$k_1 w_1 = 10$		
0	0	—	—	0	0
1	0	—	—	0	0
2	0	—	—	0	0
3	0	—	—	0	0
4	0	—	—	0	0
5	0	4	—	4	1
6	0	4	—	4	1
7	0	4	—	4	1
8	0	4	—	4	1
9	0	4	—	4	1
10	0	4	8	8	2

Notice that the largest value of $k_1 = [x_1/w_1] = [10/5] = 2$.

For the second stage $(i = 2)$, the largest value of k_2 is $[x_2/w_2] = [10/8] = 1$. Thus

Stage 2:

	$f_2(k_2|x_2) = 10k_2 + f_1(x_2 - 8k_2)$		Optimum solution	
	$k_2 = 0$	$k_2 = 1$	$f_2(x_2)$	k_2^*
x_2	$k_2w_2 = 0$	$k_2w_2 = 8$		
0	$0 + 0 = 0$	—	0	0
1	$0 + 0 = 0$	—	0	0
2	$0 + 0 = 0$	—	0	0
3	$0 + 0 = 0$	—	0	0
4	$0 + 0 = 0$	—	0	0
5	$0 + 4 = 4$	—	4	0
6	$0 + 4 = 4$	—	4	0
7	$0 + 4 = 4$	—	4	0
8	$0 + 4 = 4$	$10 + 0 = 10$	10	1
9	$0 + 4 = 4$	$10 + 0 = 10$	10	1
10	$0 + 8 = 8$	$10 + 0 = 10$	10	1

Finally, for the third stage $(i = 3)$, the largest value of k_3 equals $[x_3/w_3] = [10/3] = 3$. Thus

Stage 3:

	$f_3(k_3|x_3) = 6k_3 + f_2(x_3 - 3k_3)$				Optimum solution	
	$k_3 = 0$	$k_3 = 1$	$k_3 = 2$	$k_3 = 3$	$f_3(x_3)$	k_3^*
x_3	$w_3k_3 = 0$	$w_3k_3 = 3$	$w_3k_3 = 6$	$w_3k_3 = 9$		
0	$0 + 0 = 0$	—	—	—	0	0
1	$0 + 0 = 0$	—	—	—	0	0
2	$0 + 0 = 0$	—	—	—	0	0
3	$0 + 0 = 0$	$6 + 0 = 6$	—	—	6	1
4	$0 + 0 = 0$	$6 + 0 = 6$	—	—	6	1
5	$0 + 4 = 4$	$6 + 0 = 6$	—	—	6	1
6	$0 + 4 = 4$	$6 + 0 = 6$	$12 + 0 = 12$	—	12	2
7	$0 + 4 = 4$	$6 + 0 = 6$	$12 + 0 = 12$	—	12	2
8	$0 + 10 = 10$	$6 + 4 = 10$	$12 + 0 = 12$	—	12	2
9	$0 + 10 = 10$	$6 + 4 = 10$	$12 + 0 = 12$	$18 + 0 = 18$	18	3
10	$0 + 10 = 10$	$6 + 4 = 10$	$12 + 0 = 12$	$18 + 0 = 18$	18	3

The optimal solution corresponding to $W = 10$ is thus given by ($k_1^* = 0$, $k_2^* = 0$, $k_3^* = 3$). This solution may have been obtained by simple inspection of the data but in general it will not be so obvious. ◄

▶ **Example 7·3-3** (Reliability Problem)

Consider the problem of designing an electronic device which consists of three main components. The three components are arranged in series so that a failure of one component will cause the failure of the whole device. It is thus decided that the reliability (that is, probability of no failure) of the device can be improved by installing parallel (stand-by) units on each component. The analysis is limited to the cases where each component may include 1, 2, or 3 parallel units. The total capital (in thousands of dollars) available for the design of the device is 10. The data for the reliability, R_{im_i}, and cost, c_{im_i}, for the ith component ($i = 1, 2, 3$) given m_i parallel units ($m_i = 1, 2, 3$) are tabulated below:

m_i	$i = 1$		$i = 2$		$i = 3$	
	R_{1m_1}	c_{1m_1}	R_{2m_2}	c_{2m_2}	R_{3m_3}	c_{3m_3}
1	.5	2	.7	3	.6	1
2	.7	4	.8	5	.8	2
3	.9	5	.9	6	.9	3

The objective is to determine m_i for $i = 1, 2,$ and 3 which will maximize the total reliability of the system without exceeding the allocated capital.

By definition, the total reliability, R, of a system of N series components and m_i parallel units per component i ($i = 1, 2, \ldots, N$) is given by

$$R = \prod_{i=1}^{N} R_{im_i}(c_{im_i}),$$

where $R_{im_i}(c_{im_i})$ indicates that the reliability of the ith component is a function of the cost c_{im_i} allocated to it. The problem thus becomes:

$$\text{maximize} \quad R = \prod_{i=1}^{N} R_{im_i}(c_{im_i}),$$

subject to

$$\sum_{i=1}^{N} c_{im_i} \leq C, \qquad m_i = 1, 2, 3,$$

where C is the total capital available. (Notice that the alternative $m_i = 0$ is meaningless in this case.) This problem is very similar to the budgeting problem of Example 7·3-1 with the exception that the return functions of the different components are multiplied by each other. The recursive equation will thus be developed based on a multiplicative decomposition.

Let $f_i(x_i)$ represent the reliability of components (stages) 1 through i, inclusive, given that x_i is the capital allocated to these i components,

$0 \leq x_i \leq C$. The states of the system are thus given by x_i. The recursive equation is then developed as

$$f_1(x_1) = \max_{\substack{m_1 \\ 0 \leq c_{1m_1} \leq x_1}} \{R_{1m_1}(c_{1m_1})\},$$

$$f_i(x_i) = \max_{\substack{m_i \\ 0 \leq c_{im_i} \leq x_i}} \{R_{im_i}(c_{im_i}) \cdot f_{i-1}(x_i - c_{im_i})\}, \qquad i = 2, 3, \ldots, N.$$

The tabular computations for the above example are thus given by:

Stage 1:

x_1	$f_1(m_1\|x_1) = R_{1m_1}(c_{1m_1})$			Optimum solution	
	$m_1 = 1$	$m_1 = 2$	$m_1 = 3$	$f_1(x_1)$	m_1^*
	$R_{1m_1} = .5$ $c_{1m_1} = 2$	$R_{1m_1} = .7$ $c_{1m_1} = 4$	$R_{1m_1} = .9$ $c_{1m_1} = 5$		
0	—	—	—	—	—
1	—	—	—	—	—
2	.5	—	—	.5	1
3	.5	—	—	.5	1
4	.5	.7	—	.7	2
5	.5	.7	.9	.9	3
6	.5	.7	.9	.9	3
7	.5	.7	.9	.9	3
8	.5	.7	.9	.9	3
9	.5	.7	.9	.9	3
10	.5	.7	.9	.9	3

Stage 2:

x_2	$f_2(m_2\|x_2) = R_{2m_2}(c_{2m_2}) \cdot f_1(x_2 - c_{2m_2})$			Optimum solution	
	$m_2 = 1$	$m_2 = 2$	$m_2 = 3$	$f_2(x_2)$	m_2^*
	$R_{2m_2} = .7$ $c_{2m_2} = 3$	$R_{2m_2} = .8$ $c_{2m_2} = 5$	$R_{2m_2} = .9$ $c_{2m_2} = 6$		
0	—	—	—	—	—
1	—	—	—	—	—
2	—	—	—	—	—
3	$.7 \times (-) = -$	—	—	—	—
4	$.7 \times (-) = -$	—	—	—	—
5	$.7 \times .5 = .35$	$.8 \times (-) = -$	—	.35	1
6	$.7 \times .5 = .35$	$.8 \times (-) = -$	$.9 \times (-) = -$	.35	1
7	$.7 \times .7 = .49$	$.8 \times .5 = .40$	$.9 \times (-) = -$	.49	1
8	$.7 \times .9 = .63$	$.8 \times .5 = .40$	$.9 \times .5 = .45$	.63	1
9	$.7 \times .9 = .63$	$.8 \times .7 = .56$	$.9 \times .5 = .45$	.63	1
10	$.7 \times .9 = .63$	$.8 \times .9 = .72$	$.9 \times .7 = .63$	.72	2

Notice that while some of the values of x_2 satisfy the capital requirements of stage 2, they do not provide enough capital for stage 1. This means that $m_1 = 0$ which is an infeasible solution and hence it is discarded. Such cases are indicated by $(-)$ in the above table.

Stage 3:

	$f_3(m_3\|x_3) = R_{3m_3}(c_{3m_3}) \cdot f_2(x_3 - c_{3m_3})$					Optimum solution	
	$m_3 = 1$		$m_3 = 2$		$m_3 = 3$		
x_3						$f_3(x_3)$	m_3^*
	$R_{3m_3} = .6$ $c_{3m_3} = 1$		$R_{3m_3} = .8$ $c_{3m_3} = 2$	$R_{3m_3} = .9$ $c_{3m_3} = 3$			
0	—		—		—		—	—
1	$.6 \times (-) = -$		—		—		—	—
2	$.6 \times (-) = -$		$.8 \times (-) = -$		—		—	—
3	$.6 \times (-) = -$		$.8 \times (-) = -$		$.9 \times (-) = -$		—	—
4	$.6 \times (-) = -$		$.8 \times (-) = -$		$.9 \times (-) = -$		—	—
5	$.6 \times (-) = -$		$.8 \times (-) = -$		$.9 \times (-) = -$		—	—
6	$.6 \times .35 = .210$		$.8 \times (-) = -$		$.9 \times (-) = -$		.210	1
7	$.6 \times .35 = .210$		$.8 \times .35 = .280$		$.9 \times (-) = -$		.280	2
8	$.6 \times .49 = .294$		$.8 \times .35 = .280$		$.9 \times .35 = .315$		.315	3
9	$.6 \times .63 = .378$		$.8 \times .49 = .392$		$.9 \times .35 = .315$		.392	2
10	$.6 \times .63 = .378$		$.8 \times .63 = .504$		$.9 \times .49 = .441$		.504	2

The optimal solution is given by $m_1^* = 3$, $m_2^* = 1$, $m_3^* = 2$ with a corresponding reliability, $R^* = .504$. ◀

▶ **Example 7·3-4** (Optimal Subdivision Problem)

Consider the mathematical problem of dividing a quantity q (> 0) into N parts. The objective is to determine the optimum subdivision of q which will maximize the product of the N parts.

The dynamic programming formulation of this problem is similar to that of the reliability problem (Example 7·3-3). Let y_i be the ith part of q ($i = 1, 2, \ldots, N$), then the problem becomes:

$$\text{maximize} \quad p = \prod_{i=1}^{N} y_i,$$

subject to

$$\sum_{i=1}^{N} y_i = q,$$

$$y_i \geq 0, \quad i = 1, 2, \ldots, N.$$

Each part i may be regarded as a stage. The alternatives at each stage are infinite in this case since y_i may assume any nonnegative value which satisfies $\sum_{i=1}^{N} y_i = q$. This means that y_i is continuous. The states x_i of the system at stage i may be defined as the portion of q allocated to parts 1 through i, inclusive. It follows that $0 \le x_i \le q$. The recursive equation of the problem is then given by,

$$f_1(x_1) = \max_{y_1 = x_1} \{y_1\},$$

$$f_i(x_i) = \max_{0 \le y_i \le x_i} \{y_i \cdot f_{i-1}(x_i - y_i)\}, \qquad i = 2, 3, \ldots, N.$$

Since the variables y_i are continuous, tabular computations are not suitable in this case and the problem must be solved in a closed form. Thus for $i = 1$,

$$f_1(x_1) = x_1,$$

which means that $y_1^* = x_1$.

For $i = 2$,

$$f_2(y_2|x_2) = y_2 \cdot f_1(x_2 - y_2)$$

$$= y_2(x_2 - y_2).$$

Hence, for $0 \le y_2 \le x_2$, to obtain optimal y_2

$$\frac{\partial f_2(y_2 \mid x_2)}{\partial y_2} = x_2 - 2y_2 = 0,$$

which gives

$$y_2^* = \frac{x_2}{2},$$

and hence

$$f_2(x_2) = \max_{0 \le y_2 \le x_2} f_2(y_2 \mid x_2) = \left(\frac{x_2}{2}\right)^2.$$

(Notice that the second partial derivative is negative indicating a sufficient condition for a maximum).[3]
For $i = 3$,

$$f_3(y_3 \mid x_3) = y_3 \cdot f_2(x_3 - y_3)$$

$$= y_3 \cdot \left(\frac{x_3 - y_3}{2}\right)^2.$$

---

[3] See Chapter 16 for a complete presentation of the necessary and sufficient conditions in classical optimization methods.

Again

$$\frac{\partial f_3(y_3 \, x_3)}{\partial y_3} = x_3^2 + 3y_3^2 - 4x_3 \, y_3 = 0.$$

This yields $y_3 = x_3$ or $x_3/3$. Since only $y_3^* = x_3/3$ satisfies the sufficiency conditions for a maximum, then

$$f_3(x_3) = \max_{0 \le y_3 \le x_3} f_3(x_3 \mid x_3) = \left(\frac{x_3}{3}\right)^3.$$

Thus, given x_3, $y_3^* = x_3/3$. This leaves $x_2 = x_3 - x_3/3 = \frac{2}{3}x_3$ for the first two parts. According to the optimal policy at the second stage

$$y_2^* = \frac{x_2}{2} = \frac{1}{2}\frac{(2x_3)}{3} = \frac{x_3}{3}.$$

Hence

$$y_1^* = \frac{2}{3}x_3 - \frac{1}{3}x_3 = \frac{x_3}{3}.$$

The above calculations for stages 1, 2, and 3 suggest that, in general, given the state x_i for stage i, then

$$y_1^* = y_2^* = \cdots = y_i^* = \frac{x_i}{i}$$

with

$$f_i(x_i) = \left(\frac{x_i}{i}\right)^i.$$

This result can be proved by induction as follows.

$$f_{i+1}(x_{i+1}) = \max_{0 \le y_{i+1} \le x_{i+1}} \{y_{i+1} \cdot f_i(x_{i+1} - y_{i+1})\}$$

$$= \max_{0 \le y_{i+1} \le x_{i+1}} \left\{ y_{i+1} \left(\frac{x_{i+1} - y_{i+1}}{i}\right)^i \right\}.$$

Again, using calculus, $y_{i+1}^* = (x_{i+1}/i + 1)$ and the proof is complete. Thus for the case where $x_N = q$,

$$y_1^* = y_2^* = \cdots = y_N^* = \frac{q}{N} \quad \blacktriangleleft$$

Note: The above result can be used to develop the so-called *Cauchy inequality*. The development is presented here for later use in Chapter 17 and may be skipped at this point without loss of continuity.

Since,

$$f_N(q) = \left(\frac{q}{N}\right)^N = \left(\frac{\sum_{i=1}^{N} y_i}{N}\right)^N$$

and

$$f_N(q) = \max_{y_i} \prod_{i=1}^{N} y_i \geq \prod_{i=1}^{N} y_i,$$

hence

$$\prod_{i=1}^{N} y_i \leq \left(\frac{\sum_{i=1}^{N} y_i}{N}\right)^N,$$

or

$$\sqrt[N]{\prod_{i=1}^{N} y_i} \leq \frac{\sum_{i=1}^{N} y_i}{N}.$$

This shows that the geometric mean of N numbers is always less than their arithmetic mean except when $y_1 = y_2 = \ldots = y_N$ where they become equal. This inequality is known as *Cauchy's geometric-arithmetic mean* inequality.

§ 7·4
Forward and Backward Computations in Dynamic Programming

The recursive equations of the examples in Section 7·3 were solved by finding f_i in the order

$$f_1 \to f_2 \to \ldots \to f_N,$$

where f_1 and f_N are the initial and final functions of the recursive equation, respectively. This type of computation is referred to as the *forward* computational procedure. The recursive equation may also be formulated differently such that the solution is obtained by finding

$$f_N \to f_{N-1} \to \ldots \to f_1.$$

In this case, the method of computation is referred to as the *backward* computational procedure.[4]
    The question now is: When would either procedure arise? The reader will recall from the discussion in Section 7·2 on the budgeting problem that the

---

[4] The common notation in dynamic programming defines f_i as the optimum return such that i is the *number* of *remaining* stages (or the *number* of stages *to go*). This book adopts a more convenient notation for the beginning reader whereby f_i defines the optimum returns for stage i and all the previously considered stages. In other words, i identifies a specific stage and not the number of stages remaining for consideration.

states of the system at stage i $(i = 1, 2, \ldots, N)$ can be defined either as the capital allocated to stage i and the *preceding* $(i - 1)$ stages or as the capital allocated to stage i and the *succeeding* $(N - i)$ stages. Pictorially, the two cases are illustrated as shown in Figure 7–3. It is noted that in the first case one would start the solution by finding f_1 while in the second case the solution is started by finding f_N. It can thus be concluded that forward and backward computations arise depending on the definition of the states of the system.

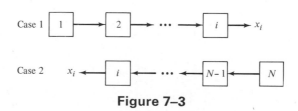

Figure 7–3

Conceptually, the two procedures should yield equivalent results. However, from the computational point of view, the backward method is usually more efficient than the forward method. This occurs in the forward method usually because of the complexity of making state transformations between two consecutive stages. Fortunately, this problem was not encountered in any of the examples of Section 7·3 (where forward computations were used) basically because the transformation of states from the ith stage to $(i - 1)$st stage was simple. For example, in the budgeting problem (Example 7·3-1), given x_i and c_{im_i}, the optimal return from the previous stages, f_{i-1}, is dependent only on $x_{i-1} = (x_i - c_{im_i})$ which is a very simple transformation from x_i to x_{i-1}. Consequently, f_i can be computed easily. The difficulty encountered with the forward method can best be illustrated by the following highly simplified, but instructive, example.

▶ **Example 7·4-1**

A farmer owns k number of sheep. Once every year, over the next N years, he will be faced with the decision of how many to sell and how many to keep. If he sells, his profit per sheep is estimated by p_i in year i. If he keeps, the number of sheep kept in year i will be doubled in year $i + 1$. It is assumed that he will sell completely at the end of N years.

In this problem each period represents a stage. Notice that, unlike the problems of Section 7·3, the stages here are defined by the chronological sequence of the periods so that stage 1 corresponds to period 1, stage 2 corresponds to period 2 and so on. Before defining the states, it may be more convenient to visualize the problem as a decision tree as shown in Figure 7–4. Let x_i be the number kept in the ith year and let y_i be the number sold in the same year. Define $z_i = x_i + y_i$, then from the conditions of the problem,

$$z_1 = 2x_0 = 2k,$$

$$z_i = 2x_{i-1}, \qquad i = 2, 3, \ldots, N.$$

The states of the system at stage i may be described by z_i, the number of sheep available at the end of stage i for allocation to stages $i, i + 1, \ldots,$ and N; or by x_i, the number of sheep available at the beginning of stage $i + 1$ after the decisions at stages $1, 2, \ldots,$ and i have been made.

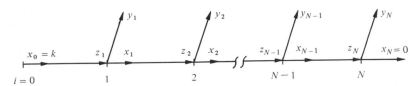

Figure 7–4

Consider the first definition and let $f_i(z_i)$ represent the optimum profit for stages $i, i + 1, \ldots,$ and N given z_i. Thus the recursive equation for this case is given by

$$f_N(z_N) = \max_{y_N = z_N \leq 2^N k} \{p_N y_N\},$$

$$f_i(z_i) = \max_{0 \leq y_i \leq z_i \leq 2^i k} \{p_i y_i + f_{i+1}(2(z_i - y_i))\}, \qquad i = 1, 2, \ldots, N-1,$$

where y_i and z_i are nonnegative integers, for all i. Notice that y_i, the amount sold at the end of period i, must be less than or equal to z_i. The upper limit on z_i is $2^i k$ (where k is the initial size of the flock) which will occur if no sales take place; that is, if all $y_i = 0$. The alternatives at each stage i thus correspond to $y_i = 0, 1, 2, \ldots, 2^i k$. Notice that the recursive equation computes f_i from f_{i+1} and hence the order of computations is given by

$$f_N \rightarrow f_{N-1} \rightarrow \cdots \rightarrow f_1,$$

which, by definition, is of the backward type.

The second definition of the states, x_i, will now be used to develop another recursive equation. Let $g_i(x_i)$ represent the optimum profit accumulated from stages $1, 2, \ldots,$ and i given x_i (where x_i is the size of the flock at the beginning of stage $i + 1$). The recursive equation becomes

$$g_1(x_1) = \max_{y_1 = 2k - x_1} \{p_1 y_1\},$$

$$g_i(x_i) = \max_{\substack{y_i \leq 2^i k - x_i \\ \left(\frac{y_i + x_i}{2}\right), \text{ integer}}} \left\{p_i y_i + g_{i-1}\left(\frac{y_i + x_i}{2}\right)\right\}, \qquad i = 2, \ldots, N,$$

where y_i and z_i are nonnegative integers, for all i. The solution of this recursive equation is obtained by finding

$$g_1 \to g_2 \to \ldots \to g_N,$$

which follows the forward computational procedure.

A comparison between the two procedures shows that in the forward procedure the transformation of states between two consecutive stages is more difficult to handle than in the backward case. For example, in the backward case, given z_i and y_i at stage i, state transformation from stage i to stage $i + 1$ is simply given by $z_{i+1} = 2(z_i - y_i)$ which shows that $f_i(z_i)$ can be computed easily. On the other hand, in the forward case, given x_i and y_i, the transformation from stage i to stage $i - 1$ is more complex. This follows since $x_{i-1} = (y_i + x_i/2)$ must be an integer as fractional values will be meaningless. This means that in addition to selecting integer values of x_i and y_i which satisfy the constraint

$$y_i \leq 2^i k - x_i,$$

the two values must also satisfy the integrality condition resulting from state transformation. This example illustrates the difficulty that may be associated with the forward method. ◄

§ 7·5
The Problem of Dimensionality in Dynamic Programming

In all the dynamic programming problems that have been presented so far, the states of the system have been described by one variable only. In general, these states may consist of n (≥ 1) variables in which case the dynamic programming model is said to have a multidimensional state vector.

An increase in the state variables signifies an increase in the number of evaluations for the different alternatives at each stage. This is especially true in the case of tabular computations. Since most dynamic programming computations are done on the digital computers, such an increase in the state variables may tax the computer memory and increase the computation time. This problem is known as the "problem of dimensionality" (or the "curse of dimensionality" as called by R. Bellman) and it presents a serious obstacle in solving medium- and large-size dynamic programming problems.

To illustrate the concept of multidimensional states, consider the following example.

► **Example 7·5-1**
In a house-to-house advertising campaign, D dollars and M man-hours are available for conducting the canvass. Assuming there are N possible districts, the net return from the ith district is estimated by $R_i(d_i, m_i)$, where d_i is the amount of dollars spent and m_i is the amount of man-hours devoted

to the district. The objective is to find the optimal assignment of D and M to each of the N districts which will maximize the total returns.

Using the backward recursive equation, the states of the system at any stage i should be described by the amount of capital and man-hours that are allocated to stage i, $i + 1$, ..., and N. This means that the states should be represented by a two-dimensional vector (D_i, M_i) where D_i and M_i represent the capital and man-hours, respectively, available at stage i for stages i, $i + 1$, ..., N. Let $f_i(D_i, M_i)$ be the optimal return for stages i through N, inclusive, given D_i and M_i. The recursive equation is thus given by

$$f_N(D_N, M_N) = \max_{\substack{0 \le d_N = D_N \\ 0 \le m_N = M_N}} \{R_N(d_N, m_N)\},$$

$$f_i(D_i, M_i) = \max_{\substack{0 \le d_i \le D_i \\ 0 \le m_i \le M_i}} \{R_i(d_i, m_i) + f_{i+1}(D_i - d_i, M_i - m_i)\},$$

$$i = 1, 2, \ldots, N - 1.$$

The above example shows that the computations of $f_i(D_i, M_i)$ and (d_i^*, m_i^*) become more difficult in this case since one has to account for all the feasible combinations of d_i and m_i. This gives rise to the problem of computational infeasibility especially in tabular computations where the entries of the tables (three dimensional in the above example) become too large for available computer storage. In addition the computation time may become excessively long. For example, suppose D_i and M_i assume discrete values only in the range $(0, 10)$. Thus an equivalent problem with one state variable will have 10(stages) $\times$ 10(alternatives) $= 100$ entries per table while for the two-dimensional state problem each table will have $10 \times 10 \times 10 = 1000$ entries. This shows that for such a small problem, the storage requirements on the computer will be increased by approximately 10 times. This will also affect the computation time roughly by an equivalent amount. In some instances, the computation time may be too large for the solution to be of any practical value.

It is noticed that the computer storage requirements and computation time increase rather rapidly with the number of state variables at each stage. Some ramifications and approximation methods have been explored, however, which may partially compensate for the effect of the increase in the number of state variables (see Nemhauser [4]). The bulk of these computational difficulties still persists, however, and will probably continue to do so irrespective of the tremendous advancement in the capabilities of modern digital computers. ◀

§ 7·6

Solution of Linear Programming Problems by Dynamic Programming

The general linear programming problem:

$$\text{maximize} \quad x_0 = c_1 x_1 + c_2 x_2 + \cdots + c_n x_n,$$

subject to

$$a_{11}x_1 + a_{12}x_2 + \cdots + a_{1n}x_n \leq b_1,$$

$$a_{21}x_1 + a_{22}x_2 + \cdots + a_{2n}x_n \leq b_2,$$

$$\vdots \qquad\qquad \vdots \quad \vdots$$

$$a_{m1}x_1 + a_{m2}x_2 + \cdots + a_{mn}x_n \leq b_m,$$

$$x_1 \geq 0, \quad x_2 \geq 0, \ldots, x_n \geq 0,$$

can be formulated as a dynamic programming model. Each activity $j(j = 1, 2, \ldots, n)$ may be regarded as a stage. The level of the activity, x_j (≥ 0), represents the decision variables (alternatives) at stage j. Since x_j is continuous, each stage possesses an infinite number of alternatives within the feasible space.

The linear programming problem is an allocation problem. Thus, similar to the examples of Section 7·2, the states may be defined as the amounts of resources to be allocated to the current stage and the succeeding stages. (This will result in a backward recursive equation.) Since there are m resources, the states must be represented by an m-dimensional vector. (In the examples of Section 7·2, each problem has one constraint and hence one state variable.)

Let $(B_{1j}, B_{2j}, \ldots, B_{mj})$ be the states of the system at stage j in accordance with the above definition; that is, the amounts of resources $1, 2, \ldots,$ and m, respectively, allocated to stage $j, j + 1, \ldots,$ and n. Using the backward recursive equation let $f_j(B_{1j}, B_{2j}, \ldots, B_{mj})$ be the optimum value of the objective function for stages (activities) $j, j + 1, \ldots,$ and n given the states $B_{1j}, \ldots, B_{mj}$. Thus

$$f_n(B_{1n}, B_{2n}, \ldots, B_{mn}) = \max_{\substack{0 \leq a_{in}x_n \leq B_{in} \\ i = 1, 2, \ldots, m}} \{c_n x_n\},$$

$$f_j(B_{1j}, B_{2j}, \ldots, B_{mj})$$

$$= \max_{\substack{0 \leq a_{ij}x_j \leq B_{ij} \\ i = 1, \ldots, m}} \{c_j x_j + f_{j+1}(B_{1j} - a_{1j}x_j, \ldots, B_{mj} - a_{mj}x_j)\},$$

$$j = 1, 2, \ldots, n - 1,$$

where it is understood that $0 \leq B_{ij} \leq b_i$ for all i and j.

The fact that the problem is multidimensional makes the computation quite difficult. Fortunately, it is not necessary to use tabular computations here since the variables are continuous. This means that the computations can be made in a more compact form.

To illustrate the use of the above recursive equation, consider the following problem.

▶ **Example 7·6-1**

Consider the following linear programming problem.

$$\text{Maximize} \quad x_0 = 2x_1 + 5x_2,$$

subject to

$$2x_1 + x_2 \le 430,$$

$$2x_2 \le 460,$$

$$x_1 \ge 0, \qquad x_2 \ge 0.$$

Because there are two resources, the states of the equivalent dynamic programming model are described by two variables only. Let (v_j, w_j) describe the states at stage j ($j = 1, 2$). Thus,

$$f_2(v_2, w_2) = \max_{\substack{0 \le x_2 \le v_2 \\ 0 \le 2x_2 \le w_2}} \{5x_2\}.$$

Since $x_2 \le \min\{v_2, w_2/2\}$ and $f_2(x_2|v_2, w_2) = 5x_2$, then

$$f_2(v_2, w_2) = \max_{x_2} f_2(x_2 \,|\, v_2, w_2)$$

$$= 5 \min\left(v_2, \frac{w_2}{2}\right)$$

and $x_2^* = \min (v_2, w_2/2)$.

Now,

$$f_1(v_1, w_1) = \max_{0 \le 2x_1 \le v_1} \{2x_1 + f_2(v_1 - 2x_1, w_1)\}$$

$$= \max_{0 \le 2x_1 \le v_1} \left\{2x_1 + 5 \min\left(v_1 - 2x_1, \frac{w_1}{2}\right)\right\}.$$

Since this is the last stage, then, $v_1 = 430$, $w_1 = 460$. Thus, $x_1 \le v_1/2 = 215$, and

$$f_1(x_1 \,|\, v_1, w_1) = f_1(x_1 \,|\, 430, 460)$$

$$= 2x_1 + 5 \min\left(430 - 2x_1, \frac{460}{2}\right),$$

$$= 2x_1 + \begin{cases} 5(230), & \text{for } 0 \le x_1 \le 100 \\ 5(430 - 2x_1), & \text{for } 100 \le x_1 \le 215 \end{cases}$$

$$= \begin{cases} 2x_1 + 1150, & 0 \le x_1 \le 100 \\ -8x_1 + 2150, & 100 \le x_1 \le 215. \end{cases}$$

Hence, for the given ranges of x_1,

$$f_1(v_1, w_1) = f_1(430, 460) = \max_{x_1}(2x_1 + 1150, -8x_1 + 2150)$$

$$= 2(100) + 1150$$

$$= -8(100) + 2150$$

$$= 1350,$$

which is achieved at $x_1^* = 100$.

To obtain x_2^*, it is noticed that

$$v_2 = v_1 - 2x_1 = 430 - 200 = 230,$$

$$w_2 = w_1 - 0 \quad = 460,$$

and hence,

$$x_2^* = \min\left(v_2, \frac{w_2}{2}\right) = \min(230, 460/2) = 230.$$

Thus the optimal solution is $x_0^* = 1350$, $x_1 = 100$, $x_2 = 230$. ◄

The above simple example shows the inherent difficulties of using dynamic programming to solve linear programming problems. These difficulties will become more serious as the number of constraints (states) increases (problem of dimensionality). Increasing the number of stages will also cause great inconvenience since it is necessary to keep track of all the conditional values of the objective function over the feasible range of the corresponding variables and in terms of the variables of the states. Finally, the computational feasibility of the dynamic programming approach is highly questionable when it comes to solving linear programming problems which include different types of constraints ($\leq$, $=$, and $\geq$).

SELECTED REFERENCES

1. BELLMAN, R. and S. DREYFUS, *Applied Dynamic Programming*, Princeton, N.J.: Princeton University Press, 1962.
2. HADLEY, G., *Nonlinear and Dynamic Programming*, Reading, Massachusetts: Addison-Wesley, 1964.
3. JACOBS, O. L. R., *An Introduction to Dynamic Programming*, London: Chapman and Hall Ltd., 1967.
4. NEMHAUSER, G., *Introduction to Dynamic Programming*, New York: Wiley, 1966.

PROBLEMS

☐ **7-1** A student is faced with the problem of selecting ten elective courses from four different departments. He must choose at least one course from each department. His objective is to "allocate" the ten courses to the four departments so as to maximize his "knowledge" in the four fields. He realizes that if he takes over a certain number of courses in one department, his knowledge about the subject will not increase appreciably either because the material becomes too complicated for his comprehension or because the courses repeat themselves. He thus measures his learning ability as a function of the number of courses he takes in each department on a 100 point scale and produces the following chart.

Department	Number of courses									
	1	2	3	4	5	6	7	8	9	10
I	25	50	60	80	100	100	100	100	100	100
II	20	70	90	100	100	100	100	100	100	100
III	40	60	80	100	100	100	100	100	100	100
IV	10	20	30	40	50	60	70	80	90	100

It is assumed that the above course groupings satisfy the prerequisites for each department.

Formulate the problem as a dynamic programming model and find the solution.

☐ **7-2** Consider the problem of deciding on the size of the labor force in a company over the next five time-periods. Let the *minimum* amount of labor b_i required for the five periods be given by 5, 7, 8, 4, and 6 for $i = 1, 2, 3, 4$, and 5, respectively. Let $y_i (\geq b_i)$ be the actual labor force available for the ith period. If y_i exceeds b_i, an excess cost of

$$C_1(y_i - b_i) = 3(y_i - b_i)$$

is incurred. On the other hand, if y_{i-1} is less than y_i, a hiring cost of

$$C_2(y_i - y_{i-1}) = \begin{cases} 4 + 2(y_i - y_{i-1}), & y_i > y_{i-1} \\ 0 & , \text{ otherwise} \end{cases}$$

is incurred.

Formulate the problem as a dynamic programming model and find the optimal solution if the initial employment is given by $y_0 = 5$. How is the solution affected if $y_0 = 3$?

☐ **7-3** Consider the problem of determining the economic lot sizes for four different items. It is assumed that the demand occurs at a constant rate over time. The stock for the ith item is replenished instantaneously upon request in lots of sizes Q_i. There is a limited storage space, however, which is equal to A ft^2. Each unit of item i occupies d_i ft^2. The objective is to determine the Q_i's which optimize the per unit cost of holding the inventory and of ordering subject to the storage area constraint. The cost function may be written in terms of Q_i as

$$TC = \sum_{i=1}^{4} \left(\frac{a_i}{Q_i} + b_i Q_i \right), \qquad Q_i > 0,$$

where a_i and b_i are fixed constants to be determined from the data of the problem.

Formulate the problem as a dynamic programming model then solve using the following data:

i	a_i	b_i	d_i
1	2	5	2
2	6	2	$1\frac{1}{2}$
3	3	7	2
4	2	5	1

Assume Q_i is discrete, and let $A = 10$. Find the solution for $A = 7$.

☐ **7-4** Indicate the difficulty in solving Problem 7-3 when Q_i is continuous.

☐ **7-5** Formulate the following problem as a dynamic programming model.

$$\text{Maximize} \quad x_0 = (x_1 + 2)^2 + x_2 x_3 + (x_4 - 5)^2,$$

subject to

$$x_1 + x_2 + x_3 + x_4 \le 5,$$

$$x_i, \text{ nonnegative integer}$$

Find the optimum solution. What is the optimum solution if the right-hand side of the constraint is 3 instead of 5?

☐ **7-6** Solve the following problem by dynamic programming.

$$\text{Minimize} \quad \sum_{i=1}^{10} y_i^2,$$

subject to

$$\prod_{i=1}^{10} y_i = 8,$$

$$y_i \ge 0.$$

☐ **7-7** An equipment-rental business is considering the investment of an initial capital C in buying two types of equipment. If x is the amount of money invested in Type I, the corresponding return at the end of the first year is $g_1(x)$ while the return from Type II is $g_2(C - x)$. The company's policy is to salvage any equipment after one year. In this case the salvage values for Type I and Type II at period t are $p_t x$ and $q_t (C - x)$, respectively, where $0 < p_t < 1$ and $0 < q_t < 1$. At the end of each year the company reinvests the returns from salvaging the equipment. This is repeated over the next N years with the same return functions, g_1 and g_2, holding for every year.

Formulate the problem as a dynamic programming model using the backward method, then solve using the following data for $N = 5$.

t	1	2	3	4	5
p_t	.5	.9	.4	.5	.9
q_t	.6	.1	.5	.7	.5

Assume $C = \$10,000$, $g_1(z) = .5z$ and $g_2(z) = .7z$.

☐ **7-8** Solve Problem 7-7 assuming that 80 per cent of the profit of period t is reinvested in period $t + 1$.

☐ **7-9** Solve Problem 7-7 for $N = 3$, $g_1(z) = .6(z - 1)^2$, $g_2(z) = .5z^2$ and $C = \$10,000$. Use the values of p_t and q_t for the first three periods in Problem 7-7 above.

☐ **7-10** Formulate the dynamic recursive equation for the problem

$$\min_{\substack{y_i \\ i = 1, 2, \ldots, n}} \quad \{\max(f(y_1), f(y_2), \ldots, f(y_n))\},$$

subject to

$$\sum_{i=1}^{n} y_i = C,$$

$$y_i \geq 0.$$

Then solve assuming $n = 3$, $C = 10$ and

$$f(y_1) = y_1 - 2,$$

$$f(y_2) = 5y_2 + 3,$$

$$f(y_3) = y_3 + 5.$$

☐ **7-11** Solve Example 7·4-1 using both the forward and the backward formulations. Assume $x_0 = 2$, $N = 3$, and $p_1 = 16$, $P_2 = 4$, $P_3 = 4$.

☐ **7-12** A man invests his money in a savings account. At the end of each year he decides how much money he will spend and how much he will re-invest. Assuming that the interest rate on the money is $\alpha(\alpha > 1)$ and that the satisfaction he derives from spending an amount y_i in period i is measured by $g(y_i)$, formulate the problem as a dynamic programming model using both the forward and backward formulations. Assuming that the initial capital available is C and $g(y_i) = by_i$, where b is a constant, find the optimal solution to the problem.

☐ **7-13** Solve Problem 7-12 assuming $g(y_i) = b\sqrt{y_i}$.

☐ **7-14** Consider the following equipment replacement problem over N years. A new equipment costs C dollars and its salvage value T years hence is given by $S(T) = N - T$ for $N \geq T$ and zero for $N < T$. The annual profit for a T-year old equipment is $P(T) = N^2 - T^2$, for $N \geq T$, and zero otherwise.

Formulate the problem as a dynamic programming model then solve assuming $N = 3$, $C = 10$ and that the present equipment is two years old.

☐ **7-15** Solve Problem 7-14 assuming $P(T) = N/1 + T$, $C = 6$, $N = 4$, and that the equipment is one year old.

☐ **7-16** Solve Example 7·5-1 numerically assuming $N = 3$, $D = 5$, and $M = 5$. The function $R_i(d_i, m_i)$ for $i = 1, 2$, and 3 is given by

d_i	$R_i(d_i, m_i)$														
	m_1					m_2					m_3				
	1	2	3	4	5	1	2	3	4	5	1	2	3	4	5
1	10	4	3	5	16	7	6	10	10	6	7	9	8	20	25
2	5	15	12	4	7	10	8	30	5	4	9	7	2	34	30
3	7	10	1	12	9	20	15	24	7	3	11	13	14	32	22
4	10	6	7	10	3	4	17	22	9	15	12	40	16	7	40
5	9	8	9	18	2	1	19	20	8	20	10	15	20	50	23

☐ **7-17** Consider the cargo-loading problem presented in Example 7·3-2. Suppose that in addition to the weight limitation W, there is also the volume limitation R.

Formulate the problem as a dynamic programming model assuming that r_i is the volume per unit of item i. The remaining information is the same as in Example 7·3-2.

☐ **7-18** Consider the transportation problem (Chapter 5) with m sources and n destinations. Let a_i be the amount available at source i, $i = 1, 2, \ldots, m$, and let b_j be the amount demanded at destination j, $j = 1, 2, \ldots, n$. Assuming that the cost of transporting x_{ij} units from source i to destination j is $h_{ij}(x_{ij})$, formulate the problem as a dynamic programming model.

☐ **7-19** Solve the following linear programming problem using dynamic programming. Assume all the variables to be nonnegative integers.

$$\text{Maximize} \quad x_0 = 8x_1 + 7x_2,$$

subject to

$$2x_1 + x_2 \le 8,$$
$$5x_1 + 2x_2 \le 15,$$
$$x_1 \ge 0, \; x_2 \ge 0 \text{ and integers.}$$

☐ **7-20** Solve the following linear programming problem using dynamic programming.

$$\text{Maximize} \quad x_0 = 4x_1 + 14x_2,$$

subject to

$$2x_1 + 7x_2 \le 21,$$
$$7x_1 + 2x_2 \le 21,$$
$$x_1 \ge 0, \; x_2 \ge 0.$$

☐ **7-21** Solve the following nonlinear problem using dynamic programming

$$\text{Maximize} \quad x_0 = 7x_1^2 + 6x_1 + 5x_2^2,$$

subject to

$$x_1 + 2x_2 \le 10,$$
$$x_1 - 3x_2 \le 9,$$
$$x_1 \ge 0, \; x_2 \ge 0.$$

CHAPTER 8

The Linear Programming Problem in Matrix Form

§ 8·1
Introduction

In Chapters 3 and 4 the basic computational techniques of linear programming were presented. Several questions were left unanswered mainly because of the lack of adequate theory. This chapter will thus be concerned with the development of the basic theory of linear programming. With this theory, it will be possible to introduce a number of additional techniques which include the revised simplex method, the decomposition algorithm, and the bounded variables algorithm. The parametric programming problem introduced in the next chapter will also be based on the theory developed here.

§ 8·2
Mathematical Definitions[1]

§ 8·2·1
Basic Solutions

Consider the set of m independent linear equations in r unknowns ($m < r$),

$$A X = b,$$

where X represents a vector of r unknowns. The reader will recall that a " basic solution " for this system was defined informally in Section 3·2 as the solution obtained by setting ($r - m$) variables equal to zero and then solving for the remaining m variables *provided* the resulting solution exists and is unique. These conditions now can be formally defined as follows.

---

[1] The reader with no background in matrix algebra is expected to review Appendix A before proceeding with this chapter.

Let

$$A = (P_1, P_2, \ldots, P_r),$$

where P_j, $j = 1, 2, \ldots, r$, represents the jth column-vector of A. Then, by setting the variables corresponding to any $(r - m)$ vectors equal to zero, the solution of the remaining variables exists and is unique if, and only if, their associated vectors are *linearly independent*. In other words, the square matrix comprising these vectors must be *nonsingular*. In this case, the m linearly independent vectors are said to comprise a *basis*, and the resulting solution of the m variables is called a *basic* solution.

§ 8·2·2
Convex Combination

Given the points

$$X^{(i)} = (x_1^i, x_2^i, \ldots, x_n^i), \qquad i = 1, 2, \ldots, K,$$

in n-dimensional space, then for $0 \leq \lambda_i \leq 1$ and $\sum_{i=1}^{K} \lambda_i = 1$,

$$X = \sum_{i=1}^{K} \lambda_i X^{(i)}$$

is called a (linear) *convex combination* of $X^{(i)}$.

§ 8·2·3
Convex Set

A set C in n-dimensional space is said to be *convex* if every point on the line joining any two distinct points in C is also in C. Mathematically, this means that if $X^{(1)}$ and $X^{(2)}$ are two *distinct* points in C, then their convex combinations

$$X = \lambda X^{(1)} + (1 - \lambda) X^{(2)}, 0 \leq \lambda \leq 1;$$

must also be in C.

To illustrate, in Figure 8–1 the sets (1) and (2) are convex while the set (3) is nonconvex.

(1)   Convex   (2)   Convex   (3)   Nonconvex

Figure 8–1

§ 8·2·4
Extreme Points of a Convex Set

A point **S** in a convex set **C** is called an *extreme point* if **S** *cannot* be expressed as a convex combination of any two *distinct* points in **C**. For example, in Figure 8–1, the convex set (1) has an infinite number of extreme points while the convex set (2) has only four extreme points.

§ 8·2·5
Convex Hull

Given a set of points, a *convex hull* is the *smallest* convex set containing this set of points. For example, in the two-dimensional space, given the five points $X^{(1)}$, $X^{(2)}$, $X^{(3)}$, $X^{(4)}$, and $X^{(5)}$ as shown in Figure 8–2 the dotted lines represent the boundaries of the convex hull for these five points.

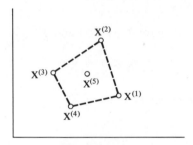

Figure 8–2

The *edge* of a convex hull is defined as the line joining two of its *adjacent* extreme points. Notice that in Figure 8–2, the two extreme points $X^{(1)}$ and $X^{(2)}$ are adjacent while $X^{(1)}$ and $X^{(3)}$ are not adjacent.

§ 8·3
Matrix Definition of the Linear Programming Problem

The general linear programming problem in the standard form can always be expressed as follows:

$$\text{maximize}\quad x_0 = C\,X,$$

subject to

$$(A, I)\,X = P_0\,,\quad P_0 \geq 0,$$

$$X \geq 0,$$

where

$$\mathbf{X} = (x_1, x_2, \ldots, x_{m+n})^T,$$
$$\mathbf{C} = (c_1, c_2, \ldots, c_{m+n}),$$
$$\mathbf{P}_0 = (b_1, b_2, \ldots, b_m)^T,$$

$$\mathbf{A} = \begin{bmatrix} a_{11} & a_{12} & \cdots & a_{1n} \\ a_{21} & a_{22} & \cdots & a_{2n} \\ \vdots & \vdots & & \vdots \\ a_{m1} & a_{m2} & \cdots & a_{mn} \end{bmatrix},$$

$\mathbf{I}$ is the m-identity matrix.

The constraints $(\mathbf{A}, \mathbf{I}) \mathbf{X} = \mathbf{P}_0$ may also be written as,

$$\sum_{j=1}^{m+n} x_j \mathbf{P}_j = \mathbf{P}_0,$$

where $\mathbf{P}_j$ represents the jth column-vector of the matrix $(\mathbf{A}, \mathbf{I})$. This form will be useful in proving the theorems of Section 8·4.

The vector $\mathbf{X}$ is assumed to include the decision variables, the slack variables, and the artificial variables, if any. For convenience, the same symbol, x, is used to represent all three types of variables. The vector $\mathbf{C}$ gives the corresponding coefficients of the objective function. For example, if the variable is slack, its corresponding $\mathbf{C}$-element is zero.

Notice that the identity matrix $\mathbf{I}$ can always be made to appear as shown in the constraint equation. This is done by adding slack or artificial variables as necessary and rearranging their positions so that they always constitute the last m columns with their constraint coefficients appearing in an identity matrix form. This means that with the above form, the last m variables of $\mathbf{X}$ must correspond to the starting solution.

The above form will be used throughout this chapter and will thus be illustrated by an example to make sure that the concepts are clear.

▶ **Example 8·3-1**
Consider the problem:

$$\text{maximize} \quad x_0 = 2x_1 + 3x_2 + 4x_3,$$

subject to

$$x_1 + x_2 + x_3 \geq 5,$$
$$x_1 + 2x_2 \qquad = 7,$$
$$5x_1 - 2x_2 + 3x_3 \leq 9,$$

$$x_1 \geq 0, \quad x_2 \geq 0, \quad x_3 \geq 0.$$

This problem appears in matrix form as:

$$\text{maximize} \quad x_0 = (2, 3, 4, 0, -M, -M, 0) \begin{bmatrix} x_1 \\ x_2 \\ x_3 \\ x_4 \\ x_5 \\ x_6 \\ x_7 \end{bmatrix},$$

subject to

$$\begin{pmatrix} 1 & 1 & 1 & -1 & 1 & 0 & 0 \\ 1 & 2 & 0 & 0 & 0 & 1 & 0 \\ 5 & -2 & 3 & 0 & 0 & 0 & 1 \end{pmatrix} \begin{bmatrix} x_1 \\ x_2 \\ x_3 \\ x_4 \\ x_5 \\ x_6 \\ x_7 \end{bmatrix} = \begin{pmatrix} 5 \\ 7 \\ 9 \end{pmatrix},$$

$$x_j \geq 0, \quad \text{all } j.$$

Thus

$$\mathbf{X} = (x_1, x_2, x_3, x_4, x_5, x_6, x_7)^T,$$
$$\mathbf{C} = (2, 3, 4, 0, -M, -M, 0),$$
$$\mathbf{P}_0 = (5, 7, 9)^T,$$
$$\mathbf{A} = \begin{pmatrix} 1 & 1 & 1 & -1 \\ 1 & 2 & 0 & 0 \\ 5 & -2 & 3 & 0 \end{pmatrix}.$$

Notice that x_4 is the slack variable for the first constraint while x_5 is an artificial variable. Their corresponding coefficients in the objective function are 0 and $-M$, respectively. Similarly, x_6 and x_7 are the artificial variable and the slack variable for the second and third constraints, respectively. The variable x_5, x_6, and x_7 thus constitute the starting solution. It is noted that the constraint coefficients of the slack variable x_4 are now part of the matrix $\mathbf{A}$. ◄

§ 8·4
Optimal Solution of the Linear Programming Problem

In Section 3·2, it is stated without proof that a candidate for the optimum solution must correspond to a basic feasible solution of the linear programming problem. This section will prove this result. Because of the number of new ideas and theorems which will be presented here, Figure 8–3 will be

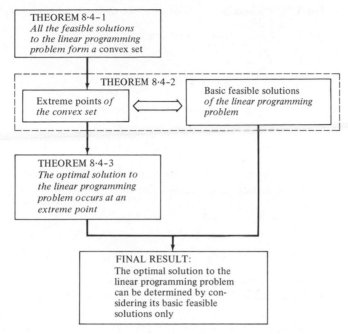

Figure 8–3

used to outline the general development of this section and to relate between the different theorems in a logical sequence. The reader may find it convenient to refer to this figure as he advances through this section.

The proofs in this section may be outlined as follows. The first theorem (Theorem 8·4-1) proves that the solution space of the linear programming problem constitutes a convex set. By definition, this set must have extreme points (provided the set is not empty). The second theorem (Theorem 8·4-2) then proves that every extreme point of the indicated set must correspond to a basic feasible solution of the linear programming problem, and *vice versa*. Finally, the third theorem (Theorem 8·4-3) proves that the optimum solution to a linear programming problem must occur at an extreme point. Since by Theorem 8·4-2 these extreme points are completely defined by the basic feasible solutions of the problem, the final result is that the optimal solution of the problem can be obtained by considering its basic feasible solutions only. This result ascertains the statement of Section 3·2.

Theorem 8·4-1: *The set* $\mathbf{Q}$ *of all feasible solutions of the system,*

$$(\mathbf{A}, \mathbf{I})\mathbf{X} = \mathbf{P}_0$$
$$\mathbf{X} \geq \mathbf{0},$$

defined in Section 8·3 is convex.

PROOF: Let $X^{(1)} \geq 0$ and $X^{(2)} \geq 0$ be any two distinct points in Q; that is,

$$(A, I)X^{(1)} = P_0$$

and

$$(A, I)X^{(2)} = P_0 .$$

Define a new point $X^{(0)}$ as the convex combination of $X^{(1)}$ and $X^{(2)}$. This means that

$$X^{(0)} = \lambda X^{(1)} + (1 - \lambda)X^{(2)}, 0 \leq \lambda \leq 1.$$

By definition, Q is convex if $X^{(0)}$ is also in Q. To show this is true, one must show that $X^{(0)}$ satisfies all the constraints of the problem. Thus,

$$
\begin{aligned}
(A, I)X^{(0)} &= (A, I)\{\lambda X^{(1)} + (1 - \lambda)X^{(2)}\} \\
&= \lambda(A, I)X^{(1)} + (1 - \lambda)(A, I)X^{(2)} \\
&= \lambda P_0 + (1 - \lambda)P_0 = P_0
\end{aligned}
$$

Since $0 \leq \lambda \leq 1$, and since $X^{(1)}$ and $X^{(2)}$ are nonnegative then $X^{(0)}$ is also non-negative. This means that $X^{(0)}$ is in Q and consequently Q is convex. ◄

In general the convex set Q is either (1) empty, (2) unbounded, or (3) closed. The *empty* set occurs when the constraints of the set cannot be satisfied simultaneously. In this case the system yields no solution. An *unbounded* set implies that the solution space is not constrained in at least one direction. Finally, a *closed* set implies that the solution space is a *convex polyhedron* since it is defined by the intersections of a finite number of linear constraints.

In the following discussion, it will be assumed that Q is closed. It is shown in Section 3·6 that the simplex method has the power to detect empty and unbounded solution spaces when they occur. Consequently, these latter cases will not be considered explicitly in the following proofs.

Theorem 8·4-2:   *A necessary and sufficient condition for a point* $X \geq 0$ *in* Q *to be an extreme point is that* X *is a* basic feasible *solution satisfying the system*

$$(A, I)X = P_0$$

$$X \geq 0.$$

PROOF: The proof will be given in two parts using contradiction. The first part proves the sufficiency condition while the second part proves the necessity condition. Before doing this, the following definition must be introduced.

Let X_B be a basic feasible solution. Then by definition there must be n non-basic variables at zero level associated with it. Suppose that the elements of

X corresponding to X_B are so arranged such that the last n elements are equal to zero; that is

$$X^T = (X_B^T, 0),$$

and assume that the vectors of the matrix (A, I) have been arranged accordingly such that the first m column-vectors correspond to X_B; that is, (A, I) is replaced by (B, R) where B is the *basis* including the column-vectors of (A, I) corresponding to X_B. Then

$$(B, R)\begin{pmatrix} X_B \\ 0 \end{pmatrix} = P_0,$$

or

$$BX_B = P_0.$$

By the definition of basic solutions, B must be nonsingular, hence

$$X_B = B^{-1}P_0.$$

Now, to show that a basic feasible solution is sufficient for defining an extreme point, one must show that this solution cannot be expressed as a convex combination of any two other distinct points in Q. Suppose there existed two such points $X^{(1)} \geq 0$ and $X^{(2)} \geq 0$ in Q such that

$$X = \lambda X^{(1)} + (1 - \lambda)X^{(2)}, \quad 0 < \lambda < 1.$$

(Notice the strict inequality on the values of λ.) From the definition of X given above and since $0 < \lambda < 1$, it follows that the last n elements of $X^{(1)}$ and $X^{(2)}$ must also be equal to zero. Let $X_B^{(1)}$ and $X_B^{(2)}$ represent the first m elements of $X^{(1)}$ and $X^{(2)}$, respectively. Because $X^{(1)}$ and $X^{(2)}$ are in Q, then

$$BX_B^{(1)} = P_0,$$

and

$$BX_B^{(2)} = P_0,$$

or

$$X_B^{(1)} = X_B^{(2)} = B^{-1}P_0 = X_B.$$

This shows that $X = X^{(1)} = X^{(2)}$ which leads to contradiction. Consequently, X cannot be expressed as a convex combination of any two distinct points in Q and it must be an extreme point.

Now, consider the necessity condition. Suppose X is an extreme point. To show that X corresponds to a basic solution one must show first that the vectors associated with the positive elements of X are independent. Next, one must show that the number of independent vectors associated with an extreme point is equal to m (that is, equal to the number of independent equations). Consider the first part. Assume that the k vectors associated with *postive* x_j are arranged such that

$$\sum_{j=1}^{k} x_j \mathbf{P}_j = \mathbf{P}_0.$$

If $\mathbf{P}_1, \mathbf{P}_2, \ldots, \mathbf{P}_k$ are not independent they must be dependent. Thus there must exist some scalar β_j such that

$$\sum_{j=1}^{k} \beta_j \mathbf{P}_j = \mathbf{0},$$

with at least one $\beta_j \neq 0$.

For some arbitrary $\delta > 0$, it is possible to establish the equalities,

$$\sum_{j=1}^{k} x_j \mathbf{P}_j \pm \delta \sum_{j=1}^{k} \beta_j \mathbf{P}_j = \mathbf{P}_0,$$

or

$$\sum_{j=1}^{k} (x_j \pm \delta \beta_j) \mathbf{P}_j = \mathbf{P}_0.$$

Thus, the two points,

$$\mathbf{X}^{(1)} = (x_1 + \delta \beta_1, \ldots, x_k + \delta \beta_k, 0, \ldots, 0),$$

and

$$\mathbf{X}^{(2)} = (x_1 - \delta \beta_1, \ldots, x_k - \delta \beta_k, 0, \ldots, 0),$$

satisfy the constraints $(\mathbf{A}, \mathbf{I})\mathbf{X} = \mathbf{P}_0$. In addition, since $x_j > 0$, then by selecting δ such that,

$$0 < \delta < \min_j \left\{ \frac{x_j}{|\beta_j|} \right\},$$

the first k elements of $\mathbf{X}^{(1)}$ and of $\mathbf{X}^{(2)}$ will always be positive. Since the remaining elements in $\mathbf{X}^{(1)}$ and $\mathbf{X}^{(2)}$ are zero, it follows that $\mathbf{X}^{(1)}$ and $\mathbf{X}^{(2)}$ lie in $\mathbf{Q}$.

The above argument indicates that $\mathbf{X}$ can be expressed as a convex combination of the two distinct points $\mathbf{X}^{(1)}$ and $\mathbf{X}^{(2)}$ in $\mathbf{Q}$ by selecting $\lambda = \frac{1}{2}$; that is,

$$\mathbf{X} = \tfrac{1}{2}\mathbf{X}^{(1)} + \tfrac{1}{2}\mathbf{X}^{(2)}.$$

This contradicts the assumption that $\mathbf{X}$ is an extreme point. Consequently, for $\mathbf{X}$ to be an extreme point, the vectors, $\mathbf{P}_1, \mathbf{P}_2, \ldots,$ and $\mathbf{P}_k$ must be linearly independent.

It is now shown that the number of independent vectors associated with the extreme point $\mathbf{X}$ must be equal to m. Since there are m equation in the system, there can be no more than m independent vectors. Now, if $k = m$; that is, *nondegenerate* extreme point, then by definition, there is a unique basic solution corresponding to the extreme point. On the other hand, if $k < m$; that is, a *degenerate* extreme point, then one can select $(m - k)$ additional vectors from the matrix $(\mathbf{A}, \mathbf{I})$ with their corresponding variables equal to zero. The resulting set of vectors are necessarily independent. For suppose they are not, this implies that more than m vectors in $(\mathbf{A}, \mathbf{I})$ are dependent. This is not true since $\mathbf{I}$ is nonsingular. Thus, the resulting m vectors are independent. This completes the proof of this theorem. ◄

The above theorem indicates that every extreme point corresponds to a basic solution and conversely every basic solution corresponds to an extreme point. It can thus be concluded that the number of extreme point of the set $\mathbf{Q}$ is finite and that it cannot exceed the number of its basic solutions. That is, the number of extreme points is limited by

$$\binom{m + n}{m} = \frac{(m + n)!}{n!\,m!}.$$

It is noted that a degenerate extreme point may have more than one basic solution corresponding to it while a nondegenerate extreme point will correspond to one basic solution only. This point is best illustrated by an example.

▶ **Example 8·4-1**

Consider the following system of linear equations.

$$\begin{matrix} \mathbf{P}_1 & \mathbf{P}_2 & \mathbf{P}_3 & \mathbf{P}_4 \end{matrix}$$

$$\begin{pmatrix} 2 & 3 & 1 & 0 \\ 1 & 2 & 0 & 1 \end{pmatrix} \begin{pmatrix} x_1 \\ x_2 \\ x_3 \\ x_4 \end{pmatrix} = \begin{pmatrix} 6 \\ 4 \end{pmatrix}$$

with all $x_j \geq 0$.

By Theorem 8·4-2 above, the number of extreme points for this system is limited by

$$\binom{4}{2} = 6.$$

Let $\mathbf{X}^T = (x_1, x_2, x_3, x_4)$ define a possible extreme point. Then, Table 8–1 gives all the extreme points of the above system.

Although there are five basic *feasible* solutions, the number of extreme points is three. These are given by $(0, 2, 0, 0)$, $(3, 0, 0, 1)$, and $(0, 0, 6, 4)$. The first extreme point is degenerate and it corresponds to the basic solutions

Table 8–1

No.	Vectors combination	$X^T = (x_1, \quad x_2, \quad x_3, \quad x_4)$	Is X an extreme point?
1	(P_1, P_2)	$(0, \quad 2, \quad 0, \quad 0)$	yes, degenerate
2	(P_1, P_3)	$(4, \quad 0, \quad -2, \quad 0)$	no, $x_3 < 0$
3	(P_1, P_4)	$(3, \quad 0, \quad 0, \quad 1)$	yes, nondegenerate
4	(P_2, P_3)	$(0, \quad 2, \quad 0, \quad 0)$	yes, degenerate
5	(P_2, P_4)	$(0, \quad 2, \quad 0, \quad 0)$	yes, degenerate
6	(P_3, P_4)	$(0, \quad 0, \quad 6, \quad 4)$	yes, nondegenerate

$(P_1, P_2,)$, (P_2, P_3), and (P_2, P_4). The second and the third extreme points are nondegenerate and they correspond to the basic solutions (P_1, P_4) and (P_3, P_4), respectively. ◄

Theorem 8·4-3:   *The optimum solution of the linear programming problem,*

$$\text{maximize} \quad x_0 = CX,$$

subject to

$$(A, I)X = P_0,$$
$$X \geq 0,$$

when it is finite must occur at an extreme point of its feasible space Q. *If the optimum solution occurs at more than one extreme point, the value of the objective function will be the same for all the convex combinations of these extreme points.*

PROOF: Let $X^{(i)}$, $i = 1, 2, \ldots, k$ be the extreme points of the feasible space and let

$$x_0^* = \max_i \{CX^{(i)}\} = CX^{(m)},$$

where $X^{(m)}$ is the extreme point at which the value of the objective function is maximum ($= x_0^*$).

Now, consider a point $X^{(0)}$ in Q which is not an extreme point and let $x_0^{(0)}$ be the corresponding value of the objective function. Then,

$$x_0^{(0)} = CX^{(0)}.$$

Since $X^{(0)}$ is not an extreme point, it can be expressed as a convex combination of the extreme points of the feasible space Q. (Notice that Q is assumed to be a closed set.) That is,

$$X^{(0)} = \sum_{i=1}^{k} \lambda_i X^{(i)}, \quad \lambda_i \geq 0, \quad \sum_{i=1}^{k} \lambda_i = 1.$$

Thus, substituting,

$$x_0^{(0)} = \mathbf{C}\mathbf{X}^{(0)} = \mathbf{C}\left(\sum_{i=1}^{k} \lambda_i \mathbf{X}^{(i)}\right)$$

$$= \sum_{i=1}^{k} \lambda_i(\mathbf{C}\mathbf{X}^{(i)}) \le \mathbf{C}\mathbf{X}^{(m)}.$$

Since

$$\mathbf{C}\mathbf{X}^{(m)} = x_0^*,$$

it follows that $x_0^{(0)} \le x_0^*$. This means that at the optimum solution, the extreme point solution is at least as good as any other feasible solution in **Q**.

Now to show that the second part of the theorem is true, let $\mathbf{X}^{(j)}, j = 1, 2, \ldots, r, (r \le k)$, be the extreme points of the feasible space at which the objective function assumes the same optimum value. That is,

$$x_0^* = \mathbf{C}\mathbf{X}^{(j)}, \quad j = 1, 2, \ldots, r.$$

Let

$$\mathbf{X} = \sum_{j=1}^{r} \lambda_j \mathbf{X}^{(j)}, \quad \lambda_j > 0, \quad \sum_{j=1}^{r} \lambda_j = 1$$

be the convex combination of $\mathbf{X}^{(j)}$, then

$$\mathbf{C}\mathbf{X} = \mathbf{C}\left(\sum_{j=1}^{r} \lambda_j \mathbf{X}^{(j)}\right)$$

$$= \sum_{j=1}^{r} \lambda_j(\mathbf{C}\mathbf{X}^{(j)})$$

$$= x_0^*.$$

This completes the proof of the theorem.   ◄

As indicated in Figure 8–3, Theorems 8·4-1, 8·4-2 and 8·4-3 now give the formal proof that the optimal solution to the linear programming problem can be obtained by considering its basic feasible solutions only. Using this result, the next section shows how the most promising basic solutions can be selected for consideration for the optimal solution.

§ 8·5
Derivation of the Simplex Method Conditions

As stated in Section 3·2, the simplex method does not investigate all possible basic solutions. Rather, the two conditions called the *feasibility* and the *optimality* conditions are invoked to select the most promising candidates for the optimum solution. The idea of these conditions was introduced in

Section 3·3. In this section the two conditions will be treated rigorously from the mathematical point of view. This mathematical development will be the basis for introducing the important additional techniques given in Section 8·6.

§ 8·5·1
Condition for Selecting the Leaving Vector P$_r$—The Feasibility Condition

Consider the linear programming problem defined in Section 8·3. Let the *ordered* vectors of the matrix $(\mathbf{A}, \mathbf{I})$ corresponding to the *current* basic feasible variables, $\mathbf{X}_B$, be designated by $\mathbf{P}_1, \mathbf{P}_2, \ldots, \mathbf{P}_m$. Using the notation in Section 8·4, the basic matrix $\mathbf{B}$ is expressed as

$$\mathbf{B} = (\mathbf{P}_1, \mathbf{P}_2, \ldots, \mathbf{P}_m).$$

This means that,

$$\sum_{k=1}^{m} x_k \mathbf{P}_k = \mathbf{B}\mathbf{X}_B = \mathbf{P}_0,$$

or

$$\mathbf{X}_B = \mathbf{B}^{-1}\mathbf{P}_0 \geq 0.$$

Thus, the value of the basic variable x_k is given by the kth element of the column-vector $\mathbf{B}^{-1}\mathbf{P}_0$. This may be written as, $x_k = (\mathbf{B}^{-1}\mathbf{P}_0)_k$.

Now, to show how a new basic feasible solution can be generated from the current one, let $\mathbf{P}_j$ be a new vector selected from the remaining n nonbasic vectors of $(\mathbf{A}, \mathbf{I})$ and let x_j be its corresponding variable. Since, by definition, $\mathbf{P}_1, \mathbf{P}_2, \ldots, \mathbf{P}_m$ are linearly independent, it is possible to express $\mathbf{P}_j$ as a linear combination of these vectors. Thus, a scalar α_k^j (the superscript j corresponds to the new vector $\mathbf{P}_j$) can be selected with at least one nonzero value such that

$$\sum_{k=1}^{m} \alpha_k^j \mathbf{P}_k = \mathbf{P}_j,$$

Or letting

$$\boldsymbol{\alpha}^j = (\alpha_1^j, \alpha_2^j, \ldots, \alpha_m^j)^T,$$

then

$$\mathbf{B}\boldsymbol{\alpha}^j = \mathbf{P}_j$$

or

$$\boldsymbol{\alpha}^j = \mathbf{B}^{-1}\mathbf{P}_j.$$

Let θ be any real number. Thus

$$\theta \mathbf{B}\alpha^j = \theta \mathbf{P}_j.$$

Since

$$\mathbf{B}\mathbf{X}_B = \mathbf{P}_0,$$

then by subtraction

$$\mathbf{B}(\mathbf{X}_B - \theta\alpha^j) \mid \theta \mathbf{P}_j - \mathbf{P}_0.$$

This indicates that the new $(m + 1)$ vector

$$\mathbf{X}' = \begin{pmatrix} \mathbf{X}_B - \theta\alpha^j \\ \theta \end{pmatrix} = \begin{pmatrix} \mathbf{B}^{-1}\mathbf{P}_0 - \theta\alpha^j \\ \theta \end{pmatrix},$$

is a solution to the given linear programming problem with the new variable $x_j = 0$. However, it is nonbasic since it includes $(m + 1)$ variables. In order to obtain a new *basic feasible* solution, the scalar θ must be selected so that one of the old basic variables is set equal to zero; that is, becomes nonbasic. In the meantime, all the new elements of $\mathbf{X}'$ must remain nonnegative. This means that,

$$(x_k - \theta\alpha_k^j) \geq 0, \quad k = 1, 2, \ldots, m$$

and

$$x_j = \theta \geq 0.$$

Since $x_k \geq 0$, then $(x_k - \theta\alpha_k^j)$ may turn negative only if $\alpha_k^j > 0$. Thus, in considering the feasibility of the problem one should consider those variables having positive α_k^j only. In this case, the old basic variable to be set equal to zero should be selected such that

$$\theta = \min_k \left\{ \frac{x_k}{\alpha_k^j}, \quad \alpha_k^j > 0 \right\}$$

$$= \min_k \left\{ \frac{(\mathbf{B}^{-1}\mathbf{P}_0)_k}{\alpha_k^j}, \quad \alpha_k^j > 0 \right\}$$

$$= \frac{(\mathbf{B}^{-1}\mathbf{P}_0)_r}{\alpha_r^j}, \quad \alpha_r^j > 0,$$

where $k = r$ corresponds to the basic variable yielding the minimum ratio.

The above formula indicates that θ becomes critical only if there exists at least one $\alpha_k^j > 0$ for the selected vector $\mathbf{P}_j$. When this occurs, the old basic variable x_r corresponding to θ becomes nonbasic $(= 0)$ in the new solution. In other words, the variables x_j and x_r (or the vectors $\mathbf{P}_j$ and $\mathbf{P}_r$) become the *entering* and *leaving* variables (or vectors), respectively. If the same (minimum) value of θ occurs for more than one variable x_k, the new basic solution will be degenerate since at least one basic variable will assume zero value in the next iteration. Notice also that under the given condition, $\theta = 0$ only if $x_r = 0$ and $\alpha_r^j > 0$. This means that if a basic variable x_r is equal to zero and if its $\alpha_r^j \le 0$, the corresponding ratio must be disregarded when deciding on the critical value of θ.

It is important to notice that if *all* $\alpha_k^j \le 0$, the new variables $(x_k - \theta\alpha_k^j)$ will always be nonnegative for *any* value of $\theta \ge 0$ and hence no variables can be dropped from the solution. This means that the new solution will always be nonbasic and that its variables can be increased indefinitely. In this case the solution space is said to be unbounded. (See Example 3·6-3.)

§ 8·5·2
Condition for Selecting the Entering Vector P$_j$—The Optimality Condition

In the previous section, it is shown how a new basic feasible solution may be generated by introducing a new vector $\mathbf{P}_j$ and dropping an old vector $\mathbf{P}_r$. This section introduces the *optimality* condition which selects the nonbasic vector $\mathbf{P}_j$.

Consider the linear programming problem defined in Section 8·3. Let

$$\mathbf{C}_B = (c_1, c_2, \ldots, c_m)$$

be the ordered vector of coefficients in the objective function corresponding to the current basic solution $\mathbf{X}_B = \mathbf{B}^{-1}\mathbf{P}_0$. Define

$$z_j = \mathbf{C}_B \alpha^j,$$

where, as given in the previous section,

$$\alpha^j = \mathbf{B}^{-1}\mathbf{P}_j.$$

Then the following theorem holds.

Theorem 8·5-1:   *Given the current basic feasible solution* $\mathbf{X}_B = \mathbf{B}^{-1}\mathbf{P}_0$, *the nonbasic vector* $\mathbf{P}_j$ *is a promising candidate for entering the solution provided* $(z_j - c_j) < 0$. *When* $(z_j - c_j) \ge 0$ *for all the nonbasic vectors*, $\mathbf{P}_j$, *the current solution is optimal.*

PROOF: From Section 8·5·1, the introduction of x_j into the solution yields

$$\mathbf{X}' = \begin{pmatrix} \mathbf{X}_B - \theta\alpha^j \\ \theta \end{pmatrix},$$

where the choice of θ causes one of the old basic variables to become non-basic (at zero level). Let x_0 be the current value of the objective function ($= C_B X_B$) and define x_0' as the new value after x_j is introduced. Thus,

$$x_0' = (C_B, c_j) X'$$

$$= (C_B, c_j)\left(\frac{X_B - \theta\alpha^j}{\theta}\right)$$

$$= C_B X_B - \theta(C_B \alpha^j - c_j)$$

$$= x_0 - \theta(z_j - c_j),$$

or,

$$x_0' - x_0 = -\theta(z_j - c_j).$$

Now, since $\theta \geq 0$, then if $(z_j - c_j) < 0$, this can never worsen the value of x_0' as compared with the value of x_0. On the other hand, if $(z_j - c_j) \geq 0$, the new value of x_0' can never improve over the value of x_0. This completes the proof of the theorem. ◄

It is noticed that given the condition $(z_j - c_j) < 0$, the value of x_0' will improve only if $x_j = \theta > 0$. This means that the new solution must be non-degenerate. If $x_j = \theta = 0$, then the new solution is degenerate and the value of x_0' will remain the same as the value of x_0. This case was discussed in Section 3·6·1.

Notice that when $(z_j - c_j)$ is negative *and* the resulting value of x_j is unbounded; that is, θ could be any nonnegative value, then the value of x_0' will be unbounded and consequently the problem will have no finite solution.

The concept of alternative solutions can also be explained at this point. When $(z_j - c_j) = 0$ for a nonbasic P_j in the *optimal* iteration, it is possible to introduce P_j to obtain a new basic solution which will yield the same value of x_0. This result is self-evident from the relationship between x_0 and x_0' given above.

The given optimality condition can be extended to the minimization problem simply by requiring that $(z_j - c_j)$ be strictly positive for the entering variable. When all $z_j - c_j \leq 0$, the optimal solution is obtained. The proof of this case is left as an exercise for the reader.

▶ **Example 8·5-1**

Consider Example 3·4-1. This problem will be solved using the matrix procedure introduced above. The reader should compare this method with the tableau method used in Example 3·4-1. Little investigation should reveal that the two methods are essentially the same. The tabular form yields a more compact solution, however.

After adding the slack variables x_4, x_5, and x_6 to Example 3·4-1, its new matrix form becomes:

$$\text{maximize} \quad x_0 = (3, 2, 5, 0, 0, 0)\begin{bmatrix} x_1 \\ x_2 \\ x_3 \\ x_4 \\ x_5 \\ x_6 \end{bmatrix},$$

subject to

$$\begin{pmatrix} 1 & 2 & 1 & | & 1 & 0 & 0 \\ 3 & 0 & 2 & | & 0 & 1 & 0 \\ 1 & 4 & 0 & | & 0 & 0 & 1 \end{pmatrix}\begin{bmatrix} x_1 \\ x_2 \\ x_3 \\ x_4 \\ x_5 \\ x_6 \end{bmatrix} = \begin{pmatrix} 430 \\ 460 \\ 420 \end{pmatrix},$$

$$x_j \geq 0, \quad \text{all } j.$$

Select the vectors $\mathbf{P}_4$, $\mathbf{P}_5$, and $\mathbf{P}_6$ corresponding to the slacks for the starting solution. Thus

$$\mathbf{X}_B = (x_4, x_5, x_6)^T.$$

Since

$$\mathbf{B} = \begin{pmatrix} 1 & 0 & 0 \\ 0 & 1 & 0 \\ 0 & 0 & 1 \end{pmatrix}, \quad \text{then} \quad \mathbf{B}^{-1} = \begin{pmatrix} 1 & 0 & 0 \\ 0 & 1 & 0 \\ 0 & 0 & 1 \end{pmatrix}.$$

Thus

$$\mathbf{X}_B = \begin{pmatrix} x_4 \\ x_5 \\ x_6 \end{pmatrix} = \mathbf{B}^{-1}\mathbf{P}_0 = \begin{pmatrix} 1 & 0 & 0 \\ 0 & 1 & 0 \\ 0 & 0 & 1 \end{pmatrix}\begin{pmatrix} 430 \\ 460 \\ 420 \end{pmatrix} = \begin{pmatrix} 430 \\ 460 \\ 420 \end{pmatrix},$$

with all the other variables equal to zero.

By definition

$$\mathbf{C}_B = (c_4, c_5, c_6) = (0, 0, 0),$$

hence

$$x_0 = \mathbf{C}_B\mathbf{X}_B = 0.$$

First Iteration: The nonbasic vectors for the above solution include $\mathbf{P}_1$, $\mathbf{P}_2$, and $\mathbf{P}_3$. In order to determine which vector should enter the solution, it will be necessary to compute the corresponding $(z_j - c_j)$. This requires that $\boldsymbol{\alpha}^j$ be computed first. Thus, for $\mathbf{P}_1$

$$\boldsymbol{\alpha}^1 = \begin{pmatrix} \alpha_4^1 \\ \alpha_5^1 \\ \alpha_6^1 \end{pmatrix} = \mathbf{B}^{-1}\mathbf{P}_1 = \begin{pmatrix} 1 & 0 & 0 \\ 0 & 1 & 0 \\ 0 & 0 & 1 \end{pmatrix}\begin{pmatrix} 1 \\ 3 \\ 1 \end{pmatrix} = \begin{pmatrix} 1 \\ 3 \\ 1 \end{pmatrix},$$

for $\mathbf{P}_2$,

$$\boldsymbol{\alpha}^2 = \begin{pmatrix} \alpha_4^2 \\ \alpha_5^2 \\ \alpha_6^2 \end{pmatrix} = \mathbf{B}^{-1}\mathbf{P}_2 = \begin{pmatrix} 1 & 0 & 0 \\ 0 & 1 & 0 \\ 0 & 0 & 1 \end{pmatrix}\begin{pmatrix} 2 \\ 0 \\ 4 \end{pmatrix} = \begin{pmatrix} 2 \\ 0 \\ 4 \end{pmatrix},$$

and for $\mathbf{P}_3$,

$$\boldsymbol{\alpha}^3 = \begin{pmatrix} \alpha_4^3 \\ \alpha_5^3 \\ \alpha_6^3 \end{pmatrix} = \mathbf{B}^{-1}\mathbf{P}_3 = \begin{pmatrix} 1 & 0 & 0 \\ 0 & 1 & 0 \\ 0 & 0 & 1 \end{pmatrix}\begin{pmatrix} 1 \\ 2 \\ 0 \end{pmatrix} = \begin{pmatrix} 1 \\ 2 \\ 0 \end{pmatrix}.$$

Thus, from the formula

$$z_j - c_j = \mathbf{C}_B\boldsymbol{\alpha}_j - c_j,$$

one gets

Nonbasic vector $\mathbf{P}_j$	c_j	$(\alpha_4^j, \alpha_5^j, \alpha_6^j)$	z_j	$z_j - c_j$
$\mathbf{P}_1$	3	(1, 3, 1)	0	-3
$\mathbf{P}_2$	2	(2, 0, 4)	0	-2
$\mathbf{P}_3$	5	(1, 2, 0)	0	-5 ←

$\mathbf{P}_3$ has the most negative $z_j - c_j$, hence x_3 should be the entering variable. Now, to determine the leaving variable, consider

$$\theta = \min_{k=4,\,5,\,6} \left\{ \frac{x_k}{\alpha_k^3},\ \alpha_k^3 > 0 \right\}$$

$$= \min\left\{ \frac{430}{1}, \frac{460}{2}, - \right\} = 230.$$

This corresponds to $k = 5$. Hence x_5 must leave the solution. The new basic solution becomes (notice that x_3, the entering variable, replaces x_5, the leaving variable),

$$\mathbf{X}_B = (x_4, x_3, x_6)^T$$
$$= (430 - \theta\alpha_4^3, \theta, 420 - \theta\alpha_6^3)^T$$
$$= (200, 230, 420)^T$$

and

$$\mathbf{C}_B = (c_4, c_3, c_6)$$
$$= (0, 5, 0).$$

The new value of x_0 is $\{0 - \theta(z_3 - c_3)\} = \{0 - 230(-5)\} = 1150$. The same value can be obtained from

$$x_0 = \mathbf{C}_B\mathbf{X}_B = (0, 5, 0)\begin{pmatrix}200\\230\\420\end{pmatrix} = 1150.$$

Second Iteration: Since $\mathbf{P}_1$, $\mathbf{P}_2$, and $\mathbf{P}_5$ are the nonbasic vectors, their corresponding $z_j - c_j$ must now be computed. Thus,

$$\mathbf{B} = (\mathbf{P}_4 \quad \mathbf{P}_3 \quad \mathbf{P}_6)$$

$$= \begin{pmatrix}1 & 1 & 0\\0 & 2 & 0\\0 & 0 & 1\end{pmatrix}.$$

(Notice the order of the vectors.) Taking the inverse (see Section A·2·7),

$$\mathbf{B}^{-1} = \begin{pmatrix}1 & -1/2 & 0\\0 & 1/2 & 0\\0 & 0 & 1\end{pmatrix}$$

and a table similar to that of the first iteration can now be constructed. That is,

Nonbasic vector $\mathbf{P}_j$	c_j	$(\alpha_4^j, \alpha_3^j, \alpha_6^j)$	z_j	$z_j - c_j$
$\mathbf{P}_1$	3	$(-1/2, \ 3/2, \ 1)$	15/2	9/2
$\mathbf{P}_2$	2	$(2, \quad 0, \quad 4)$	0	$-2 \ \leftarrow$
$\mathbf{P}_5$	0	$(-1/2, \ 1/2, \ 0)$	5/2	5/2

Hence x_2 should enter the solution.

To determine the leaving variable, consider

$$\theta = \min_{k=4, \, 3, \, 6}\left\{\frac{x_k}{\alpha_k^2}, \ \alpha_k^2 > 0\right\}$$

$$= \min\left\{\frac{200}{2}, \frac{}{}, \frac{420}{4}\right\} = 100,$$

which corresponds to $k = 4$. Thus, x_4 must leave the solution. The new basic solution becomes

$$\begin{aligned} \mathbf{X}_B &= (x_2, x_3, x_6)^T \\ &= (\theta, 230 - \theta\alpha_3^2, 420 - \theta\alpha_6^2) \\ &= (100, 230, 20) \end{aligned}$$

and

$$\begin{aligned} \mathbf{C}_B &= (c_2, c_3, c_6) \\ &= (2, 5, 0). \end{aligned}$$

The new value of x_0 is $1150 - \theta(z_2 - c_2) = 1150 - 100(-2) = 1350$.

Third Iteration: The new basic vectors are $\mathbf{P}_2$, $\mathbf{P}_3$, and $\mathbf{P}_6$. Thus

$$\begin{aligned} \mathbf{B} &= (\mathbf{P}_2 \quad \mathbf{P}_3 \quad \mathbf{P}_6) \\ &= \begin{pmatrix} 2 & 1 & 0 \\ 0 & 2 & 0 \\ 4 & 0 & 1 \end{pmatrix}. \end{aligned}$$

Computing the inverse, one gets

$$\mathbf{B}^{-1} = \begin{pmatrix} 1/2 & -1/4 & 0 \\ 0 & 1/2 & 0 \\ -2 & 1 & 1 \end{pmatrix}.$$

Thus for the nonbasic vectors $\mathbf{P}_1$, $\mathbf{P}_4$, and $\mathbf{P}_5$, one obtains

Nonbasic vector $\mathbf{P}_j$	c_j	$(\alpha_2^j, \alpha_3^j, \alpha_6^j)$	z_j	$z_j - c_j$
$\mathbf{P}_1$	3	$(-1/4, 3/2, 2)$	7	4
$\mathbf{P}_4$	0	$(1/2, 0, -2)$	1	1
$\mathbf{P}_5$	0	$(-1/4, 1/2, 1)$	2	2

Since all $(z_j - c_j) > 0$, the current solution is optimal. Thus the optimal solution is $x_1 = 0$, $x_2 = 100$, $x_3 = 230$, $x_4 = 0$, $x_5 = 0$, $x_6 = 20$, and $x_0 = 1350$.

It is noticed that the above method yields essentially the same type of computation as the tableau form presented in Example 3·4-1. Investigation of the tableau form will show that by carrying out the simple row operations to create an identity matrix for the basic vectors, one is automatically solving for α_k^j for the nonbasic vectors and also for the new values of the basic variables. This is the reason why it is possible in the tableau form to determine the minimum ratio (θ) by taking the ratio of the right-hand side to corresponding elements of the left-hand side of the tableau. Finally, the x_0-equation coefficients in the tableau form always give the values of ($z_j - c_j$). The reader can verify these results by comparing between the methods of solution used in the above example and in Example 3·4-1. However, in the next section, the matrix version of the tableau form will be developed. From this, it will be possible to see directly the relationship between the two methods.   ◄

§ 8·6
Matrix Version of the Simplex Tableau Form

The general linear programming problem was defined in Section 8·3 as:

$$\text{maximize } x_0 = \mathbf{CX},$$

subject to

$$(\mathbf{A}, \mathbf{I})\mathbf{X} = \mathbf{P}_0,$$

$$\mathbf{X} \geq 0.$$

Let $\mathbf{C} = (\mathbf{C}_\mathrm{I}, \mathbf{C}_\mathrm{II})$, where $\mathbf{C}_\mathrm{II}$ represent the vector of the coefficients of the objective function corresponding to the *starting* solution of the problem. To illustrate this point, in Example 8·3-1 the $\mathbf{C}$-vector is given by

$$\mathbf{C} = (2, 3, 4, 0, -M, -M, 0).$$

Since x_5, x_6, and x_7 constitute the starting solution then

$$\mathbf{C}_\mathrm{I} = (2, 3, 4, 0),$$

$$\mathbf{C}_\mathrm{II} = (-M, -M, 0).$$

Combining x_0 and $\mathbf{X}$ in one vector, the above problem appears in the tableau form as

$$\left(\begin{array}{c|c|c} 1 & -\mathbf{C}_\mathrm{I} & -\mathbf{C}_\mathrm{II} \\ \hline 0 & \mathbf{A} & \mathbf{I} \end{array} \right) \left(\begin{array}{c} x_0 \\ \hline \mathbf{X}_\mathrm{I} \\ \mathbf{X}_\mathrm{II} \end{array} \right) = \left(\begin{array}{c} 0 \\ \hline \mathbf{P}_0 \end{array} \right),$$

where

$$\mathbf{X} = \begin{pmatrix} \mathbf{X}_\mathrm{I} \\ \mathbf{X}_\mathrm{II} \end{pmatrix},$$

and $\mathbf{X}_\mathrm{II}$ is the starting solution vector.

At any iteration, the current basic solution $\mathbf{X}_B$ is given in terms of the current basic matrix $\mathbf{B}$ by

$$\mathbf{BX}_B = \mathbf{P}_0.$$

Similarly

$$x_0 = C_B X_B.$$

where C_B as defined in Section 8·5·2 is the vector representing the coefficients of X_B in the objective function.

Combining the above two sets of equations, this gives

$$\begin{pmatrix} 1 & -C_B \\ 0 & B \end{pmatrix} \begin{pmatrix} x_0 \\ X_B \end{pmatrix} = \begin{pmatrix} 0 \\ P_0 \end{pmatrix}.$$

Let

$$M = \begin{pmatrix} 1 & -C_B \\ 0 & B \end{pmatrix}.$$

Since B is nonsingular, the inverse of M must exist. Using the formulas developed in Section A·2·7 for the inversion of a partitioned matrix, it can be shown that

$$M^{-1} = \begin{pmatrix} 1 & C_B B^{-1} \\ 0 & B^{-1} \end{pmatrix}.$$

Thus, the current solution is given by

$$\begin{pmatrix} x_0 \\ X_B \end{pmatrix} = M^{-1} \begin{pmatrix} 0 \\ P_0 \end{pmatrix} = \begin{pmatrix} C_B B^{-1} P_0 \\ B^{-1} P_0 \end{pmatrix}.$$

The corresponding general tableau for the current solution can be obtained by pre-multiplying both sides of the original tableau by M^{-1}; that is

$$\begin{pmatrix} 1 & C_B B^{-1} \\ 0 & B^{-1} \end{pmatrix} \begin{pmatrix} 1 & -C_I & -C_{II} \\ 0 & A & I \end{pmatrix} \begin{pmatrix} X_0 \\ X_I \\ X_{II} \end{pmatrix} = \begin{pmatrix} 1 & C_B B^{-1} \\ 0 & B^{-1} \end{pmatrix} \begin{pmatrix} 0 \\ P_0 \end{pmatrix}$$

or

$$\left(\begin{array}{c|c|c} 1 & C_B B^{-1} A - C_I & C_B B^{-1} - C_{II} \\ \hline 0 & B^{-1} A & B^{-1} \end{array} \right) \begin{pmatrix} X_0 \\ X_I \\ X_{II} \end{pmatrix} = \begin{pmatrix} C_B B^{-1} P_0 \\ B^{-1} P_0 \end{pmatrix}.$$

Hence at any iteration the matrix tableau equivalent to the tableau form of Chapter 3 is given by

Basic	x_0	X_I^T	X_{II}^T	Solution
x_0	1	$C_B B^{-1} A - C_I$	$C_B B^{-1} - C_{II}$	$C_B B^{-1} P_0$
X_B	0	$B^{-1} A$	B^{-1}	$B^{-1} P_0$

It is obvious from the above tableau that by carrying out the row operations as indicated in Chapter 3, the matrix under the starting solution will directly give $\mathbf{B}^{-1}$ (cf. Section A·2·7). This, of course, assumes that the *starting* solution has its constraint coefficients in the form of an identity matrix; a condition which can always be satisfied.

It will now be shown using the matrix version of the tableau form that the computations of Chapter 3 are exactly the same as those of Section 8·5.

1. *The values of* α^j. It was shown in Section 8·5 that for any nonbasic vector $\mathbf{P}_j$,

$$\alpha^j = \mathbf{B}^{-1}\mathbf{P}_j.$$

Since $\mathbf{P}_j$ is a vector of $(\mathbf{A}, \mathbf{I})$, then for all the vectors of $(\mathbf{A}, \mathbf{I})$,

$$\{\alpha^j\} = \mathbf{B}^{-1}(\mathbf{A}, \mathbf{I}) = (\mathbf{B}^{-1}\mathbf{A}, \mathbf{B}^{-1}),$$

which is the same as the constraint coefficients in the above tableau form. This means that, at any iteration, the constraints coefficients of the tableau yield the values of α^j directly. This point can be illustrated by comparing the values of α^j obtained in Example 8·5-1 and the corresponding constraint coefficients in the tableau-form solution of the same problem which is given in Example 3·4-1.

2. *The values of* $z_j - c_j$. Since by definition,

$$z_j = \mathbf{C}_B\alpha^j = \mathbf{C}_B\mathbf{B}^{-1}\mathbf{P}_j,$$

then for all the variables of the problem

$$\{z_j\} = \mathbf{C}_B\mathbf{B}^{-1}(\mathbf{A}, \mathbf{I}) = [\mathbf{C}_B\mathbf{B}^{-1}\mathbf{A}, \mathbf{C}_B\mathbf{B}^{-1}].$$

Thus,

$$\{z_j - c_j\} = (\mathbf{C}_B\mathbf{B}^{-1}\mathbf{A}, \mathbf{C}_B\mathbf{B}^{-1}) - (\mathbf{C}_I, \mathbf{C}_{II})$$
$$= (\mathbf{C}_B\mathbf{B}^{-1}\mathbf{A} - \mathbf{C}_I), (\mathbf{C}_B\mathbf{B}^{-1} - \mathbf{C}_{II}),$$

which is the same as the objective equation coefficients of the tableau form. Again this result is illustrated by comparing the computations of Examples 3·4-1 and 8·5-1.

It is noticed from the above discussion that once the inverse matrix $\mathbf{B}^{-1}$ for the current iteration is known, it will be possible to determine all the elements of the current tableau using the original information of the problem. This important point will be used in the next section to develop more computationally efficient techniques for solving the linear programming problem. In Section 8·8, it will be shown that the above relationships are the key points for establishing the primal-dual relationships which were introduced in Section 4·4.

§ 8·7
Efficient Computational Techniques for the Linear Programming Problem

In spite of the recent tremendous advancement in the computational power and memory size of the digital computers, there are still some large linear programming models which cannot be handled conveniently by the digital computers. New computational techniques have thus been developed to overcome some of these difficulties. This section introduces the three most prominent techniques which include *the revised simplex method, the decomposition algorithm*, and *the bounded variables algorithm*.

§ 8·7·1
The Revised Simplex Method

The solution of Example 8·5-1 using the matrix definition of the problem is based mainly on identifying B^{-1} for the current iteration. Although this procedure is not as compact as the one presented in Chapter 3, it offers the advantage of ultimately dealing with the basic matrix B only rather than with the entire tableau. This should have a direct effect on the storage space which the problem occupies on the computer memory.

Savings in the computational time of the problem are also realized by observing the relationship between the basic matrices of the subsequent iterations. Let $B_{current}$ and B_{next} be the basic matrices of the current and the next iterations, respectively. It is noticed that B_{next} is obtained from $B_{current}$ by replacing the leaving vector by the entering vector (see Section 8·5). Using this relationship and given $B_{current}^{-1}$ it is possible through the use of a special formula (which will be derived later) to obtain B_{next}^{-1} directly without having to invert B_{next}. The elimination of the inversion at each iteration should generally lead to savings in the computational time of the problem.

The above remark serves as the key point in the development of the *revised simplex method*. The basic steps of the new technique are essentially the same as those given in Example 8·5-1 except that B_{next}^{-1} is obtained directly from $B_{current}^{-1}$ rather than from the raw data. Once B_{next}^{-1} is determined, the next solution is obtained from (see Section 8·6)

$$\begin{pmatrix} x_0 \\ X_B \end{pmatrix} = M_{next}^{-1} \begin{pmatrix} 0 \\ P_0 \end{pmatrix},$$

where

$$M_{next}^{-1} = \begin{pmatrix} 1 & C_B B_{next}^{-1} \\ 0 & B_{next}^{-1} \end{pmatrix}.$$

The important point now is to show how B_{next}^{-1} can be determined from the knowledge of $B_{current}^{-1}$ together with the entering and the leaving vectors.

The procedure is actually part of the general theory of matrix algebra (see References 1 and 2, Appendix A). Consequently, only the procedure, rather than its theoretical development, will be presented here.

Let the identity matrix $\mathbf{I}_m$ be represented as

$$\mathbf{I}_m = (\mathbf{e}_1, \mathbf{e}_2, \ldots, \mathbf{e}_m)$$

where $\mathbf{e}_i$ is a unit column-vector with a one-element at the ith place and zero-elements elsewhere. Let $\mathbf{e}_r$ be the unit vector representing the leaving variable x_r. Given x_j is the entering variable, then $\mathbf{B}_{\text{next}}^{-1}$ can be computed from the formula

$$\mathbf{B}_{\text{next}}^{-1} = \mathbf{E}\mathbf{B}_{\text{current}}^{-1},$$

where

$$\mathbf{E} = (\mathbf{e}_1, \ldots, \mathbf{e}_{r-1}, \boldsymbol{\xi}, \mathbf{e}_{r+1}, \ldots, \mathbf{e}_m)$$

and

$$\boldsymbol{\xi} = \begin{bmatrix} -\alpha_1^j/\alpha_r^j \\ -\alpha_2^j/\alpha_r^j \\ \vdots \\ +1/\alpha_r^j \\ \vdots \\ -\alpha_m^j/\alpha_r^j \end{bmatrix}$$

where the values of $\boldsymbol{\alpha}^j$ are given by $(\mathbf{B}_{\text{current}}^{-1} \mathbf{P}_j)$ as shown in Section 8·5·1. In other words, $\mathbf{E}$ is obtained from $\mathbf{I}_m$ by replacing its rth column-vector by $\boldsymbol{\xi}$. The determination of $\boldsymbol{\xi}$ can be achieved systematically as shown below.

	Leaving vector $\mathbf{e}_r$		*Entering vector* $\boldsymbol{\alpha}^j$		*Multiplier*		*New vector* $\boldsymbol{\xi}$
rth place	$\begin{bmatrix} 0 \\ \vdots \\ (1) \\ \vdots \\ 0 \end{bmatrix}$	$\rightarrow$	$\begin{bmatrix} \alpha_1^j \\ \vdots \\ (\alpha_r^j) \\ \vdots \\ \alpha_m^j \end{bmatrix}$	$\rightarrow$	$\begin{bmatrix} -1/\alpha_r^j \\ \vdots \\ +1/\alpha_r^j \\ \vdots \\ -1/\alpha_r^j \end{bmatrix}$	$\rightarrow$	$\begin{bmatrix} -\alpha_1^j/\alpha_r^j \\ \vdots \\ +1/\alpha_r^j \\ \vdots \\ -\alpha_m^j/\alpha_r^j \end{bmatrix}.$

The given relationship between $\mathbf{B}_{\text{current}}^{-1}$ and $\mathbf{B}_{\text{next}}^{-1}$ can be applied generally to any nonsingular matrices. It is important to observe, however, that the vector $\boldsymbol{\xi}$ of the matrix $\mathbf{E}$ is formed from the elements of $\boldsymbol{\alpha}$ corresponding to the entering vector rather than from the original elements. Thus, in general, given $\mathbf{D}$ and $\mathbf{D}^{-1}$, if the jth column $\mathbf{P}_j$, of $\mathbf{D}$, is changed to $\mathbf{P}_j'$, then $\boldsymbol{\xi}$ must be constructed from $\mathbf{D}^{-1}\mathbf{P}'_j$. To illustrate this case numerically, consider the matrix

$$\mathbf{D} = \begin{pmatrix} 3 & 4 & 0 \\ 1 & 4 & 0 \\ -1 & 4 & 1 \end{pmatrix}.$$

Its inverse is given by

$$\mathbf{D}^{-1} = \begin{pmatrix} 1/2 & -1/2 & 0 \\ -1/8 & 3/8 & 0 \\ 1 & -2 & 1 \end{pmatrix}.$$

Suppose the first column of $\mathbf{D}$ is changed to $\mathbf{P}'_1 = (1, 2, 3,)^T$. The new inverse is obtained as follows:

$$\boldsymbol{\alpha}^1 = \mathbf{D}^{-1}\mathbf{P}'_1 = \begin{pmatrix} 1/2 & -1/2 & 0 \\ -1/8 & 3/8 & 0 \\ 1 & -2 & 1 \end{pmatrix} \begin{pmatrix} 1 \\ 2 \\ 3 \end{pmatrix} = \begin{pmatrix} -1/2 \\ 5/8 \\ 0 \end{pmatrix}.$$

The vector ξ is thus given by

$$\xi = \begin{bmatrix} +\dfrac{1}{(-1/2)} \\[2ex] -\dfrac{5/8}{(-1/2)} \\[2ex] -\dfrac{0}{(-1/2)} \end{bmatrix} = \begin{bmatrix} -2 \\[2ex] 5/4 \\[2ex] 0 \end{bmatrix}.$$

Letting $\mathbf{D}_1^{-1}$ represent the new inverse, this is given as

$$\mathbf{D}_1^{-1} = \mathbf{E}\mathbf{D}^{-1} = \begin{pmatrix} -2 & 0 & 0 \\ 5/4 & 1 & 0 \\ 0 & 0 & 1 \end{pmatrix} \begin{pmatrix} 1/2 & -1/2 & 0 \\ -1/8 & 3/8 & 0 \\ 1 & -2 & 1 \end{pmatrix} = \begin{pmatrix} -1 & 1 & 0 \\ 1/2 & -1/4 & 0 \\ 1 & -2 & 1 \end{pmatrix}.$$

It is noted that $\mathbf{B}^{-1}$ for the first iteration in the simplex method is always given by an identity matrix. Consequently, throughout all the iterations of the revised simplex method, it will not be necessary to invert any matrices.

The above calculations call for computing $\mathbf{B}_{next}^{-1}$ first, from which $\mathbf{M}_{next}^{-1}$ can then be computed. However, $\mathbf{M}_{next}^{-1}$ can be obtained directly from $\mathbf{M}_{current}^{-1}$ by using a small modification in the matrix $\mathbf{E}$. Let $\mathbf{E}_0$ be the modified version of $\mathbf{E}$, then

$$\mathbf{M}_{next}^{-1} = \mathbf{E}_0 \, \mathbf{M}_{current}^{-1},$$

where

$$\mathbf{E}_0 = \begin{pmatrix} 1 & 0\cdots 0 & -(z_i - c_j)/\alpha_r^j & 0 & \cdots 0 \\ 0 & \mathbf{e}_1 \cdots \mathbf{e}_{r-1} & \xi & \mathbf{e}_{r+1} & \cdots \mathbf{e}_m \end{pmatrix}.$$

This is actually equivalent to $(m + 1)$-identity matrix with its $(r + 1)$st column replaced by

$$\xi_0 = \begin{pmatrix} -(z_j - c_j)/\alpha_r^j \\ \xi \end{pmatrix}.$$

When the formula for M_{next}^{-1} is used, it will be necessary to determine M^{-1} for the starting solution which is computed from

$$M_{\text{starting}}^{-1} = \begin{pmatrix} 1 & C_B \\ 0 & I \end{pmatrix}.$$

This, of course, assumes that B_{starting}^{-1} is an identity matrix, which is always true.

The revised simplex method procedure is now summarized in three basic steps:

Step 1.   Determination of the entering vector P_j.
From Section 8·5,

$$(z_j - c_j) = C_B B^{-1} P_j - c_j$$

$$= (1, C_B B^{-1}) \begin{pmatrix} -c_j \\ P_j \end{pmatrix},$$

so that the vector having the most negative $(z_j - c_j)$ should enter the solution. Otherwise, if all $(z_j - c_j)) \geq 0$, the optimal solution is attained.

Step 2.   Determination of the leaving vector P_r.
Given the entering vector P_j and the current basic solution $x_k = (B^{-1}P_0)_k$ $k = 1, 2, \ldots, m$, then

$$\alpha^j = B^{-1} P_j.$$

The leaving vector must correspond to,

$$\theta = \min_k \left\{ \frac{(B^{-1}P_0)_k}{\alpha_k^j}, \alpha_k^j > 0 \right\}.$$

If all $\alpha_k^j \leq 0$, the problem has no bounded solution.

Step 3.   Determination of the next basic solution.
Determine E_0 as explained above, then

$$M_{\text{next}}^{-1} = E_0 M_{\text{current}}^{-1},$$

and the next basic solution is given by

$$\begin{pmatrix} x_0 \\ X_B \end{pmatrix} = M_{\text{next}}^{-1} \begin{pmatrix} 0 \\ P_0 \end{pmatrix}.$$

Go to Step 1.

▶ **Example 8·7-1**

Consider the same problem of Example 3·4-1. This problem was solved again in Example 8·5-1 and will now be resolved using the revised simplex method. The reader is encouraged to compare between the three methods to see why the revised method may be computationally more advantageous. Notice, however, that the only difference between this method and the method of Example 8·5-1 occurs in the method of computing B_{next}^{-1} (or M_{next}^{-1}).

The starting basic solution is given by

$$\mathbf{X}_B = \begin{pmatrix} x_4 \\ x_5 \\ x_6 \end{pmatrix} = \begin{pmatrix} 430 \\ 460 \\ 420 \end{pmatrix}.$$

Since

$$\mathbf{C}_B = (0, 0, 0)$$

and

$$\mathbf{B}^{-1} = \begin{pmatrix} 1 & 0 & 0 \\ 0 & 1 & 0 \\ 0 & 0 & 1 \end{pmatrix},$$

then

$$\mathbf{C}_B\mathbf{B}^{-1} = (0, 0, 0)$$

and

$$\mathbf{M}^{-1} = \begin{pmatrix} 1 & \mathbf{C}_B\mathbf{B}^{-1} \\ \mathbf{0} & \mathbf{B}^{-1} \end{pmatrix} = \begin{pmatrix} 1 & 0 & 0 & 0 \\ 0 & 1 & 0 & 0 \\ 0 & 0 & 1 & 0 \\ 0 & 0 & 0 & 1 \end{pmatrix}.$$

First Iteration:

Step 1. Computations of $(z_j - c_j)$ for $\mathbf{P}_1$, $\mathbf{P}_2$, and $\mathbf{P}_3$.

$$\{z_j - c_j\} = (1, \mathbf{C}_B\mathbf{B}^{-1}) \begin{pmatrix} -c_1 & -c_2 & -c_3 \\ \mathbf{P}_1 & \mathbf{P}_2 & \mathbf{P}_3 \end{pmatrix}$$

$$= (1, 0, 0, 0) \begin{pmatrix} -3 & -2 & -5 \\ 1 & 2 & 1 \\ 3 & 0 & 3 \\ 1 & 4 & 0 \end{pmatrix} = (-3, -2, -5)$$

where $(1, \mathbf{C}_B\mathbf{B}^{-1})$ is obtained directly from the top row of $\mathbf{M}^{-1}$. Hence $\mathbf{P}_3$ enters the solution.

Step 2. Determination of the leaving vector given the entering vector $\mathbf{P}_3$.

$$\alpha^3 = \begin{pmatrix} \alpha_4^3 \\ \alpha_5^3 \\ \alpha_6^3 \end{pmatrix} = \mathbf{B}^{-1}\mathbf{P}_3 = \begin{pmatrix} 1 & 0 & 0 \\ 0 & 1 & 0 \\ 0 & 0 & 1 \end{pmatrix}\begin{pmatrix} 1 \\ 2 \\ 0 \end{pmatrix} = \begin{pmatrix} 1 \\ 2 \\ 0 \end{pmatrix}.$$

Hence, for $k = 4, 5$, and 6,

$$\theta = \min\left\{\frac{430}{1}, \frac{460}{2}, -\right\} = 230,$$

which corresponds to $\mathbf{P}_5$. Thus $\mathbf{P}_5$ leaves the solution.

Step 3. Determination of the new solution.

$$\xi_0 = \begin{pmatrix} -(z_3 - c_3)/\alpha_5^3 \\ -\alpha_4^3/\alpha_5^3 \\ +1/\alpha_5^3 \\ -\alpha_6^3/\alpha_5^3 \end{pmatrix} = \begin{pmatrix} -(-5/2) \\ -1/2 \\ +1/2 \\ -0/2 \end{pmatrix} = \begin{pmatrix} 5/2 \\ -1/2 \\ 1/2 \\ 0 \end{pmatrix}.$$

Then

$$\mathbf{E}_0 = \begin{pmatrix} 1 & 0 & 5/2 & 0 \\ 0 & 1 & -1/2 & 0 \\ 0 & 0 & 1/2 & 0 \\ 0 & 0 & 0 & 1 \end{pmatrix},$$

and

$$\mathbf{M}_{\text{next}}^{-1} = \mathbf{E}_0\mathbf{M}_{\text{current}}^{-1}$$

$$= \begin{pmatrix} 1 & 0 & 5/2 & 0 \\ 0 & 1 & -1/2 & 0 \\ 0 & 0 & 1/2 & 0 \\ 0 & 0 & 0 & 1 \end{pmatrix}\begin{pmatrix} 1 & 0 & 0 & 0 \\ 0 & 1 & 0 & 0 \\ 0 & 0 & 1 & 0 \\ 0 & 0 & 0 & 1 \end{pmatrix} = \begin{pmatrix} 1 & 0 & 5/2 & 0 \\ 0 & 1 & -1/2 & 0 \\ 0 & 0 & 1/2 & 0 \\ 0 & 0 & 0 & 1 \end{pmatrix}.$$

This directly gives $\mathbf{C}_B\mathbf{B}^{-1} = (0, 5/2, 0)$. The new solution is then

$$\begin{pmatrix} x_0 \\ \mathbf{X}_B \end{pmatrix} = \begin{pmatrix} x_0 \\ x_4 \\ x_3 \\ x_6 \end{pmatrix} = \begin{pmatrix} 1 & 0 & 5/2 & 0 \\ 0 & 1 & -1/2 & 0 \\ 0 & 0 & 1/2 & 0 \\ 0 & 0 & 0 & 1 \end{pmatrix}\begin{pmatrix} 0 \\ 430 \\ 460 \\ 420 \end{pmatrix} = \begin{pmatrix} 1150 \\ 200 \\ 230 \\ 420 \end{pmatrix}.$$

Second Iteration:

Step 1. Computations of $(z_j - c_j)$ for $\mathbf{P}_1$, $\mathbf{P}_2$, and $\mathbf{P}_5$.

$$\{z_j - c_j\} = (1, 0, 5/2, 0)\begin{pmatrix} -3 & -2 & 0 \\ 1 & 2 & 0 \\ 3 & 0 & 1 \\ 1 & 4 & 0 \end{pmatrix} = (9/2, -2, 5/2),$$

and $\mathbf{P}_2$ should enter the solution.

Step 2. Determination of the leaving vector given the entering vector $\mathbf{P}_2$.

$$\boldsymbol{\alpha}^2 = \begin{pmatrix} \alpha_4^2 \\ \alpha_3^2 \\ \alpha_6^2 \end{pmatrix} = \begin{pmatrix} 1 & -1/2 & 0 \\ 0 & 1/2 & 0 \\ 0 & 0 & 1 \end{pmatrix}\begin{pmatrix} 2 \\ 0 \\ 4 \end{pmatrix} = \begin{pmatrix} 2 \\ 0 \\ 4 \end{pmatrix}.$$

Hence, for $k = 4, 3$, and 6,

$$\theta = \min\left\{\frac{200}{2}, \frac{}{}, \frac{420}{4}\right\} = 100.$$

This corresponds to the leaving vector $\mathbf{P}_4$.

Step 3. Determination of the new solution.

$$\xi_0 = \begin{pmatrix} -(z_2 - c_2)/\alpha_4^2 \\ +1/\alpha_4^2 \\ -\alpha_3^2/\alpha_4^2 \\ -\alpha_6^2/\alpha_4^2 \end{pmatrix} = \begin{pmatrix} -(-2/2) \\ 1/2 \\ -0/2 \\ -4/2 \end{pmatrix} = \begin{pmatrix} 1 \\ 1/2 \\ 0 \\ -2 \end{pmatrix}$$

$$\mathbf{M}_{next}^{-1} = \begin{pmatrix} 1 & 1 & 0 & 0 \\ 0 & 1/2 & 0 & 0 \\ 0 & 0 & 1 & 0 \\ 0 & -2 & 0 & 1 \end{pmatrix}\begin{pmatrix} 1 & 0 & 5/2 & 0 \\ 0 & 1 & -1/2 & 0 \\ 0 & 0 & 1/2 & 0 \\ 0 & 0 & 0 & 1 \end{pmatrix} = \begin{pmatrix} 1 & 1 & 2 & 0 \\ 0 & 1/2 & -1/4 & 0 \\ 0 & 0 & 1/2 & 0 \\ 0 & -2 & 1 & 1 \end{pmatrix}$$

and

$$\begin{pmatrix} x_0 \\ \mathbf{X}_B \end{pmatrix} = \begin{pmatrix} x_0 \\ x_2 \\ x_3 \\ x_6 \end{pmatrix} = \begin{pmatrix} 1 & 1 & 2 & 0 \\ 0 & 1/2 & -1/4 & 0 \\ 0 & 0 & 1/2 & 0 \\ 0 & -2 & 1 & 1 \end{pmatrix}\begin{pmatrix} 0 \\ 430 \\ 460 \\ 420 \end{pmatrix} = \begin{pmatrix} 1350 \\ 100 \\ 230 \\ 20 \end{pmatrix}$$

Third Iteration:

Step 1. Computation of $(z_j - c_j)$ for $\mathbf{P}_1, \mathbf{P}_4$, and $\mathbf{P}_5$.

$$\{z_j - c_j\} = (1, 1, 2, 0)\begin{pmatrix} -3 & 0 & 0 \\ 1 & 1 & 0 \\ 3 & 0 & 1 \\ 1 & 0 & 0 \end{pmatrix} = (4, 1, 2)$$

Since all $(z_j - c_j) > 0$, the last solution is optimal. ◄

§ 8·7·2
The Decomposition Algorithm

Situations exist where the special structure of a large linear programming problem may allow the determination of the optimal solution by first decomposing the problem into small subproblems and then solving those subproblems almost independently. The procedure, when applicable, has the advantage of making it possible to handle large scale problems which otherwise may be computationally infeasible. A typical situation occurs when each of the activities involved has its own exclusive resources; in the meantime, common resources exist which are shared between all the activities. This means that the problem includes two types of resources: common constraints and independent constraints.

Let $D_j, j = 1, 2, \ldots, n$, be the technological matrix of the jth activity and let X_j represent the vector of the corresponding variables. Let the resources of the jth activity be given by the vector b_j. It follows that each set of independent constraints can be written as[2]

$$D_j X_j = b_j, \qquad j = 1, 2, \ldots, n.$$

For the common constraints, let A_j be the technological matrix of the jth activity and let b_0 be its corresponding common resources vector. This gives,

$$A_1 X_1 + A_2 X_2 + \cdots + A_n X_n = b_0$$

Let C_j represent the vector of the objective function coefficients for the jth activity. Thus the complete problem becomes:

$$\text{maximize} \quad x_0 = C_1 X_1 + C_2 X_2 + \cdots + C_n X_n,$$

subject to

$$A_1 X_1 + A_2 X_2 + \cdots + A_n X_n = b_0,$$
$$D_1 X_1 \qquad\qquad\qquad = b_1,$$
$$D_2 X_2 \qquad\qquad\quad = b_2,$$
$$\ddots \qquad \vdots$$
$$D_n X_n = b_n,$$
$$X_j \geq 0, \quad \text{for all } j.$$

It is noted that if the size of the matrix A_j is $(r_0 \times m_j)$ and that of D_j is $(r_j \times m_j)$, then the problem has $\sum_{j=0}^{n} r_j$ constraints and $\sum_{j=1}^{n} m_j$ variables.

---

[2] It is assumed that the slack variables are added as necessary to change inequality constraints into equalities. In this case, the resulting slacks and coefficients are assumed to be part of X_j and D_j, respectively.

The *decomposition principle* as applied to the above problem will now be discussed. It is assumed that each of the convex sets

$$\mathbf{D}_j \mathbf{X}_j = \mathbf{b}_j, \ \mathbf{X}_j \geq \mathbf{0}, \qquad j = 1, 2, \ldots, n,$$

is bounded. Thus, if $\hat{\mathbf{X}}_j^k$, $k = 1, 2, \ldots, K_j$, are the extreme points of the *j*th set, then every point $\mathbf{X}_j$ in this set can be expressed as a convex combination of these extreme points. This means that for $\beta_j^k \geq 0$, and $\sum_{k=1}^{K_j} \beta_j^k = 1$,

$$\mathbf{X}_j = \sum_{k=1}^{K_j} \beta_j^k \hat{\mathbf{X}}_j^k, \qquad j = 1, 2, \ldots, n.$$

These new equations imply the complete solution space enclosed by the sets $\mathbf{D}_j \mathbf{X}_j = \mathbf{b}_j$ and $\mathbf{X}_j \geq 0, j = 1, 2, \ldots, n$. It is thus possible to eliminate the constraints of the subproblems and to reformulate the original problem in the following equivalent form:

$$\text{maximize } x_0 = \sum_{k=1}^{K_1} \mathbf{C}_1 \hat{\mathbf{X}}_1^k \beta_1^k + \sum_{k=1}^{K_2} \mathbf{C}_2 \hat{\mathbf{X}}_2^k \beta_2^k + \cdots + \sum_{k=1}^{K_n} \mathbf{C}_n \hat{\mathbf{X}}_n^k \beta_n^k,$$

subject to

$$\sum_{k=1}^{K_1} \mathbf{A}_1 \hat{\mathbf{X}}_1^k \beta_1^k + \sum_{k=1}^{K_2} \mathbf{A}_2 \hat{\mathbf{X}}_2^k \beta_2^k + \cdots + \sum_{k=1}^{K_n} \mathbf{A}_n \hat{\mathbf{X}}_n^k \beta_n^k = \mathbf{b}_0,$$

$$\sum_{k=1}^{K_1} \beta_1^k = 1,$$

$$\sum_{k=1}^{K_2} \beta_2^k = 1,$$

$$\vdots$$

$$\sum_{k=1}^{K_n} \beta_n^k = 1,$$

and $\beta_j^k \geq 0$ for all j and k.

It is noticed that since $\hat{\mathbf{X}}_j^k$ are the "known" extreme points of the set $\mathbf{D}_j \mathbf{X}_j = \mathbf{b}_j, \ \mathbf{X}_j \geq 0$, the new decision variables of the modified problem become β_j^k. Once the optimal values of β_j^k, for all j and k, are determined, the optimal solution to the original problem is obtained by recognizing that

$$\mathbf{X}_j = \sum_{k=1}^{K_j} \beta_j^k \hat{\mathbf{X}}_j^k.$$

The new problem has $(r_0 + n)$ constraints as compared with $\sum_{j=0}^{n} r_j$ in the original problem. On the other hand, the number of variables is increased depending on the total number of extreme points for the different subproblems. The modified problem, however, is computationally more attractive since the computational effort in any linear programming problem is mainly dependent on the number of constraints rather than the number of variables.

The decomposition principle outlined above may suggest, at the first thought, that all the extreme points $\hat{\mathbf{X}}_j^k$ must be determined before the optimal values of β_j^k are obtained. This is not the case. In fact, given an initial basic feasible solution for the modified problem, it is possible at every succeeding iteration to determine systematically the extreme points as they are required. This point will now be explained using the *decomposition algorithm*. It should be noted first that this algorithm is based mainly on the revised simplex method procedure presented in the preceding section.

Let $\mathbf{B}$ be the basic matrix associated with the current basic solution of the *modified* problem and $\mathbf{C}_B$ be the vector of the corresponding coefficients in the objective function. Thus, using the revised simplex procedure the current solution is optimal if for all $\mathbf{P}_j^k$ not in the basic solution,

$$z_j^k - c_j^k = \mathbf{C}_B\mathbf{B}^{-1}\mathbf{P}_j^k - c_j^k \geq 0,$$

where, from the definition of the modified problem,

$$c_j^k = \mathbf{C}_j\hat{\mathbf{X}}_j^k$$

and

$$\mathbf{P}_j^k = \begin{array}{c} r_0\left\{ \vphantom{\begin{bmatrix}A_j\hat{\mathbf{X}}_j^k\\0\\\vdots\end{bmatrix}} \right. \\ \\ n\left\{ \vphantom{\begin{bmatrix}1\\\vdots\\0\end{bmatrix}} \right. \end{array} \begin{bmatrix} A_j\hat{\mathbf{X}}_j^k \\ 0 \\ \vdots \\ 1 \\ \vdots \\ 0 \end{bmatrix} \leftarrow (r_0 + j)\text{th place.}$$

It is noticed from the special structure of $\mathbf{P}_j^k$ that the expression for $(z_j^k - c_j^k)$ can be simplified as follows. Let

$$\mathbf{B}^{-1} = (\overbrace{\mathbf{R}_0}^{r_0}\mid\overbrace{\mathbf{V}_1, \mathbf{V}_2, \ldots, \mathbf{V}_j, \ldots, \mathbf{V}_n}^{n}),$$

where $\mathbf{R}_0$ is the matrix of size $(r_0 + n) \times r_0$ consisting of the first r_0 columns of $\mathbf{B}^{-1}$, and $\mathbf{V}_j$ is the $(r_0 + j)$th column of the same matrix $\mathbf{B}^{-1}$. Thus

$$(z_j^k - c_j^k) = (\mathbf{C}_B\mathbf{R}_0\mathbf{A}_j\hat{\mathbf{X}}_j^k + \mathbf{C}_B\mathbf{V}_j) - \mathbf{C}_j\hat{\mathbf{X}}_j^k$$

$$= (\mathbf{C}_B\mathbf{R}_0\mathbf{A}_j - \mathbf{C}_j)\hat{\mathbf{X}}_j^k + \mathbf{C}_B\mathbf{V}_j.$$

If the current solution is not optimal, the vector $\mathbf{P}_j^k$ having the smallest $(z_j^k - c_j^k) < 0$ (most negative) is selected to enter the solution. The important point here is that $z_j^k - c_j^k$ cannot be evaluated numerically until all the elements of $\mathbf{P}_j^k$ are known. On the other hand, $\mathbf{P}_j^k$ cannot be evaluated numerically until the corresponding extreme point $\hat{\mathbf{X}}_j^k$ is known. This leads to the key point that the evaluation of $(z_j^k - c_j^k)$ (and hence the selection of the entering variable) depends on the determination of $\hat{\mathbf{X}}_j^k$. The trick here is that instead of determining all the extreme points for all the n sets, the problem can be reduced to determining the one extreme point, $\hat{\mathbf{X}}_j^{k*}$, in every set j which will yield the smallest $(z_j^k - c_j^k)$. Let

$$\rho_j = \min_k \{z_j^k - c_j^k\} = z_j^{k*} - c_j^{k*},$$

and let $\rho = \min_j \{\rho_j\}$. If $\rho < 0$, then the variable β_j^k corresponding to ρ is selected as the entering variable. Otherwise, if $\rho \geq 0$, then the optimal solution is attained.

It will be shown now how $\hat{\mathbf{X}}_j^{k*}$ can be determined. Recall that $\hat{\mathbf{X}}_j^{k*}$ is an extreme point of the set $\mathbf{D}_j \mathbf{X}_j = \mathbf{b}_j$, $\mathbf{X}_j \geq \mathbf{0}$. This means that the determination of $\hat{\mathbf{X}}_j^{k*}$ reduces to solving the linear programming problem:

$$\text{minimize} \quad z_j - c_j,$$

subject to

$$\mathbf{D}_j \mathbf{X}_j = \mathbf{b}_j,$$

$$\mathbf{X}_j \geq \mathbf{0}.$$

The superscript k is supressed for the following reason. Since by assumption the set $\mathbf{D}_j \mathbf{X}_j = \mathbf{b}_j$, $\mathbf{X}_j \geq \mathbf{0}$, is bounded, it follows that the minimum value of $(z_j - c_j)$ is also bounded and must occur at an extreme point of the set. (See Theorem 8·4-3.) This automatically gives the required extreme point, $\hat{\mathbf{X}}_j^{k*}$.

Now, as shown previously

$$z_j^k - c_j^k = (\mathbf{C}_B \mathbf{R}_0 \mathbf{A}_j - \mathbf{C}_j)\hat{\mathbf{X}}_j^k + \mathbf{C}_B \mathbf{V}_j.$$

Since $\mathbf{C}_B \mathbf{V}_j$ is a constant independent of k, the above linear programming problems become:

$$\text{minimize} \quad w_j = (\mathbf{C}_B \mathbf{R}_0 \mathbf{A}_j - \mathbf{C}_j)\mathbf{X}_j,$$

subject to

$$\mathbf{D}_j \mathbf{X}_j = \mathbf{b}_j,$$

$$\mathbf{X}_j \geq \mathbf{0},$$

for $j = 1, 2, \ldots, n$. It thus follows that

$$\rho_j = w_j^* + \mathbf{C}_B \mathbf{V}_j,$$

where w_j^* is the optimum value of w_j. As stated above, the variable β_j^k corresponding to $\rho = \min_j \{\rho_j\}$ is then selected to enter the solution. (Notice that the extreme point corresponding to β_j^k is automatically known at this point.)

The next step now is to determine the leaving variable. This is accomplished in the usual manner using the feasibility condition of the revised simplex method. The procedure is then repeated until ρ becomes nonnegative, in which case the optimal solution to the original problem will be given by

$$\mathbf{X}_j^* = \sum_{k=1}^{K_j} \beta_j^{k*} \hat{\mathbf{X}}_j^{k*}, \qquad j = 1, 2, \ldots, n,$$

where β_j^{k*} are the optimal values of the modified problem and $\hat{\mathbf{X}}_j^{k*}$ are their corresponding extreme points.

The decomposition algorithm can now be summarized in the following steps:

Step 1: Reduce the original problem to the modified form in terms of the new variables β_j^k.

Step 2: Find an initial basic feasible solution to the modified problem. If such solution is not immediately obvious, invoke the artificial variables technique (see Section 3·5) to secure an initial basis.

Step 3: For the current iteration, find $\rho_j = w_j^* + \mathbf{C}_B V_j$ for each sub-problem j and then determine $\rho = \min_j\{\rho_j\}$. If $\rho \geq 0$, the current solution is optimal and the process is terminated; otherwise,

Step 4: Introduce the variable β_j^k corresponding to ρ into the basic solution. Determine the leaving variable using the feasibility condition and then compute the next $\mathbf{B}^{-1}$ using the revised simplex method technique. Go to Step 3.

▶ **Example 8·7-2**

Consider the following linear programming problem:

$$\text{maximize } x_0 = x_1 + 2x_2 + x_3 + 3x_4,$$

subject to

$$x_1 + x_2 + x_3 + x_4 \leq 200,$$
$$x_1 + 2x_2 + x_3 + 3x_4 \geq 400,$$
$$x_1 + 2x_2 \qquad\qquad \leq 100,$$
$$4x_1 + 6x_2 \qquad\qquad \leq 300,$$
$$3x_3 + 6x_4 \leq 600,$$
$$x_4 \geq 20,$$

$$x_j \geq 0, \text{ for all } j.$$

The constraints of the above problem can be changed to the equality type by augmenting the problem with the nonnegative slack variables $S_1, S_2, S_3, S_4,$

S_5, and S_6. The augmented problem can thus be summarized as shown below.

x_1	x_2	S_3	S_4	x_3	x_4	S_5	S_6	S_1	S_2	
1	2	0	0	1	3	0	0	0	0	
1	1	0	0	1	1	0	0	0	1	200
1	2	0	0	1	3	0	0	−1	0	400
1	2	1	0							100
4	6	0	1							300
				3	6	1	0			600
				0	1	0	−1			20

By definition, the above problem can be decomposed into two subproblems, $j = 1, 2$. Thus for $j = 1$,

$$X_1 = (x_1, x_2, S_3, S_4)^T$$

$$C_1 = (1, 2, 0, 0),$$

$$A_1 = \begin{pmatrix} 1 & 1 & 0 & 0 \\ 1 & 2 & 0 & 0 \end{pmatrix},$$

$$D_1 = \begin{pmatrix} 1 & 2 & 1 & 0 \\ 4 & 6 & 0 & 1 \end{pmatrix},$$

$$b_1 = \begin{pmatrix} 100 \\ 300 \end{pmatrix},$$

and for $j = 2$,

$$X_2 = (x_3, x_4, S_5, S_6)^T,$$

$$C_2 = (1, 3, 0, 0),$$

$$A_2 = \begin{pmatrix} 1 & 1 & 0 & 0 \\ 1 & 3 & 0 & 0 \end{pmatrix},$$

$$D_2 = \begin{pmatrix} 3 & 6 & 1 & 0 \\ 0 & 1 & 0 & -1 \end{pmatrix},$$

$$b_2 = \begin{pmatrix} 600 \\ 20 \end{pmatrix}.$$

The slack variables (S_1, S_2) do not constitute a subproblem in the sense given above. Consequently, these variables must be treated separately as will be shown later.

Let R_1, R_2, R_3 be artificial variables. The modified problem together with a starting solution is given by

	β_1^1	β_1^2	⋯	$\beta_1^{K_1}$	β_2^1	β_2^2	⋯	$\beta_2^{K_2}$	S_1	S_2	R_1	R_2	R_3	
	$C_1\hat{X}_1^1$	$C_1\hat{X}_1^2$	⋯	$C_1\hat{X}_1^{K_1}$	$C_2\hat{X}_2^1$	$C_2\hat{X}_2^2$	⋯	$C_2\hat{X}_2^{K_2}$	0	0	$-M$	$-M$	$-M$	
	$A_1\hat{X}_1^1$	$A_1\hat{X}_1^2$	⋯	$A_1\hat{X}_1^{K_1}$	$A_2\hat{X}_2^1$	$A_2\hat{X}_2^2$	⋯	$A_2\hat{X}_2^{K_2}$	0	①	0	0	0	200
									-1	0	①	0	0	400
	1	1	⋯	1	0	0	⋯	0	0	0	0	①	0	1
	0	0	⋯	0	1	1	⋯	1	0	0	0	0	①	1

Subproblem 1 (columns β_1)   Subproblem 2 (columns β_2)   Starting basic solution (columns S_2, R_1, R_2, R_3)

The starting basic solution is given by

$$\mathbf{X}_B = \begin{pmatrix} S_2 \\ R_1 \\ R_2 \\ R_3 \end{pmatrix} = \begin{pmatrix} 200 \\ 400 \\ 1 \\ 1 \end{pmatrix},$$

and the corresponding basic matrix is

$$\mathbf{B} = \begin{pmatrix} 1 & 0 & 0 & 0 \\ 0 & 1 & 0 & 0 \\ 0 & 0 & 1 & 0 \\ 0 & 0 & 0 & 1 \end{pmatrix} = \mathbf{B}^{-1}.$$

Hence

$$\mathbf{R}_0 = \begin{pmatrix} 1 & 0 \\ 0 & 1 \\ 0 & 0 \\ 0 & 0 \end{pmatrix}, \quad \mathbf{V}_1 = \begin{pmatrix} 0 \\ 0 \\ 1 \\ 0 \end{pmatrix}, \quad \mathbf{V}_2 = \begin{pmatrix} 0 \\ 0 \\ 0 \\ 1 \end{pmatrix},$$

and

$$\mathbf{C}_B = (0, -M, -M, -M), \quad \text{and} \quad \mathbf{C}_B \mathbf{R}_0 = (0, -M).$$

First Iteration:

Consider the first subproblem ($j = 1$). The corresponding linear programming problem is:

$$\text{minimize} \quad w_1 = (\mathbf{C}_B \mathbf{R}_0 \mathbf{A}_1 - \mathbf{C}_1)\mathbf{X}_1,$$

subject to

$$\mathbf{D}_1 \mathbf{X}_1 = \mathbf{b}_1,$$

$$\mathbf{X}_1 \geq \mathbf{0}.$$

Thus,

$$w_1 = \left[(0, -M) \begin{pmatrix} 1 & 1 & 0 & 0 \\ 1 & 2 & 0 & 0 \end{pmatrix} - (1, 2, 0, 0) \right] \begin{pmatrix} x_1 \\ x_2 \\ S_3 \\ S_4 \end{pmatrix}$$

$$= -(M+1)x_1 - 2(M+1)x_2,$$

and the problem becomes:

$$\text{minimize} \quad w_1 = -(M+1)x_1 - 2(M+1)x_2,$$

subject to

$$\begin{pmatrix} 1 & 2 & 1 & 0 \\ 4 & 6 & 0 & 1 \end{pmatrix} \begin{pmatrix} x_1 \\ x_2 \\ S_3 \\ S_4 \end{pmatrix} = \begin{pmatrix} 100 \\ 300 \end{pmatrix},$$

$$x_1 \geq 0, \quad x_2 \geq 0, \quad S_3 \geq 0, \quad S_4 \geq 0.$$

The optimal solution of this problem can be obtained using the regular simplex method. This gives

$$\hat{\mathbf{X}}_1^1 = \begin{pmatrix} 0 \\ 50 \\ 0 \\ 0 \end{pmatrix}, \, w_1^* = -100M - 100.$$

Since $C_B V_1 = -M$, then $\rho_1 = w_1^* + C_B V_1 = -101M - 100$.
For the second subproblem $(j = 2)$,

$$w_2 = \left[(0, -M) \begin{pmatrix} 1 & 1 & 0 & 0 \\ 1 & 3 & 0 & 0 \end{pmatrix} - (1, 3, 0, 0) \right] \begin{pmatrix} x_3 \\ x_4 \\ S_5 \\ S_6 \end{pmatrix}$$

$$= -(M + 1)x_3 - 3(M + 1)x_4,$$

and the corresponding problem becomes:

$$\text{minimize} \quad w_2 = -(M + 1)x_3 - 3(M + 1)x_4,$$

subject to

$$\begin{pmatrix} 3 & 6 & 1 & 0 \\ 0 & 1 & 0 & -1 \end{pmatrix} \begin{pmatrix} x_3 \\ x_4 \\ S_5 \\ S_6 \end{pmatrix} = \begin{pmatrix} 600 \\ 20 \end{pmatrix},$$

$$x_3 \geq 0, \quad x_4 \geq 0, \quad S_5 \geq 0, \quad S_6 \geq 0.$$

This gives the optimal solution

$$\hat{\mathbf{X}}_2^1 = \begin{pmatrix} 0 \\ 100 \\ 0 \\ 80 \end{pmatrix}, \, w_2^* = -300M - 300.$$

Since $C_B V_2 = -M$, then $\rho_2 = w_2^* + C_B V_2 = -301M - 300$.

It follows from the solutions of the first and second subproblems that

$$\rho = \min\{\rho_1, \rho_2\} = -301M - 300 < 0,$$

corresponding to $j = 2$. However, before determining the entering variable, it is noticed that ρ evaluates $(z_j - c_j)$ for the two subproblems only. This means that $(z_j - c_j)$ must also be evaluated for *all* the nonbasic variables which are not included in the subproblems. Thus for the slack variable S_1,

$$z_{S_1} - c_{S_1} = C_B B^{-1} P_{S_1} - c_{S_1}.$$

Since $C_B B^{-1} = (0, -M, -M, -M)$,

$$P_{S_1} = \begin{pmatrix} 0 \\ -1 \\ 0 \\ 0 \end{pmatrix},$$

and

$$c_{S_1} = 0,$$

then

$$z_{S_1} - c_{S_1} = M > 0.$$

This means that S_1 cannot enter the solution. Thus, since $\rho < 0$ corresponds to $j = 2$, the variable β_2^1 (corresponding to $\hat{X}_2^1$) must enter the solution.

The leaving variable is determined by applying the feasibility condition of the revised simplex method. It is noticed that

$$P_2^1 = \begin{pmatrix} A_2 \hat{X}_2^1 \\ 0 \\ 1 \end{pmatrix} = \left[\begin{pmatrix} 1 & 1 & 0 & 0 \\ 1 & 3 & 0 & 0 \end{pmatrix} \begin{pmatrix} 0 \\ 100 \\ 0 \\ 80 \end{pmatrix} \right] = \begin{bmatrix} 100 \\ 300 \\ 0 \\ 1 \end{bmatrix}.$$

Thus α for P_2^1 is given by

$$\alpha = \begin{pmatrix} \alpha_{S_2} \\ \alpha_{R_1} \\ \alpha_{R_2} \\ \alpha_{R_3} \end{pmatrix} = B^{-1} P_2^1 = \begin{pmatrix} 100 \\ 300 \\ 0 \\ 1 \end{pmatrix}.$$

and

$$\theta = \min_{S_2, R_1, R_2, R_3} \left\{ \frac{200}{100}, \frac{400}{300}, \frac{-}{-}, \frac{1}{1} \right\} = 1.$$

Thus R_3 leaves the solution.

Now to determine the new basic solution, the formula introduced in Section 8·7·1 is used to determine B_{next}^{-1}. This means,

$$B_{next}^{-1} = EB_{current}^{-1}$$

$$= \begin{bmatrix} 1 & 0 & 0 & -100 \\ 0 & 1 & 0 & -300 \\ 0 & 0 & 0 & 0 \\ 0 & 0 & 0 & 1 \end{bmatrix} \begin{bmatrix} 1 & 0 & 0 & 0 \\ 0 & 1 & 0 & 0 \\ 0 & 0 & 1 & 0 \\ 0 & 0 & 0 & 1 \end{bmatrix} = \begin{bmatrix} 1 & 0 & 0 & -100 \\ 0 & 1 & 0 & -300 \\ 0 & 0 & 1 & 0 \\ 0 & 0 & 0 & 1 \end{bmatrix}.$$

Hence

$$X_B = \begin{pmatrix} S_2 \\ R_1 \\ R_2 \\ \beta_2^1 \end{pmatrix} = B^{-1} \begin{pmatrix} 200 \\ 400 \\ 1 \\ 1 \end{pmatrix} = \begin{pmatrix} 100 \\ 100 \\ 1 \\ 1 \end{pmatrix}.$$

The modified coefficients of β_2^1 in the objective function is given by

$$c_2^1 = C_2 \hat{X}_2^1 = 300.$$

Second Iteration:

$$R_0 = \begin{pmatrix} 1 & 0 \\ 0 & 1 \\ 0 & 0 \\ 0 & 0 \end{pmatrix}, \quad V_1 = \begin{pmatrix} 0 \\ 0 \\ 1 \\ 0 \end{pmatrix}, \quad V_2 = \begin{pmatrix} -100 \\ -300 \\ 0 \\ 1 \end{pmatrix}$$

$$C_B = (0, -M, -M, 300),$$

$$C_B R_0 = (0, -M).$$

For $j = 1$

$$w_1 = -(M + 1)x_1 - 2(M + 1)x_2.$$

Thus the corresponding optimal solution of the first subproblem is the same as in first iteration and is given by

$$\hat{X}_1^2 = \begin{pmatrix} 0 \\ 50 \\ 0 \\ 0 \end{pmatrix}, \quad w_1^* = -100M - 100.$$

Hence $\rho_1 = w_1^* + C_B V_1 = -100M - 100 - M = -101M - 100$.
    For $j = 2$

$$w_2 = -(M + 1)x_3 - 3(M + 1)x_4.$$

Again, this is the same as in the last iteration and the solution is given by

$$\hat{X}_2^2 = \begin{pmatrix} 0 \\ 100 \\ 0 \\ 80 \end{pmatrix}, \quad w_2^* = -300M - 300.$$

Since $C_B V_2 = 300M + 300$, hence $\rho_2 = 0$.

Finally, $z_{S_1} - c_{S_1} = M > 0$. Thus $\rho = \rho_1 < 0$ indicating that β_1^2 (corresponding to $\hat{X}_1^2$) must enter the solution.

For the leaving variable,

$$P_1^2 = \begin{pmatrix} A_1 X_1^2 \\ 1 \\ 0 \end{pmatrix} = \begin{bmatrix} \begin{pmatrix} 1 & 1 & 0 & 0 \\ 1 & 2 & 0 & 0 \end{pmatrix} \begin{pmatrix} 0 \\ 50 \\ 0 \\ 0 \end{pmatrix} \\ 1 \\ 0 \end{bmatrix} = \begin{pmatrix} 50 \\ 100 \\ 1 \\ 0 \end{pmatrix},$$

and

$$\alpha = B^{-1} P_1^2 = \begin{pmatrix} 50 \\ 100 \\ 1 \\ 0 \end{pmatrix}.$$

Thus

$$\theta = \min_{S_2, R_1, R_2, \beta_2^1} \left\{ \frac{100}{50}, \frac{100}{100}, \frac{1}{1}, - \right\} = 1.$$

Hence either R_1 or R_2 can leave the solution.

Let R_2 be the leaving variable, then

$$B_{next}^{-1} = \begin{bmatrix} 1 & 0 & -50 & 0 \\ 0 & 1 & -100 & 0 \\ 0 & 0 & 1 & 0 \\ 0 & 0 & 0 & 1 \end{bmatrix} \begin{bmatrix} 1 & 0 & 0 & -100 \\ 0 & 1 & 0 & -300 \\ 0 & 0 & 1 & 0 \\ 0 & 0 & 0 & 1 \end{bmatrix} = \begin{bmatrix} 1 & 0 & -50 & -100 \\ 0 & 1 & -100 & -300 \\ 0 & 0 & 1 & 0 \\ 0 & 0 & 0 & 1 \end{bmatrix}$$

and

$$X_B = \begin{pmatrix} S_2 \\ R_1 \\ \beta_1^2 \\ \beta_2^1 \end{pmatrix} = B^{-1} \begin{pmatrix} 200 \\ 400 \\ 1 \\ 1 \end{pmatrix} = \begin{pmatrix} 50 \\ 0 \\ 1 \\ 1 \end{pmatrix}.$$

The modified coefficient of β_1^2 in the objective function is given by
$c_1^2 = C_1 \hat{X}_1^2 = 100$.

Third Iteration:

$$R_0 = \begin{pmatrix} 1 & 0 \\ 0 & 1 \\ 0 & 0 \\ 0 & 0 \end{pmatrix}, \quad V_1 = \begin{pmatrix} -50 \\ -100 \\ 1 \\ 0 \end{pmatrix}, \quad V_2 = \begin{pmatrix} -100 \\ -300 \\ 0 \\ 1 \end{pmatrix}$$

$$C_B = (0, -M, 100, 300), \quad C_B R_0 = (0, -M).$$

For $j = 1$, computing w_1 from the above information gives

$$w_1 = -(M + 1)x_1 - 2(M + 1)x_2,$$

and thus the solution is the same as in the last two iterations, that is,

$$\hat{X}_1^3 = \begin{pmatrix} 0 \\ 50 \\ 0 \\ 0 \end{pmatrix}, \quad w_2^* = -100M - 100.$$

Now $C_B V_1 = 100M + 100$, hence $\rho_1 = 0$.
  Similarly, for $j = 2$, computing w_2 gives

$$w_2 = -(M + 1)x_3 - 3(M + 1)x_4,$$

which is the same as in the previous iterations. Thus the solution remain the same. That is,

$$\hat{X}_2^3 = \begin{pmatrix} 0 \\ 100 \\ 0 \\ 80 \end{pmatrix}, \quad w_2^* = -300M - 300.$$

But since $C_B V_2 = 300M + 300$, it follows that $\rho_2 = 0$.
  For S_1, $z_{S_1} - c_{S_1} = M > 0$. Since $\rho = 0$, this implies that the current solution is optimal. Thus the optimal solution to the modified problem is

$$X_B = \begin{pmatrix} S_2 \\ R_1 \\ \beta_1^2 \\ \beta_2^1 \end{pmatrix} = \begin{pmatrix} 50 \\ 0 \\ 1 \\ 1 \end{pmatrix}.$$

(Notice that the optimal solution includes the artificial variable R_1; yet since $R_1 = 0$, the optimal solution exists and is given by X_B above.) Now the optimal solution to the original problem is given by

$$X_1^* = \begin{pmatrix} x_1 \\ x_2 \\ S_3 \\ S_4 \end{pmatrix} = \sum_{k=1}^{K_1} \beta_1^k \hat{X}_1^k$$

$$= \beta_1^2 \hat{X}_1^2 = (1)\begin{pmatrix} 0 \\ 50 \\ 0 \\ 0 \end{pmatrix} = \begin{pmatrix} 0 \\ 50 \\ 0 \\ 0 \end{pmatrix},$$

$$X_2^* = \begin{pmatrix} x_3 \\ x_4 \\ S_5 \\ S_6 \end{pmatrix} = \sum_{k=1}^{K_2} \beta_2^k \hat{X}_2^k$$

$$= \beta_2^1 \hat{X}_2^1 = (1)\begin{pmatrix} 0 \\ 100 \\ 0 \\ 80 \end{pmatrix} = \begin{pmatrix} 0 \\ 100 \\ 0 \\ 80 \end{pmatrix},$$

and

$$S_2 = 50.$$

with all the remaining variables equal to zero. In other words, $x_1 = 0$, $x_2 = 50$, $x_3 = 0$, $x_4 = 100$, and $x_0 = 500$ is the optimal solution to the problem. ◀

§ 8·7·3
Bounded Variables

Applications of linear programming exists where, in addition to the regular constraints, some (or all) variables are bounded from above and below. In this case, the problem appears as:

$$\text{maximize} \quad x_0 = \mathbf{CX},$$

subject to

$$(\mathbf{A, I})\mathbf{X} = \mathbf{P}_0,$$

$$\mathbf{L} \le \mathbf{X} \le \mathbf{U},$$

where

$$\mathbf{U} = \begin{pmatrix} \mu_1 \\ \mu_2 \\ \vdots \\ \mu_{n+m} \end{pmatrix}, \quad \text{and} \quad \mathbf{L} = \begin{pmatrix} \ell_1 \\ \ell_2 \\ \vdots \\ \ell_{n+m} \end{pmatrix}, \quad \mathbf{U} \ge \mathbf{L} \ge 0.$$

For the unbounded variables, the corresponding elements of $\mathbf{L}$ and $\mathbf{U}$ are 0 and ∞, respectively.

The given problem can be solved using the regular simplex method in which case the constraints are put in the form

$$(\mathbf{A}, \mathbf{I})\mathbf{X} = \mathbf{P}_0,$$

$$\mathbf{X} + \mathbf{X}' = \mathbf{U},$$

$$\mathbf{X} - \mathbf{X}'' = \mathbf{L},$$

$$\mathbf{X} \geq \mathbf{0},$$

$$\mathbf{X}' \geq \mathbf{0},$$

$$\mathbf{X}'' \geq \mathbf{0},$$

where $\mathbf{X}'$ and $\mathbf{X}''$ are slack variables. This problem includes $3(m + n)$ variables and $3m + 2n$ constraint equations. It will be shown now that the size of this problem can be reduced considerably through the use of special techniques which will ultimately reduce the constraints to the set

$$(\mathbf{A}, \mathbf{I})\mathbf{X} = \mathbf{P}_0.$$

Consider first the lower bound constraints. These constraints present no problem since their effect can be accounted for by using the substitution,

$$\mathbf{X} = \mathbf{L} + \mathbf{X}'',$$

to eliminate $\mathbf{X}$ from all the remaining constraints. The new variables of the problem thus become $\mathbf{X}'$ and $\mathbf{X}''$. There is no fear in this case that $\mathbf{X}$ may violate the nonnegativity constraint since both $\mathbf{L}$ and $\mathbf{X}''$ are nonnegative.

The real problem occurs with the upper bounded variables. A substitution similar to that of the lower bound case is illegitimate since there is no guarantee that

$$\mathbf{X} = \mathbf{U} - \mathbf{X}'$$

will remain nonnegative. This difficulty is overcome by using a different procedure. Consider the problem without the lower bounds. This is given by

$$\text{maximize} \quad x_0 = \mathbf{CX},$$

subject to

$$(\mathbf{A}, \mathbf{I})\mathbf{X} = \mathbf{P}_0,$$

$$\mathbf{X} + \mathbf{X}' = \mathbf{U},$$

$$\mathbf{X} \geq \mathbf{0},$$

$$\mathbf{X}' \geq \mathbf{0}.$$

Rather than including the constraints

$$\mathbf{X} + \mathbf{X}' = \mathbf{U}$$

in the simplex tableau, their effect will be accounted for by modifying the feasibility condition of the simplex method. The optimality condition, on the other hand, will remain the same as in the regular simplex method.

The basic idea for modifying the feasibility condition involves a recognition of the fact that a variable becomes infeasible if it becomes negative or if it exceeds its upper bound. The nonnegativity condition is treated exactly as in the regular simplex method. The upper bound condition requires special provisions which will allow a basic variable to become nonbasic at its upper bound. (Compare with the regular simplex method where all the nonbasic variables are at zero level.) Also, when a nonbasic variable is selected to enter the solution, its entering value should not exceed its upper bound. Thus, in developing the new feasibility condition, two main points must be considered

(a) The nonnegativity and upper bound constraints for the entering variable.
(b) The nonnegativity and upper bound constraints for those basic variables that may be affected by introducing the entering variable.

To develop the above ideas mathematically, consider the linear programming problem without the upper bounds. At every iteration, one guarantees that the solution is feasible as follows. Let x_j be a nonbasic variable at *zero* level which is selected to enter the solution. (Later it is shown that every nonbasic variable can always be put at zero level.) Let $(\mathbf{X}_B)_i = (\mathbf{X}_B^*)_i$ be the ith variable of the current basic solution $\mathbf{X}_B$. Thus according to the theory in Section 8·5·1, introducing x_j into the solution gives

$$(\mathbf{X}_B)_i = (\mathbf{X}_B^*)_i - \alpha_i^j x_j$$

where α_i^j is the ith element of $\boldsymbol{\alpha}^j = \mathbf{B}^{-1}\mathbf{P}_j$ and $\mathbf{P}_j$ is the vector of $(\mathbf{A}, \mathbf{I})$ corresponding to x_j.

Now following the guidelines given above, x_j remains feasible if

$$0 \le x_j \le \mu_j, \tag{i}$$

while $(\mathbf{X}_B)_i$ remains feasible if

$$0 \le (\mathbf{X}_B^*)_i - \alpha_i^j x_j \le \mu_i, \qquad i = 1, 2, \ldots, m. \tag{ii}$$

Since the introduction of x_j into the solution implies that it must be nonnegative, condition (i) is taken care of by observing the upper bound on x_j. Next, consider condition (ii). From the nonnegativity condition,

$$(\mathbf{X}_B)_i = (\mathbf{X}_B^*)_i - \alpha_i^j x_j \ge 0,$$

it follows that only $\alpha_i^j > 0$ may cause $(\mathbf{X}_B)_i$ to be negative. Let θ_1 represent the maximum value of x_j resulting from this condition. Thus,

$$\theta_1 = \min_i \left\{ \frac{(\mathbf{X}_B^*)_i}{\alpha_i^j}, \ \alpha_i^j > 0 \right\}.$$

This actually is the same as the feasibility condition of the regular simplex method.

In order to guarantee that $(\mathbf{X}_B)_i$ will not exceed its upper bound, it is necessary that

$$(\mathbf{X}_B)_i = (\mathbf{X}_B^*)_i + (-\alpha_i^j)x_j \leq \mu_i.$$

This condition can be violated if α_i^j is negative. Thus, letting θ_2 represent the maximum value of x_j resulting from this condition, then

$$\theta_2 = \min_i \left\{ \frac{\mu_i - (\mathbf{X}_B^*)_i}{-\alpha_i^j}, \ \alpha_i^j < 0 \right\}.$$

Let θ denote the maximum value of x_j which does not violate any of the above conditions. Then

$$\theta = \min\{\theta_1, \theta_2, \mu_j\}.$$

It is noticed that an old basic variable $(\mathbf{X}_B)_i$ can be dropped from the solution (become nonbasic) only if the introduction of the entering variable x_j at level θ causes $(\mathbf{X}_B)_i$ to be zero or to be at its upper bound. This means that if $\theta = \mu_j$, then x_j cannot be made basic since no $(\mathbf{X}_B)_i$ can be dropped from the solution and thus it should remain nonbasic at its upper bound. (If $\theta = \mu_j = \theta_1 = \theta_2$, the tie may be broken arbitrarily.)

In the above derivation, the entering variable, x_j, is assumed to be at zero level before it is introduced into the solution. To maintain the validity of the above results, every nonbasic variable, x_k, at upper bound can be put at zero level using the substitution

$$x_k = \mu_k - x_k',$$

where, as indicated previously, $0 \leq x_k' \leq \mu_k$. This substitution ensures that all the nonbasic variables are at zero level.

Using the above ideas, the changes in the current basic solution can be effected as follows. Let $(\mathbf{X}_B)_r$ be the variable corresponding to $\theta = \min\{\theta_1, \theta_2, \mu_j\}$, then

1. If $\theta = \theta_1$, $(\mathbf{X}_B)_r$ is dropped from the solution and x_j is introduced using the regular row operations of the simplex method.

2. If $\theta = \theta_2$, $(\mathbf{X}_B)_r$ is dropped and x_j is introduced; then $(\mathbf{X}_B)_r$ being nonbasic at its upper bound must be substituted out by using $(\mathbf{X}_B)_r = \mu_r - (\mathbf{X}_B)_r'$.

3. If $\theta = \mu_j$, x_j is substituted at its upper bound $(\mu_j - x_j)$ while remaining nonbasic.

The upper bounding technique is now illustrated by an example.

▶ **Example 8·7-3**
Consider the following problem.

$$\text{Maximize} \quad x_0 = 3x_1 + 5y + 3x_3,$$

subject to

$$x_1 + 2y + 2x_3 \le 14,$$
$$2x_1 + 4y + 3x_3 \le 23,$$
$$0 \le x_1 \le 4,$$
$$2 \le y \le 5,$$
$$0 \le x_3 \le 3.$$

Since y has a positive lower bound, it must be substituted at its lower bound. Let $y = x_2 + 2$, then $0 \le x_2 \le 3$ and the above problem reduces to

Starting tableau:

Basic	x_0	x_1	x_2	x_3	S_1	S_2	Solution
x_0	①	-3	-5	-2	0	0	10
S_1	0	1	2	2	①	0	10
S_2	0	2	4	3	0	①	15

First Iteration:

Select x_2 as the entering variable $(z_2 - c_2 = -5)$. Thus

$$\alpha^2 = \binom{2}{4} > 0$$

and

$$\theta_1 = \min\{10/2,\ 15/4\} = 3.75$$

Since all $\alpha_i^2 > 0$, it follows that $\theta_2 = \infty$. Consequently,

$$\theta = \min\{3.75,\ \infty,\ 3\} = 3.$$

Because $\theta = \mu_2$, x_2 is substituted at its upper limit but it remains non-basic. Thus putting $x_2 = \mu_2 - x_2' = 3 - x_2'$, the new tableau becomes

Basic	x_0	x_1	x_2'	x_3	S_1	S_2	Solution
x_0	①	-3	5	-2	0	0	25
S_1	0	1	-2	2	①	0	4
S_2	0	2	-4	3	0	①	3

Second Iteration:

Select x_1 as the entering variable ($z_1 - c_1 = -3$). Thus,

$$\alpha^1 = \begin{pmatrix} 1 \\ 2 \end{pmatrix},$$

$$\theta_1 = \min\{4/1,\ 3/2\} = 3/2, \quad \text{corresponding to } S_2$$
$$\theta_2 = \infty.$$

Hence $\theta = \min\{3/2,\ \infty,\ 4\} = 3/2$ corresponding to θ_1. Thus introduce x_1 and drop S_2. This yields

Basic	x_0	x_1	x_2'	x_3	S_1	S_2	Solution
x_0	①	0	-1	$2\frac{1}{2}$	0	$3/2$	$59/2$
S_1	0	0	0	$1/2$	①	$-1/2$	$5/2$
x_1	0	①	-2	$3/2$	0	$1/2$	$3/2$

Third Iteration:

Select x_2' as the entering variable. Since

$$\alpha^2 = \begin{pmatrix} 0 \\ -2 \end{pmatrix} \le 0,$$

$$\theta_1 = \infty,$$

$$\theta_2 = \left(\frac{4 - \frac{3}{2}}{-(-2)} \right) = \frac{5}{4}, \quad \text{corresponding to } x_1.$$

Thus,

$$\theta = \min\{\infty, 5/4, 3\} = 5/4.$$

Since $\theta = \theta_2$, introduce x_2' into basis and drop x_1 then substitute it out at its upper bound $(4 - x_1')$. Thus removing x_1 and introducing x_2', the table becomes

Basic	x_0	x_1'	x_2'	x_3	S_1	S_2	Solution
x_0	①	$-\frac{1}{2}$	0	$\frac{7}{4}$	0	$\frac{5}{4}$	$115/4$
S_1	0	0	0	$\frac{1}{2}$	①	$-\frac{1}{2}$	$\frac{5}{4}$
x_2'	0	$-\frac{1}{2}$	①	$-\frac{3}{4}$	0	$-\frac{1}{4}$	$-\frac{3}{4}$

Now substituting for $x_1 = 4 - x_1'$, the final tableau becomes

Basic	x_0	x_1'	x_2'	x_3	S_1	S_2	Solution
x_0	①	$1/2$	0	$7/4$	0	$5/4$	$123/4$
S_1	0	0	0	$1/2$	①	$-1/2$	$5/2$
x_2'	0	$1/2$	①	$-3/4$	0	$-1/4$	$5/4$

which is now optimal and feasible.

The optimal solution in terms of the original variables $x_1, x_2,$ and x_3 is found as follows. Since $x_1' = 0$, it follows that $x_1 = 4$. Also, since $x_2' = 5/4$, then $x_2 = 3 - 5/4 = 7/4$ and $y = 2 + 7/4 = 15/4$. Finally x_3 equals 0. These values yield $x_0 = 123/4$ as shown in the optimal tableau. ◄

It might be beneficial at this point to study the effect of the upper bounding technique on the development of the simplex tableau. Specifically, it is required to define $\{z_j - c_j\}$ and the value of the current basic solution at every iteration. This will be presented here in matrix notation.

Let $\mathbf{X}_u$ represent the basic *and* nonbasic variable which are at their upper bound. Also, let $\mathbf{X}_z$ be the remaining basic *and* nonbasic variables. Suppose that the ordered vectors of $(\mathbf{A}, \mathbf{I})$ corresponding to $\mathbf{X}_z$ and $\mathbf{X}_u$ are given, respectively, by the matrices $\mathbf{D}_z$ and $\mathbf{D}_u$ and let the vector $\mathbf{C}$ of the objective function be partitioned correspondingly so that

$$\mathbf{C} = (\mathbf{C}_z, \mathbf{C}_u).$$

The linear programming problem at any iteration reduces the set of equations

$$\begin{pmatrix} 1 & -C_z & -C_u \\ 0 & D_z & D_u \end{pmatrix} \begin{pmatrix} x_0 \\ X_z \\ X_u \end{pmatrix} = \begin{pmatrix} 0 \\ P_0 \end{pmatrix}.$$

Instead of dealing with two types of variables, namely X_z and X_u, it is more convenient to have one type only by putting X_u at zero level using the substitution,

$$X_u = U_u - X'_u,$$

where U_u is a subset of U representing the upper bounds for the variables in X_u. This gives,

$$\begin{pmatrix} 1 & -C_z & C_u \\ 0 & D_z & -D_u \end{pmatrix} \begin{pmatrix} x_0 \\ X_z \\ X'_u \end{pmatrix} = \begin{pmatrix} C_u U_u \\ P_0 - D_u U_u \end{pmatrix}.$$

The optimality and the feasibility conditions can be developed more easily now since all the nonbasic variables are of the same type. It should be noted, however, that it is still necessary to check that no basic or nonbasic variable will exceed its upper bound.

Define X_B as the basic variables of the current iteration and let C_B represent the elements corresponding to X_B in C. Also, let B be the basic matrix corresponding to X_B.

Given

$$M = \begin{pmatrix} 1 & -C_B \\ 0 & B \end{pmatrix},$$

then as shown in Section 8·6, the inverse is given by

$$M^{-1} = \begin{pmatrix} 1 & C_B B^{-1} \\ 0 & B^{-1} \end{pmatrix}.$$

Since at the current iteration all the nonbasic variables included in X_z and X'_u are at zero level, it follows that

$$M \begin{pmatrix} x_0 \\ X_B \end{pmatrix} = \begin{pmatrix} C_u U_u \\ P_0 - D_u U_u \end{pmatrix},$$

or

$$\begin{pmatrix} x_0 \\ X_B \end{pmatrix} = M^{-1} \begin{pmatrix} C_u U_u \\ P_0 - D_u U_u \end{pmatrix}$$

$$= \begin{pmatrix} C_u U_u + C_B B^{-1}(P_0 - D_u U_u) \\ B^{-1}(P_0 - D_u U_u) \end{pmatrix}$$

This gives the complete solution at the current iteration.

Let

$$P'_0 = P_0 - D_u U_u.$$

The complete simplex tableau corresponding to the any iteration is obtained by premultiplying both sides of the original set of equations by M^{-1} (compare with Section 8·6). This yields the tableau

Basic	x_0	X_z^T	$X_u'^T$	Solution
x_0	1	$C_B B^{-1} D_z - C_z$	$-C_B B^{-1} D_u + C_u$	$C_B B^{-1} P'_0 + C_u U_u$
X_B	0	$B^{-1} D_z$	$-B^{-1} D_u$	$B^{-1} P'_0$

The arrangement of this tableau is the same as the one presented in Section 8·6. For the x_0-equation, the left-hand side coefficients yield $(z_j - c_j)$, the optimality indicator, for all the nonbasic variables X_z and X_u' while its right-hand side yields the corresponding value of x_0. The constraint coefficients $B^{-1}(D_z, -D_u)$ will by definition give the corresponding $\{\alpha\}$ for the indicated nonbasic variables. Finally, the right-hand side of the constraint equations, $B^{-1} P'_0$, gives directly the values of X_B.

§ 8·8
The Dual Problem in Matrix Form

Consider the primal linear programming problem in the canonical form (see Section 2·3).

$$\text{Maximize} \quad x_0 = CX,$$

subject to

$$AX \leq P_0,$$
$$X \geq 0.$$

Its associated dual problem can be determined as indicated in Section 4·2 as follows. Let

$$Y = (y_1, y_2, \ldots, y_m)$$

be the row-vector defining the dual variables. Hence the dual problem is given by

$$\text{minimize} \quad y_0 = YP_0$$

subject to

$$YA \geq C$$
$$Y \geq 0.$$

Next consider the primal problem in the standard forms defined in Section 8·6. That is,

$$\text{maximize} \quad x_0 = C_I X_I + C_{II} X_{II},$$

subject to

$$(A, I)\begin{pmatrix} X_I \\ X_{II} \end{pmatrix} = P_0; P_0 \geq 0,$$

$$X_I \geq 0,$$

$$X_{II} \geq 0,$$

where X_{II} corresponds to the starting solution. It was indicated in Section 4·2 that an *equality* constraint in one problem corresponds to an unrestricted variable in the other problem. Thus the dual problem for the standard form is given by:

$$\text{minimize} \quad y_0 = Y P_0,$$

subject to

$$YA \geq C_I,$$

$$Y \geq C_{II}.$$

The vector Y is unrestricted in sign except, of course, as may be imposed by the constraints of the dual. For example, if one of the variables in the *starting* solution (X_{II}) is slack, its corresponding element in C_{II} is zero and hence this variable must be nonnegative.

If, on the other hand, the primal problem is given by:

$$\text{maximize} \quad x_0 = CX,$$

subject to

$$AX \leq P_0,$$

where the vector X is unrestricted in sign, its associated dual is given by:

$$\text{minimize} \quad y_0 = Y P_0,$$

subject to

$$YA = C,$$

$$Y \geq 0.$$

Notice that all dual constraints are equations except for the nonnegativity constraints which are inequalities.

Given the above matrix definition of the primal and dual problems, the following properties can now be proved. Assume, for convenience, that the primal problem is given in the standard form defined above. There is no loss in generality here since any problem can be put in this form.

Property I. Given any two feasible solutions X and Y for the primal and dual problems respectively, the value y_0 of the dual (minimization) problem acts as upper bound on the value of x_0 of the primal (maximization) problem. When $x_0 = y_0$, the corresponding feasible solutions are necessarily the optimal solutions to the two problems.

To prove this property, it is noticed that,

$$\mathbf{Y}\left[(\mathbf{A}, \mathbf{I}) \begin{pmatrix} \mathbf{X_I} \\ \mathbf{X_{II}} \end{pmatrix} \right] = \mathbf{Y}\mathbf{P_0} = y_0 .$$

Also

$$[\mathbf{Y}(\mathbf{A}, \mathbf{I})]\begin{pmatrix} \mathbf{X_I} \\ \mathbf{X_{II}} \end{pmatrix} = [\mathbf{YA}, \mathbf{Y}]\begin{pmatrix} \mathbf{X_I} \\ \mathbf{X_{II}} \end{pmatrix} \geq [\mathbf{C_I}, \mathbf{C_{II}}]\begin{pmatrix} \mathbf{X_I} \\ \mathbf{X_{II}} \end{pmatrix}$$

$$= \mathbf{C_I}\mathbf{X_I} + \mathbf{C_{II}}\mathbf{X_{II}} = x_0 .$$

Since the left-hand sides are equal, it follows that

$$y_0 \geq x_0 .$$

The above proof can be easily extended to the canonical form.

Since x_0 and y_0 are associated with the maximization and the minimization problems, respectively, then the optimal values of x_0 and y_0 which satisfy the inequality

$$x_0 \leq y_0 ,$$

must be such that

$$\max x_0 = \min y_0 .$$

This relationship assumes that both problems have finite optimal solution. (If one problem has a finite optimal solution, the optimal solution to the other problem must also be finite.) Property III shows that when one problem has an unbounded (infinite) solution, the other problem will have an infeasible solution. In this case no finite optimal solution exists.

Property II. If a finite optimal solution exists for the primal problem, its optimal dual solution will be given by $\mathbf{Y}^* = \mathbf{C_B}\mathbf{B}^{-1}$ where $\mathbf{C_B}$ and $\mathbf{B}^{-1}$ correspond to the optimal basic solution of the primal.

This property will be proved by showing that,

1. The solution $\mathbf{Y}^* = \mathbf{C_B}\mathbf{B}^{-1}$ yields the optimum value of the objective function obtained in the primal problem.
2. The same solution satisfies all the constraints of the dual problem.

The first point follows immediately since by definition,

$$y_0^* = Y^*P_0.$$

Putting $Y^* = C_B B^{-1}$, this gives directly the same value of x_0^*.

The second point is verified from the optimal conditions of the primal problem. Since for the optimal primal, $(z_j - c_j) \geq 0$ for all the variables, then by definition

$$\{z_j - c_j\} = \{C_B B^{-1} A - C_I, C_B B^{-1} - C_{II}\} \geq 0.$$

This means that,

$$C_B B^{-1} A - C_I \geq 0,$$

and

$$C_B B^{-1} - C_{II} \geq 0.$$

Putting $Y^* = C_B B^{-1}$, then

$$Y^* A \geq C_I,$$

and

$$Y^* \geq C_{II}.$$

This shows that the dual constraints are satisfied by the solution $Y^* = C_B B^{-1}$.

It is indicated in Section 4·3 that the optimal values of the dual variables can be obtained from the coefficients of the objective equation corresponding to the starting solution. The reason for this should be clear now since these coefficients are equal to $C_B B^{-1} - C_{II}$. Notice that when the corresponding element of C_{II} is not equal to zero (that is, the case of nonslack starting variables), this element must be added to the coefficient of the objective equation before the corresponding value of the dual variable can be obtained.

Property III. At any iteration of the primal, by substituting $Y = C_B B^{-1}$ in the dual problem, the differences between the left-hand and the right-hand sides of the dual constraints is equal to $\{z_j - c_j\}$ in the primal iteration.

The dual constraints are defined as

$$YA \geq C_I,$$
$$Y \geq C_{II}.$$

The differences between the left and the right sides are thus given by

$$Y(A, I) - (C_I, C_{II}).$$

Putting $Y = C_B B^{-1}$, the above differences reduce to

$$[(C_B B^{-1} A - C_I), (C_B B^{-1} - C_{II})],$$

which is equal to $\{z_j - c_j\}$ of the primal.

It is noted that at the optimal iteration $Y = C_B B^{-1}$ gives the optimal dual values. At the other iterations $C_B B^{-1}$ do not give the dual solution. Rather these values are called the simplex multipliers (see Section 4·4). They actually represent infeasible dual solutions. This result is ascertained by the fact that at the nonoptimal primal iterations, some $(z_j - c_j) < 0$ which means that the corresponding dual constraints are not satisfied by the values $C_B B^{-1}$. At the optimal primal solution, all $(z_j - c_j) \geq 0$, and hence $Y = C_B B^{-1}$ represents a feasible (optimal) solution to the dual problem. This means that while the primal problem is seeking optimality the dual problem is seeking feasibility.

It is now possible to explain why an unbounded primal problem will result in an infeasible dual problem. Recall that the primal solution is unbounded if there exist a nonbasic variable x_j for which $(z_j - c_j) < 0$ and $\alpha^j \leq 0$. In this case, x_j cannot be introduced into the solution and hence $(z_j - c_j)$ will always remain less than zero. From the above property, this would mean that the corresponding dual constraints will always remain unsatisfied and hence infeasible.

SELECTED REFERENCES

1. GARVIN, W., *Introduction to Linear Programming*, New York: McGraw-Hill, 1960
2. GASS, S., *Linear Programming*, New York: McGraw-Hill, second edition, 1964.
3. HADLEY, G., *Linear Programming*, Reading, Massachusetts: Addison-Wesley, 1962.
4. SIMMONARD, M., *Linear Programming*, translated by W. Jewell, Englewood Cliffs, N.J.: Prentice-Hall, 1966.

PROBLEMS

☐ **8-1** Given the general linear programming problem with m equations and $(m + n)$ unknowns, what is the maximum number of *adjacent* extreme points which can be reached from a nondegenerate extreme point of the corresponding convex set?

☐ **8-2** For the following system of linear equations determine all the extreme points and their corresponding basic solutions.

$$3x_1 + 6x_2 + 5x_3 + x_4 \qquad = 12,$$
$$2x_1 + 4x_2 + x_3 \qquad + 2x_5 = 8,$$

where $x_j \geq 0$, for all j.

☐ **8-3** Prove that the optimal solution for the following problem occurs at an extreme point.

$$\text{Minimize} \quad x_0 = \mathbf{CX},$$

subject to

$$\mathbf{AX} \geq \mathbf{P}_0,$$

$$\mathbf{X} \geq \mathbf{0}.$$

☐ **8-4** In applying the feasibility condition of the simplex method, suppose $x_r = 0$ is a basic variable and that x_j is the entering variable. Why is it necessary to have $\alpha_r^j > 0$ in order for x_r to be the leaving variable? What is the fallacy if $\alpha_r^j \leq 0$?

☐ **8-5** In applying the feasibility condition of the simplex method, what are the conditions for a degenerate solution to appear for the first time in the next iteration? For continuing to obtain a degenerate solution in the next iteration? For removing degeneracy in the next iteration? Express the answer mathematically.

☐ **8-6** What are the relationships between extreme points and basic solutions under each of the following conditions, (a) nondegeneracy, and (b) degeneracy. What is the maximum possible number of simplex iterations that can be performed at the same extreme point?

☐ **8-7** Consider the problem, max $x_0 = \mathbf{CX}$ subject to $\mathbf{AX} \leq \mathbf{P}_0$, where $\mathbf{P}_0 \geq \mathbf{0}$ and $\mathbf{X} \geq \mathbf{0}$. Suppose that the entering vector $\mathbf{P}_j$ is such that at least one element of α^j is greater than zero. If $\mathbf{P}_j$ is replaced by $\beta\mathbf{P}_j$, where β is a positive scalar, and provided that x_j remains the entering variable; find the relationships between the values of x_j corresponding to $\mathbf{P}_j$ and $\beta\mathbf{P}_j$.

☐ **8-8** Answer Problem 8-7 if, in addition, $\mathbf{P}_0$ is replaced by $\gamma\mathbf{P}_0$, where γ is a positive scalar.

☐ **8-9** Prove Theorem 8·5-1 for the minimization case showing that a nonbasic vector $\mathbf{P}_j$ will improve the current solution only if $(z_j - c_j)$ is greater than zero.

☐ **8-10** Consider the linear programming problem defined in Problem 8-7. After obtaining the optimum solution it is suggested that a nonbasic variable x_j can be made basic (profitable) by reducing the requirements per unit of x_j for the different resources to $1/\beta$ of their original values, where β is a scalar greater than 1. Since the requirements per unit are reduced, it is expected that the profit per unit of x_j will be reduced to $1/\beta$ of its original value. Will these changes make x_j a profitable variable? What should be recommended in order for x_j to be an attractive variable?

□ **8-11** In view of Problem 8-10, give an economic interpretation of the quantity $(z_j - c_j)$. Specifically, what is the interpretation of z_j?

□ **8-12** Consider a linear programming problem in which the variable x_k is unrestricted in sign. Prove that by replacing x_k by $x_k^+ - x_k^-$, where x_k^+ and x_k^- are nonnegative variables, then in any of the simplex iterations (including the optimum) it is never possible to have *both* x_k^+ and x_k^- as *basic* variables, nor is it possible that these two variables can replace one another in an *alternative* optimum solution.

□ **8-13** Solve Example 3·5-1 using the matrix method of Section 8·5-2. Compare this method with the tableau method.

□ **8-14** Consider the matrix version of the tableau form given in Section 8·6. Suppose that the starting feasible solution consists of all-slack variables. Show that the "mechanical" method introduced in Section 3·3 automatically computes $z_j - c_j$ for all the nonbasic variables in the starting tableau.

□ **8-15** In Problem 8-14 suppose that the starting solution consists of all-artificial variables. Give the corresponding starting tableau in matrix form. Show that the "mechanical" method used in Section 3·5 automatically computes $z_j - c_j$ for all the nonbasic variables in the starting tableau.

□ **8-16** Consider the problem

$$\text{minimize} \quad x_0 = \mathbf{CX}$$

subject to

$$\mathbf{AX} \geq \mathbf{P}_0,$$

$$\mathbf{X} \geq \mathbf{0}.$$

Develop the matrix version of the dual simplex tableau introduced in Section 4·5. Verify the answer by applying it to the last tableau of the example in Section 4·5.

□ **8-17** The inverse of the matrix,

$$\mathbf{A} = \begin{bmatrix} 2 & 1 & 0 \\ 0 & 2 & 0 \\ 4 & 0 & 1 \end{bmatrix},$$

is given by

$$\mathbf{A}^{-1} = \begin{bmatrix} 1/2 & -1/4 & 0 \\ 0 & 1/2 & 0 \\ -2 & 1 & 1 \end{bmatrix}.$$

If the second and third columns of $\mathbf{A}$ are replaced by $(5, -1, 4)^T$ and $(1, 2, 1)^T$, find the new inverse using the method introduced in Section 8·7·1.

☐ **8-18** Solve by the revised simplex method:

$$\text{maximize} \quad x_0 = 6x_1 - 2x_2 + 3x_3,$$

subject to

$$2x_1 - x_2 + 2x_3 \le 2,$$
$$x_1 \quad\;\; + 4x_3 \le 4,$$
$$x_1, x_2, x_3 \ge 0.$$

☐ **8-19** Solve by the revised simplex method:

$$\text{maximize} \quad x_0 = 2x_1 + x_2 + 2x_3,$$

subject to

$$4x_1 + 3x_2 + \;\; 8x_3 \le 12,$$
$$4x_1 + \;\; x_2 + 12x_3 \le \;\; 8,$$
$$4x_1 - \;\; x_2 + \;\; 3x_3 \le \;\; 8,$$
$$x_1, x_2, x_3 \ge 0.$$

☐ **8-20** Solve by the revised simplex method:

$$\text{minimize} \quad x_0 = 2x_1 + x_2,$$

subject to

$$3x_1 + \;\; x_2 = 3,$$
$$4x_1 + 3x_2 \ge 6,$$
$$x_1 + 2x_2 \le 3,$$
$$x_1, x_2 \ge 0.$$

☐ **8-21** Apply the decomposition principle to the following problem:

$$\text{maximize} \quad x_0 = 6x_1 + 7x_2 + 3x_3 + 5x_4 + x_5 + x_6,$$

subject to

$$x_1 + x_2 + \;\; x_3 + x_4 + x_5 + \;\; x_6 \le 50,$$
$$x_1 + x_2 \qquad\qquad\qquad\qquad \le 10,$$
$$x_2 \qquad\qquad\qquad\qquad\quad \le \;\; 8,$$
$$5x_3 + x_4 \qquad\qquad \le 12,$$
$$x_5 + \;\; x_6 \ge \;\; 5,$$
$$x_5 + 5x_6 \le 50,$$

with all $x_j \ge 0$.

☐ **8-22** Solve by the decomposition algorithm:

$$\text{maximize} \quad x_0 = x_1 + 3x_2 + 5x_3 + 2x_4,$$

subject to

$$
\begin{aligned}
2x_1 + x_2 &\le 9, \\
5x_1 + 3x_2 + 4x_3 &\ge 10, \\
x_1 + 4x_2 &\le 8, \\
x_3 - 5x_4 &\le 4, \\
x_3 + x_4 &\le 10,
\end{aligned}
$$

with all $x_j \ge 0$.

☐ **8-23** Indicate the necessary changes in the decomposition algorithm in order to apply it to minimization problems. Then solve the following problem:

$$\text{minimize} \quad x_0 = 5x_1 + 3x_2 + 8x_3 - 5x_4,$$

subject to

$$
\begin{aligned}
x_1 + x_2 + x_3 + x_4 &\ge 25, \\
5x_1 + x_2 &\le 20, \\
5x_1 - x_2 &\ge 5, \\
x_3 + x_4 &= 20,
\end{aligned}
$$

with all $x_j \ge 0$.

☐ **8-24** Solve using the decomposition algorithm:

$$\text{minimize} \quad y_0 = 10y_1 + 2y_2 + 4y_3 + 8y_4 + y_5,$$

subject to

$$
\begin{aligned}
y_1 + 4y_2 - y_3 &\ge 8, \\
2y_1 + y_2 + y_3 &\ge 2, \\
3y_1 + y_4 + y_5 &\ge 4, \\
y_1 + 2y_4 - y_5 &\ge 10,
\end{aligned}
$$

with all $y_j \ge 0$. (Hint: Consider the dual of the above problem.)

☐ **8-25** Solve using the lower and upper bounding techniques:

$$\text{maximize} \quad x_0 = 4x_1 + 2x_2 + 6x_3,$$

subject to

$$
\begin{aligned}
4x_1 - x_2 &\le 9, \\
- x_1 + x_2 + 2x_3 &\le 8, \\
-3x_1 + x_2 + 4x_3 &\le 12, \\
\end{aligned}
$$
$$1 \le x_1 \le 3, \quad 0 \le x_2 \le 5, \quad 0 \le x_3 \le 2.$$

☐ **8-26** Verify that the elements of the tableaus in the second and optimal iterations of Example 8·7-3 satisfy the matrix definition of the simplex tableau with upper bounding.

☐ **8-27** Solve the transportation problem introduced in Section 5·2·2 assuming that $x_{23} \leq 10$ and $x_{14} \leq 3$.

☐ **8-28** Given the linear programming problem:

$$\text{maximize}\quad x_0 = \mathbf{CX}$$

subject to

$$(\mathbf{A}, \mathbf{I})\mathbf{X} = \mathbf{P}_0,$$
$$\mathbf{X} \geq 0,$$

where $\mathbf{X}$ is an $(m + n)$ column-vector. Let $\{\mathbf{P}_1, \mathbf{P}_2, \ldots, \mathbf{P}_m\}$ be the vectors corresponding to a *basic* solution and let $\{c_1, c_2, \ldots, c_m\}$ be the coefficients in the objective function associated with these vectors. If $\{c_1, \ldots, c_m\}$ is changed to $\{d_1, \ldots, d_m\}$, show that $(z_j - c_j)$ for the *basic* variables will remain equal to zero and interpret the result.

☐ **8-29** For the linear programming problem defined in 8-28, let the given basis be the optimal basis. Prove that for any vector,

$$\mathbf{P}_k = \begin{bmatrix} a_{1k} \\ a_{2k} \\ \vdots \\ a_{mk} \end{bmatrix}, k = 1, 2, \ldots, m + n,$$

the following relationship holds.

$$\sum_{j=1}^{m} c_j \alpha_j^k = \sum_{i=1}^{m} y_i^* a_{ik},$$

where
  α_j^k is as defined in the chapter,
  y_i^* is the corresponding optimal dual value.

☐ **8-30** Given the primal linear programming problem:

$$\text{maximize}\quad x_0 = \mathbf{CX},$$

subject to

$$\mathbf{DX} = \mathbf{P}_0,$$
$$\mathbf{X} \geq 0.$$

(a) Write the complete dual problem.
(b) Find the relationship between the values of the objective function in the primal and dual problems.

☐ **8-31** In Problem 8-30, write the complete dual problem if all the variables were unrestricted in sign.

□ **8-32** Write the dual problem for Problem 8-16 and then show how its solution can be obtained directly from the (optimal) feasible dual simplex tableau. Illustrate the answer by applying it to the example in Section 4·5.

□ **8-33** Consider the primal problem:

$$\text{maximize} \quad x_0 = \mathbf{CX},$$

subject to

$$\mathbf{AX} \le \mathbf{P}_0,$$
$$\mathbf{X} \ge \mathbf{0}.$$

Let $\mathbf{S}$ be the slack variables corresponding to the above primal and let $\mathbf{Y}$ be the dual variables. Prove that for any pair of the optimal primal and dual solutions

$$y_i S_i = 0; \quad i = 1, 2, \ldots, m,$$

and give an interpretation for the result. (Hint: This is the so-called "complementary slackness" theorem. See Section 4·4, Property II.)

□ **8-34** Consider the linear programming problem:

$$\text{minimize} \quad x_0 = \sum_{j=1}^{n} c_j^0 x_j,$$

subject to

$$\sum_{j=1}^{n} a_{ij} x_j = b_i, \quad i = 1, 2, \ldots, m,$$

$$x_j \ge 0, \text{ for all } j.$$

Let $(x_1^0, \ldots, x_n^0)$ be the optimal solution to the above problem and let $(x_1', \ldots, x_n')$ be its optimal solution if c_j^0 is replaced by c_j', for all j. Prove that

$$\sum_{j=1}^{n} (c_j' - c_j^0)(x_j' - x_j^0) \le 0.$$

If $c_j' < c_j^0$, for $j = k$ and $c_j' = c_j^0$, for $j \ne k$, what can be said about x_k' as compared with x_k^0?

□ **8-35** Consider the linear programming problem:

$$\text{minimize} \quad x_0 = \mathbf{CX},$$

subject to

$$\mathbf{AX} = \mathbf{P}_0^0,$$
$$\mathbf{X} \ge \mathbf{0}.$$

Let $\mathbf{X}^0$ be the optimal solution to the above problem and let $\mathbf{Y}^0$ be its corresponding optimal dual solution. If $\mathbf{X}^*$ is the optimal solution when $\mathbf{P}_0^0$ is replaced by $\mathbf{P}_0^*$, prove that

$$\mathbf{C}(\mathbf{X}^0 - \mathbf{X}^*) \le \mathbf{Y}^0(\mathbf{P}_0^0 - \mathbf{P}_0^*).$$

CHAPTER 9

Parametric Linear Programming

§ 9·1
Introduction

In Chapter 4, sensitivity or postoptimality analysis as applied to the linear programming problem was investigated. The objective there was to study the effect of discrete changes in the coefficients of the linear programming problem on the optimal solution. In this chapter, a similar type of analysis is presented. This is the so-called *parametric linear programming*. It investigates the behavior of the optimal solution as a result of *predetermined linear* variations in the parameters of the problem. The analysis is based mainly on the same primal-dual relationships presented in Section 4·4 and which are summarized in matrix form in Section 8·8. Like the sensitivity analysis techniques, the purpose of parametric linear programming is to minimize the additional computational effort required to obtain the indicated results.

To illustrate the application of parametric linear programming, suppose that the maximum amounts of resources for a certain problem vary linearly with time as shown in Figure 9–1. One is thus interested in the points in time at which new optimal basic solutions occur. A similar investigation may also be required for the remaining parameters of the problem such as changes in the profit (or cost) coefficients with time. It should be noted that the analysis in all these cases is restricted to linear variations only since the nonlinear variations do not yield neat mathematical results.

Define the linear programming problem before parameterization as:

$$\text{maximize} \quad x_0 = \mathbf{CX},$$

subject to

$$(\mathbf{A}, \mathbf{I})\mathbf{X} = \mathbf{P}_0,$$

$$\mathbf{X} \geq \mathbf{0}.$$

286

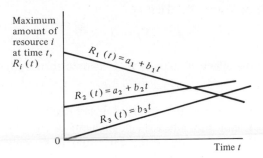

Figure 9–1

The following four types of linear variations will be investigated,

1. Variations in $\mathbf{C}$.
2. Variations in $\mathbf{P}_0$.
3. Variations in the coefficients of the nonbasic vector $\mathbf{P}_j$.
4. Simultaneous variations in $\mathbf{C}$ and $\mathbf{P}_0$.

Let θ define the parameter of variation. Thus the linear functions of the above coefficients may be defined as

$$^{\theta}\mathbf{C} = {}^{0}\mathbf{C} + \theta\mathbf{E} = ({}^{0}c_1, \ldots, {}^{0}c_{m+n}) + \theta(e_1, \ldots, e_{m+n})$$

and

$$^{\theta}\mathbf{P}_0 = {}^{0}\mathbf{P}_0 + \theta\mathbf{b} = \begin{bmatrix} {}^{0}P_{01} \\ {}^{0}P_{02} \\ \vdots \\ {}^{0}P_{0m} \end{bmatrix} + \theta \begin{bmatrix} b_1 \\ b_2 \\ \vdots \\ b_m \end{bmatrix}.$$

The parameter θ is assumed to be nonnegative. There is no loss in generality here, however, since the same analysis is equally applicable to $\theta \leq 0$. Notice that $^{0}\mathbf{C}$ and $^{0}\mathbf{P}_0$ are obtained from the above functions by letting $\theta = 0$. Notice also that the elements of $^{0}\mathbf{C}$, $\mathbf{E}$, $^{0}\mathbf{P}_0$, and $\mathbf{b}$ are known constants.

The parametric analysis presented here will be limited to maximization problems only. It is a trivial task, however, to change the analysis to minimization problems.

§ 9·2
Linear Variations in the C-vector

The first step is to solve the problem for $\theta = 0$. This means that the above linear programming problem is solved with $\mathbf{C} = {}^{0}\mathbf{C}$. Let

$$^{0}\mathbf{X}_B = {}^{0}\mathbf{B}^{-1}\mathbf{P}_0$$

be the corresponding optimal solution. Thus, at the optimal iteration,

$$^{0}z_j - {}^{0}c_j \geq 0,$$

for all the nonbasic vectors $\mathbf{P}_j$. That is,

$$^0\mathbf{C}_B{}^0\mathbf{B}^{-1}\mathbf{P}_j - {}^0c_j \geq 0,$$

for all nonbasic $\mathbf{P}_j$.

Next, consider the effect of changes in $\mathbf{C}$ as described by the function,

$$^\theta\mathbf{C} = {}^0\mathbf{C} + \theta\mathbf{E}.$$

From the matrix definition of the simplex tableau (Section 8·6), it is seen that any variations in $\mathbf{C}$ can only affect the coefficients of the objective function; that is, $(z_j - c_j)$. Thus, in studying the variations in $\mathbf{C}$, only the optimality of the problem needs to be checked.

The procedure now is to determine the consecutive values of θ at which the optimal basic solution changes. These will be referred to as *critical values* and are assumed to be measured from the *zero* datum. Thus initiating the procedure by starting with $^0\mathbf{X}_B$, the optimal solution at $\theta = 0$, let $\theta = \alpha$ and $\theta = \beta$ be two *consecutive* critical values, $(\alpha \leq \beta)$. It is assumed that the optimal basic solution at $\theta = \alpha$ is already known and is given by $^\alpha\mathbf{X}_B$. The determination of the next critical value $\theta = \beta$ is then achieved as follows.

The basic solution $^\alpha\mathbf{X}_B$ will remain optimal for some range of $\theta \geq \alpha$ as long as the condition $^\theta z_j - {}^\theta c_j \geq 0$ corresponding to this solution is satisfied for all j. Now, to determine a convenient expression for $^\theta z_j - {}^\theta c_j$, consider for $\theta \geq \alpha$,

$$^\theta\mathbf{C}_B = {}^0\mathbf{C}_B + \theta\mathbf{E}_B$$

$$= {}^0\mathbf{C}_B + \alpha\mathbf{E}_B + (\theta - \alpha)\mathbf{E}_B$$

$$= {}^\alpha\mathbf{C}_B + (\theta - \alpha)\mathbf{E}_B.$$

Similarly, for $\theta \geq \alpha$,

$$^\theta c_j = {}^\alpha c_j + (\theta - \alpha)e_j.$$

(Notice that $\mathbf{E}_B$ and $^0\mathbf{C}_B$ should have been subscripted to read $\mathbf{E}_{B_\alpha}$ and $^0\mathbf{C}_{B_\alpha}$, thus reflecting the fact that their specific elements must correspond to the basic variables at $\theta = \alpha$. This complicates the notation, however, and hence the subscript α is suppressed with the understanding that its implication still holds.) Consequently,

$$^\theta z_j - {}^\theta c_j = \{^\alpha\mathbf{C}_B + (\theta - \alpha)\mathbf{E}_L\}\,^\alpha\mathbf{B}^{-1}\mathbf{P}_j - \{^\alpha c_j + (\theta - \alpha)e_j\}$$

$$= (^\alpha z_j - {}^\alpha c_j) + (\theta - \alpha)(\mathbf{E}_B\,^\alpha\mathbf{B}^{-1}\mathbf{P}_j - e_j).$$

Since $^\alpha z_j - {}^\alpha c_j \geq 0$, it follows from the condition $^\theta z_j - {}^\theta c_j \geq 0$ that,

1. If $(\mathbf{E}_B\,^\alpha\mathbf{B}^{-1}\mathbf{P}_j - e_j) \geq 0$, for all j, then the condition $^\theta z_j - {}^\theta c_j \geq 0$ is satisfied for all $\theta \geq \alpha$. In this case, $^\alpha\mathbf{X}_B$ remains optimal for all $\theta \geq \alpha$.

2. If $(\mathbf{E}_B\,^\alpha\mathbf{B}^{-1}\mathbf{P}_j - e_j) < 0$, for at least one j, there exists a critical value, $\theta = \beta$, which is given by,

$$\beta = \alpha + \min_j\left[\frac{-(^\alpha z_j - {}^\alpha c_j)}{(\mathbf{E}_B\,^\alpha\mathbf{B}^{-1}\mathbf{P}_j - e_j)}\,\middle|\,\mathbf{E}_B\,^\alpha\mathbf{B}^{-1}\mathbf{P}_j - e_j < 0\right].$$

Let x_k be the nonbasic variable corresponding to β as defined above. Then $z_k - c_k = 0$ at $\theta = \beta$. This means that at $\theta = \beta$, there exists an *alternative* solution; while for $\theta > \beta$ the basic solution $^\alpha\mathbf{X}_B$ ceases to be optimal. This follows since $z_k - c_k$ will become negative. Thus, at $\theta = \beta$ the regular simplex method is invoked to introduce the variable x_k. This yields the *alternative* optimal solution $^\beta\mathbf{X}_B$ at $\theta = \beta$. The above procedure is then repeated on $^\beta\mathbf{X}_B$ to obtain the succeeding critical value; that is, the range over which $^\beta\mathbf{X}_B$ remains optimal.

▶ **Example 9·2-1**

Consider the parametric problem,

$$\text{maximize} \quad x_0 = (3 - 6\theta)x_1 + (2 - 2\theta)x_2 + (5 + 5\theta)x_3,$$

subject to

$$x_1 + 2x_2 + x_3 \le 430,$$
$$3x_1 \qquad + 2x_3 \le 460,$$
$$x_1 + 4x_2 \qquad \le 420,$$

with all $x_j \ge 0$.

Thus,

$$^\theta\mathbf{C} = {}^0\mathbf{C} + \theta\mathbf{E}$$

$$= (3, 2, 5) + \theta(-6, -2, 5).$$

At $\theta = 0$, the above problem becomes identical to Example 3·4-1. Hence, the optimal tableau in this case is given by,

Basic	x_0	x_1	x_2	x_3	x_4	x_5	x_6	Solution
x_0	①	4	0	0	1	2	0	1350
x_2	0	$-1/4$	①	0	1/2	$-1/4$	0	100
x_3	0	3/2	0	①	0	1/2	0	230
x_6	0	2	0	0	-2	1	①	20

where x_4, x_5, and x_6 are slack variables. Hence,

$$^0\mathbf{X}_B = \begin{bmatrix} x_2 \\ x_3 \\ x_6 \end{bmatrix} = \begin{bmatrix} 100 \\ 230 \\ 20 \end{bmatrix},$$

and

$$^0\mathbf{B}^{-1} = \begin{bmatrix} 1/2 & -1/4 & 0 \\ 0 & 1/2 & 0 \\ -2 & 1 & 1 \end{bmatrix}.$$

Consider now the determination of the first critical value, $\theta = \theta'$. Since (x_2, x_3, x_6) are basic at $\theta = 0$, it follows that

$$^\theta\mathbf{C}_B = {}^0\mathbf{C}_B + \theta\mathbf{E}_B$$

$$= (2, 5, 0) + \theta(-2, 5, 0),$$

and

$$\mathbf{E}_B{}^0\mathbf{B}^{-1} = (-2, 5, 0) \begin{bmatrix} 1/2 & -1/4 & 0 \\ 0 & 1/2 & 0 \\ -2 & 1 & 1 \end{bmatrix} = (-1, 3, 0).$$

Now, for the nonbasic variables x_1, x_4, x_5,

$$\mathbf{E}_B{}^0\mathbf{B}^{-1}(\mathbf{P}_1, \mathbf{P}_4, \mathbf{P}_5) - (e_1, e_4, e_5)$$

$$= (-1, 3, 0) \begin{bmatrix} 1 & 1 & 0 \\ 3 & 0 & 1 \\ 1 & 0 & 0 \end{bmatrix} - (-6, 0, 0)$$

$$= (14, -1, 3).$$

Since only $(\mathbf{E}_B{}^0\mathbf{B}^{-1}\mathbf{P}_4 - e_4) < 0$, then

$$\theta' = \frac{-({}^0z_4 - {}^0c_4)}{(\mathbf{E}_B{}^0\mathbf{B}^{-1}\mathbf{P}_4 - e_4)} = \frac{-(1)}{-1} = 1$$

is the first critical value for θ. (Notice that ${}^0z_4 - {}^0c_4$ is obtained from the optimal tableau corresponding to $\theta = 0$.)

It follows that ${}^0\mathbf{X}_B$ remains optimal for $0 \le \theta \le \theta'$. At $\theta = \theta'$, x_4 is introduced into the solution and a new basic solution is obtained. This yields,

Basic	x_0	x_1	x_2	x_3	x_4	x_5	x_6	Solution
x_0	①	18	0	0	0	5	0	2300
x_4	0	$-1/2$	2	0	①	$-1/2$	0	200
x_3	0	$3/2$	0	①	0	$1/2$	0	230
x_6	0	1	4	0	0	0	①	420

In the above table, the new constraint coefficients are obtained by using the regular row transformation operation. However, the coefficients of the objective equation must be computed as follows,

$$^{\theta'}z_j - {}^{\theta'}c_j = (^0z_j - {}^0c_j) + \theta'(E_B\,{}^0B^{-1}P_j - e_j).$$

Thus,

$$^{\theta'}z_1 - {}^{\theta'}c_1 = 4 + 1(14) = 18,$$

$$^{\theta'}z_4 - {}^{\theta'}c_4 = 1 + 1(-1) = 0,$$

$$^{\theta'}z_5 - {}^{\theta'}c_5 = 2 + 1(3) = 5.$$

The next step now is to compute the second critical value $\theta = \theta''$. From the optimal tableau corresponding to $\theta = \theta'$, one gets,

$$^{\theta'}B^{-1} = \begin{bmatrix} 1 & -1/2 & 0 \\ 0 & 1/2 & 0 \\ 0 & 0 & 1 \end{bmatrix}.$$

Since x_4, x_3 and x_6 are the new basic variables at $\theta = \theta'$, then,

$$^{\theta}C_B = (0, 5, 0) + \theta(0, 5, 0).$$

Thus,

$$E_B = (0, 5, 0)$$

and

$$E_B\,{}^{\theta'}B^{-1} = (0, 5, 0)\begin{bmatrix} 1 & -1/2 & 0 \\ 0 & 1/2 & 0 \\ 0 & 0 & 1 \end{bmatrix} = (0, 5/2, 0).$$

Now, for the nonbasic variables x_1, x_2, and x_5,

$$E_B\,{}^{\theta'}B^{-1}(P_1, P_2, P_5) - (e_1, e_2, e_5)$$

$$= (0, 5/2, 0)\begin{bmatrix} 1 & 2 & 0 \\ 3 & 0 & 1 \\ 1 & 4 & 0 \end{bmatrix} - (-6, -2, 0)$$

$$= (27/2, 2, 5/2).$$

Again, $\{^{\theta'}z_j - {}^{\theta'}c_j\} = (18, 0, 5)$ is obtained directly from optimal tableau at $\theta = \theta'$. However, since all

$$E_B\,{}^{\theta'}B^{-1}P_j - e_j, \qquad j = 1, 2, 5,$$

are nonnegative, [$= (27/2, 2, 5/2)$], this means that there is no new critical value for θ. Consequently, $^{\theta'}X_B$, the optimal solution at $\theta = \theta'$, remains basic, feasible and optimal for all $\theta \ge \theta'$; that is, for all $\theta \ge 1$.

The use of the given formula to determine the critical values of θ is suitable for automatic computations. The same result can be obtained directly from the original condition $(^{\theta}z_j - {}^{\theta}c_j) \geq 0$. Again, in this case all critical values are measured from the zero datum directly.

To illustrate this direct procedure, consider the determination of θ'' for the above example.

$$^{\theta}\mathbf{C}_B\,{}^{\theta'}\mathbf{B}^{-1} = (0,\, 5 + 5\theta,\, 0)\begin{bmatrix} 1 & -1/2 & 0 \\ 0 & 1/2 & 0 \\ 0 & 0 & 1 \end{bmatrix} = \left(0,\, \frac{5+5\theta}{2},\, 0\right).$$

Consequently, for the nonbasic vectors, $\mathbf{P}_1$, $\mathbf{P}_2$, and $\mathbf{P}_5$,

$$(^{\theta}z_j - {}^{\theta}c_j) = {}^{\theta}\mathbf{C}_B\,{}^{\theta'}\mathbf{B}^{-1}(\mathbf{P}_1, \mathbf{P}_2, \mathbf{P}_5) - (^{\theta}c_1, {}^{\theta}c_2, {}^{\theta}c_5)$$

$$= \left(0,\, \frac{5+5\theta}{2},\, 0\right)\begin{bmatrix} 1 & 2 & 0 \\ 3 & 0 & 1 \\ 1 & 4 & 0 \end{bmatrix} - (3 - 6\theta,\, 2 - 2\theta,\, 0)$$

$$= \left(\frac{9+27\theta}{2},\, -2 + 2\theta,\, \frac{5+5\theta}{2}\right).$$

This shows that $(^{\theta}z_j - {}^{\theta}c_j)$ is nonnegative for all $\theta \geq 1$, which is the same result as obtained using the automatic formula.

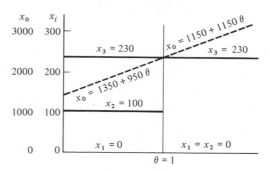

Figure 9–2

The behavior of the optimal solution for $\theta \geq 0$ can be summarized graphically as shown in Figure 9–2. Notice that for $0 \leq \theta \leq 1$, the basic variables are given by $\mathbf{X}_B = (x_2, x_3, x_6)^T$. Thus,

$$x_0 = {}^{\theta}\mathbf{C}_B{}^{0}\mathbf{B}^{-1}\mathbf{P}_0$$

$$= {}^{\theta}\mathbf{C}_B{}^{0}\mathbf{X}_B$$

$$= (2 - 2\theta,\, 5 + 5\theta,\, 0)\begin{bmatrix} 100 \\ 230 \\ 20 \end{bmatrix}$$

$$= (1350 + 950\theta).$$

For $\theta \geq 1$, $\mathbf{X}_B = (x_4, x_3, x_6)^T$, hence

$$x_0 = (0, 5 + 5\theta, 0) \begin{bmatrix} 200 \\ 230 \\ 420 \end{bmatrix} = (1150 + 1150\theta).$$

It is interesting to notice that because x_1 and x_2 are having decreasing profit coefficients with θ, the two variables are soon discarded from the solution. The variable x_3, on the other hand, stays in the solution since its profit coefficient increases with θ. ◄

§ 9·3
Linear Variations in the P_0-vector

The parameterized vector ${}^\theta\mathbf{P}_0$ is defined by

$$^\theta\mathbf{P}_0 = {}^0\mathbf{P}_0 + \theta\mathbf{b},$$

where ${}^0\mathbf{P}_0$ and $\mathbf{b}$ are two vectors with known elements.

The first step is to solve the problem for $\theta = 0$. If ${}^0\mathbf{X}_B$ is the corresponding optimal solution, then

$$^0\mathbf{X}_B = {}^0\mathbf{B}^{-1}\,{}^0\mathbf{P}_0 \geq 0.$$

From the theory in Chapter 8 it follows that variations in the $\mathbf{P}_0$-vector can only affect the feasibility of the problem. Consequently, only the feasibility of the problem needs to be checked.

The procedure for determining the critical values of θ is initiated by using the solution ${}^0\mathbf{X}_B$ obtained at $\theta = 0$. Let α and β be two *consecutive* critical values of θ, $(\alpha \leq \beta)$, where it is assumed that the basic solution at $\theta = \alpha$ is already known and is given by ${}^\alpha\mathbf{X}_B$. Thus, the next critical value $\theta = \beta$ is determined as follows.

The basic solution ${}^\alpha\mathbf{X}_B$ will remain feasible for some range of $\theta \geq \alpha$ as long as the condition ${}^\alpha\mathbf{B}^{-1}\,{}^\theta\mathbf{P}_0 \geq 0$ is satisfied. Now,

$$^\alpha\mathbf{B}^{-1}\,{}^\theta\mathbf{P}_0 = {}^\alpha\mathbf{B}^{-1}({}^0\mathbf{P}_0 + \alpha\mathbf{b}) + (\theta - \alpha)\,{}^\alpha\mathbf{B}^{-1}\mathbf{b}$$

$$= {}^\alpha\mathbf{B}^{-1}\,{}^\alpha\mathbf{P}_0 + (\theta - \alpha)\,{}^\alpha\mathbf{B}^{-1}\mathbf{b}.$$

Let $({}^\alpha\mathbf{B}^{-1}\,{}^\alpha\mathbf{P}_0)_i$ and $({}^\alpha\mathbf{B}^{-1}\mathbf{b})_i$ be the ith elements of ${}^\alpha\mathbf{B}^{-1}\,{}^\alpha\mathbf{P}_0$ and ${}^\alpha\mathbf{B}^{-1}\mathbf{b}$, respectively. Since ${}^\alpha\mathbf{B}^{-1}\,{}^\alpha\mathbf{P}_0 \geq 0$, it follows from the condition ${}^\alpha\mathbf{B}^{-1}\,{}^\theta\mathbf{P}_0 \geq 0$ that

1. If $({}^\alpha\mathbf{B}^{-1}\mathbf{b})_i \geq 0$, for all i, then ${}^\alpha\mathbf{X}_B$ remains feasible for all $\theta \geq \alpha$.
2. If $({}^\alpha\mathbf{B}^{-1}\mathbf{b})_i < 0$, for at least on i, there exists a critical value, $\theta = \beta$, which is given by

$$\beta = \alpha + \min_i \left[\frac{-({}^\alpha\mathbf{B}^{-1}\mathbf{P}_0)_i}{({}^\alpha\mathbf{B}^{-1}\mathbf{b})_i} \,\middle|\, ({}^\alpha\mathbf{B}^{-1}\mathbf{b})_i < 0 \right].$$

Thus, for $\theta > \beta$, $^{\alpha}\mathbf{X}_B$ will no longer be feasible. At $\theta = \beta$, an alternative basic solution, $^{\beta}\mathbf{X}_B$, can be obtained by using the *dual* simplex method. Since the variable corresponding to β above will be the first to go infeasible, it must be selected as the leaving variable at $\theta = \beta$.

The above procedure is now repeated on $^{\beta}\mathbf{X}_B$ to obtain a new critical value of θ; that is, the range of θ over which $^{\beta}\mathbf{X}_B$ remains feasible.

▶ **Example 9·3-1**

Consider the same problem of Example 9·2-1 except that $\mathbf{C}$ is not parameterized. Instead, $\mathbf{P}_0$ is parameterized as shown below.

$$\text{Maximize} \quad x_0 = 3x_1 + 2x_2 + 5x_3,$$

subject to

$$x_1 + 2x_2 + x_3 \le 430 + 100\theta,$$

$$3x_1 + 2x_3 \le 460 - 200\theta,$$

$$x_1 + 4x_2 \le 420 + 400\theta,$$

with all x_j being nonnegative.

For $\theta = 0$, the optimal solution is the same as in Example 9·2-1. For $\theta > 0$,

$$^{\theta}\mathbf{P}_0 = \begin{bmatrix} 430 \\ 460 \\ 420 \end{bmatrix} + \theta \begin{bmatrix} 100 \\ -200 \\ 400 \end{bmatrix}.$$

Thus,

$$^{\theta}\mathbf{B}^{-1}\mathbf{b} = \begin{bmatrix} 1/2 & -1/4 & 0 \\ 0 & 1/2 & 0 \\ -2 & 1 & 1 \end{bmatrix} \begin{bmatrix} 100 \\ -200 \\ 400 \end{bmatrix} = \begin{bmatrix} 100 \\ -100 \\ 0 \end{bmatrix}.$$

Since from the optimal tableau at $\theta = 0$,

$$^{0}\mathbf{X}_B = {}^{0}\mathbf{B}^{-1}\,{}^{0}\mathbf{P}_0 = \begin{bmatrix} 100 \\ 230 \\ 20 \end{bmatrix},$$

then

$$\theta' = \frac{-230}{-100} = 2.3.$$

This means that $^{0}\mathbf{X}_B = (x_2, x_3, x_6)^T$ remains basic and feasible for $0 \le \theta \le \theta'$. At $\theta = \theta'$,

$$^{\theta'}\mathbf{P}_0 = \begin{bmatrix} 430 \\ 460 \\ 420 \end{bmatrix} + 2.3 \begin{bmatrix} 100 \\ -200 \\ 400 \end{bmatrix} = \begin{bmatrix} 660 \\ 0 \\ 1340 \end{bmatrix},$$

and the corresponding basic solution is given by

$$\theta' X_B = {}^0B^{-1}\,\theta' P_0 = \begin{bmatrix} 330 \\ 0 \\ 20 \end{bmatrix}.$$

The table corresponding to this solution is then given by

Basic	x_0	x_1	x_2	x_3	x_4	x_5	x_6	Solution
x_0	①	4	0	0	1	2	0	1320
x_2	0	$-1/4$	①	0	1/2	$-1/4$	0	330
x_3	0	3/2	0	①	0	1/2	0	0
x_6	0	2	0	0	-2	①	1	20

Applying the dual simplex method, the variable x_3 should leave the solution since its value becomes negative for $\theta > \theta'$. It is noted, however, that all the constraints coefficients corresponding to the second constraint are non-negative. This means that the problem has no feasible solution for $\theta > \theta'$ and consequently the analysis should stop at this point. The above results can be summarized graphically as shown in Figure 9-3. ◀

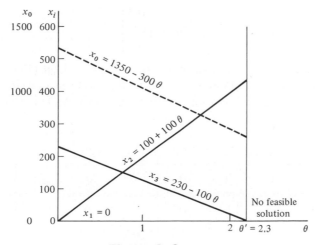

Figure 9–3

▶ **Example 9·3-2**

To illustrate the case where there is a feasible solution beyond θ', suppose in Example 9·3-1 that $^{\theta}P_0$ is given by

$$^{\theta}P_0 = \begin{bmatrix} 430 \\ 460 \\ 420 \end{bmatrix} + \theta \begin{bmatrix} 1 \\ -4 \\ -4 \end{bmatrix}.$$

Then at $\theta = 0$, the optimal solution of Example 9·3-1 still holds.

To determine the first critical value, θ', consider,

$$^{0}B^{-1}b = \begin{bmatrix} 1/2 & -1/4 & 0 \\ 0 & 1/2 & 0 \\ -2 & 1 & 1 \end{bmatrix} \begin{bmatrix} 1 \\ -4 \\ -4 \end{bmatrix} = \begin{bmatrix} 3/2 \\ -2 \\ -10 \end{bmatrix},$$

$$^{0}B^{-1}\,{}^{\theta}P_0 = \begin{bmatrix} 100 \\ 230 \\ 20 \end{bmatrix}.$$

Thus,

$$\theta' = \min\left(-, \frac{-230}{-2}, \frac{-20}{-10}\right) = 2,$$

which corresponds to the basic variable x_6. Consequently, the solution

$$\begin{bmatrix} x_2 \\ x_3 \\ x_6 \end{bmatrix} = {}^{0}B^{-1}({}^{\theta}P_0 + \theta b) = \begin{bmatrix} 100 \\ 230 \\ 20 \end{bmatrix} + \theta \begin{bmatrix} 3/2 \\ -2 \\ -10 \end{bmatrix}$$

will remain basic for $0 \le \theta \le \theta'$.

At $\theta = \theta'$,

$$^{\theta'}X_B = \begin{bmatrix} 103 \\ 226 \\ 0 \end{bmatrix}.$$

This will represent the new right-hand side of the optimal tableau at $\theta = 0$. Thus applying the dual simplex method to the modified tableau, x_4 and x_6 become the entering and leaving variables, respectively. This yields the new tableau,

Basic	x_0	x_1	x_2	x_3	x_4	x_5	x_6	Solution
x_0	(1)	5	0	0	0	5/2	1/2	1336
x_2	0	1/4	(1)	0	0	0	1/4	103
x_3	0	3/2	0	(1)	0	1/2	0	226
x_4	0	-1	0	0	(1)	-1/2	-1/2	0

Next, θ'' is determined. Consider

$$^{\theta'}\mathbf{B}^{-1\,\theta'}\mathbf{P}_0 = {}^{\theta'}\mathbf{X}_B = \begin{bmatrix} 103 \\ 226 \\ 0 \end{bmatrix}$$

and

$$^{\theta'}\mathbf{B}^{-1}\mathbf{b} = \begin{bmatrix} 0 & 0 & 1/4 \\ 0 & 1/2 & 0 \\ 1 & -1/2 & -1/2 \end{bmatrix} \begin{bmatrix} 1 \\ -4 \\ -4 \end{bmatrix} = \begin{bmatrix} -1 \\ -2 \\ 5 \end{bmatrix}.$$

Hence,

$$\theta'' = \theta' + \min\left[\frac{-103}{-1}, \frac{-226}{-2}, \frac{\quad}{\quad} \right] = 2 + 103 = 105.$$

This means that for $\theta' \le \theta \le \theta''$, the solution below remains feasible. That is,

$$\begin{bmatrix} x_2 \\ x_3 \\ x_4 \end{bmatrix} = {}^{\theta'}\mathbf{B}^{-1\,\theta'}\mathbf{P}_0 + (\theta - \theta')^{\theta'}\mathbf{B}^{-1}\mathbf{b}$$

$$= \begin{bmatrix} 103 \\ 226 \\ 0 \end{bmatrix} + (\theta - \theta')\begin{bmatrix} -1 \\ -2 \\ 5 \end{bmatrix}$$

$$= \begin{bmatrix} 103 \\ 226 \\ 0 \end{bmatrix} + (\theta - 2)\begin{bmatrix} -1 \\ -2 \\ 5 \end{bmatrix} = \begin{bmatrix} 105 \\ 230 \\ -10 \end{bmatrix} + \theta\begin{bmatrix} -1 \\ -2 \\ 5 \end{bmatrix}.$$

At $\theta = \theta''$,

$$^{\theta''}\mathbf{X}_B = \begin{pmatrix} 0 \\ 20 \\ 515 \end{pmatrix}.$$

represents the new right-hand side for the last tableau. Applying the dual simplex method, the variable x_2 leaves the solution. However, since all the constraint coefficients (α^j) corresponding to the first constraint are non-negative, the problem has no feasible solution for $\theta > \theta''$.

Here also, as in Section 9·2, the formulas given for computing the critical values are mainly suitable for automatic calculations. The same results can be obtained using the original condition $\mathbf{B}^{-1\,\theta}\mathbf{P}_0 \ge 0$. In this case, all the critical values are directly measured from the zero datum.

To illustrate this procedure, consider the determination of θ'' in this example.

$$^{\theta}\mathbf{B}^{-1\,\theta}\mathbf{P}_0 = \begin{bmatrix} 0 & 0 & 1/4 \\ 0 & 1/2 & 0 \\ 1 & -1/2 & -1/2 \end{bmatrix}\begin{bmatrix} 430 + \theta \\ 460 - 4\theta \\ 420 - 4\theta \end{bmatrix} = \begin{bmatrix} 105 - \theta \\ 230 - 2\theta \\ -10 + 5\theta \end{bmatrix} \ge \begin{bmatrix} 0 \\ 0 \\ 0 \end{bmatrix}$$

Hence,

$$\theta'' = \min\left[\frac{105}{1}, \frac{230}{2}, \frac{}{}\right] = 105,$$

as obtained previously. ◄

§ 9·4
Linear Variations in the Nonbasic Vector P_j of A

The analysis in this section is restricted to the study of variations in non-basic vectors only. The problem becomes complicated when $\mathbf{P}_j$ is a basic vector since in this case the basis $\mathbf{B}$ (and hence its inverse) changes. This means that $\mathbf{B}$ may no longer be a basis, or if a basis, it may cease to be optimal.

Let the parameterized nonbasic vector be given by

$$^\theta\mathbf{P}_j = {}^0\mathbf{P}_j + \theta\mathbf{b}_j.$$

The procedure again is to solve the problem for $\theta = 0$. It is seen by Property III, Section 8·8, that a change in a nonbasic vector, $\mathbf{P}_j$, can only affect $(z_j - c_j)$ for this vector. Consequently one needs to check the optimality of the vector $\mathbf{P}_j$ only.

It is important to notice that, unlike the previous cases in Sections 9·2 and 9·3, the analysis for the present case cannot be extended to cover the entire range of θ. This follows since after the first critical value, θ', is reached (assuming it is finite), the vector $\mathbf{P}_j$ will become basic for $\theta > \theta'$ and thus not susceptible to the present analysis. Consequently, the following analysis will only show how θ' is determined.

Consider $^0\mathbf{X}_B$, the optimal basic solution at $\theta = 0$. This solution will remain basic as long as

$$^\theta z_j - c_j = \mathbf{C}_B{}^0\mathbf{B}^{-1}{}^\theta\mathbf{P}_j - c_j$$

remains nonnegative. (Notice that $\mathbf{C}$ is not parameterized.) This means that

$$^\theta z_j - c_j = \mathbf{C}_B{}^0\mathbf{B}^{-1}({}^0\mathbf{P}_j + \theta\mathbf{b}_j) - c_j \geq 0,$$

or

$$\theta(\mathbf{C}_B{}^0\mathbf{B}^{-1}\mathbf{b}_j) \geq -(\mathbf{C}_B{}^0\mathbf{B}^{-1}{}^0\mathbf{P}_j - c_j).$$

Since $^0z_j - c_j = (\mathbf{C}_B{}^0\mathbf{B}^{-1}{}^0\mathbf{P}_j - c_j)$ is nonnegative due to the fact that the solution at $\theta = 0$ is optimal, then

1. If $\mathbf{C}_B{}^0\mathbf{B}^{-1}\mathbf{b}_j \geq 0$, for all j, then $^0\mathbf{X}_B$ remains optimal for all $\theta \geq 0$.
2. If $\mathbf{C}_B{}^0\mathbf{B}^{-1}\mathbf{b}_j < 0$, for at least one j, there exists the critical value,

$$\theta' = \min_j\left[\frac{-({}^0z_j - c_j)}{\mathbf{C}_B{}^0\mathbf{B}^{-1}\mathbf{b}_j}\,\middle|\,\mathbf{C}_B{}^0\mathbf{B}^{-1}\mathbf{b}_j < 0\right],$$

above which $^0\mathbf{X}_B$ ceases to be optimal. At $\theta = \theta'$, the problem has an altern-ative optimal solution which may be obtained by introducing the nonbasic vector $\mathbf{P}_j$ corresponding to θ' into the solution.

▶ **Example 9·4-1**

Consider the following problem,

$$\text{maximize} \quad x_0 = 3x_1 + 2x_2 + 5x_3,$$

subject to

$$(1 + \theta)x_1 + 2x_2 + \quad x_3 \leq 430,$$
$$(3 - \theta)x_1 \quad\quad\quad + 2x_3 \leq 460,$$
$$x_1 + 4x_2 \quad\quad\quad \leq 420,$$

with all x_j being nonnegative.

At $\theta = 0$, the optimal is the same as in Example 9·2-1. For $\theta > 0$,

$$(^\theta z_1 - c_1) = (1, 2, 0) \begin{bmatrix} 1 + \theta \\ 3 - \theta \\ 1 \end{bmatrix} - 3 \geq 0$$

or

$$4 - \theta \geq 0,$$

hence,

$$\theta' = 4. \quad ◄$$

§ 9·5
Simultaneous Linear Variations in $\mathbf{P}_0$, $\mathbf{C}$, and $\mathbf{P}_j$

The procedures introduced in the above three sections can be combined to study the effect of *simultaneous* variations in $\mathbf{P}_0$, $\mathbf{C}$, and $\mathbf{P}_j$. It is still assumed that these variations are linear functions of the same parameter θ. In such cases there will be two types of critical values for θ. The first type, θ_1, controls the optimality of the problem while the second type, θ_2, controls its feasibility. One would thus select

$$\theta_3 = \min\{\theta_1, \theta_2\}$$

as the critical value satisfying both the optimality and the feasibility conditions of the problem. The new solution will then be obtained using the regular simplex method if $\theta_3 = \theta_1$ or the dual simplex method if $\theta_3 = \theta_2$.[1] The

---

[1] If $\theta_1 = \theta_2 \ (= \theta_3)$, the problem becomes both nonoptimal and infeasible at the same time. In such a case, a technique, called the *primal-dual algorithm*, must be used. This is mainly developed to treat infeasible nonoptimal problems. See Hadley [1], (257–266), for a complete description of this technique.

process then continues until the entire range $\theta \geq 0$ is covered. It must be noted, however, that the variations in $\mathbf{P}_j$ are limited to the nonbasic vectors only. As indicated in Section 9·4, as soon as $\mathbf{P}_j$ becomes basic, the given analysis will no longer be applicable.

The parametric programming problem can also be extended to the general case where the variations in $\mathbf{P}_0$, $\mathbf{C}$, and $\mathbf{P}_j$ occur with different linear parameters (α, β, and γ_j, say). Although the same theory still holds, the problem becomes much more difficult since the search for the critical values will occur in two or more dimensions. This indicates that such type of problem does not lend itself neatly to mathematical analysis.

SELECTED REFERENCES

1. HADLEY, G., *Linear Programming*, Reading, Massachusetts: Addison-Wesley, 1962.
2. SIMMONARD, M., *Linear Programming*, translated by W. Jewell, Englewood Cliffs, N.J.: Prentice-Hall, 1966.

PROBLEMS

☐ **9-1**   Solve Example 9·2-1 assuming that the objective function is given by

$$x_0 = (3 + 3\theta)x_1 + 2x_2 + (5 - 6\theta)x_3,$$

where θ is a nonnegative parameter.

☐ **9-2**   Solve Example 9·3-1 assuming that the right-hand side of the constraints is given by

$$ {}^{\theta}\mathbf{P}_0 = \begin{bmatrix} 430 \\ 460 \\ 420 \end{bmatrix} + \theta \begin{bmatrix} 500 \\ 100 \\ -200 \end{bmatrix}, $$

where θ is a nonnegative parameter.

☐ **9-3**   Suppose that the parameterization of x_0 and $\mathbf{P}_0$ given in Problems 9-1 and 9-2 are considered simultaneously. Study the variations in the optimal solution with θ.

☐ **9-4**   Consider Example 3·5-1 (Chapter 3). Suppose that the objective function becomes:

$$\text{minimize} \quad x_0 = (2 - \theta)x_1 + (1 - 3\theta)x_2 + (3 - \theta)x_3,$$

where x_3 is an additional variable with its constraint coefficients being given in the original problem by 1, 2, and 5, respectively. Study the variations in the optimal solution with θ. Assume $\theta \geq 0$.

□ **9-5** In Problem 9-4 suppose instead that the right-hand side of the constraints is given by,

$$^{\theta}\mathbf{P}_0 = \begin{bmatrix} 3 \\ 6 \\ 3 \end{bmatrix} + \theta \begin{bmatrix} 3 \\ 2 \\ 4 \end{bmatrix}.$$

Study the variation in the optimal solution with θ. Assume $\theta \geq 0$.

□ **9-6** Suppose that the parameterization of x_0 and $\mathbf{P}_0$ as given in Problems 9-4 and 9-5 are considered simultaneously. Study the variation in the optimal solution with the parameter θ.

□ **9-7** Consider the problem:

maximize $x_0 = (2 + \theta)x_1 + (4 - \theta)x_2 + (4 - 2\theta)x_3 - (3 - 3\theta)x_4$,

subject to

$$x_1 + x_2 + x_3 \quad\quad = 4 - \theta,$$
$$2x_1 + 4x_2 \quad\quad + x_4 = 8 - \theta,$$
$$x_1, x_2, x_3, x_4 \geq 0.$$

where θ is a nonnegative parameter. Obtain the optimal solution for $\theta = 0$ using x_3 and x_4 for the starting basic solution. Then study the variation of the optimal solution with θ.

□ **9-8** The following linear programming problem

maximize $x_0 = 3x_1 + 6x_2$,

subject to

$$x_1 \quad\quad \leq 4,$$
$$3x_1 + 2x_2 \leq 18,$$
$$x_1, x_2 \geq 0,$$

has the solution,

Basic	x_0	x_1	x_2	x_3	x_4	Solution
x_0	①	6	0	0	3	54
x_3	0	1	0	①	0	4
x_2	0	3/2	①	0	1/2	9

where x_3 and x_4 are slack variables.

Let

$$^\theta \mathbf{P}_0 = \begin{bmatrix} 4 \\ 18 \end{bmatrix} + \theta \begin{bmatrix} 8 \\ -24 \end{bmatrix},$$

$$^\theta \mathbf{P}_1 = \begin{bmatrix} 1 \\ 3 \end{bmatrix} + \theta \begin{bmatrix} 2 \\ -3 \end{bmatrix},$$

and

$$^\theta c_2 = 6 - 4\theta,$$

while c_1 and $\mathbf{P}_2$ remain as given in the original problem.

If the above parametric functions are introduced *simultaneously*, find the range of θ for which the above solution remains basic, feasible, and optimal. Assume $\theta \geq 0$.

☐ **9-9** In Problem 9-8, suppose

$$x_0 = (3 + \alpha)x_1 + (6 - \alpha)x_2$$

and

$$^\beta \mathbf{P}_1 = \begin{bmatrix} 1 + \beta \\ 3 - \beta \end{bmatrix},$$

while $\mathbf{P}_0$ remains unparameterized, where α and β are real parameters. Find the relationship between α and β which will always keep the solution in Problem 9-8 optimal.

☐ **9-10** Consider the unparameterized version of Problem 9-8. Suppose that the objective function and the right-hand side vary with the parameter θ according to

$$x_0 = (3 + \theta - \theta^2)x_1 + (6 - 2\theta - \theta^2)x_2,$$

$$^\theta \mathbf{P}_0 = \begin{bmatrix} 4 + \theta^2 \\ 18 - 2\theta^2 \end{bmatrix}.$$

Study the variation in the optimal solution with the parameter $\theta(\theta \geq 0)$. What are the difficulties involved in dealing with the nonlinear functions?

☐ **9-11** Consider the following problem.

$$\text{Maximize} \quad x_0 = (4 - 10\theta)x_1 + (8 - 4\theta)x_2,$$

subject to

$$x_1 + x_2 \leq 4,$$

$$2x_1 + x_2 \leq 3 - \theta,$$

$$x_1, x_2 \geq 0.$$

Study the variations in the optimal solution with the parameter θ, where $-\infty < \theta < \infty$. Notice that θ may assume negative values in this case.

□ **9-12** The analysis in this chapter has always assumed that the optimal solution of the problem at $\theta = 0$ is obtained using the regular simplex method. In some problems, however, it may be more convenient to obtain such an optimal solution using the dual simplex method of Section 4·5. Indicate how parametric analysis can be carried out in this case. (Hint: Use the results of Problem 8-16.)

□ **9-13** In the problem introduced in Section 4·5 (Dual Simplex Method), suppose that the objective function is given by

$$x_0 = (2 + \theta)x_1 + (1 + 4\theta)x_2 \,.$$

Study the variation the optimal solution with $\theta, \theta \geq 0$.

□ **9-14** In Problem 9-13, suppose instead that the right-hand side of the constraints in given by

$$^{\theta}\mathbf{P}_0 = \begin{bmatrix} 3 + 2\theta \\ 6 - \theta \\ 3 - 4\theta \end{bmatrix}.$$

Study the variation in the optimal solution with $\theta, \theta \geq 0$.

□ **9-15** The parametric programming analysis in this chapter assumes that an optimal basic solution exists at $\theta = 0$. Show that the selection of $\theta = 0$ as a datum is arbitrary and that any datum $\theta = \theta_0$ at which a basic optimal solution exists can be used to initiate the parametric analysis.

CHAPTER 10

Integer Linear Programming

§ 10·1
Introduction

There exists a class of linear programming problems where all or some of the variables in the optimal solution are restricted to nonnegative integer values. These problems are referred to as "all-integer" or "mixed" problems depending, respectively, on whether all or some of the variables are constrained to integral values.

Although the regular simplex method may yield an integer solution to a special class of linear programming problems (such as the transportation problem), there is actually no guarantee that such a condition will be satisfied in general. In the meantime, it is generally inaccurate to obtain an integer optimal solution by rounding the optimal values resulting from applying the simplex method to the problem. In fact, in some cases the deviation from the "exact" optimal integer values (as a result of rounding) may become large enough to yield an infeasible solution.

The need for a systematic procedure which will identify the optimal *integer* solution was recognized by several researchers in the field. This, however, remained only an idea until 1958 when R. E. Gomory developed the cutting plane algorithms for treating both the "all-integer" and the "mixed" problems. These alogrithms are proved to converge to the optimal integer solution in a finite number of iterations. Although the cutting plane algorithm makes use of the familiar dual simplex method; it mainly introduces the clever idea of constructing "secondary" constraints which, when added to the optimum (noninteger) solution, will effectively "cut" (hence the name "cutting plane") the solution space toward the required result. Successive application of these constraints should gradually force the noninteger optimum solution toward the desired "all-integer" or "mixed" optimal solutions.

Another important approach for solving both the all-integer and the mixed problems has originated from the straightforward idea of enumerating all feasible integer solutions. This has given rise to the so-called branch-and-bound technique. In this respect, A. H. Land and A. G. Doig (1960) have developed a general algorithm for solving both all-integer and mixed linear programming problems. Egon Balas (1965) has also introduced an interesting enumerative algorithm for linear programming problems with binary (zero or one) variables only.

Although several algorithms have been developed for the integer programming problem, the presentation in this chapter will be limited to the models indicated above. Section 10·2 introduces Gomory's cutting plane algorithms for both the all-integer and the mixed problems. Section 10·3 develops the Land-Doig algorithms. Finally, the Balas algorithm is presented in Section 10·4. Section 10·5 then presents some applications of integer programming.

§ 10·2
Gomory's Cutting Plane Algorithms

The concept of the cutting plane will first be illustrated by an example. Consider the linear programming problem:

$$\text{maximize} \quad x_0 = 7x_1 + 9x_2,$$

subject to

$$-x_1 + 3x_2 \leq 6,$$

$$7x_1 + x_2 \leq 35,$$

$$x_1 \geq 0, \quad x_2 \geq 0, \quad \text{and integers.}$$

The optimal solution (ignoring the integrality condition) is shown graphically in Figure 10–1. This is given by $x_0 = 63$, $x_1 = 4\frac{1}{2}$ and $x_2 = 3\frac{1}{2}$ which is noninteger.

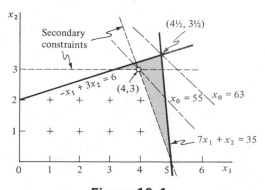

Figure 10–1

Consider first the case of all-integer optimal solution. The idea is to change the convex set of the solution space so that the appropriate extreme point becomes an all-integer point. Such changes in the boundaries of the solution space should result still in a convex set. Also this change should be made without "slicing off" *any* of the feasible *integer* solutions of the original problem. Figure 10–1 shows how two (arbitrarily-selected) secondary constraints are added to the problem with the new extreme point (4,3) giving the all-integer optimal solution. Notice that the area sliced off the original solution space (shaded area) does not include any integer values.

The idea of the cutting plane is applied to the mixed problem using the same principle. In this case, however, the new constraints are imposed such that only the constrained variables are forced toward integrality.

The main objective now is to show how these secondary constraints can be developed in a systematic way.

§ 10·2·1
The All-Integer Algorithm

A basic requirement for the application of this algorithm is that all the co-efficients and the right-hand side constant of each constraint must be in integer form. For example, the constraint,

$$x_1 + \frac{1}{3} x_2 \le \frac{13}{2},$$

must be transformed to

$$6x_1 + 2x_2 \le 39,$$

where no fractions are present. The latter is achieved by multiplying both sides of the original constraint by the least common multiple of the denominators. Clearly, such transformation does not affect the solution space of the problem.

The above requirement is imposed since, as will be shown later, the all-integer algorithm does not differentiate between the regular and slack variables of the problem in the sense that all of these variables must be integers. The presence of the fractional coefficients in the constraints thus may not allow the slack variables to be integers. The difficulty here is that the developed algorithm will not be applicable even though the problem may possess a feasible integer solution. (See Problem 10-1 for an illustration of this case.)

The details of the all-integer algorithm will be discussed now. First, the problem is solved as a regular linear programming problem; that is, disregarding the integrality condition. If the optimal solution happens to be all-integer, there is nothing more to be done. Otherwise, the secondary constraints which will force the solution toward an all-integer point are developed as follows. Let the final optimal tableau for the noninteger solution be given by

Basic	x_0	$x_1 \cdots x_i \cdots x_m$	$w_1 \cdots w_j \cdots w_n$	Solution
x_0	①	$0 \cdots 0 \cdots 0$	$\overline{c}_1 \cdots \overline{c}_j \cdots \overline{c}_n$	β_0
x_1	0	① $\cdots 0 \cdots 0$	$\alpha_1^1 \cdots \alpha_1^j \cdots \alpha_1^n$	β_1
⋮	⋮	⋮ ⋮ ⋮ ⋮	⋮ ⋮ ⋮	⋮
x_i	0	$0 \cdots$ ① $\cdots 0$	$\alpha_i^1 \cdots \alpha_i^j \cdots \alpha_i^n$	β_i
⋮	⋮	⋮ ⋮ ⋮ ⋮	⋮ ⋮ ⋮	⋮
x_m	0	$0 \cdots 0 \cdots$ ①	$\alpha_m^1 \cdots \alpha_m^j \cdots \alpha_m^n$	β_m

The variables x_i ($i = 1, 2, \ldots, m$) represent the basic variables while the variables w_j ($j = 1, 2, \ldots, n$) are the nonbasic variables. These variables have been arranged as such for convenience of presentation.

Consider the ith equation where the variable x_i assumes a noninteger value. This is given by,

$$x_i = \beta_i - \sum_{j=1}^{n} \alpha_i^j w_j, \ \beta_i \text{ is noninteger.}$$

Let

$$\beta_i = [\beta_i] + f_i,$$
$$\alpha_i^j = [\alpha_i^j] + f_{ij},$$

where $N = [a]$ is the largest integer such that $N \leq a$. It follows that $0 < f_i < 1$ and $0 \leq f_{ij} < 1$; that is, f_i is a strictly positive fraction while f_{ij} is a nonnegative fraction. For example,

a	$[a]$	$f = a - [a]$
$1\frac{1}{2}$	1	1/2
$-2\frac{1}{3}$	-3	2/3
-1	-1	0
$-2/5$	-1	3/5

Now, substituting in the equation for x_i, then

$$f_i - \sum_{j=1}^{n} f_{ij} w_j = x_i - [\beta_i] + \sum_{j=1}^{n} [\alpha_i^j] w_j.$$

Now, for all the variables x_i and w_j to be integer values, the right-hand side of the above equation must be an integer. This implies that the left-hand side

$$\left(f_i - \sum_{j=1}^{n} f_{ij} w_j \right)$$

must also be an integer. Since $0 < f_i < 1$ and $\sum_{j=1}^{n} f_{ij} w_j \geq 0$, it follows that the integrality condition is satisfied if,

$$\left(f_i - \sum_{j=1}^{n} f_{ij} w_j \right) \leq 0.$$

This is true because $(f_i - \sum_{j=1}^{n} f_{ij} w_j) \leq f_i < 1$. But since $(f_i - \sum_{j=1}^{n} f_{ij} w_j)$ is an integer, then it can be either a zero or a negative integer.

The last constraint can be put in the form

$$S_i = \sum_{j=1}^{n} f_{ij} w_j - f_i,$$

where S_i is a nonnegative slack variable which by definition must be an integer. This constraint equation defines the so-called Gomory cutting plane. From the last tableau, $w_j = 0$ and thus $S_i = -f_i$ which is infeasible. This means that the new constraint is not satisfied by the given solution. The dual simplex method must then be used to clear this infeasibility. This in effect is equivalent to cutting off the solution space toward the optimal integer solution.

The new tableau after adding the Gomory constraint will thus become

Basic	x_0	x_1 $\cdots$ x_i $\cdots$ x_m	w_1 $\cdots$ w_j $\cdots$ w_n	S_i	Solution
x_0	①	0 $\cdots$ 0 $\cdots$ 0	$\overline{c}_1$ $\cdots$ $\overline{c}_j$ $\cdots$ $\overline{c}_n$	0	β_0
x_1	0	① $\cdots$ 0 $\cdots$ 0	α_1^1 $\cdots$ α_1^j $\cdots$ α_1^n	0	β_1
$\vdots$	$\vdots$	$\vdots$ $\quad$ $\vdots$ $\quad$ $\vdots$	$\vdots$ $\quad$ $\vdots$ $\quad$ $\vdots$	$\vdots$	$\vdots$
x_i	0	0 $\cdots$ ① $\cdots$ 0	α_i^1 $\cdots$ α_i^j $\cdots$ α_i^n	0	β_i
$\vdots$	$\vdots$	$\vdots$ $\quad$ $\vdots$ $\quad$ $\vdots$	$\vdots$ $\quad$ $\vdots$ $\quad$ $\vdots$	$\vdots$	$\vdots$
x_m	0	0 $\cdots$ 0 $\cdots$ ①	α_m^1 $\cdots$ α_m^j $\cdots$ α_m^n	0	β_m
S_i	0	0 $\cdots$ 0 $\cdots$ 0	$-f_{i1} \cdots -f_{ij} \cdots -f_{in}$ ①		$-f_i$

If the new solution (after applying the dual simplex method) is all-integer, the process ends. Otherwise, a new Gomory's constraint is constructed from the *resulting* tableau and the dual simplex method is used again to clear the infeasibility. This procedure is repeated as necessary until an all-integer solution is achieved. However, if at any iteration, the dual simplex algorithm indicates that no feasible solution exists, then the problem has no feasible *integer* solution.

The above algorithm might indicate, at the first thought, that the number of additional constraints can become very large especially if the solution converges slowly. This is not true. In fact, the total number of constraints in the *augmented* problem does not exceed the number of variables in the original problem; that is, $m + n$. This follows since if the augmented problem includes more than $n + m$ constraints, then one or more of the slack variables, S_i, associated with the additional constraints must become basic. This shows that the equation associated with such a basic S_i must be dropped from the tableau indicating that the corresponding constraint is redundant.

The given algorithm has two basic disadvantages: (1) The round-off errors that evolve in automatic calculations may yield the wrong optimal integer solution. Although this can be overcome by separately storing the numerators and the denominators of the different fractions (hence avoiding decimal calculations), the sizes of the associated numbers may exceed the available capacity of the computer. (2) The solution of the problem remains infeasible in the sense that no *integer* solution can be obtained until the optimal integer solution is reached. This means that there will be no "good" integer solution in store if the calculations are stopped prematurely prior to the attainment of the optimal (integer) solution.

The first difficulty was overcome by the development of an "all-integer integer" algorithm also due to Gomory.[1] The algorithm starts with an initial all-integer tableau (that is, all the coefficients are integers) suitable for the application of the dual simplex algorithm. A special additional constraint is then constructed such that its addition to the tableau will preserve the integrality of all the coefficients. Another advantage here is that the additional constraint is constructed such that it can be abandoned after it is used. The fact that the solution remains infeasible until the integer optimal solution is reached still presents a disadvantage.

The second difficulty is receiving special attention. Encouraging results have been reported by F. Glover for the development of a cutting plane algorithm which starts integer and feasible but nonoptimal.[2] The iterations continue to be feasible and integral until the optimum solution is reached. In this respect, this algorithm is primal-feasible as compared with Gomory's algorithms which are dual-feasible.

▶ **Example 10·2-1**

Consider the same problem which was solved graphically at the beginning of Section 10·2. The optimal noninteger tableau is given by

Basic	x_0	x_1	x_2	x_3	x_4	Solution
x_0	①	0	0	28/11	15/11	63
x_2	0	0	①	7/22	1/22	$3\frac{1}{2}$
x_1	0	①	0	$-1/22$	3/22	$4\frac{1}{2}$

[1] R. E. Gomory, "All-Integer Integer Programming Algorithm," in Muth and Thompson (Eds.), *Industrial Scheduling*, Prentice-Hall, Englewood Cliffs, N.J., 1963, Chapter 13.

[2] F. Glover, "A New Foundation for a Simplified Primal Integer Programming Algorithm," *Operations Research*, Vol. 16, 1968, pp. 727–740.

Since this solution is noninteger, a Gomory constraint must be added to the tableau. Generally, any of the constraint equations corresponding to a noninteger solution can be selected to generate the said constraint. However, as a rule of thumb, it is preferable to generate it from the equation corresponding to $\max_i(f_i)$. Thus, in the above problem, since both equations have the same value of f_i, that is, $f_1 = f_2 = \frac{1}{2}$, either one of the two equations is used. Consider the x_2-equation above. This gives

$$x_2 + \frac{7}{22}x_3 + \frac{1}{22}x_4 = 3\tfrac{1}{2}$$

or

$$x_2 + \left(0 + \frac{7}{22}\right)x_3 + \left(0 + \frac{1}{22}\right)x_4 = \left(3 + \frac{1}{2}\right).$$

Hence, the corresponding Gomory constraint is given by

$$S_1 - \frac{7}{22}x_3 - \frac{1}{22}x_4 = -\frac{1}{2}.$$

This gives the new tableau

Basic	x_0	x_1	x_2	x_3	x_4	S_1	R.H.S.
x_0	①	0	0	28/11	15/11	0	63
x_2	0	0	①	7/22	1/22	0	$3\tfrac{1}{2}$
x_1	0	①	0	−1/22	3/22	0	$4\tfrac{1}{2}$
S_1	0	0	0	−7/22	−1/22	①	−1/2

Applying the dual simplex method, this yields,

Basic	x_0	x_1	x_2	x_3	x_4	S_1	Solution
x_0	①	0	0	0	1	8	59
x_2	0	0	①	0	0	1	3
x_1	0	①	0	0	1/7	−1/7	$4\tfrac{4}{7}$
x_3	0	0	0	①	1/7	−22/7	$1\tfrac{4}{7}$

The solution is still noninteger. A new Gomory constraint is thus constructed. Selecting the x_1-equation to generate the cutting plane, then

$$x_1 + \left(0 + \frac{1}{7}\right)x_4 + \left(-1 + \frac{6}{7}\right)S_1 = \left(4 + \frac{4}{7}\right),$$

which gives

$$S_2 - \frac{1}{7}x_4 - \frac{6}{7}S_1 = -\frac{4}{7}.$$

Adding this constraint to the last iteration, one gets

Basic	x_0	x_1	x_2	x_3	x_4	S_1	S_2	R.H.S.
x_0	①	0	0	0	1	8	0	59
x_2	0	0	①	0	0	1	0	3
x_1	0	①	0	0	1/7	$-1/7$	0	$4\frac{4}{7}$
x_3	0	0	0	①	1/7	$-22/7$	0	$1\frac{4}{7}$
S_2	0	0	0	0	$-1/7$	$-6/7$	①	$-4/7$

The dual simplex method now yields

Basic	x_0	x_1	x_2	x_3	x_4	S_1	S_2	Solution
x_0	①	0	0	0	0	2	7	55
x_2	0	0	①	0	0	1	0	3
x_1	0	①	0	0	0	-1	1	4
x_3	0	0	0	①	0	-4	1	1
x_4	0	0	0	0	①	6	-7	4

which gives the optimal integer solution $x_0 = 55$, $x_1 = 4$, $x_2 = 3$.

The reader can verify graphically that the addition of the above Gomory constraints effectively "cut" the solution space as desired. Thus the first constraint,

$$S_1 - \frac{7}{22}x_3 - \frac{1}{22}x_4 = -\frac{1}{2},$$

can be expressed in terms of x_1 and x_2 only by using the appropriate substitution. This gives

$$S_1 + x_2 = 3,$$

or

$$x_2 \leq 3.$$

Similarly, for the second constraint,

$$S_2 - \frac{1}{7}x_4 - \frac{6}{7}S_1 = -\frac{4}{7},$$

the equivalent constraint in terms of x_1 and x_2 is

$$x_1 + x_2 \leq 7.$$

Plotting these two constraints on Figure 10–1, it is seen that the addition of these two constraints will result in the new (optimal) extreme point (4,3). ◄

§ 10·2·2
The Mixed Algorithm

Let x_k be a variable of the mixed problem which is constrained to integral values. Again, as in the all-integer case, consider the x_k-equation in the optimal (noninteger) solution. This is given by

$$x_k = \beta_k - \sum_{j=1}^{n} \alpha_k^j w_j,$$

$$= [\beta_k] + f_k - \sum_{j=1}^{n} \alpha_k^j w_j,$$

or

$$x_k - [\beta_k] = f_k - \sum_{j=1}^{n} \alpha_k^j w_j.$$

Notice that w_j may not be restricted to integral values in this case. Consequently, it is not possible to use the same constraint developed for the all-integer problem. It is now shown, however, that the development of the constraint for the mixed problem is based on the same idea presented in the preceding section.

Consider the above equation for x_k. Let

$J^+ =$ the set of subscripts, j, for which $\alpha_k^j \geq 0$
$J^- =$ the set of subscripts, j, for which $\alpha_k^j < 0$.

Then the equation for x_k can be written as

$$\sum_{j \in J^+} \alpha_k^j w_j + \sum_{j \in J^-} \alpha_k^j w_j = f_k + ([\beta_k] - x_k).$$

The right-hand side may be *either* nonnegative *or* negative. Consider the case, where

$$f_k + ([\beta_k] - x_k) \geq 0.$$

Since $0 < f_k < 1$, then in order for x_k to be integral,

$$f_k + ([\beta_k] - x_k) = f_k + p, \quad p = 0, \quad \text{or } 1, \quad \text{or } 2, \ldots.$$

It thus follows that,

$$\sum_{j \in J^+} \alpha_k^j w_j + \sum_{j \in J^-} \alpha_k^j w_j \geq f_k.$$

Since the second element in the left-hand side is nonpositive, an inequality which implies the above information can then be given by

$$\sum_{j \in J^+} \alpha_k^j w_j \geq f_k. \tag{i}$$

Next, consider the case where,

$$f_k + ([\beta_k] - x_k) < 0.$$

Since $0 < f_k < 1$, then for x_k to be an integer,

$$f_k + ([\beta_k] - x_k) = f_k - q, \quad q = 1, \text{ or } 2, \text{ or } 3, \ldots.$$

This means that

$$\sum_{j \in J^+} \alpha_k^j w_j + \sum_{j \in J^-} \alpha_k^j w_j \leq f_k - 1,$$

or

$$\sum_{j \in J^-} \alpha_k^j w_j \leq f_k - 1.$$

Consequently since $f_k - 1 < 0$, it follows that

$$\sum_{j \in J^-} \left(\frac{1}{f_k - 1} \right) \alpha_k^j w_j \geq 1. \tag{ii}$$

Noting that *either* (i) or (ii) above must be satisfied, and multiplying both sides of (ii) by f_k, one obtains

$$\sum_{j \in J^+} \alpha_k^j w_j + \left(\frac{f_k}{f_k - 1} \right) \sum_{j \in J^-} \alpha_k^j w_j \geq f_k$$

which implies both (i) and (ii).

Now, introducing the slack variable S_k, then

$$S_k - \left\{ \sum_{j \in J^+} \alpha_k^j w_j + \left(\frac{f_k}{f_k - 1} \right) \sum_{j \in J^-} \alpha_k^j w_j \right\} = -f_k.$$

This is the required Gomory constraint which must be satisfied before x_k becomes an integer. Since for the current optimal solution $w_j = 0$, for all j, then

$$S_k = -f_k.$$

Thus by adding this constraint to the last tableau and applying the dual simplex method, this constraint will cut effectively in the solution space. The procedure is repeated as necessary until the optimal mixed integer solution is obtained.

It is noted that stronger constraints can be constructed if more than one variable must be integral. In this case the Gomory constraint is given by

$$S_k = -f_k + \sum_{j=1}^{n} \lambda_j w_j,$$

where

$$\lambda_j = \begin{cases} \alpha_k^j, & \text{if } \alpha_k^j \geq 0 \text{ and } w_j \text{ is nonintegral.} \\[2mm] \dfrac{f_k}{f_k - 1} \alpha_k^j, & \text{if } \alpha_k^j < 0 \text{ and } w_j \text{ is nonintegral.} \\[2mm] f_{kj}, & \text{if } f_{kj} \leq f_k \text{ and } w_j \text{ is integral.} \\[2mm] \dfrac{f_k}{1 - f_k}(1 - f_{kj}), & \text{if } f_{kj} > f_k \text{ and } w_j \text{ is integral.} \end{cases}$$

The derivation of this formula is found in [7].

▶ **Example 10·2-2**

Consider the same problem given in Example 10·2-1. Suppose it is required that x_1 be restricted to nonnegative integer values. Thus, from the x_1-equation,

$$x_1 - \frac{1}{22} x_3 + \frac{3}{22} x_4 = \left(4 + \frac{1}{2}\right),$$

$$J^- = \{3\}, \quad J^+ = \{4\}, \quad f_1 = \tfrac{1}{2}.$$

Hence the cutting plane is given by

$$S_1 - \left\{ \frac{3}{22} x_4 + \left(\frac{\tfrac{1}{2}}{\tfrac{1}{2} - 1} \right)\left(-\frac{1}{22} \right) x_3 \right\} = -\frac{1}{2},$$

or

$$S_1 - \frac{1}{22} x_3 - \frac{3}{22} x_4 = -\frac{1}{2}.$$

Adding this to the last tableau, then

Basic	x_0	x_1	x_2	x_3	x_4	S_1	R.H.S.
x_0	①	0	0	28/11	15/11	0	63
x_2	0	0	①	7/22	1/22	0	$3\frac{1}{2}$
x_1	0	①	0	$-1/22$	3/22	0	$4\frac{1}{2}$
S_1	0	0	0	$-1/22$	$-3/22$	①	$-\frac{1}{2}$

Now, applying the dual simplex method, this yields,

Basic	x_0	x_1	x_2	x_3	x_4	S_1	Solution
x_0	①	0	0	23/11	0	10	58
x_2	0	0	①	10/33	0	$-1/3$	$3\frac{1}{3}$
x_1	0	①	0	$-1/11$	0	1	4
x_4	0	0	0	1/3	①	$-22/3$	11/3

which yields the optimal solution $x_0 = 58$, $x_1 = 4$, and $x_2 = 3\frac{1}{3}$ with x_1 an integer as required. ◄

§ 10·3
Branch and Bound Algorithms

This section considers the Land and Doig algorithms for solving both the all-integer and mixed problems. Section 10·3·1 gives the algorithm as originally introduced by Land and Doig. Section 10·3·2 then presents a modification of the same algorithm which makes it more amenable to computer coding. The reason for giving these techniques the name "branch-and-bound" will be made clear later in the section.

§ 10·3·1
Land-Doig Algorithm

Consider the problem,

$$\text{maximize} \quad z = \mathbf{C}'\mathbf{X} + \mathbf{C}''\mathbf{Y}$$

subject to

$$\mathbf{A}'\mathbf{X} + \mathbf{A}''\mathbf{Y} = \mathbf{P}_0$$
$$\mathbf{X} \geq \mathbf{0}, \quad \text{and integers,}$$
$$\mathbf{Y} \geq \mathbf{0},$$

where

$$\mathbf{X} = (x_1, x_2, \ldots, x_p)^T,$$
$$\mathbf{Y} = (y_1, y_2, \ldots, y_q)^T.$$

The elements of the vectors $\mathbf{C}'$, $\mathbf{C}''$, $\mathbf{A}'$ $\mathbf{A}''$, and $\mathbf{P}_0$ define the different co-efficients of the problem.

The above problem defines a mixed integer programming problem in which the elements of the vector $\mathbf{X}$ are limited to integer values. Naturally, if an all-integer problem is desired, then all the variables must belong to the vector $\mathbf{X}$. For later references, let (P) define the above problem without the integrality condition on the elements of $\mathbf{X}$.

In Gomory's cutting plane algorithm, the above mixed problem is solved by adding "secondary" constraints which gradually create a new solution space with its optimal extreme point satisfying the integrality condition of all the variables in $\mathbf{X}$. The Land-Doig algorithm, on the other hand, is based on making successive parallel shifts in the objective hyperplane toward the interior of the solution space such that each new shift will coincide with an integer value of at least one variable in $\mathbf{X}$. These successive shifts are made in an orderly manner so that it is never possible to by-pass a *superior* integer point (in $\mathbf{X}$) in the solution space. Thus, let z^1, z^2, $\ldots$, and z^k represent the values of z corresponding to the first, second, $\ldots$, and kth shifts in the objective hyperplane. The optimum solution is reached at the kth shift (iteration) if, for the first time, all the variables in $\mathbf{X}$ assume integer values.

The objective now is to show how these shifts in the objective hyperplane can be effected. The procedure advanced by Land and Doig is started by finding the optimal solution to (P); that is, the optimal solution to the original problem neglecting the integrality condition. If it is integral, the process ends. Otherwise, let z^0 be the corresponding value of the objective function. Select a (integer-constrained) variable x_r for consideration and let x_r^* be its optimal (fractional) value corresponding to z^0.

The first shift in the objective hyperplane, specified by z^1, is determined by considering the two neighboring values of x_r^*; that is, $[x_r^*]$ and $[x_r^*] + 1$, where $[x_r^*]$ is the largest integer value included in x_r^*. Let z_r^m and z_r^M be the optimal values of z corresponding to the linear programming problem (P) subject to the additional constraints $x_r = [x_r^*]$ and $x_r = [x_r^*] + 1$, respectively. (The subscript r is used with z to indicate that x_r is the variable being considered for integrality.) It then follows that,

$$z^1 = \max\{z_r^m, z_r^M\}.$$

The above definitions are illustrated graphically in Figure 10–2 by two different cases in the two-dimensional space. The reader will also find these illustrations helpful in following the discussion to be presented below. Thus, in Figure 10–2, given x_2 is an integer-constrained variable, Case (a) illustrates the situation where $z_2^m < z_2^M$, and hence $z^1 = z_2^M$. Case (b), on the other hand, shows that $z_2^M < z_2^m$, hence $z^1 = z_2^m$.

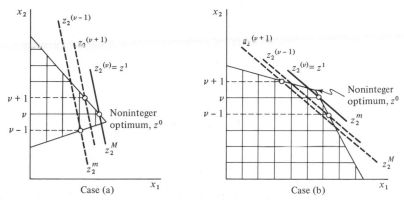

Case (a)   Case (b)

Figure 10–2

It must be noted that in order for x_r to be an integer, z^1 will represent the upper bound on the value of z since no larger value can be obtained under this condition. In other words, by shifting the objective hyperplane parallel to itself from $z = z^0$ to $z = z^1$, one is certain that *no* integer values of x_r are included within this range.

The determination of z^1 can be achieved systematically using the concept of a decision tree. The first node in this tree is represented by z^0. Two branches corresponding to $x_r = [x_r^*]$ and $x_r = [x_r^*] + 1$ must emanate from this node. The end nodes of these two branches will be identified with z_r^m and z_r^M, respectively. This yields either one of the two trees shown in Figure 10–3 depending on whether $z^1 = z_r^M$ [Case (a)] or $z^1 = z_r^m$ [Case (b)]. It is now said that the nodes associated with z^0 and z^1 have been *labelled*. In general, a node will be labelled if it defines the next shift in the objective hyperplane.

Notice that in Figure 10–3, z^0 is the highest node in the tree thus representing the *largest* value of z. The value of z at the other nodes will thus be measured on the vertical scale relative to the value of z^0. This means that the lower the node, the smaller will be its corresponding value of z. Notice also that any branch in the tree will necessarily be associated with an integer value of one of the variables in **X**.

It should be noted that the node z^0 is now reserved for the variable x_r. In general, as will be shown later, every node will be identified with one (integer-constrained) variable only. It is possible, however, that the same variable may be defined at more than one node.

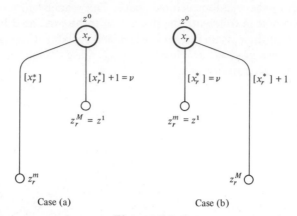

Case (a)   Case (b)

Figure 10–3

The typical decision trees in Figure 10–3 (and the determination of z^1) give the initialization step in the Land-Doig algorithm. Suppose now that the solution corresponding to z^1 does not satisfy the integrality condition for all the variables in **X**. The objective hyperplane must then be shifted (parallel to itself) to a new value (node) $z = z^2$ in search for a possible integer solution.

Rather than discussing the specific case of determining z^2, the general procedure for determining z^k, given z^{k-1}, will be introduced first. Specific examples will then be introduced to illustrate its application.

Consider first the following definitions. As stated above, z^{k-1} represents the last labelled node. (For example, in Figure 10–3, z^1 represents such a node.) Let x_j be a variable that assumes a fractional value at z^{k-1} and define (P_j) as the optimization problem yielding the optimum solution at z^{k-1}. Thus, (P_j) is equivalent to the original problem (P) *and* all the integrality constraints leading from the node z^0 to the node z^{k-1}. (For example, in Figure 10–3, if x_s is the variable selected at z^1 for integrality, then (P_s) is equivalent to (P) and $x_r = [x_r^*] + 1$ or $x_r = [x_r^*]$ for cases (a) and (b), respectively.) Let x_i be the variable associated with the node at the *top-end* of the branch leading to the last labelled node, z^{k-1}, and let $x_i = v$ define such a branch. (For example, in Figure 10–3, x_r defines the variable associated with z^0, the node at the top-end of the branch leading to z^1. The value of v is given by $[x_r^*] + 1$ and $[x_r^*]$ for cases (a) and (b), respectively.) In general, as will be shown later, x_i need not be associated with z^{k-2}. Finally, define (P_i) in a similar way to (P_j) as the optimization problem yielding the optimum solution at the node associated with x_i.

The principal idea underlying the determination of z^k is that the corresponding branch must emanate from a *labelled* node. Thus, by keeping track of the next best branch (in terms of the value of z) at each labelled node, one automatically guarantees the proper selection of z^k (that is, no superior integer solution will be by-passed in going from z^{k-1} to z^k). Investigation shows that attention should be paid mainly to the two nodes associated with x_i and x_j defined above, since these are the only two nodes where changes in the next best branch *may* occur. The remaining *labelled* nodes will not be affected and hence they automatically have their next best branches in store.

Consider first the node associated with x_i. The structure of the tree necessarily indicates that *either* $x_i = v - 1$ *or* $x_i = v + 1$ must be present in the tree, where $x_i = v$, as given above, defines the branch leading to z^{k-1}. Thus, depending on which branch is already in the tree, the other branch must be added. The corresponding optimum values of z will be referred to as $z_i^{(v-1)}$ and $z_i^{(v+1)}$ and are obtained by solving (P_i) given $x_i = v - 1$ and $x_i = v + 1$, respectively. The point here is that because of the special properties of the original problem (P) (convex solution space and linear objective function), the branch that is next best to $x_i = v$ will always be in store as long as both $x_i = v - 1$ and $x_i = v + 1$ are present in the tree.

Next consider the last labelled node, z^{k-1}, and its associated variable x_j. Let $x_j = x_j^*$ represent the optimal (fractional) value at z^{k-1}. Since this node does not yet have any branches associated with it, its best branch is included in the tree by adding the two branches $x_j = [x_j^*]$ and $x_j = [x_j^*] + 1$. The optimum values of z corresponding to these two branches will be referred to as z_j^m and z_j^M, respectively. These are obtained by optimizing (P_j) subject to the respective constraints, $x_j = [x_j^*]$ and $x_j = [x_j^*] + 1$. Notice that this application is similar to determining z_r^m and z_r^M at z^0.

Having added the three branches indicated above (one at the x_i-node and two at the x_j-node), the next node to be labelled, z^k, is then selected from among *all* the *un*labelled nodes. This will be the node having the *largest* value of $z \leq z^{k-1}$.

The above discussion involves two basic procedures which must be applied whenever a new node is to be labelled. These will be referred to as the *augmentation* and the *exploration* procedures. The augmentation procedure defines the branch $x_i = v - 1$ (or $v + 1$) associated with the node at the top-end of the branch $x_i = v$. Notice that the end effect of the augmentation procedure is that the two branches on both sides of $x_i = v$ must be present in the tree. The name of the procedure indicates that a new branch is being "augmented" to the tree at a previously-labelled node. The exploration procedure adds the two branches $x_j = [x_j^*]$ and $x_j = [x_j^*] + 1$ to the tree. The name of the procedure indicates that the last labelled node is being "explored" for the possibility of identifying an integer solution.

To illustrate the application of the above two procedures, consider the decision trees in Figure 10–4, [Cases (a) and (b)]. Since z^1 is the last labelled node, the augmentation procedure is applied at z^0, the node immediately above z^1. The branch $x_r = v$ is the one leading to z^1. Hence, in Case (a), the branch $x_r = v + 1$ must be added to the tree while in Case (b), the branch $x_r = v - 1$ must be added. The addition of these branches will result in the

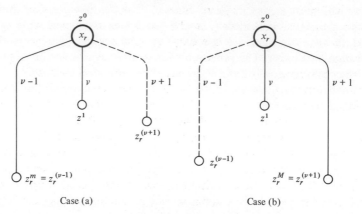

Case (a)   Case (b)

Figure 10–4

new trees in Figure 10-4. (The new branches are indicated by dotted lines.) The values of $z_r^{(v+1)}$ and $z_r^{(v-1)}$ are obtained by optimizing (P) subject to $x_r = v + 1$ and $x_r = v - 1$, respectively. It is assumed that the relative values of $z_r^{(v+1)}$ and $z_r^{(v-1)}$ are as shown in Figure 10-4.

The exploration procedure is now applied at z^1. Let x_s be the variable associated with this node. Two branches, $x_s = [x_s^*]$ and $x_s = [x_s^*] + 1$ are added with their relative optimum values of z being given by z_s^m and z_s^M, respectively. The values of z_s^m and z_s^M are obtained by solving (P_s) subject to $x_s = [x_s^*]$ and $x_s = [x_s^*] + 1$, respectively. Suppose the tree in Case (a) of Figure 10-4 is considered and that the relative values of z_s^m and z_s^M are found to be as shown in Figure 10–5 (where the new branches are again

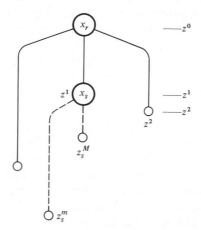

Figure 10–5

indicated by dotted lines). Then z^2, the node to be labelled next, is selected from among all the unlabelled nodes (shown in small circles) as the one having the largest value of z. The result of this selection is shown in Figure 10–5. The determination of z^2 now signifies the start of a new iteration.

Again, if the solution at z^2 is integral, the process ends. Otherwise, a new shift $z = z^3$ must be determined. Let x_t be the fractional variable selected at z^2. The branch leading to z^2 happened to be associated with x_r. Thus, let $x_r = v$ define this branch. The augmentation procedure is applied now. Since $x_r = v - 1$ is already in the tree, a new branch $x_r = v + 1$ must be added. Notice that this branch originates from z^0, the node at the top-end of the branch leading to the current node, z^2. This illustrates the case where it is not necessary for such a branch to emanate from the *last explored* node. The augmentation procedure is followed by the application of the exploration procedure. Thus, the two branches, $x_t = [x_t^*]$ and $x_t = [x_t^*] + 1$ are added at z^2. The end result here is the determination of z^3, the node having the largest value of z among all the unlabelled nodes. Figure 10–6 illustrates the result of

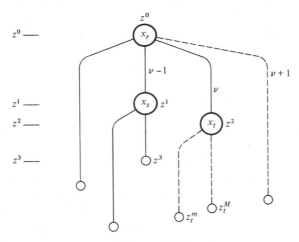

Figure 10–6

applying these two procedures to the tree in Figure 10–5. The value of z^3 is thus as shown in the figure. Notice that z^3 does not correspond to any of the branches that were added to the tree by the last applications of the augmentation and exploration procedures. This illustrates the reason why the next node to be labelled must be selected from among *all* the *un*labelled nodes in the tree.

An important remark must be made here. Consider any node that has been explored and identify the branch emanating from this node which corresponds to $\max\{z_i^m, z_i^M\}$, where i identifies the variable x_i associated with the node. Let $x_i = x_i^{\max}$ define the branch corresponding to $\max\{z_i^m, z_i^M\}$. It follows that the branches $x_i = x_i^{\max} + q, q = 1, 2, \ldots$, will yield optimum values of z which are necessarily monotone nonincreasing with q. A similar result applies for the branches $x_i = x_i^{\text{max}} - q$. This, of course, assumes that q is selected such that $x_i = x_i^{\text{max}} \pm q$ is feasible. The reason for the above result is that the solution space of the original problem (P) is convex and its objective function is linear. (The reader can visualize this point better by referring to the graphical examples in Figure 10–2.) This should explain why the augmentation and the exploration procedures are sufficient for identifying the next labelled node such that no superior integer solution is by-passed.

It must be noted that in applying either the augmentation or the exploration procedure, the new branches may yield infeasible solutions. In this case, such branches must be discarded. Moreover, for future considerations, any integer value (originating from the same node) beyond the ones that have proved infeasible will also yield infeasible solutions. In particular, if the application of the exploration procedure at the first node, z^0, yields no feasible solution for both branches, then the associated variable cannot be restricted to an integer value.

The above procedure is repeated successively always selecting the next largest value of z. As indicated previously, at iterations $1, 2, \ldots,$ and k these upper bounds take on the successive values $z^1, z^2, \ldots,$ and z^k. Then by definition,[3]

$$z^0 \geq z^1 \geq z^2 \geq \cdots \geq z^k$$

The procedure will terminate at the kth node if it corresponds to a solution having all the elements in $\mathbf{X}$ in integer form or if all the branches terminate with infeasible solutions.

The above discussion indicates that branches can be added to the tree only by applying the exploration and augmentation procedures. It might be convenient here to summarize the general rules of the two procedures.

Exploration Procedure. At the kth iteration, given the optimal value of the variable x_j at the node z^k is equal to x_j^*, two branches $x_j = [x_j^*]$ and $x_j = [x_j^*] + 1$ must emanate from this node. The values of z_j^m and z_j^M corresponding to these branches are computed by optmizing the problem (P_j) subject to the respective constraints, $x_j = [x_j^*]$ and $x_j = [x_j^*] + 1$, where (P_j) is equivalent to (P) and all the integrality conditions specified by the branches leading from the node z^0 to the node z^k. Each application of this procedure adds two branches to the tree.

Augmentation Procedure. Given that the node z^k is to be explored, let $x_i = v$ define the branch leading to z^k. A new branch corresponding to $x_i = v - 1$ *or* $x_i = v + 1$ must originate from the node at the top-end of the branch $x_i = v$ (this is not necessarily z^{k-1}) such that the branches representing

---

[3] The equality sign will occur when the objective hyperplane coincides with several integer *feasible* solutions. Under such a condition, the corresponding successive upper bounds of z will be equal.

the integers on both sides of $x_i = v$ are present in the tree. The value of $z_i^{(v-1)}$ (or $z_i^{(v+1)}$) corresponding to the added branch is obtained by optimizing (P_i) subject to $x_i = v - 1$ (or, $v + 1$), where (P_i) is equivalent to (P) and all the integrality constraints specified by the branches leading from the node z^0 to the node associated with x_i. Each application of this procedure adds one branch to the tree.

It is possible now to summarize the basic steps of the Land-Doig algorithm:

Step 0:   Obtain the optimum solution to (P); that is, disregarding the integrality constraints. If the resulting solution is integral for all the variables in **X**, the process ends. Otherwise, the first node z^0 is labelled and an integer-constrained variable is selected for investigation. Then pass to step 1.

Step 1:   Apply the exploration procedure to the last labelled node. Then pass to step 2.

Step 2:   At the kth iteration, label the node z^k as the one having the largest z ($\leq z^{k-1}$) among *all* the *un*labelled nodes. If the solution corresponding to z^k satisfies the integrality condition for all the variables in **X**, the process ends. Otherwise, select an integer-constrained variable at z^k for investigation. Then pass to step 3.

Step 3:   Apply the augmentation procedure to the node at the top-end of the branch leading to z^k. Then go to step 1.

It is clear from the above presentation that the addition of new branches may occur at any node in the tree. Although in writing a computer code for this algorithm the maximum possible number of branches at each node is limited (provided the solution space is bounded), accounting for all possible branches of the problem will put a severe demand on the memory of the computer. This basic disadvantage is a limiting factor in the use of this algorithm. It is shown in Section 10·3·2 that such a difficulty may be overcome partially by introducing a simple modification in the algorithm.

The concept of branching and bounding must be clear now. At each iteration, new branches are added to the tree in an intelligent manner so that it is never possible to by-pass a promising integer solution. The new node to be labelled next must satisfy the condition that its corresponding z yield the next largest upper *bound* for the value of the objective function among all the unlabelled nodes. This guarantees eliminating inferior nodes from explicit consideration thus leading to computational efficiency.

Notice that, unlike the Gomory algorithms, the Land-Doig algorithm does not result in an enlarged problem. In fact, at any node, the constraints of the branches leading to this node are substituted out in the constraints of the original problem (P) and hence are never considered explicitly. This yields new problems with a smaller number of variables which are thus computationally more efficient in general. This is a basic advantage of the branch and bound algorithms. Another advantage is that it is often possible to secure a "good" integer feasible solution before the true optimum is achieved. In the Gomory's algorithms, solutions remain nonintegral until the optimum integral solution is reached.

▶ **Example 10·3-1**

Consider the same problem of Example 10·2-1. This is given by:

$$\text{maximize} \quad z = 7x_1 + 9x_2,$$

subject to

$$-x_1 + 3x_2 \le 6,$$

$$7x_1 + x_2 \le 35,$$

$$x_1, x_2 \ge 0 \text{ and integers.}$$

Step 0: The solution of (P) is given by $z^0 = 63$, $x_1^* = 4\frac{1}{2}$ and $x_2^* = 3\frac{1}{2}$. (See Example 10·2-1.) Since this solution is nonintegral, z^0 is labelled as the first node in the tree.

Step 1: The exploration procedure is applied to x_1 at z^0. Thus, z_1^m and z_1^M are computed by solving (P) subject to the additional constraints $x_1 = [x_1^*] = 4$ and $x_1 = [x_1^*] + 1 = 5$, respectively.[4] The optimal solution for $x_1 = 4$ is given by $z_1^m = 58$ and $x_2 = 10/3$; and for $x_1 = 5$ it is given by $z_1^M = 35$ and $x_2 = 0$. The two branches $x_1 = 4$ and $x_1 = 5$ are now added at the node z^0. (See Figure 10–7.)

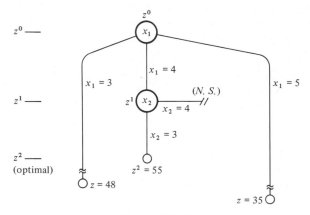

Figure 10–7

---

[4] The solution can be obtained graphically in this case. In general, the simplex procedure is used after substituting out the value of x_1 in the entire problem and then solving for the remaining variables.

Step 2: Consider

$$z^1 = \max\{z_1^m, z_1^M\} = 58.$$

This corresponds to the branch $x_1 = 4$ in Figure 10–7. The corresponding solution shows that $x_2 = \frac{10}{3}$; that is, noninteger, and hence x_2 must be considered for integrality.

Step 3: The augmentation procedure is now applied to the node immediately above z^1; that is, z^0. Figure 10–7 shows that the branch $x_1 = 3$ must be added to the tree. Thus solving (P) subject to $x_1 = 3$, this yields $z_1^{(3)} = 48$ and $x_2 = 3$.

Step 1: The exploration procedure is applied at the node z^1 to the variable x_2. Since at this node $x_2^* = \frac{10}{3}$, two branches are added by considering z_2^m and z_2^M corresponding to $x_2 = [x_2^*] = 3$ and $x_2 = [x_2^*] + 1 = 4$, respectively. The constraint of the branch $x_2 = 4$ yields no feasible solution (N.S.) and hence it is discarded.

Step 2: The next node to be labelled must be the one having the largest $z \le z^1$ among all the unlabelled nodes. This is associated with the branch $x_2 = 3$ which yields $z^2 = 55$. Since the solution corresponding to this node is all-integer, the process ends. Thus, the optimum solution is given by $x_1 = 4$, $x_2 = 3$ and $z = 55$ which, of course, is the same as in Example 10·2-1. ◀

§ 10·3·2
Modified Land-Doig (Dakin's) Algorithm

In the above section it was indicated that a major limitation on the use of the original Land-Doig algorithm is that it does not lend itself efficiently to computer coding. This limitation was overcome by R. J. Dakin[5] who introduced a simple modification to the algorithm which guarantees exactly two branches at each node. Rather than forcing the variables at each node to take exact integral values, Dakin suggests that bounds can be used to cover the entire range of each of the variables.

Let x_r be an integer-constrained variable which assumes a fractional value x_r^* at the last labelled node. Then the range,

$$[x_r^*] < x_r < [x_r^*] + 1$$

is inadmissible. Consequently, two branches may emanate from this node which represent the two nonoverlapping constraints,

$$x_r \le [x_r^*]$$

---

[5] R. J. Dakin, "A Tree-Search Algorithm for Mixed Integer Programming Problems," *The Computer Journal*, 1966, pp. 250–255.

and

$$x_r \geq [x_r^*] + 1.$$

By considering these two branches at each node, one actually is accounting for all possible branches that may be generated for the variable x_r in the original Land-Doig algorithm. This means that the application of the augmentation procedure will not be necessary in this case. The search stops when *all* the branches in the tree have terminated either with an integer solution or with a solution that violates the constraints of (P). The best solution is then selected from among all the feasible solutions.

It should be noted that the above additional constraints need not be considered explicitly in the problem since the bounded variables method (Section 8·7·3) may be used. Also it may not be necessary to exhaust all the branches of the tree before the optimal integer solution is attained. This follows from the fact that once a feasible (integer) solution is obtained for one of the branches, its corresponding x_0-value is used as a lower bound ($= x_0'$, say), so that any new branch yielding an x_0-value less than x_0' must be discarded. The value of x_0' will be changed, of course, if a better solution is encountered. It is obvious in this case that the computational effort may be reduced appreciably if one can start with a good estimate of x_0'.

▶ **Example 10·3-2**

Consider the same problem of Example 10·3-1. The tree corresponding to this example is shown in Figure 10–8.

The calculations in the figure are self-explanatory and may be summarized as shown in Table 10–1.

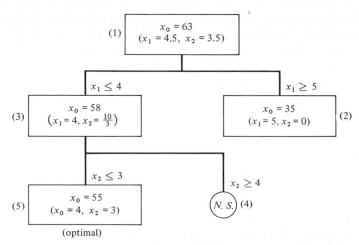

Figure 10–8

Table 10–1

Node	Solution			Additional constraints	Type of solution	
	x_0	x_1	x_2			
1	63	9/2	7/2	—	Original problem	
2	35	5	0	$x_1 \geq 5$	Integer	$\leftarrow x_0'$
3	58	4	10/3	$x_1 \leq 4$	Noninteger	
4	—	—	—	$x_1 \leq 4$ $x_2 \geq 4$	No solution	
5	55	4	3	$x_1 \leq 4$ $x_2 \leq 3$	Integer (optimal)	

§ 10·4
Balas' Zero-One Algorithm

Egon Balas (1965) has developed an algorithm for solving linear programming problems with binary (zero or one) variables only. This algorithm is mainly applicable where the variables reduce to the "yes-no" type. For example, in the capital budgeting problem where several new projects are competing for limited capital, the final choice resolves to either accepting or rejecting each of the new projects. Thus, if project j is represented by the variable x_j, then $x_j = 0$ may signify rejection, in which case $x_j = 1$ signifies acceptance.

The general approach of the algorithm is to start the problem with an optimal (actually better-than-optimal) and infeasible solution. A procedure is then developed which forces the solution toward feasibility while keeping the solution optimal all the time. This reasoning suggests that the algorithm may be based on the dual simplex method. This is true only as far as the starting solution is concerned.[6] The rules for selecting the entering variable are completely different, however. Also, there are no leaving variables in the sense employed in the dual method.

---

[6] Balas suggests that the procedure is based on what he calls "*pseudo* dual simplex method" since it actually makes no use of the basic criteria of the dual method.

Consider the linear programming problem,

$$\text{maximize (or minimize) } x_0 = (c_1', c_2', \ldots, c_n') \begin{bmatrix} x_1' \\ x_2' \\ \vdots \\ x_n' \end{bmatrix},$$

subject to

$$\begin{bmatrix} a_{11}' & a_{12}' & \cdots & a_{1n}' \\ a_{21}' & a_{22}' & \cdots & a_{2n}' \\ \vdots & \vdots & & \vdots \\ a_{m1}' & a_{m2}' & \cdots & a_{mn}' \end{bmatrix} \begin{bmatrix} x_1' \\ x_2' \\ \vdots \\ x_n' \end{bmatrix} \begin{matrix} = \\ \le \\ \ge \end{matrix} \begin{bmatrix} b_1' \\ b_2' \\ \vdots \\ b_m' \end{bmatrix},$$

$$x_j' = 0 \quad \text{or} \quad 1, \quad j = 1, 2, \ldots, n.$$

This problem can always be put in the following form which will be used for developing the algorithm.

$$\text{Minimize } z = (c_1, c_2, \ldots, c_n) \begin{bmatrix} x_1 \\ x_2 \\ \vdots \\ x_n \end{bmatrix},$$

subject to

$$\begin{bmatrix} a_{11} & a_{12} & \cdots & a_{1n} & 1 & 0 \cdots 0 \\ a_{21} & a_{22} & \cdots & a_{2n} & 0 & 1 \cdots 0 \\ \vdots & \vdots & & \vdots & \vdots & \vdots \\ a_{m1} & a_{m2} & \cdots & a_{mn} & 0 & 0 \cdots 1 \end{bmatrix} \begin{bmatrix} x_1 \\ x_2 \\ \vdots \\ x_n \\ S_1 \\ S_2 \\ \vdots \\ S_m \end{bmatrix} = \begin{bmatrix} b_1 \\ b_2 \\ \vdots \\ b_m \end{bmatrix},$$

$$x_j = 0 \quad \text{or} \quad 1, \quad j = 1, 2, \ldots, n,$$

$$S_i \ge 0, \quad i = 1, 2, \ldots, m,$$

where $c_j \ge 0$, for all j. In matrix form, this appears as:

$$\text{minimize } z = \mathbf{CX}, \quad \mathbf{C} \ge \mathbf{0},$$

subject to

$$\mathbf{AX} + \mathbf{S} = \mathbf{b},$$

$$\mathbf{S} \ge \mathbf{0},$$

$$x_j = 0 \quad \text{or} \quad 1, \quad j = 1, 2, \ldots, n.$$

The transformation in the constraints can be seen immediately by following the elementary operations for the canonical form of linear programming which have been introduced in Section 2·3·1. On the other hand, the objective functions can always be put in the given form by first converting it into the minimization form and then using the substitution

$$x_j = \begin{cases} x_j', & \text{for } c_j' \geq 0. \\ 1 - x_j', & \text{for } c_j' < 0. \end{cases}$$

This substitution must also be made simultaneously in the constraints.

The new definition indicates that the "transformed" problem starts optimal but infeasible.[7] As in the dual simplex method, the starting solution can be written as

$$z_0 = 0, \quad \mathbf{S}^0 = \mathbf{b},$$

with all $x_j = 0$. The starting solution

$$\mathbf{S}^0 = \mathbf{b}$$

is an infeasible basic solution by definition.

The above infeasible starting solution plays a key role in the development of the algorithm. However, before introducing the exact rules of the procedure, it is necessary to introduce some basic definitions which will be used later in the discussion.

Given the binary variables $x_1, x_2, \ldots, x_n$ of the problem, a *partial solution*, J, is defined as a subset of these n variables with each element being assigned a binary value. Thus, for $n = 4$, the subset $J = \{x_1 = 0, x_3 = 1\}$ is a partial solution. Any variables not included in a partial solution are called *free* variables and, unless otherwise specified, are assumed equal to zero. Thus, in the given example, x_2 and x_4 are free variables. These variables are called "free" since one has the choice of either leaving them at zero level or elevating their value to one.

A *completion* of a partial solution J is defined as the complete set of variables which includes J together with a binary specification of its free variables. Thus, for the above partial solution, $J = \{x_1 = 0, x_3 = 1\}$, the possible completions are given by

Completion	$(x_1,$	$x_2,$	$x_3,$	$x_4)$
1	(0,	0,	1,	0)
2	(0,	0,	1,	1)
3	(0,	1,	1,	0)
4	(0,	1,	1,	1)

Notice that in all the completions $x_1 = 0$ and $x_3 = 1$ as specified by the corresponding partial solution.

---

[7] If the starting solution happens to be both optimal and feasible, then there is nothing more to be done and the starting solution becomes the optimal solution.

Rather than using the above 0–1 representation for a solution set, it is more convenient to use the symbols j and $-j$ to represent $x_j = 1$ and the $x_j = 0$, respectively. For example, the first completion given above may be written as $(-1, -2, +3, -4)$. Such a notation has the advantage of identifying the variables associated with the binary value. This is especially useful as will be seen later since the elements of a solution may not be presented in a natural order.

The basic idea of the Balas algorithm will be explained now. Given that the starting solution $\mathbf{S}^0 = \mathbf{b}$ is infeasible, the corresponding partial solution is given by $J_0 = \varnothing$. This indicates that all x_j are free variables each with zero value. The procedure then calls for augmenting the set J_0 with one of the free variables x_j which will now enter the solution at level 1. The condition here is that the resulting partial solution, J_1, should force $\mathbf{S}^0$ toward the feasible region. (The specific rules for testing this point will be presented later.) If, however, no such variable can be found for augmenting J_0, then the problem has no feasible solution.

Given the new partial solution J_1, new augmentations with one free variable at a time will result in a series of partial solution $J_1, J_2, \ldots, J_t$. It is possible, as these partial solutions are generated, that one of its completions will result in feasible values for $\mathbf{S}$; that is $\mathbf{S} \geq \mathbf{0}$. When this is encountered for the first time, the corresponding value of the objective function is kept in store as the best feasible value so far attained. Let such a value be referred to as $z_{\min}$. Thus, at a later iteration, a *feasible* solution that does not yield a better value than $z_{\min}$ must be discarded. On the other hand, if a feasible solution yields a better value than $z_{\min}$, then $z_{\min}$ should be adjusted accordingly. In other words, $z_{\min}$ acts as an (adjustable) upper bound on the value of the objective function. Conventionally, before the first feasible solution is attained, $z_{\min}$ is taken equal to ∞.

When a completion of a partial solution yields a feasible solution with a better value than $z_{\min}$, or when it is impossible to find a completion which will improve the infeasibility in the current solution then it can be concluded that the given partial solution has been *fathomed*. This means that all the completions of this partial solution have been *implicitly* accounted for (or enumerated) and hence may not be reinvestigated in future iterations.

The *implicit enumeration* referred to above represents an important concept in the Balas algorithm. This makes it possible to investigate *explicitly* only a small number of the 2^n possible solutions while automatically accounting for all the remaining solutions. To clarify this concept, consider a partial solution J of a given problem. If J has no completion which yields a feasible solution to the problem, then such completions must be discarded in future investigations. On the other hand, if the completion of J resulting from putting all the free variables equal to zero yields a better value of z (that is, a value $< z_{\min}$), then any other completion in which one (or more) free variable assumes a value other than zero can never improve the value of z.

This follows since the coefficients, c_j, of the (modified) objective function are nonnegative and thus the addition of a new variable at level one cannot yield a better value of z. It becomes necessary then that all such completions be discarded in future iterations. As mentioned above, when J has no feasible completion or when it yields a better feasible completion, it is said that J has been fathomed. The question as to how fathoming can be achieved will be presented later in detail.

The above discussion indicates that it is not fruitful to investigate the remaining completions of a fathomed partial solution J. One must thus ensure that such completions will be excluded from further considerations. A procedure, called "backtracking," has been developed for this purpose. The general idea of this procedure is to generate a new partial solution which differs from the immediately preceding one by one element. (The exact details of backtracking will be presented later.) Thus, any completion of the new partial solution cannot repeat any of the previously considered ones.

The new partial solution must now be attempted for fathoming as outlined above. When this is accomplished, a new partial solution is generated again using the backtracking procedure. Since there is a finite number of possible solutions to the problem (namely, 2^n), successive applications of the backtracking procedure should enumerate (implicitly or explicitly) *all* the possible solutions of the problem. It thus follows that after backtracking is completed, the solution corresponding to $z_{\min}$ will represent the optimal solution to the problem. If $z_{\min}$ is still equal to ∞, this would mean that none of the 2^n solutions is feasible.

It is now possible to present the exact rules of the Balas algorithm. These rules are categorized under three major steps:

Step 1: Determine the entering variable, x_k.
Step 2: Determine the new solution, S_i.
Step 3: Backtrack and determine the optimal solution (when it exists).

Each of these steps will be discussed in detail. First, the following definitions must be introduced.

At any iteration t, let

N = set of subscripts of all the x_j-variables.
J_t = set of subscripts of the x_j-variables that have been assigned a binary specification; that is, the set corresponding to a partial solution. $J_0 = \varnothing$, by definition.
$N - J_t$ = set of "free" variables which are not included in the partial solution and hence may be considered to enter the solution. (All free variables are equal to zero.)
N_t = set of subscripts of the x_j-variables, selected from $(N - J_t)$, which are candidates for improving the current solution. This will be called the *improving set* of variables.

Step 1. Determination of the Entering Variable, x_k

Given the two sets N and J_t for the current (tth) iteration, the entering variable is determined from among the "free" variables (whose subscripts are included in $N - J_t$). This is accomplished at two levels. The first level determines the set N_t of the promising candidate variables by excluding all the nonpromising free variables. The exclusion at this level is based on the two criteria, Feasibility Condition I and Optimality Condition I. The objective of Feasibility Condition I is to eliminate all the free variables that do not result in forcing at least one negative slack variable, S_i, toward the feasible region. Optimality Condition I, on the other hand, excludes all the free variables which may result in a value of the objective function, z_t, which is worse than $z_{\min}$.

The second level also introduces two conditions. Feasibility Condition II which checks the possibility of obtaining a feasible solution ($\mathbf{S} \geq 0$) if all the promising variables in N_t were assigned the value 1. If this test fails, then the set N_t cannot improve the solution. If the test does not fail, the search passes to Optimality Condition II which selects the most promising variable from N_t to enter the solution. Such a variable should be the one that results in the least total infeasibility in the problem. This infeasibility is measured according to an empirical rule which will be introduced later.

Notice that, unlike the simplex method of linear programming, the optimality and feasibility conditions are used for the sole purpose of selecting an entering variable.

The above conditions will be considered now in detail.

Feasibility Condition I

For any free variable x_r such that $r \in (N - J_t)$, if $a_{ir} \geq 0$ for *all* i corresponding to $S_i < 0$, this would mean that by introducing $x_r (= 1)$, the new values of S_i will be given by

$$S_i^{t+1} = S_i^t - (a_{ir}), \quad a_{ir} \geq 0, \quad S_i^t < 0,$$

which does not force any negative S_i toward the feasible space. Let the corresponding set of indices for such variables be specified by E_t. Then any $j \in E_t$ should be excluded as a nonpromising variable.

Next, Optimality Condition I is considered.

Optimality Condition I

Given $z_{\min}$ as defined above, let

$$z_t = \sum_{j \in J_t} c_j x_j$$

be the value of the objective function corresponding to the current (infeasible) solution. A "free" variable x_{j*}, such that $j^* \in (N - J_t)$, cannot improve the solution if by adding it (setting it equal to 1), the resulting new value of the objective function, $c_{j*} + z_t$, becomes greater than z_{min}. This means that any "free" variable x_{j*} satisfying the inequality,

$$c_{j*} + z_t \geq z_{min},$$

should not be considered for entering the solution.

Let D_t be the set of subscripts including all such $j*$. Then N_t, the improving set of subscripts, is given by

$$N_t = N - J_t - (E_t \cup D_t).$$

In essence then, the set N_t is obtained by deleting the set E_t from $(N - J_t)$ and then deleting the *nonredundant* elements of D_t from $N - J_t - E_t$.

If the set N_t is void ($= \emptyset$), then the present partial solution, J_t, has no better feasible completion. In this case, J_t is said to have been fathomed. The search now moves to the backtracking procedure of Step 3 for a consideration of another partial solution. Otherwise, Feasibility Condition II is invoked.

Feasibility Condition II

Consider the ith constraint,

$$a_{i1}x_1 + a_{i2}x_2 + \cdots + a_{in}x_n + S_i = b_i$$

where $S_i < 0$. The variables x_j, such that $j \in N_t$ and such that their coefficients $a_{ij} < 0$, will represent a promising combination if, when simultaneously assigned the value 1, a feasible solution for all S_i would result. If this test fails for any *negative* S_i, this means that the indicated combination, N_t, cannot bring feasibility to the solution and hence it should be discarded. In other words, if for *any* $S_i < 0$, the condition,

$$\sum_{\substack{j \in N_t \\ a_{ij} < 0}} a_{ij} > S_i^t,$$

is satisfied, then N_t should be abandoned. This again is equivalent to having $N_t = \emptyset$; that is, J_t is fathomed. In this case, the search moves to the backtracking procedure of Step 3. Otherwise, Optimality Condition II is checked.

Optimality Condition II

Define

$$v_j^t = \sum_{\text{all } i} \min(0, S_i^t - a_{ij}),$$

and compute v_j^t for all $j \in N_t$. The quantity v_j^t may be regarded as a measure of the total infeasibility in S^{t+1} after x_j is set equal to one. The entering variable x_k is thus selected as the one yielding the least amount of infeasibility. That is, the one yielding,

$$v_k^t = \max_{j \in N_t} \{v_j^t\}$$

It is noted that this condition is purely empirical and may be replaced if a stronger condition can be constructed.

The new partial solution, J_{t+1}, is now obtained by augmenting J_t by $\{+k\}$; that is

$$J_{t+1} = J_t \cup \{+k\}$$

$$= \{J_t, +k\}.$$

The next step at this point is to branch to Step 2 for the determination of the new solution **S** as well as the new value of $z_{\min}$ (if any).

Step 2. Determination of the New Solution
Given J_{t+1} as determined from Step 1, then

$$S_i^{t+1} = S_i^t - a_{ik},$$

$$z_{t+1} = z_t + c_k.$$

Now,

(a) if $S_i^{t+1} \geq 0$, for all i, then set

$$z_{\min} = z_{t+1}.$$

This means that J_{t+1} is fathomed and the algorithm moves to the backtracking procedure of Step 3. Otherwise,

(b) if *any* $S_i^{t+1} < 0$, go to Step 1 for a new augmentation of J_{t+1}.

Step 3. Backtracking and Determination of Optimal Solution
Although a procedure for considering all 2^n solutions was devised by Balas in his algorithm, Balas' method for this part is quite cumbersome. This follows from the fact that it requires a great amount of explicit recordings which should be retained from all previous iterations of the solution. This is especially inconvenient when the problem is solved on the computer. The indicated difficulty was overcome using the idea of backtracking which was introduced by F. Glover [4] and implemented for the Balas algorithm by A. Geoffrion [3].

As mentioned previously, the backtracking procedure is invoked after a partial solution J_t is fathomed; that is, after it becomes evident that all the completions of J_t have been considered. In order *not* to encounter any of the previously-enumerated solutions, the backtracking procedure generates a new partial solution by replacing the last element in J_t by its complement. Consequently, any completion to the new partial solution is a new completion which has not been considered previously. As indicated earlier, the backtracking procedure will terminate only after all 2^n solutions have implicitly (or explicitly) enumerated.

The basic rules of backtracking will now be presented.[8] Consider a specific problem with $n = 10$. Suppose that at the tth iteration, the partial solution J_t appears as

$$J_t = \{+2, +5, +3, +7\}.$$

The positive subscripts ($j = 2, 3, 5, 7$) were initiated by the process of augmentation introduced in Step 1.

Suppose that J_t is fathomed. The backtracking procedure is initiated by checking the last (right-justified) element of J_t. If it is positive, then it is made negative indicating that the corresponding variable is set equal to zero. If it is negative, then the right-most positive element is made negative and all the elements to its right are deleted from the set. Thus for the above set, since the last element is positive, the new partial solution becomes,

$$J_{t+1} = \{+2, +5, +3, -7\}.$$

The procedure now is to attempt fathoming J_{t+1} using Steps 1 and 2. Suppose that $J_{t+1} = \{+2, +5, +3, -7\}$ is fathomed. This again would require the application of backtracking. Since now the last element of J_{t+1} is negative, the new partial solution J_{t+2} is obtained by making the right-most positive element of J_{t+1} negative and then deleting all the elements to its right. This gives

$$J_{t+2} = \{+2, +5, -3\},$$

which again should be attempted for fathoming.

If, on the other hand, J_{t+1} cannot be fathomed, then (according to Step 1) it must be augmented by a new free variable with value 1. Let this variable be x_8, say. This yields

$$J_{t+2} = \{+2, +5, +3, -7, +8\}.$$

An attempt to fathom J_{t+2} must be made now. If it cannot be fathomed still, then it must be augmented again by a new free variable with value 1. This process is repeated until at some later trial t^*, J_{t^*} is fathomed.

The above process is repeated as necessary. The backtracking procedure is complete when _all_ the elements of a _fathomed_ partial solution are negative. At this point all 2^n solutions of the problem have been implicitly (or explicitly) enumerated.

The given three steps complete all the rules for the Balas algorithm. Because there are several choices at each step, it is helpful to summarize the algorithm in the form of a flowchart. This is shown in Figure 10–9. It is

---

[8] No attempt is made here to introduce the validity proof for this procedure. The interested reader is referred to Geoffrion's work where he proves that this procedure "leads to a nonredundant sequence of partial trial solutions which does not terminate before all 2^n solutions have been (implicitly) enumerated." [3], p. 9.

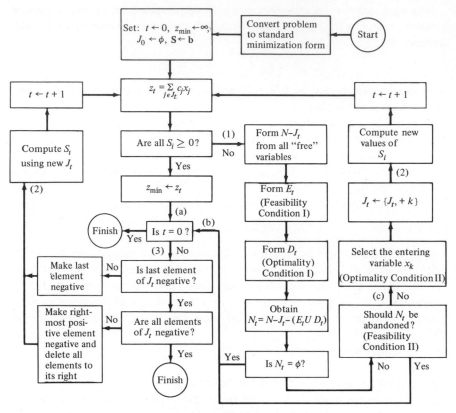

Figure 10–9

**Flowchart for the Balas Algorithm with
Implicit Enumeration**

noted in this figure that Branches (a) and (b) are the indicators that a partial
solution is fathomed. Branch (a) indicates the attainment of a better feasible
solution and Branch (b) shows that there exists no better feasible completion.
If the fathoming occurs at iteration $t = 0$, then the process ends either with
a feasible solution having all $x_j = 0$ [Branch (a)], or with no feasible solution
[Branch (b)]. Branch (c), on the other hand, represents the augmentation of
a nonfathomed partial solution by a free variable x_k. Finally, Branches (1),
(2), and (3) correspond to the starting points of Steps (1), (2), and (3) for the
algorithm.

▶ **Example 10·4-1**

Consider the linear programming problem:

$$\text{maximize} \quad x_0 = 3x_1' + 2x_2' - 5x_3' - 2x_4' + 3x_5',$$

subject to

$$x_1' + x_2' + x_3' + 2x_4' + x_5' \le 4,$$

$$7x_1' \qquad + 3x_3' - 4x_4' + 3x_5' \le 8,$$

$$11x_1' - 6x_2' \qquad + 3x_4' - 3x_5' \ge 3,$$

$$x_j' = 0 \quad \text{or} \quad 1, \quad j = 1, 2, \dots, 5.$$

This problem can be put in the standard minimization form by substituting

$$x_j' = \begin{cases} 1 - x_j, & j = 1, 2, 5 \\ x_j, & j = 3, 4. \end{cases}$$

Thus, the new problem becomes,

$$
\begin{bmatrix}
3 & 2 & 5 & 2 & 3 & 0 & 0 & 0 \\
-1 & -1 & 1 & 2 & -1 & 1 & 0 & 0 \\
-7 & 0 & 3 & -4 & -3 & 0 & 1 & 0 \\
11 & -6 & 0 & -3 & -3 & 0 & 0 & 1
\end{bmatrix}
\begin{bmatrix}
x_1 \\ x_2 \\ x_3 \\ x_4 \\ x_5 \\ S_1 \\ S_2 \\ S_3
\end{bmatrix}
=
\begin{bmatrix}
z_0 \\ 1 \\ -2 \\ -1
\end{bmatrix}.
$$

Starting Iteration:

$$z_{\min} = \infty,$$

$$J_0 = \varnothing,$$

$$(S_1^0, S_2^0, S_3^0) = (1, -2, -1).$$

Since

$$N = \{1, 2, 3, 4, 5\},$$

and

$$J_0 = \varnothing,$$

hence

$$N - J_0 = \{1, 2, 3, 4, 5\}.$$

Applying Feasibility Condition I, the variable x_3 should be excluded since for $S_2 < 0$ and $S_3 < 0$, a_{23} and a_{33} are ≥ 0. This means that

$$E_0 = \{3\}.$$

Now, from Optimality Condition I, since $z_{\min} = \infty$, no x_j can be excluded and

$$D_0 = \varnothing.$$

It follows that

$$N_0 = \{1, 2, 3, 4, 5\} - \{3\} = \{1, 2, 4, 5\}.$$

Since $N_0 \neq \varnothing$, Feasibility Condition II is checked. Thus,

$$S_2: \quad -7-4-3 = -14 < -2,$$
$$S_3: \quad -6-3-3 = -12 < -1,$$

which shows that N_0 cannot be abandoned. Next consider Optimality Condition II,

$$v_1^0 = 0 + 0 + (-1 - 11) = -12$$
$$v_2^0 = 0 + (-2 + 0) + 0 = -2$$
$$v_4^0 = (1 - 2) + 0 + 0 = -1$$
$$v_5^0 = 0 + 0 + 0 + 0 = \boxed{0}.$$

Since

$$\max_{j \in N_0}\{-12, -2, -1, 0\} = 0,$$

corresponding to x_5, it follows that $k = 5$. This gives

$$J_1 = \{+5\}.$$

First Iteration:
The new solution is given by

$$(S_1^1, S_2^1, S_3^1) = \{1 + 1, -2 + 3, -1 + 3\}$$
$$= (2, 1, 2),$$

and

$$z_1 = 3.$$

Since $\mathbf{S} > \mathbf{0}$, it follows that

$$z_{min} = z_1 = 3.$$

The search now goes to Step 3 for backtracking. This yields

$$J_2 = \{-5\}.$$

The corresponding solution is given by

$$(S_1^2, S_2^2, S_3^2) = (1, -2, -1),$$

and

$$z_2 = 0.$$

Second Iteration:

$$N - J_2 = \{1, 2, 3, 4, 5\} - \{5\} = \{1, 2, 3, 4\}.$$

Again, x_3 is excluded by Feasibility Condition I; that is,

$$E_2 = \{3\}.$$

Now, consider

$$z_{min} - z_2 = 3 - 0 = 3.$$

Since x_1 and x_3 have their $c_j \geq z_{min} - z_2$, then

$$D_2 = \{1, 3\},$$

and it follows that

$$N_2 = N - J_2 - \{E_2 \cup D_2\},$$
$$= \{1, 2, 3, 4\} - \{3\} \cup \{1, 3\},$$
$$= \{2, 4\} \neq \varnothing.$$

Thus, applying Feasibility Condition II,

$$S_2: \quad -4 < -2,$$
$$S_3: \quad -6 - 3 = -9 < -1,$$

and hence N_2 cannot be abandoned. Next, consider Optimality Condition II,

$$v_2^2 = 0 + (-2 - 0) + 0 = -2,$$
$$v_4^2 = (1 - 2) + 0 + 0 \quad = \boxed{-1}.$$

Hence $k = 4$, and the new partial solution is given by

$$J_3 = \{-5, +4\}.$$

The corresponding solution is

$$(S_1^3, S_2^3, S_3^3) = (1 - 2, -2 + 4, -1 + 3)$$
$$= (-1, 2, 2),$$

and

$$z_3 = 2.$$

Third Iteration:

$$N - J_3 = \{1, 2, 3\}$$

Again, one gets

$$E_3 = \{3\}.$$

Now, since $z_{min} - z_3 = 3 - 2 = 1$, it follows that

$$D_3 = \{1, 2, 3\}.$$

This gives

$$N_3 = \{1, 2, 3\} - \{3 \cup (1, 2, 3)\} = \varnothing.$$

Since N_3 is void, backtracking is invoked. Thus

$$J_4 = \{-5, -4\},$$

and the corresponding solution is

$$(S_1^4, S_2^4, S_3^4) = (1, -2, -1),$$

and

$$z_4 = 0.$$

Fourth Iteration:

$$N - J_4 = \{1, 2, 3\}$$

Again, one gets

$$E_4 = \{3\}.$$

Since

$$z_{min} - z_4 = 3 - 0 = 3,$$

it follows that

$$D_4 = \{1, 3\}.$$

This means that

$$N_4 = \{1, 2, 3\} - \{3 \cup (1, 3)\}$$
$$= \{2\}.$$

From Feasibility Condition II, one gets.

$$S_2 : \quad 0 \nless -2,$$
$$S_3 : \quad -6 < -1.$$

Since the condition is violated for S_2, N_4 should be abandoned. Because all the elements of J_4 are negative, backtracking is complete and the process ends.

The value $z_{min} = 3 \ (< \infty)$ corresponds to z_1. Hence the optimal solution corresponds to the first iteration; that is, J_1. This is given by

$$x_j = \begin{cases} 1, & j = 5 \\ 0, & j = 1, 2, 3, 4 \end{cases}$$

and

$$z = 3.$$

Transferring this to the original problem, this yields

$$x_j' = \begin{cases} 1, & j = 1, 2 \\ 0, & j = 3, 4, 5 \end{cases}$$

and

$$x_0 = 5. \quad \blacktriangleleft$$

§ 10·4·1
Zero-One Polynomial Programming by the Balas Method

Consider the problem

$$\text{maximize} \quad x_0 = f(x_1, \ldots, x_n),$$

subject to

$$g_i(x_1, \ldots, x_n) \le b_i, \quad i = 1, 2, \ldots, m,$$

$$x_j = 0 \text{ or } 1, \quad j = 1, 2, \ldots, n$$

Assume that f and g_i are polynomials with the kth term being generally represented by $d_k \prod_{j=1}^{n_k} x_j^{a_{kj}}$ where a_{kj} is a nonnegative constant exponent and d_k is a constant.

A procedure was developed by L. J. Watters[9] to convert the above seemingly highly nonlinear problem into a linear form which can be solved as a zero-one linear programming problem. This procedure recognizes the fact that since x_j is a binary variable, then $x_j^{a_{kj}} = x_j$ for any positive exponent a_{kj}. (If $a_{kj} = 0$, then obviously the variable x_j will not be present in the kth term.) This means that the kth term can be written as $d_k \prod_{j=1}^{n_k} x_j$.

Let $y_k = \prod_{j=1}^{n_k} x_j$, then y_k is also a binary variable and the kth term of the polynomial reduces to the linear term $d_k y_k$. However, in order to ensure that $y_k = 1$ when all $x_j = 1$ and zero otherwise, the following constraints must be added for each y_k,[10]

$$\sum_{j=1}^{n_k} x_j - (n_k - 1) \le y_k \tag{i}$$

$$\frac{1}{n_k} \sum_{j=1}^{n_k} x_j \ge y_k \tag{ii}$$

---

[9] L. J. Watters, "Reduction of Integer Polynomial Programming Problems to Zero-One Linear Programming Problems," _Operations Research_, Vol. 15, No. 6, 1967. pp. 1171–1174.

[10] A more efficient procedure which does not require the addition of these constraints and which deals directly with the converted linear system of the polynomial problem has been developed by H. Taha, "A Balasian-Based Algorithm for Zero-One Polynomial Programming," Research Report, University of Arkansas, May 1970. This procedure extends the Balas algorithm to the polynomial problem in a straightforward manner.

Thus, if all $x_j = 1$, $\sum_{j=1}^{n_k} x_j = n_k$ and constraint (i) yields $y_k \geq 1$ while constraint (ii) gives $y_k \leq 1$; that is, $y_k = 1$. On the other hand, if at least one $x_j = 0$, then $\sum_{j=1}^{n_k} x_j < n_k$ and constraints (i) and (ii) respectively yield $y_k \geq -(n_k - 1)$ and $y_k < 1$ with the only feasible value being given by $y_k = 0$.

To illustrate the procedure consider the numerical example,

$$\text{maximize} \quad x_0 = 2x_1 x_2 x_3^2 + x_1^2 x_2,$$

subject to

$$5x_1 + 9x_2^2 x_3 \leq 15.$$

Suppressing the exponents and letting $y_1 = x_1 x_2 x_3$, $y_2 = x_1 x_2$ and $y_3 = x_2 x_3$, the problem becomes,

$$\text{maximize} \quad x_0 = 2y_1 + y_2$$

subject to

$$5x_1 + 9y_3 \leq 15$$

$$x_1 + x_2 + x_3 - 2 \leq y_1,$$

$$\tfrac{1}{3}(x_1 + x_2 + x_3) \geq y_1,$$

$$x_1 + x_2 - 1 \leq y_2,$$

$$\tfrac{1}{2}(x_1 + x_2) \geq y_2,$$

$$x_2 + x_3 - 1 \leq y_3,$$

$$\tfrac{1}{2}(x_2 + x_3) \geq y_3,$$

with y_1, y_2, y_3, x_1, x_2, and x_3 being binary variables.

The above procedure can be used, at least in theory, to convert *any* polynomial integral (not necessarily binary) program into a binary linear program. The idea here is to first represent every integral variable by an equivalent system of binary variables. Once this is done, the application of the above procedure becomes straightforward.

To show how an integral variable x_j can be represented by an equivalent system of binary variables, assume $x_j \leq a_j < \infty$, where the upper bound a_j can be determined from the constraints of the associated problem. Let y_k^j be a binary variable. It follows that

$$x_j = \sum_{k=0}^{N} 2^k y_k^j$$

where N is the smallest integer such that $(a_j + 1)/2 \leq 2^N$. By selecting such a value for N, one guarantees that all the feasible integer values less than or equal to a_j are represented in the solution.

The use of the above substitution for x_j in the original problem will automatically convert it into a binary problem. The application of Watters' scheme will effect the desired linear transformation.

§ 10·5
Some Applications of Integer Programming

In this section, a number of applications of integer programming (all-integer and mixed) are presented. Some of these applications are concerned with the direct formulation of the problem. A more important contribution will be the use of integer programming to reformulate "ill-constructed" models into the standard format of integer programming. In this case, the available techniques can be used to solve problems that otherwise may be very difficult to tackle.

§ 10·5·1
Travelling Salesman Problem

In this well-known problem it is assumed that there are n towns with known distances between any two of them. A salesman wants to start from a given town, visit each town once, and then return to his starting point. The objective is to minimize his total travelling time. Clearly, starting from a given town the salesman will have a total of $(n - 1)!$ possible round trips. Since each trip goes through all towns, the optimal solution must be independent of the selection of a starting point.

Although this problem may be solved by exhaustive enumeration, it can also be formulated as a zero-one integer programming problem. First, the problem can be represented as a network (see Section 5·4) where the nodes and the arcs represent the towns and the distances between them, respectively. Suppose in a four-town problem, a round trip of the salesman is given by the arcs

$$(4, 3), (3, 2), (2, 1), (1, 4).$$

These arcs, taken in order, will be referred to as the first, second, third, and fourth *directed* arcs for the trip. Thus, in general, the kth directed arc will represent the kth leg of the trip. Obviously, for each trip there must be n such directed arcs.

Let

$$x_{ijk} = \begin{cases} 1, & \text{if the } k\text{th directed arc is from town } i \text{ to town } j, \\ 0, & \text{if otherwise}, \end{cases}$$

where i, j, and k are integers that vary between 1 and n. The constraints of the problem can be classified under four types:

1. Only one directed arc may be assigned to a specific k, thus,

$$\sum_{\substack{i \\ i \neq j}} \sum_{j} x_{ijk} = 1, \quad k = 1, 2, \ldots, n.$$

2. Only one other town may be reached from a specific town i, thus

$$\sum_j \sum_k x_{ijk} = 1, \quad i = 1, 2, \ldots, n.$$

3. Only one other town can initiate a directed arc to a specified town j, thus

$$\sum_i \sum_k x_{ijk} = 1, \quad j = 1, 2, \ldots, n.$$

4. Given the kth directed arc ends at some specific town j, the $(k + 1)$st directed arc must start at the same town j, thus

$$\sum_{\substack{i \\ i \neq j}} x_{ijk} = \sum_{\substack{r \\ r \neq j}} x_{jr(k+1)}, \quad \text{for all } j \text{ and } k.$$

This constraint ensures that the round trip will consist of connected segments (directed arcs).

The objective function is thus:

$$\text{minimize} \quad x_0 = \sum_i \sum_j \sum_k d_{ij} x_{ijk}, \quad i \neq j$$

where d_{ij} is the distance from town i to town j.

The travelling salesman problem has several practical applications. An important application occurs in sequencing several jobs on a single processing facility where the set-up time for a given job is dependent on which job immediately precedes this one. Since the processing time per job can be assumed constant, the problem reduces to determining the sequence which minimizes the sum of the total set-up times. This problem is equivalent to that of the travelling salesman since a job can be thought of as a city with the set-up times replacing the distances between the different cities.

Although, the travelling salesman problem can, in principle, be solved by the Balas, Gomory, or Land-Doig Algorithms, a special algorithm based on the idea of "branch-and-bound" was developed by Little *et al*[11] to handle the problem efficiently. This algorithm is not presented here, however.

§ 10·5·2
Job-Shop Scheduling Problem[12]

Consider the sequencing problem involving the completion of n different operations on a *single* machine in the minimum possible time. Each end product goes through a sequence of different operations whose order must be

---

[11] J. D. C. Little, *et al*, "An Algorithm for the Travelling Salesman Problem," *Operations Research*, 11, 1963, 979–989.

[12] This model is based on A. S. Manne, "On the Job-Shop Scheduling Problem," *Operations Research*, 8, 1960, 219–223.

preserved. Also each of these end products may have to meet some delivery date.

The problem thus has three types of constraints,

1. sequencing constraints.
2. noninterference constraints.
3. delivery date constraints.

The second type of constraints ascertains that no two operations can be processed (on one machine) simultaneously.

Consider the first type of constraints. Let x_j be the time (beginning from the zero datum) for starting operation j. Let a_j be the processing time required to finish operation j. Thus, if operation i is to precede operation j, then

$$x_i + a_i \leq x_j.$$

Similarly, if both operations i and j must precede operation k, then

$$x_i + a_i \leq x_k$$

and

$$x_j + a_j \leq x_k.$$

These two constraints obviously do not include any precedence relationship between operations i and j. This, however, can be incorporated in a similar way.

Consider next the noninterference constraints. In order for operations i and j not to occupy the machine simultaneously, then; *either*

$$x_i - x_j \geq a_j,$$

or

$$x_j - x_i \geq a_i,$$

depending, respectively, on whether j precedes i or i precedes j in the optimal solution.

The presence of the "either-or" constraints poses a problem since the model is no longer in the linear programming format (that is, the either-or constraint results in a nonconvex solution space). This difficulty is overcome by introducing the binary (0 or 1) variable y_{ij}. Let M be a very large positive number. Then the above two constraints are equivalent to

$$My_{ij} + (x_i - x_j) \geq a_j,$$

and

$$M(1 - y_{ij}) + (x_j - x_i) \geq a_i.$$

The significance of the new transformation can now be explained. If in the optimal solution $y_{ij} = 0$, the second constraint becomes redundant since, regardless of the values of x_i and x_j, the presence of the constant M as indicated will make it redundant. In the meantime, the first constraint remains effective. Similarly if $y_{ij} = 1$, the second, but not the first, constraint becomes effective. The introduction of the binary variable y_{ij} has thus reduced these constraints to the normal form where it is possible to use mixed integer linear programming.

Returning to the problem of formulation, the delivery dates can be met by adding the following constraints. Suppose that operation j must be completed by time d_j, then

$$x_j + a_j \le d_j.$$

Now, if t is the total time required to finish all n operations, then the objective is

$$\text{minimize} \quad x_0 = t,$$

subject to

$$x_j + a_j \le t, \quad j = 1, 2, \ldots, n$$

together with the sequencing, noninterference and delivery constraints developed above.

This problem may be solved first as a regular linear programming problem with

$$0 \le y_{ij} \le 1.$$

The mixed algorithms given above are then used to force y_{ij} to take the values zero or one.

§ 10·5·3
Fixed Charge Problem

Consider the production planning problem where it is required to produce at least N units of a certain product on n different machines. Let x_j be the number of units produced on machine j, $j = 1, 2, \ldots, n$. The production cost function for the jth machine is given by

$$C_j(x_j) = \begin{cases} K_j + c_j x_j, & x_j > 0, \\ 0, & x_j = 0, \end{cases}$$

where K_j is the set-up cost for machine j. The model for this problem is given by:

$$\text{minimize} \quad x_0 = \sum_{j=1}^{n} C_j(x_j),$$

subject to

$$\sum_{j=1}^{n} x_j \geq N,$$

$$x_j \geq 0, \text{ and integer.}$$

The objective function in the above model is nonlinear because of the presence of the fixed charge K_j. This problem may be overcome using mixed integer programming.

Let M be a very large number that exceeds the capacity of any of the machines and let y_j be a binary variable. The above model thus reduces to:

$$\text{minimize} \quad x_0 = \sum_{j=1}^{n} K_j y_j + \sum_{j=1}^{n} c_j x_j,$$

subject to

$$\sum_{j=1}^{n} x_j \geq N,$$

$$x_j \leq M y_j, \text{ all } j,$$

$$x_j \geq 0, \text{ and integer,}$$

$$y_j = 0 \text{ or } 1, \text{ for all } j,$$

which can then be solved in the regular way.

With the above formulation it is clear that,

1. If $x_j > 0$, then y_j must be equal to 1 (rather than zero), otherwise the constraint,

$$x_j \leq M y_j,$$

is not satisfied.

2. If $x_j = 0$, then y_j may be either zero or one. However, because non-trivial K_j is positive, minimization of the objective function should give $y_j = 0$ to ensure optimality.

The idea of introducing the binary variable y_j and the large positive constant M can be successfully extended to encompass two important cases, (1) the solution requires that any k out of m constraints must hold, and (2) the right-hand side of the constraint may assume one of several discrete values. Consider the first case. Let the m constraints of the problem be put in the form

$$\sum_{j} a_{ij} x_j \leq b_i, \quad i = 1, 2, \ldots, m.$$

Out of these m constraints only k $(<m)$ must be effective. Thus the equivalent formulation becomes

$$\sum_j a_{ij} x_j \leq b_i + M y_i, \quad i = 1, 2, \ldots, m,$$

$$\sum_{i=1}^{m} y_i = m - k,$$

$$y_i = 0 \text{ or } 1, \quad i = 1, 2, \ldots, m.$$

This shows that exactly $(m - k)$ of the y_i-variables will be equal to 1. In this case, their corresponding constraints will be nonbinding since the right-hand sides will be too large to be restrictive.

The second case assumes that the right-hand side of the constraint,

$$\sum_j a_{ij} x_j = b_i,$$

(that is, b_i) takes one of the exclusive values, $b_i^1, \ldots, b_i^r$. Thus, letting y_i^k be a binary variable, $k = 1, 2, \ldots, r$, the above constraint becomes equivalent to,

$$\sum_j a_{ij} x_j - \sum_{k=1}^{r} b_i^k y_i^k = 0,$$

$$\sum_{k=1}^{r} y_i^k = 1,$$

$$y_i^k = 0 \text{ or } 1, \quad k = 1, 2, \ldots, r.$$

§ 10·5·4
Nonlinear Objective Function Problem

Consider the nonlinear objective function:

$$\text{minimize} \quad x_0 = \sum_{j=1}^{n} f_j(x_j),$$

subject to

$$\sum_{j=1}^{n} a_{ij} x_j = b_i, \quad i = 1, 2, \ldots, m,$$

$$x_j \geq 0, \quad \text{all } j,$$

where $f_j(x_j)$ is a nonlinear function in x_j. The point now is to convert the objective function into a linear form by approximating each $f_j(x_j)$ over its permissible domain. A typical linear approximation for each $f(x)$ is given in Figure 10–10.

The points (a_k, b_k), $k = 1, 2, \ldots, K$ are called the *breaking points* which join the linear segments approximating the function $f(x)$. Let t_k represent a nonnegative weight associated with the kth breaking point such that

$$\sum_{k=1}^{K} t_k = 1.$$

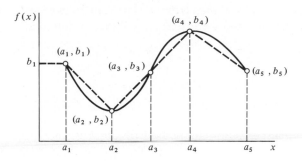

Figure 10–10

Linear Approximation of a Nonlinear Function

Suppose that additional constraints are imposed as necessary so that all t_k but $t_{k'}$ and $t_{k'+1}$ are set equal to zero. In this case, any point on the line joining the breaking points $(a_{k'}, b_{k'})$ and $(a_{k'+1}, b_{k'+1})$ can be defined by appropriately specifying $t_{k'}$ and $t_{k'+1}$. This means that such a point will be the weighted average of $(a_{k'}, b_{k'})$ and $(a_{k'+1}, b_{k'+1})$.

With the above point in mind, it follows that $f(x)$ and x can be approximated by

$$f(x) = \sum_{k=1}^{K} b_k t_k,$$

where

$$x = \sum_{k=1}^{K} a_k t_k.$$

This means that the new variables of the problem are given by t_k.

The necessary additional constraints which guarantee a valid approximation are

$$0 \leq t_1 \quad \leq y_1,$$
$$0 \leq t_2 \quad \leq y_1 + y_2,$$
$$0 \leq t_3 \quad \leq \quad y_2 + y_3,$$
$$0 \quad \vdots \qquad\qquad\qquad \ddots$$
$$0 \leq t_{K-1} \leq \qquad\qquad\qquad y_{K-2} + y_{K-1},$$
$$0 \leq t_K \quad \leq \qquad\qquad\qquad y_{K-1},$$

$$\sum_{k=1}^{K} t_k = 1,$$

$$\sum_{k=1}^{K-1} y_k = 1,$$

$$y_k = 0 \text{ or } 1, \text{ for all } k.$$

Suppose now that $y_{k'} = 1$, then from the last constraint above all other $y_k = 0$. The immediately preceding constraints will then ensure that

$$0 \le t_{k'} \le y_{k'} = 1$$

and

$$0 \le t_{k'+1} \le y_{k'} = 1$$

The remaining constraints should thus yield $t_k \le 0$ and hence all other $t_k = 0$ as required.

The above approximation can be used to substitute the corresponding values of x and $f(x)$ in the original problem. The additional constraints should also be added to ensure the validity of the approximation. It is obvious in this case that the size of the problem may increase beyond computational feasibility. The main point here, however, is to show how integer programming could assist in reformulating the problem into a manageable form. (See Section 17·2 for further discussion on this problem.)

SELECTED REFERENCES

1. BALAS, E., "An Additive Algorithm for Solving Linear Programs with Zero-One Variables," *Operations Research*, 13, 517–546, (1965).
2. BALINSKI, M., "Integer Programming: Methods, Uses, Computations," *Management Science*, 12, 253–313, (1961).
3. GEOFFRION, A., "Integer Programming by Implicit Enumeration and Balas' Method," *The Rand Corporation*, RM-4783-PR, February, 1966.
4. GLOVER, F., "A Multiphase-Dual Algorithm for the Zero-One Integer Programming Problems," *Operations Research*, 13, 879–919, (1965).
5. LAND, A., and A. DOIG, "An Automatic Method for Solving Discrete Programming Problems," *Econometrica*, 28, 497–520, (1960).
6. PETERSON, C., "Computational Experience with Variants of the Balas Algorithm Applied to the Selection of R&D Projects," *Management Science*, 13, 736–784, (1967).
7. SIMMONARD, M., *Linear Programming*, translated by W. Jewell, Englewood Cliffs, N.J.: Prentice-Hall, 1966, Chaps. 8 and 9.

PROBLEMS

□ **10-1**   Consider the problem:

$$\text{maximize} \quad x_0 = x_1 + 2x_2,$$

subject to

$$x_1 + \frac{1}{2} x_2 \le \frac{13}{4},$$

x_1, x_2 nonnegative integers.

Show that Gomory's all-integer algorithm does not yield a feasible solution to this problem unless the coefficients *and* the right-hand side of the constraint are integers, then find the optimal solution.

□ **10-2** Solve by the Gomory algorithm,

$$\text{maximize} \quad x_0 = 4x_1 + 6x_2 + 2x_3,$$

subject to

$$4x_1 - 4x_2 \le 5,$$
$$-x_1 + 6x_2 \le 5,$$
$$-x_1 + x_2 + x_3 \le 5,$$
$$x_1, x_2, x_3 \ge 0 \text{ and integers.}$$

Compare between the solutions obtained by rounding the optimal non-integer solution and the optimal integer solution.

□ **10-3** Solve by the Gomory algorithm,

$$\text{maximize} \quad x_0 = 3x_1 + x_2 + 3x_3,$$

subject to

$$-x_1 + 2x_2 + x_3 \le 4,$$
$$4x_2 - 3x_3 \le 2,$$
$$x_1 - 3x_2 + 2x_3 \le 3,$$
$$x_1, x_2, x_3 \ge 0 \text{ and integers.}$$

Compare between the solutions obtained by rounding the optimal non-integer solution and the optimal integer solution.

□ **10-4** Solve Problem 10-2 assuming that x_1 and x_3 are the only integer variables. Use Gomory's mixed algorithm.

□ **10-5** Solve Problem 10-3 assuming that x_1 and x_3 are the only integer variables. Use Gomory's mixed algorithm.

□ **10-6** Show graphically that the following problem has no feasible integer solution.

$$\text{Maximize} \quad x_0 = 2x_1 + x_2,$$

subject to

$$10x_1 + 10x_2 \le 9,$$
$$10x_1 + 5x_2 \ge 1,$$
$$x_1, x_2 \ge 0 \text{ and integers.}$$

Verify this result algebraically using

(a) The Gomory algorithm.
(b) The Land-Doig algorithm.

☐ **10-7** Solve Example 10·3-1 starting with the variable x_2, instead of x_1, at the node z^0.

☐ **10-8** Consider the problem,

$$\text{maximize } x_0 = x_1 + x_2,$$

subject to

$$2x_1 + 5x_2 \leq 16,$$

$$6x_1 + 5x_2 \leq 30,$$

$$x_1, x_2 \geq 0 \text{ and integers.}$$

Find the noninteger solution graphically. Using the Land-Doig and Dakin algorithms, show graphically the successive parallel changes in the x_0-value which will lead to the optimal integer solution.

☐ **10-9** Solve Problem 10-5 using both Land-Doig's and Dakin's algorithms. Compare the two methods.

☐ **10-10** Consider the cargo-loading (or knapsack) problem discussed in Problem 7-17 (chapter 7). Suppose five items are to be loaded on the vessel. The weight w_i and the volume r_i per unit of the different items as well as their corresponding values v_i are tabulated below.

Item i	w_i	r_i	v_i
1	5	1	4
2	8	8	7
3	3	6	6
4	2	5	5
5	7	4	4

The maximum cargo weight and volume are given by $W = 112$ and $R = 109$, respectively. It is required to determine the most valuable cargo-load in discrete units of each item.

Formulate the problem as an integer programming model and then solve using both Land-Doig's and Dakin's algorithms. Compare the two methods.

☐ **10-11** In Problem 10-3, suppose all the variables are restricted to binary values only. Find the solution to the problem using the Balas Algorithm.

☐ **10-12** In Problem 10-6, assume that x_1 and x_2 are binary variables. Show how the Balas algorithm can be used to discover that the problem has no feasible (integer) solution.

☐ **10-13** Consider the capital budgeting problem where five projects are being considered for execution over the next three years. The expected returns for each project and the yearly expenditures (in thousands of dollars) are shown below. Assume that each approved project will be executed over the three-year period.

Project	Expenditures for			Returns
	Year 1	Year 2	Year 3	
1	5	1	8	20
2	4	7	10	40
3	3	9	2	20
4	7	4	1	15
5	8	6	10	30
Maximum available funds	25	25	25	—

The objective is to select the projects which will maximize the total returns.

Formulate the problem as a zero-one integer programming problem and solve by Balas' algorithm.

☐ **10-14** Suggest some modifications which will render stronger exclusion tests (that is, optimality and feasibility conditions) for the Balas algorithm.

☐ **10-15** Consider a four-city travelling salesman problem. The distances between the cities are indicated below.

	City j			
	1	2	3	4
City i 1	0	1	5	4
2	7	0	3	1
3	5	—	0	2
4	4	1	2	0

It is assumed that city 2 cannot be reached from city 3.

Write the explicit functions describing the constraints and the objective of the problem.

□ **10-16** Solve the following problem.

$$\text{Maximize} \quad x_0 = x_1 + 2x_2 + 5x_3,$$

subject to

$$|-x_1 + 10x_2 - 3x_3| \geq 15,$$

$$2x_1 + x_2 + x_3 \leq 10,$$

$$x_1, x_2, x_3 \geq 0.$$

□ **10-17** Using mixed integer programming, show how the nonconvex solution spaces (shaded areas) indicated below can be transformed to fit into the regular form.

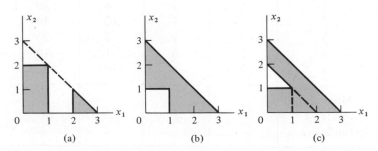

(a)   (b)   (c)

Using mixed integer programming find the optimum solution which maximizes $x_0 = 2x_1 + 3x_2$ subject to the solution space given in case (a) above. (Hint: use the concept of "either-or" constraints.)

□ **10-18** Consider the production planning problem where it is required to produce 2000 units of a certain product on three different machines. The set-up costs, the production costs per unit and the maximum production capacity for each machine are tabulated below.

Machine	Set-up cost	Production cost/unit	Capacity (no. of units)
1	100	10	600
2	300	2	800
3	200	5	1200

The objective is to minimize the total production cost of the required lot.

Formulate the problem as an integer programming problem and find the solution.

□ **10-19** In an oil well drilling problem there are two attractive drilling sites for reaching four targets (or possible oil wells). The preparation costs at each site and the cost of drilling from site i to target j ($i = 1, 2$; $j = 1, 2, 3, 4$) are given below.

Site	Drilling cost to target				Preparation cost
	1	2	3	4	
1	2	1	8	5	5
2	4	6	3	1	6

The objective is to determine the best site for each target so that the total cost is minimized.

Formulate the problem as an integer programming model and suggest a method for obtaining the solution.

□ **10-20** Consider the job-shop scheduling problem which involves eight operations on a single machine with a total of two end products. The sequencing of these eight operations is shown in the network below. Let b_j be the processing time for the jth operation, $j = 1, 2, \ldots, 8$. Delivery dates for products 1 and 2 are restricted by d_1 and d_2 time units measured from the zero datum. Since each operation requires a special machine set-up, it is assumed that any operation once started must be completed before a new operation can be undertaken.

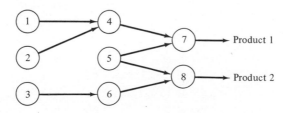

Formulate the problem as a mixed integer programming model in order to minimize the total scheduling time on the machine while satisfying all the pertinent constraints.

□ **10-21** Solve the following problem assuming that only one of the given constraints holds.

$$\text{Maximize} \quad x_0 = x_1 + 2x_2 - 3x_3,$$

subject to

$$20x_1 + 15x_2 - x_3 \leq 10,$$

$$12x_1 - 3x_2 + 4x_3 \leq 20,$$

x_1, x_2, x_3 are binary variables.

□ **10-22** Using mixed integer programming show how the solution space indicated below (shaded area) can be expressed to fit into the proper format of mixed integer linear programming.

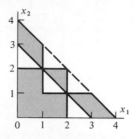

□ **10-23** Consider the nonlinear problem

$$\text{minimize} \quad x_0 = x_1^2 + x_2^3 - x_2,$$

subject to

$$x_1 + x_2 \le 5,$$

$$x_1 \ge 0, \quad x_2 \ge 0.$$

Approximate the problem into an equivalent linear problem.

CHAPTER 11

Project Scheduling by PERT-CPM

§ 11·1
Introduction

A *project* defines a combination of interrrelated activities which must be executed in a certain order before the entire task can be completed. The activities are interrelated in a logical sequence in the sense that the execution of some activities cannot start until some others are completed. An activity in a project is usually viewed as a job requiring time and resources for its completion. In general, a project is a one-time effort in which the same sequence of activities may not be repeated.

Until recently, the scheduling of a project (over time) was done with little or no planning. The best known "planning" tool then was the so-called (Gantt) bar chart which specifies the start and finish times for each activity on a horizontal time scale. The disadvantage here is that the interdependency between the different activities (which mainly controls the progress of the project) cannot be determined from the bar chart. The growing complexities of today's projects have demanded more systematic and more effective planning techniques with the objective of optimizing the efficiency of executing the project. Efficiency here implies effecting the utmost reduction in the time required to complete the project while accounting for the economic feasibility of using available resources.

Project management has evolved as a new field with the development of two "analytic" techniques for planning, scheduling and controlling of projects. These are the Critical Path Method (CPM) and the Project Evaluation and Review Technique (PERT). The two techniques were developed by two different groups almost simultaneously (1956–1958). CPM was first developed by E. I. du Pont de Nemours Company as an application to construction projects and was later extended to a more advanced status by Mauchly Asssociates.

PERT, on the other hand, was developed by the U.S. Navy for scheduling the research and development activities for the Polaris missile program.

PERT and CPM are basically time-oriented methods in the sense that they both lead to the determination of a time schedule for the project. Although the two methods were developed almost independently, they are strikingly similar. Perhaps the most important difference is that originally in CPM the time estimates for the different activities were assumed to be deterministic while in PERT these were described probabilistically. Today, PERT and CPM actually comprise one technique and the differences, if any, are only historical. Consequently, both techniques will be referred to as "project scheduling" techniques.

Project scheduling by PERT-CPM consists of three basic phases: planning, scheduling and controlling.

The planning phase is initiated by breaking down the project into distinct activities. The time estimates for these activities are then determined and a network (or arrow) diagram is constructed with each of its arcs (arrows) representing a distinct activity. The entire arrow diagram gives a graphic representation of the interdependencies between the activities of the project. The construction of the arrow diagram as a planning phase yields the advantage of studying the different jobs in details, perhaps suggesting improvements before the project is actually executed. More important will be its use to develop the schedule for the project.

The ultimate objective of the scheduling phase is to construct a time chart showing the start and finish times for each activity as well as its relationship to the other activities of the project. In addition, the schedule must pinpoint the critical (in view of time) activities which require special attention if the project is to be completed on time. For the noncritical activities the schedule must show the amount of slack or float times which can be used advantageously when such activities are delayed or when limited resources are to be utilized effectively.

The final phase in project management is controlling. This includes the use of the arrow diagram and the time chart for making periodic progress reports. The network may thus be updated and analyzed and, if necessary, new courses of action are determined for the remaining portion of the project.

This chapter presents the basics of the above three phases. Section 11·2 discusses the rules for constructing the arrow diagram. The method of preparing the data for the construction of the time chart is given in Section 11·3. Section 11·4 explains the method of constructing the time chart as well as the method of allocating limited resources to the different activities. (The latter is known as *resource leveling*.) Section 11·5 then presents the aspects of probability and cost as applied to project scheduling. A discussion of project control is given in Section 11·6. Finally, Section 11·7 presents the mathematical formulation of project scheduling techniques as a linear programming model. This section is presented for the theoretical interest and may be skipped without loss of continuity.

§ 11·2
Arrow (Network) Diagram Representation

The first step in project scheduling is the construction of the arrow diagram which represents the interdependencies and the precedence relationships between the activities of the project. An arrow is commonly used to represent an activity with its head indicating the direction of progress in the project. The precedence relationship between the activities is specified using the concept of events. An *event* represents a point in time signifying the completion of some activities and the beginning of new ones. Thus activities originating from a certain event cannot start until the activities terminating in the same event have been completed. In network theory terminology (see Section 5·4), each activity is represented by a directed arc while each event is represented by a node. As in other network models, the length of the arc need not be proportional to the duration of the activity nor does it have to be drawn as a straight line.

Figure 11–1 (a) shows an example of a typical representation of an activity (i, j) with its tail event i and its head event j.

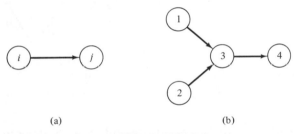

(a)   (b)

Figure 11–1

Figure 11–1(b) shows another example where activities (1, 3) and (2, 3) must be completed before activity (3, 4) can start. Notice that the direction of progress in each activity can be specified by assigning a smaller number to the tail event as compared to the number of its head event. This procedure is especially convenient for automatic computations and hence will be adopted throughout this chapter.

The rules for constructing the arrow diagram will be summarized now.

Rule 1: Each activity is represented by one and only one arrow in the network.
This means that no single activity can be represented twice in the network. This is to be differentiated from the case where one activity is broken down into segments. In this case, each segment may be represented by a separate arrow. For example, in laying down a pipe, this may be done in sections rather than as one job.

Rule 2: *No two activities can be identified by the same end events.* A situation like this may arise when two or more activities can be performed concurrently. An example of this case is shown in Figure 11–2(a) where activities *A* and *B* have the same end events. The procedure here is to introduce a *dummy* activity either between *A* and one of the end events or between *B* and one of the end events. The modified representations, after introducing the dummy *D*, are shown in Figure 11–2(b). As a result of using the dummy *D*, activities *A* and *B* can now be identified by unique end events. It must be noted that a dummy activity does not consume any time or resources.

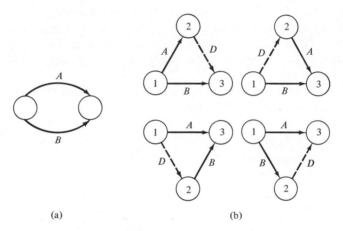

(a)   (b)

Figure 11–2

Dummy activities are also useful in establishing logic relationships in the arrow diagram which otherwise cannot be represented correctly. Suppose in a certain project that jobs *A* and *B* must precede *C*. On the other hand, job *E* is preceded by job *B* only. Figure 11–3(a) shows the incorrect way; since, although the relationship between *A*, *B*, and *C* are correct, the diagram implies that *E* must be preceded by both *A* and *B*. The correct representation using the dummy *D* is shown in Figure 11–3(b). Since *D* consumes no time (or resources) it is obvious that the indicated precedence relationships are satisfied.

Rule 3: *In order to ensure the correct precedence relationship in the arrow diagram the following questions must be checked as every activity is added to the network.*

   (i) *What activities must be completed immediately before this activity can start?*
  (ii) *What activities must follow this activity?*
 (iii) *What activities must occur concurrently with this activity?*

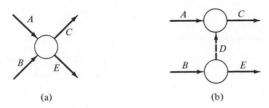

Figure 11–3

This rule is self-explanatory. It actually allows for checking (and rechecking) the precedence relationships as one progresses in the development of the network.

An example is now introduced to illustrate the use of the above rules.

▶ **Example 11·2-1**

Construct the arrow diagram comprising activities A, B, C, ..., and L such that the following relationships are satisfied.

1. A, B and C, the first activities of the project, can start simultaneously.
2. A and B precede D.
3. B precedes E, F, and H.
4. F and C precede G.
5. E and H precede I and J.
6. C, D, F, and J precede K.
7. K precedes L.
8. I, G, and L are the terminal activities of the project.

The resulting arrow diagram is shown in Figure 11–4. It is noted that the dummy activities D_1 and D_2 are used to establish correct precedence relationships while D_3 is used to identify activities E and H with unique end events. The events of the project are now numbered such that their ascending order will indicate the direction of progress in the project. ◀

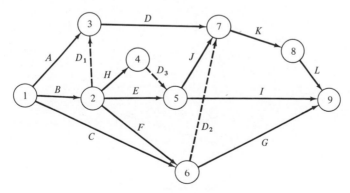

Figure 11–4

§ 11·3
Critical Path Calculations

The application of PERT-CPM should ultimately yield a schedule specifiying the start and completion dates of each activity. The arrow diagram represents the first step toward achieving that goal. Because of the interaction among the different activities, the determination of the start and completion times requires special computations. These calculations are performed directly on the arrow diagram using simple arithmetic. The end result here is to classify the activities of the project into *critical* and *noncritical*. As mentioned previously, an activity is said to be critical if a delay in its start will cause a delay in the completion date of the entire project. A noncritical activity, on the other hand, is such that the time between its earliest start and its latest completion dates (as allowed by the project) is longer than its actual duration. In this case, the noncritical activity is said to have a *slack* or *float* time.

The advantage of pinpointing the critical activities and of determining the floats will be discussed in Section 11·4. This section will mainly present the methods for obtaining this information.

§ 11·3·1
Determination of the Critical Path

A critical path defines a chain of critical activities which connect the start and end events of the arrow diagram. In other words the critical path identifies all the critical activities of the project. The method of determining such a path is best illustrated by a numerical example.

▶   **Example 11·3-1**
Consider the network in Figure 11–5 which starts at node 1 and terminates at node 6. The time required to perform each activity is indicated on the arrows.

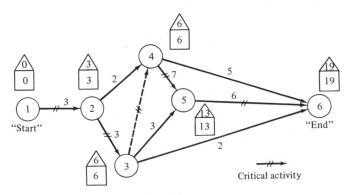

Fig. 11–5

The critical path calculations include two phases. The first phase is called the *forward pass* where the calculations begin from the " start " node and move toward the " end " node. At each node a number is computed representing the earliest occurrence time of the corresponding event. These numbers are shown in the above network in squares, $\square$. The second phase, called the *backward pass*, begins the calculations from the " end " node and moves toward the " start " node. The number computed at each node (shown in triangles, $\triangle$) represents the latest occurrence time of the corresponding event. The solution starts now by the forward pass.

Let ES_i be the *earliest start* time of all the activities emanating from event i. Thus ES_i represents the earliest occurrence time of event i. Now if $i = 1$ is the " start " event, then conventionally for the critical path calculations, $ES_1 = 0$. Let D_{ij} be the duration of activity (i, j). The forward pass calculations are thus obtained from the formula,

$$ES_j = \max_i \{ES_i + D_{ij}\}, \quad \text{for all defined } (i, j) \text{ activities,}$$

where $ES_1 = 0$. This formula says that in order to compute ES_j for event j, ES_i for the tail events i of *all* the incoming activities (i, j) must be computed first.

Applying the forward pass calculations to the above network, $ES_1 = 0$ is shown in Figure 11–5 in the square above event 1. Moving to event 2, since there is only one incoming activity $(1, 2)$, with $D_{12} = 3$, then

$$ES_2 = ES_1 + D_{12} = 0 + 3 = 3.$$

This is entered in the square associated with event 2. The next event to be considered is 3. (Notice that event 4 cannot be considered at this point since ES_3 (event 3) is not yet known.) Thus,

$$ES_3 = ES_2 + D_{23} = 3 + 3 = 6.$$

The value of ES_4 can now be obtained. Since there are two incoming activities, namely $(2, 4)$ and $(3, 4)$ then

$$ES_4 = \max_{i=2, 3} \{ES_i + D_{i4}\} = \max\{3 + 2, 6 + 0\} = 6.$$

This is entered now in the square associated with event 4.

The procedure continues in the same manner until ES_i is computed for all i. Thus,

$$ES_5 = \max_{i=3, 4} \{ES_i + D_{i5}\} = \max\{6 + 3, 6 + 7\} = 13,$$

$$ES_6 = \max_{i=3, 4, 5} \{ES_i + D_{i6}\} = \max\{6 + 2, 6 + 5, 13 + 6\} = 19.$$

These calculations complete the forward pass.

The backward pass starts from the "end" event and proceeds backward to the "start" event. The objective of this phase is to compute LC_i, the *latest completion* time for all the activities coming into event i. Thus, if $i = n$ is the "end" event, then $LC_n = ES_n$ initiates the backward pass. In general, for any node i,

$$LC_i = \min_j \{LC_j - D_{ij}\}, \quad \text{for all defined } (i, j) \text{ activities.}$$

Applying this to the given network the values of LC are entered in the triangles ($\triangle$) associated with each event. Thus

$$LC_6 = ES_6 = 19,$$

$$LC_5 = LC_6 - D_{56} = 19 - 6 = 13,$$

$$LC_4 = \min_{j=5,\,6} \{LC_j - D_{4j}\} = \min\{13 - 7, 19 - 5\} = 6,$$

$$LC_3 = \min_{j=4,\,5,\,6} \{LC_j - D_{3j}\} = \min\{6 - 0, 13 - 3, 19 - 2\} = 6,$$

$$LC_2 = \min_{j=3,\,4} \{LC_j - D_{2j}\} = \min\{6 - 3, 6 - 2\} = 3,$$

$$LC_1 = LC_2 - D_{12} = 3 - 3 = 0.$$

This completes the backward pass calculations.

The critical path activities can now be identified using the results of the forward and the backward passes. An activity (i, j) is said to lie on the critical path if it satisfies the following three conditions,

(i) $ES_i = LC_i$,
(ii) $ES_j = LC_j$,
(iii) $ES_j - ES_i = LC_j - LC_i = D_{ij}$,

These conditions actually indicate that there is no float time between the earliest start (completion) and the latest start (completion) of the activity. Thus, this activity must be critical. In the arrow diagram these activities are characterized by the fact that the numbers in $\square$ and $\triangle$ are the same at each of the head and the tail events *and* that the difference between the number in $\square$ (or $\triangle$) at the head event and the number in $\square$ (or $\triangle$) at the tail event is equal to the duration of the activity.

Applying this to the given network it follows that activities (1, 2), (2, 3), (3, 4), (4, 5), and (5, 6) define its critical path. This is actually the shortest possible time to complete the project. Notice that activities (2, 4), (3, 5), (3, 6), and (4, 6) satisfy conditions (i) and (ii) for critical activities but not condition (iii). Hence, they are not critical. Notice also that the critical path must form a chain of *connected* activities which spans the network from its "start" event to its "end" event. ◄

§ 11·3·2
Determination of the Floats

Following the determination of the critical path, the floats for the noncritical activities must be computed. Naturally, a critical activity must have a zero float. In fact this is the main reason it is critical.

Before showing how floats are determined, it is necessary first to define two new times which are associated with each activity. These are the *latest start* (LS) and the *earliest completion* (EC) times. These are given for activity (i, j) by

$$LS_{ij} = LC_j - D_{ij},$$

$$EC_{ij} = ES_i + D_{ij}.$$

There are two important types of floats; the *total float* (TF) and the *free float* (FF). The total float, TF_{ij}, for activity (i, j) is defined by the difference between the maximum time available to perform the activity $(= LC_j - ES_i)$ and its duration $(= D_{ij})$; that is,

$$TF_{ij} = LC_j - ES_i - D_{ij},$$

$$= LC_j - EC_{ij},$$

$$= LS_{ij} - ES_i.$$

The free float, on the other hand, is defined by assuming that all the activities start as early as possible. In this case, FF_{ij} for activity (i, j) is the excess of available time $(= ES_j - ES_i)$ over its duration $(= D_{ij})$; that is,

$$FF_{ij} = ES_j - ES_i - D_{ij}.$$

The critical path calculations together with the floats for the noncritical activities can be summarized in the convenient form shown in Table 11–1. The information in columns (1), (2), (3), and (6) are obtained from the network calculations of Example 11·3-1. The remaining information can be determined using the above formulas.

Table 11–1 gives a typical summary of the critical path calculations. It includes all the information necessary to construct the time chart. Notice that a critical activity, and only a critical activity, must have zero *total* float. The free float must also be zero when the total float is zero. The converse is not true, however, in the sense that a *non*critical activity may have zero free float. The above table shows that the total float is the same as the free float. This happened to occur mainly because all the events of the project are on the critical path. In general, this will not be true. It must be noted that the free float is seldom used in the construction of the time chart. Its main use comes in considering the cost aspect of project scheduling (see Section 11·5).

Table 11–1

Activity	Duration	Earliest		Latest		Total float	Free float
		Start $\square$	Completion	Start	Completion $\triangle$		
(i, j) (1)	D_{ij} (2)	ES_i (3)	EC_{ij} (4)	LS_{ij} (5)	LC_j (6)	TF_{ij} (7)	FF_{ij} (8)
$(1, 2)$	3	0	3	0	3	0*	0
$(2, 3)$	3	3	6	3	6	0*	0
$(2, 4)$	2	3	5	4	6	1	1
$(3, 4)$	0	6	6	6	6	0*	0
$(3, 5)$	3	6	9	10	13	4	4
$(3, 6)$	2	6	8	17	19	11	11
$(4, 5)$	7	6	13	6	13	0*	0
$(4, 6)$	5	6	11	14	19	8	8
$(5, 6)$	6	13	19	13	19	0*	0

*Critical activity.

§11·4

Construction of the Time Chart and Resource Leveling

The end product of network calculations is the construction of the time chart (or schedule). This time chart can be converted easily into a calender time schedule convenient for use by the personnel who will execute the project.

The construction of the time chart must be made within the limitations of the available resources. This means that it may not be possible to execute concurrent activities because of the limitations on manpower and equipment. This is where the total floats for the noncritical activity may become useful. By shifting a noncritical activity (back and forth) between its ES and LC limits, one may be able to adjust the maximum resource requirements. In any case, even in the absence of limited resources, it is a common practice to use the total floats to level the resources over the duration of the entire project. In essence this would mean a more steady work force as compared to the case where the work force (and equipment) would change from one day to the next.

The procedure for constructing the time chart will be illustrated by Example 11·4-1. Example 11·4-2 will then show how resource leveling can be effected for the same project of Example 11·4-1.

▶ **Example 11·4-1**

In this example the time chart for the project given in Example 11·3-1 will be constructed.

The information necessary to construct the time chart is summarized in Table 11–1. The first step now is to consider the scheduling of the critical activities. Next, the noncritical activities are considered by indicating their *ES* and *LC* time limits on the chart. It is a common practice to show the critical activities with solid lines indicating that they must be completed on time if the project is not to be delayed. The time ranges for the noncritical activities are shown by dotted lines indicating that such activities may be scheduled anywhere within those ranges.

Figure 11–6 shows the time chart corresponding to Example 11·3-1. Notice that the dummy activity (3, 4) is shown by a vertical line indicating that it requires zero time. The numbers shown with the noncritical activities represent their durations. If resources are not an effective factor, then each noncritical activity should be scheduled as early as possible. This allows taking the utmost advantage of the float in case the execution of any of these activities is delayed unexpectedly. ◀

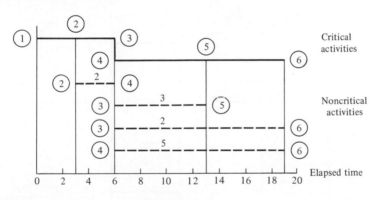

Figure 11–6

▶ **Example 11·4-2**

In Example 11·4-1 suppose the following manpower requirements are specified for the different activities. It is required to develop a time schedule which will level the manpower requirements during the project duration.

Activity	Number of men	Activity	Number of men
1, 2	5	3, 6	1
2, 3	7	4, 5	2
2, 4	3	4, 6	5
3, 5	2	5, 6	6

Figure 11–7(a) shows the manpower requirements over time if the non-critical activities are scheduled as early as possible while Figure 11–7(b) shows the requirements if these activities are scheduled as late as possible. The dotted line shows the requirements for the critical activities which obviously must be satisfied if the project is to be completed on time.

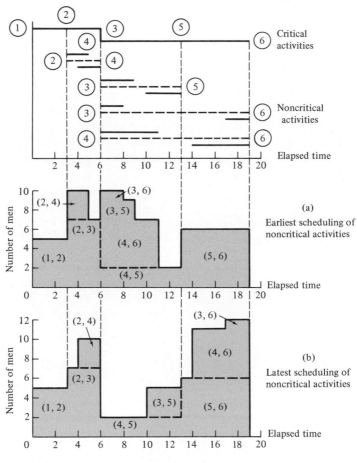

Figure 11–7

It is noticed that the project requires at least 7 men as indicated by the requirements of the critical activity (2, 3). The earliest scheduling of the noncritical activities results in a maximum requirement of 10 men while the latest scheduling of the same activities sets the maximum requirements at 12 men. This illustrates that the maximum requirements depend on how the total float of the noncritical activities are utilized. In Figure 11–7 it is obvious, however, that regardless of how the floats are allocated the maximum requirement cannot be less than 10 men. This follows since the range for activity (2, 4) happened to coincide with the time for the critical activity (2, 3). The manpower requirement using the earliest scheduling can be improved, however, by rescheduling activity (3, 5) at its latest possible time and activity (3, 6) right after activity (4, 6) is completed. This new requirement is shown in Figure 11–8. Notice that the new schedule has now resulted in a smoother allocation of resources.

In some projects the objective may be specified as keeping the maximum resource utilization below a certain limit rather than merely leveling the resources. If this cannot be accomplished by rescheduling the noncritical activities, it will be necessary to expand the time for some of the critical activities provided of course that this would result in a decrease in the required resources. This however, may still necessitate that some jobs be executed in segments rather than as one entity. ◀

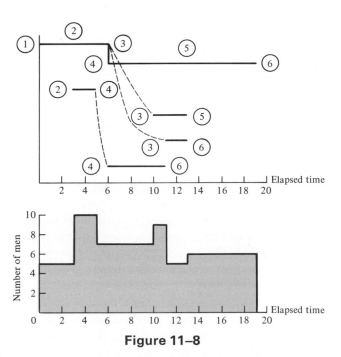

Figure 11–8

It must be noted that due to mathematical complexity, no technique has yet been developed which will yield the *optimum* solution to the resource leveling problem; that is, minimization of the maximum required resources for the project at any point in time. Rather, heuristic programs similar to the one outlined above are actually used. These programs are based mainly on taking advantage of the different floats for the noncritical activities.

§11·5
Probability and Cost Considerations in Project Scheduling

The analysis in Sections 11·2, 11·3, and 11·4 is basic to the scheduling of any project. This development, however, does not take into account the case where the time estimates for the different activities are probabilistic. Also, the above treatment does not consider explicitly the cost aspect of equivalent schedules. This section will thus present both the probability and cost aspects in detail.

§11·5·1
Probability Considerations in Project Scheduling[1]

Probability considerations are incorporated in project scheduling by assuming that the time estimate for each activity is based on three different values:

$a = $ The optimistic time which will be required if the execution of the activity goes extremely well.
$b = $ The pessimistic time which will be required if everything goes badly.
$m = $ The most likely time which will be required if execution occurs under normal conditions.

It is noticed that the range specified by the optimistic and pessimistic estimates (a and b, respectively) supposedly must enclose every possible estimate of the duration of the activity. The most likely estimate, m, need not coincide with the midpoint $(a + b)/2$ and may occur to its left or to its right. Because of these properties it was *intuitively* justified that the duration for each activity may follow the so-called Beta distribution with its unimodal point occurring at m and its end points occurring at a and b. Figure 11–9 shows the three cases of the Beta distribution in which it is; (i) symmetric, (ii) skewed to the left, and (iii) skewed to the right.

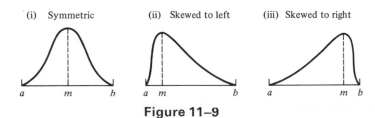

Figure 11–9

---

[1] This section requires a knowledge of elementary probability theory. See Chapter 12.

The expressions for the mean, $\bar{D}$, and variance, V, of the Beta distribution are developed as follows[2]. The midpoint $(a + b)/2$ is assumed to weigh half as much as the most likely point m. Thus, $\bar{D}$ is the arithmetic mean of $(a + b)/2$ and $2m$; that is,

$$\bar{D} = \frac{\dfrac{a + b}{2} + 2m}{3} = \frac{a + b + 4m}{6}.$$

On the other hand, the range (a, b) is assumed to enclose about six standard deviations of the distribution. This follows since about 90 per cent or more of *any* probability density function lies within three standard deviations of its mean. Thus,

$$V = \left(\frac{b - a}{6}\right)^2.$$

Having determined the values of $\bar{D}$ for the different activities, the network calculations given in Sections 11·2, 11·3, and 11·4 can now be applied directly with $\bar{D}$ replacing the single estimate D. It is possible now, however, to estimate the probability of occurrence of each event in the network.

Let μ_i be the earliest occurrence time of event i. Since the times of the activities summing up to i are random variables, then μ_i is also a random variable. Assuming that all the activities in the network are statistically independent, the mean and variance of μ_i are obtained as follows. If there is only one path leading from the "start" event to event i, then $E\{\mu_i\}$ is given by the sum of the expected durations, $\bar{D}$, for the activities along this path and $\text{Var}\{\mu_i\}$ is the sum of the variances of the same activities. Complications arise, however, where there are more than one path leading to the same event. In this case, if the *exact* $E\{\mu_i\}$ and $\text{Var}\{\mu_i\}$ are to be computed one must develop first the statistical distribution for the longest of the different paths (that is, the distribution of the maximum of several random variables) and then find its expected value and its variance. This is rather difficult in general and a simplifying

---

[2] Severe criticism has been given to the validity of the Beta distribution assumption. It has been shown that the expressions for $\bar{D}$ and V developed below cannot be satisfied for the Beta distribution unless certain restrictive relationships between a, b, and m exist. (See F. Grubbs, "Attempts to Validate Certain PERT Statistics or 'Picking on PERT'," *Operations Research*, Vol. 10, No. 6, pp. 912–915.) It will be noted, however, that the developments of the expressions for $\bar{D}$ and V are based on intuitive arguments regardless of the original Beta distribution assumption. Later it will be shown that the basic analysis of the network is based on the central limit theorem which assumes normality regardless of the original distributions. In that respect, whether the real distribution is Beta or not seems to be unimportant. The question as to whether $\bar{D}$ and V are the true measures of the original (unknown) distribution still remains unanswered, however.

assumption is introduced which computes $E\{\mu_i\}$ and $\text{Var}\{\mu_i\}$ as equal to those of the path leading to event i and having the largest sum of *expected* activity durations. If two or more paths have the same $E\{\mu_i\}$, then the one with the largest $\text{Var}\{\mu_i\}$ is selected since it reflects greater uncertainty and hence more conservative results. To summarize, $E\{\mu_i\}$ and $\text{Var}\{\mu_i\}$ are given for the selected path by

$$E\{\mu_i\} = ES_i,$$

$$\text{Var}\{\mu_i\} = \sum_k V_k,$$

where k defines the activities along the longest path leading to i. The idea now is that μ_i is the sum of independent random variables and hence according to the central limit theorem (see Section 12·6), μ_i is approximately normally-distributed with the mean, $E\{\mu_i\}$, and variance $\text{Var}\{\mu_i\}$. Since μ_i represents the earliest occurrence time, then event i will meet a certain scheduled time, ST_i, with probability

$$P\{\mu_i \le ST_i\} = P\left\{\frac{\mu_i - E\{\mu_i\}}{\sqrt{\text{Var}\{\mu_i\}}} \le \frac{ST_i - E\{\mu_i\}}{\sqrt{\text{Var}\{\mu_i\}}}\right\}$$

$$= P\{z \le K_i\}$$

where z is the standard normal distribution with mean zero and variance one and

$$K_i = \frac{ST_i - E\{\mu_i\}}{\sqrt{\text{Var}\{\mu_i\}}}.$$

It is a common practice to compute the probability that event i will occur no . later than its LC_i. Such probabilities will thus represent the chance that the succeeding events will occur within the (ES_i, LC_i) duration.

▶ **Example 11·5-1**

Consider the project of Example 11·3-1. To avoid repeating the critical path calculations, the values of a, b, and m shown in Table 11–2 are selected such that $\bar{D}_{ij}$ will have the same value as its corresponding D_{ij} in Example 11·3-1.

Table 11–2

Activity (i, j)	Estimated Times (a, b, m)	Activity (i, j)	Estimated Times (a, b, m)
(1, 2)	(2, 8, 2)	(3, 6)	(1, 3, 2)
(2, 3)	(1, 11, 1.5)	(4, 5)	(6, 8, 7)
(2, 4)	(.5, 7.5, 1)	(4, 6)	(3, 11, 4)
(3, 5)	(1, 7, 2.5)	(5, 6)	(4, 8, 6)

The mean $\bar{D}_{ij}$ and variance V_{ij} for the different activities are computed as shown in Table 11–3.

Table 11–3

Activity	$\bar{D}_{ij}$	V_{ij}	Activity	$\bar{D}_{ij}$	V_{ij}
(1, 2)	3	1.00	(3, 6)	2	0.11
(2, 3)	3	2.80	(4, 5)	7	0.11
(2, 4)	2	1.36	(4, 6)	5	1.78
(3, 5)	3	1.00	(5, 6)	6	0.44

The results of this example can be summarized as shown in Table 11–4. The information in the "ST_i"-column is given as part of the input data.

Table 11–4

Event	Path	$E\{\mu_i\}$	$\mathrm{Var}\{\mu_i\}$	ST_i	K_i	$P\{z \le K_i\}$
1	—	—	—	—	—	—
2	(1, 2)	3	1.00	2	−1.000	0.159
3	(1, 2, 3)	6	3.80	5	−0.512	0.304
4	(1, 2, 3, 4)	6	3.80	6	0.000	0.500
5	(1, 2, 3, 4, 5)	13	3.91	17	2.020	0.978
6	(1, 2, 3, 4, 5, 6)	19	4.35	20	0.480	0.684

It is possible in the above project to replace ST_i by LC_i to obtain the probabilities that none of the activities will be delayed beyond its latest occurrence time. However, since all the events of the project lie on the critical path, all such probabilities will be equal to 0.5. This follows since for event i on the critical path $E\{\mu_i\} = EC_i = LC_i = ST_i$, hence, $K_i = 0$ for all i.

In Table 11–4 the information under the "path"-column is obtained directly from the network. This defines the longest path from event 1 to event i. Again, in this example, because *all* the events lie on the critical path, it follows that such paths are defined by the critical path up to the designated event. In general, one must select the longest path leading to the event. For example, without the prior knowledge that event 5 lies on the critical path, the path to this event is selected as the longest of $\{(1, 2, 3, 5); (1, 2, 4, 5); (1, 2, 3, 4, 5)\}$.

After computing $E\{\mu_i\}$ and $\mathrm{Var}\{\mu_i\}$, the calculations of K_i and $P\{z \le K_i\}$ are straightforward. The probabilities associated with the realization of each event can then be computed. Such information should give more insight as to where resources are needed most in order to avoid delays in the execution of the project. ◄

§ 11·5·2
Cost considerations in Project Scheduling

The cost aspect is included in project scheduling by defining the cost-duration relationship for each activity in the project. Costs here are defined to include direct elements only. This means that indirect costs such as administrative or supervision costs cannot be included. The effect of the indirect costs will be included in the final analysis, however. Figure 11–10 shows a typical straight-line relationship which is used with most projects. The point (D_n, C_n) represents the duration D_n and its associated cost C_n if the activity is executed under *normal* conditions. The duration D_n can be compressed by increasing the allocated resources and hence by increasing the direct costs. There is a certain limit, however, beyond which no further reduction in the duration can be effected. This is called *crash* time. At this point any increase in resources will only increase the costs without reducing the duration. The crash point is indicated in Figure 11–10 by the point (D_c, C_c).

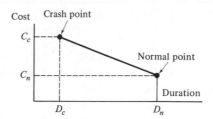

Figure 11–10

The straight-line relationship is used mainly for convenience since such a relationship can be determined for each activity from the knowledge of the normal and crash points only; that is, (D_n, C_n) and (D_c, C_c), respectively. It must be noted that any other type of nonlinear relationships will cause complications in the calculations and hence are disregarded from consideration. There is one exceptional case, however, where the nonlinear relationship can be approximated by a *piecewise* linear curve as shown in Figure 11–11. Under such conditions, the activity can be broken down into a number of subactivities each corresponding to one of the line segments. Notice the increasing slopes of the line segments as one moves from the normal point to the crash point. If this condition is not satisfied, then the original activity cannot be broken into smaller ones as indicated.

After defining the cost-time relationships for all the activities, the idea now is to consider the project with all the activities at their normal durations. The critical path corresponding to normal durations is then computed and the associated (direct) costs of the project are recorded. The next step is to consider reducing the duration of the project. Since such a reduction can be effected only if the duration of a critical activity is reduced, attention must be

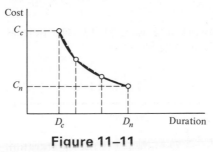

Figure 11–11

paid to such activities alone. In order to achieve a reduction in the duration at the least possible cost, one must compress the critical activity having the smallest cost-time slope as much as possible.

The amount by which an activity can be compressed is limited by its crash time. However, there are other limits which must be taken into account before the exact compression amount can be determined. The details of these limits will be discussed in Example 11·5-2.

Assuming that the selected activity has been properly compressed, the result of this compression is a new schedule perhaps with a new critical path. The cost associated with the new schedule must be greater than the immediately preceding schedule. The new schedule must now be considered for compression by selecting the (uncrashed) critical activity with the least slope. The procedure is repeated until all the critical activities are at their crash times. The final result of the above calculations is a cost-time curve for the different schedules and their corresponding costs. A typical curve is shown by a solid line in Figure 11–12. This, as indicated earlier, represents the direct costs only.

It is logical to assume that as the duration of the project increases, the *in*direct costs must also increase. This is shown in Figure 11–12 by a dotted curve. The sum of these two costs (direct + indirect) gives the total cost of the project. The optimum schedule must thus correspond to the minimum total cost.

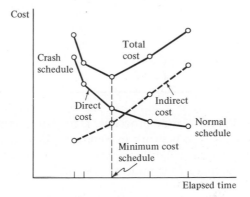

Figure 11–12

▶ **Example 11·5-2**

Consider the network in Figure 11–13. The normal and crash points for each activity are given in Table 11–5.

Table 11–5

Activity (i, j)	Normal Duration	Normal Cost	Crash Duration	Crash Cost
(1, 2)	8	100	6	200
(1, 3)	4	150	2	350
(2, 4)	2	50	1	90
(2, 5)	10	100	5	400
(3, 4)	5	100	1	200
(4, 5)	3	80	1	100

It is required to compute the different minimum-cost schedules that can occur between normal and crash times.

As mentioned earlier, the analysis in this problem is mainly dependent on the cost-time slopes for the different activities. These are computed using the formula

$$\text{slope} = \frac{C_c - C_n}{D_n - D_c}.$$

Thus the slopes for the activities of the above network are summarized below

Activity	Slope
(1, 2)	50
(1, 3)	100
(2, 4)	40
(2, 5)	60
(3, 4)	25
(4, 5)	10

The first step in the calculation procedure is to assume that all the activities occur at normal times. The network in Figure 11–13 shows the critical path calculations under normal conditions. Activities (1, 2) and (2, 5) constitute the critical path. The time of the project is 18 and its associated (normal) cost is 580.

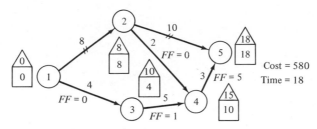

Figure 11–13

The second step now is to reduce the time of the project by compressing (as much as possible) the critical activity with the least slope. For the network in Figure 11–13 there are only two critical activities [(1, 2) and (2, 5)] with activity (1, 2) having the smaller slope ($= 50$). Thus activity (1, 2) is selected for compression. According to the time-cost curve this activity can be compressed by two time units; a limit which is specified by its crash point (henceforth called "crash limit"). It must be noted, however, that compressing a critical activity to its crash point would not necessarily mean that the duration of the entire project will be reduced by an equivalent amount. This follows since as the critical activity is compressed a *new* critical path may develop. At this point one must discard the old critical activity and pay attention to the activities of the new critical path.

One way of predicting whether a new critical path will develop before a crash point is reached is to consider the free floats for the noncritical activities. By definition, these free floats are independent of the start times of the other activities. Thus if during the compression of a critical activity, a *positive* free float becomes zero, then the said critical activity is not to be compressed without further checking since there is a *possibility* that this zero free float activity may become critical. This means that in addition to the "crash limit" one must also consider the "free float limit."

To determine the free float limit, one needs first to reduce the duration of the critical activity selected for compression by *one* time unit. Then, by recomputing the free floats for all the noncritical activities, one will note which of these activities have reduced their *positive* free floats by *one* time unit. The smallest free float (before reduction) of all such activities determines the required free float limit.

Applying this to the network of Figure 11–13, the free floats (FF) are shown on the respective activities. Now, reducing activity (1, 2) by one time unit, it follows that only the free float of activity (3, 4) will drop from one to zero. The free float of activity (4, 5) will remain unchanged at 5. This means that the FF-limit $= 1$. Since the crash limit for (1, 2) $= 2$, its "compression limit" is equal to the minimum of its crash limit and its FF-limit; that is $\min(2, 1) = 1$. The new schedule is shown in Figure 11–14. The corresponding project time is

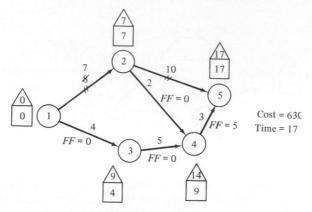

Figure 11–14

17 and its associated cost is equal to that of the previous schedule plus the additional cost of the compressed time, that is, $580 + (18 - 17) \times 50 = 630$. Notice that although the free float is binding, the critical path remains the same. This illustrates that it is *not* always true that a new critical path will arise when the compression limit is specified by the FF-limit.

Since activity (1, 2) is still the best candidate for compression, its corresponding crash and FF-limits are computed. Notice, however, that the crash limit for activity (1, 2) is equal to 1. In such a case it is not necessary to compute the FF-limit since one is guaranteed that any positive FF is at least equal to 1. Consequently, activity (1, 2) is compressed by one unit thus reaching its crash limit. The resulting computations are shown in Figure 11–15 which also shows that the critical path remains unchanged. The time of the project is 16 and its associated cost is $630 + (17 - 16) \times 50 = 680$.

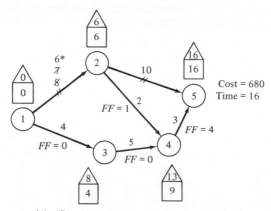

*signifies that activity has reached its crash limit

Figure 11–15

Continuing in the same manner, activity (1, 2) can no longer be compressed. Hence, activity (2, 5) is selected for compression. Now

$$\text{crash limit} = 10 - 5 = 5,$$
$$FF\text{-limit} = 4, \quad \text{(corresponding to activity (4, 5))}$$
$$\text{compression limit} = \min(5, 4) = 4.$$

The resulting computations are shown in Figure 11–16. Notice that there are two critical paths now, (1, 2, 5) and (1, 3, 4, 5). The time for the new project is 12 and its cost is $680 + (16 - 12) \times 60 = 920$.

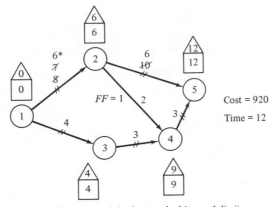

*signifies that activity has reached its crash limit

Figure 11–16

The appearance of two critical paths indicates that in order to reduce the time of the project, it will be necessary to reduce the time of the two critical paths simultaneously. The previous rule for selecting the critical activities to be compressed still applies here. Thus for the path (1, 2, 5), activity (2, 5) can be compressed by one time unit. For the path (1, 3, 4, 5), activity (4, 5) has the least slope and its crash limit is 2. Thus, the crash limit for the two paths is equal to min (1, 2) = 1. The FF-limit is determined for this case by taking the minimum of the FF-limits obtained by considering each critical path separately. However, since the crash limit is equal to 1, then by the same argument given above the FF-limit need not be computed.

The new schedule is shown in Figure 11–17. Its time is 11 and its cost is $920 + (12 - 11) \times (25 + 60) = 1005$.

The two critical paths of the project remain the same. Since all the activities on the critical path (1, 2, 5) are at crash time, it is no longer possible to reduce the time of the project. The schedule in Figure 11–17 thus gives the crash schedule.

The summary of the above computations is given in Figure 11–18. This

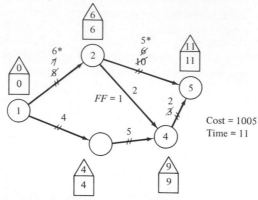

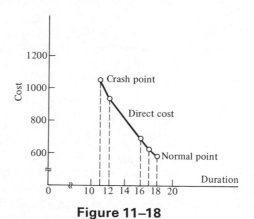

Cost = 1005
Time = 11

* signifies that activity has reached its crash limit

Figure 11–17

Figure 11–18

represents the direct cost of the project. By adding the indirect costs corresponding to each schedule one can compute the minimum total cost (or optimum) schedule. ◄

The above example summarizes all the rules for compressing activities under the given conditions. There is a case, however, where one may have to expand an already compressed activity before the duration of the entire project can be reduced. Figure 11–19 illustrates a typical case. There are three critical paths, namely (1, 2, 3, 4), (1, 2, 4), and (1, 3, 4). Activity (3, 4) has been compressed from its normal time 8 to its present time 5. It is clear that the duration of the given project may be reduced by simultaneously reducing

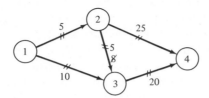

Figure 11–19

one of the activities on each of the critical paths (1, 2, 4) and (1, 3, 4) or by simultaneously compressing activities (1, 2) and (3, 4) and expanding activity (2, 3). The alternative to be selected here is the one having the smallest *net* sum of slopes. Notice that if activities (1, 2) and (3, 4) are compressed and activity (2, 3) is expanded, the so-called *net* sum of slopes is given by the sum of the slopes for activities (1, 2) and (3, 4) *minus* the slope for activity (2, 3). In all other cases where there are no expandable activities, the net sum is equal to the sum of the slopes of the compressed activities.

It is noticed that if expansion is necessary, then in addition to the crash limit and the FF-limit, the expansion limit must also be taken into account. This is equal to the normal time of the activity minus its present compressed time. Consequently, the compression limit is the minimum of the crash limit, the FF-limit, and the expansion limit.

An Alternative Procedure for Detecting New Critical Paths

In Example 11·5-2 ,the FF-limit was used to detect the possibility of having new critical paths. Thus, if the FF-limit is large and is equal to the compression limit, one can reduce the duration of the project in large steps. In essence, this has the advantage that the number of schedules computed between the normal and crash points is kept to a minimum. This could possibly mean that the *main* computations of the project are kept to a minimum. It is noticed, however, that the determination of the FF-limits requires additional computations which increase especially with the increase in the number of critical paths in the project. Consequently, there is no guarantee that the use of the FF-limit method would yield minimum computations.

Another method has thus been developed which completely eliminates the need for the FF-limit.[3] It is indicated in Example 11·5-2 that if the crash limit is equal to 1, then there is no need for computing the FF-limit since it is a fact that any positive FF is at least equal to 1. The new procedure thus calls for reducing the duration of the project by one time unit at each cycle of the computations. This is done again by compressing the activity having the least slope. The procedure is repeated on the new schedule (and the new critical

---

[3] There exist other more efficient methods for effecting minimum computations between the normal and crash schedules. The rules for such methods are somewhat complex, however. See, for example, Chapter 7 of [4].

path(s), if any) until crash schedule is attained. Notice that the new method compresses the project duration by one time unit each cycle. Thus, if there are n time units between normal and crash schedules, one should expect a total of n cycles of computations.

There is no conclusive evidence as to which method is computationally more efficient. However, for hand computations the non-FF-limit method seems more convenient. The reader is asked in Problem 11–7 to resolve Example 11·5-2 using the new method and hence compare the amount of computations in each cycle.

§ 11·6
Project Control

There is a tendency among some PERT-CPM users to think that the arrow diagram can be discarded as soon as the time schedule is developed. This is not so. In fact, an important use of the arrow diagram occurs during the execution phase of the project. It seldom happens that the planning phase will develop a time schedule that can be followed exactly during the execution phase. Quite often some of the jobs are delayed or expedited as compared to their time schedule. This naturally depends on the actual work conditions. As soon as such disturbances occur in the original plan it becomes necessary to develop a new time schedule for the remaining portion of the project. This section thus outlines a procedure for monitoring and controlling the project during the execution phase.

It is important to follow the progress of the project on the arrow diagram rather than on the time schedule alone. The time schedule is mainly used to check if each activity is on time. The effect of a delay in a certain activity on the remaining portion of the project can best be traced on the arrow diagram.

Suppose now that as the project progresses over time, it is discovered that the delay in some activities necessitates the development of a completely new schedule. How can this be effected using the present arrow diagram? The immediate requirement is to update the arrow diagram by assigning zero values to the duration of the activities that have already been completed. Those activities that only have been partially completed are assigned times equivalent to their unfinished portions. Changes in the arrow diagram such as addition or deletion of any future activities must also be made. By repeating the usual computations on the arrow diagram with its new time elements one can determine the new time schedule and consequently possible change in the duration of the project. Such information is used until it is further necessary to update the time schedule. In real situations, a large number of revisions of the time schedule are usually required at the early stages of the execution phase. This is then followed by the stable period in which little revisions of the current schedule are required.

§ 11·7
Representation of the CPM-PERT Problem as a Linear Programming Model

The determination of the critical path for a given project is equivalent to the determination of the longest path or route in the network representing the project. In Chapter 5 it was indicated how a linear programming model (the transshipment model) can be used to obtain the shortest path in a network. (See Problem 5-11.) The same procedure can be adapted to obtain the longest path in a network by replacing the minimization criterion of the shortest route problem by an equivalent maximization criterion.

Another equivalent linear programming formulation can also be constructed to determine the critical path in a network. To illustrate this case, consider the specific network shown in Figure 11–20. Let t_j be the occurrence time of

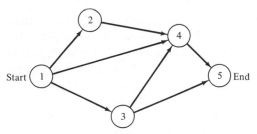

Figure 11–20

event $j, j = 1, 2, \ldots, 5$. Let D_{ij} be the duration of activity (i, j). The objective here is to determine the ealiest start time for each activity. This is equivalent to determining the smallest occurrence time for event 5 subject to the appropriate constraints. Thus, the equivalent linear programming model becomes:

$$\text{minimize} \quad Y_0 = t_5,$$

subject to

$$t_2 - t_1 \geq D_{12},$$
$$t_3 - t_1 \geq D_{13},$$
$$t_4 - t_1 \geq D_{14},$$
$$t_4 - t_2 \geq D_{24},$$
$$t_4 - t_3 \geq D_{34},$$
$$t_5 - t_3 \geq D_{35},$$
$$t_5 - t_4 \geq D_{45},$$

where t_1 can arbitrarily be set equal to zero. Notice that the above formulation automatically guarantees that none of the variables t_j will be negative so that there is no need to include the constraint $t_j \geq 0$ explicitly.

In the above formulation there are as many constraints as the number of activities. Thus, in general, for a network with N events, the linear programming model becomes:

$$\text{minimize} \quad Y_0 = t_N,$$

subject to

$$t_j - t_i \geq D_{ij}, \quad i < j,$$

for all defined activities, (i, j).

Another problem in critical path scheduling which can be solved by linear programming is that of determining the *minimum* (direct) cost schedules as a function of the project duration. This problem was discussed fully in Section 11·5·2. Define

$$S_{ij} = \frac{C_c(i, j) - C_n(i, j)}{D_n(i, j) - D_c(i, j)}$$

as the slope of the straight line representing the cost–duration relationship for activity (i, j). The symbols C_c, C_n, D_c, D_n were defined in Section 11·5·2 as the costs and durations corresponding to the crash and normal points on the cost-duration relationships. Again, let t_j be the occurrence time of event j as defined above, where $j = 1$ is the "start" event and $j = N$ is the "end" event. Define θ' and θ'' as the earliest start times for event N given that all the activities are at their crash and normal durations, respectively. This means that $\theta' < \theta''$. Let x_{ij} be the duration of activity (i, j), then $D_c(i, j) \leq x_{ij} \leq D_n(i, j)$. The objective function of the problem may be written as:

$$\text{minimize} \quad Z_0 = \sum_{(i, j)} \{S_{ij} D_c(i, j) + C_c(i, j) - S_{ij} x_{ij}\}.$$

Since

$$\sum_{(i, j)} S_{ij} D_c(i, j) + C_c(i, j)$$

is a constant, then the objective function is equivalent to:

$$\text{minimize} \quad Z_0' = - \sum_{(i, j)} S_{ij} x_{ij},$$

or

$$\text{maximize} \quad Z_0'' = \sum_{(i, j)} S_{ij} x_{ij}.$$

Let θ be the occurrence time of event N, then the constraints of the problem are then given by

$$D_c(i, j) \leq x_{ij} \leq D_n(i, j),$$
$$t_j - t_i \leq x_{ij}, \quad i < j,$$
$$t_N = \theta,$$

where these constraints hold for all defined activities, (i, j).

Notice that, by definition, $\theta' \leq \theta \leq \theta''$, where θ' and θ'' are given values as defined above. Thus solving the problem for $\theta = \theta'$, the parametric programming technique (Chapter 9) can be used to find all the minimum cost durations that exist between the extreme values, θ' and θ''. Using the results of parametric programming, a direct cost-duration relationship similar to the one given in Figure 11–12 can be constructed.

The parametric programming model will now be illustrated by a numerical example.

▶ **Example 11·7-1**

Consider the network presented in Example 11·5-2. The equivalent parametric programming model is given by:

$$\text{maximize} \quad Z_0 = 50x_{12} + 100x_{13} + 40x_{24} + 60x_{25} + 25x_{34} + 10x_{45},$$

subject to

$$6 \leq x_{12} \leq 8,$$
$$2 \leq x_{13} \leq 4,$$
$$1 \leq x_{24} \leq 2,$$
$$5 \leq x_{25} \leq 10,$$
$$1 \leq x_{34} \leq 5,$$
$$1 \leq x_{45} \leq 3,$$
$$t_2 - t_1 \geq x_{12},$$
$$t_3 - t_1 \geq x_{13},$$
$$t_4 - t_2 \geq x_{24},$$
$$t_5 - t_2 \geq x_{25},$$
$$t_4 - t_3 \geq x_{34},$$
$$t_5 - t_4 \geq x_{45},$$
$$t_5 = \theta.$$

To obtain the limits θ' and θ'', one computes the earliest start time for activity 5 assuming all activities are at their crash and normal durations, respectively. Thus, as shown in Figure 11–13, $\theta'' = 18$. Replacing the normal durations by their equivalent crash durations, this gives $\theta' = 11$. This means that $11 \leq \theta \leq 18$. The constraint $t_5 = \theta$ may thus be put in the parameterized form as

$$t_5 = \theta' + \beta,$$
$$= 11 + \beta,$$

where $0 \leq \beta \leq \theta'' - \theta'$; that is, $0 \leq \beta \leq 7$.

The solution of this model should essentially yield the same results in Example 11·5-2. It is noticed that for practical purposes, the procedure given in Example 11·5-2 is more efficient. The advantage of the linear programming model is realized, however, when the cost-duration curve for each activity is nonconvex in which case the procedure of Example 11·5-2 cannot be used. By using the general procedure of Section 10·5·4 for approximating any nonlinear function by a piecewise-linear function, one can use the mixed integer programming algorithm (Chapter 10) to obtain the optimal solution to the problem. The computational feasibility of the procedure remains questionable, however, due to the inefficiency of the mixed integer programming algorithms. There is another approximating method called the *restricted basis method*, which (based on the same type of linear approximation) can handle this type of problem without having to use the mixed integer programming algorithm explicitly. This method will be presented in Section 17·2. ◄

This section has presented a brief introduction to the relationship between CPM-PERT and linear programming. These linear programming models can be solved in a much easier way using network flow theory (see Section 5·4) by considering their corresponding dual problems. This, however, is not presented here and the interested reader should consult References [1] and [3] for the details. Appendix 7–1 of [4] also includes some discussion on the same problem.

SELECTED REFERENCES

1. FULKERSON, D., "A Network Flow Computation for Project Cost Curve," *Management Science*, Vol. 7, No. 2 (1961).
2. KELLEY, J., "Critical Path Planning and Scheduling: Mathematical Basis," *Operations Research*, Vol. 9, No. 3 (1961).
3. KELLEY, J., "The Critical Path Method: Resources Planning and Scheduling," in *Industrial Scheduling*, Muth and Thompson (Eds.), Chapter 21, Englewood Cliffs, N.J.: Prentice-Hall, 1963.
4. MODER, J., and C. PHILLIPS, *Project Management with CPM and PERT*, New York: Reinhold, 1964.
5. O'BRIEN, J., *CPM in Construction Management*, New York: McGraw-Hill, 1965.
6. SHAFFER, L., J. RITTER, and W. MEYER, *The Critical Path Method*, New York: McGraw-Hill, 1965.

PROBLEMS

☐ **11-1** Construct the arrow diagram comprising activities A, B, C, ..., and P, which satisfies the following precedence relationships.

(i) A, B, and C, the first activities of the project can start simultaneously.

(ii) Activities D, E, and F start immediately after A is completed.

(iii) Activities I and G start after both B and D are completed.

(iv) Activity *H* starts after both *C* and *G* are completed.

(v) Activities *K* and *L* succeed activity *I*.

(vi) Activity *J* succeeds both *E* and *H*.

(vii) Activities *M* and *N* succeed *F* but cannot start until *E* and *H* are completed.

(viii) Activity *O* succeeds *M* and *I*.

(ix) Activity *P* succeeds *J*, *L*, and *O*.

(x) Activities *K*, *N*, and *P* are the terminal jobs of the project.

☐ **11-2** Determine the critical path(s) for each of the following projects.

Project a:

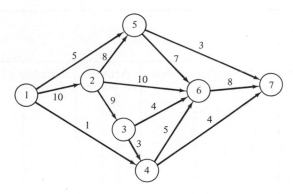

Project b:

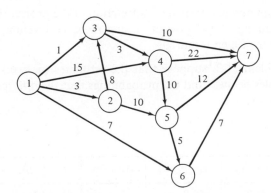

☐ **11-3** In Problem 11-2 compute the total and free floats and summarize the critical path calculations using the format in Table 11–1.

☐ **11-4** In problem 11-2, using the results of Problem 11-3, construct the corresponding time charts assuming no limits on the resources.

☐ **11-5** Suppose in Problem 11-2 the following manpower requirements are specified for the different activities of projects (a) and (b),

Project (a)

Activity	Number of men	Activity	Number of men
1, 2	5	3, 6	9
1, 4	4	4, 6	1
1, 5	3	4, 7	10
2, 3	1	5, 6	4
2, 5	2	5, 7	5
2, 6	3	6, 7	2
3, 4	7		

Project (b)

Activity	Number of men	Activity	Number of men
1, 2	1	3, 7	9
1, 3	2	4, 5	8
1, 4	5	4, 7	7
1, 6	3	5, 6	2
2, 3	1	5, 7	5
2, 5	4	6, 7	3
3, 4	10		

Find the minimum number of men (as a function of the project time) required during the scheduling of the project. Using resource leveling, estimate the maximum number of men required.

☐ **11-6** In Problem 11-2, suppose that the estimates (a, b, m) are given as shown in the tables below. Find the probabilities that the different events will occur without delay.

Project (a)

Activity	(a, b, m)	Activity	(a, b, m)
1, 2	(5, 8, 6)	3, 6	(3, 5, 4)
1, 4	(1, 4, 3)	4, 6	(4, 10, 8)
1, 5	(2, 5, 4)	4, 7	(5, 8, 6)
2, 3	(4, 6, 5)	5, 6	(9, 15, 10)
2, 5	(7, 10, 8)	5, 7	(4, 8, 6)
2, 6	(8, 13, 9)	6, 7	(3, 5, 4)
3, 4	(5, 10, 9)		

Project (b)

Activity	(a, b, m)	Activity	(a, b, m)
1, 2	(1, 4, 3)	3, 7	(12, 14, 13)
1, 3	(5, 8, 7)	4, 5	(10, 15, 12)
1, 4	(6, 9, 7)	4, 7	(8, 12, 10)
1, 6	(1, 3, 2)	5, 6	(7, 11, 8)
2, 3	(3, 5, 4)	5, 7	(2, 8, 4)
2, 5	(7, 9, 8)	6, 7	(5, 7, 6)
3, 4	(10, 20, 15)		

☐ **11-7** Solve Example 11·5-2 without using the *FF*-limit method; that is, by compressing the project duration by one unit at a time, and compare with the results of Example 11·5-2.

☐ **11-8** In Problem 11-2, given the data below for the direct costs of the normal and crash durations, find the different minimum cost schedules between the normal and crash points.

Project (a)

Activity (i, j)	Normal		Crash	
	Duration	Cost	Duration	Cost
1, 2	5	100	2	200
1, 4	2	50	1	80
1, 5	2	150	1	180
2, 3	7	200	5	250
2, 5	5	20	2	40
2, 6	4	20	2	40
3, 4	3	60	1	80
3, 6	10	30	6	60
4, 6	5	10	2	20
4, 7	9	70	5	90
5, 6	4	100	1	130
5, 7	3	140	1	160
6, 7	3	200	1	240

Project (b)

Activity (i, j)	Normal		Crash	
	Duration	Cost	Duration	Cost
1, 2	4	100	1	400
1, 3	8	400	5	640
1, 4	9	120	6	180
1, 6	3	20	1	60
2, 3	5	60	3	100
2, 5	9	210	7	270
3, 4	12	400	8	800
3, 7	14	120	12	140
4, 5	15	500	10	750
5, 6	11	160	8	240
5, 7	8	70	5	110
6, 7	10	100	2	180

☐ **11-9** Express the projects of Problem 11-8 in the form of parametric programming problems.

Part 2

Probability, Inventory, and Queueing

CHAPTER 12

Review of Probability Theory

§ 12·1
Introduction

The material in this chapter is by no means exhaustive of probability theory. Rather, it provides the basic background necessary for the continuity of the presentation in this book. The reader interested in further details about the subject should consult the references cited at the end of this chapter.

§ 12·2
Outcomes, Sample Space, and Events

Before a formal definition of probability can be given, it is necessary first to introduce the concepts of outcomes, sample space and events. From the viewpoint of probability theory, an *experiment* represents the act of performing something the output of which is subject to chance (unknown) variation. Such output is usually referred to as the *outcome* of the experiment. The number of these outcomes may be finite or infinite depending on the nature of the experiment. For example, consider the experiment of rolling a die. The outcomes in this case are finite and are represented by the six faces of the die; that is, 1, 2, 3, 4, 5, and 6. On the other hand, if the experiment is concerned with measuring the time between successive failures of an electronic component, the outcomes in this case are given by the time-to-failure which may assume any nonnegative real value.

A *sample space* defines the set including *all* possible outcomes of the experiment. For example in the die-rolling experiment, the sample space consists of $\{1, 2, 3, 4, 5, 6\}$. Similarly, if t represents the interfailure time of the electronic components then its sample space is given by $\{0 \leq t < \infty\}$. Again, from the definition of outcomes, a sample space may be finite or infinite depending on whether the number of outcomes is finite or infinite, respectively.

An *event* is a collection of outcomes from within the sample space. For example, one may consider the event that a rolled die will turn up a "six" in which case the occurrence of the event is associated with an outcome of 6; or the event that the sum of the faces turned up in two consecutive rolls is equal to five in which case the event is realized when the consecutive outcomes are either (4, 1), (3, 2), (2, 3), or (1, 4). In the case of electronic component failure, one may consider the event that the interfailure time is less than or equal to some real constant T.

§ 12-3
Laws of Probability

Having introduced the concepts of outcomes, sample space, and events in the previous section, the definition of *probability* is now in order. The probability of an event E (usually written as $P\{E\}$) is a *non*negative real number which after observing a sufficiently large number of trials, is taken equal to the fraction of trials for which the outcomes successfully describe E. Mathematically, this means that if n is the total number of trials out of which there are m trials describing E, then

$$P\{E\} = \lim_{n \to \infty} \frac{m}{n}.$$

Clearly,

$$0 \leq P\{E\} \leq 1,$$

where $P\{E\} = 0$ signifies that the event is impossible while $P\{E\} = 1$ signifies that it is certain. For example, the probability associated with the event that a rolled die will turn up a "seven" is zero (impossible) while the probability of the event that a tossed coin will turn up a head *or* a tail is one (certain).

The basic probability laws will now be introduced. Consider the two events E and F. The notation $E \cap F$ (or simply EF) means that both E *and* F occur simultaneously, while the notation $E \cup F$ (or simply $E + F$) signifies that E *or* F (or both) occurs. Using these notations, the basic probability laws are given by:

(i) $\quad P\{E + F\} = P\{E\} + P\{F\} - P\{EF\}$

(ii) $\quad P\{E \mid F\} = \dfrac{P\{EF\}}{P\{F\}}, \quad P\{F\} > 0$

These laws, of course, imply that any probability is measured on the zero–one scale.

The first law is called the *addition law* and it states that the probability that E *or* F (or both) occurs is equal to the probability of E occurring plus the probability of F occurring minus the probability of both E *and* F occurring. If E and F are *mutually exclusive*; that is, the occurrence of one event signifies the nonoccurrence of the other, then

$$P\{EF\} = 0.$$

In this case,

$$P\{E + F\} = P\{E\} + P\{F\}.$$

In general, one can deduce that if $E_1, E_2, \ldots, E_n$ are mutually exclusive then

$$P\{E_1 + E_2 + \cdots + E_n\} = P\{E_1\} + P\{E_2\} + \cdots + P\{E_n\}.$$

The second law is called the *conditional probability law*. It computes the probability of event E occurring given that F has occurred. If event F is contained in event E and if $P\{F\} > 0$, then

$$P\{E \mid F\} = \frac{P\{E\}}{P\{F\}}.$$

Two events E and F are said to be *independent* if,

$$P\{E \mid F\} = P\{E\}.$$

Hence, from the conditional probability law, E and F are independent if, and only if,

$$P\{EF\} = P\{E\}\, P\{F\}.$$

In general, events $E_1, E_2, \ldots, E_n$ are independent if, and only if, for all combinations $1 \leq i < j < k < \cdots < n$ the following conditions are satisfied simultaneously,

$$P\{E_i E_j\} = P\{E_i\}P\{E_j\},$$

$$P\{E_i E_j E_k\} = P\{E_i\}P\{E_j\}P\{E_k\},$$

$$\vdots$$

$$P\{E_1 E_2 \ldots E_n\} = P\{E_1\}P\{E_2\} \ldots P\{E_n\}.$$

It is noted that two mutually exclusive events, E and F, are independent if and only if

$$P\{EF\} = P\{E\}\, P\{F\} = 0,$$

which can only occur if

$$P\{E\} = 0 \quad \text{and/or} \quad P\{F\} = 0.$$

§ 12·4
Random Variables and Probability Distributions

The outcomes of an experiment are said to be represented by a random variable if these outcomes are themselves numerical or if they have real numbers assigned to them. For example, in the die-rolling experiment, the corresponding random variable is represented by the set of outcomes $\{1, 2, 3, 4, 5, 6\}$; while in the coin-tossing experiment the outcomes, head (H) or tail (T), can be represented as a random variable by assigning 0 to H and 1 to T. In a sense then a random variable is a real-valued function which maps the sample space onto the real line.

A random variable may be discrete or continuous depending, of course, on the nature of the outcomes. For example, in the coin-tossing or the die-rolling experiments, the random variables are discrete, while in the component-failure experiment, the random variable is continuous.

Associated with the random variable x is a function $f(x)$ which assigns a probability measure to this random variable. This function is called *probability density function* (p.d.f.). Thus if x is a continuous random variable on the range $(-\infty, +\infty)$, then its p.d.f. $f(x)$ must satisfy the following two conditions

$$\text{(i)} \quad f(x) \geq 0, \quad -\infty < x < \infty,$$

$$\text{(ii)} \quad \int_{-\infty}^{+\infty} f(x)\, dx = 1.$$

Similarly, if x is a discrete random variable, then its p.d.f. $P(x)$ must satisfy the conditions,

$$\text{(i)} \quad P(x) \geq 0, \quad \text{for all } x,$$

$$\text{(ii)} \quad \sum_{\text{all } x} P(x) = 1.$$

The first condition in both the continuous and discrete distributions indicates that a p.d.f. cannot assume negative values (otherwise the probability of some events occurring may be negative). The second condition, on the other hand, shows that the probability of the entire space occurring must be equal to 1.0.

▶ **Example 12·4-1**

To illustrate the above properties of a p.d.f., consider the continuous function,

$$f(x) = \begin{cases} a, & 0 \leq x \leq 10, \\ 0, & \text{otherwise.} \end{cases}$$

In order for $f(x)$ to be a p.d.f., the condition,

$$\int_{-\infty}^{\infty} f(x)\, dx = 1,$$

must be satisfied. This is true for the above function if

$$\int_{0}^{10} a\, dx = 1,$$

or

$$a = 1/10.$$

Since $a > 0$, it follows that $f(x) \geq 0$. This indicates that $f(x)$ satisfies the conditions for a p.d.f.

Similarly, for the die-rolling experiment, the associated probabilities of the discrete random variables are given by

x	1	2	3	4	5	6
$P(x)$	1/6	1/6	1/6	1/6	1/6	1/6

which clearly satisfy the conditions of a p.d.f. ◄

Another useful probability measure is the so-called *cumulative density function* (C.D.F.). Consider the continuous case first. Let $F(x)$ represent the C.D.F. for the continuous random variable x, $-\infty < x < \infty$. For any real number a, $F(a)$ defines the probability that $x \leq a$. This is given in terms of the p.d.f. $f(x)$ by

$$F(a) = P\{x \leq a\},$$

$$= \int_{-\infty}^{a} f(x)\, dx.$$

Thus $F(a)$ represents the area under $f(x)$ enclosed by the range $-\infty < x < a$.

Notice that for the continuous random variable x,

$$P\{x = a\} = 0,$$

since the enclosed area is zero. On the other hand, given two real numbers a and b such that $-\infty < a < b < \infty$, the probability of the event $a \leq x \leq b$ (or $a < x < b$) occurring is given by:

$$P\{a \leq x \leq b\} = \int_{a}^{b} f(x)\, dx,$$

$$= \int_{-\infty}^{b} f(x)\, dx - \int_{-\infty}^{a} f(x)\, dx,$$

$$= F(b) - F(a).$$

This case is illustrated graphically in Figure 12–1. It is clear that the said probability is equal to the area under $f(x)$ enclosed in the range $a \leq x \leq b$.

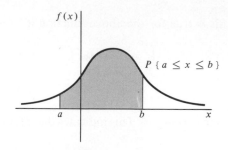

Figure 12–1

The C.D.F. $F(a)$ has the following important properties.

(i) $\displaystyle \lim_{a \to \infty} F(a) = \lim_{a \to \infty} \int_{-\infty}^{a} f(x)\, dx = 1.$

(ii) $\displaystyle \lim_{a \to -\infty} F(a) = \lim_{a \to -\infty} \int_{-\infty}^{a} f(x)\, dx = 0.$

(iii) $F(a)$ is monotone nondecreasing function of a.

A typical C.D.F. is illustrated in Figure 12–2. The vertical scale of $F(x)$ should thus give directly the probability that x is less than a certain value.

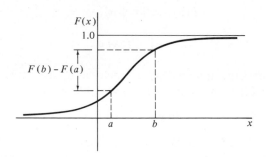

Fig. 12–2

From the relationship between $f(x)$ and $F(x)$, it follows that

$$f(x) = \frac{d}{dx} F(x).$$

Thus, the probability law of the random variable x is in general defined completely by either $f(x)$ or $F(x)$.

Similar definitions can be made for the C.D.F. in the discrete case simply by replacing $f(x)$ by $P(x)$ in all the above properties. This will naturally require changing integration sign into summation sign while differentiation may be replaced by differences. Notice, however, the distinct difference in the discrete case where the probability of a single value occurring is not necessarily equal to zero. Notice also that for a discrete random variable, the C.D.F. is in the form of a step function since the p.d.f. is defined at discrete values only.

▶ **Example 12·4-2**
Consider the same problems of Example 12·4-1. For the continuous p.d.f.,

$$f(x) = \begin{cases} \dfrac{1}{10}, & 0 \le x \le 10, \\ 0, & \text{otherwise.} \end{cases}$$

Then the C.D.F.,

$$F(x) = \int_0^x f(u)\, du,$$

$$= \int_0^x \frac{1}{10}\, du = \frac{x}{10}, \qquad 0 \le x \le 10.$$

This function is illustrated graphically in Figure 12–3.

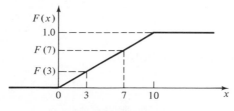

Figure 12–3

Suppose now that one wants to compute $P\{3 \le x \le 7\}$ then,

$$P\{3 \le x \le 7\} = F(7) - F(3)$$

$$= \frac{7}{10} - \frac{3}{10} = \frac{4}{10},$$

as could be seen directly from Figure 12–3.
Again consider the discrete random variable x with the following p.d.f.,

x	1	2	3	4	5	6
$P(x)$	1/6	1/6	1/6	1/6	1/6	1/6

Then

$$F(x) = \sum_{u=1}^{u=x} \frac{1}{6} = \frac{x}{6}, \qquad x = 1, 2, \dots, 6$$

which is shown graphically in Figure 12–4. ◄

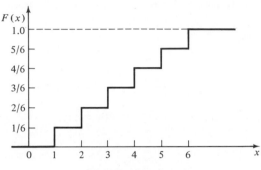

Figure 12–4

Having introduced the basic properties of probability distributions, the remainder of this section will be devoted to the presentation of some important discrete and continuous density functions. The utilization of these functions is often encountered in the analysis of inventory and waiting line models.

§ 12·4·1
Discrete Probability Distributions

§ 12·4·1·1
Independent Bernoulli Trials Distributions

Perhaps the simplest form of a p.d.f. comes as a result of the so-called independent Bernoulli trials with each trial having exactly two outcomes. These two outcomes may be classified as "success" (S) or "failure" (F). Examples of such trials occur in the coin-tossing experiment where the outcome is a head (S), or a tail (F), or in testing a product where the outcome is defective (F) or nondefective (S).

Let the random variable describing the two outcomes F and S be 0 and 1, respectively. The corresponding p.d.f. may be written as

$$P\{x = 0\} = p,$$
$$P\{x = 1\} = q = 1 - p,$$

where $0 \le q \le 1$.

Consider now the case of n independent Bernoulli trials each with the same p. The probability of a *particular* combination of outcomes with k failures (F) and $n - k$ successes (S) is

$$p^k q^{n-k}, \qquad 0 \le k \le n.$$

This follows directly from the fact that all n trials are independent. For example, if $n = 5$, the probability that the first trial is F and the remaining four trials are S is equal to pq^4.

Consider next the probability that the *number of failures* in n independent Bernoulli trials is equal to k, where n is specified in advance. In this case *all* the distinct combinations having k failures (regardless of their order of occurrence in the n trials) should be considered in computing this probability. Under the given conditions, there are

$$\binom{n}{k} = \frac{n!}{k!(n-k)!}$$

such distinct combinations. Since as shown above, the probability of each combination is $p^k q^{n-k}$, then by the addition law of probability (Section 12·3),

$$P\{x = k\} = \binom{n}{k} p^k q^{n-k}, \qquad k = 0, 1, 2, \ldots, n.$$

This is the *binomial distribution* with parameters n and p and it satisfies the conditions for p.d.f. since

(i) $P\{x = k\} \ge 0, \qquad$ for all $k = 0, 1, 2, \ldots, n,$

(ii) $\sum\limits_{k=0}^{n} P\{x = k\} = \sum\limits_{k=0}^{n} \binom{n}{k} p^k q^{n-k},$

$$= (p + q)^n = 1.$$

Another important distribution which comes from Bernoulli independent trials is the *negative binomial* (or *Pascal*) distribution. It is noticed in the binomial distribution that the number of trials n is specified in advance and that the random variable is given by the number of failures. In the negative binomial, the random variable will be given by the number of independent trials until a fixed number of failures occur. Let j and c represent the number of trails and the fixed number of failures, respectively. The probability of j trials until c failures occur is thus the product of

(i)   probability of $c - 1$ failures in $j - l$ trials

$$= \binom{j-1}{c-1} p^{c-1} q^{j-c},$$

(ii)   probability of a failure on the jth trial $= p$.

Thus the negative binomial p.d.f. is given by

$$P\{x = j\} = \binom{j-1}{c-1} p^c q^{j-c}, \qquad j = c, c+1, c+2, \ldots.$$

A special case of the negative binomial distribution is the *geometric* distribution which occurs when $c = 1$; that is,

$$P\{x = j\} = pq^{j-1}, \qquad j = 1, 2, 3, \ldots.$$

It is noted that the negative binomial and geometric distribution can be regarded, in a sense, as describing the "time" until a certain number of failures occur. This is seen by assuming that there is a fixed time associated with each trial.

§ 12·4·1·2
Poisson Distribution

Consider the random variable x which includes nonnegative integer values only; that is, $k = 0, 1, 2, \ldots$. The p.d.f.

$$P\{x = k\} = \frac{\lambda^k e^{-\lambda}}{k!}, \qquad k = 0, 1, 2, \ldots,$$

where $\lambda > 0$, is called the *Poisson* distribution. A typical application of the Poisson distribution occurs in analyzing waiting line problems where customers arrive randomly at a facility for service. In certain situations, the number of arrivals and of departures to and from the facility can be described by the Poisson distribution.

Under certain conditions, the Poisson distribution can be used as an approximation to the binomial distribution. Using the same symbols introduced above, let $p \to 0$ and $n \to \infty$ such that $np \to \lambda > 0$. Then, under these conditions, the binomial p.d.f. becomes,

$$P\{x = k\} = \binom{n}{k} \left(\frac{\lambda}{n}\right)^k \left(1 - \frac{\lambda}{n}\right)^{n-k}$$

$$= \frac{n!}{k!(n-k)!} \left(\frac{\lambda}{n}\right)^k \left(1 - \frac{\lambda}{n}\right)^{n-k}.$$

It can be shown that as $n \to \infty$,

$$\frac{n!}{(n-k)!} \to n^k,$$

$$\left(1 - \frac{\lambda}{n}\right)^{-k} \to 1,$$

and

$$\left(1 - \frac{\lambda}{n}\right)^n \to e^{-\lambda}.$$

Hence

$$P\{x = k\} \to \frac{\lambda^k e^{-\lambda}}{k!}, \qquad k = 0, 1, 2, \ldots,$$

is the Poisson distribution. This indicates that if n is large and p is small such that $\lambda = np > 0$, the Poisson distribution can be used as an approximation to the binomial distribution.

§ 12·4·2
Continuous Probability Distributions

§ 12·4·2·1
Normal Distribution

The most well-known continuous p.d.f. is the so-called *normal* distribution with its density function given by

$$f(x) = \frac{1}{\sqrt{2\pi\sigma^2}} \exp\left\{-\frac{(x - \mu)^2}{2\sigma^2}\right\}, \qquad -\infty < x < \infty,$$

where μ and σ are given parameters. The C.D.F. of the normal distribution is defined by

$$F(x) = \int_{-\infty}^{x} \frac{1}{\sqrt{2\pi\sigma^2}} \exp\left\{-\frac{(y - \mu)^2}{2\sigma^2}\right\} dy.$$

Typical p.d.f. and C.D.F. of the normal distribution are shown in Figure 12–5. Notice that the p.d.f. $f(x)$ is symmetrical around $x = \mu$.

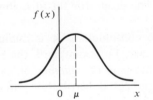
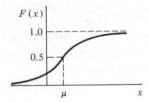

Figure 12–5

It should be noted that the expression for the C.D.F., $F(x)$, cannot be obtained in a closed form which is suitable for computations. Normal tables are available, however, which give the values of $F(x)$ as a function of x. These tables are based on the following *standard* form of the normal p.d.f.,

$$\phi(z) = \frac{1}{\sqrt{2\pi}} \exp\left\{-\frac{z^2}{2}\right\}, \qquad -\infty < z < \infty,$$

with its parameters given by $\mu = 0$ and $\sigma = 1$. The corresponding C.D.F. is thus given by

$$\Phi(z) = \int_{-\infty}^{z} \frac{1}{\sqrt{2\pi}} \exp\left\{-\frac{y^2}{2}\right\} dy.$$

The standard form is obtained from the regular form by making the substitution

$$z = \frac{x - \mu}{\sigma}.$$

This means that any normal random variable x can be transformed to the standard form given above.

The normal distribution can be used as an approximation to the binomial distribution. Specifically, it can be proved for the binomial distribution that, given a fixed p, then as $n \to \infty$,

$$\sum_{k=a}^{b} \binom{n}{k} p^k q^{n-k} \to \frac{1}{\sqrt{2\pi}} \int_{(a-\mu-1/2)/\sigma}^{(b-\mu+1/2)/\sigma} \exp\left(-\frac{y^2}{2}\right) dy,$$

where $\mu = np$ and $\sigma = \sqrt{npq}$.

§ 12·4·2·2
Exponential Distribution

An important distribution which is often encountered in waiting line theory is the exponential distribution with its p.d.f. given by

$$f(x) = \mu e^{-\mu x}, \quad x > 0,$$

where $\mu \ (> 0)$ is a given parameter. The graph for this distribution is illustrated in Figure 12–6.

The exponential distribution in the continuous case is analogous to the geometric distribution in the discrete case. For example, if the random variable in the geometric distribution represents the *number* of trials before a failure occurs, its equivalence in the exponential distribution will represent the

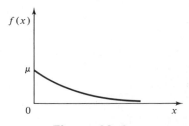

Figure 12–6

time-to-failure. In fact, it can be proved that as $p \rightarrow 0$ and the inter-trial time $\rightarrow 0$, the geometric distribution will in the limit tend to the exponential distribution.

Another important relationship exists between the Poisson distribution and the exponential distribution. If the Poisson distribution describes the *number* of failures per unit time, the exponential distribution will represent the *time* between two successive failures. In effect then, the exponential distribution can be derived from the Poisson distribution (see, for example, Section 14·3·3).

§ 12·4·2·3
Gamma Distribution

Given n identically distributed and independent exponential random variables, the distribution of the *sum* of these random variables gives rise to the so-called *gamma* or *Erlang* distribution with its p.d.f. given by

$$f(x) = \frac{\mu(\mu x)^{n-1} e^{-\mu x}}{(n-1)!}, \qquad x > 0.$$

(See Example 12·9-1 for a proof of this formula.) Notice that by putting $n = 1$, the above p.d.f. reduces to the exponential p.d.f..

It is indicated in Section 12·4·2·2 that the exponential distribution is analogous to the geometric distribution. In a similar way, the gamma distribution (sum of exponential random variables) is analogous to the negative binomial (sum of geometric random variables).

§ 12·5
Joint Probability Distributions

In Section 12·4, only distributions with one random variable have been introduced. There are situations, however, where there are two or more outcomes which are distinct in nature. In this case, the process may be described by a corresponding number of random variables.

In general, the notations $f(x_1, x_2, \ldots, x_n)$ and $P(x_1, x_2, \ldots, x_n)$ are used to describe the so-called *joint* p.d.f. of n random variables in the continuous and the discrete cases, respectively. These functions must satisfy the following conditions. For the continuous case,

(i) $f(x_1, \ldots, x_n) \geq 0$, $\qquad -\infty < x_i < \infty$, $\quad i = 1, 2, \ldots, n$,

(ii) $\displaystyle\int_{-\infty}^{+\infty} dx_1 \int_{-\infty}^{+\infty} dx_2 \cdots \int_{-\infty}^{+\infty} dx_n\, f(x_1, x_2, \ldots, x_n) = 1$,

and for the discrete case

(i) $P(x_1, x_2, \ldots, x_n) \geq 0$, $\qquad$ for all x_i, $\quad i = 1, 2, \ldots, n$,

(ii) $\displaystyle\sum_{\text{all } x_1} \sum_{\text{all } x_2} \cdots \sum_{\text{all } x_n} P(x_1, x_2, \ldots, x_n) = 1$.

The C.D.F. of a joint distribution can also be defined as

$$F(x_1, x_2, \ldots, x_n) = \begin{cases} \int_{-\infty}^{x_1} du_1 \int_{-\infty}^{x_2} du_2 \cdots \int_{-\infty}^{x_n} du_n \, f(u_1, u_2, \ldots, u_n), \\ \qquad \qquad \qquad \qquad \qquad \qquad \text{continuous case} \\[4pt] \sum_{u_1 \le x_1} \sum_{u_2 \le x_2} \cdots \sum_{u_n \le x_n} P(u_1, u_2, \ldots, u_n), \\ \qquad \qquad \qquad \qquad \qquad \qquad \text{discrete case.} \end{cases}$$

This definition indicates that,

$$F(-\infty, \ldots, x_n) = 0,$$
$$F(\infty, \ldots, \infty) = 1.$$

By a reciprocal operation, it follows for the continuous case that the joint p.d.f. is obtained from the joint C.D.F. using

$$f(x_1, \ldots, x_n) = \frac{\partial^n}{\partial x_1 \cdots \partial x_n} F(x_1, \ldots, x_n).$$

In the discrete case, the difference operation replaces the differentiation.

The probability that $a_i \le x_i \le b_i$, $i = 1, 2, \ldots, n$ (where a_i and b_i are given constants which are defined on the range of the ith random variable) can be determined from

$$P\{a_1 \le x_1 \le b_1, \ldots, a_n \le x_n \le b_n\} = \begin{cases} \int_{a_1}^{b_1} dx_1 \cdots \int_{a_n}^{b_n} dx_n \, f(x_1, \ldots, x_n), \\ \qquad \qquad \qquad \qquad \qquad \text{continuous case,} \\[4pt] \sum_{x_1 = a_1}^{b_1} \cdots \sum_{x_n = a_n}^{b_n} P(x_1, \ldots, x_n), \\ \qquad \qquad \qquad \qquad \qquad \text{discrete case.} \end{cases}$$

Notice that this probability is *not* in general equal to

$$F(b_1, \ldots, b_n) - F(a_1, \ldots, a_n).$$

▶ **Example 12·5-1**

Consider the joint p.d.f.

$$f(x_1, x_2) = \begin{cases} 2(x_1 + x_2 - 2x_1 x_2), & 0 \le x_1 \le 1, \quad 0 \le x_2 \le 1, \\ 0, & \text{otherwise.} \end{cases}$$

This is a p.d.f. since

(i) $f(x_1, x_2) = 2(x_1 + x_2 - 2x_1 x_2) = 2\{x_1(1 - x_2) + x_2(1 - x_1)\}.$

This shows that for $0 \le x_1, x_2 \le 1, f(x_1, x_2)$ is nonnegative.

(ii) $\displaystyle\int_0^1 \int_0^1 f(x_1, x_2) \, dx_1 \, dx_2 = \int_0^1 \int_0^1 2(x_1 + x_2 - 2x_1 x_2) \, dx_1 \, dx_2$

$$= 1.$$

The probability that $0 \leq x_1 \leq \frac{1}{2}$ and $0 \leq \,\leq x_2 \leq \frac{1}{4}$ is given by

$$P\left\{0 \leq x_1 \leq \frac{1}{2}, 0 \leq x_2 \leq \frac{1}{4}\right\} = \int_0^{1/2} \int_0^{1/4} 2(x_1 + x_2 - 2x_1 x_2) \, dx_2 \, dx_1$$

$$= \frac{5}{64}.$$

The C.D.F. is now given by

$$F(x_1, x_2) = \int_0^{x_1} \int_0^{x_2} 2(u_1 + u_2 - 2u_1 u_2) \, du_1 \, du_2$$

$$= x_1^2 x_2 + x_1 x_2^2 - x_1^2 x_2^2$$

Notice that $F(0, 0) = 0$ and $F(1, 1) = 1$. ◄

§ 12·5·1
Marginal Distribution

Given the continuous joint p.d.f. $f(x_1, \ldots, x_n)$, the *marginal* distribution of any random variable x_i is defined by

$$f_i(x_i) = \int_{-\infty}^{+\infty} dx_1 \cdots \int_{-\infty}^{+\infty} dx_{i-1} \int_{-\infty}^{+\infty} dx_{i+1} \cdots \int_{-\infty}^{+\infty} dx_n \, f(x_1, \ldots, x_n)$$

$$= \frac{\partial}{\partial x_i} F(\infty, \ldots, \infty, x_i, \infty, \ldots, \infty).$$

Similarly, in the discrete case

$$P_i(x_i) = \sum_{\text{all } x_1} \cdots \sum_{\text{all } x_{i-1}} \sum_{\text{all } x_{i+1}} \cdots \sum_{\text{all } x_n} P(x_1, \ldots, x_n).$$

▶ **Example 12·5-2**
Consider the same problem of Example 12·5-1.

$$f_1(x_1) = \int_0^1 2(x_1 + x_2 - 2x_1 x_2) \, dx_2 = 1, \qquad 0 \leq x_1 \leq 1$$

$$f_2(x_2) = \int_0^1 2(x_1 + x_2 - 2x_1 x_2) \, dx_1 = 1, \qquad 0 \leq x_2 \leq 1$$

Notice that $f_1(x_1)$ and $f_2(x_2)$ satisfy the conditions of a p.d.f. ◄

§ 12·5·2
Conditional Distribution and Independence

Consider the joint p.d.f. $f(x_1, x_2)$. The conditional p.d.f. of the random variable x_1 given the random variable x_2 is defined as

$$f(x_1 \mid x_2) = \frac{f(x_1, x_2)}{f_2(x_2)}, \qquad f_2(x_2) > 0,$$

where

$$f_2(x_2) = \int_{-\infty}^{\infty} f(x_1, x_2) \, dx_1$$

is the marginal p.d.f. of x_2.

In general, given $f(x_1, \ldots, x_n)$, the conditional p.d.f. of $(x_1, x_2, \ldots, x_{n-1})$ given x_n is

$$f(x_1, x_2, \ldots, x_{n-1} \mid x_n) = \frac{f(x_1, x_2, \ldots, x_n)}{f_n(x_n)}, \qquad f_n(x_n) > 0,$$

where

$$f_n(x_n) = \int_{-\infty}^{+\infty} dx_1 \int_{-\infty}^{+\infty} dx_2 \cdots \int_{-\infty}^{+\infty} dx_{n-1} f(x_1, \ldots, x_n).$$

A similar definition can be established for the discrete case.

The conditional p.d.f. must satisfy the two conditions of a regular p.d.f., namely,

(i) $f(x_1, \ldots, x_{n-1} \mid x_n) \geq 0, \quad -\infty < x_i < \infty, \quad i = 1, 2, \ldots, n,$

(ii) $\displaystyle\int_{-\infty}^{+\infty} dx_1 \cdots \int_{-\infty}^{+\infty} dx_{n-1} f(x_1, \ldots, x_{n-1} \mid x_n) = 1.$

The conditional C.D.F. can also be defined as

$$F(x_1, \ldots, x_{n-1} \mid x_n) = \int_{-\infty}^{x_1} du_1 \cdots \int_{-\infty}^{x_{n-1}} du_{n-1} f(u_1, \ldots, u_{n-1} \mid x_n).$$

It is said that n random variables $x_1, \ldots, x_n$ are *independent* if, and only if, the joint p.d.f. is equal to the *product* of the marginal distributions of the random variables. That is,

$$f(x_1, \ldots, x_n) = f_1(x_1) f_2(x_2) \cdots f_n(x_n)$$

$$= \prod_{i=1}^{n} f_i(x_i),$$

where $f_i(x_i)$ is the marginal distribution of the random variable x_i.

Now, if x_1 and x_2 are two independent random variables, then

$$f(x_1 \mid x_2) = \frac{f(x_1, x_2)}{f_2(x_2)}$$

$$= \frac{f_1(x_1) f_2(x_2)}{f_2(x_2)}$$

$$= f_1(x_1),$$

which shows that in the case of independence, the conditional p.d.f. is equal to the marginal p.d.f.

▶ **Example 12·5-3**

Consider the same problem of Example 12·5-1. It was shown in Example 12·5-2 that

$$f_1(x_1) = \begin{cases} 1, & 0 \le x_1 \le 1, \\ 0, & \text{otherwise}, \end{cases}$$

$$f_2(x_2) = \begin{cases} 1, & 0 \le x_2 \le 1, \\ 0, & \text{otherwise}. \end{cases}$$

Since $f(x_1, x_2) \ne f_1(x_1) \cdot f_2(x_2)$, this means that x_1 and x_2 are not independent. Again, the conditional density function of x_1 given x_2 is obtained as

$$f(x_1 \mid x_2 = t) = \frac{f(x_1, t)}{f_2(t)}$$

$$= \frac{2(x_1 + t - 2tx_1)}{1}$$

$$= 2(x_1 + t - 2tx_1), \qquad 0 \le x_1 \le 1.$$

Notice that $f(x_1 \mid t) \ge 0$ and that

$$\int_0^1 f(x_1 \mid t)\, dx_1 = 2 \int_0^1 (x_1 + t - 2tx_1)\, dx_1$$

$$= 2 \left[\frac{x_1^2}{2} + tx_1 - tx_1^2 \right]_0^1$$

$$= 1,$$

regardless of the value of t $(0 \le x_2 = t \le 1)$. This shows that $f(x_1 \mid t)$ is a p.d.f. ◀

§ 12·6
Expectation and Moments of a Random Variable

It was shown in the previous sections how distribution functions are used to specify discrete and continuous random variables. It is often desirable to summarize the characteristics of a probability distribution by a number of meaningful measures from which general conclusions can be drawn about the random variable. These measures are usually specified by what is called the *expected value* of certain functions of the random variable. This section will give the definition and derivation of these measures.

§ 12·6·1
Definition of Expectation

Let x be a random variable and define $h(x)$ as any function of x. Define $E\{h(x)\}$ as the *expected* value of $h(x)$ with respect to the probability distributions of x. Thus,

$$E\{h(x)\} = \begin{cases} \displaystyle\int_{-\infty}^{+\infty} h(x)f(x)\,dx, & x \text{ continuous,} \\[2mm] \displaystyle\sum_{\text{all }x} h(x)P(x), & x \text{ discrete.} \end{cases}$$

The above definition can be extended to the case of a function of n random variables $h(x_1, \ldots, x_n)$. Thus

$$E\{h(x_1, \ldots, x_n)\} = \begin{cases} \displaystyle\int_{-\infty}^{+\infty} dx_1 \cdots \int_{-\infty}^{+\infty} dx_n\, h(x_1, \ldots, x_n)f(x_1, \ldots, x_n), \\ \hspace{6cm} x \text{ continuous,} \\[2mm] \displaystyle\sum_{\text{all }x_1} \cdots \sum_{\text{all }x_n} h(x_1, \ldots, x_n)P(x_1, \ldots, x_n), \\ \hspace{6cm} x \text{ discrete.} \end{cases}$$

It can be seen from the basic definition of expectation that, for any constant b.

$$E\{b\} = b,$$

$$E\{bh(x_1, \ldots, x_n)\} = b\, E\{h(x_1, \ldots, x_n)\},$$

$$E\{b \pm h(x_1, \ldots, x_n)\} = b \pm E\{h(x_1, \ldots, x_n)\}.$$

§ 12·6·2
Mean, Variance, and Moments

In summarizing the data of a single random variable, x, two measures are commonly used. These are the mean, $E\{x\}$, and the variance, $\text{Var}\{x\}$. The mean is a measure of central tendency of the distribution while the variance is a measure of dispersion of the distribution around its mean.

The mean of distribution is defined by substituting $h(x) = x$ in the expectation formula given in Section 12·6·1. Thus

$$E\{x\} = \begin{cases} \displaystyle\int_{-\infty}^{+\infty} xf(x)\,dx = \int_{-\infty}^{+\infty} x\,dF(x), & x \text{ continuous,} \\[2mm] \displaystyle\sum_{\text{all }x} xP(x), & x \text{ discrete.} \end{cases}$$

Another definition of the mean which is sometimes useful when dealing with *nonnegative* continuous random variables is obtained as follows. Let

$$H(x) = 1 - F(x),$$

then

$$E\{x\} = \int_0^\infty x \, dF(x)$$

$$= \int_0^\infty x \, d[1 - H(x)]$$

$$= -\left[xH(x)\right]_0^\infty + \int_0^\infty H(x) \, dx$$

$$= \int_0^\infty H(x) \, dx.$$

This definition will be used in the development in Section 14·4·2.

The above definitions of the mean can be extended to the important case where the random variable x is defined as

$$x = b_1 x_1 + b_2 x_2 + \cdots + b_n x_n,$$

where b_i is a constant and x_i is a random variable, $i = 1, 2, \ldots, n$. Then,

$$E\{x\} = E\{b_1 x_1 + \cdots + b_n x_n\}$$

$$= \int_{-\infty}^{+\infty} dx_1 \cdots \int_{-\infty}^{+\infty} dx_n (b_1 x_1 + \cdots + b_n x_n) f(x_1, \ldots, x_n),$$

$$= b_1 \int_{-\infty}^{+\infty} x_1 f_1(x_1) \, dx_1 + \cdots + b_n \int_{-\infty}^{+\infty} x_n f_n(x_n) \, dx_n,$$

$$= b_1 E\{x_1\} + \cdots + b_n E\{x_n\}.$$

This shows that "E" can be considered as linear operator in this case. For the special case where $b_i = 1$, $i = 1, 2, \ldots, n$, the expected value of the sum of n variables is equal to the sum of their respective expected values. Notice that the assumption of independence is not required in this case.

Suppose now that x is the product of n random variables; that is,

$$x = x_1 x_2 \ldots x_n,$$

then

$$E\{x\} = \int_{-\infty}^{+\infty} dx_1 \cdots \int_{-\infty}^{+\infty} dx_n (x_1 \cdots x_n) f(x_1, \ldots, x_n).$$

If $x_1, x_2, \ldots, x_n$ are independent then

$$f(x_1, x_2, \ldots, x_n) = f_1(x_1)f_2(x_2)\ldots f_n(x_n)$$

and

$$E\{x_1 x_2 \cdots x_n\} = \int_{-\infty}^{+\infty} x_1 f_1(x_1)\, dx_1 \cdots \int_{-\infty}^{+\infty} x_n f_n(x_n)\, dx_n$$

$$= E\{x_1\}E\{x_2\} \cdots E\{x_n\}.$$

Thus, the expected value of the product of *independent* random variables is the product of their expected values.

The variance of a distribution, on the other hand, is obtained by substituting $h(x) = (x - E\{x\})^2$ in the expectation formula given in Section 12·6·1, Thus,

$$\text{Var}\{x\} = E\{(x - E\{x\})^2\}$$
$$= E\{x^2 - 2xE\{x\} + (E\{x\})^2\}$$
$$= E\{x^2\} - 2E\{x\}E\{x\} + (E\{x\})^2$$
$$= E\{x^2\} - (E\{x\})^2,$$

which is obtained using the properties of expectation. Notice that $\text{Var}\{x\}$ is readily determined as soon as $E\{x^2\}$ and $E\{x\}$ are determined.

The quantity $E\{x^2\}$ is called the second moment of the distribution around zero. In general the nth moment (n, an integer, > 0) around zero is defined by putting $h(x) = x^n$ in the expectation formula. That is,

$$E\{x^n\} = \int_{-\infty}^{+\infty} x^n f(x)\, dx.$$

Although these moments can be determined from the given expression, it is usually simpler to use another method called the moment generating function. This is explained in the next section.

Before showing how the variance of

$$x = b_1 x_1 + b_2 x_2 + \cdots + b_n x_n$$

is obtained in terms of those of $x_1, x_2, \ldots, x_n$, it is necessary to introduce the definition of a *covariance*. Given two random variables x_1 and x_2, the covariance of x_1 and x_2 is defined as

$$\text{Cov}\{x_1, x_2\} = E\{(x_1 - E\{x_1\})(x_2 - E\{x_2\})\}$$
$$= E\{(x_1 x_2 - x_1 E\{x_2\} - x_2 E\{x_1\} + E\{x_1\}E\{x_2\})\}$$
$$= E\{x_1 x_2\} - E\{x_1\}E\{x_2\}.$$

If x_1 and x_2 are independent, then as shown previously,

$$E\{x_1 x_2\} = E\{x_1\}E\{x_2\},$$

hence

$$\text{Cov}\{x_1, x_2\} = 0.$$

However, the converse is not true in general, that is, if $\text{Cov}\{x_1, x_2\} = 0$, this does not mean that x_1 and x_2 are independent.

The covariance of any two random variables x_1 and x_2 can be expressed in terms of their variances as follows

$$\text{Cov}\{x_1, x_2\} = \rho_{12}\sqrt{\text{Var}\{x_1\}\text{Var}\{x_2\}}$$

or

$$\rho_{12} = \frac{\text{Cov}\{x_1, x_2\}}{\sqrt{\text{Var}\{x_1\}\,\text{Var}\{x_2\}}},$$

where ρ_{12} is called the *correlation* coefficient of x_1 and x_2. It can be proved that $|\rho_{12}| \leq 1$. When $\rho_{12} = \pm 1$, this means that x_1 and x_2 are linearly related, with probability one. Notice that when x_1 and x_2 are *independent*, $\rho_{12} = 0$.

It is now possible to obtain the variance of

$$x = b_1 x_1 + b_2 x_2 + \cdots + b_n x_n$$

in terms of the variances of x_i, $i = 1, 2, \ldots, n$. Consider first the case where $x = b_1 x_1 + b_2 x_2$. Then

$$
\begin{aligned}
\text{Var}\{x\} &= E\{(b_1 x_1 + b_2 x_2 - b_1 E\{x_1\} - b_2 E\{x_2\})^2\}, \\
&= b_1^2 E\{(x_1 - E\{x_1\})^2\} + b_2^2 E\{(x_2 - E\{x_2\})^2\} \\
&\quad + 2b_1 b_2 E\{(x_1 - E\{x_1\})(x_2 - E\{x_2\})\}, \\
&= b_1^2 \,\text{Var}\{x_1\} + b_2^2 \,\text{Var}\{x_2\} + 2b_1 b_2 \,\text{Cov}\{x_1, x_2\}.
\end{aligned}
$$

If x_1 and x_2 are independent *or* uncorrelated, then

$$\text{Var}\{x\} = b_1^2 \,\text{Var}\{x_1\} + b_2^2 \,\text{Var}\{x_2\}.$$

In a similar way, it can be proved that for

$$x = b_1 x_1 + \cdots + b_n x_n,$$

$$\text{Var}\{x\} = \sum_{i=1}^{n}\left[b_i^2 \,\text{Var}\{x_i\} + 2\sum_{j=i+1}^{n} b_i b_j \,\text{Cov}\{x_i, x_j\}\right].$$

Again, if $x_1, \ldots, x_n$ are independent or *pairwise* uncorrelated, then

$$\text{Var}\{x\} = \sum_{i=1}^{n} b_i^2 \,\text{Var}\{x_i\}.$$

§ 12·7
Moment Generating Function

Evaluation of the moments $E\{x^n\}$ of a probability distribution can be made directly from the definition in Section 12·6·2. The moment generating function (m.g.f.) is another transformation method which can be used to generate these moments. Let $M_x(t)$ be the m.g.f. of the random variable x, where t is a parameter greater than zero. Thus, given $f(x)$, the p.d.f. of x,

$$M_x(t) = E\{e^{tx}\} = \begin{cases} \displaystyle\int_{-\infty}^{+\infty} e^{tx}f(x)\, dx, & x \text{ continuous,} \\ \displaystyle\sum_{\text{all } x} e^{tx}P(x), & x \text{ discrete.} \end{cases}$$

It is clear that

$$M_x(0) = \int_{-\infty}^{+\infty} f(x)\, dx = \sum_{\text{all } x} P(x) = 1,$$

and that,

$$\left[\frac{\partial}{\partial t}M_x(t)\right]_{t=0} = \int_{-\infty}^{\infty} xf(x)\, dx = \sum_{\text{all } x} xP(x) = E\{x\}.$$

In general, it can be shown by induction that

$$E\{x^n\} = \left[\frac{\partial^n}{\partial t^n}M_x(t)\right]_{t=0}.$$

In the case where all the moments of the distribution exist,[1] it is possible to express $M_x(t)$ in the form of a power series. This is achieved as follows

$$M_x(t) = E\{e^{tx}\} = E\left\{\sum_{n=0}^{\infty}\frac{t^n x^n}{n!}\right\}$$

$$= \sum_{n=0}^{\infty}\left(\frac{t^n}{n!}\right)E\{x^n\}.$$

If the expression for the m.g.f. can be put in this form, the general expression for the nth moment becomes immediately available.

---

[1] There are some probability distributions for which the moments, and hence the m.g.f., are not defined. For example, for the *Cauchy* distribution,

$$f(x) = \frac{1}{\pi(1 + x^2)}, \qquad -\infty < x < \infty$$

$E\{x^n\}$ does not exist for all $n \geq 1$, and hence its m.g.f. is not defined. Another transformation function can be defined, however, which is proved to exist for any p.d.f. This is called the *characteristic* function and is defined by

$$\Psi_x(\rho) = E\{e^{i\rho x}\}, \quad i = \sqrt{-1}, \quad \rho > 0$$

The characteristic function is used to obtain the moments in much the same way as the moment generating function. Its application is more general, however, since it can be used to derive the p.d.f.

It must be noted that the m.g.f. for any p.d.f., when it exists, is unique. This means that if the m.g.f.'s of two random variables are identical, their p.d.f.'s are necessarily the same.

▶ **Example 12·7-1**

For the gamma distribution

$$f(x) = \frac{\mu(\mu x)^{n-1} e^{-\mu x}}{(n-1)!}, \qquad x > 0,$$

the m.g.f. is given by

$$M_x(t) = \int_0^\infty e^{tx} \frac{\mu(\mu x)^{n-1} e^{-\mu x}}{(n-1)!}\, dx,$$

$$= \left(\frac{\mu}{\mu - t}\right)^n \int_0^\infty \frac{(\mu - t)[(\mu - t)x]^{n-1} e^{-(\mu - t)x}}{(n-1)!}\, dx,$$

$$= \left(\frac{\mu}{\mu - t}\right)^n.$$

By definition,

$$E\{x\} = \frac{\partial M_x(0)}{\partial t} = \frac{n}{\mu}.$$

Also,

$$E\{x^2\} = \frac{\partial^2 M(0)}{\partial t^2} = \left(\frac{n}{\mu^2}\right) - \left(\frac{n^2}{\mu^2}\right).$$

Hence

$$\mathrm{Var}\{x\} = \frac{n}{\mu^2}.$$

Since the exponential distribution is obtained from the gamma distribution by putting $n = 1$, then the m.g.f. for the exponential distribution is

$$M_x(t) = \frac{\mu}{\mu - t}.$$

The m.g.f. for the exponential distribution can be put in a power series form as follows

$$\frac{\mu}{\mu - t} = \frac{1}{1 - (t/\mu)} = \sum_{n=0}^\infty \left(\frac{t^n}{n!}\right)\frac{n!}{\mu^n}.$$

Thus, from the power series definition of the m.g.f.,

$$E\{x^n\} = \left(\frac{n!}{\mu^n}\right)$$

or

$$E\{x\} = \frac{1}{\mu}$$

and

$$E\{x^2\} = \frac{2}{\mu^2}.$$

Hence

$$\text{Var}\{x\} = \frac{2}{\mu^2} - \left(\frac{1}{\mu}\right)^2 = \frac{1}{\mu^2}. \quad \blacktriangleleft$$

The concept of the m.g.f. can also be extended to the sum of *independent* random variables. Let

$$y = \sum_{i=1}^{k} x_i$$

be a random variable which is defined as the sum of k *independent* random variables x_i. The m.g.f. of y as a function of x is given by

$$M_y(t) = E\{e^{ty}\} = E\{e^{t(x_1 + x_2 + \dots + x_k)}\}.$$

Since $x_1, x_2, \dots, x_k$ are independent random variables, then

$$M_y(t) = E\{e^{tx_1}\}E\{e^{tx_2}\} \cdots E\{e^{tx_k}\}$$

$$= \prod_{i=1}^{k} M_{x_i}(t),$$

where $M_{x_i}(t)$ is the m.g.f. of x_i. This means that the m.g.f. of the sum of independent random variables is equal to the product of their m.g.f.'s.

▶ **Example 12·7-2**

Let $x_1, x_2, \dots, x_n$ be n *independent* and exponentially distributed random variables with parameters $\mu_1, \mu_2, \dots, \mu_n$ respectively. Let $y = \sum_{i=1}^{n} x_i$. As shown in Example 12·7-1,

$$M_{x_i}(t) = \frac{\mu_i}{\mu_i - t},$$

hence,

$$M_y(t) = \prod_{i=1}^{n} \left(\frac{\mu_i}{\mu_i - t}\right).$$

For the case where all the exponential distributions are identical with the same parameter μ, then

$$M_y(t) = \left(\frac{\mu}{\mu - t}\right)^n.$$

This is the m.g.f. of a gamma distribution with mean n/μ and variance n/μ^2. (See Example 12·7-1.) Since the m.g.f. is unique, this shows that the sum of independent and identically distributed exponential random variables is gamma distributed. ◄

§ 12·8
Central Limit Theorem

Consider the random variable S_n which is defined as the sum of n independent and identically distributed random variables $x_1, x_2, \ldots, x_n$. That is,

$$S_n = x_1 + x_2 + \cdots + x_n.$$

The *central limit theorem* proves the remarkable result that as n becomes large ($n \to \infty$), the distribution of S_n tends toward normality *regardless* of the original distribution of $x_1, \ldots, x_n$. Mathematically, this theorem is expressed as follows. Let the mean and variance of x_i be constant and given by μ and σ^2, respectively. Then, $E\{S_n\} = n\mu$ and $\text{Var}\{S_n\} = n\sigma^2$. Thus, the central limit theorem indicates that,

$$\lim_{n \to \infty} P\{S_n \le s\} = \lim_{n \to \infty} P\left\{\frac{S_n - n\mu}{\sigma\sqrt{n}} \le \frac{s - n\mu}{\sigma\sqrt{n}}\right\}$$

$$= \frac{1}{\sqrt{2\pi}} \int_{-\infty}^{z} \exp\left(-\frac{y^2}{2}\right) dy,$$

where $z = (s - n\mu)/\sigma\sqrt{n}$. This means that S_n is approximately normal with mean $n\mu$ and variance $n\sigma^2$.

§ 12·9
Convolutions

Consider the case of two continuous random variables x and y with a joint p.d.f. $f(x, y)$ where $-\infty < x < \infty$ and $-\infty < y < \infty$. It is required to determine the p.d.f. of $s = x + y$. This will be accomplished by considering the C.D.F. of s, $G(s)$. Thus,

$$G(s) = P\{x + y \le s\}$$

$$= \iint_{\{x+y \le s\}} f(x, y)\, dx\, dy, \qquad -\infty < x < \infty, -\infty < y < \infty.$$

Making the necessary changes in the limits of integration, and noting that $-\infty < x < \infty$ and $-\infty < y < \infty$, then

$$G(s) = \int_{-\infty}^{+\infty} \left\{ \int_{-\infty}^{s-x} f(x, y)\, dy \right\} dx.$$

The p.d.f. of s, $g(s)$, is then obtained by differentiating $G(s)$ with respect to s.[2] Hence,

$$g(s) = \int_{-\infty}^{+\infty} f(x, s - x)\, dx.$$

If x and y are independent, then $f(x, y) = f_1(x)f_2(y)$ and the resulting p.d.f of s, denoted by $g_c(s)$, is given by

$$g_c(s) = \int_{-\infty}^{+\infty} f_1(x)f_2(s - x)\, dx.$$

The operation of obtaining the density function of the sum of two *independent* random variables is called *convolution* and the resulting p.d.f. is usually indicated as $g_c = f_1 * f_2$. The convolution operation can also be extended to the discrete case in essentially the same way. Namely.

$$P_c(s) = \sum_{\text{all } x} P_1(x)P_2(s - x).$$

An important case of convolution occurs when the random variables are positive only. In this case the limits of integration in the convolution formula must be nonnegative. This means that if $y = s - x$ is to be nonnegative, x cannot exceed s. Thus

$$G_c(s) = \int_0^s \left\{ \int_0^{s-x} f_2(y)\, dy \right\} f_1(x)\, dx.$$

Again, by differentiation, this gives

$$g_c(s) = \int_0^s f_1(x)f_2(s - x)\, dx.$$

It is noted for the case where it is required to obtain the convolution of three or more random variables, that the above formulas can be applied recursively until the density function of the total sum is obtained. For example, let

$$s = x_1 + x_2 + \cdots + x_n$$

---

[2] Given

$$H(y) = \int_{a(y)}^{b(y)} f(x, y)\, dx$$

then

$$\frac{dH(y)}{dy} = \int_{a(y)}^{b(y)} \frac{\partial f(x, y)}{\partial y}\, dx + f(b(y), y)\frac{db(y)}{dy} - f(a(y), y)\frac{da(y)}{dy}.$$

where $x_1, x_2, \ldots, x_n$ are independent random variables. Thus, to obtain the p.d.f. of s, one starts first by obtaining the p.d.f. of $s_2 = x_1 + x_2$. Next consider $s_3 = s_2 + x_3$ and continue in the same manner until $s = s_{n-1} + x_n$ is obtained.

▶ **Example 12·9-1**

Consider the exponential distribution,

$$f(x) = \mu e^{-\mu x}, \qquad x > 0.$$

It will now be shown that the n-fold convolution of the above exponential random variable is a gamma distribution with mean n/μ and variance n/μ^2.

Let $s_n = x_1 + x_2 + \cdots + x_n$. Consider first $s_2 = x_1 + x_2$. From the convolution formula for positive random variables, one gets

$$f_2(s_2) = \int_0^{s_2} \mu e^{-\mu x_2} \mu e^{-\mu(s_2 - x_2)} \, dx_2$$

$$= \mu^2 s_2 \, e^{-\mu s_2}.$$

Again, letting $s_3 = s_2 + x_3$, and applying the same formula, then

$$f_3(s_3) = \int_0^{s_3} \mu^2 s_2 \, e^{-\mu s_2} (\mu e^{-\mu(s_3 - s_2)}) \, ds_2$$

$$= \frac{\mu^3 s_3^2 \, e^{-\mu s_3}}{2!}.$$

Continuing in the same manner, it can be shown by induction that for $s_n = s$,

$$f_n(s) = \frac{\mu^n s^{n-1} e^{-\mu s}}{(n-1)!}, \qquad s > 0.$$

This is a gamma distribution with mean n/μ and variance n/μ^2. This result, obtained by convolution, ascertains the same conclusion obtained by the m.g.f. (see Example 12·7-2). ◀

▶ **Example 12·9-2**

The discrete density function of the weekly demand on a certain commodity is given by

x	0	1	2
$P(x)$	.1	.4	.5

where x is the number of units demanded per week. Assuming that this distribution is the same for every week (stationary) and that they are statistically independent, find the distribution of the demand for two weeks.

The application of the convolution formula for the discrete case yields,

$$P(0) = P_1(0)P_2(0) = .1 \times .1 = .01,$$

$$P(1) = P_1(0)P_2(1) + P_1(1)P_2(0)$$
$$= .1 \times .4 + .4 \times .1 = .08,$$

$$P(2) = P_1(0)P_2(2) + P_1(1)P_2(1) + P_1(2)P_2(0)$$
$$= .1 \times .5 + .4 \times .4 + .5 \times .1 = .26,$$

$$P(3) = P_1(1)P_2(2) + P_1(2)P_2(1)$$
$$= .4 \times .5 + .5 \times .4 = .40,$$

$$P(4) = P_1(2)P_2(2) = .5 \times .5 = .25.$$

Thus

$x_1 + x_2$	0	1	2	3	4
$P(x_1 + x_2)$	.01	.08	.26	.40	.25

◄

§ 12-10
Stochastic Processes

Consider the discrete points in time $\{t_k\}$, for $k = 1, 2, \ldots$, and let ξ_{t_k} be the random variable which characterizes the state of the system at t_k. The family of random variables $\{\xi_{t_k}\}$ is said to form a *stochastic process*. It is noticed that the states at time t_k actually represent the (exhaustive and mutually exclusive) outcomes of the system at that time. The number of states may thus be finite or infinite. For example, the Poisson distribution

$$P_n(t) = \frac{e^{-\lambda t}(\lambda t)^n}{n!}, \qquad n = 0, 1, 2, \ldots,$$

represents a stochastic process with an infinite number of states. Here the random variable n represents the number of occurrences between 0 and t (assuming the system starts at time 0). The states of the system at any time t are thus given by $n = 0, 1, 2, \ldots$.

Another example is represented by the coin-tossing game which continues over a number of trials k. Each trial may be viewed as a point in time. The resulting sequence of trials forms a stochastic process. The state of the system at any trial are represented by the occurrence of either a head or a tail.

It is not the purpose of this section to introduce the general theory of stochastic processes. Rather, a summary of an important class of stochastic systems is presented. These include the so-called *Markov process* and *Markov chains*. A Markov chain is actually a special case of Markov processes. It is mainly used to study the short- and long-run behavior of certain stochastic systems. Markov processes and chains will be especially useful in dealing with queueing (or waiting line) theory which will be presented in Chapters 14 and 15.

§12·10·1
Markov Processes

A _Markov process_ is a stochastic system for which the occurrence of a future state depends on the immediately preceding state and only on it. Thus if $t_0 < t_1 < \cdots < t_n$ $(n = 0, 1, 2, \ldots)$ represents points in time, then the family of random variables $\{\xi_{t_n}\}$ is a Markov process if it possesses the following _Markovian property_.

$$P\{\xi_{t_n} = x_n \mid \xi_{t_{n-1}} = x_{n-1}, \ldots, \xi_{t_0} = x_0\} = P\{\xi_{t_n} = x_n \mid \xi_{t_{n-1}} = x_{n-1}\},$$

for all possible values of $\xi_{t_0}, \xi_{t_1}, \ldots, \xi_{t_n}$.

The probability $p_{x_{n-1}, x_n} = P\{\xi_{t_n} = x_n \mid \xi_{t_{n-1}} = x_{n-1}\}$ is called the _transition_ probability. It represents the _conditional_ probability of the system being in x_n at t_n, given that it was in x_{n-1} at t_{n-1}. This probability is also referred as _one-step_ transition probability since it describes the system between t_{n-1} and t_n. An m-step transition probability is thus defined by

$$p_{x_n, x_{n+m}} = P\{\xi_{t_{n+m}} = x_{n+m} \mid \xi_{t_n} = x_n\}.$$

§ 12·10·2
Markov Chains

Let $E_1, E_2, \ldots, E_j, \ldots$ $(j = 1, 2, \ldots)$ represent the exhaustive and mutually exclusive outcomes (states) of the system at any time. Initially at time t_0, the system may be in any of these states. Let $\{a_j^{(0)}\} = \{a_0^{(0)}, a_1^{(0)}, \ldots, a_j^{(0)}, \ldots\}$ be the absolute probability distribution that the system is in state E_j at t_0. Assume further that the system is Markovian.

Define

$$p_{ij} = P\{\xi_{t_n} = j \mid \xi_{t_{n-1}} = i\}$$

as the one-step transition probability of going from state i at t_{n-1} to state j at t_n and assume that these probabilities are fixed over time. Thus, the transition probabilities from state E_i to state E_j can be more conveniently arranged in a matrix form as follows:

E_i \ E_j	0	1	2	3	$\cdots$
0	p_{00}	p_{01}	p_{02}	p_{03}	$\cdots$
1	p_{10}	p_{11}	p_{12}	p_{13}	$\cdots$
2	p_{20}	p_{21}	p_{22}	p_{23}	$\cdots$
3	p_{30}	p_{31}	p_{32}	p_{33}	$\cdots$
$\vdots$	$\vdots$	$\vdots$	$\vdots$	$\vdots$	

$\mathbf{P} = t_{n-1}$, with t_n labeling the columns.

The matrix $\mathbf{P}$ is called a *homogeneous* transition or stochastic matrix. It is homogeneous because all the transition probabilities p_{ij} are fixed and independent of time. It is noticed that p_{ij} must satisfy the conditions,

$$\sum_j p_{ij} = 1, \quad \text{for all } i,$$

$$p_{ij} \geq 0, \quad \text{for all } i \text{ and } j.$$

The definition of a *Markov chain* is now in order. *A transition matrix* $\mathbf{P}$ *together with the initial probabilities* $\{a_j^{(0)}\}$ *associated with the states* E_j *completely define a Markov chain.* One usually thinks of a Markov chain as defining the transitional behavior of a system over equally-spaced intervals of time. There are some situations, however, where the time spacings are dependent on the characteristics of the system and hence may not be equal. This case is referred to as *imbedded* Markov chains.

§ 12·10·2·1
Absolute and Transition Probabilities

Given $\{a_j^{(0)}\}$ and $\mathbf{P}$ of a Markov chain, it is possible to determine the absolute probabilities of the system after a specified number of transitions. Let $\{a_j^{(n)}\}$ be the absolute probabilities of the system after n transitions; that is at t_n. The general expression of $\{a_j^{(n)}\}$ in terms of $\{a_j^{(0)}\}$ and $\mathbf{P}$ can be found as follows

$$a_j^{(1)} = a_1^{(0)} p_{1j} + a_2^{(0)} p_{2j} + a_3^{(0)} p_{3j} + \cdots$$
$$= \sum_i a_i^{(0)} p_{ij}.$$

Again

$$a_j^{(2)} = \sum_i a_i^{(1)} p_{ij}$$

$$= \sum_i \left(\sum_k a_k^{(0)} p_{ki} \right) p_{ij}$$

$$= \sum_k a_k^{(0)} \left(\sum_i p_{ki} p_{ij} \right)$$

$$= \sum_k a_k^{(0)} p_{kj}^{(2)},$$

where

$$p_{kj}^{(2)} = \sum_i p_{ki} p_{ij}$$

is the *two-step* or *second-order* transition probability; that is, the probability of going from state k to state j in exactly two transitions.

Similarly, it can be shown by induction that

$$a_j^{(n)} = \sum_i a_i^{(0)} \left(\sum_k p_{ik}^{(n-1)} p_{kj} \right)$$

$$= \sum_i a_i^{(0)} p_{ij}^{(n)},$$

where $p_{ij}^{(n)}$ is the n-step or n-order transition probability which is given by the recursive formula,

$$p_{ij}^{(n)} = \sum_k p_{ik}^{(n-1)} p_{kj}.$$

In general, for all i and j

$$p_{ij}^{(n)} = \sum_k p_{ik}^{(n-m)} p_{kj}^{(m)}, \qquad 0 < m < n.$$

These equations are known as *Chapman-Kolomogorov equations*.

The elements of a higher transition matrix $\|p_{ij}^{(n)}\|$ can be obtained directly by matrix multiplication. Thus

$$\|p_{ij}^{(2)}\| = \|p_{ij}\| \, \|p_{ij}\| = \mathbf{P}^2,$$

$$\|p_{ij}^{(3)}\| = \|p_{ij}^{(2)}\| \, \|p_{ij}\| = \mathbf{P}^3,$$

and, in general,

$$\|p_{ij}^{(n)}\| = \mathbf{P}^{n-1}\mathbf{P} = \mathbf{P}^n.$$

Hence, if the absolute probabilities are defined in vector form as

$$\mathbf{a}^{(n)} = \{a_1^{(n)}, a_2^{(n)}, a_3^{(n)}, \dots\},$$

then

$$\mathbf{a}^{(n)} = \mathbf{a}^{(0)}\mathbf{P}^n.$$

▶ **Example 12·10-1**

Consider the following Markov chain with two states,

$$\mathbf{P} = \begin{pmatrix} .2 & .8 \\ .6 & .4 \end{pmatrix},$$

with $\mathbf{a}^{(0)} = (.7 \quad .3)$. Determine $\mathbf{a}^{(1)}$, $\mathbf{a}^{(4)}$, and $\mathbf{a}^{(8)}$.

$$\mathbf{P}^2 = \begin{bmatrix} .2 & .8 \\ .6 & .4 \end{bmatrix} \begin{bmatrix} .2 & .8 \\ .6 & .4 \end{bmatrix} = \begin{bmatrix} .52 & .48 \\ .36 & .64 \end{bmatrix},$$

$$\mathbf{P}^4 = \mathbf{P}^2\mathbf{P}^2 = \begin{bmatrix} .52 & .48 \\ .36 & .64 \end{bmatrix} \begin{bmatrix} .52 & .48 \\ .36 & .64 \end{bmatrix} \cong \begin{bmatrix} .443 & .557 \\ .417 & .583 \end{bmatrix},$$

$$\mathbf{P}^8 = \mathbf{P}^4\mathbf{P}^4 = \begin{bmatrix} .443 & .577 \\ .417 & .583 \end{bmatrix} \begin{bmatrix} .443 & .557 \\ .417 & .583 \end{bmatrix} \cong \begin{bmatrix} .4281 & .5719 \\ .4274 & .5726 \end{bmatrix}.$$

Thus

$$\mathbf{a}^{(1)} = (.7 \quad .3)\begin{bmatrix} .2 & .8 \\ .6 & .4 \end{bmatrix} = (.32 \quad .68),$$

$$\mathbf{a}^{(4)} = (.7 \quad .3)\begin{bmatrix} .443 & .557 \\ .417 & .583 \end{bmatrix} = (.435 \quad .565),$$

$$\mathbf{a}^{(8)} = (.7 \quad .3)\begin{bmatrix} .4281 & .5719 \\ .4274 & .5726 \end{bmatrix} = (.4279 \quad .5721).$$

Notice the interesting result that the rows of $\mathbf{P}^8$ tend to be identical. Notice also that $\mathbf{a}^{(8)}$ tends to be identical with the rows of $\mathbf{P}^8$. This result has to do with the long-run properties of Markov chains. This property, as will be shown in Section 12·10·2·3, implies that the long-run absolute probabilities are independent of $\mathbf{a}^{(0)}$. In this case, the resulting probabilities are known as the *steady state* probabilities. ◄

§ 12·10·2·2
Classification of States in Markov Chains

In using Markov chain analysis, one may be interested in studying the behavior of the system over a short period of time. In this case, the absolute probabilities are computed as shown in the previous section. A more important study, however, would involve the long-run behavior of the system; that is, when the number of transitions tends to infinity. In such a case, the analysis given in the previous section becomes inadequate and a systematic procedure which will predict the long-run behavior of the system becomes necessary. This section introduces a number of definitions concerning the classification of states in Markov chains. These classifications will be useful in studying the long-run behavior of the system.

Irreducible Markov Chain

A Markov chain is said to be *irreducible* if every state E_j can be reached from every other state E_i after a finite number of transitions; that is, for $i \neq j$,

$$P_{ij}^{(n)} > 0,$$

for $1 \leq n < \infty$. In this case, it is said that all the states of the chain *communicate*.

Closed Set and Absorbing States

In a Markov chain, a set C of states is said to be *closed* if the system, once in one of the states of C, will remain in C indefinitely. A special example of a closed set is a single state E_j with transition probability $p_{jj} = 1$. In this case, E_j is called an *absorbing state*. It is seen by definition that all the states of an irreducible chain must form a closed set and that no other subset can be closed. It is also noticed that the closed set C must satisfy all the conditions of a Markov chain and hence it may be studied independently.

▶ **Example 12·10-2**
Consider the following Markov chain,

$$\mathbf{P} = \quad \begin{array}{c|cccc} \diagdown E_j \\ E_i \diagdown & 0 & 1 & 2 & 3 \\ \hline 0 & 1/2 & 1/4 & 1/4 & 0 \\ 1 & 0 & 0 & 1 & 0 \\ 2 & 1/3 & 0 & 1/3 & 1/3 \\ 3 & 0 & 0 & 0 & 1 \end{array}$$

This chain is illustrated graphically in Figure 12–7. The figure shows that the four states do *not* constitute an irreducible chain since States 0, 1, and 2 cannot be reached from State 3. State 3, by itself, forms a closed set and hence it is absorbing. One can also say that State 3 forms an irreducible chain. ◀

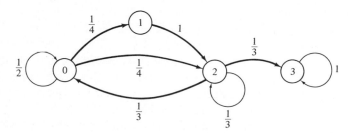

Figure 12–7

First Return Times
An important concept in Markov chains theory is the *first return* time. Given the system is initially in state E_j, the system may return to E_j *for the first time* at the nth step; $n \geq 1$. The number of steps before the system returns to E_j is called the first return time.

Let $f_{jj}^{(n)}$ denote the probability that the first return to E_j occurs at the nth step. Then given the transition matrix

$$\mathbf{P} = \|p_{ij}\|,$$

an expression for $f_{jj}^{(n)}$ can be determined as follows:

$$p_{jj} = f_{jj}^{(1)},$$

$$p_{jj}^{(2)} = f_{jj}^{(2)} + f_{jj}^{(1)}p_{jj},$$

or

$$f_{jj}^{(2)} = p_{jj}^{(2)} - f_{jj}^{(1)}p_{jj}.$$

Using induction it can be proved in general that

$$p_{jj}^{(n)} = f_{jj}^{(n)} + \sum_{m=1}^{n-1} f_{jj}^{(m)} p_{jj}^{(n-m)},$$

which yields the required expression,

$$f_{jj}^{(n)} = p_{jj}^{(n)} - \sum_{m=1}^{n-1} f_{jj}^{(m)} p_{jj}^{(n-m)}.$$

The probability of *at least* one return to state E_j is then given by

$$f_{jj} = \sum_{n=1}^{\infty} f_{jj}^{(n)}.$$

Thus the system is certain to return to j if $f_{jj} = 1$. In this case, if μ_{jj} defines the mean return (recurrence) time, then

$$\mu_{jj} = \sum_{n=1}^{\infty} n f_{jj}^{(n)}.$$

If, on the other hand, $f_{jj} < 1$, then it is not certain that the system will return to E_j and consequently $\mu_{jj} = \infty$.

The states of a Markov chain can thus be classified based on the definition of the first return times.

(i)   A state is transient if $f_{jj} < 1$; that is, $\mu_{jj} = \infty$.

(ii) A state is *recurrent* (persistent) if $f_{jj} = 1$.

(iii) A recurrent state is *null* if $\mu_{jj} = \infty$ and *nonnull* if $\mu_{jj} < \infty$ (finite).

(iv) A state is *periodic* with period t if, for $t(> 1)$, the greatest integer with this property, a return is possible only in $t, 2t, 3t, \ldots$, steps. This means that $p_{jj}^{(n)} = 0$ whenever n is not divisible by t.

(v)   A recurrent state is *ergodic* if it is nonnull and aperiodic (not periodic).

Ergodic Markov Chains

An *irreducible* Markov chain is ergodic if all its states are ergodic. In this case the absolute probability distribution

$$\mathbf{a}^{(n)} = \mathbf{a}^{(0)} \mathbf{P}^n$$

always converges uniquely to a limiting distribution as $n \to \infty$, where the limiting distribution is independent of the initial probabilities $\mathbf{a}^{(0)}$.

The following theorem is now in order.

Theorem 1.   *All the states in an irreducible infinite Markov chain may belong to one, and only one, of the following three classes: transient state, recurrent null state, or recurrent nonnull state. In every case all the states communicate and they have the same period. For the special case where the chain has a finite number of states, the chain cannot consist of transient states only nor can it contain any null states.*

The proof of this theorem can be found in Feller [1], Vol. I, p. 355.

§ 12·10·2·3
Limiting Distribution of Irreducible Chains

It was shown in Example 12·10-1 that as the number of transitions increase, the absolute probability tends to be independent of the initial distribution. This was referred to as the long-run property of Markov chains. In this section, determination of the limiting (long-run) distribution of an *irreducible* chain will be presented. The discussion will be restricted to the aperiodic type, since this is the only type needed in this text. In addition, the analysis of the periodic case is rather involved.

The existence of a limiting distribution in an irreducible aperiodic chain depends on the class of its states. Thus considering the three classes given in Theorem 1 above, the following theorem can be stated. (See Feller [1], Vol. I, p. 357 for the proof).

> **Theorem 2.** *In an irreducible aperiodic Markov chain,*
>
> (a) *If the states are all transient or all null, then $p_{ij}^{(n)} \to 0$ as $n \to \infty$ for all i and j and no limiting distribution exists.*
>
> (b) *If all the states are ergodic, then*
>
> $$\lim_{n \to \infty} a_j^{(n)} = \beta_j, \qquad j = 0, 1, 2, \ldots$$
>
> *where β_j is the limiting (steady state) distribution. The probabilities β_j exist uniquely and are independent of $a_j^{(0)}$. In this case β_j can be determined from the set of equations[3]*
>
> $$\beta_j = \sum_i \beta_i \, p_{ij},$$
>
> $$1 = \sum_j \beta_j.$$
>
> *The mean recurrence time for state j is then given by*
>
> $$\mu_{jj} = \frac{1}{\beta_j}.$$

▶ **Example 12·10-3**
Consider Example 12·10-1.
To determine its steady state probability distribution, one has

$$\beta_1 = .2\beta_1 + .6\beta_2$$

$$\beta_2 = .8\beta_1 + .4\beta_2,$$

$$1 = \beta_1 + \beta_2.$$

---

[3] Notice that one of the equations $\beta_j = \sum_i \beta_i p_{ij}$ is redundant.

Noting that one of the first two equations is redundant, the solution of these equations yields $\beta_1 = 0.4286$ and $\beta_2 = 0.5714$. These results are very close to the values of $\mathbf{a}^{(8)}$ (and the rows of $\mathbf{P}^8$) in Example 12·10-1.

Now,

$$\mu_{11} = \frac{1}{\beta_1} = 2.3,$$

$$\mu_{22} = \frac{1}{\beta_2} = 1.75,$$

so that the mean recurrent time for the first state is 2.3 steps and for the second state is 1.75 steps. ◄

▶ **Example 12·10-4**

Consider the following Markov chain with three states.

$$
\mathbf{P} = \begin{matrix} & \begin{matrix} 0 & \quad 1 & \quad 2 \end{matrix} \\ \begin{matrix} 0 \\ 1 \\ 2 \end{matrix} & \begin{bmatrix} 1/2 & 1/4 & 1/4 \\ 1/2 & 1/4 & 1/4 \\ 0 & 1/2 & 1/2 \end{bmatrix} \end{matrix}.
$$

This is called a doubly-stochastic matrix since

$$\sum_{i=1}^{s} p_{ij} = \sum_{j=1}^{s} p_{ij} = 1,$$

where s is the number of states. In such cases, the steady state probabilities are $\beta_j = 1/s$ for all j. Thus for the above matrix,

$$\beta_0 = \beta_1 = \beta_2 = 1/3. \quad ◄$$

§ 12·11
The z-Transform

An important transformation function which is used with nonnegative discrete random variables is the so-called z-transform. Let n be a discrete random variable defined over a set of nonnegative integers and let p_n be its p.d.f. Let the notation $Z(p_n) \equiv P(z)$ represent the z-transform of p_n. Thus, the z-transform is defined by

$$Z(p_n) = P(z) = \sum_{n=0}^{\infty} p_n z^n,$$

where z is determined such that $Z(p_n)$ converges. Since $\sum_{n=0}^{\infty} p_n = 1$, $Z(p_n)$ will always converge for $|z| \le 1$. It should be noted that the z-transform for a given p.d.f. is unique.

The z-transform, like the moment generating function (Section 12·7) can be used to determine the moments of the random variable n. A more important contribution will be the use of the z-transform to determine the p.d.f. of n. The following sections will investigate these points in detail.

§ 12·11·1
Characteristics of the z-Transform

Given $P(z)$, the z-transform for p_n as defined above, and defining

$$P^{(n)}(z) = \frac{\partial^n P(z)}{\partial z^n},$$

the following properties can be established.

Property 1:

$$P(0) = p_0.$$

Property 2:

$$P(1) = \sum_{n=0}^{\infty} p_n = 1.$$

Property 3:

$$p_n = \frac{1}{n!} P^{(n)}(0).$$

Property 3 can be established as follows

$$P(z) = p_0 + p_1 z + p_2 z^2 + \cdots.$$

Hence

$$P^{(1)}(z) = p_1 + 2p_2 z + 3p_3 z^2 + \cdots,$$

which yields

$$P^{(1)}(0) = p_1 = 1!\,p_1.$$

Again

$$P^{(2)}(z) = 2p_2 + 3 \cdot 2p_3 z + 4 \cdot 3p_4 z^2 + \cdots,$$

which gives

$$P^{(2)}(0) = 2p_2 = 2!\,p_2.$$

Similarly

$$P^{(3)}(0) = 3 \cdot 2p_3 = 3!\,p_3.$$

Continuing in the same manner, Property 3 can be proved by induction.

Property 4:

$$E\{n\} = P^{(1)}(1).$$
$$\text{Var}\{n\} = P^{(2)}(1) + P^{(1)}(1) - \{P^{(1)}(1)\}^2.$$

This property is derived as follows.

$$P^{(1)}(1) = p_1 + 2p_2 + 3p_3 + \cdots$$

$$= \sum_{n=1}^{\infty} np_n = E\{n\}.$$

Again,

$$p^{(2)}(1) = 2p_2 + 3.2p_3 + 4.3p_4 + \cdots$$

$$= \sum_{n=2}^{\infty} n(n-1)p_n$$

$$= \sum_{n=2}^{\infty} n^2 p_n - \sum_{n=2}^{\infty} np_n$$

$$= E\{n^2\} - E\{n\}.$$

Thus,

$$\text{Var}\{n\} = E\{(n - E\{n\})^2\}$$
$$= E\{n^2\} - (E\{n\})^2$$
$$= P^{(2)}(1) + P^{(1)}(1) - \{P^{(1)}(1)\}^2.$$

It is seen from Property 3 that once the z-transform is known, P_n is completely defined. Property 4 also shows that the mean and variance of n can be derived from the z-transform.

§ 12·11·2
Special Cases of the z-Transform

This section will present some useful relationships which are often encountered in the derivations of the z-transform. It must be noted first that the z-transform is a general mathematical operation which applies to any nonnegative *sequence* of which a nonnegative random variable represents a special case. Thus in the following analysis, p_n and q_n will be thought of as general nonnegative sequences.

1. The z-transform of p_{n-1}.

$$Z(p_{n-1}) = \sum_{n=0}^{\infty} p_{n-1}z^n$$

$$= z \sum_{k=0}^{\infty} p_k z^k$$

$$= zZ(p_n)$$

$$= zP(z).$$

2. The z-transform of p_{n+1}.

$$Z(p_{n+1}) = \sum_{n=0}^{\infty} p_{n+1} z^n$$

$$= \frac{1}{z} \left(\sum_{n=0}^{\infty} p_{n+1} z^{n+1} \right)$$

$$= \frac{1}{z} \left(\sum_{k=0}^{\infty} p_k z^k - p_0 \right)$$

$$= \frac{1}{z} (Z(p_n) - p_0)$$

$$= \frac{1}{z} (P(z) - p_0).$$

3. The z-transform of $(p_n + q_n)$.

$$Z(p_n + q_n) = \sum_{n=0}^{\infty} (p_n + q_n) z^n$$

$$= Z(p_n) + Z(q_n)$$

$$= P(z) + Q(z).$$

4. The z-transform of bp_n, where b is a constant.

$$Z(bp_n) = \sum_{n=0}^{\infty} bp_n z^n$$

$$= bZ(p_n)$$

$$= bP(z).$$

5. The z-transform of the convolution of p_n and q_n. Let

$$y_n = q_n * p_n = q_0 p_n + q_1 p_{n-1} + \cdots + q_{n-1} p_1 + q_n p_0 .$$

Then,

$$Z(y_n) = \sum_{n=0}^{\infty} y_n z^n$$

$$= q_0 p_0 + (q_0 p_1 + q_1 p_0) z + (q_0 p_2 + q_1 p_1 + q_2 p_0) z^2 + \cdots$$

$$= \{ q_0 (p_0 + p_1 z + p_2 z^2 + \cdots)$$

$$+ q_1 z (p_0 + p_1 z + p_2 z^2 + \cdots)$$

$$+ q_2 z^2 (p_0 + p_1 z + p_2 z^2 + \cdots)$$

$$+ \cdots \}$$

$$= (q_0 + q_1 z + q_2 z^2 + \cdots)(p_0 + p_1 z + p_2 z^2 + \cdots)$$

$$= Z(q_n) Z(p_n)$$

$$= Q(z) P(z).$$

Thus the z-transform of the convolution of two p.d.f.'s is the product of their z-transforms.

The power of the z-transform is realized when dealing with the situations where p_n is expressed implicitly by difference or differential equations such as in queueing theory analysis (see Chapters 14 and 15). For such cases, the expression for $P(z)$ is first derived from the given equations, then using Property 3, Section 12·11·1, the expression for p_n can be obtained. There are some cases, however, where the general expression for p_n can be obtained by taking the inverse of $P(z)$; that is, $p_n = Z^{-1}\{P(z)\}$. Tables of the inverse z-transform have thus been prepared for this purpose. A short list of some important cases which will be used in the next chapters is included in Table 12–1. An illustration of the use of these tables is given in Example 12.11-2 below.

Table 12–1
z-Transform Functions and Their Inverses *

Formula	$P(z) = \sum\limits_{n=0}^{\infty} p_n z^n$	$Z^{-1}\{P(z)\} = p_n$
1	$z^k Q(z)$	$p_n = \begin{cases} 0 & ,n < k \\ q_{n-k}, & n \geq k \end{cases}$
2	$z^{-k}Q(z) - \sum\limits_{j=0}^{k-1} q_j\, z^{j-k}$	q_{n+k}
3	$Q(a^b z)$	$a^{bn} q_n$
4	$\{(1-z)Q(z) - q_0\}z^{-1}$	$q_{n+1} - q_n$
5	$a/(1-z)$	a
6	$z/(1-z)^2$	n
7	$1/(1-az)$	a^n
8	$1/(1-az)^{k+1}$	$\binom{n+k}{k} a^n$
9	$(a+bz)^m$	$\binom{m}{n} b^n a^{m-n}$
10	$-\ln(1-az)$	a^n/n
11	e^{az}	$\dfrac{a^n}{n!}$
12	a^z	$(\ln a)^n/n!$

* This table is excerpted from C. Beightler, L. Mitten, and G. Nemhauser, "A Short Table of z-Transform and Generating Function," *Operations Research,* Vol. 9, No. 4, 574–578, (1961).

▶ **Example 12·11-1**

Consider the z-transform of a Poisson distribution with parameter λ. That is,

$$p_n = \frac{\lambda^n e^{-\lambda}}{n!}, \qquad n = 0, 1, 2, \dots.$$

The z-transform is given by

$$P(z) = \sum_{n=0}^{\infty} \frac{\lambda^n e^{-\lambda}}{n!} z^n$$

$$= \frac{e^{-\lambda}}{e^{-\lambda z}} \sum_{n=0}^{\infty} \frac{(\lambda z)^n e^{-\lambda z}}{n!}$$

$$= e^{\lambda(z+1)}.$$

Hence,

$$E\{n\} = P^{(1)}(1) = [\lambda e^{\lambda(z-1)}]_{z=1} = \lambda.$$

Similarly,

$$P^{(2)}(1) = [\lambda^2 e^{\lambda(z-1)}]_{z=1} = \lambda^2.$$

Thus

$$\mathrm{Var}\{n\} = P^{(2)}(1) + P^{(1)}(1) - \{P^{(1)}(1)\}^2$$

$$= \lambda^2 + \lambda - \lambda^2 = \lambda. \quad ◀$$

▶ **Example 12·11-2**

Consider the z-transform of the convolution of the two Poisson distributions,

$$p_n = \frac{\lambda_1^n e^{-\lambda_1}}{n!}, \qquad n = 0, 1, 2, \dots$$

and

$$q_n = \frac{\lambda_2^n e^{-\lambda_2}}{n!}, \qquad n = 0, 1, 2, \dots.$$

Let

$$y_n = q_n * p_n.$$

Hence, from Section 12·11·2,

$$Z(y_n) = Q(z)P(z).$$

From Example 12·11-1,

$$Q(z) = e^{\lambda_2(z-1)},$$

$$P(z) = e^{\lambda_1(z-1)},$$

or

$$Z(y_n) = e^{\{(\lambda_1 + \lambda_2)(z-1)\}}.$$

From Table 12–1, Formula 11 gives,

$$Z^{-1}\{e^{az}\} = \frac{a^n}{n!}$$

Thus

$$y_n = Z^{-1}\{e^{\{(\lambda_1 + \lambda_2)(z-1)\}}\}$$

$$= e^{-(\lambda_1 + \lambda_2)} Z^{-1}\{e^{(\lambda_1 + \lambda_2)z}\}$$

$$= \frac{e^{-(\lambda_1 + \lambda_2)}(\lambda_1 + \lambda_2)^n}{n!}, \qquad n = 0, 1, 2, \ldots.$$

This shows that the convolution of two (independent) Poisson distributions with parameters λ_1 and λ_2 is also Poisson with parameter $(\lambda_1 + \lambda_2)$. ◄

SELECTED REFERENCES

1. FELLER, W., *An Introduction to Probability Theory and Its Applications*, New York: Wiley, Vols. I and II, 1966.
2. PARZEN, E., *Modern Probability Theory and Its Applications*, New York: Wiley, 1960.
3. PARZEN, E., *Stochastic Processes*, San Francisco: Holden-Day, 1962.
4. TAKÁCS, L., *Stochastic Processes*, New York: Wiley, 1960.

PROBLEMS

☐ **12-1**   Derive the relationships

(a) $P\{E + F\} = P\{E\} + P\{F\} - P\{EF\}$
(b) $P\{ABC\} = P\{A\}P\{B \mid A\}P\{C \mid AB\}$.

☐ **12-2**   Find the value of k so that

$$f(x) = \begin{cases} \dfrac{k}{x^2}, & 10 \le x \le 20, \\ \\ 0, & \text{otherwise,} \end{cases}$$

is a p.d.f.

☐ **12-3**   Given a random variable j which assumes the values $c, c + 1, c + 2, \ldots$, where c is a positive integer, show that

$$P\{x = j\} = \binom{j-1}{c-1} p^c (1 - p)^{j-c}, \qquad 0 < p < 1$$

is a proper density function. (This is the Pascal distribution introduced in Section 12·4·1·1.)

☐ **12-4**   A random variable t has the following C.D.F.

$$F(t) = \begin{cases} 1 - e^{-2t}, & t \geq 0, \\ 0, & t < 0. \end{cases}$$

Find

(a)   the corresponding p.d.f.
(b) $P\{5 < t < 10\}$.
(c) $P\{t = 10)$.
(d) $P\{t < 5 \text{ or } t > 10\}$.
(e) $P\{3 < t < 5 \text{ and } 6 < t < 7\}$.

☐ **12-5**   Show that

$$\int_{-\infty}^{+\infty} \exp(-x^2/2)\, dx = \sqrt{2\pi}\,.$$

☐ **12-6**   Show that the geometric distribution (Section 12·4·1·1) approaches the exponential distribution as $p \to 0$ and the intertrial time $\to 0$.

☐ **12-7**   Show that

$$f(x, y) = \begin{cases} \exp(-x - y), & x > 0, \quad y > 0, \\ 0, & \text{otherwise}, \end{cases}$$

is a density function, then find

(a)   the marginal distributions of x and y.
(b)   the C.D.F., $F(x, y)$.
(c) $P\{1 < x < 10, 5 < y < 7\}$.

☐ **12-8**   In Problem 12-7, show that x and y are independent.

☐ **12-9**   Given

$$f(x_1, x_2) = \begin{cases} k(1 - x_1 - x_2), & 0 < x_2 < 1 - x_1, \quad 0 < x_1 < 1, \\ 0, & \text{otherwise}. \end{cases}$$

(a)   Find the value of k which will make $f(x_1, x_2)$ a p.d.f.
(b)   Find the conditional p.d.f. $g(x_1 \mid x_2)$ and then show that x_1 and x_2 are not independent.

☐ **12-10**   For the uniform p.d.f.,

$$f(x) = \begin{cases} \dfrac{1}{b - a}, & a < x < b, \\ 0, & \text{otherwise}, \end{cases}$$

find the mean and variance.

☐ **12-11**   In Problem 12-9, find $E\{x_1 \mid x_2\}$.

☐ **12-12**   Given $x_1, x_2, \ldots, x_n$ are identically distributed and independent random variables each with mean μ and variance σ^2, find the expected value of S^2, where

$$S^2 = \left(\frac{\sum_{i=1}^{n} (x_i - \bar{x})^2}{n} \right)$$

and

$$n\bar{x} = \sum_{i=1}^{n} x_i.$$

☐ **12-13**   Given the two random variables x_1 and x_2 with the correlation coefficient ρ_{12}, prove that $|\rho_{12}| \leq 1$.

☐ **12-14**   Consider the two random variables x_1 and x_2. Assuming that x_1^2 and x_2^2 have a zero correlation coefficient, find $\mathrm{Var}\{x_1 x_2\}$.

☐ **12-15**   The nth moment of the random variable x is given by $E\{x^n\} = n!$. Find its m.g.f. and show that it coincides with the m.g.f. of an exponential distribution with parameter 1.

☐ **12-16**   Show that the sum of two independent Poisson distributions with parameters λ_1 and λ_2 is also Poisson with parameter $(\lambda_1 + \lambda_2)$. Use the m.g.f procedure.

☐ **12-17**   Find the m.g.f. of a binomial distribution with parameters (p, n). Then find its mean and variance.

☐ **12-18**   Using the m.g.f., find the general expression for the nth moment of a normal distribution with mean zero and variance one.

☐ **12-19**   If x_1 and x_2 are independent and have uniform distributions on the interval $(0, 1)$, find the p.d.f. of $x_1 + x_2$.

☐ **12-20**   Let $x_1, x_2, \ldots, x_n, \ldots$, be independent continuous random variables with identical exponential p.d.f. Define m such that

$$x_1 + x_2 + \cdots + x_m \leq t \leq x_1 + x_2 + \cdots + x_{m+1}.$$

Find the discrete p.d.f. of m.

☐ **12-21**   Consider the following p.d.f. of the discrete random variable x which represents the monthly demand on a certain item.

x	0	1	2	3
$p(x)$	0.1	0.2	0.3	0.4

Assuming that the monthly demands are independent and identical, find the p.d.f. for a two-month demand.

□ **12-22** Classify the following Markov chains and find their stationary distributions.

$$\text{(i)} \quad \begin{bmatrix} 1/4 & 1/4 & 1/2 \\ 1/4 & 3/4 & 0 \\ 1/2 & 0 & 1/2 \end{bmatrix}$$

$$\text{(ii)} \quad \begin{bmatrix} q & p & 0 & 0 & 0 \\ q & 0 & p & 0 & 0 \\ q & 0 & 0 & p & 0 \\ q & 0 & 0 & 0 & p \\ 1 & 0 & 0 & 0 & 0 \end{bmatrix}, \quad p + q = 1.$$

□ **12-23** Find the mean recurrence time for each state of the following Markov chain.

$$\begin{bmatrix} 1/3 & 1/3 & 1/3 \\ 1/2 & 1/4 & 1/4 \\ 1/5 & 3/5 & 1/5 \end{bmatrix}$$

□ **12-24** Find the z-transform of a binomial distribution with parameters (p, n). From this determine its mean and variance.

□ **12-25** Solve for x_n in terms of y_n using the z-transform.

$$x_n = ax_{n-1} + by_n, \quad n = 2, 3, \ldots$$

$$x_1 = y_1, \quad x_0 = 0.$$

CHAPTER 13

Inventory Models

§ 13·1
Definition of the Inventory Problem

An inventory problem exists when it is necessary to stock physical goods or commodities for the purpose of satisfying demand over a specified time horizon (finite or infinite). Almost every business must carry out stocks of goods in order to ensure smooth and efficient running of its operation. Decisions regarding how much should be ordered for stocking and when should it be ordered are typical of every inventory problem. The required demand may be satisfied by stocking once for the entire time horizon or by stocking separately for every time unit during the horizon. The two cases may be regarded as overstocking (with respect to one time unit), or understocking (with respect to the entire horizon), respectively.

An overstock would require higher invested capital per unit time but less frequent occurrence of shortages and placement of orders. An understock, on the other hand, would decrease the invested capital per unit time but would increase the frequency of ordering as well as the risk of running out of stock. Obviously, the two extremes are costly. The above decisions regarding the quantity ordered and the time at which it is ordered may thus be based on the minimization of an appropriate cost function which balances the total costs resulting from overstocking and understocking.

Before developing the decision models, it is necessary first to explore the basic characteristics of an inventory system which may affect the developments of such models.

1. *Economic Parameters:* These parameters usually describe the following types.
(a) *Setup cost.* This involves the fixed charge associated with the placement of an order or with the initial preparation of a production system. The setup cost is usually assumed independent of the quantity ordered or produced.

438

(b) *Purchase price or production cost.* Such a parameter is of special interest when " quantity discounts " or " price breaks " can be secured for orders above a certain quantity or when large production runs may result in a decrease in the production cost. Under these conditions, the order quantity must be adjusted to take advantage of these price breaks.

(c) *Selling price.* In some inventory situations, the demand on the commodity may be affected by the quantity stocked. In such cases, the decision model is based on a profit maximization criterion which includes the revenue from selling the commodity. Unit selling price may be constant or variable depending, for example, on whether quantity discount is allowed.

(d) *Holding cost.* This represents the cost of carrying inventory in storage. It includes the interest on invested capital, storage costs, handling costs, depreciation costs, etc. Holding costs usually are assumed to vary directly with the level of inventory as well as the length of time the item is held in stock.

(e) *Shortage cost.* These are the penalty costs that are incurred as a result of running out of stock when the commodity is needed. They generally include the costs due to loss in customers' goodwill and due to potential loss in income. In the case where the unfilled demand for the commodity can be satisfied at a later date (backlog case), these costs are usually assumed to vary directly with both the shortage quantity and the delay time. On the other hand, if the unfilled demand is lost (no-backlog case), shortage costs become proportional to shortage quantity only.

2. *Demand:* The demand pattern of a commodity may be either deterministic or probabilistic. In the deterministic case, it is assumed that the quantities needed over subsequent periods of time are known with certainty. This may be expressed over *equal* periods of time in terms of known constant demands or in terms of known variable demands. The two cases are referred to as *static* and *dynamic* demands, respectively.

Probabilistic demand occurs when the demand over a certain period of time is not known with certainty but its pattern can be described by a known probability distribution. In this case, the probability distribution may be either *stationary* or *nonstationary* over time. These are equivalent to static and dynamic demands in the deterministic case, respectively.

The demand for a given period of time may be satisfied *instantaneously* at the beginning of the period or *uniformly* during that period. The effect of instantaneous and uniform demands should reflect directly on the total cost of holding inventory.

3. *Ordering Cycle:* This is concerned with the time measurement of the inventory situation. An ordering cycle may be identified by the time period between two successive placements of orders. The latter may be initiated in one of two ways:

(a) *Continuous review* where a record of the inventory level is updated continuously until a certain lower limit is reached at which point a new order is placed.

(b) *Periodic review* where orders are placed usually at equally spaced intervals of time.

4. *Delivery Lags or Lead Times:* When an order is placed, it may be delivered instantaneously or it may require some time before delivery is effected. The time between the placement of an order and its receipt is called delivery lag or lead time. In general, delivery lags may be deterministic or probabilistic.

5. *Stock Replenishment:* Although an inventory system may operate with delivery lags, the actual replenishment of stock may occur instantaneously or uniformly. Instantaneous replenishment occurs in case the stock is purchased from outside sources. On the other hand, uniform replenishment may occur when the product is manufactured locally within the organization. This means that a system may operate with positive delivery lag and also with uniform stock replenishment. This case, however, is not generally considered in developing inventory models.

6. *Time Horizon:* The time horizon defines the time period over which the inventory level will be controlled. This horizon may be finite or infinite depending on the nature of the demand for the commodity.

7. *Number of Supply Echelons:* An inventory system may consist of several (rather than one) stocking points. In some cases these stocking points are organized such that one point acts as a source of supply for some other points. This type of operation may be repeated at different levels so that a demand point will again become a new supply point. Such a situation is usually referred to as a multiechelon system.

8. *Number of Items:* An inventory system may involve more than one item (commodity). This case will be of interest only if some kind of interaction exists between the different items. For example, the items may compete for limited floor space or limited total capital. Such an interaction must lead to a special formulation of the inventory model.

The above characteristics represent the basic elements for developing different inventory models. This chapter will present a variety of inventory models under different conditions of these characteristics. These models will be categorized broadly as deterministic and probabilistic models signifying deterministic and probabilistic demands, respectively.

It must be noted that the present development of inventory models has been mostly limited to the single-item single-echelon system. This occurs because it is very difficult to study the other cases analytically. For this reason, the models presented in this chapter will be limited mainly to the indicated type.

§ 13·2
Symbols

The following common symbols will be used in connection with the inventory models presented in this chapter.

c = purchase price per unit (of inventory)
r = selling price or revenue per unit, $r > c$
K = setup cost per order
h = holding cost per unit per unit time
p = shortage (penalty) cost per unit per unit time for the backlog case and per unit only for the no-backlog case.
x = initial stock on hand before an order is placed
y = amount on hand after an order is received
$y - x$ = amount ordered
ξ = amount demanded during an order cycle.

§ 13·3
Deterministic Models

As mentioned above a deterministic model implies that the demand is known with certainty. Such models are usually referred to as *Economic Lot Size Models*. In this section both static and dynamic cases will be considered. The reader will notice that the static models are based on *infinite* time horizons while the dynamic models are restricted to *finite* time horizons only. It will be shown later that this restriction follows from the nature of the model formulation.

§ 13·3·1
Single-Item Static Model

Consider the production-inventory situation where production occurs at constant rate α units per unit time. The consumption (demand) of the product also occurs at a constant rate β ($< \alpha$) units per unit time with no shortage allowed. It is assumed that both production and consumption can occur simultaneously. Since β is smaller than α, the production system should be stopped after the net level of inventory has reached a certain limit. This limit should satisfy all the demand during the remaining time period of the production cycle; that is, until a new cycle is started. It thus follows that the inventory will build up uniformly during the production time at the rate $(\alpha - \beta)$. Pictorially, the inventory fluctuations will occur as shown in Figure 13–1 where t_0 represents the total time per production cycle. The demand ξ during t_0 is thus equal to βt_0.

Assuming that the initial stock, x, is zero, Figure 13–1 shows that the quantity y represents the total amount produced per cycle during the production time t_1. Because production and consumption occur simultaneously during t_1, the net level of inventory at the end of t_1 is $z < y$. The amount z thus satisfies the demand during $t_2 = t_0 - t_1$.

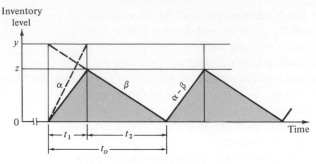

Figure 13–1

It is noted that the production cycle time ($= t_0$) is determined by *continuously reviewing* the level of inventory with time. However, because α and β are constants, t_0 also becomes constant. This means that there is a new production run every t_0 time units and the system may also be regarded as a *periodic review* model.

The optimal value of y will now be computed. Let $TC(y)$ be total cost of inventory per production cycle. This cost includes the setup and the holding costs only since no shortages are allowed. Thus, from the geometry of Figure 13–1,

$$z = t_1(\alpha - \beta)$$

$$= \frac{y}{\alpha}(\alpha - \beta)$$

$$= y\left(1 - \frac{\beta}{\alpha}\right).$$

Then,

$$\text{holding cost per cycle} = \frac{z}{2}(t_1 + t_2)h$$

$$= \frac{hy}{2}\left(1 - \frac{\beta}{\alpha}\right)t_0.$$

Given the setup cost is equal to K then,

$$TC(y) = K + \frac{hy}{2}\left(1 - \frac{\beta}{\alpha}\right)t_0.$$

Now, letting $TCU(y)$ be the total cost per unit time, then

$$TCU(y) = \frac{TC(y)}{t_0}.$$

Using the substitution

$$t_0 = \frac{y}{\beta},$$

then

$$TCU(y) = \frac{K\beta}{y} + \frac{h}{2}\left(1 - \frac{\beta}{\alpha}\right)y.$$

The optimum value of y is obtained by equating the first derivative of the last expression to zero. Thus

$$-\frac{K\beta}{y^2} + \frac{h}{2}\left(1 - \frac{\beta}{\alpha}\right) = 0$$

or

$$y^* = \sqrt{\frac{2K\beta}{h\left(1 - \frac{\beta}{\alpha}\right)}}.$$

Hence

$$t_0^* = \sqrt{\frac{2K}{\beta h\left(1 - \frac{\beta}{\alpha}\right)}}$$

and

$$TCU(y^*) = \sqrt{2\beta h K\left(1 - \frac{\beta}{\alpha}\right)}.$$

In the case where the stock is replenished by purchasing rather than by producing the item, it can be assumed that such a replenishment takes place *instantaneously* (rather than uniformly) as shown in Figure 13–2. This means that $\alpha = \infty$ (or $t_1 = 0$), and the results for this model can be obtained by letting $\alpha \to \infty$ in the above model. This gives,

$$y^* = \sqrt{\frac{2K\beta}{h}}$$

$$t_0^* = \sqrt{\frac{2K}{\beta h}}$$

$$TCU(y^*) = \sqrt{2K\beta h}.$$

The effect of shortage can also be included in the original model. Assuming that the unfilled demand is backlogged, the inventory fluctuations of the shortage case are shown in Figure 13–3.

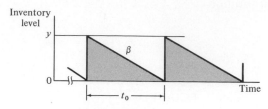

Figure 13–2

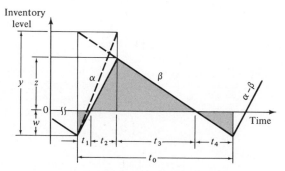

Figure 13–3

Let w be the maximum shortage quantity. Since

$$z = y\left(1 - \frac{\beta}{\alpha}\right) - w,$$

$$t_0 = \frac{y}{\beta},$$

$$t_1 = \frac{w}{\alpha - \beta},$$

$$t_2 = \frac{z}{\alpha - \beta},$$

$$t_3 = \frac{z}{\beta},$$

$$t_4 = \frac{w}{\beta},$$

then

$$TC(z, w) = K + h\frac{z}{2}(t_2 + t_3) + p\frac{w}{2}(t_1 + t_4)$$

$$= K + \frac{hz^2 + pw^2}{2\beta\left(1 - \dfrac{\beta}{\alpha}\right)}.$$

Substituting for z, the total cost *per unit time* is given by

$$TCU(y, w) = \frac{K\beta}{y} + \frac{h\left\{y\left(1 - \frac{\beta}{\alpha}\right) - w\right\}^2 + pw^2}{2\left(1 - \frac{\beta}{\alpha}\right)y}.$$

Now, taking the first partial derivatives of the last expression with respect to y and w and equating to zero, this gives, respectively,

$$-\frac{K\beta}{y^2} + h\left(\frac{1}{2}\left(1 - \frac{\beta}{\alpha}\right) - \frac{w^2}{2y^2\left(1 - \frac{\beta}{\alpha}\right)}\right) - \frac{pw^2}{2y^2\left(1 - \frac{\beta}{\alpha}\right)} = 0$$

and

$$h\left(\frac{w}{y\left(1 - \frac{\beta}{\alpha}\right)} - 1\right) + \frac{pw}{y\left(1 - \frac{\beta}{\alpha}\right)} = 0.$$

Solving these two equations, this gives

$$y^* = \sqrt{\frac{2K\beta(p + h)}{ph\left(1 - \frac{\beta}{\alpha}\right)}},$$

$$w^* = \sqrt{\frac{2K\beta h\left(1 - \frac{\beta}{\alpha}\right)}{p(p + h)}},$$

$$t_0^* = \frac{y^*}{\beta},$$

and

$$TCU(y^*, w^*) = \sqrt{\left(\frac{2Khp\beta}{p + h}\right)\left(1 - \frac{\beta}{\alpha}\right)}.$$

Again, it is noticed that when the stock is replenished instantaneously; that is, $\alpha = \infty$ or $t_1 + t_2 = 0$, then taking the limits of the above results as $\alpha \to \infty$ gives

$$y^* = \sqrt{2K\beta\left(\frac{1}{h} + \frac{1}{p}\right)},$$

$$w^* = \sqrt{\frac{2K\beta h}{p(p + h)}},$$

and

$$TCU(y^*, w^*) = \sqrt{\frac{2Khp\beta}{p+h}}.$$

Furthermore, by letting $p \to \infty$ (no shortage), the above results should reduce to those of the no-shortage case.

§ 13·3·2
Single-Item Static Model with Price Breaks

In the models of Section 13·3·1, the production (purchasing) cost per unit, c, is neglected in the analysis because it is constant and hence should not affect the level of inventory. It often happens in the inventory models that the purchasing price per unit depends on the quantity purchased. This usually occurs in the form of discrete price breaks or quantity discounts. In such cases, the purchasing price should be considered in the inventory model.

Consider the inventory model with instantaneous stock replenishment and no shortage. Assume that the cost per unit is c_1 for $y < q$ and c_2 for $y \geq q$, where $c_1 > c_2$ and q is a constant. The total cost per cycle will now include the purchasing cost in addition to the setup cost and the holding cost.

Thus, for $y < q$,

$$TCU_1(y) = \beta c_1 + \frac{K\beta}{y} + \frac{h}{2} y$$

and for $y \geq q$,

$$TCU_2(y) = \beta c_2 + \frac{K\beta}{y} + \frac{h}{2} y.$$

These two functions are shown graphically in Figure 13–4. Disregarding the effect of price breaks for the moment, let y_m be the quantity at which the minimum values of TCU_1 and TCU_2 occur. It is evident that,

$$y_m = \sqrt{\frac{2K\beta}{h}}.$$

Now, including the effect of the price break, the solid curves in Figure 13–4 represents the total cost function for the entire range of y. Define $y = q_1$ ($> y_m$) such that,

$$TCU_1(y_m) = TCU_2(q_1).$$

The solution of the problem depends mainly on whether $q \leq y_m$ or $q > y_m$. If $q \leq y_m$, then it is evident from Figure 13–4 that $y^* = y_m$ and $TCU(y^*) = TCU_2(y_m)$. If $q > y_m$, then two cases must be considered,

(i) $q < q_1$: In this case, it is clear from the figure that for $q \leq y < q_1$,

$$TCU_2(y) < TCU_1(y_m).$$

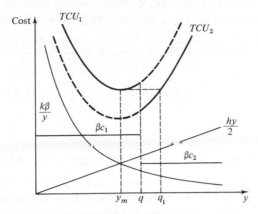

Figure 13–4

This means that $y^* = q$ and $TCU(y^*) = TCU_2(q)$.

(ii) $q \geq q_1$: The figure shows that $y^* = y_m$ and that $TCU(y^*) = TCU_1(y_m)$. The above results can be summarized as

$$TCU(y^*) = \begin{cases} TCU_2(y_m), & q \leq y_m \\ TCU_2(q), & y_m < q < q_1 \\ TCU_1(y_m), & y_m < q_1 \leq q. \end{cases}$$

This model represents one case of the price break situations. A more generalized model can be considered with several price breaks. The same idea may be extended, in certain cases, to breaks in holding and setup costs.

To illustrate the application of this model, consider the following situation; $K = 10$, $h = 1$, $\beta = 5$, $c_1 = 2$, $c_2 = 1$, and $q = 15$. First compute y_m, thus

$$y_m = \sqrt{\frac{2K\beta}{h}} = \sqrt{\frac{2 \times 10 \times 5}{1}} = 10.$$

Since $y_m < q$, it is necessary to check whether q is less than q_1. The value of q_1 is computed from

$$TCU_1(y_m) = TCU_2(q_1)$$

or

$$c_1\beta + \frac{K\beta}{y_m} + \frac{hy_m}{2} = c_2\beta + \frac{K\beta}{q_1} + \frac{hq_1}{2}.$$

Substituting, this yields,

$$2 \times 5 + \frac{10 \times 5}{10} + \frac{1 \times 10}{2} = 1 \times 5 + \frac{10 \times 5}{q_1} + \frac{1 \times q_1}{2}$$

or

$$q_1^2 - 30q_1 + 100 = 0.$$

This yields $q_1 = 26.18$ or $q_1 = 3.82$. By definition, q_1 must be selected as the larger value. Now, since $q_1 > q$, it follows that $y^* = q = 15$ and

$$TCU(y^*) = TCU_2(15) = c_2\beta + \frac{K\beta}{15} + \frac{h \times 15}{2}$$

$$= 1 \times 5 + \frac{10 \times 5}{15} + \frac{1 \times 15}{2} = 15.83.$$

§ 13-3-3
Multiple-Item Static Model with Storage Limitation

This model considers the inventory system including n (> 1) items which are competing for a limited storage space. This limitation represents an interaction between the different items which can be included in the model as a constraint.

Let the maximum storage area available for the n items be equal to A and let the storage area requirements per unit of the ith item be equal to a_i. Thus, if y_i is the amount ordered of the ith item, the storage requirements constraint becomes

$$\sum_{i=1}^{n} a_i y_i \leq A.$$

Assume that each item is replenished instantaneously and that there are no quantity discounts. Assume further that no shortages are allowed. Let β_i, K_i, and h_i be, respectively, the demand rate per unit time, the setup cost and the holding cost per unit per unit time corresponding to the ith item. The inventory costs associated with each item should be essentially the same as in the case of an equivalent single-item model. The problem thus becomes:

$$\text{minimize} \quad TCU(y_1, \ldots, y_n) = \sum_{i=1}^{n} \left(\frac{K_i\beta_i}{y_i} + \frac{h_i y_i}{2}\right),$$

subject to

$$\sum_{i=1}^{n} a_i y_i \leq A,$$

$$y_i > 0.$$

The general solution of this problem is obtained by the Lagrange multipliers method.[1] However, before this is done, it is necessary to check whether the constraint is active. This means that if the unconstrained value of y_i given by,

$$y_i^* = \sqrt{\frac{2K_i\beta_i}{h_i}}$$

---

[1] See Chapter 16 for a complete analysis of the Lagrangian method.

satisfy the storage constraint, the constraint is said to be inactive and hence can be neglected.

If, on the other hand, the constraint is not satisfied by the above values of y_i^*, then it must be active. In this case, new optimal values of y_i must be found which will satisfy the storage constraint in *equality* sense. This is accomplished by first formulating the Lagrangian function. Thus,

$$L(\lambda, y_1, y_2, \ldots, y_n) = TCU(y_1, \ldots, y_n) - \lambda\left(\sum_{i=1}^{n} a_i y_i - A\right)$$

$$= \sum_{i=1}^{n} \left(\frac{K_i \beta_i}{y_i} + \frac{h_i y_i}{2}\right) - \lambda\left(\sum_{i=1}^{n} a_i y_i - A\right),$$

where $\lambda < 0$ is the Lagrange multiplier.

The optimum values of y_i and λ can be found by equating the respective first partial derivatives to zero. This gives,

$$\frac{\partial L}{\partial y_i} = -\frac{K_i \beta_i}{y_i^2} + \frac{h_i}{2} - \lambda a_i = 0,$$

$$\frac{\partial L}{\partial \lambda} = -\sum_{i=1}^{n} a_i y_i + A = 0.$$

The second equation implies that y_i^* must satisfy the storage constraint in equality sense.

From the first equation,

$$y_i^* = \sqrt{\frac{2K_i \beta_i}{h_i - 2\lambda^* a_i}}.$$

Notice that y_i^* is dependent on λ^*, the optimal value of λ. Notice also that for $\lambda^* = 0$, y_i^* gives the solution of the unconstrained case.

The value λ^* can be found by systematic trial and error. Since by definition $\lambda < 0$ for the above minimization case, then by trying successive negative values of λ the value of λ^* should result in simultaneous values of y_i^* which satisfy the given constraint in equality sense. Thus determination of λ^* will automatically determine y_i^*. This procedure will now be illustrated by an example.

▶ **Example 13·3-1**
Consider the inventory problem with three items ($n = 3$). The parameters of the problem are shown in the table below.

Item i	K_i	β_i	h_i	a_i
1	$10	2 units	$0.3	1 ft^2
2	5	4	0.1	1
3	15	3	0.2	1

Assume that the total available storage area is given by $A = 25$ ft^2.
Given the formula

$$y_i^* = \sqrt{\frac{2K_i \beta_i}{h_i - 2\lambda^* a_i}},$$

the following table can be constructed.

λ	y_1	y_2	y_3	$\sum_{i=1}^{3} a_i y_i - A$
0	11.2	20.0	21.2	$+27.4$
-0.05	10.0	14.1	17.3	$+16.4$
-0.10	9.0	11.5	14.9	$+10.4$
-0.15	8.2	10.0	13.4	$+ 6.6$
-0.20	7.6	8.9	12.2	$+ 3.7$
-0.25	7.1	8.2	11.3	$+ 1.6$
-0.30	6.7	7.6	10.6	$- 0.1$

It is noted that for $A = 25$ ft^2, the storage constraint is satisfied in equality
sense for some value of λ between -0.25 and -0.3. This value is equal to
λ^* and may be estimated by linear interpolation. The corresponding values of
y_i should thus yield y_i^* directly. It is noted from the table that λ^* must be very
close to -0.3 and hence the optimal y_i^* are approximately given by

$$y_1^* = 6.7, \quad y_2^* = 7.6, \quad \text{and} \quad y_3^* = 11.6.$$

Notice that if $A \geq 52.4$, then the unconstrained values of y_i corresponding
to $\lambda = 0$ should yield y_i^*. In this case the constraint is inactive and should be
neglected. ◄

§ 13·3·4
Single-Item N-Period Dynamic Model

In the static models discussed above, it is assumed that the demands are constant over equal periods of time. This assumption may not be realistic in some
inventory systems. In this model, it will be assumed that the demand, although
known with certainty, may vary from one period to the next. It is also assumed
that the inventory level is reviewed *periodically* rather than continuously.
Although delivery lag (expressed as a fixed number of periods) may be allowed,
the model assumes that the stock is replenished instantaneously at the beginning of the concerned period. Finally it is assumed that no shortages are
allowed.

The development of dynamic deterministic models is limited to the study of finite time horizons. This limitation stems from the fact that the numerical solution of these models requires the use of the dynamic programming technique (see Chapter 7) which *in this case* is feasible only for a finite number of periods (stages). This is not a serious limitation, however, since distant future demands will have a little effect on the decisions of the present finite time horizon. In addition, in most situations it may not be practical to assume that the item will be held in stock indefinitely.

Define for period i, $i = 1, 2, \ldots, N$,

z_i = amount ordered,
ξ_i = amount demanded,
x_i = entering inventory (at the beginning of period i),
h_i = holding cost per unit of inventory carried forward from period i to period $i + 1$,
K_i = setup cost,
$c_i(z_i)$ = marginal purchasing (production) cost function given z_i.

Let

$$C_i(z_i) = \delta_i K_i + c_i(z_i).$$

where

$$\delta_i = \begin{cases} 0, & z_i = 0, \\ 1, & z_i > 0. \end{cases}$$

It is noticed that $c_i(z_i)$ will be of interest in the development of the model only if the unit purchasing cost varies from one period to the next or if there are price breaks.

Since no shortages are allowed, the objective will be to determine the optimal values of z_i which minimize the sum of the setup costs, the purchasing costs and the holding costs for all N periods. The holding costs will be based on the amount of inventory carried forward from period i to period $i + 1$; that is, based on

$$x_{i+1} = x_i + z_i - \xi_i.$$

It must be noted that in this presentation, the holding cost at period i is assumed directly proportional to the end of period inventory *only for simplicity*. (The proportionality constant is equal to h_i.) The model can be readily extended to cover *any* holding cost function $H_i(x_{i+1})$ by replacing $h_i x_{i+1}$ by $H_i(x_{i+1})$.

The development of the dynamic programming model for this problem will be simplified by first depicting the problem schematically as shown in Figure 13–5. Each period represents a stage. Using the backward recursive equation, the states of the system at stage i may be defined as the amount of entering

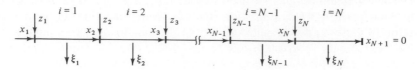

Figure 13–5

inventory, x_i. Let $f_i(x_i)$ be the minimum inventory cost for periods $i, i + 1, \ldots$, and N. The complete recursive equations are given by,

$$f_N(x_N) = \min_{\substack{z_N + x_N = \xi_N \\ z_N \geq 0}} \{C_N(z_N)\},$$

$$f_i(x_i) = \min_{\substack{\xi_i \leq x_i + z_i \leq \xi_i + \cdots + \xi_N \\ z_i \geq 0}} \{C_i(z_i) + h_i(x_i + z_i - \xi_i) + f_{i+1}(x_i + z_i - \xi_i)\},$$

$$i = 1, 2, \ldots, N - 1.$$

The forward recursive equation can be developed by defining the states at stage i as the amount of inventory at the end of period i. From Figure 13–5, these states are equivalent to x_{i+1}. Notice that at any stage the values of x_{i+1} are limited by,

$$0 \leq x_{i+1} \leq \xi_{i+1} + \cdots + \xi_N.$$

This means that at the extreme case, the amount z_j in period $j \leq i$ may be ordered large enough so that the remaining inventory x_{i+1} will satisfy the demand for all the remaining periods.

Let $f_i(x_{i+1})$ be the minimum inventory cost for periods $1, 2, \ldots,$ and i given x_{i+1}, the amount of inventory at the end of period i. The complete recursive equations are then given by

$$f_1(x_2) = \min_{0 \leq z_1 \leq \xi_1 + x_2} \{C_1(z_1) + h_1 x_2\},$$

$$f_i(x_{i+1}) = \min_{0 \leq z_i \leq \xi_i + x_{i+1}} \{C_i(z_i) + h_i x_{i+1} + f_{i-1}(x_{i+1} + \xi_i - z_i)\}.$$

$$i = 2, 3, \ldots, N.$$

From the forward and backward formulations of the model, it is noticed that the two algorithms are computationally equivalent. This follows from the fact that the *state transformations* are basically the same in both cases. (See Section 7·4.) However, the forward algorithm, as indicated later, will prove useful in developing an important special case of the above model. The following numerical example will thus be used to illustrate the computational procedure of the forward algorithm. The procedure for the backward algorithm will be left as an exercise for the reader. (See Problem 13-10.)

▶ **Example 13·3-2**

Consider a three period inventory situation with discrete units and dynamic deterministic demand. The data for the problem are given below.

Period i	Demand ξ_i	Setup cost K_i	Holding cost h_i
1	3 units	\$3.00	\$1.00
2	2	7.00	3.00
3	4	6.00	2.00

The entering inventory x_1 to period 1 is equal to 1. Let the marginal purchasing function be given by

$$c_i(z_i) = \begin{cases} 10z_i, & 0 \le z_i \le 3, \\ 30 + 20(z_i - 3), & z_i \ge 4. \end{cases}$$

This means that the price per unit is 10 for the first three units and 20 for any number of units in excess of that.

Using the forward algorithm, then,

Stage 1: $\xi_1 = 3$, $0 \le x_2 \le 2 + 4 = 6$

			$f_1(z_1 \mid x_2) = C_1(z_1) + h_1 x_2$						Optimal solution	
		$z_1 = 2$	3	4	5	6	7	8		
x_2	$h_1 x_2$	$C_1(z_1) = 23$	33	53	73	93	113	133	$f_1(x_2)$	z_1^*
0	0	23							23	2
1	1		34						34	3
2	2			55					55	4
3	3				76				76	5
4	4					97			97	6
5	5						118		118	7
6	6							139	139	8

Notice that since $x_1 = 1$, the smallest value of z_1 is $\xi_1 - x_1 = 3 - 1 = 2$.

Stage 2: $\xi_2 = 2$, $0 \le x_3 \le 4$

| | | | \multicolumn{7}{c}{$f_2(z_2 \mid x_3) = C_2(z_2) + h_2 x_3 + f_1(x_3 + \xi_2 - z_2)$} | \multicolumn{2}{c}{Optimal solution} |

		$z_2 = 0$	1	2	3	4	5	6		
x_3	$h_2 x_3$	$C_2(z_2) = 0$	17	27	37	57	77	97	$f_2(x_3)$	z_2^*
0	0	$0 + 55$ $= 55$	$17 + 34$ $= 51$	$27 + 23$ $= 50$					50	2
1	3	$3 + 76$ $= 79$	$20 + 55$ $= 75$	$30 + 34$ $= 64$	$40 + 23$ $= 63$				63	3
2	6	$6 + 97$ $= 103$	$23 + 76$ $= 99$	$33 + 55$ $= 88$	$43 + 34$ $= 77$	$63 + 23$ $= 86$			77	3
3	9	$9 + 118$ $= 127$	$26 + 97$ $= 123$	$36 + 76$ $= 112$	$46 + 55$ $= 101$	$66 + 34$ $= 100$	$86 + 23$ $= 109$		100	4
4	12	$12 + 139$ $= 151$	$29 + 118$ $= 147$	$39 + 97$ $= 136$	$49 + 76$ $= 125$	$69 + 55$ $= 124$	$89 + 34$ $= 123$	$109 + 23$ $= 132$	123	5

Stage 3: $\xi_3 = 4$, $x_4 = 0$

| | | \multicolumn{5}{c}{$f_3(z_3 \mid x_4) = C_3(z_3) + h_3 x_4 + f_2(x_4 + \xi_3 - z_3)$} | \multicolumn{2}{c}{Optimal solution} |

		$z_3 = 0$	1	2	3	4		
x_4	$h_3 x_4$	$C_3(z_3) = 0$	16	26	36	56	$f_3(x_4)$	z_3^*
0	0	$0 + 123$ $= 123$	$16 + 100$ $= 116$	$26 + 77$ $= 103$	$36 + 63$ $= 99$	$56 + 50$ $= 106$	99	3

The solution is given as

Period i	1	2	3
z_i^*	2	3	3

which costs a total of $99. ◄

Special Case with Constant or Decreasing Marginal Costs

The above dynamic programming model can be used under *any* conditions for the cost functions. An important special case of this model occurs when for period i both the purchasing (production) cost *per unit* and the holding cost *per unit* are *constant* or *decreasing* functions of z_i and x_{i+1}, respectively. In this case, the cost function is said to yield constant or decreasing *marginal* cost. Typical illustrations of such cost functions are shown in Figure 13–6. Mathematically, these functions are said to be concave. Case (a) shows the situation where there is a constant marginal cost. Case (b) is typical of

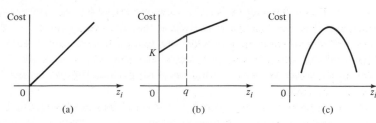

Figure 13–6

many production (or purchasing) cost functions. Thus, regardless of the amount produced, a setup cost K is charged. A constant marginal cost is then incurred and if a "quantity discount" or "price break" is allowed at $z_i = q$, the marginal cost for $z_i > q$ becomes smaller. Finally Case (c) illustrates a general concave function.

Under the conditions stipulated above, it can be proved that[2]

1. Given the initial inventory $x_1 = 0$, then at any period i of the N-period model, it is optimal to have a positive quantity z_i^* *or* a positive entering inventory x_i^* but not both; that is, $z_i^* x_i^* = 0$.[3]

2. The amount z_i ordered at any period i is optimal only if it is zero *or* if it satisfies the *exact* demand of one or more succeeding periods. These succeeding periods are such that if the demand in period $i + m (< N)$ is satisfied by z_i^* then the demands for periods $i, i + 1, \ldots,$ and $i + m - 1$ must also be satisfied by z_i^*.

The first property (theorem) implies that for any period i it is not economical to bring in inventory and to place an order at the same time. For suppose that the *least* marginal cost of acquiring and holding *one* additional unit from a previous period i' to the present period i'' ($i' < i''$) is b' while the marginal cost of ordering one more unit at i'' is b''. If $b'' \le b'$, the amount ordered at i'' can be increased to cover the exact demand at i'' without any increase in the associated total costs as compared with the case where this demand is satisfied from period i'. This follows because of the nonincreasing marginal costs. Hence having $x_{i''} z_{i''} = 0$ will yield a solution which *at least* is as good as any other solution. On the other hand, if $b'' > b'$, it is more economical to increase the order in i' to cover the exact demand in i'' so that the amount ordered in i'' is

---

[2] For details of the proofs, see H. Wagner and T. Whitin, "Dynamic Version of the Economic Lot Size Model," *Management Science*, Vol. 5, No. 1, 89–96, (1958). The original proofs by Wagner and Whitin, however, were developed under the restrictive assumption that the per unit purchasing costs are *constant* and *identical* for all the periods. This was later improved by A. F. Veinott, Jr., of Stanford University, to include concave cost functions for each period.

[3] In this special case, the initial inventory, x_1, can always be taken equal to zero. Since, if $x_1 > 0$, this amount can be written off from the demands of the successive periods until it is exhausted. Under such conditions, the periods for which the demands have been satisfied are still included in the problem; this time with zero demands. In such a case it is possible to have both z_i and x_i equal to zero.

equal to zero. This follows again for the same reason of having nonincreasing marginal costs. The implication here then is that the condition $x_i z_i = 0$ will not yield any worse solution provided the marginal costs are constant or decreasing and the initial inventory is zero. The second property which calls for ordering the exact amount for one or more periods follows immediately from the first property.

The above properties, when applicable, will result in a more simplified computational procedure which is still based on the general dynamic programming algorithms presented above. This point will be explained now using the forward algorithm.

Since by the second property the amount of inventory at the end of period i, that is x_{i+1}, must satisfy the exact requirements of one or more periods, it follows that the number of the states of the system at any period is determined by the number of succeeding periods (rather than by the number of units demanded in the succeeding periods as in the general model). For example, if $N = 5$ with demands 10, 15, 20, 50, and 70, respectively, then at the *end* of the third period (stage), the number of the states (x_4) in the general model will be $50 + 70 + 1 = 121$ while in the new model it will reduce to three (the remaining number of periods plus one) since x_4 could be 0, 50, or 120 only. A similar argument using the first property will also show that the number of alternatives z_i are much smaller in the new model. This indicates that the computational effort is reduced tremendously in the new model.

The new model will now be illustrated by an example.

▶ **Example 13·3-3**

Consider the following 4-period model with the given data.

Period i	ξ_i	K_i
1	76	$98
2	26	114
3	90	185
4	67	70

The holding cost per unit per period is constant and equal to $1.00. Also the purchasing cost per unit is equal to $2.00 for all the periods. The initial inventory x_1 is assumed equal to 15 units. Notice that the per unit holding and purchasing costs are taken the same over all the periods only for simplicity.

The solution is obtained using the same procedure of forward dynamic programming except that the number of states, x_{i+1}, and the number of alternatives, z_i, will be determined according to the new properties. Since $x_1 = 15$, the demand for the first period is decreased by an equivalent amount and thus it becomes equal to $76 - 15 = 61$.

Stage 1: $\xi_1 = 61$

$$f_1(z_1|x_2) = C_1(z_1) + h_1 x_2$$

		$z_1 = 61$	87	177	244	Optimal Solution	
x_2	$h_1 x_2$	$C_1(z_1) = 220$	272	452	586	$f_1(x_2)$	z_1^*
0	0	220	—	—	—	220	61
26	26	—	298	—	—	298	87
116	116	—	—	568	—	568	177
183	183	—	—	—	769	769	244
Order in 1 for:		1	1,2	1,2,3	1,2,3,4		

Stage 2: $\xi_2 = 26$

$$f_2(z_2 \mid x_3) = C_2(z_2) + h_2 x_3 + f_1(x_3 + \xi_2 - z_2)$$

		$z_2 = 0$	26	116	183	Optimal Solution	
x_3	$h_2 x_3$	$C_2(z_2) = 0$	166	346	480	$f_2(x_3)$	z_2^*
0	0	$0 + 298 = 298$	$166 + 220 = 386$	—	—	298	0
90	90	$90 + 568 = 658$	—	$436 + 220 = 656$	—	656	116
157	157	$157 + 769 = 926$	—	—	$637 + 220 = 857$	857	183
Order in 2 for:		—	2	2,3	2,3,4		

Stage 3: $\xi_3 = 90$

$$f_3(z_3 \mid x_4) = C_3(z_3) + h_3 x_4 + f_2(x_4 + \xi_3 - z_3)$$

x_4	$h_3 x_4$	$z_3 = 0$	90	157		Optimal Solution	
		$C_3(z_3) = 0$	365	499		$f_3(x_4)$	z_3^*
0	0	$0 + 656 = 656$	$365 + 298 = 663$	—		656	0
67	67	$67 + 857 = 924$	—	$566 + 298 = 864$		864	157
Order in 3 for:		—	3	3,4			

Stage 4: $\xi_4 = 67$

$$f_4(z_4 \mid x_5) = C_4(z_4) + h_4 x_5 + f_3(x_5 + \xi_4 - z_4)$$

				Optimal Solution	
x_5	$h_4 x_5$	$z_4 = 0$	67	$f_4(x_5)$	z_4^*
		$C_4(z_4) = 0$	204		
0	0	$0 + 864 = 864$	$204 + 656 = 860$	860	67
Order in 4 for:		—	4		

The optimal policy is thus given by

Period i	1	2	3	4
z_i^*	61	116	0	67

at a total cost of \$860. ◀

A special case of the above *concave* cost model occurs when the production cost for a period is defined by the linear function

$$C_i(z_i) = K_i + c_i z_i, \qquad i = 1, 2, \ldots, N,$$

provided that $c_{i+1} \leq c_i$, for all i; that is, $c_1 \geq c_2 \geq \cdots \geq c_N$. Under this new condition, the forward algorithm for the concave cost model can be modified such that further savings in computations are possible. To avoid confusion, the names "original" and "modified" algorithms will be used to refer to the forward algorithms associated, respectively, with the above concave cost model and the model to be presented below.

It is noticed in the original algorithm that each stage i computes the optimal policy by considering ordering in period i for future periods up to and including period j; that is, $i \leq j \leq N$. The modified algorithm, on the other hand, defines each stage i such that for period i, the optimal policy is determined by considering ordering in each of the preceding periods, k, for periods up to and including period i; $1 \leq k \leq i$. This is expressed mathematically as[4]

$$f_i = \min \begin{cases} C_1 + h_1(\xi_2 + \cdots + \xi_i) + \cdots + h_{i-1}\xi_i, & \text{(order in 1)} \\ C_2 + h_2(\xi_3 + \cdots + \xi_i) + \cdots + h_{i-1}\xi_i + f_1, & \text{(order in 2)} \\ \vdots \\ C_{i-1} + h_{i-1}\xi_i + f_{i-2}, & \text{(order in } i-1) \\ C_i + f_{i-1}, & \text{(order in } i) \end{cases}$$

where

f_i = minimum total cost for periods 1 through i, inclusive, $i = 1, 2, \ldots, N$

C_k = total ordering cost (setup + purchasing) for ordering in period k the amount $z_k = \xi_k + \cdots + \xi_i$ for periods k through i, $k \leq i$.

To start with, and without taking advantage of the special feature of the cost function $C_i(z_i)$, it is noticed that the number of computations in the

---

[4] In the modified model, the state of the system, x_i, is suppressed since this corresponds directly to the number of the preceding periods; that is, i. The same reasoning could have been used also with the original model.

modified model is less than that in the original one.[5] This follows because the modified model does not consider explicitly the case where no orders are placed at the different stages. The computations using the modified algorithm may be further reduced by making use of the following theorem.

Planning Horizon Theorem: *In the modified forward algorithm, if for period i^* the minimum cost occurs such that the demand at i^* is satisfied by ordering in a previous period $i^{**} < i^*$, then for all future periods $i > i^*$, it is sufficient to compute the optimal program based on ordering in periods i^{**}, $i^{**} + 1, \ldots$, and i only. In particular, if the optimal policy calls for ordering in i^* for the same period i^* (that is, $i^* = i^{**}$), then for any future period $i > i^*$ it will always be optimal to order in i^* regardless of the future demands. In this case, i^* is said to mark the beginning of a planning horizon.*

The above theorem implies two important concepts.

(i) During the course of computations, the calculations may be truncated so that the entries for periods $i < i^{**}$ need not be considered. This should lead to computational savings.

(ii) For the special case where $i^* = i^{**}$, in addition to truncating the computations at i^*, the problem will possess the property that future periods starting with i^* can be considered completely independently of all the previous periods. Moreover, it will always be optimal to order in i^* regardless of future demands.

Notice that when i^{**} is strictly less than i^*, it is not always true that ordering will occur in i^{**}. Indeed, future demands may call for a change in the optimal policy. In this case it will not be possible to break down the problem into independent planning horizons. For the purpose of distinction, i^{**} will be referred to as the starting period of a *subhorizon* whenever $i^{**} < i^*$.

The above ideas will be illustrated now by an example.

▶ **Example 13·3-4**

Consider a 6-period inventory model with the following data

i	ξ_i	K_i	h_i
1	10	20	1
2	15	17	1
3	7	10	1
4	20	20	3
5	13	5	1
6	25	50	1

---

[5] The maximum number of entries are given by $\{N(N+1) + (N-1)N\}/2 = N^2$ in the original table and by $N(N+1)/2$ in the modified one.

The purchasing cost per unit is equal to 2 for all the periods of the model.

The computations for this example are summarized in Table 13–1. These are carried out on a row-by-row basis starting with row 1. Each column represents a decision alternative defining the period k in which the demands for periods $k, k + 1, \ldots,$ and i are filled, $1 \leq k \leq i$. Each row, on the other hand, represents the limiting period up to which the demand is filled. Thus, for each i, the optimum value f_i, as defined for the modified algorithm, is obtained by considering all the feasible decision alternatives k ($\leq i$) and then selecting the alternative yielding minimum cumulative costs. For example, if $i = 3$, then one can order in 1 for 1, 2, and 3 or in 2 for 2 and 3, or in 3 for 3. This shows that the entries of the table above its main diagonal are infeasible since no backorders are allowed.

To illustrate the use of planning horizons (and subhorizons), notice that in row 3, f_3 occurs under period 2. This means that it is optimal at this point to order for period 3 (and period 2) in period 2. This is equivalent to saying that $i^{**} = 2$ and $i^* = 3$. According to the above theorem, for all $i > 3$ the calculations can go back only to period 2. Period 2 thus marks the beginning of a *sub*horizon. Moving to row 4, it is noticed that f_4 occurs under period 4 signifying that it is optimal to order for period 4 in period 4. This means that $i^{**} = i^* = 4$ and hence $i = 4$ marks the beginning of a planning horizon. Thus in the succeeding rows the entries under periods 1, 2, 3 should not be computed. Continuing in this manner, Table 13–1 shows that another planning horizon commences in period 5 with the result that in the computations in row 6 only the entries under periods 5 and 6 need be computed. Thus periods 1, 4, and 5 mark the beginnings of the three planning horizons of the problem. The advantages of the planning horizon theorem must now be clear since all the blank entries below the main diagonal of the table represent computational savings.

The optimal solution is obtained by considering the last row in Table 13–1. f_6 indicates that it is optimal to order in 5 the amount $z_5 = 38$ for 5 and 6. Thus moving to row 4 ($= 5 - 1$), f_4 requires ordering $z_4 = 20$ for a period 4 alone. Again in row 3 ($= 4 - 1$), f_3 calls for ordering in 2 the amount $z_2 = 22$ for 2 and 3. Finally, the amount $z_1 = 10$ is ordered in period 1. The total cost is 274 for the entire problem. ◄

§ 13·3·5
N-Period Dynamic Production Scheduling Model

Consider the problem of scheduling production over N successive periods. The demands for the different periods are variable but deterministic. These demands may be met either by fluctuating inventory while keeping production constant or by fluctuating production while keeping inventory constant, or by a combination of both. Fluctuations in production can be achieved by working overtime while fluctuation in inventory may be met by holding positive stock

Table 13–1

Order in period k for periods up to and including i

		$k = 1$	$k = 2$	$k = 3$	$k = 4$	$k = 5$	$k = 6$
$i = 1$	(1)†	20					
	(2)	$10 \times 2 = 20$					
	(3)	0					
	(4)	0					
		—					
		$f_1 \rightarrow 40^*$					
$i = 2$	(1)	20	17				
	(2)	$(10 + 15) \times 2 = 50$	$15 \times 2 = 30$				
	(3)	$15 \times 1 = 15$	0				
	(4)	0	$f_1 = 40$				
		—	—				
		$f_2 \rightarrow 85^*$	87				
$i = 3$	(1)	20	17	10			
	(2)	$(10 + 15 + 7) \times 2 = 64$	$(15 + 7) \times 2 = 44$	$7 \times 2 = 14$			
	(3)	$22 \times 1 + 7 \times 1 = 29$	$7 \times 1 = 7$	0			
	(4)	0	$f_1 = 40$	$f_2 = 85$			
		—	—	—			
		113	$f_3 \rightarrow 108^*$	109			
$i = 4$	(1)		17	10	20		
	(2)		$(15 + 7 + 20) \times 2 = 84$	$(7 + 20) \times 2 = 54$	$20 \times 2 = 40$		
	(3)		$27 \times 1 + 20 \times 1 = 47$	$20 \times 1 = 20$	0		
	(4)		$f_1 = 40$	$f_2 = 85$	$f_3 = 108$		
			—	—	—		
			188	169	$f_4 \rightarrow 168^*$		

Table 13–1—continued

		$k=1$	$k=2$	$k=3$	$k=4$	$k=5$	$k=6$
$i=5$	(1)				20	5	
	(2)				$(20+13)\times2 = 66$	$13\times2 = 26$	
	(3)				$13\times3 = 39$	0	
	(4)				$f_3 = 108$	$f_4 = 168$	
					$\overline{233}$	$f_5 \to 199^*$	
$i=6$	(1)					5	50
	(2)					$(13+25)\times2 = 76$	$25\times2 = 50$
	(3)					$25\times1 = 25$	0
	(4)					$f_4 = 168$	$f_5 = 199$
						$f_6 \to 274^*$	$\overline{299}$

† (1) Setup cost   (2) Purchasing cost   (3) Holding cost   (4) Optimum total cost from previous periods.

on hand or by allowing backlog of the unfilled demand. The objective here is to determine the production schedule for all N periods which will minimize the total relevant costs.

This model assumes that the setup cost in every period is equal to zero. In general, shortages are allowed except that all the backlogged demand must be filled by the Nth period. It will be shown now that this situation can be represented as a transportation model. (See Chapter 5.) In particular, by noting the special characteristics of the model for the case where no shortage is allowed, the problem can be solved in an easy way without having to apply the iterative procedure of the transportation technique.

Define the following symbols for period i, $i = 1, \ldots, N$.

c_i = production cost per unit during regular time.
d_i = production cost per unit during overtime, $c_i < d_i$.
h_i = holding cost per unit forwarded from period i to period $i + 1$.
p_i = shortage cost per unit demanded in period i and filled in period $i + 1$.
a_{Ri} = production capacity (in number of units) during regular time.
a_{Ti} = production capacity (in number of units) during overtime.
b_i = demand (in number of units).

Notice that c_i, the per-unit production cost during regular time is less than d_i, the per-unit production cost during overtime. This is shown graphically in Figure 13–7(a). The situation may be generalized to the case where there are

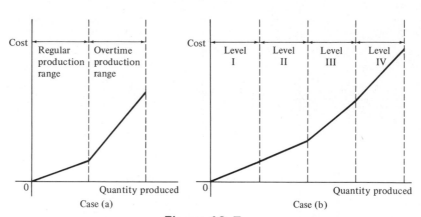

Figure 13–7

k levels of production such that the per-unit production cost increases with the level of production. A typical illustration is shown in Figure 13–7(b). Under such conditions, the production cost function is said to have increasing marginal costs. Mathematically, the function is said to be convex.

The above restriction on the production cost function must be maintained, otherwise the model to be developed below will not be applicable. This point will be justified later after the details of the model have been presented.

First, consider the case where no shortage is allowed in the system. Using the terminology of the transportation model (Chapter 5), the "sources" are represented by the regular and overtime productions for the different periods. The "destinations," on the other hand, are given by the demands for the respective periods. The per-unit "transportation" cost from any source to any destination is represented by the corresponding per-unit production plus holding costs.

The complete cost matrix for the equivalent transportation model (assuming no shortages) is given in Table 13–2.

Table 13–2

Demand Period j

		1	2	3	$\cdots$	N	Surplus	a_i
	R_1	c_1	$c_1 + h_1$	$c_1 + h_1 + h_2$		$c_1 + h_1 + \cdots + h_{N-1}$	0	a_{R1}
1	T_1	d_1	$d_1 + h_1$	$d_1 + h_1 + h_2$		$d_1 + h_1 + \cdots + h_{N-1}$	0	a_{T1}
	R_2	////	c_2	$c_2 + h_2$		$c_2 + h_2 + \cdots + h_{N-1}$	0	a_{R2}
2	T_2	////	d_2	$d_2 + h_2$		$d_2 + h_2 + \cdots + h_{N-1}$	0	a_{T2}
$\vdots$								$\vdots$
	R_N	////	////	////		c_N	0	a_{RN}
N	T_N	////	////	////		d_N	0	a_{TN}
	b_j	b_1	b_2	b_3	$\cdots$	b_N	S	

(left margin label: Production Period i)

The surplus column is used to balance the transportation model; that is, $S = \sum_i a_i - \sum_j b_j$. This is based on the reasonable assumption that the demand is always less than the production capacity of the system. (Notice that the cost per unit in the surplus column is equal to zero.) Since no shortage is allowed, the production in period i cannot be used to satisfy the demands for periods $1, 2, \ldots,$ and $i - 1$. This is shown in the above table by shaded squares which is actually equivalent to assigning a very large per unit cost to each one of them.

Because no backorders are allowed in this model, it is necessary to include the restriction that for every period, k, the cumulative amount of demand up to and including that period must not exceed the corresponding cumulative amount of production; that is,

$$\sum_{i=1}^{k} (a_{Ri} + a_{Ti}) \geq \sum_{j=1}^{k} b_j,$$

for $k = 1, 2, \ldots, N$.

The solution of the problem is greatly simplified by its formulation as a transportation model. Since the demand at period i should be satisfied before those at periods $i + 1, i + 2, \ldots,$ and N are satisfied, and because of the special condition imposed on the production cost function, it will not be necessary even to use the regular transportation algorithm in solving the problem. Instead, the demand for period 1 is first satisfied by successively assigning as much amount as possible to the cheapest entries of the first column (period 1). The new values of a_i are then updated to reflect the *remaining* capacities for the different periods. Next, period 2 is considered and its demand is satisfied in the cheapest possible way within the new capacity limitations. The process is continued until the demand for period N is satisfied.[6]

It is important to notice that because of the increasing marginal costs in the production cost function, the regular production capacity will be exhausted before the overtime production can start. If this condition is not satisfied, the transportation model will not be applicable since this might yield meaningless results (such as using overtime production before regular production is exhausted).

The no-shortage model will now be illustrated by a numerical example.

▶ **Example 13·3-5**

Consider a four-period production scheduling problem with the following data.

Period i	Capacity (units)		Demand (units) b_i
	a_{Ri}	a_{Ti}	
1	100	50	120
2	150	80	200
3	100	100	250
4	200	50	200
Totals	550	280	770

---

[6] For a proof of the optimality of this procedure, see S. M. Johnson, "Sequential Production Planning Over Time at Minimum Cost," *Management Science*, Vol. 3, No. 4, 435–437 (1957).

The production costs are assumed identical for all the periods; that is, $c_i = 2$ and $d_i = 3$, for all i. The holding cost also is assumed constant for all the periods and is given by $h_i = 0.1$, for all i. Notice that the cost functions are taken identical for all the periods only for simplicity.

The equivalent transportation model is shown in Table 13–3. The number in

Table 13–3

j

		1	2	3	4	Surplus	a_i
1	R_1	2 100	2.1	2.2	2.3	0	~~100~~
	T_1	3 20	3.1	3.2 20	3.3	0 10	~~50~~ ~~30~~ ~~10~~
2	R_2	/////	2 150	2.1	2.2	0	~~150~~
	T_2	/////	3 50	3.1 30	3.2	0	~~80~~ ~~30~~
3	R_3	/////	/////	2 100	2.1	0	~~100~~
	T_3	/////	/////	3 100	3.1	0	~~100~~
4	R_4	/////	/////	/////	2 200	0	~~200~~
	T_4	/////	/////	/////	3	0 50	~~50~~
	b_j	~~120~~ ~~20~~	~~200~~ ~~50~~	~~250~~ ~~150~~ ~~50~~ ~~20~~	~~200~~	~~60~~ ~~10~~	

i (labels the row groups 1–4 on the left side)

the top-right corner of each square represents the "transportation" costs while those in the middle of the squares represent the solution.

Notice the logic of the solution. For column 1, square $(R_1, 1)$ has the smallest cost per unit ($= 2$). The maximum amount that can be assigned to this square is 100 units which exhausts the supply of R_1. The remaining demand units for period 1 can be satisfied by assigning 20 units to square $(T_1, 1)$. This leaves a supply of 30 units for T_1. Next, consider column 2. Square $(R_2, 2)$ has the smallest cost ($= 2$). A maximum of 150 units can be assigned to it which will exhaust the R_2-supply. The next smallest cost in column 2 occurs in Square $(R_1, 2)$. Since the R_1-supply is equal to zero now, square $(T_2, 2)$ having the next smallest cost element in the same column must be considered. By assigning 50 units to this square, the demand for period 2 is satisfied. This leaves 30 units in the T_2-supply. The indicated procedure is continued until the demand for period 4 (column 4) is satisfied.

The reader can verify that the above solution is optimal by invoking the optimality condition of the transportation algorithm. (See Section 5·2·2.) This is accomplished in the usual manner by computing the simplex multipliers for the present solution and then checking for optimality. (See Problem 13-15.) Notice, however, that the given "optimal" solution is degenerate. ◄

Consider now a generalization of the above model in which shortages are allowed. It is assumed that backlogged demand must be filled by the end of the N-period horizon.

Table 13–3 can be modified readily to include the effect of backlogging. This is achieved by introducing the appropriate unit "transportation" costs in the blocked routes. For example, defining p_i as the shortage cost per unit demanded in period i and filled in period $i + 1$, the unit transportation cost corresponding to squares $(R_N, 1)$ and $(T_N, 1)$ are given by $\{c_N + p_1 + p_2 + \cdots + p_{N-1}\}$ and $\{d_N + p_1 + \cdots + p_{N-1}\}$, respectively.

It would seem reasonable to assume that the solution procedure used with the no-shortage case above would also be applicable to the new situation where shortage is allowed. Unfortunately, this is not true. To justify this claim, the following numerical example is designed to show that the preceding procedure may generally yield an inferior solution.

▶ **Example 13·3-6**
Consider a three-period model where regular and overtime production are used. The production capacities for the three periods are shown below.

Period	Production capacity	
	Regular	Overtime
1	15	10
2	15	0
3	20	15

The production cost per unit is the same for all the periods and is given by 5 for the regular production and 10 for the overtime production. The holding and shortage costs per unit are also constant for all the periods and are given by 1 and 2, respectively. The demands for the three periods are 20, 35, and 15, respectively.

The equivalent transportation model is given in Table 13–4. Notice that period 2 has no overtime production since its corresponding capacity is equal to zero.

Table 13–4

i		j = 1	2	3	Surplus	a_i	
1	R_1	5 15	6	7	0	15	
	T_1	10	11 5	12	0 5	10	
2	R_2	7 5	5 10	6	0	15	Total cost = 505
3	R_3	9	7 20	5	0	20	
	T_3	14	12	10 15	0	15	
	b_j	20	35	15	5		

Table 13–4 also shows the solution of the problem which is obtained using the above procedure. Thus, for column 1, 15 units are assigned to $(R_1, 1)$ and 5 units to $(R_2, 1)$ (Notice in this case that the cheapest route is selected from among *all* the entries of the column under consideration.) Next, consider column 2. Assign 10 units to $(R_2, 2)$, 20 units to $(R_3, 2)$, and 5 units to $(T_1, 2)$. Finally in column 3, assign 15 units to $(T_3, 3)$. The total cost associated with the schedule is $(5 \times 15 + 5 \times 7 + 5 \times 11 + 10 \times 5 + 20 \times 7 + 15 \times 10) = 505$.

It can be shown that the solution in Table 13–4 does not satisfy the optimality condition of the transportation algorithm. In fact Table 13–5 gives the optimal solution to this problem. The associated total cost in this case is $(15 \times 5 + 5 \times 10 + 5 \times 11 + 15 \times 5 + 5 \times 7 + 10 \times 12 + 15 \times 5) = 485.$ ◄

The above example show that the simple procedure of satisfying the demands for the successive periods does not yield an optimum solution for the shortage model. Consequently, one would have to apply the general transportation algorithm in order to obtain the optimum solution.

Table 13–5

		j				
		1	2	3	Surplus	a_i
1	R_1	5 15	6	6	0	15
	T_1	10 5	11 5	12	0	10
i 2	R_2	7	5 15	6	0	15
3	R_3	9	7 5	5 15	0	20
	T_3	14	12 10	10	0 5	15
	b_j	20	35	15	5	

Total cost = 485

§ 13·4
Probabilistic Models

This section deals with single-item inventory models in which demand is described by a known probability distribution. It will be assumed that all demand distributions are stationary and independent over time. The models developed here are mainly of the periodic-review type. These will be categorized under single- and multiple-period cases. However, in order to give the reader some appreciation of the type of analysis used in the continuous-review problem, the last model in this section will be developed for one such case. In general the analysis in the continuous case is more complex.

§ 13·4·1
Single-Period Models

The single-period inventory models occur in situations where the item is ordered once only to satisfy the demand of a specific period of time. For example, a style item becomes obsolete after a certain period of time and hence should not be reordered. In this section, the single-period models will be investigated under different conditions including mainly instantaneous and uniform demand, and setup and no setup cases. It will be assumed that stock replenishment occurs instantaneously. The optimal inventory level will be derived based on the minimization of the expected inventory costs. These include the ordering costs (setup + purchasing or production costs), the holding costs, and the shortage costs. Notice that because the demand is probabilistic the purchasing (production) cost per unit, although constant, becomes an effective factor in the cost function.

The same symbols introduced in Section 13·2 will be used again throughout this section. In addition $\phi(\xi)$ will be used to represent the p.d.f. of the demand ξ per period.

§ 13·4·1·1
Instantaneous Demand, No Setup Cost Model

In the models with instantaneous demand, it is assumed that the total demand is filled at the beginning of the period. Thus depending on the amount demanded, ξ, the inventory position right after the demand occurs may be either positive (surplus) or negative (shortage). These two cases are shown in Figure 13–8 (a and b).

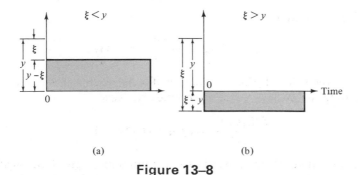

(a)   (b)

Figure 13–8

It is clear from Figure 13–8 that, given y, the amount on hand after an order is received, the holding inventory is generally given by

$$H(y) = \begin{cases} y - \xi, & \text{for } \xi < y, \\ 0, & \text{for } \xi \ge y, \end{cases}$$

while the shortage inventory is given by

$$G(y) = \begin{cases} 0, & \text{for } \xi < y, \\ \xi - y, & \text{for } \xi \ge y. \end{cases}$$

Given x, the amount on hand before an order is placed, then in the absence of a setup cost and assuming y is continuous, the expected inventory costs, $E\{C(y)\}$, for the period is given by

$$E\{C(y)\} = \text{Ordering cost} + E\{\text{holding cost}\} + E\{\text{shortage cost}\}$$

$$= c(y - x) + h \int_0^\infty H(y)\phi(\xi) \, d\xi + p \int_0^\infty G(y)\phi(\xi) \, d\xi$$

$$= c(y - x) + h\left\{\int_0^y (y - \xi)\phi(\xi) \, d\xi + 0\right\}$$

$$+ p\left\{0 + \int_y^\infty (\xi - y)\phi(\xi) \, d\xi\right\}$$

$$= c(y - x) + h \int_0^y (y - \xi)\phi(\xi) \, d\xi + p \int_y^\infty (\xi - y)\phi(\xi) \, d\xi.$$

The optimal value of y is obtained by equating the first derivative of $E\{C(y)\}$ to zero.[7] Thus

$$\frac{\partial E\{C(y)\}}{\partial y} = c + h \int_0^y \phi(\xi) \, d\xi - p \int_y^\infty \phi(\xi) \, d\xi = 0.$$

Since

$$\int_y^\infty \phi(\xi) \, d\xi = 1 - \int_0^y \phi(\xi) \, d\xi,$$

the above equation gives

$$\int_0^{y^*} \phi(\xi) \, d\xi = \frac{p - c}{p + h} = q, \quad \text{say.}$$

Notice that the value of y^* is defined only if $p \geq c$. If $p < c$, this is interpreted as discarding the inventory system completely. Now,

$$\frac{\partial^2 E\{C(y)\}}{\partial y^2} = (h + p)\phi(y^*) > 0,$$

which shows that y^* corresponds to a minimum point. Graphically, the function $E\{C(y)\}$ should appear as shown in Figure 13–9. In such cases the function $E\{C(y)\}$ is said to be convex. Since y^* is unique, it must give a global minimum. The adopted policy is thus called a *single critical number policy*.

According to the above condition, the value of y^* is selected such that the probability that $\xi \leq y^*$ is equal to

$$q = \frac{p - c}{p + h}, \quad p > c.$$

The optimal ordering policy given x on hand before an order is received is given by:

$$\text{if } y^* > x, \quad \text{order } y^* - x,$$
$$\text{if } y^* \leq x, \quad \text{do not order.}$$

---

[7] See footnote on page 418.

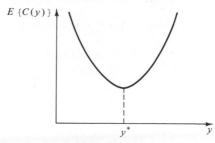

Figure 13–9

▶ **Example 13·4-1**

Consider the one-period model with $h = \$0.5$, $p = \$4.5$ and $c = \$0.5$. The demand density function is given by

$$\phi(\xi) = \begin{cases} \dfrac{1}{10}, & 0 \le \xi \le 10, \\ 0, & \xi > 10. \end{cases}$$

Thus, the critical ratio is given by

$$q = \frac{p - c}{p + h} = \frac{4.5 - .5}{4.5 + .5} = .8$$

and

$$P\{\xi \le y^*\} = \int_0^{y^*} \phi(\xi)\, d\xi = \int_0^{y^*} \frac{1}{10}\, d\xi = \frac{y^*}{10}$$

or

$$y^* = 8.$$

The above solution is illustrated graphically as shown in Figure 13–10. ◀

Suppose now that demand occurs in discrete units rather than in continuous units. Then

$$E\{C(y)\} = c(y - x) + h \sum_{\xi=0}^{y} (y - \xi)\phi(\xi) + p \sum_{\xi=y+1}^{\infty} (\xi - y)\phi(\xi).$$

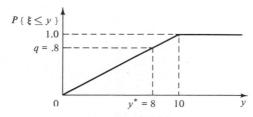

Figure 13–10

In the discrete case, the necessary conditions for a minimum are given by

$$E\{C(y-1)\} \geq E\{C(y)\},$$

and

$$E\{C(y+1)\} \geq E\{C(y)\}.$$

Thus

$$E\{C(y-1)\} = c(y-1-x) + h\sum_{\xi=0}^{y-1}(y-1-\xi)\phi(\xi) + p\sum_{\xi=y}^{\infty}(\xi-y+1)\phi(\xi)$$

$$= c(y-x) + h\sum_{\xi=0}^{y-1}(y-\xi)\phi(\xi) + p\sum_{\xi=y}^{\infty}(\xi-y)\phi(\xi)$$

$$- h\sum_{\xi=0}^{y-1}\phi(\xi) + p\sum_{\xi=y}^{\infty}\phi(\xi) - c$$

$$= E\{C(y)\} + p - c - (h+p)\sum_{\xi=0}^{y-1}\phi(\xi).$$

Therefore,

$$E\{C(y-1)\} - E\{C(y)\} = p - c - (h+p)P\{\xi \leq y-1\} \geq 0,$$

or

$$P\{\xi \leq y-1\} \leq \frac{p-c}{p+h}.$$

Similarly, it can be shown from the condition,

$$E\{C(y+1)\} \geq E\{C(y)\},$$

that

$$P\{\xi \leq y\} \geq \frac{p-c}{p+h}.$$

Thus, y^* must satisfy

$$P\{\xi \leq y^*-1\} \leq \frac{p-c}{p+h} \leq P\{\xi \leq y^*\}$$

▶ **Example 13·4-2**

Consider the single-period model with $h = \$1.00$, $p = \$4.00$ and $c = \$2.00$. The demand density function is given by

ξ	$\phi(\xi)$
0	.10
1	.20
2	.25
3	.20
4	.15
5	.10

The critical ratio is

$$q = \frac{p - c}{p + h} = \frac{4 - 2}{4 + 1} = 0.4.$$

The optimal solution is obtained by constructing the following table.

y	$P\{\xi \le y\}$
0	.10
1	.30
2	.55 $\leftarrow q = .4$
3	.75
4	.90
5	1.00

Thus,

$$P\{\xi \le 1\} = 0.3 < 0.4 < 0.55 = P\{\xi \le 2\}.$$

Hence, the optimal value is given by $y^* = 2$. ◄

§ 13·4·1·2
Uniform Demand, No Setup Cost Model

In this case, demand occurs uniformly (rather than instantaneously) during the period as shown in Figure 13–11.

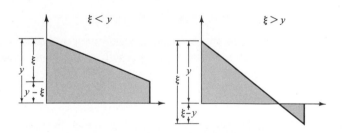

Average holding inventory = $y - \frac{\xi}{2}$ Average holding inventory = $\frac{y^2}{2\xi}$

Average shortage inventory = 0   Average shortage inventory = $\frac{(\xi - y)^2}{2\xi}$

(a)   (b)

Figure 13–11

The expected total cost for this model is thus given by (assuming y is a continuous variable),

$$E\{C(y)\} = c(y - x) + h\left\{\int_0^y \left(y - \frac{\xi}{2}\right)\phi(\xi)\,d\xi + \int_y^\infty \frac{y^2}{2\xi}\,\phi(\xi)\,d\xi\right\}$$
$$+ p\int_y^\infty \frac{(\xi - y)^2}{2\xi}\,\phi(\xi)\,d\xi.$$

Taking the first derivative and equating it to zero, one gets,

$$c + h\left(\int_0^y \phi(\xi)\,d\xi + \int_y^\infty \frac{y}{\xi}\,\phi(\xi)\,d\xi\right) - p\int_y^\infty \left(\frac{\xi - y}{\xi}\right)\phi(\xi)\,d\xi = 0,$$

or

$$\int_0^{y^*} \phi(\xi)\,d\xi + y^*\int_{y^*}^\infty \frac{\phi(\xi)}{\xi}\,d\xi = \frac{p - c}{p + h} = q.$$

This policy is also of the single critical number type since $E\{C(y)\}$ is convex in this case.

▶ **Example 13·4-3**

Consider the same problem of Example 13·4-1. Since

$$\phi(\xi) = \frac{1}{10}, \qquad 0 \le \xi \le 10,$$

then

$$\int_0^{y^*} \frac{1}{10}\,d\xi + y^*\int_{y^*}^{10} \frac{1}{10\xi}\,d\xi = .8,$$

or

$$\frac{1}{10}(y^* - y^* \ln y^* + 2.3y^*) = 0.8,$$

or

$$3.3y^* - y^* \ln y^* - 8 = 0.$$

The solution of this equation is obtained by trial and error and is given by $y^* = 4.5$. Notice the difference between this result and the one given in the case of instantaneous demand. ◀

§ 13·4·1·3
Instantaneous Demand, Setup Cost Model—(*s-S* Policy)

Consider the same model as in Section 13·4·1·1 with the exception that the setup cost, K, will be taken into account. Let $E\{\bar{C}\{y\}\}$ be the total expected cost of the system inclusive of the setup cost. Thus

$$E\{\bar{C}(y)\} = K + c(y - x) + h\int_0^y (y - \xi)\phi(\xi)\,d\xi + p\int_y^\infty (\xi - y)\phi(\xi)\,d\xi$$
$$= K + E\{C(y)\}.$$

The minimum value of $E\{C(y)\}$ was shown in Section 13·4·1·1 to occur at y^* satisfying,

$$\int_0^{y^*} \phi(\xi)\, d\xi = \frac{p - c}{p + h}.$$

Since K is constant, the minimum value of $E\{\bar{C}(y)\}$ must also occur at y^*. By comparison with Figure 13–9, the function $E\{C(y)\}$ and $E\{\bar{C}(y)\}$ must appear as shown in Figure 13–12.

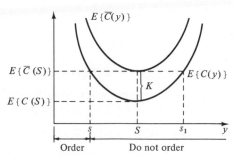

Figure 13–12

The new symbols s and S are defined in the figure for later use in the analysis. The value of S is equal to y^* while the value of s is determined from

$$E\{C(s)\} = E\{\bar{C}(S)\}$$

$$= K + E\{C(S)\},$$

such that $s < S$. (Notice that this equation must yield another value, $s_1 > S$, which can be disregarded.)

The question now is: given x, the amount on hand before the order is placed, how much should be ordered, if any? This question is investigated under three conditions.

$$\text{(i)} \quad x < s.$$
$$\text{(ii)} \quad s \leq x \leq S.$$
$$\text{(iii)} \quad x > S.$$

Case 1: $x < s$

Since x implies no ordering, its equivalent cost is given by $E\{C(x)\}$. If any additional amount $y - x$, $(y > x)$, is ordered, the corresponding cost given y is $E\{\bar{C}(y)\}$ which includes the setup cost K. Thus it follows from Figure 13–12 that for all $x < s$

$$\min_{y > x} E\{\bar{C}(y)\} = E\{\bar{C}(S)\} < E\{C(x)\}.$$

This implies that the optimal inventory level must reach $y^* = S$ and the amount ordered is thus equal to $S - x$.

Case 2: $s \leq x \leq S$

Again, from Figure 13–12

$$E\{C(x)\} \leq \min_{y > x} E\{\bar{C}(y)\} = E\{\bar{C}(S)\}.$$

Thus, it is no more costly not to order in this case. Hence $y^* = x$.

Case 3: $x > S$

From Figure 13–12, for $y > x$.

$$E\{C(x)\} < E\{\bar{C}(y)\},$$

which again indicates that it is less costly not to order and $y^* = x$.

The above policy is called the *s-S* policy and is summarized as follows:

if $x < s$,   order $S - x$,

if $x \geq s$,   do not order.

Notice that the optimality of the *s-S* policy is mainly dependent on the fact that the cost function is convex. In general, when this property is not satisfied, the *s-S* policy will cease to be optimal.

▶ **Example 13·4-4**
Consider the same problem of Example 13·4-1 and let $K = \$25$.
Since $y^* = 8$, hence $S = 8$. To determine the value of s, consider

$$E\{C(y)\} = .5(y - x) + .5 \int_0^y \frac{1}{10} (y - \xi) \, d\xi + 4.5 \int_y^{10} \frac{1}{10} (\xi - y) \, d\xi$$

$$= .5(y - x) + 0.05 \left[y\xi - \frac{\xi^2}{2} \right]_0^y + .45 \left[\frac{\xi^2}{2} - \xi y \right]_y^{10}$$

$$= 0.25y^2 - 4.0y + 22.5 - 0.5x.$$

So that from the equation

$$E\{C(s)\} = K + E\{C(S)\},$$

$$0.25 s^2 - 4.0s + 22.5 - 0.5x = 25 + 0.25 S^2 - 4.0 S + 22.5 - 0.5x.$$

Putting $S = 8$, this equation reduces to

$$s^2 - 16 s - 36 = 0.$$

This equation gives

$$s = -2 \text{ or } 18.$$

The value of $s = 18$ (which is greater than S) should be disregarded. Since the remaining value less than S is negative ($= -2$), this means that s has no feasible value (notice that $E\{C(y)\}$ is defined for nonnegative values of y only). The optimal solution thus calls for not ordering at all. Clearly this does not follow the s-S policy since s is undefined.[8] The current situation is illustrated graphically in Figure 13–13. This usually occurs when the cost function is flat or when the setup cost K is large compared with the other costs. ◀

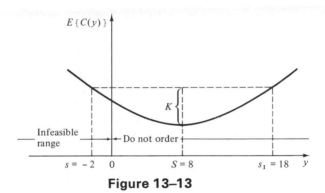

Figure 13–13

§ 13·4·2
Multiperiod Models

In Section 13·4·1, only single-period models have been considered. In this section, probabilistic models will be considered for the multiperiod (finite or infinite) case under different combinations of the following conditions.

(i) Backlogging and no backlogging of demand.
(ii) Zero and positive delivery lags.

The models will be developed mainly for the finite period case. Models with infinite periods will be derived from the finite case by taking the limit as the number of periods tends to infinity. It will be assumed that there is no setup cost at any period. The inclusion of setup costs in the multiperiod case generally leads to computationally infeasible solutions. As will be shown below, all the multiperiod models are formulated by dynamic programming.

Although in all previous inventory models the optimal policy was determined by minimizing a cost function, the optimal inventory level will be determined in this section based on the maximization of a profit function. The objective here is to familiarize the reader with the application of the maximization (profit) criterion as an alternative to the minimization (cost) criterion.

---

[8] Conventionally, if $s < 0$, then s is set equal to zero and the given s–S policy becomes applicable.

Unlike the single-period models, a multiperiod model should take into account the discounted value of money. Thus if α (< 1) is the discount factor per period, then an amount of money, S, n periods hence ($n \geq 1$) is equivalent to $\alpha^n S$ now.

§ 13·4·2·1
Backlog, Zero Delivery Lag Model

Let the finite planning horizon be limited to N periods. Define

$f_i(x_i)$ = maximum total expected profit for periods i, $i + 1$, ..., N, given x_i is the amount on hand before an order is placed in the ith period.

Using the symbols of Section 13·2, the problem can be formulated as a (backward) dynamic programming model as follows:

$$f_i(x_i) = \max_{y_i \geq x_i}\left(-c(y_i - x_i) + \int_0^{y_i} [r\xi - h(y_i - \xi)]\phi(\xi)\,d\xi \right.$$

$$+ \int_{y_i}^{\infty} [ry_i + \alpha r(\xi - y_i) - p(\xi - y_i)]\phi(\xi)\,d\xi$$

$$\left. + \alpha \int_0^{\infty} f_{i+1}(y - \xi)\phi(\xi)\,d\xi \right), \qquad i = 1, 2, \ldots, N.$$

with $f_{N+1}(y_N - \xi) \equiv 0$. Notice that x_i may be negative since the unfilled demand is backlogged. Notice, also, that the quantity $[\alpha r(\xi - y_i)]$ in the second integral expression is included for the following reason. The amount $(\xi - y_i)$ represents the unfilled demand in the ith period which must be filled in the $(i + 1)$st period. The discounted return is thus $[\alpha r(\xi - y_i)]$.

The above recursive equation can basically be solved using the computational technique of dynamic programming. However, this procedure is extremely difficult in this case (see Problem 13-31). An important case can be analyzed, however, by letting $N \to \infty$. This yields the infinite period model with its recursive equation given by

$$f(x) = \max_{y \geq x}\left(-c(y - x) + \int_0^{y} [r\xi - h(y - \xi)]\phi(\xi)\,d\xi \right.$$

$$\left. + \int_{y}^{\infty} [ry + \alpha r(\xi - y) - p(\xi - y)]\phi(\xi)\,d\xi + \alpha \int_0^{\infty} f(y - \xi)\phi(\xi)\,d\xi \right),$$

where x and y are the inventory levels for each period before and after an order is received, respectively.

The optimal policy for the infinite period case is of the single critical number type. Thus

$$\frac{\partial(\,\cdot\,)}{\partial y} = -c - h \int_0^y \phi(\xi)\, d\xi + \int_y^\infty [(1-\alpha)r + p]\phi(\xi)\, d\xi$$

$$+ \alpha \int_0^\infty \frac{\partial f(y-\xi)}{\partial y}\, \phi(\xi)\, d\xi = 0.$$

The value of

$$\frac{\partial f(y-\xi)}{\partial y}$$

is determined as follows. If there are δ (> 0) units more on hand at the start of the next period, the profit for the next period will increase by $c\delta$, for this much less has to be ordered. This means that

$$\frac{\partial f(y-\xi)}{\partial y} = c.$$

The above equation thus becomes,

$$-c - h \int_0^y \phi(\xi)\, d\xi + \left((1-\alpha)r + p\right)\left(1 - \int_0^y \phi(\xi)\, d\xi\right) + \alpha c \int_0^\infty \phi(\xi)\, d\xi = 0.$$

This reduces to

$$\int_0^{y^*} \phi(\xi)\, d\xi = \frac{p + 1(-\alpha)(r-c)}{p + h + (1-\alpha)r}.$$

The optimal policy for each period given its entering inventory x is:

$$\text{if } x < y^*, \qquad \text{order } (y^* - x)$$

$$\text{if } x \geq y^*, \qquad \text{do not order.}$$

It is stated here, without proof, that if in the finite model y_i^* represents the optimal inventory level for period i, then the following relationship is always satisfied.

$$y_N^* \leq y_{N-1}^* \leq \cdots \leq y_i^* \leq \cdots \leq y_1^* \leq y^*,$$

where y^* is the single critical value in the infinite model. This means that in the finite model the optimal policy calls for ordering less as one comes closer to the end of the horizon. In the meantime, none of the critical values y_i^* can exceed the optimal value y^* in the infinite model.

§ 13·4·2·2
No-Backlog, Zero Delivery Lag Model

This model is similar to the backlog case except when the demand ξ exceeds the inventory level y_i in which case the next period will start with $x_{i+1} = 0$. This means that the unfilled demand is lost and hence does not result in any revenue.

The N-period (finite) recursive equation for the no backlog case is thus given by

$$f_i(x_i) = \max_{y_i \geq x_i}\left(-c(y_i - x_i) + \int_0^{y_i} [r\xi - h(y_i - \xi)]\phi(\xi)\,d\xi \right.$$

$$+ \int_{y_i}^{\infty} [ry_i - p(\xi - y_i)]\phi(\xi)\,d\xi + \alpha\left[\int_0^{y_i} f_{i+1}(y_i - \xi)\phi(\xi)\,d\xi\right.$$

$$\left.\left. + \int_{y_i}^{\infty} f_{i+1}(0)\phi(\xi)\,d\xi\right]\right), \qquad i = 1, 2, \ldots \ N,$$

with $f_{N+1} \equiv 0$.

The dynamic programming solution for this problem is also difficult to obtain. The corresponding infinite period model is easy to solve, however, since it is of the single critical number type. Thus letting $N \to \infty$ as in the backlog case, then,

$$f(x) = \max_{y \geq x}\left(-c(y - x) + \int_0^y [r\xi - h(y - \xi)]\phi(\xi)\,d\xi \right.$$

$$\left. + \int_y^{\infty} [ry - p(\xi - y)]\phi(\xi)\,d\xi + \alpha\left[\int_0^y f(y - \xi)\phi(\xi)\,d\xi + \int_y^{\infty} f(0)\phi(\xi)\,d\xi\right]\right).$$

Taking the first derivative and equating to zero, then

$$-c - h\int_0^y \phi(\xi)\,d\xi + (r + p)\int_y^{\infty} \phi(\xi)\,d\xi + \alpha\int_0^y \frac{\partial f(y - \xi)}{\partial y}\phi(\xi)\,d\xi = 0.$$

Since as in the backlog case,

$$\frac{\partial f(y - \xi)}{\partial y} = c,$$

then

$$\int_0^{y^*} \phi(\xi)\,d\xi = \frac{r + p - c}{h + r + p - \alpha c}.$$

It must be noted that in this model, as in the previous one, the relationship,

$$y_N^* \leq y_{N-1}^* \leq \cdots \leq y_i^* \leq \cdots \leq y_1^* \leq y^*,$$

still holds true; where y_i^* corresponds to the optimal inventory level of period i in the finite model.

§ 13·4·2·3
Backlog, Positive Delivery Lag Model

In this model it is assumed that an order placed at the beginning of period i will be received k periods later; that is, at period $i + k$, $k \geq 1$. The delivery lag, k, is assumed constant for all the periods.

Let $z, z_1, \ldots, z_{k-1}$ be the amounts due in (as a result of previous decisions) at the beginning of periods $i, i+1, \ldots,$ and $i+k-1$. (See Figure 13–14.)

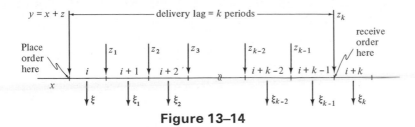

Figure 13–14

Let $y = x + z$ be the amount of inventory at the beginning of period i where x is the entering inventory (possibly negative because of backlogging) to period i. At period i, the decision variable is represented by z_k, the amount ordered now to be received k periods later.

Define $f_i(y, z_1, \ldots, z_{k-1})$ as the present worth of the maximum expected profit for periods $i, i+1, \ldots,$ and N; given $y, z_1, \ldots,$ and z_{k-1}. Thus,

$$f_i(y, z_1, \ldots, z_{k-1})$$

$$= \max_{z_k \geq 0} \left\{ -cz_k + L(y) + \alpha \int_0^\infty f_{i+1}(y + z_1 - \xi, z_2, \ldots, z_k)\phi(\xi)\, d\xi \right\},$$

$$i = 1, 2, \ldots, N,$$

where $f_{N+1} \equiv 0$, and

$$L(y) = \int_0^y (r\xi - h(y - \xi))\phi(\xi)\, d\xi + \int_y^\infty (ry + (\alpha r - p)(\xi - y))\phi(\xi)\, d\xi.$$

$L(y)$ represents the expected revenue minus the holding and penalty costs for period i.

It will be shown now that the optimal policy for this model can be expressed in terms of $(y + z_1 + \cdots + z_{k-1})$. This is advantageous computationally since it reduces the dimensions of the state of the system to one only.

Consider first the special case of a finite horizon consisting of k periods starting with period i. Since z_k is received at the beginning of period $i+k$, it will have no effect on the holding and penalty costs or the revenue during the k-period horizon. Let C_k represent the present worth of the expected revenue during the k-period horizon exclusive of the ordering cost cz_k. Thus

$$C_k = L(y) + \alpha E\{L(y + z_1 - \xi)\} + \alpha^2 E\{L(y + z_1 + z_2 - \xi - \xi_1)\}$$

$$+ \cdots + \alpha^{k-1} E\left\{ L\left(y + \sum_{j=1}^{k-1} z_j - \xi - \sum_{j=1}^{k-2} \xi_j \right) \right\},$$

where ξ is the demand for period i and ξ_j is the demand for period $i + j$. The operator "E" is the expectation operator.

Since all the demands are independent and identically distributed, each with p.d.f. $\phi(\xi)$, the random variable $\eta_m = \xi + \xi_1 + \cdots + \xi_{m-1}$, $m = 2$, $3, \ldots, k - 1$, is the m-fold convolution of ξ. (See Section 12·9.) Let $\phi_m(\eta_m)$ be the p.d.f. of η_m, then

$$E\left\{ L\left(y + \sum_{j=1}^{m} z_j - \xi - \sum_{j=1}^{m-1} \xi_j \right) \right\} = \int_0^\infty L\left(y + \sum_{j=1}^{m} z_j - \eta_m \right) \phi_m(\eta_m) \, d\eta_m.$$

It is noticed that the expression for C_k is a constant independent of z_k.

In order to compute the net revenue for period $i + k$, let

$$u = y + (z_1 + \cdots + z_{k-1}) + z_k,$$

and

$$v = y + (z_1 + \cdots + z_{k-1}) = u - z_k.$$

Now, $\eta_{k+1} = \xi + \xi_1 + \cdots \xi_k$ represents the demand for periods $i, i + 1, \ldots,$ and $i + k$. The holding and shortage inventories for period $i + k$ are thus given by $(u - \eta_{k+1})$ and $(\eta_{k+1} - u)$, respectively. Consequently, the net revenue (not accounting for the ordering cost cz_k) for period $i + k$ is given by

$$L_{k+1}(u) = \left[\int_0^u \{ r\eta_{k+1} - h(u - \eta_{k+1}) \} \phi_{k+1}(\eta_{k+1}) \, d\eta_{k+1} \right.$$

$$\left. + \int_u^\infty \{ ru + (\alpha r - p)(\eta_{k+1} - u) \} \phi_{k+1}(\eta_{k+1}) \, d\eta_{k+1} - A \right],$$

where A is a constant representing the expected revenue for periods i, $i + 1, \ldots,$ and $i + k - 1$.

Let $g_i(v)$ define the optimal expected profit for periods $i + k, \ldots,$ and N; then,

$$g_i(v) = \max_{u \geq v} \left\{ -c(u - v) + \alpha^k L_{k+1}(u) + \int_0^\infty g_{i+1}(u - \xi) \phi(\xi) \, d\xi \right\}.$$

Now, the expected optimum revenue for periods $i, i + 1, \ldots,$ and N is equal to the *sum* of the expected optimum revenues for periods $i, i + 1, \ldots, i + k - 1$ and for periods $i + k, i + k + 1, \ldots, N; N \geq k$. Since $v = y + z_1 + \cdots + z_{k-1}$, then by definition the above statement implies that

$$f_i(y, z_1, \ldots, z_{k-1}) = C_k + g_i(y + z_1 + \cdots + z_{k-1}).$$

Since C_k is a constant, the optimization problem using f_i must be equivalent to the optimization problem using g_i. The advantage here is that the new problem is described by one state $v = y + z_1 + \cdots + z_{k-1}$ which is computationally more attractive. It is noticed now that the solution of the modified problem is essentially the same as that of the zero lag case discussed in Section 13·4·2·1.

As $N \to \infty$, the modified problem becomes

$$g(v) = \max_{u \geq v}(-c(u - v) + \alpha^k L_{k+1}(u) + \alpha E\{g(u - \xi)\})$$

This, as shown in Section 13·4·2·1, yields a unique optimal value u^* which can be obtained from,

$$\frac{\partial(\cdot)}{\partial u} = -c + \alpha^k L'_{k+1}(u) + \alpha c = 0.$$

This gives,

$$\int_0^{u^*} \phi_{k+1}(\eta_{k+1}) \, d\eta_{k+1} = \frac{p + (1 - \alpha)(r - c\alpha^{-k})}{h + p + (1 - \alpha)r}.$$

The optimal policy at any period i is:

$$\text{if } u^* \geq v, \qquad \text{order } u^* - v,$$

$$\text{if } u^* < v, \qquad \text{do not order.}$$

Notice that at period i, the value of v is already known. (See the definition of v given above.) Notice also that for $k = 0$; that is, no delivery lag, the above result reduces to the same one given for the zero delivery lag model (Section 13·4·2·1).

§ 13·4·2·4
No Backlog, Positive Delivery Lag Model

Using the same symbols as in Section 13.4.2.3, the model for the no backlog case becomes,

$$f_i(y, z_1, \ldots, z_{k-1}) = \max_{z_k \geq 0}\left[-cz_k + \int_0^y \{r\xi - h(y - \xi)\}\phi(\xi) \, d\xi \right.$$

$$+ \int_y^\infty \{ry - p(\xi - y)\}\phi(\xi) \, d\xi$$

$$+ \alpha \int_0^y f_{i+1}(y - \xi + z_1, z_2, \ldots, z_k)\phi(\xi) \, d\xi$$

$$\left. + \alpha \int_y^\infty f_{i+1}(z_1, z_2, \ldots, z_k)\phi(\xi) \, d\xi \right], \qquad i = 1, 2, \ldots, N,$$

with $f_{N+1} \equiv 0$.

In general, the dynamic programming solution of this model is very difficult for $k > 1$ since this results in a dimensionality problem that increases with k.

§ 13·4·3
A Continuous Review Model

This section introduces a probabilistic model in which the stock is reviewed continuously and an order of size y is placed every time the stock level reaches a certain reorder point R. The model is studied over an infinite time horizon. The objective here is to determine the optimum values of y and R which minimize the total inventory costs per unit time. In this model, a unit of time will be taken to represent one year.

The inventory fluctuations corresponding to this situation are depicted in Figure 13–15. A cycle is defined as the time period between two successive

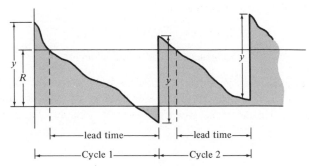

Figure 13–15

arrivals of orders. It is assumed that the lead time between the placement of an order and its receipt is stochastic and that the unfilled demand during this lead time is backlogged. The distribution of the demand during a lead time is assumed independent of the time at which it occurs. It is also assumed that the demand during a lead time is never larger than R so that there is no more than one outstanding order at a time.

Let

$r(x \mid t)$ = conditional p.d.f. of demand x during lead time t, $x > 0$,
$s(t)$ = p.d.f. of lead time t, $t > 0$,
$f(x)$ = absolute p.d.f. of demand x during lead time,
     $= \int_0^\infty r(x \mid t)s(t)\, dt$,
y = amount *ordered* per cycle,
D = expected total demand per year.

The total annual cost for this model includes the average setup cost, the expected holding cost and the expected shortage cost. The average setup cost is given by (DK/y) where (D/y) represents the approximate number of orders per year and K is the setup cost per order.

The expected holding cost is calculated based on the expected net inventory level at the beginning and at the end of a cycle. The expected stock level at the end of an inventory cycle is equal to $E\{R - x\}$. At the beginning of the cycle (right after an order of size y is received), the expected stock level is equal to $y + E\{R - x\}$. This means that the average inventory per cycle (and hence per year) is given by

$$\bar{H} = \frac{(y + E\{R - x\}) + E\{R - x\}}{2}$$

$$= (y/2) + E\{R - x\}.$$

Now, given $f(x)$ as defined above, then

$$E\{R - x\} = \int_0^\infty (R - x)f(x)\, dx$$

$$= R - E\{x\}.$$

Notice that the expression for $\bar{H}$ neglects the case where $R - E\{x\}$ is negative (shortage quantity). This is one of the simplifying approximations of the model.

Finally, let S be the shortage quantity per cycle, then

$$S(x) = \begin{cases} 0, & x \leq R \\ x - R, & x > R. \end{cases}$$

Consequently the expected shortage quantity per cycle is

$$\bar{S} = \int_0^\infty S(x)f(x)\, dx$$

$$= \int_R^\infty (x - R)f(x)\, dx.$$

Since there are approximately (D/y) orders per year, the expected annual shortage is then equal to $(D\bar{S}/y)$.

Summarizing all the above information, the total annual cost of the system is given by

$$TAC(y, R) = \frac{DK}{y} + h\left(\frac{y}{2} + R - E\{x\}\right) + \frac{pD\bar{S}}{y}.$$

Notice that the shortage cost $(pD\bar{S}/y)$ is assumed proportional to the shortage quantity only without taking the shortage time into account. This again is another simplifying approximation in the model since in the case of backlog it is generally assumed that shortage cost is also a function of the shortage time.

The solution for y^* and R^* is obtained by equating to zero the partial derivatives of $TAC(y, R)$ with respect to y and R. Thus,

$$\frac{\partial TAC}{\partial y} = -\left(\frac{DK}{y^2}\right) + \frac{h}{2} - \frac{pD\bar{S}}{y^2} = 0,$$

$$\frac{\partial TAC}{\partial R} = h - \left(\frac{pD}{y}\right)\int_R^\infty f(x)\,dx = 0.$$

From the first equation,

$$y^* = \sqrt{\frac{2D(K + p\bar{S})}{h}},\tag{1}$$

and from the second equation,

$$\int_{R^*}^\infty f(x)\,dx = \frac{hy^*}{pD}.\tag{2}$$

An explicit general solution for y^* and R^* is not possible in this case. It is thus necessary to use a convenient numerical analysis method to solve Equations (1) and (2) above. The following procedure, due to Hadley and Whitin [2], is proved to converge in a finite number of iterations, provided a solution exists.

In Equation (1) above, it is noticed that $\bar{S}$ is *at least* equal to zero. This shows that the *smallest* value of y^* is equal to $\sqrt{2DK/h}$, which is achieved when $\bar{S} = 0$ (or $R \to \infty$). Now, at $R = 0$, Equation (1) gives,

$$y^* = \hat{y} = \sqrt{\frac{2D(K + pE\{x\})}{h}},$$

while Equation (2) gives

$$y^* = \tilde{y} = \frac{pD}{h}.$$

It can be proved ([2], pp. 169–174) that if $\tilde{y} \geq \hat{y}$, then the optimal values y^* and R^* exist and are unique. In such a case, these values are computed as follows. Compute the first trial value of y^* as $y_1 = \sqrt{2DK/h}$. Next use Equation (2) to compute the value of R_1 corresponding to y_1. Using R_1, a new trial value, y_2, is obtained from Equation (1). Next, R_2 is computed from Equation (2) using y_2. This procedure is repeated until two successive values of R are approximately equal. At this point, the last value computed for y and R will yield y^* and R^*, respectively.

▶ **Example 13·4-5**
Let $K = 100$, $D = 1000$, $p = 10$, and $h = 2$ and assume that the demand during a lead time follows a uniform distribution over the range 0 to 100. The objective is to find the optimal values y^* and R^*.

To check whether the problem has a feasible solution, consider

$$\hat{y} = \sqrt{\frac{2D(K + pE\{x\})}{h}}$$

$$= \sqrt{\frac{2 \times 1000(100 + 10 \times 50)}{2}}$$

$$= 774.5$$

and

$$\tilde{y} = \frac{pD}{h} = \frac{10 \times 1000}{2} = 5000.$$

Since $\tilde{y} > \hat{y}$, a unique solution for y^* and R^* exists.
To compute the optimal solution, consider

$$\bar{S} = \int_R^\infty (x - R)f(x)\, dx$$

$$= \int_R^{100} (x - R)\frac{1}{100}\, dx$$

$$= \frac{R^2}{200} - R + 50. \tag{i}$$

From Equation (1)

$$y^* = \sqrt{\frac{2D(K + p\bar{S})}{h}}$$

$$= \sqrt{\frac{2 \times 1000(100 + 10\bar{S})}{2}}$$

$$= \sqrt{100{,}000 + 10{,}000\bar{S}}, \tag{ii}$$

where $\bar{S}$ is as given by (i) above. From Equation (2)

$$\int_{R^*}^{100} \frac{1}{100}\, dx = \frac{2y^*}{10 \times 1000},$$

or

$$R^* = 100 - \frac{y^*}{50}. \tag{iii}$$

Equation (iii) will be used to compute R_i for a given value of y_i, while Equation (ii) will be used to compute y_{i+1} for a given value of R_i.

Iteration 1:

$$y_1 = \sqrt{\frac{2DK}{h}}$$

$$= \sqrt{\frac{2 \times 1000 \times 100}{2}}$$

$$= 316$$

Thus, from (iii)

$$R_1 = 100 - \frac{316}{50} = 93.68.$$

Iteration 2:

From (i)

$$\bar{S} = \frac{R_1^2}{200} - R_1 + 50 = .19971,$$

and from (ii)

$$y_2 = \sqrt{100,000 + 10,000 \times .19971} = 319.5.$$

Hence from (iii)

$$R_2 = 100 - \frac{319.5}{50} = 93.61.$$

Iteration 3:

From (i)

$$\bar{S} = \frac{R_2^2}{200} - R_2 + 50 = .20416,$$

and from (ii)

$$y_3 = \sqrt{100,000 + 10,000 \times .20416} = 319.8.$$

Thus from (iii)

$$R_3 = 100 - \frac{319.8}{50} = 93.604.$$

Since R_2 and R_3 are approximately equal, the approximate optimal solution is given by

$$R^* \cong 93.604, \qquad y^* \cong 319.8 \quad \blacktriangleleft$$

SELECTED REFERENCES

1. ARROW, K. J., S. KARLIN, and H. SCARF, *Studies in Mathematical Theory of Inventory and Production*, Stanford, California: Stanford University Press, 1958.
2. HADLEY, G. and T. WHITIN, *Analysis of Inventory Systems*, Englewood Cliffs, N.J.: Prentice-Hall, 1963.

PROBLEMS

☐ **13-1** A product is produced at the rate of 50 items per day. The demand occurs at the rate of 30 items per day. Given that

setup cost per order = $100,
holding cost per unit per unit time = $.05,

find the economic lot size and the associated total cost per cycle assuming that no shortage is allowed.

☐ **13-2** Repeat Problem 13-1 assuming that the product is purchased; that is, the stock is replenished instantaneously upon request.

☐ **13-3** In Problem 13-1 suppose that shortage is allowed. If it is decided to use a lot size of 600 units, what is the implied shortage cost per unit under optimal conditions?

☐ **13-4** A stock of one product can be replenished instantaneously upon order. Demand occurs at the constant rate of 50 items per unit time. A fixed cost of $400 is incurred each time an order is placed. Although shortage is allowed, it is the company's policy that the shortage quantity does not exceed 20 units. In the meantime, because of budget limitation, no more than 200 units can be ordered at a time. Find the relationship between the implied holding cost and shortage cost per unit under optimal conditions.

☐ **13-5** In Problem 13-2 suppose that quantity discount is allowed so that the purchasing cost per unit is 10 for any quantity less than or equal to $q = 300$ and 8 for any quantity above this limit. Find the economic lot size. What is the economic lot size if instead the breaking point occurs at $q = 500$?

☐ **13-6** In the deterministic model with instantaneous stock replenishment, no shortage, and constant demand rate; suppose that the holding cost per unit is given by h_1 for quantities below q and h_2 for quantities above q, $h_1 > h_2$. Find the economic lot size in this case.

☐ **13-7** Four different items are kept in store for continuous use in a certain manufacturing process. The demand rates are constant for the four items. Shortage is not allowed and the stock may be replenished instantaneously upon request. Let D_i be the annual amount demanded for the ith item, $i = 1, 2, 3, 4$. Using the regular symbols introduced in the chapter, the data of the problem are given by

Item i	K_i	β_i	h_i	D_i
1	100	10	.1	10,000
2	50	20	.2	5,000
3	90	5	.2	7,500
4	20	10	.1	5,000

Find the economic lot sizes for the four products assuming that the total number of orders per year (for the four items) cannot exceed 200 orders.

☐ **13-8** Solve Problem 13-7 assuming that there is a limit $C = \$10,000$ on the amount of capital to be invested in the inventory at any time. Let c_i be the cost per unit of the ith item where $c_i = 10, 5, 10, 10$, for $i = 1, 2, 3, 4$, respectively. Disregard the restriction on the number of orders per year.

☐ **13-9** Solve Example 13·3-2 assuming an initial inventory $x_1 = 4$.

☐ **13-10** Solve Example 13·3-2 using the backward recursive equation of dynamic programming.

☐ **13-11** Solve the following 4-period deterministic inventory problem.

Period i	Demand ξ_i	Setup cost K_i	Holding cost h_i
1	5	5	1
2	7	7	1
3	11	9	1
4	3	7	1

The purchasing cost per unit is 1 for the first 6 units and 2 for any number in excess of that.

☐ **13-12** Solve the following 10-period deterministic inventory problem.

Period i	Demand ξ_i	Purchasing cost c_i	Holding cost h_i	Setup cost K_i
1	150	6	1	100
2	100	6	1	100
3	20	4	2	100
4	40	4	1	200
5	70	6	2	200
6	90	8	3	200
7	130	4	1	300
8	180	4	4	300
9	140	2	2	300
10	50	6	1	300

Assume an initial inventory of 50 units.

□ **13-13** Solve the following 5-period deterministic inventory problem using the modified forward algorithm.

Period i	Demand ξ_i	Holding cost h_i	Setup cost K_i
1	50	1	80
2	70	1	70
3	100	1	60
4	30	1	80
5	60	1	60

The ordering cost function specifies a cost of 20 per unit for the first 30 items and 10 per unit for any additional units (quantity discount).

□ **13-14** Solve Problem 13-12 assuming a constant purchasing cost $c_i = 6$ for all the periods. Identify the planning horizons and the subhorizons for the problem.

□ **13-15** Show that the solution of Example 13·3-5 is optimal by showing that the optimality condition of the transportation technique (Section 5·2·2) is satisfied for the given solution.

□ **13-16** An item is manufactured to meet a known demand for four periods. The following table summarizes the costs and demand information for the problem.

Production range in number of units	Production cost per unit in			
	Period 1	Period 2	Period 3	Period 4
1 to 3	1	2	2	3
4 to 11	1	4	5	4
12 to 15	2	4	7	5
16 to 25	5	6	10	7
Holding cost per unit to next period	2	5	3	—
Total demand	11	4	17	29

Find the optimal solution indicating the number of units to be produced in each of the four periods. Suppose 10 additional units are needed in period 4, in which periods should they be produced?

☐ **13-17** The demand for a certain product for the next five periods may be filled by regular production, overtime production and subcontracting. Subcontracting can only be used if the overtime capacity is not sufficient. The following data give the supply and demand figures for the five periods.

Period i	Maximum number of supply units			Demand
	Regular time	Overtime	Subcontracting	
1	100	50	30	153
2	40	60	80	300
3	90	80	70	159
4	60	50	20	134
5	70	50	100	203

The production cost is the same for each period and is given by 1, 2, and 3 per unit for the regular time, overtime, and subcontracting, respectively. The holding cost from period i to period $i + 1$ is 0.5. A penalty cost of 2 per unit per period is incurred for late delivery. Find the optimal solution. (Hint: This problem requires the use of backordering.)

□ **13-18** The demand for an item during a single period occurs according to a negative exponential distribution with mean 10. Assuming that the demand occurs instantaneously at the beginning of the period and that the per unit holding and penalty costs for the period are 1 and 3, respectively. The purchasing costs is 2 per unit. Find the optimal order quantity given an initial inventory of 2 units. What is the optimal order quantity if the initial inventory is 5 units?

□ **13-19** For the discrete case derivation given in Section 13·4·1·1, prove that at the optimal solution

$$P\{\xi \leq y\} \geq \frac{p-c}{p+h}.$$

□ **13-20** Solve Problem 13-18 assuming that the demand occurs according to a Poisson distribution with mean 10.

□ **13-21** The purchasing cost per unit of a product is $10 and its holding cost per unit per period is $1. If the order quantity is 4 units, find the permissible range of p under optimal conditions given the following demand p.d.f.

ξ	0	1	2	3	4	5	6	7	8
$\phi(\xi)$	.05	.1	.1	.2	.25	.15	.05	.05	.05

□ **13-22** Suppose in Problem 13-18 it is found that the penalty cost p cannot be estimated easily. Consequently, it is decided to determine the order quantity such that the probability of shortage is at most equal to 0.1. What is the order quantity in this case? Assuming that all the remaining parameters are as given in Problem 13-18, what is the implied penalty cost under optimal conditions?

□ **13-23** Consider a one period inventory model with zero setup cost and zero initial inventory. Let c be the ordering cost per unit and let r and v be the selling price and salvage value per unit, respectively ($v < c < r$). The demand ξ is described by a *discrete* p.d.f., $\phi(\xi)$. Find the expression for the total *profit* equation as a function of the ordering quantity and derive the condition for selecting the optimal value. Assume zero holding and penalty costs.

□ **13-24** Solve Problem 13-18 assuming that the demand occurs uniformly over the period.

□ **13-25** Solve Problem 13-20 assuming that the demand occurs uniformly over the period. First derive the condition for the optimal order quantity given discrete demand units.

□ **13-26** Solve Problem 13-21 assuming that the demand occurs uniformly over the period.

☐ **13-27** Find the optimal ordering policy for a one period model with instantaneous demand given that the demand occurs according to the following p.d.f.,

$$\phi(\xi) = \begin{cases} 1/5, & 5 \le \xi \le 10, \\ 0, & \text{otherwise.} \end{cases}$$

The cost parameters are $h = 1.0$, $p = 5.0$, and $c = 3.0$ and the setup cost is $K = 5.0$. Assume an initial inventory of 10 units. What is the general ordering policy in this case?

☐ **13-28** Repeat Problem 13-27 assuming

$$\phi(\xi) = \begin{cases} e^{-\xi}, & \xi > 0, \\ 0, & \text{otherwise,} \end{cases}$$

and a zero initial inventory.

☐ **13-29** In the single period model of Section 13·4·1·1, suppose instead that the profit is to be maximized. Given r is the selling price per unit and using the information in Section 13·4·1·1, develop an expression for the total expected *profit* and find the optimal order quantity.

Suppose $r = 3$, $c = 2$, $p = 4$, $h = 1$. If a setup cost $K = 10$ is included in the above problem, find the optimal ordering policy given that the p.d.f. of demand is uniform for $0 \le \xi \le 10$.

☐ **13-30** Consider a one period model where it is desired to maximize the expected profit per period. The demand occurs instantaneously at the *end* of the period. Let r and v be the per unit selling price and salvage value respectively. Using the same notation of the chapter, develop the expression for the expected profit and then find the optimal solution. Assume that the unfilled demand at the end of the period is lost.

☐ **13-31** Consider a *two* period probabilistic inventory model with backlog and zero delivery lag. Let the demand p.d.f. be given by

$$\phi(\xi) = \begin{cases} 1/10, & 0 \le \xi \le 10, \\ 0, & \text{otherwise.} \end{cases}$$

The cost parameters per unit are

> selling price $= 2$,
> purchasing price $= 1$,
> holding cost $= 0.1$,
> penalty cost $= 3$,
> discount factor $= 0.8$.

Find the optimal ordering policy which will maximize the expected profit over the two periods. Use the dynamic programming formulation.

☐ **13-32**   By expanding the recursive equation for the infinite horizon model in Section 13·4·2·1, show that $f(x)$ is concave. Hence there exists a single critical number y^* for all the periods.

☐ **13-33**   Consider an infinite horizon probabilistic inventory model for which the demand p.d.f. per period is given by

$$\phi(\xi) = \begin{cases} 0.08\xi, & 0 \le \xi \le 5, \\ 0, & \text{otherwise.} \end{cases}$$

The per unit parameters of the problem are

$$\begin{aligned} &\text{selling price} = 10, \\ &\text{purchasing price} = 8, \\ &\text{penalty cost} = 1, \\ &\text{discount factor} = 0.9. \end{aligned}$$

Find the optimal ordering policy which maximizes the expected profit given that the unfilled demand is backlogged and that the delivery lag is equal to zero.

☐ **13-34**   Solve Problem 13-31 assuming no backlog.

☐ **13-35**   Solve Problem 13-33 assuming no backlog.

☐ **13-36**   Consider an infinite horizon inventory model. Rather than developing the optimal policy based on maximization of profit, it is developed based on minimization of expected costs. Using the regular symbols in the chapter, find the expected cost expression and then derive the optimal solution. Assume,

$$\begin{aligned} &\text{holding cost for } x \text{ units} = hx^2, \\ &\text{penalty cost for } x \text{ units} = px^2. \end{aligned}$$

Also assume that there is no delivery lag and that all the unfilled demand is backlogged.

Show that for the special case where $h = p$, the optimal solution is independent of the specific p.d.f. of the demand.

☐ **13-37**   Repeat Problem 13-36 assuming no backlog of the unfilled demand. In this case, however, when $h = p$, the optimal solution still depends on the p.d.f. of the demand.

☐ **13-38**   Consider a five-period probabilistic inventory model with backlogged demand. Given there is a delivery lag of three periods and the p.d.f. of the demand per period is negative exponential with mean one, give a detailed procedure of how the order quantities for periods 4 and 5 can be determined. Assume, for simplicity, that the receipts for periods 1, 2, and 3 are all equal to zero and that the initial inventory at the beginning of period 1 is equal to x_1.

☐ **13-39** Consider an infinite horizon probabilistic inventory model with the following p.d.f. for the demand per period,

$$\phi(\xi) = \begin{cases} e^{-\xi}, & \xi > 0, \\ 0, & \text{otherwise.} \end{cases}$$

If the parameters are $r = 10$, $c = 5$, $p = 15$, $h = 1$, and $\alpha = 0.9$, find the optimal policy assuming that backlog is allowed and that there is a delivery lag of exactly two periods.

☐ **13-40** Find the expected cost in Problem 13-36 assuming no backlog and a delivery lag of exactly two periods.

☐ **13-41** Solve Example 13·4-5 assuming that the p.d.f. of the demand during lead time is given by

$$f(x) = \begin{cases} 1/50, & 0 \le x \le 50, \\ 0, & \text{otherwise.} \end{cases}$$

All the other parameters remain the same as in the Example.

☐ **13-42** Find the optimal solution for the continuous review model of Section 13·4·3 assuming $f(x)$ is normal with mean 100 and variance 4. Assume that $D = 10,000$, $h = 2$, $p = 4$, and $K = 20$.

☐ **13-43** In problem 13-41 suppose

$$f(x) = \begin{cases} 1/10, & 20 \le x \le 30, \\ 0, & \text{otherwise,} \end{cases}$$

with all the other parameters remaining unchanged. Compare the values of R^* and y^* in this problem with those of Problem 13-41 and interpret the result. (Hint: In both problems $E\{x\}$ is the same but the variance in this problem is smaller.)

CHAPTER 14

Queueing Theory

§ 14·1
Introduction

A queueing situation is basically characterized by a flow of customers arriving randomly at one or more service facilities. The customer upon arrival at the facility may be serviced immediately or, if willing, may have to experience waiting time until the facility is made available. The service time allocated to each customer may be fixed or random depending on the type of service.

Situations of this type exist in every-day life. A typical example occurs in a barbershop. Here the arriving individuals are the customers and the barbers are the servers. Another example is represented by letters arriving at a typist's desk. Again, the letters represent the customers and the typist represents the server. A third example is illustrated by a machine breakdown situation. A broken machine represents a customer calling for the service of a repairman. It is noticed from these examples that the term "customer" may be interpreted in a variety of ways. It is also noticed that a service may be performed either by moving the server to the customer or the customer to the server.

Such service facilities are difficult to schedule "optimally" because of the presence of the randomness element in the arrival and service patterns. A mathematical theory has thus evolved which provides means for analyzing such situations. This is queueing (or waiting line) theory which is based on describing the arrival and/or departure (service) patterns by the appropriate probability distributions. Operating characteristics of the queueing situation are then derived using the results of probability theory. Examples of these characteristics are the expected waiting time until a customer completes his service or the percentage of idle time per server. The availability of such measures enables the analyst to make inferences concerning the operation of the system. The parameters of the system (such as the service rate) may then be adjusted to ensure a more effective utilization both from the viewpoint of the customer and the server.

It is often desirable to base decisions concerning the effectiveness of a queueing situation on some type of cost analysis. For example, an increase in the number of servers in the system would eventually decrease the expected waiting time but would also increase the cost of service. On the other hand, a decrease in the number of servers would increase the expected waiting time time but would also decrease the cost of service. Thus, if one can express the expected waiting time in monetary values, it is possible to select the "optimum" number of servers (or service rate) which minimizes the sum of the costs of service and waiting time. Although this approach is theoretically sound, difficulties generally arise in practice when estimating the cost per unit waiting time. In most cases, these costs are so subtle that a reliable estimate is practically impossible. With such cases, one may have to resort to another criterion for reaching a decision. This point is discussed in more detail in Section 14·9.

The above discussion indicates that queueing theory cannot be categorized as an optimization technique. Rather, it is an analytical tool which provides the analyst with more effective information about the problem. The procedure for dealing with a queueing problem may thus be summarized in the following four steps.

1. Define and relate the variables of the situation in order to describe the problem.
2. Derive the associated distributions based on available data and using the appropriate statistical tests.
3. Use the distributions to develop the operating characteristics which describe the system as a whole.
4. Improve the performance of the system through the use of the appropriate decision models and based on the operating characteristics of the situation.

In this chapter, the main attention is directed toward developing queueing models under different conditions of arrival and departure. This will begin by presenting the basic axioms governing the behavior of elementary queueing models. These axioms lead to the so-called Poisson queues in which arrivals and departures occur according to Poisson distributions. Other models which do not strictly follow the basic Poisson axioms (called non-Poisson queues) will also be presented.[1] The presentation of the queueing models will be followed by a discussion of the queueing decision models and the use of simulation as an alternative tool to mathematical modeling. The last section will then present a case study of a practical queueing situation. This case study will encompass all the basic steps of analyzing a real queueing problem.

Experience has shown that a lack of knowledge of the basic assumptions and derivations of queueing formulas usually leads to erroneous applications.

---

[1] A more sophisticated analysis of non-Poisson queues based on Markov chains theory will also be presented in Chapter 15.

This chapter will thus follow the procedure of first presenting the basic model together with a summary of its main results. The method of deriving these results will then be presented separately so that the interested reader may be able to follow the details of the derivation. These derivations may be skipped, however, without any loss of continuity.

§ 14·2
Basic Definitions and Notations

Figure 14–1 depicts the basic elements of a queueing system. A queueing system is defined to include the waiting line (or queue) and the service channels. Thus the number of customers in the *system* at any point in time is given by the number in *queue* plus the number in *service*. Several basic definitions and notations will now be introduced for use throughout this chapter.

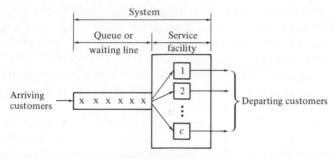

Figure 14–1

Schematic Representation of a Queueing System with *c* Parallel Servers.

§ 14·2·1
Characteristics of Queueing Models

A queueing system is specified completely by six main characteristics.

1. Input or arrival (interarrival) distribution.
2. Output or departure (service) distribution.
3. Service channels.
4. Service discipline.
5. Maximum number of customers allowed in the system.
6. Calling source.

Each of these characteristics will now be explained.

The arrival and departure distributions determine the pattern by which the *number* of customers arrive at and leave from the system, respectively.

Arrivals can also be described using the *interarrival* time which defines the time period between two successive arrivals. Similarly, departures can be described using the service (inter-departure) time which defines the time between the commencements of two successive services. These distributions are usually determined by sampling from the actual situation (see Section 14·10 for an illustration).

Service channels may be arranged in parallel or in series or as a more complex combination of both. This naturally depends on the design of the service mechanism of the system. In the case of parallel channels, several customers may be serviced simultaneously. For the series channels, a customer must pass successively through all the channels before his service is completed. A queueing model is called a one-server model when the system has one server only and a multiple-server model when the system has a number of parallel channels each with one server. Models can also be constructed for series and network-like situations. The analysis in these last cases, however, is not as simple as in the single-server and the multiple-server models.

Service discipline is a rule for selecting customers from the queue to start service. The most common discipline is the "first come, first served" rule where customers are admitted to start service in the strict order of their arrivals. Other disciplines include, "last come, first served" rule, "random selection" rule, and "priority selection" rule. The last case occurs when an arriving customer is given higher priority for service over some of the other customers that are already in the system.

The maximum number in the system can be either finite or infinite depending on the design of the facility. For example, in some facilities, only a limited number of customers are allowed to wait in the system. In this case newly arriving customers are not permitted to join the queue as long as its maximum limit has been reached. This case is to be differentiated from the case of *balking* where a customer refuses to join the queue because it is too long.

Finally, the calling source (or population) represents an important factor in queueing theory analysis since the arrival pattern is dependent on the source from which these arrivals are generated. The calling source generating the arrivals may be finite or infinite. A finite source exists when the occurrence of an arrival affects the rate of arrival of potential future customers. An example occurs in machine repair situations where there are a total of M machines. Before any machine is broken, the calling source will consist of M potential customers. Once a machine is broken, it becomes a calling customer and hence incapable of generating another call until it is serviced (repaired). Distinction must be made between this and another case where the "cause" for generating the calls is limited, yet this limited cause is capable of generating an infinite number of arrivals. For example, in a typing pool, the number of users is limited, yet each user could theoretically generate an infinite number of arrivals (typing material).

§ 14·2·2
Kendall's Notation for Representing Queueing Models

D. Kendall (1953) has introduced a useful notation for multiple-server queueing models which describes the first three characteristics given in Section 14·2·1 above; namely, the arrival distribution, the departure distribution, and the number of parallel service channels. Later, A. Lee (1966) added the fourth and the fifth characteristics to the notation; that is, the service discipline and the maximum number in the system. In this book, the Kendall Lee notation will be augmented by the sixth characteristic describing the calling source. The complete notation thus appears in the following symbolic form:

$$(a/b/c):(d/e/f)$$

where,

"a" represents the arrival (or interarrival) distribution,
"b" represents the departure (or service time) distribution,
"c" represents the number of parallel service channels in the system,
"d" represents the service discipline,
"e" represents the maximum number allowed in the system (in service + waiting),
"f" represents the calling source.

The following conventional codes are usually used to replace the symbols "a", "b" and "d",

Symbols "a" and "b"

$M \equiv$ Poisson arrival or departure distributions (or equivalently exponential interarrival or service times distributions).
$D \equiv$ Deterministic interarrival or service times.
$E_k \equiv$ Erlangian or gamma interarrival or service time distribution.
$GI \equiv$ General independent distribution of arrivals (or interarrival times).
$G \equiv$ General distribution of departures (or service times).

Symbol "d"

$FCFS \equiv$ First come, first served.
$LCFS \equiv$ Last come, first served.
$SIRO \equiv$ Service in random order.
$GD \equiv$ General service discipline.

The symbol "c" is replaced by any positive number representing the number of parallel servers. The symbols "e" and "f" represent finite or infinite numbers in the system and calling source, respectively.

To illustrate the use of this notation, consider, $(M/M/c):(FCFS/N/\infty)$. This denotes Poisson arrival (exponential interarrival), Poisson departure (exponential service time), c parallel servers, "first come, first served" service discipline, a maximum allowable number N in the system, and an infinite calling source.

It is noticed that this notation is not suitable for describing complex models such as queues in series or network queues. It will be suitable, however, for the purpose of the material presented here and the reader should find it helpful in comparing the different models.

§ 14·2·3
Definition of Transient and Steady States

Queueing theory analysis involves the study of a system's behavior over time. A system is said to be in "transient state" when its operating characteristics (behavior) are dependent on time. This usually occurs at the early stages of the operation of the system where its behavior is still dependent on the initial conditions. However, since one is mostly interested in the "long-run" behavior of the system, most attention in queueing theory analysis has been directed toward "steady state" results. A steady state condition is said to prevail when the behavior of the system becomes independent of time.

A necessary condition for the steady state to be reached is that the elapsed time since the start of the operation becomes sufficiently large (in mathematical terms, this is equivalent to saying that the elapsed time tends to infinity). This condition, however, is not sufficient since the parameters of the system may not permit the existence of a steady state. This means that the parameters of the system must also be checked. For example, in some situations if the arrival rate of the system is larger than its service rate, a steady state cannot be reached regardless of the length of the elapsed time. In fact, in this case the queue length will increase with time and theoretically it could build up to infinity.

In this text only the steady state analysis will be considered. Although transient state solutions are available for some models, the complex mathematical tools required to derive these solutions are beyond the scope of this book. The difference-differential equations which can be used for deriving transient solutions will be presented, however.

§ 14·2·4
Symbols

The following symbols will be used in connection with queueing models. The reader is reminded that a queueing *system* is defined to include both the *queue* and the *service channels*. (See Figure 14–1.)

$n =$ number of units in the *system*.

$p_n(t) =$ transient state probabilities of exactly n customers in the system at time t assuming that the system has started its operation at time zero.

$p_n =$ steady state probabilities of exactly n customers in the system.

$\lambda =$ mean arrival rate (number of customers arriving per unit time).

$\mu =$ mean service rate per busy server (number of customers served per unit time).

$c =$ number of parallel servers.

$\rho = \dfrac{\lambda}{\mu} =$ traffic intensity.

$\dfrac{\rho}{c} =$ utilization factor for c service facilities.

$w(\tau) =$ p.d.f. of waiting time in the system.

$W_s =$ expected waiting time per customer in the system.

$W_q =$ expected waiting time per customer in the queue.

$L_s =$ expected number of customers in the system.

$L_q =$ expected number of customers in the queue.

§ 14·2·5
Relationships between W_s, W_q, L_s, and L_q

It can be proved[2] under rather general conditions of arrival, departure, and service discipline that the formulas,

$$L_s = \lambda W_s$$

and

$$L_q = \lambda W_q,$$

will hold in general. These formulas act as key points in establishing the strong relationships between W_s, W_q, L_s, and L_q which can be found as follows. By definition,

$$W_q = W_s - \frac{1}{\mu}.$$

Thus, multiplying both sides by λ and substituting from the above formulas, one gets

$$L_q = L_s - \rho.$$

---

[2] J. D. C. Little, "A Proof of the Queueing Formula: $L = \lambda W$," *Operations Research*, 9, 383–387 (1961). See also, W. S. Jewell, "A Simple Proof of $L = \lambda W$," *Operations Research*, 15, 1109–1116 (1967).

This means that in general a knowledge of one of the four expected values (together with λ and μ) should immediately yield the other three values.

In queueing models, it is usually easier to determine L_s (or L_q) from the knowledge of p_n; namely

$$L_s = \sum_{n=0}^{\infty} n p_n$$

and

$$L_q = \sum_{n=c}^{\infty} (n - c)p_n .$$

On the other hand, a direct evaluation of W_s and W_q may not be as simple. In this case, given L_s (or L_q), the above general formulas can be used to determine W_s and W_q.

The given relationships do not hold directly for the special cases where arrivals occur with a rate λ but not all arrivals join the system (for example, in the cases where the maximum allowable queue length is reached, no new arrivals are allowed to join the queue). However, by redefining λ to include only those arrivals that join the system, these relationships can be made to hold. Thus, letting λ_{eff} define the effective arrival rate, the value of λ_{eff} can be conveniently determined from

$$L_q = L_s - \frac{\lambda_{\text{eff}}}{\mu}$$

or

$$\lambda_{\text{eff}} = \mu(L_s - L_q).$$

(In some models, it may be possible to determine λ_{eff} directly from the parameters of the problem.) Once λ_{eff} is known, then from the general formulas,

$$W_s = \frac{L_s}{\lambda_{\text{eff}}}$$

$$W_q = \frac{L_q}{\lambda_{\text{eff}}} .$$

§ 14·3
Axiomatic Derivation of the Arrivals and Departures Distributions for Poisson Queues

In this section, the arrival and departure distributions for Poisson queues are derived. First, the basic axioms governing this type of queue will be stated.

§ 14·3·1
Basic Axioms

Axiom 1: Given $N(t)$ the number of arrivals or departures during the time interval $(0, t)$, the probability process describing $N(t)$ has stationary independent increments.

This axiom is explained as follows. Given h, a positive increment, then for $t_0 < t_1 < \cdots < t_k$, $(k + 1)$ points in time, the two random variables $\{N(t_{i+1}) - N(t_i)\}$ and $\{N(t_{i+1} + h) - N(t_i + h)\}$, $i = 0, 1, \ldots, k - 1$, are independent and identically distributed.

Axiom 2: In any interval of time $h > 0$, there is a positive probability of arrival (departure) but this probability is not certain; that is, $0 < P\{N(h) = 1\} < 1$.

Axiom 3: In a sufficiently small interval of time, at most one arrival (departure) can occur; that is, $P\{N(h) \geq 2\} = 0$.

These axioms will be used now to derive the distributions of arrivals and departures.

§ 14·3·2
Distribution of Arrivals (Pure Birth Model)

In this model it is assumed that only arrivals are allowed at the rate λ per unit time. This case is sometimes referred to as the pure birth model. It is assumed that there is no one in the system at $t = 0$. The arrivals distribution can thus be developed as follows.

The above axioms imply that the probability of one arrival during $h\,(> 0)$, a small increment in time, is equal to $\lambda h + 0(h^2)$, where $0(h^2)$ is a term of much smaller order of magnitude than λh and hence will tend to zero as $h \to 0$.[3] By Axiom 3, the probability of more than one arrival approaches zero as $h \to 0$. This means that the probability of no arrivals during h is approximately equal to $(1 - \lambda h)$, where by Axiom 2, $0 < 1 - \lambda h < 1$.

Consider the probabilities $p_n(t)$ and $p_n(t + h)$ of n customers in the system at times t and $t + h$, respectively. Figure 14–2 shows all possible changes in the number in the system between times t and $t + h$. Thus, for $n > 0$, the system will have n customers at $t + h$ if, (a) there are n customers at t and no arrivals occur during h, or (b) there are $n - 1$ customers at t and one arrival occurs during h. For $n = 0$, the system will have no customers at

---

[3] Consider $p_0(t + h)$. By Axiom 1, $p_0(t + h) = p_0(t) \cdot p_0(h)$, where $p_0(h) > 0$ by Axiom 2. This yields the general solution $p_0(t) = \exp(-\lambda t)$, where λ is a positive constant. (See Ref. [3] of Chapter 12, pp. 121–123, for the proof.) Thus,

$$p_0(h) = 1 - \lambda h + (\lambda h)^2 / 2! - \ldots = 1 - \lambda h + 0\,(h^2)$$

And by Axiom 3, $p_1(h) = 1 - p_0(h) = \lambda h + 0\,(h^2)$.

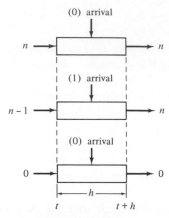

(0) arrival

$n \longrightarrow$ ☐ $\longrightarrow n$

(1) arrival

$n-1 \longrightarrow$ ☐ $\longrightarrow n$

(0) arrival

$0 \longrightarrow$ ☐ $\longrightarrow 0$

$\longleftarrow h \longrightarrow$

$t \qquad\qquad t+h$

Figure 14–2

$t + h$ if there are no customers at t and no arrivals occur during h. Since by Axiom 1, all the probabilities are independent and identically distributed, then

$$p_n(t + h) \cong p_n(t)(1 - \lambda h) + p_{n-1}(t)\lambda h, \quad n > 0,$$
$$p_0(t + h) \cong p_0(t)(1 - \lambda h), \quad n = 0.$$

Rearranging the terms, one gets

$$\frac{p_n(t + h) - p_n(t)}{h} \cong -\lambda p_n(t) + \lambda p_{n-1}(t),$$

$$\frac{p_0(t + h) - p_0(t)}{h} \cong -\lambda p_0(t).$$

Taking the limits as $h \to 0$, then

$$p_n'(t) = -\lambda p_n(t) + \lambda p_{n-1}(t),$$
$$p_0'(t) = -\lambda p_0(t),$$

where $p_n'(t)$ is the first derivative $p_n(t)$ with respect to time, t.

The resulting equations are called difference-differential equations and their solution is given by

$$p_n(t) = \frac{(\lambda t)^n e^{-\lambda t}}{n!}, \qquad n = 0, 1, 2, \ldots,$$

which is Poisson with its expected value being equal to (λt). This means that under the basic axioms of Section 14·3·1, arrivals occur according to a Poisson distribution.

Derivation of the Results[4]

The above two differential equations can be solved directly by induction (see Problem 14-4). The z-transform introduced in Section 12·11 will be used, however, to solve these two equations. Thus, applying this to the first equation, one gets

$$\sum_{n=1}^{\infty} p_n'(t)z^n = - \sum_{n=1}^{\infty} \lambda p_n(t)z^n + \sum_{n=1}^{\infty} \lambda p_{n-1}(t)z^n.$$

Adding the second equation, then

$$\sum_{n=0}^{\infty} p_n'(t)z^n = - \sum_{n=0}^{\infty} \lambda p_n(t)z^n + \sum_{n=1}^{\infty} \lambda p_{n-1}(t)z^n.$$

Letting

$$P(z, t) = \sum_{n=0}^{\infty} p_n(t)z^n$$

then

$$P'(z, t) = \frac{d}{dt} \sum_{n=0}^{\infty} p_n(t)z^n = \sum_{n=0}^{\infty} p_n'(t)z^n.$$

The z-transform equation thus becomes,

$$P'(z, t) = -\lambda P(z, t) + \lambda z P(z, t)$$

or

$$\frac{dP(z, t)}{P(z, t)} = \lambda(z - 1)\, dt.$$

Solving this differential equation in t, this gives

$$P(z, t) = Be^{\lambda(z-1)t},$$

where B is a constant. Since

$$P(z, 0) = p_0(0) = 1,$$

then $B = 1$. This yields

$$P(z, t) = e^{\lambda(z-1)t}.$$

Using the inverse z-transform (Table 12–1, Formula 11), then

$$Z^{-1}\{P(z, t)\} = Z^{-1}\{e^{\lambda(z-1)t}\}$$

$$= e^{-\lambda t}Z^{-1}\{e^{\lambda tz}\}.$$

---

[4] In this model and the subsequent models, derivation of the results may be skipped without loss of continuity.

This gives,

$$p_n(t) = \frac{e^{-\lambda t}(\lambda t)^n}{n!}, \qquad n = 0, 1, 2, \ldots,$$

which is Poisson with its mean and variance equal to (λt).

§ 14·3·3
Distribution of Interarrival Times

Interarrival times are defined as the time intervals between two successive arrivals. Given the arrival distribution is Poisson, one can derive the inter-arrival times as follows. Let $f(t)$, $t > 0$, be the p.d.f. of interarrival times and define $F(t)$ as the C.D.F. of $f(t)$. Thus

$$F(t) = \int_0^t f(u)\,du.$$

Having no arrivals during the interval $(0, t)$ is equivalent to having an inter-arrival time greater than t. This means,

$$p_0(t) = \int_t^\infty f(u)\,du,$$

$$= 1 - \int_0^t f(u)\,du$$

$$= 1 - F(t).$$

From the results of Section 14·3·2, since

$$p_0(t) = e^{-\lambda t},$$

then,

$$e^{-\lambda t} = 1 - F(t).$$

Differentiating $F(t)$ with respect to t gives

$$f(t) = \begin{cases} \lambda e^{-\lambda t}, & t > 0, \\ 0, & t \leq 0. \end{cases}$$

This shows that for Poisson arrivals, the distribution of interarrival time is exponential with mean $1/\lambda$ and variance $1/\lambda^2$.

The exponential distribution has the unique property that, at any point in time, the time until the next arrival occurs is independent of the time that has elapsed since the occurrence of the last arrival. This is equivalent to saying that

$$P\{t > T + S \,|\, t > S\} = P\{t > T\}.$$

To show this, consider

$$P\{t > T + S \mid t > S\} = \frac{P\{t > T + S, t > S\}}{P\{t > S\}}$$

$$= \frac{P\{t > T + S\}}{P\{t > S\}}$$

$$= \frac{e^{-\lambda(T+S)}}{e^{-\lambda S}}$$

$$= e^{-\lambda T},$$

which is independent of S. This property is usually referred to as "lack of memory" or "forgetfulness" of the exponential distribution.

§ 14·3·4
Distribution of Departures (Pure Death Model)

In this model it is assumed that there are N customers in the system at $t = 0$. It is also assumed that no arrivals can occur in the system. Departures occur at the rate μ per unit time. The objective then is to derive the distribution of departures from this system based on the axioms of Section 14·3·1.

For small $h > 0$, $\mu h + 0(h^2)$ gives the probability of one departure during h. Using the same argument as in Section 14·3·2, the term $0(h^2) \to 0$ as $h \to 0$ and hence it can be neglected. It again follows that the probability of no departure is approximately $1 - \mu h$. Hence

$$p_N(t + h) \cong p_N(t)(1 - \mu h), \qquad\qquad n = N,$$

$$p_n(t + h) \cong p_n(t)(1 - \mu h) + p_{n+1}(t)\mu h, \qquad 0 < n < N,$$

$$p_0(t + h) \cong p_0(t) \cdot 1 + p_1(t)\mu h, \qquad\qquad n = 0.$$

Rearranging the terms and taking the limits as $h \to 0$, this gives

$$p_N'(t) = -\mu p_N(t), \qquad\qquad n = N,$$

$$p_n'(t) = -\mu p_n(t) + \mu p_{n+1}(t), \qquad 0 < n < N,$$

$$p_0'(t) = \mu p_1(t), \qquad\qquad n = 0.$$

The solution of these equations yields

$$p_n(t) = \frac{(\mu t)^{N-n} e^{-\mu t}}{(N - n)!}, \qquad n = 1, 2, \ldots, N,$$

$$p_0(t) = 1 - \sum_{n=1}^{N} p_n(t),$$

which is a truncated Poisson distribution.

Derivation of the Results:

Because the z-transform does not yield a simple solution for this case, the above three equations will be solved by induction.

From the equation for $n = N$,

$$p'_N(t) = -\mu p_N(t),$$

which gives the solution,

$$p_N(t) = Be^{-\mu t}, \quad B \text{ constant.}$$

From initial conditions $p_N(0) = 1$, hence $B = 1$, or

$$p_N(t) = e^{-\mu t}$$

From the equation for $0 < n < N$, letting $n = N - 1$ and substituting for $p_N(t) = e^{-\mu t}$, then

$$p'_{N-1}(t) = -\mu p_{N-1}(t) + \mu p_N(t)$$
$$= -\mu p_{N-1}(t) + \mu e^{-\mu t}.$$

Again, solving this differential equation, one gets[5]

$$p_{N-1}(t) = e^{-\mu t}\left(\int \mu e^{-\mu t}e^{\mu t}dt + B\right)$$
$$= (\mu t + B)e^{-\mu t}$$

Since $p_{N-1}(0) = 0$, $B = 0$, and

$$p_{N-1}(t) = \mu t e^{-\mu t}.$$

Similarly, for $n = N - 2$,

$$p'_{N-2}(t) + \mu p_{N-2}(t) = \mu^2 t e^{-\mu t},$$

which after accounting for the initial conditions gives,

$$p_{N-2}(t) = \frac{e^{-\mu t}(\mu t)^2}{2!}.$$

In general, it can be proved by induction that,

$$p_{N-i}(t) = \frac{e^{-\mu t}(\mu t)^i}{i!}, \quad i = 0, 1, \ldots, N - 1,$$

---

[5] The general differential equation of the form

$$y' + a(t)y = b(t)$$

has the solution

$$y = e^{-\int a(t)dt}\{\int b(t)e^{\int a(t)dt}dt + \text{Constant}\}$$

or, letting $N - i = n$, then

$$p_n(t) = \frac{(\mu t)^{N-n} e^{-\mu t}}{(N-n)!}, \qquad n = 1, 2, \ldots, N.$$

For $n = 0$ the differential equation,

$$p_0'(t) = \mu p_1(t) = \mu \frac{(\mu t)^{N-1} e^{-\mu t}}{(N-1)!},$$

will give by successive integration by parts,

$$p_0(t) = 1 - \sum_{n=1}^{N} \frac{(\mu t)^{N-n} e^{-\mu t}}{(N-n)!}$$

$$= 1 - \sum_{n=1}^{N} p_n(t).$$

This result also follows since,

$$\sum_{n=0}^{N} p_n(t) = 1.$$

§ 14·3·5
Distribution of Service Times

Let $g(t)$ be the p.d.f. of service times. To derive $g(t)$ for the Poisson departure case, it is noticed that the probability of no services during the period $(0, T)$ is equivalent to the probability of having no departures during the same period. Thus

$$P\{\text{service time, } t > T\} = P\{\text{no departures during } T\},$$

or

$$1 - \int_0^T g(t)\, dt = p_N(T) = e^{-\mu T}.$$

Hence

$$\int_0^T g(t)\, dt = 1 - e^{-\mu T}.$$

This gives by differentiation,

$$g(t) = \begin{cases} \mu e^{-\mu t}, & t > 0, \\ 0, & t \le 0, \end{cases}$$

which shows that the service time distribution is exponential with mean $1/\mu$ and variance $1/\mu^2$.

§ 14·4
Poisson Queueing Models

The results of Section 14·3 indicate that the given axioms lead to Poisson arrivals (exponential interarrival time) and exponential service time (Poisson departures). These, as mentioned earlier, are the distributions describing Poisson queues. In this section, a number of Poisson queues with different characteristics are presented. These characteristics will be summarized for each model using Kendall's notation presented in Section 14·2·2.

§ 14·4·1
$(M/M/1) : (FCFS/\infty/\infty)$

This model, called birth and death model, combines the pure birth and pure death models given in Section 14·3·2 and 14·3·4. This means that arrivals and departures will be allowed in this model. The model, as indicated by Kendall's notation, assumes that there is only one server and that the queue length and the calling source are unlimited.

The difference-differential equations describing this model are derived as follows. The probability that there are n (> 0) in the system at time $t + h$ is approximately the sum of

  (i) $P\{n$ in the system at t, and no arrivals and no departures during $h\}$

$$\cong p_n(t)\{(1 - \lambda h)(1 - \mu h)\},$$

  (ii) $P\{n$ in the system at t, and one arrival and one departure during $h\}$

$$\cong p_n(t)\{(\lambda h)(\mu h)\},$$

  (iii) $P\{n - 1$ in the system at t, and one arrival and no departures during $h\}$

$$\cong p_{n-1}(t)\{(\lambda h)(1 - \mu h)\},$$

  (iv) $P\{n + 1$ in the system at t, and no arrivals and one departure during $h\}$

$$\cong p_{n+1}(t)\{(1 - \lambda h)(\mu h)\}.$$

Thus, adding the four probabilities and realizing that the terms in h^2 imply the occurrence of two simultaneous events during h and hence will tend to zero as h becomes sufficiently small, then, for $n > 0$,

$$p_n(t + h) \cong p_n(t)\{1 - \lambda h - \mu h\} + p_{n-1}(t)(\lambda h) + p_{n+1}(t)(\mu h).$$

Similarly, for $n = 0$

$$p_0(t + h) \cong p_0(t)\{(1 - \lambda h) \cdot 1\} + p_1(t)(\mu h)(1 - \lambda h)$$

$$= p_0(t)(1 - \lambda h) + p_1(t)(\mu h).$$

Taking the limits as $h \to 0$, the above two equations give

$$p'_n(t) = \lambda p_{n-1}(t) + \mu p_{n+1}(t) - (\lambda + \mu)p_n(t), \qquad n > 0,$$

$$p'_0(t) = -\lambda p_0(t) + \mu p_1(t), \qquad\qquad\qquad n = 0.$$

The solution of the above two equations should yield $p_n(t)$, the transient probabilities. As mentioned earlier, these results require complex mathematical tools and consequently they will not be presented here. The reader may refer to Saaty [4] for the detailed derivation of $p_n(t)$.

The steady state solution can be proved to exist as $t \to \infty$ when $\lambda < \mu$; that is,

$$\rho = \frac{\lambda}{\mu} < 1.$$

Consequently, assuming that this restriction holds, the steady state equations are obtained by recognizing that as $t \to \infty$, $p'_n(t) \to 0$ and $p_n(t) \to p_n$, for $n = 0, 1, 2, \ldots$. This immediately yields,

$$-\lambda p_0 + \mu p_1 = 0, \qquad n = 0,$$

$$\lambda p_{n-1} + \mu p_{n+1} - (\lambda + \mu)p_n = 0, \qquad n > 0.$$

The solution of these difference equations yields

$$p_n = (1 - \rho)\rho^n, \qquad n = 0, 1, 2, \ldots,$$

where $\rho = \lambda/\mu < 1$. This is a geometric distribution with mean,

$$E\{n\} = \frac{\rho}{1 - \rho},$$

and variance,

$$\mathrm{Var}\{n\} = \frac{\rho}{(1 - \rho)^2}.$$

The measures L_s, L_q, W_s, and W_q are derived from the general formulas of Section 14·2·4 and are given by

$$L_s = E\{n\} = \frac{\rho}{1 - \rho},$$

$$L_q = L_s - \frac{\lambda}{\mu} = \frac{\rho^2}{1 - \rho},$$

$$W_s = \frac{L_s}{\lambda} = \frac{1}{\mu(1 - \rho)},$$

$$W_q = \frac{L_q}{\lambda} = \frac{\rho}{\mu(1 - \rho)}.$$

An alternative method for deriving W_s is given in Section 14·4·1·1.

Derivation of the Results:

The above difference equations can be written as

$$(\rho + 1)p_n = \rho p_{n-1} + p_{n+1}, \qquad n > 0,$$
$$(\rho + 1)p_0 = p_0 + p_1, \qquad n = 0.$$

The z-transform for the two equations is given by

$$(\rho + 1)P(z) = \rho z P(z) + \frac{1}{z} P(z) + \left(\frac{z-1}{z}\right)p_0.$$

This yields

$$P(z) = \left\{\frac{z}{(z-1) - \rho z(z-1)}\right\}\left\{\frac{z-1}{z}\right\}p_0$$

$$= \left\{\frac{1}{1 - \rho z}\right\}p_0.$$

From Table 12–1, the inverse z-transform is given by

$$Z^{-1}\{P(z)\} = p_0 Z^{-1}\left\{\frac{1}{1 - \rho z}\right\}$$

$$= p_0 \rho^n,$$

or

$$p_n = p_0 \rho^n, \qquad n = 0, 1, 2, \ldots.$$

The value of p_0 is determined by recognizing that $\sum_{n=0}^{\infty} p_n = 1$. Thus

$$p_0 \sum_{n=0}^{\infty} \rho^n = p_0 \frac{1}{1 - \rho} = 1$$

or

$$p_0 = (1 - \rho).$$

It is noticed that $\sum_{n=0}^{\infty} \rho^n$ converges only if $\rho < 1$ which ascertains the steady state requirements mentioned earlier. This finally gives

$$p_n = (1 - \rho)\rho^n, \qquad n = 0, 1, 2, \ldots.$$

The mean $E\{n\} = L_s$ can be obtained from the basic definition of the expected value or from the properties of the z-transform. From Section 12·11·1 (Property 4),

$$E\{n\} = P'(1)$$

$$= p_0\left\{\frac{\rho}{(1 - \rho z)^2}\right\}\Bigg|_{z=1} = \frac{\rho p_0}{(1 - \rho)^2}.$$

Since $p_0 = (1 - \rho)$, hence

$$L_s = E\{n\} = \frac{\rho}{1 - \rho}.$$

§ 14·4·1·1
Waiting Time Distribution for *FCFS* Service Discipline

Let τ be the amount of time a person *just arriving* must wait in the *system*; that is, until his service is completed. Based on *FCFS* service discipline, if an arriving customer finds n persons ahead of him in the system, then,

$$\tau = t_1' + t_2 + \cdots + t_{n+1}$$

where t_1' is the time for the customer actually in service to complete his service and $t_2, t_3, \ldots, t_n$ are the service times for the $n - 1$ customers in queue. The time t_{n+1} thus represents the service time for the arriving customer.

Let $w(\tau \mid n + 1)$ be the conditional p.d.f. of τ given n customers in the system ahead of the arriving customer. Since t_i, for all i, is exponentially distributed, then by the forgetfulness property, t_1' will also have the same exponential distribution as $t_2, t_3, \ldots$, and t_{n+1}. Consequently, τ is the sum of $n + 1$ identically distributed and independent exponential distributions. This means that $w(\tau \mid n + 1)$ is gamma distributed with parameters $(\mu, n + 1)$ (see Example 12·9–1). Thus,

$$w(\tau) = \sum_{n=0}^{\infty} w(\tau \mid n + 1)p_n$$

$$= \sum_{n=0}^{\infty} \frac{\mu(\mu\tau)^n e^{-\mu\tau}}{n!} (1 - \rho)\rho^n$$

$$= (1 - \rho)\mu e^{-\mu\tau} \sum_{n=0}^{\infty} \frac{(\lambda\tau)^n}{n!}$$

$$= \mu(1 - \rho)e^{-\mu(1-\rho)\tau}, \qquad \tau > 0,$$

which is an exponential distribution with mean

$$E\{\tau\} = \frac{1}{\mu(1 - \rho)}.$$

The mean $E\{\tau\}$ is actually equal to W_s, the expected waiting time in the system.

§ 14·4·2
$(M/M/1):(SIRO/\infty/\infty)$

In this section, the same model as in Section 14·4·1 will be considered with the exception that the service discipline will follow the *SIRO*-rule ("Service in Random Order") instead of the *FCFS*-rule. It is noticed first that the derivation of p_n for the $(M/M/1):(FCFS/\infty/\infty)$ model does not depend on any specific service discipline. It can thus be concluded that for the *SIRO*-rule case,

$$p_n = (1 - \rho)\rho^n \qquad n = 0, 1, 2, \ldots.$$

Consequently, whether the service discipline follows the *SIRO*-rule or the *FCFS*-rule, the expected number in the system $L_s \, (= E\{n\})$ will be the same for the two cases. In fact, L_s will remain the same for any service discipline provided, of course, p_n remains unchanged. It thus follows that $W_s = L_s/\lambda$ under the *SIRO*-rule is the same as under the *FCFS*-rule and hence it is given by

$$W_s = \frac{1}{\mu(1 - \rho)}.$$

The above result is verified below by deriving the waiting time distribution based on the explicit use of the *SIRO*-discipline. Although it is not easy to derive a convenient form for the p.d.f. of the waiting time, the analysis can be used to show that the expected waiting time is the same as that under the *FCFS*-rule. The same result can be extended to any queue discipline as long as p_n remains unchanged. Specifically, this result applies to the three most common disciplines, *FCFS*, *LCFS*, and *SIRO*. It does not apply, however, to queueing models with priorities since such service discipline results in a change of the structure of the model and hence in a different expression for p_n (see Section 14·6). The only difference between the three service disciplines (*FCFS*, *LCFS*, and *SIRO*) thus occurs in the distribution of the waiting time where the probabilities of long and short waiting times change depending upon the discipline used. This means that while the expected value of the distribution remains the same, its variance changes.

Following the above discussion, the symbol *GD* (general discipline) will be used to represent the disciplines *FCFS*, *LCFS*, and *SIRO*. If, however, the waiting time distribution is derived, then the specific discipline governing the model will be indicated. Also in the case of priority queues, the exact discipline will be specified.

Derivation of the Results:

The expected value of the waiting time in the system will now be derived based on the *SIRO*-rule. It is more convenient, however, to compute W_q first from which W_s can be readily determined using the formulas of Section 14·2·5.

Let $R(T|n)$ be the probability that a specified customer which arrived when there were *n other* customers in the *queue*, is still in the queue time T later.[6] It can be arbitrarily assumed that the customer arrived at time $t = 0$. Thus, mathematically,

$$R(T|n) = P\{\xi > T \mid n \text{ customers are in the } queue \text{ at } t = 0\},$$

---

[6] Contrary to the general notation of the chapter where *n* is used to represent the number in the *system*, *n* will be used in this derivation to describe the number in the *queue*.

where ξ is the random variable describing the waiting time in the queue. The changes in R will now be studied given that the specified customer joins the queue at instant $t = h$ later instead of at $t = 0$. The following events may thus occur during h.

(i) An additional customer arrives with probability λh and the probability the specified customer waits at least $T - h$ is $R(T - h\,|\,n + 1)$. This event thus occurs with probability $(\lambda h)\,R(T - h\,|\,n + 1)$.

(ii) A customer finishes service with probability (μh), one of the *other* customers (selected randomly) begins service with probability $(n/n + 1)$, and the specified customer waits at least $(T - h)$ with probability $R(T - h\,|\,n - 1)$. Thus, the probability of this event is

$$(\mu h)\left(\frac{n}{n+1}\right)R(T - h\,|\,n - 1).$$

(iii) No arrivals and no services with probability $\{1 - (\lambda + \mu)h\}$ and the specified customer waits at least $(T - h)$ with probability $R(T - h\,|\,n)$. This event occurs with probability $\{1 - (\lambda + \mu)h\}R(T - h\,|\,n)$.

Combining these probabilities, one gets

$$R(T\,|\,n) = (\lambda h)R(T - h\,|\,n + 1) + \left(\frac{n}{n+1}\right)(\mu h)R(T - h\,|\,n - 1)$$

$$+ \{1 - (\lambda + \mu)h\}R(T - h\,|\,n), \qquad n > 0.$$

$$R(T\,|\,0) = (\lambda h)R(T - h\,|\,1) + \{1 - (\lambda + \mu)h\}R(T - h\,|\,0), \qquad n = 0.$$

Rearranging the terms and taking the limits as $h \to 0$, gives,

$$R'(T\,|\,n) = \left(\frac{n}{n+1}\right)\mu R(T\,|\,n - 1) + \lambda R(T\,|\,n + 1) - (\lambda + \mu)R(T\,|\,n) \qquad n > 0,$$

$$R'(T\,|\,0) = \lambda R(T\,|\,1) - (\lambda + \mu)R(T\,|\,0), \qquad n = 0.$$

Let $R(T)$ be the (absolute) probability that the specified customer waits at least T in the queue (before starting service). Then following an argument similar to the one in Section 14·4·1·1, one gets

$$R(T) = \sum_{n=0}^{\infty} p_{n+1}R(T\,|\,n).$$

(Notice that having n customers in the *queue* is equivalent to having $(n + 1)$ customers in the system.) Thus substituting for p_{n+1}, then

$$R(T) = (1 - \rho)\sum_{n=0}^{\infty} \rho^{n+1}R(T\,|\,n),$$

The explicit determination of $R(T\,|\,n)$ from the above differential equations is not at all simple. However, the expected waiting time in the queue, W_q, can be determined as follows. By definition (see Section 12·6·2)

$$W_q = \int_0^\infty R(T)\, dt$$

$$= (1 - \rho) \sum_{n=0}^\infty \rho^{n+1} \int_0^\infty R(T \mid n)\, dT.$$

Now, multiplying both sides of the above differential equations by

$$\frac{(n + 1)\rho^{n+1}}{\mu}$$

and then summing over n from 0 to ∞, then

$$\frac{1}{\mu} \sum_{n=0}^\infty (n + 1)\rho^{n+1} R'(T \mid n) = \sum_{n=1}^\infty n\rho^{n+1} R(T \mid n - 1) + \sum_{n=0}^\infty \rho^{n+2}(n + 1)$$

$$\times R(T \mid n + 1) - (1 + \rho) \sum_{n=0}^\infty (n + 1)\rho^{n+1} R(T \mid n).$$

Integrating both sides over T from 0 to ∞, the left member gives,

$$\frac{1}{\mu} \sum_{n=0}^\infty (n + 1)\rho^{n+1} \int_0^\infty R'(T \mid n)\, dT = \frac{1}{\mu} \sum_{n=0}^\infty (n + 1)\rho^{n+1} \int_0^\infty dR(T \mid n)$$

$$= -\frac{1}{\mu} \sum_{n=0}^\infty (n + 1)\rho^{n+1}$$

$$= -\frac{\rho}{\mu} \frac{d}{d\rho} \sum_{n=0}^\infty \rho^n$$

$$= \frac{-\rho}{\mu(1 - \rho)^2}$$

On the other hand, the right member gives

$$\sum_{n=1}^\infty n\rho^{n+1} \int_0^\infty R(T \mid n - 1)\, dT + \sum_{n=0}^\infty \rho^{n+2}(n + 1) \int_0^\infty R(T \mid n + 1)\, dT$$

$$- (1 + \rho) \sum_{n=0}^\infty (n + 1)\rho^{n+1} \int_0^\infty R(T \mid n)\, dT$$

$$= \sum_{n=0}^\infty (n + 1)\rho^{n+2} \int_0^\infty R(T \mid n)\, dT + \sum_{n=1}^\infty n\rho^{n+1} \int_0^\infty R(T \mid n)\, dT$$

$$- (1 + \rho) \sum_{n=0}^\infty (n + 1)\rho^{n+1} \int_0^\infty R(T \mid n)\, dT$$

$$= -\sum_{n=0}^\infty \rho^{n+1} \int_0^\infty R(T \mid n)\, dT$$

$$= -\frac{1}{1 - \rho} W_q,$$

where the last expression is obtained from the above definition of W_q. Thus, equating the left and the right members, this gives

$$-\frac{\rho}{\mu(1-\rho)^2} = -\frac{1}{(1-\rho)}\, W_q,$$

or

$$W_q = \frac{\rho}{\mu(1-\rho)}.$$

Hence

$$W_s = W_q + \frac{1}{\mu} = \frac{1}{\mu(1-\rho)},$$

which is the same result obtained under *FCFS* rule.

§ 14·4·3
$(M/M/1):(GD/N/\infty)$

This model is essentially the same as the model in Section 14·4·1 except that the maximum number in the system is limited to N (maximum queue length = $N - 1$). Since the waiting time distribution is not derived in this model, the GD service discipline is used to indicate that the obtained results are applicable to any of the three common service disciplines.

By comparison with the $(M/M/1):(FCFS/\infty/\infty)$, Section 14·4·1, the steady state equations for this model are given by,

$$-\rho p_0 + p_1 = 0, \qquad n = 0,$$
$$-(1 + \rho)p_n + p_{n+1} + \rho p_{n-1} = 0, \qquad 0 < n < N,$$
$$-p_N + \rho p_{N-1} = 0, \qquad n = N.$$

The solution of these difference equations is given by

$$p_n = \left(\frac{1-\rho}{1-\rho^{N+1}}\right)\rho^n, \qquad n = 0, 1, 2, \ldots, N.$$

It is noticed in this case that ρ need *not* be less than 1. This result can be verified mathematically as shown below. Intuitively, this can be interpreted as follows. The number allowed in the system is controlled by the maximum queue length, $N - 1$, and not by the relative rates of arrival and departure. Consequently, the arrival rate, λ, does not affect the steady state conditions of the system.

The expected number in the system is given by

$$L_s = \frac{\rho\{1 - (N+1)\rho^N + N\rho^{N+1}\}}{(1-\rho)(1-\rho^{N+1})}.$$

The other measures L_q, W_s, and W_q can be derived from L_s using the formulas in Section 14·2·5. It is noticed, however, that because there is a queue limit, some customers are lost. Consequently, it is necessary first to compute λ_{eff}, the effective arrival rate of the system. Since the probability that a customer is lost is given by p_N, then

$$\lambda_{\text{eff}} = \lambda(1 - p_N).$$

It follows that

$$W_q = \frac{L_q}{\lambda_{\text{eff}}} = \frac{L_q}{\lambda(1 - p_N)},$$

$$L_s = L_q + \frac{\lambda_{\text{eff}}}{\mu} = L_q + \frac{\lambda(1 - p_N)}{\mu},$$

$$W_s = W_q + \frac{1}{\mu} = \frac{L_s}{\lambda(1 - p_N)}.$$

The value of λ_{eff} can also be obtained using the formula given in Section 14·2·5, namely

$$\lambda_{\text{eff}} = \mu(L_s - L_q).$$

This is left as an exercise for the reader (see Problem 14-14).

Derivation of the Results:
The above steady state difference equations can be written as

$$(1 + \rho)p_0 = p_1 + p_0, \qquad n = 0,$$

$$(1 + \rho)p_n = p_{n+1} + \rho p_{n-1}, \qquad 0 < n < N,$$

$$(1 + \rho)p_N = \rho p_{N-1} + \rho p_N, \qquad n = N.$$

Taking the z-transform of these equations, one gets

$$(1 + \rho) \sum_{n=0}^{N} z^n p_n = \sum_{n=0}^{N-1} p_{n+1} z^n + \rho \sum_{n=1}^{N} p_{n-1} z^n + p_0 + \rho p_N z^N.$$

Since $p_n = 0$ for $n > N$, one gets after simplification,

$$(1 + \rho)P(z) = \frac{1}{z}\{P(z) - p_0\} + \rho z\{P(z) - p_N z^N\} + p_0 + \rho p_N z^N,$$

or

$$P(z) = p_0\left(\frac{1}{1 - \rho z}\right) - \rho p_N\left(\frac{z^{N+1}}{1 - \rho z}\right).$$

Taking the inverse z-transform, then from Formula 7, Table 12–1,

$$Z^{-1}\left\{\frac{p_0}{1 - \rho z}\right\} = p_0 \rho^n, \qquad n = 0, 1, 2, \ldots, N,$$

and from Formula 1 in the same table,

$$Z^{-1}\left\{\rho p_N\left(\frac{z^{N+1}}{1-\rho z}\right)\right\} = \begin{cases} 0, & n = 0, 1, 2, \ldots, N, \\ p_N \rho^{n-N}, & n = N+1, N+2, \ldots. \end{cases}$$

Thus, combining the two terms,

$$p_n = \begin{cases} p_0 \rho^n, & n = 0, 1, \ldots, N \\ p_0 \rho^n - p_N \rho^{n-N}, & n = N+1, N+2, \ldots. \end{cases}$$

Since

$$(p_0 \rho^n - p_N \rho^{n-N}) = (p_0 \rho^n - p_0 \rho^N \rho^{n-N}) = 0,$$

then,

$$p_n = p_0 \rho^n, \qquad n = 0, 1, \ldots, N.$$

The value of p_0 can be determined from[7]

$$p_0 \sum_{n=0}^{N} \rho^n = p_0\left(\frac{1 - \rho^{N+1}}{1 - \rho}\right) = 1,$$

or

$$p_0 = \left(\frac{1-\rho}{1-\rho^{N+1}}\right).$$

Hence

$$p_n = \left(\frac{1-\rho}{1-\rho^{N+1}}\right)\rho^n, \qquad n = 0, 1, 2, \ldots, N.$$

Consequently,

$$L_s = E\{n\} = \sum_{n=0}^{N} n p_n$$

$$= \frac{(1-\rho)}{(1-\rho^{N+1})} \sum_{n=0}^{N} n\rho^n$$

$$= \frac{(1-\rho)}{(1-\rho^{N+1})} \rho \frac{d}{d\rho}\left(\frac{1-\rho^{N+1}}{1-\rho}\right)$$

$$= \frac{\rho\{1 - (N+1)\rho^N + N\rho^{N+1}\}}{(1-\rho)(1-\rho^{N+1})}$$

after simplification. This expression can be derived readily from the z-transform expression. (See Problem 14-15.)

---

[7] Given $S = 1 + \rho + \rho^2 + \cdots + \rho^N$, then $\rho S = \rho + \rho^2 + \cdots + \rho^{N+1}$. Thus

$$S - S\rho = 1 - \rho^{N+1}, \quad \text{or} \quad S = \frac{1 - \rho^{N+1}}{1-\rho}.$$

Notice that the derivation does not require ρ to be less than one.

§ 14·4·4
$(M/M/c):(GD/\infty/\infty)$

So far only Poisson queues with one server have been considered. In this section, a model with c parallel servers ($c \geq 1$) is considered so that c customers may be in service at the same time. It is assumed that all the channels have the same (exponential) service distribution with mean rate μ per unit time. The derivation of the differential equations for this model is the same as in the single server model except that the probability of a service during an instant h is approximately $n\mu h$ for $n < c$ and $c\mu h$ for $n \geq c$.[8] Thus,

$$p_0(t+h) = 1 \cdot (1 - \lambda h)p_0(t) + \mu h(1 - \lambda h)p_1(t), \qquad n = 0,$$

$$p_n(t+h) = \lambda h(1 - (n-1)\mu h)p_{n-1}(t) + (n+1)\mu h(1 - \lambda h)p_{n+1}(t)$$
$$+ (1 - \lambda h)(1 - n\mu h)p_n(t), \qquad 0 < n < c,$$

$$p_c(t+h) = \lambda h(1 - (c-1)\mu h)p_{c-1}(t) + (1 - \lambda h)(c\mu h)p_{c+1}(t)$$
$$+ (1 - \lambda h)(1 - c\mu h)p_c(t), \qquad n = c,$$

$$p_n(t+h) = \lambda h(1 - c\mu h)p_{n-1}(t) + (1 - \lambda h)(c\mu h)p_{n+1}(t)$$
$$+ (1 - \lambda h)(1 - c\mu h)p_n(t), \qquad n > c.$$

Taking the limit as $h \to 0$, one gets

$$p_0'(t) = \mu p_1(t) - \lambda p_0(t), \qquad\qquad n = 0,$$

$$p_n'(t) = \lambda p_{n-1}(t) - (\lambda + n\mu)p_n(t) + (n+1)\mu p_{n+1}(t), \qquad 0 < n < c,$$

$$p_n'(t) = \lambda p_{n-1}(t) - (\lambda + c\mu)p_n(t) + c\mu p_{n+1}(t), \qquad n \geq c,$$

Assuming that the parameters of the system are such that a steady state solution exists, the steady state equations are obtained from the above differential equations as $t \to \infty$. This yields

$$-\lambda p_0 + \mu p_1 = 0, \qquad n = 0,$$

$$\lambda p_{n-1} - (\lambda + n\mu)p_n + (n+1)\mu p_{n+1} = 0, \qquad 0 < n < c,$$

$$\lambda p_{n-1} - (\lambda + c\mu)p_n + c\mu p_{n+1} = 0, \qquad n \geq c.$$

---

[8] Since the probability of one service is approximately μh, the probability that one out of n ($n \leq c$) services are completed during h follows a binomial distribution and is given by

$$\binom{n}{1}(\mu h)(1 - \mu h)^{n-1} \cong n\mu h.$$

The steady state solution is then given by

$$p_n = \begin{cases} \left(\dfrac{\rho^n}{n!}\right) p_0, & 0 \le n \le c, \\[2ex] \left(\dfrac{\rho^n}{c^{n-c}c!}\right) p_0, & n > c, \end{cases}$$

where

$$p_0 = \left\{ \sum_{n=0}^{c-1} \frac{\rho^n}{n!} + \frac{\rho^c}{c!\left(1 - \dfrac{\rho}{c}\right)} \right\}^{-1}$$

and

$$\frac{\rho}{c} < 1 \quad \text{or} \quad \frac{\lambda}{\mu c} < 1.$$

Also

$$L_q = \frac{\rho^{c+1}}{(c-1)!(c-\rho)^2} p_0$$

$$= \left(\frac{c\rho}{(c-\rho)^2}\right) p_c,$$

$$L_s = L_q + \rho,$$

$$W_q = \frac{L_q}{\lambda},$$

$$W_s = W_q + \frac{1}{\mu}.$$

It is noted that for $c = 1$, the above results reduce to those of the $(M/M/1):(GD/\infty/\infty)$ model given in Section 14·4·1.

The computations associated with this model may be tedious.[9] Morse ([4], p. 103) gives two approximations for p_0 and L_q which may be useful under the special conditions given below.

For ρ much smaller than one,

$$p_0 \to 1 - \rho,$$

$$L_q \to \frac{\rho^{c+1}}{c^2},$$

---

[9] See Appendix C for a general computer subroutine which computes the probabilities and the operating characteristics for all the Poisson models presented in this chapter.

and as $(\rho/c) \to 1$,

$$p_0 \to \frac{(c - \rho)(c - 1)!}{c^c},$$

$$L_q \to \frac{\rho}{c - \rho}.$$

Derivation of the Results:

The induction method will be used to derive the results of this model. The reader is asked in Problem 14-17 to obtain the same solution by the *z*-transform.

Let $n + 1 = k$, then for $0 < n < c$, the difference equations become

$$p_k = \frac{1}{k}\{(\rho + (k - 1))p_{k-1} - \rho p_{k-2}\}, \qquad 2 \le k \le c,$$

and also the difference equation corresponding to $n \ge c$ becomes,

$$p_k = \frac{1}{c}\{(\rho + c)p_{k-1} - \rho p_{k-2}\}, \qquad k \ge c + 1.$$

These two equations can now be used in the induction procedure.

From the difference equation for $n = 0$,

$$p_1 = \rho p_0.$$

Letting $k = 2$ in the first equation above, then

$$p_2 = \tfrac{1}{2}\{(1 + \rho)\rho p_0 - \rho p_0\}$$

$$= \frac{\rho^2}{2}\, p_0.$$

Applying induction proof to the first equation above, one finally gets,

$$p_n = \frac{\rho^n}{n!}\, p_0, \qquad 0 \le n \le c.$$

Continuing with the second equation above, then for $k = c + 1$,

$$p_{c+1} = \frac{1}{c}\{(\rho + c)p_c - \rho p_{c-1}\}.$$

Substituting for p_{c-1} and p_c in terms of p_0, then

$$p_{c+1} = \frac{p_0}{c}\left\{(\rho + c)\frac{\rho^c}{c!} - \frac{\rho^c}{(c - 1)!}\right\}$$

$$= \frac{\rho^{c+1}}{c(c!)}\, p_0.$$

Again, by induction

$$p_n = \frac{\rho^n}{c^{n-c}c!}\, p_0, \qquad n > c,$$

The value of p_0 is determined from

$$\sum_{n=0}^{\infty} p_n = \left(\sum_{n=0}^{c} \frac{\rho^n}{n!} + \sum_{n=c+1}^{\infty} \frac{\rho^n}{c^{n-c}c!} \right) p_0 = 1,$$

which gives the value of p_0 directly as

$$p_0 = \left\{ \sum_{n=0}^{c-1} \frac{\rho^n}{n!} + \frac{\rho^c}{c!} \sum_{n=c}^{\infty} \frac{\rho^{n-c}}{c^{n-c}} \right\}^{-1}$$

$$= \left\{ \sum_{n=0}^{c-1} \frac{\rho^n}{n!} + \frac{\rho^c}{c!} \sum_{j=0}^{\infty} \left(\frac{\rho}{c} \right)^j \right\}^{-1}$$

$$= \left\{ \sum_{n=0}^{c-1} \frac{\rho^n}{n!} + \frac{\rho^c}{c!} \left(\frac{1}{1 - \frac{\rho}{c}} \right) \right\}^{-1},$$

provided $(\rho/c) < 1$.

The expression for L_q is obtained as follows.

$$L_q = \sum_{n=c}^{\infty} (n - c)p_n$$

$$= \sum_{k=0}^{\infty} k p_{k+c}$$

$$= \sum_{k=0}^{\infty} \frac{k \rho^{k+c}}{c^k c!} p_0$$

$$= p_0 \frac{\rho^c}{c!} \frac{\rho}{c} \sum_{k=0}^{\infty} k \left(\frac{\rho}{c} \right)^{k-1}$$

$$= p_0 \frac{\rho^c}{c!} \frac{\rho}{c} \left(\frac{1}{\left(1 - \frac{\rho}{c}\right)^2} \right)$$

$$= \left(\frac{\rho^{c+1}}{(c-1)!(c-\rho)^2} \right) p_0$$

$$= \left(\frac{c\rho}{(c-\rho)^2} \right) p_c$$

§ 14·4·5
$(M/M/c):(GD/N/\infty)$, $c < N$

In this model, it is assumed that the maximum number in the system is limited by N, where $N > c$. The derivation of the differential equations is the same as in the $(M/M/c):(GD/\infty/\infty)$ model presented in Section 14·4·4 except that a fourth equation is needed to account for the limit on the number in the system. Thus the steady state equations are given by

$$\mu p_1 - \lambda p_0 = 0, \qquad n = 0,$$

$$(n + 1)\mu p_{n+1} + \lambda p_{n-1} - (n\mu + \lambda)p_n = 0, \qquad 0 < n < c,$$

$$c\mu p_{n+1} + \lambda p_{n-1} - (c\mu + \lambda)p_n = 0, \qquad c \le n < N,$$

$$\lambda p_{N-1} - c\mu p_N = 0, \qquad n = N.$$

The solution of these difference equations is given by

$$p_n = \begin{cases} \dfrac{\rho^n}{n!}\, p_0, & 0 \le n \le c, \\[3ex] \dfrac{\rho^n}{c!\, c^{n-c}}\, p_0, & c \le n \le N, \end{cases}$$

where

$$p_0 = \left\{ \sum_{n=0}^{c} \frac{\rho^n}{n!} + \sum_{n=c+1}^{N} \frac{\rho^n}{c!\, c^{n-c}} \right\}^{-1}$$

$$= \left\{ \sum_{n=0}^{c-1} \frac{\rho^n}{n!} + \frac{\rho^c \left(1 - \left(\dfrac{\rho}{c} \right)^{N-c+1} \right)}{c! \left(1 - \dfrac{\rho}{c} \right)} \right\}^{-1},$$

and ρ/c is not necessarily less than 1. Notice that the difference between this model and the one in Section 14·4·4 occurs only in the expression for p_0. Also,

$$L_q = p_0 \frac{\rho^{c+1}}{(c-1)!(c-p)^2} \left\{ 1 - \left(\frac{\rho}{c} \right)^{N-c} - (N-c)\left(\frac{\rho}{c} \right)^{N-c} \left(1 - \frac{\rho}{c} \right) \right\},$$

$$L_s = L_q + (c - \bar{c})$$

$$= L_q + \frac{\lambda_{\text{eff}}}{\mu},$$

$$W_q = \frac{L_q}{\lambda_{\text{eff}}},$$

$$W_s = \frac{L_s}{\lambda_{\text{eff}}},$$

where

$$\bar{c} = \text{expected number of idle servers}$$

$$= \sum_{n=0}^{c} (c - n)p_n,$$

$$\lambda_{\text{eff}} = \lambda(1 - p_N)$$

$$= \mu(c - \bar{c}).$$

Notice the interpretation of λ_{eff} in this case. Since $(c - \bar{c})$ represents the expected number of busy channels, $\mu(c - \bar{c})$ should represent the actual number served per unit time and hence the effective arrival rate.

Derivation of the Results:

The expression for p_n is determined in essentially the same way as in the previous model and consequently will not be repeated here. To obtain L_q, one has

$$L_q = \sum_{n=c+1}^{N} (n - c)p_n$$

$$= \sum_{j=1}^{N-c} j p_{j+c}$$

$$= p_0 \frac{\rho^c}{c!} \frac{\rho}{c} \sum_{j=1}^{N-c} j \left(\frac{\rho}{c}\right)^{j-1}$$

$$= p_0 \frac{\rho^{c+1}}{(c-1)!(c-p)^2} \left\{ 1 - \left(\frac{\rho}{c}\right)^{N-c} - (N - c)\left(\frac{\rho}{c}\right)^{N-c}\left(1 - \frac{\rho}{c}\right) \right\}.$$

To determine the expression for λ_{eff}, consider

$$L_q = \sum_{n=c+1}^{N} (n - c)p_n$$

$$= \sum_{n=0}^{N} n p_n - \sum_{n=0}^{c} n p_n - c\left(1 - \sum_{n=0}^{c} p_n\right)$$

$$= L_s - \left\{ c - \sum_{n=0}^{c} (c - n)p_n \right\}$$

$$= L_s - (c - \bar{c}),$$

or

$$L_s = L_q + (c - \bar{c}).$$

Consequently, from Section 14·2·5,

$$\lambda_{\text{eff}} = \mu(c - \bar{c}).$$

This means that the following equality must hold.

$$\lambda_{\text{eff}} = \mu(c - \bar{c}) = \lambda(1 - p_N).$$

(See Problem 14-29.)

§ 14·4·6
$(M/M/\infty):(GD/\infty/\infty)$

This model describes a situation with state dependent service rates where the number of servers is directly proportional to the number in the system. This situation is equivalent to a multiple server model except that the number of servers is unlimited in this case. Such situations may occur in self-service facilities.

The derivation of the differential equations for this model is essentially the same as in the model of Section 14·4·4, $(M/M/c):(GD/\infty/\infty)$, except that the probability of a single departure for all $n \geq 0$ is approximately $n\mu h$. Thus,

$$p_0'(t) = -\lambda p_0(t) + \mu p_1(t), \qquad n = 0,$$

$$p_n'(t) = -(\lambda + n\mu)p_n(t) + \lambda p_{n-1}(t) + (n + 1)\mu p_{n+1}(t), \qquad n \geq 1,$$

and the steady state difference equations (assuming a steady state solution exists) are given by

$$-\lambda p_0 + \mu p_1 = 0, \qquad n = 0,$$

$$-(\lambda + n\mu)p_n + \lambda p_{n-1} + (n + 1)p_{n+1} = 0, \qquad n \geq 1.$$

The solution for $p_n(t)$ is obtained from the first set of differential equations as

$$p_n(t) = \frac{e^{-\alpha}\alpha^n}{n!}, \qquad n = 0, 1, 2, \ldots,$$

where $\alpha = \rho(1 - e^{-\mu t})$. This is Poisson with mean $E\{n \mid t\} = \alpha$.

The steady state solution can be obtained either by taking the limit of $p_n(t)$ as $t \to \infty$ or by solving the above set of difference equations. This yields for any $\rho > 0$,

$$p_n = \frac{e^{-\rho}\rho^n}{n!}, \qquad n = 0, 1, 2, \ldots,$$

which is again Poisson with mean $E\{n\} = \rho$.

Also,

$$L_s = E\{n\} = \rho,$$

$$W_s = \frac{1}{\mu},$$

$$L_q = W_q = 0.$$

These results can also be obtained by taking the limit as $c \to \infty$ of the corresponding results in the $(M/M/c):(GD/\infty/\infty)$ model. It is noticed that there is no waiting time in the queue, W_q, and that the waiting time in the system, W_s, is equal to the service time. This is a conceivable result since the number of servers is always equal to the number of serviced customers.

Derivation of the Results:

Consider the z-transform of the differential equations representing the transient solution. Thus,

$$\sum_{n=0}^{\infty} p_n'(t)z^n = -\sum_{n=0}^{\infty} (\lambda + n\mu)p_n(t)z^n + \lambda \sum_{n=1}^{\infty} p_{n-1}(t)z^n + \mu \sum_{n=0}^{\infty} (n+1)p_{n+1}(t)z^n,$$

or

$$\frac{\partial}{\partial t} P(z, t) = -\lambda P(z, t) - \mu z \frac{\partial}{\partial z} P(z, t) + \lambda z P(z, t) + \mu \frac{\partial}{\partial z} P(z, t),$$

or

$$\frac{\partial}{\partial t} P(z, t) = \mu(1 - z)\frac{\partial}{\partial z} P(z, t) - \lambda(1 - z)P(z, t).$$

The solution of this partial differential equation under the initial condition $p_0(0) = 1$ should yield the transient solution given previously.

The steady state solution can be obtained from the above partial differential equation by recognizing that

$$\lim_{t \to \infty} \frac{\partial}{\partial t} P(z, t) = 0.$$

Thus as $t \to \infty$,

$$\frac{d}{dz} P(z) = \rho P(z).$$

This differential equation can also be obtained from the difference equations representing steady state.

Solving the last differential equation and using the z-transform property that

$$P(0) = p_0,$$

then

$$P(z) = p_0 e^{\rho z}.$$

From Formula 11, Table 12–1,

$$Z^{-1}\{e^{\rho z}\} = \frac{\rho^n}{n!}.$$

This yields

$$p_n = p_0 \frac{\rho^n}{n!} \qquad n = 0, 1, 2, \ldots.$$

and

$$p_0 = \left\{ \sum_{n=0}^{\infty} \frac{\rho^n}{n!} \right\}^{-1}$$
$$= e^{-\rho}.$$

Hence

$$p_n = \frac{e^{-\rho} \rho^n}{n!}, \qquad n = 0, 1, 2, \ldots.$$

Notice that the derivation of p_n does not require that ρ be less than one.

§ 14·4·7
$(M/M/R):(GD/K/K), K < R$

This model is usually referred to as the machine servicing model. The system has a total of K machines which are serviced by R repairmen. Once a machine is broken, it will remain so until it is serviced. Consequently, a broken machine cannot generate new calls while in service. This is equivalent to a finite calling source with a maximum limit of K potential customers.

In this model, the approximate probability of a single service during an instant h is $n\mu h$ for $n \leq R$ and $R\mu h$ for $n \geq R$. On the other hand, the probability of a single arrival during h is approximately $(K - n)\lambda h$ for $n \leq K$, where λ is defined in this case as the rate of breakdown *per machine*. Thus,

$$p_0(t + h) = p_0(t)(1 - K\lambda h) + p_1(t)\mu h\{1 - (K - 1)\lambda h\}, \qquad n = 0,$$

$$p_n(t + h) = p_n(t)\{1 - (K - n)\lambda h\}(1 - n\mu h)$$
$$+ p_{n-1}(t)\{(K - n + 1)\lambda h\}\{1 - (n - 1)\mu h\}$$
$$+ p_{n+1}(t)\{1 - (K - n - 1)\lambda h\}\{(n + 1)\mu h\}, \qquad 0 < n < R,$$

$$p_R(t + h) = p_R(t)\{1 - (K - R)\lambda h\}\{1 - R\mu h)$$

$$+ p_{R+1}(t)\{1 - (K - (R + 1))\lambda h\}(R\mu h)$$

$$+ p_{R-1}(t)\{(K - (R - 1))\lambda h\}\{1 - (R - 1)\mu h\}, \qquad n = R,$$

$$p_n(t + h) = p_n(t)\{1 - (K - n)\lambda h\}(1 - R\mu h)$$

$$+ p_{n-1}(t)\{(K - n + 1)\lambda h\}(1 - R\mu h)$$

$$+ p_{n+1}(t)\{1 - (K - n - 1)\lambda h\}(R\mu h), \qquad R < n \le K - 1,$$

$$p_K(t + h) = p_K(t)(1 - R\mu h) \cdot 1 + p_{K-1}(t)\{\lambda h(1 - R\mu h)\}, \qquad n = K.$$

Rearranging the terms and taking the appropriate limits, the steady state equations are given by,

$$K\rho p_0 = p_1, \qquad n = 0$$

$$\{(K - n)\rho + n\}p_n = (K - n + 1)\rho p_{n-1} + (n + 1)p_{n+1}, \qquad 0 < n < R$$

$$\{(K - n)\rho + R\}p_n = (K - n + 1)\rho p_{n-1} + Rp_{n+1}, \qquad R \le n \le K - 1$$

$$Rp_K = \rho p_{K-1}, \qquad n = K.$$

The steady state solution is thus given by

$$p_n = \begin{cases} \binom{K}{n}\rho^n p_0, & 0 \le n \le R \\[2ex] \binom{K}{n}\dfrac{n!\,\rho^n}{R!\,R^{n-R}}\,p_0, & R \le n \le K \end{cases}$$

where,

$$p_0 = \left\{\sum_{n=0}^{R}\binom{K}{n}\rho^n + \sum_{n=R+1}^{K}\binom{K}{n}\dfrac{n!\,\rho^n}{R!\,R^{n-R}}\right\}^{-1}.$$

The other measures are given by

$$L_q = \sum_{n=R+1}^{K}(n - R)p_n,$$

$$L_s = L_q + (R - \bar{R})$$

$$= L_q + \frac{\lambda_{\text{eff}}}{\mu},$$

$$W_q = (L_q/\lambda_{\text{eff}}),$$

$$W_s = (L_s/\lambda_{\text{eff}}),$$

where

$$\bar{R} = \text{expected number of idle repairmen}$$

$$= \sum_{n=0}^{R} (R - n)p_n,$$

$$\lambda_{\text{eff}} = \mu(R - \bar{R})$$

$$= \lambda(K - L_s).$$

The second expression for λ_{eff} is obtained as follows. Since the arrival rate given n machines in the system is $\lambda(K - n)$ (where λ is again defined as the rate of breakdown per machine), then under steady state conditions,

$$\lambda_{\text{eff}} = E\{\lambda(K - n)\}$$

$$= \lambda(K - L_s).$$

The above results apply to the case of a single repairman simply by putting $R = 1$.

Derivation of the Results:
From the first steady state difference equation,

$$p_1 = K\rho p_0.$$

Thus, letting $n = 1$ in the second difference equation, then

$$2p_2 = (K - 1)\rho p_1.$$

Using induction it can be shown that

$$(n + 1)p_{n+1} = (K - n)\rho p_n, \qquad 0 \le n < R.$$

Similarly, from the remaining two difference equations,

$$Rp_{n+1} = (K - n)\rho p_n, \qquad R \le n \le K.$$

The last two equations can be verified to give the required results for p_n.
Now,

$$L_q = \sum_{n=R+1}^{K} (n - R)p_n,$$

$$= \sum_{n=0}^{K} np_n - \left\{ R - \sum_{n=0}^{R} (R - n)p_n \right\},$$

$$= L_s - (R - \bar{R}),$$

or

$$L_s = L_q + (R - \bar{R}).$$

§ 14·5
Non-Poisson Queueing Models

The models in Section 14·4 were developed under the Poisson input-output assumptions. There exist other queueing situations, however, where arrivals and/or departures may not follow the Poisson axioms. These are called non-Poisson queues. The developments of these models are usually more complicated mainly because the Poisson axioms no longer hold. A more complete treatment of non-Poisson queues will thus be deferred until Chapter 15 where Markov chains theory is used to develop the results for $(M/G/1):(GD/\infty/\infty)$ and $(GI/M/1):(FCFS/\infty/\infty)$ models. This section, however, introduces the well-known Pollaczek-Khintchine formula for computing the expected number in the system, L_s, in a single server system with Poisson arrivals and general service time distribution. The derivation is based on the study of the $(M/G/1):(GD/\infty/\infty)$ model using elementary probability theory.

§ 14·5·1
The Pollaczek-Khintchine Formula, $(M/G/1):(GD/\infty/\infty)$

The Pollaczek-Khintchine (P-K) formula is derived for a single server situation based on the following three assumptions.

(i) Poisson arrivals with arrival rate λ.
(ii) General service time distribution with mean $E\{t\}$ and variance Var$\{t\}$.
(iii) Steady state conditions prevail with $\rho = \lambda E\{t\} < 1$.

It is shown below that under these assumptions, the (P-K) formula is given by

$$L_s = \lambda E\{t\} + \frac{\lambda^2(E^2\{t\} + \mathrm{Var}\{t\})}{2(1 - \lambda E\{t\})}.$$

Thus

$$L_q = L_s - \lambda E\{t\},$$

$$W_s = \frac{L_s}{\lambda},$$

$$W_q = \frac{L_q}{\lambda}.$$

The operating characteristics for any given service time distribution (such as gamma distributed or constant service times) can be obtained directly from the above formulas using the appropriate substitutions. It can be seen that for the exponential service time case, the above formulas reduce to those of the $(M/M/1):(GD/\infty/\infty)$ model (see Section 14·4·1).

Derivation of the Results:
Let,

$f(t)$ = service time distribution with mean $E\{t\}$ and variance $\text{Var}\{t\}$,
   n = number of customers in *the system* right after a customer departs,
   t = time to service the customer following the one that departed,
   k = number of new arrivals during t,
   n' = number of customers left behind the next departing customer.

These symbols are illustrated graphically in Figure 14–3 where T represents the time when the jth customer departs and $(T + t)$ represents the time when the next customer, $(j + 1)$st, departs. The notation $j, j + 1, \ldots$, etc., does not necessarily mean that customers are introduced into service on *FCFS* discipline. Rather, it identifies the different customers departing from the system. Thus, the results of this model should be applicable to any of the three service disciplines, *FCFS*, *LCFS*, and *SIRO*.

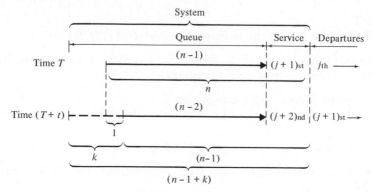

Figure 14–3

By the steady state assumption,

$$E\{n\} = E\{n'\}$$

and

$$E\{n^2\} = E\{(n')^2\}.$$

It is seen from Figure 14–3 that

$$n' = \begin{cases} k, & \text{if } n = 0, \\ n - 1 + k, & \text{if } n > 0, \end{cases}$$

Letting,

$$\delta = \begin{cases} 1, & \text{if } n = 0 \\ 0, & \text{if } n > 0 \end{cases}$$

then

$$n' = n - 1 + \delta + k.$$

Now, taking expectation of both sides,

$$E\{(n')\} = E\{n\} + E\{\delta\} + E\{k\} - 1.$$

Since $E\{n\} = E\{n'\}$, it follows that

$$E\{\delta\} = 1 - E\{k\}.$$

Also,

$$(n')^2 = \{n + (k - 1) + \delta\}^2$$

$$= n^2 + (k - 1)^2 + 2n(k - 1) + \delta^2 + 2n\delta + 2k\delta - 2\delta.$$

But by definition, $\delta^2 = \delta$ and $\delta n = 0$, hence

$$(n')^2 = n^2 + k^2 + 2n(k - 1) + \delta(2k - 1) - 2k + 1.$$

Taking expectation and realizing that $E\{(n')^2\} = E\{n^2\}$, then

$$E\{n\} = \frac{E\{k^2\} - 2E\{k\} + E\{\delta\}(2E\{k\} - 1) + 1}{2(1 - E\{k\})}.$$

Substituting for $E\{\delta\} = 1 - E\{k\}$ as obtained above, then

$$E\{n\} = \frac{E\{k^2\} - 2E\{k\} + (1 - E\{k\})(2E\{k\} - 1) + 1}{2(1 - E\{k\})}$$

$$= \frac{E\{k^2\} + E\{k\} - 2E^2\{k\}}{2(1 - E\{k\})}.$$

Now, it is necessary to determine $E\{k\}$ and $E\{k^2\}$. Since arrivals occur according to Poisson distribution, then given t,

$$E\{k \,|\, t\} = \lambda t,$$

$$E\{k^2 \,|\, t\} = (\lambda t)^2 + \lambda t.$$

Hence

$$E\{k\} = \int_0^\infty E\{k \,|\, t\} f(t) \, dt$$

$$= \int_0^\infty \lambda t f(t) \, dt$$

$$= \lambda E\{t\}.$$

Also,

$$E\{k^2\} = \int_0^\infty E\{k^2 \,|\, t\} f(t) \, dt$$

$$= \int_0^\infty \{(\lambda t)^2 + \lambda t\} f(t) \, dt$$

$$= \lambda^2 \, \text{Var}(t) + \lambda^2 E^2\{t\} + \lambda E\{t\}.$$

Thus, after simplification

$$L_s = E\{n\} = \lambda E\{t\} + \frac{\lambda^2(E^2\{t\} + \mathrm{Var}\{t\})}{2(1 - \lambda E\{t\})}.$$

Notice that $\lambda E\{t\} < 1$, otherwise L_s becomes negative and hence undefined.

§ 14·6
Queueing Models with Priorities for Service

Section 14·4·2 has investigated the effect of the three service disciplines *FCFS*, *LCFS*, and *SIRO* on the results of Poisson queueing models. This section introduces the concept of priority service discipline. It is assumed that several parallel queues are formed in front of the facility with each queue representing customers belonging to a certain priority. Let these queues be defined as queue 1, queue 2, ..., and queue m, respectively, such that queue 1 represents customers with the highest priority and queue m includes the lowest priority customers. Each queue may have its own arrival and service rates. Customers within each queue are served based on *FCFS* discipline.

Priority discipline includes two rules:

1. *Preemptive* rule where the service of a low-priority customer may be interrupted in favor of an arriving customer with higher priority.

2. *Nonpreemptive* rule where a customer, once in service, will continue until his service is completed and regardless of the priority of the arriving customer.

This section will not treat the preemptive case. Only two nonpreemptive models will be presented. These apply to single and multiple channel cases. The single channel model assumes Poisson arrival and arbitrary service distribution. In the multiple channel model both arrivals and departures are assumed to be Poisson. The symbol *NPRP* will be used with Kendall notation to represent the nonpreemptive discipline while the symbols M_i and G_i will represent Poisson and arbitrary distributions, respectively, for the ith queue.

§ 14·6·1
$(M_i/G_i/1):(NPRP/\infty/\infty)$

Let $F_i(t)$ be the C.D.F. of the arbitrary service time distribution for the ith queue $(i = 1, 2, \ldots, m)$ and let $E_i\{t\}$ and $\mathrm{Var}_i\{t\}$ be the mean and variance, respectively. Let λ_i be the arrival rate at the ith queue per unit time.

Define $L_q^{(k)}$, $L_s^{(k)}$, $W_q^{(k)}$, and $W_s^{(k)}$ in the usual manner except that they now represent the measures of the kth queue. Then, the results of this situation are given by

$$W_q^{(k)} = \frac{\sum_{i=1}^{m} \lambda_i(E_i^2\{t\} + \text{Var}_i\{t\})}{2(1 - S_{k-1})(1 - S_k)},$$

$$L_q^{(k)} = \lambda_k W_q^{(k)},$$

$$W_s^{(k)} = W_q^{(k)} + E_k\{t\},$$

$$L_s^{(k)} = L_q^{(k)} + \rho_k,$$

where

$$\rho_k = \lambda_k E_k\{t\},$$

$$S_k = \sum_{i=1}^{k} \rho_i < 1, \qquad k = 1, 2, \ldots, m,$$

$$S_0 \equiv 0.$$

Notice that W_q, the expected waiting time in the queue for *any* customer regardless of his priority, is given by

$$W_q = \sum_{k=1}^{m} \frac{\lambda_k}{\lambda} W_q^{(k)},$$

where $\lambda = \sum_{i=1}^{m} \lambda_i$ and λ_k/λ is the relative weight of $W_q^{(k)}$. A similar result applies to W_s.

Derivation of the Results:

Let $F(t)$ be the C.D.F. of the combined service time for the entire system and let the combined arrival rate be given by

$$\lambda = \sum_{i=1}^{m} \lambda_i.$$

Then $F(t)$ can be derived from

$$\lambda F(t) = \lambda_1 F_1(t) + \lambda_2 F_2(t) + \cdots + \lambda_m F_m(t).$$

This implies that the effective number serviced in the entire system is equal to the sum of the effective number serviced in the different priority queues. Consequently,

$$F(t) = \sum_{i=1}^{m} \frac{\lambda_i}{\lambda} F_i(t).$$

Let $E\{t\}$ and $\text{Var}\{t\}$ be the mean and variance corresponding to $F(t)$, then these values can be expressed in terms of $E_i\{t\}$ and $\text{Var}_i\{t\}$ as follows.

$$E\{t\} = \int_0^{\infty} t \, dF(t) = \sum_{i=1}^{m} \frac{\lambda_i}{\lambda} \int_0^{\infty} t \, dF_i(t) = \sum_{i=1}^{m} \frac{\lambda_i}{\lambda} E_i\{t\}.$$

Similarly

$$E\{t^2\} = \sum_{i=1}^{m} \frac{\lambda_i}{\lambda} (E_i^2\{t\} + \text{Var}_i\{t\}).$$

Using $E\{t\}$ and $E\{t^2\}$, Var $\{t\}$ can be obtained in terms of $E_i\{t\}$ and $\text{Var}_i\{t\}$.

Now, if a customer of the kth priority queue arrives at t_0 and starts service at time t_1, his waiting time in the queue is $T_q^{(k)} = t_1 - t_0$. Let $\xi_1, \xi_2, \ldots, \xi_k$ be the service times of the customers in queues 1 through k, inclusive, ahead of the arriving customer in queue k. During his waiting time $T_q^{(k)}$, other customers may arrive in queues 1 through $(k - 1)$. These customers will be serviced first and hence will increase the waiting time of the customer under consideration. Let $\xi_1', \xi_2', \ldots, \xi_{k-1}'$ be the service times of these customers. Thus, if ξ_0 is the time to finish the service of the customer already in service, and because each queue operates on *FCFS* discipline, then

$$T_q^{(k)} = \xi_0 + \sum_{i=1}^{k} \xi_i + \sum_{i=1}^{k-1} \xi_i'.$$

Taking the expectation of both sides and noticing that

$$E\{T_q^{(k)}\} = W_q^{(k)},$$

then

$$W_q^{(k)} = E\{\xi_0\} + \sum_{i=1}^{k} E\{\xi_i\} + \sum_{i=1}^{k-1} E\{\xi_i'\}.$$

By definition,

$$E\{\xi_i\} = \text{(expected number in the } i\text{th queue)} \times \text{(expected service time per customer)}$$
$$= L_q^{(i)} E_i\{t\}$$
$$= \lambda_i W_q^{(i)} E_i\{t\}$$
$$= \rho_i W_q^{(i)}$$

where $\rho_i = \lambda_i E_i\{t\}$. Similarly,

$$E\{\xi_i'\} = \text{(expected number of arrivals in the } i\text{th queue during } T_q^{(k)}) \times \text{(expected service time per customer)}$$
$$= E\{\lambda_i T_q^{(k)}\} E_i\{t\}$$
$$= \rho_i W_q^{(k)}.$$

Hence,

$$W_q^{(k)} = E\{\xi_0\} + \sum_{i=1}^{k} \rho_i W_q^{(i)} + W_q^{(k)} \sum_{i=1}^{k-1} \rho_i,$$

or

$$W_q^{(k)} = \frac{E\{\xi_0\} + \sum_{i=1}^{k} \rho_i W_q^{(i)}}{1 - S_{k-1}},$$

where,

$$S_k = \sum_{i=1}^{k} \rho_i.$$

Using induction on k, it can be shown that,

$$W_q^{(k)} = \frac{E\{\xi_0\}}{(1 - S_{k-1})(1 - S_k)}.$$

(Notice that S_k must be less than one, otherwise $W_q^{(k)}$ is undefined.)

Now for $k = 1$, the above result must reduce to the single channel queue described by $(M/G/1) ; (FCFS/\infty/\infty)$. That is,

$$W_q^{(1)} = W_q = \frac{E\{\xi_0\}}{1 - \lambda E\{t\}}.$$

(Notice that $S_1 = \lambda E\{t\}$ because all the arrivals and departures will be concentrated in one channel, where

$$\lambda = \sum_{i=1}^{m} \lambda_i$$

and $E\{t\}$ is the mean of $F(t)$.) But from the (P-K) formula (Section 14·5·1), one has for the given model,

$$W_q = \frac{\lambda(E^2\{t\} + \text{Var}\{t\})}{2(1 - \lambda E\{t\})}.$$

Thus, equating the two expressions, it follows that

$$E\{\xi_0\} = \frac{\lambda}{2}(E^2\{t\} + \text{Var}\{t\}).$$

Now, from the definition of $F(t)$ given earlier,

$$E^2\{t\} + \text{Var}\{t\} = E\{t^2\}$$

$$= \sum_{i=1}^{m} \frac{\lambda_i}{\lambda}(E_i^2\{t\} + \text{Var}_i\{t\}),$$

which by substitution in the expression for $E\{\xi_0\}$ will give the required result for $W_q^{(k)}$ directly.

It must be noticed that the queueing formulas presented in Section 14·2·5 are also applicable to the individual queues of the priority models. This means that for the kth queue,

$$L_q^{(k)} = \lambda_k W_q^{(k)}$$

and

$$L_s^{(k)} = \lambda W_s^{(k)}.$$

§ 14·6·2
(*Mᵢ/M/c*) : (*NPRP/∞/∞*)

This model assumes that all customers have the same service time distribution regardless of their priorities and that all c channels have identical exponential service distribution with service rate μ. The arrivals at the kth priority queue occur according to a Poisson distribution with an arrival rate λ_k, $k = 1$, $2, \ldots, m$. Thus using the same procedure as in the previous model, it can be shown for the kth queue that

$$W_q^{(k)} = \frac{E\{\xi_0\}}{(1 - S_{k-1})(1 - S_k)}, \qquad k = 1, 2, \ldots, m,$$

where $S_0 \equiv 0$ and

$$S_k = \sum_{i=1}^{k} \frac{\lambda_i}{c\mu} < 1, \qquad \text{for all } k.$$

As in the previous model, the expression for $E\{\xi_0\}$ is obtained by equating $W_q^{(1)}$ to W_q, the expected waiting time in queue for the $(M/M/c):(FCFS/\infty/\infty)$ model with $\lambda = \sum_{i=1}^{m} \lambda_i$. Thus

$$\left(\frac{E\{\xi_0\}}{1 - \dfrac{\lambda}{c\mu}} \right) = \frac{L_q}{\lambda},$$

or, letting $\rho = \lambda/\mu$, then

$$E\{\xi_0\} = \frac{(c - \rho)}{c\lambda} L_q.$$

Substituting for L_q from Section 14·4·5, then

$$E\{\xi_0\} = \left(\frac{c - \rho}{c\lambda} \right) \left(\frac{\rho^{c+1}}{(c - 1)!(c - \rho)^2} \right) \cdot \left(\frac{1}{\left(\sum_{n=0}^{c-1} \dfrac{\rho^n}{n!} + \dfrac{\rho^c}{(c - \rho)(c - 1)!} \right)} \right)$$

$$= \frac{1}{\mu c \left(\rho^{-c}(c - \rho)(c - 1)! \sum_{n=0}^{c-1} \dfrac{\rho^n}{n!} + 1 \right)}.$$

To illustrate the application of this model, consider the numerical problem where there are three priority queues with arrival rates $\lambda_1 = 2$, $\lambda_2 = 5$, and

$\lambda_3 = 10$ per unit time for queues 1, 2, and 3 respectively. Let $c = 2$ and $\mu = 10$. Thus

$$S_1 = \frac{\lambda_1}{c\mu} = \frac{2}{2 \times 10} = 0.1,$$

$$S_2 = S_1 + \frac{\lambda_2}{c\mu} = .1 + \frac{5}{2 \times 10} = 0.35,$$

$$S_3 = S_2 + \frac{\lambda_3}{c\mu} = .35 + \frac{10}{2 \times 10} = 0.85.$$

Since all $S_i < 1$, steady state can be reached.
Now, by definition

$$\rho = \frac{\lambda_1 + \lambda_2 + \lambda_3}{\mu} = \frac{17}{10} = 1.7.$$

Hence

$$E\{\xi_0\} = \frac{1}{10 \times 2\{(1.7)^{-2}(2 - 1.7)(1!)(1 + 1.7) + 1\}}$$

$$= 0.039.$$

Thus,

$$W_q^{(1)} = \frac{0.039}{(1 - 0.1)} = 0.0433,$$

$$W_q^{(2)} = \frac{0.039}{(1 - 0.1)(1 - 0.35)} = 0.0665,$$

$$W_q^{(3)} = \frac{0.039}{(1 - 0.35)(1 - 0.85)} = 0.4.$$

The waiting time in the queue for *any* customer is then given by

$$W_q = \frac{\lambda_1}{\lambda} W_q^{(1)} + \frac{\lambda_2}{\lambda} W_q^{(2)} + \frac{\lambda_3}{\lambda} W_q^{(3)}$$

$$= \frac{2}{17}(0.0433) + \frac{5}{17}(0.0665) + \frac{10}{17}(0.4)$$

$$= 0.26.$$

Finally, the expected number waiting in the queue for the entire system is given by

$$L_q = W\lambda_q = 17 \times 0.26 = 4.42.$$

§ 14·7
Queues in Series

The queueing models which have been treated in the previous sections assume that each service channel consists of one service station only. Situations exist where each service channel may consist of several stations in series. In this case, a customer must pass successively through all the stations. This situation is referred to as " queues in series" or " queues in tandem." Typical practical cases of this type may be found in multistage manufacturing systems where each product is processed through a series of operations.

The model structure for queues in series is considerably different from those of the previous models. This occurs mainly because it will not be sufficient to know how many persons are in the system but also where they are.

As an example of the analysis of queues in series, consider the simplified one-channel queueing system consisting of two series stations as shown in Figure 14–4. A customer arriving for service must go through Station 1 and

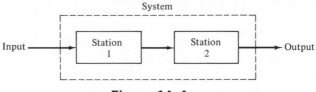

Figure 14–4

Station 2. The service times at each station are exponentially distributed with the same service rate μ. Arrivals occur according to a Poisson distribution with an arrival rate equal to λ. It is assumed that no queues are allowed in front of Station 1 or Station 2.

The construction of the model requires first that the states of the system at any point in time be identified. This is accomplished as follows. Each station may be either free or busy. Station 1 is said to be blocked if the customer in this station completes his service before Station 2 becomes free. In this case he cannot wait between the stations since this is not allowed. Let the symbols 0, 1, and b represent the free, busy, and blocked states, respectively. Let i and j represent the states of Station 1 and Station 2, then the states of the system are given by

$$\{(i, j)\} = \{(0, 0), (1, 0), (0, 1), (1, 1), (b, 1)\}.$$

Define $p_{ij}(t)$ as the probability that the system is in state (i, j) at time t. The transition probabilities between times t and $t + h$ (h is a small positive increment in time) are summarized as shown in Table 14–1. The empty squares indicate that the transitions between the indicated states at t and $t + h$ are impossible ($= 0$).

Table 14–1

States at $(t + h)$

	$(0, 0)$	$(0, 1)$	$(1, 0)$	$(1, 1)$	$(b, 1)$
$(0, 0)$	$1 - \lambda h$		λh		
$(0, 1)$	$\mu h (1 - \lambda h)$	$1 - \mu h - \lambda h$		$\lambda h(1 - \mu h)$	
$(1, 0)$		$\mu h(1 - \lambda h)$	$1 - \mu h$		
$(1, 1)$			μh	$(1 - \mu h)(1 - \mu h)$	μh
$(b, 1)$		$\mu h(1 - \lambda h)$			$1 - \mu h$

States at t (row labels)

The following equations can thus be established (neglecting the terms in h^2),

$$p_{00}(t + h) = p_{00}(t)(1 - \lambda h) + p_{01}(t)(\mu h),$$

$$p_{01}(t + h) = p_{01}(t)(1 - \mu h - \lambda h) + p_{10}(t)(\mu h) + p_{b1}(t)(\mu h),$$

$$p_{10}(t + h) = p_{00}(t)(\lambda h) + p_{10}(t)(1 - \mu h) + p_{11}(t)(\mu h),$$

$$p_{11}(t + h) = p_{01}(t)(\lambda h) + p_{11}(t)(1 - 2\mu h),$$

$$p_{b1}(t + h) = p_{11}(t)(\mu h) + p_{b1}(t)(1 - \mu h).$$

Rearranging the terms and taking the appropriate limits, the steady state equations are given by,

$$p_{01} - \rho p_{00} = 0,$$

$$p_{10} + p_{b1} - (1 + \rho)p_{01} = 0,$$

$$\rho p_{00} + p_{11} - p_{10} = 0,$$

$$\rho p_{01} - 2p_{11} = 0,$$

$$p_{11} - p_{b1} = 0.$$

One of these equations is obviously redundant. Hence adding the condition that

$$p_{00} + p_{01} + p_{10} + p_{11} + p_{b1} = 1,$$

the solution for p_{ij} is given by

$$p_{00} = \frac{2}{A},$$

$$p_{01} = \frac{2\rho}{A},$$

$$p_{10} = \frac{\rho^2 + 2\rho}{A},$$

$$p_{11} = p_{b1} = \frac{\rho^2}{A},$$

where

$$A = 3\rho^2 + 4\rho + 2.$$

The expected number in the system can then be obtained as

$$L_s = 0.p_{00} + 1(p_{01} + p_{10}) + 2(p_{11} + p_{b1})$$

$$= \frac{5\rho^2 + 4}{A}.$$

An Important Result for Serial Poisson Queues

In the above discussion a special case of queues in series is considered. This section states (without proof) a theorem which is applicable to the general case of tandem queues with Poisson properties.[10] Consider a system with k stations in series as shown in Figure 14–5. Assume that the arrivals at Station

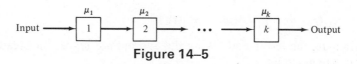

Figure 14–5

1 are generated from an infinite population according to a Poisson distribution with mean rate λ per unit time. The serviced units will move successively from one station to the next until they are discharged from station k. It is assumed that the service time distribution at each station i is exponential with mean rate μ_i per unit time, $i = 1, 2, \ldots, k$. Further it is assumed that there is no queue limit at any of the stations.

Under the above conditions, it can be proved that for all i, the output from station i (or, equivalently, the input to station $i + 1$) is Poisson with mean rate λ and that each station may be treated *independently* as an

---

[10] See Saaty [5], Sections 12–2 to 12–4, for the proof.

$(M/M_i/1):(GD/\infty/\infty)$ model. This means that for the ith station, the steady-state probabilities p_{n_i} are given by

$$p_{n_i} = (1 - \rho_i)\rho_i^{n_i}, \qquad n_i = 0, 1, 2, \ldots,$$

for $i = 1, 2, \ldots, k$; where n_i is the number in the system consisting of station i only. Naturally, the steady state results will exist only if $\rho_i = (\lambda/\mu_i) < 1$.

The same result can be extended to the case where station i includes c_i parallel servers, each with the same exponential service rate μ_i per unit time. (See Figure 14–6.) In this case each station may be treated independently as

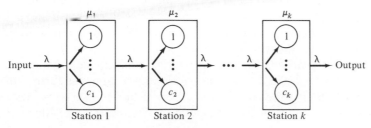

Station 1   Station 2   Station k

Figure 14–6

an $(M/M_i/c_i):(GD/\infty/\infty)$ model with mean arrival rate λ per unit time. Again, the steady state results of Section 14·4·4 will prevail only if $\lambda < c_i\mu_i$, for $i = 1, 2, \ldots, k$.

It must be noted that the above result holds true only for the infinite source model with Poisson arrivals at Station 1 and exponential service time at each station. Also it is assumed that there is no limitation on the queue length associated with each station. Consequently, this result will not hold if any of these conditions is violated.

The use of this result is illustrated by Problems 14-43, 14-44, and 14-45 as applications to production line systems.

§ 14·8
Simulation Technique

In the preceding sections different queueing models were treated analytically. Analytical solutions become rather complex when arrival and departure distributions deviate from the Poisson axioms. Simulation is thus introduced as an alternative tool to mathematical modeling and may be used when analytical solutions become too complex or impossible. Contrary to mathematical modeling where the results of the analysis yield a direct and an overall solution to the problem, simulation results are obtained by observing the system's behavior over time and accumulating the relevant statistics as the simulation progresses in time. The description of the system is generally made in terms of an exhaustive number of events which are defined as points in time signifying the termination of one or more activities and the beginning of new ones. As each event occurs, specific actions are taken which will result in the generation of new events to be considered at future points in time.

To illustrate the concept of events, consider the single channel queueing model given in Section 14·4·1. For this problem only two events are needed to describe the model completely. These are the events of arrival and departure of a customer. Let E_a and E_d represent these two events, respectively. The objective of this simulation would be to determine the output measures including the average waiting time per customer, the average number of customers waiting, and percentage of time the service facility remains idle. The input, on the other hand, should specify the patterns of arrival and departure of customers. These patterns may be described by fixed or probabilistic interarrival and service times.

Suppose for simplicity that the interarrival and service times are constant and are given by 2 and 3 time units, respectively. Suppose further that it is required to observe this system for a period of 11 time units. Table 14–2 summarizes the results of the simulation for the indicated 11 time units.

Table 14–2

Time	Customer	Event	Waiting Time
02	1	E_a	
04	2	E_a	
05	1	E_d	$5 - 4 = 1$ (customer 2)
06	3	E_a	
08	4	E_a	
08	2	E_d	$8 - 6 = 2$ (customer 3)
10	5	E_a	
11	3	E_d	$11 - 8 = 3$ (customer 4)

The table shows that the first event E_a occurs at time 2. Since the service facility can be assumed free, the arriving customer will start service immediately. His departure time is given by $2 + 3 = 5$. It is necessary at this point to indicate the arrival time of the next customer. This is given by $2 + 2 = 5$. These two events are entered in the table according to their chronological ordering. The next event to be considered is E_a for customer 2. Since the facility is occupied, this customer will join the waiting line. In the meantime, the next arrival time is generated which is equal to $4 + 2 = 6$. The event E_d occurs at time 5 and it signifies that the facility is free. Thus customer 2 can be taken out of the waiting line to start service. At this point, the waiting time for this customer is computed as $5 - 4 = 1$. The departure event of this customer is then generated and its time is given by $5 + 3 = 8$. The next event to be considered is E_a for customer 3 which occurs at time 6. This customer will join the waiting line and the next arrival will then occur at time $6 + 2 = 8$.

The above process is continued as shown in Table 14–2 until the eleven time units are covered. Notice that in carrying out the simulation, it is necessary only to generate the immediately succeeding events rather than all the events for the entire simulation period. This usually simplifies the calculations associated with the problem.

The final results of the above simple simulation can now be computed. The total waiting times calculated in the table are $1 + 2 + 3 = 6$. Since customer 5 is still waiting, his waiting time until time 11 is also included. Thus the total waiting time is equal to $6 + 1 = 7$. Consequently,

Average waiting time per customer $= \frac{7}{5} = 1.4$.
Average waiting time for those that had to wait $= \frac{7}{4} = 1.75$.
Average number waiting $= \frac{7}{11} = 0.637$.
Percentage idle time of the facility $= 0\,\%$.

Naturally, in carrying out the complex simulations, manual computations will become infeasible. However, the modern high speed digital computers with their tremendous capabilities offer the solution to this problem. In fact there are several specialized computer languages such as *GPSS* and *SIMSCRIPT* which can be used efficiently for digital simulation.

In the above example it is noticed that no attention is paid to the system until some event occurs. This type of simulation is called "variable-time increment method." There is another type where the system is observed at equal intervals of time. This is called "fixed-time increment method." In this case the system is checked regularly for *possible* occurrence of events. The major disadvantage in the last method is the possibility of making false stops when no events are occurring, which usually results in computational inefficiency. This method may be more advantageous, however, if the events are generated at a very high rate, in which case the variable-time method may become less efficient. In general, there is no conclusive evidence as to the superiority of one method over the other since each method has its own advantages and drawbacks.

§ 14·8·1
Generation of Random Deviates

Suppose in the above example the interarrival and service times were probabilistic rather than fixed; that is, described by random variables. How can this characteristic be incorporated in the model? Specifically, the answer to this question must be oriented toward the use of the digital computer as an essential tool for carrying out the simulation.

Before showing how the random deviate x for a given probability density function $f(x)$ can be generated, it is necessary first to introduce the following

Theorem: *Given any cumulative density function (C.D.F.) $F(x)$ of the random variable x, the new random variable*

$$y = F(x)$$

is uniformly distributed over the (0, 1) interval.

PROOF: The proof can be established using the following elementary probability transformation.

$$G(Y) = P\{y \le Y\} = P\{F(x) \le Y\},$$

$$= P\{x \le F^{-1}(Y)\},$$

$$= F\{F^{-1}(Y)\},$$

$$= Y.$$

Thus, the probability density function (p.d.f.) of y is given by

$$g(y) = \frac{dG(y)}{dy} = 1$$

Since by definition $0 \le y = F(x) \le 1$, then y is uniformly distributed over the (0, 1) interval. ◄

The above theorem indicates that the C.D.F. $F(x)$ is uniformly distributed over the (0, 1) interval and regardless of the distribution of x. The idea now is to generate a random number, R, on the (0, 1) interval, then by the above theorem the corresponding random deviate x for any p.d.f. $f(x)$ will be given by

$$x = F^{-1}(R).$$

This point is illustrated graphically in Figure 14–7.

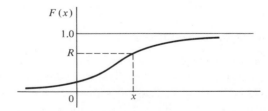

Figure 14–7

In some distributions it is possible to obtain a closed-form expression for $F^{-1}(R)$ so that the resulting formula may be used directly with the computer. For example, consider the negative exponential p.d.f.,

$$f(x) = \begin{cases} \mu e^{-\mu x}, & x > 0, \\ 0, & \text{otherwise.} \end{cases}$$

Thus,

$$R = F(x) = 1 - e^{-\mu x},$$

or

$$x = \frac{1}{\mu} \ln\left(\frac{1}{1-R}\right),$$

$$= \frac{1}{\mu} \ln\left(\frac{1}{R}\right).$$

(The last expression is justified since $1 - R$ is also a random number on the $(0, 1)$ interval.)

There are some probability density functions for which the above inversion method does not yield a closed-form expression for the random deviate. In this case one has to resort to other methods. For example, the normal random deviates can be obtained from the uniform distribution using the central limit theorem (see Section 12·8). Since R is generated from a uniform $(0, 1)$ distribution, those numbers can be used directly with the central limit theorem. Define

$$T = R_1 + R_2 + \cdots + R_n$$

as the sum of n uniform $(0, 1)$ random numbers. Thus

$$E\{T\} = n/2,$$

$$\text{Var}\{T\} = \sum_{i=1}^{n} \text{Var}(R_i)$$

$$= n/12.$$

Thus T is asymptotically normal with mean $n/2$ and variance $n/12$. Now, let

$$z = \frac{T - (n/2)}{\sqrt{(n/12)}},$$

which is normal with zero mean and unit variance.

For any normal distribution with mean μ and variance σ^2, the random deviate y corresponding to the above n random numbers is obtained by considering

$$\frac{y - \mu}{\sigma} = z = \frac{T - (n/2)}{\sqrt{n/12}}.$$

Hence

$$y = \mu + \frac{\sigma}{\sqrt{n/12}} \left(T - \frac{n}{2} \right)$$

$$= \mu + \frac{\sigma}{\sqrt{n/12}} \left(\sum_{i=1}^{n} R_i - \frac{n}{2} \right).$$

Another method which is generally useful in dealing with discrete random variables is the so-called *tabular method*. This is especially needed when the p.d.f. cannot be presented in a closed form. Consider, for example, the following p.d.f.

x	0	1	2	3
$p(x)$	.1	.3	.4	.2

The C.D.F. is given by

x	0	1	2	3
$F(x)$	.1	.4	.8	1.00

This is shown graphically in Figure 14–8.

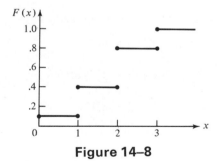

Figure 14–8

It then follows that the random numbers can be categorized to define the random deviates x uniquely as follows,

$$0 \le R \le .1, \qquad x = 0,$$
$$.1 < R \le .4, \qquad x = 1,$$
$$.4 < R \le .8, \qquad x = 2,$$
$$.8 < R \le 1.00, \qquad x = 3.$$

This generally means that for any discrete random variable x, the random deviate assumes the value j if the random number is such that

$$F(j-1) < R \leq F(j).$$

It must be noted that it is sometimes possible to exploit statistical theory to generate certain random deviates. For example, a gamma random deviate with parameters n and μ can be obtained as the sum of n random deviates each generated from an exponential distribution with mean $1/\mu$. Since the exponential random deviates can be easily determined using the inverse method, it becomes computationally attractive to generate the gamma random deviates from the exponential distribution. This method is sometimes known as the convolution method.

§ 14·8·2
Generation of Random Numbers

In Section 14·8·1, the generation of random deviates is based on the assumption that uniform $(0, 1)$ random numbers can be generated on demand. There are three methods by which these numbers can be obtained on the computer.

  (i) Store random numbers and read them into the computer as required.
  (ii) Construct an electronic device which will generate truly random numbers.
 (iii) Utilize an arithmetic operation to compute random numbers from a recursive equation.

The first method is objectionable because it is too slow and moreover, the simulation run may require more random numbers than have ever been published. The second method is extremely expensive and hence it is not practical. The last method represents the most feasible alternative. In this respect there are several arithmetic operations that can be used. One of the attractive methods is the multiplicative congruential procedure for which the recursive formula is given by[11]

$$U_{n+1} = pU_n(\text{mod } m), \qquad n = 0, 1, 2, \ldots,$$

where U_0, P, and m are parameters that are specified in advance. The sequence U_n will then give the required numbers.

It must be noted that the numbers generated by the arithmetic operations cannot be truly random. This is the reason that these are called *pseudo-random* numbers. Consequently, the generated sequence must be subjected

---

[11] The notation $x = y(\text{mod } m)$ means that $(x - y)$ is divisible by m and $0 \leq y \leq m$.

to the appropriate statistical tests before it can be used successfully in simulation models. These tests include,

(i) The chi-square test of goodness-of-fit to ensure that the numbers are generated from a $(0, 1)$ uniform distribution.
(ii) The randomness or independence test to ensure that the generated numbers are statistically independent.[12]

§ 14·8·3
Experimental Design in Simulation

The use of random numbers indicates that simulation must be regarded as a statistical experiment. Consequently, the significance of the output measures of the simulation must be tested statistically. This is done by sampling from the simulation and then applying the appropriate statistical tests. The immediate questions here are, (1) how long should be the simulation run corresponding to each sampling observation? and (2) how large is the sample size?[13] The answer to the first question has to do with the equilibrium or steady state results of the simulation. At its early stages, the system is still in transient state. The length of the simulation run should thus be long enough to by-pass this state. There is no definite solution to this problem and in general, one has to rely on experience. It is advisable, however, to start the system in a state that is similar to the steady state conditions. In general, one must also take the economic considerations into account since the longer the run, the more expensive the simulation will be.

The question of how large the sample size should be is equally difficult to answer. This comes mainly because by the very nature of simulation, observations are usually highly correlated. This makes it difficult to use the known statistical tests since these are mainly based on the assumption of independence between observations. Suggestions for overcoming this problem are to make separate independent simulation runs and to take the output of each run as representing one observation. The only problem here is that for each observation the effect of initial conditions (transient conditions) will be prominent. Another suggestion calls for making consecutive equal simulation runs so that as the simulation progresses over time, steady state is approached and, by the definition of steady state, the different runs hopefully become independent of one another.

The above discussion summarizes the main features of the simulation technique. It is noted that much progress has been made in constructing simulation

---

[12] For a description of these tests, see Donald E. Knuth, *The Art of Computer Programming: Seminumerical Algorithms*, Addison-Wesley, Reading, Massachusetts, 1969, Chapter 3.

[13] For a more complete discussion of these points, see R. Conway," Some Tactical Problems in Digital Simulation," *Management Science*, Vol. 10, No. 1, 47–61 (1963).

models. The problem of statistical verification of the results still remains largely unexplored, and its solution is still in the infant stage. In spite of these apparent difficulties, simulation represents a powerful tool which can always be used when mathematical analysis fails to work.

§ 14·9
Queueing Decision Models

This section deals with the decision-making aspect of queueing problems. Queueing decision-making is concerned with improving the performance of the system through the use of the appropriate decision models. These models are constructed using the appropriate operating characteristics and their solution ultimately determines the optimum design parameters of the system. Such design parameters may include, for example, the service rates, the number of parallel servers, or the maximum allowable queue length.

Optimization of the design parameters may be viewed in a variety of ways depending on the objective of the decision-maker. A most common viewpoint is to base the decision on a cost model which minimizes the sum of the costs of service and of waiting time per unit time. Obviously, the higher the first is, the lower the second becomes, and *vice versa*. Cost models are ideal if one can obtain reliable estimates of the necessary cost parameters. Specifically, it is usually difficult (sometimes impossible) to estimate the cost parameters associated with the waiting time. In this case one may be forced to search for another "optimality" criterion. In this section, in addition to the cost models, the so-called "aspiration-level model" will be introduced. This new model may be used when it is impractical to use the cost model.

§ 14·9·1
Cost Models

§ 14·9·1·1
Optimum Service Rate, μ

Consider the single channel model with an arrival rate λ and a service rate μ. It is assumed that the service rate μ is controllable and it is required to determine its optimum value based on an appropriate cost model.

Let

C_1 = cost per unit increase in μ per unit time,
C_2 = cost of waiting per unit waiting time per customer,
$TC(\mu)$ = total cost of waiting and service per unit time given the service rate μ.

Thus,

$$TC(\mu) = C_1\mu + C_2 L_s.$$

Notice that the cost of service per unit time is directly proportional to μ and that the cost of waiting per unit time is equal to the expected number of customers in the system multiplied by the waiting cost per customer per unit time.

Since μ is continuous, its optimum value can be obtained by differentiating $TC(\mu)$ with respect to μ. For example, for the special case of $(M/M/1):(GD/\infty/\infty)$,

$$TC(\mu) = C_1\mu + C_2\frac{\lambda}{\mu - \lambda},$$

and thus optimum μ is given by

$$\mu = \lambda + \sqrt{\frac{C_2\lambda}{C_1}}.$$

This result shows that the optimal value of the parameter μ is not only dependent on C_1 and C_2 but also on the arrival rate λ. This seems logical since if μ is independent of λ, it may cause $\rho\,(=\lambda/\mu)$ to be greater than one. Notice that in the above solution μ is always greater than λ.

It is noticed for the case where only a maximum of N customers are allowed in the system; that is, $(M/M/1):(GD/N/\infty)$, the above cost model can be modified to reflect the fact that the larger the value of N, the smaller will be the number of lost customers (those who cannot join the system because it is full) and *vice versa*. In this case N is treated as a decision variable which, together with μ, is determined by minimizing

$$TC(\mu, N) = C_1\mu + C_2 L_s + C_3 N + C_4 \lambda p_N,$$

where,

C_3 = cost per unit time per additional accommodation unit for the customers,

C_4 = cost per lost customer.

Notice that λp_N represents the number of lost customers per unit time.

A closed-form solution for this problem is not possible. Consequently, one may have to employ an appropriate numerical technique to obtain the optimal solution.

§ 14·9·1·2
Optimum Number of Servers

Consider the multiple-server model presented in Section 14·4·4. A cost model can be developed in this case for determining the optimal number of servers c. It is assumed that λ and μ are fixed in this case. A similar reasoning can be followed in developing this model as in the last model so that

$$TC(c) = cC_1 + C_2 L_s(c),$$

where,

C_1 = cost per additional server per unit time,
$L_s(c)$ = expected number in the system given c servers,

while C_2 is defined as in the previous model. (Notice that, as in the previous model, the effect of allowing a finite number in the system can be similarly included here.)

Since c is discrete, differentiation is not applicable to this case. Although optimum c can be found by direct substitution of successive values of c until the minimum of $TC(c)$ is reached, a more computationally efficient procedure can be found through the development of the necessary condition for a minimum of the given function. These are given by

$$TC(c-1) \geq TC(c)$$

and

$$TC(c+1) \geq TC(c).$$

This yields the final condition

$$L_s(c) - L_s(c+1) \leq \frac{C_1}{C_2} \leq L_s(c-1) - L_s(c).$$

The value of C_1/C_2 will now give an indication of where the search for optimum c should start.

To illustrate the use of the above condition, consider the multiple server case where $\lambda = 1.75$ and $\mu = 1$, or $\rho = 1.75$. Let $C_1 = .2$ and $C_2 = 1$, or $C_1/C_2 = .2$. The determination of optimum c is achieved by first establishing the following table (notice that $L_s(1)$ is equal to infinity since $\lambda > \mu$).

c	$L_s(c)$	$L_s(c-1) - L_s(c)$
1	∞	—
2	5.70	∞
3	0.47	5.23
4	0.09	0.38
5	0.02	$0.07 \leftarrow C_1/C_2 = .2$

Clearly

$$L_s(4) - L_s(5) = .07 < .2 < .38 = L_s(3) - L_s(4).$$

Hence optimal $c = 4$. The reader would notice that given the value of C_1/C_2, the third column calculations should give an indication of the promising range of c.

§ 14·9·2
Aspiration-Level Model[14]

The aspiration-level model recognizes the difficulty of estimating the cost parameters in cost models and hence it is based on a more straightforward analysis. It makes direct use of the operating characteristics of the system in deciding on the "optimal" values of the design parameters. Optimality here is viewed in the sense of satisfying certain aspiration levels which are set by the decision-maker. These aspiration levels are defined as the upper limits on the values of the conflicting measures which the decision-maker wishes to balance.

In the multiple server model where it is required to determine the optimum value of the number of servers, c, the two most prominent conflicting measures can be taken as

(i) The expected waiting time in the system, W_s.
(ii) The percentage of the servers' idle time, X.

These two measures represent the viewpoints of the customer and the server, respectively. Let the levels of aspiration (upper limits) for W_s and X be given by α and β, respectively. Then the level of aspiration method can be expressed mathematically as follows:

Determine the number of servers, c, such that

$$W_s \leq \alpha$$

and

$$X \leq \beta.$$

The expression for W_s is known from the analysis of the $(M/M/c):(GD/\infty/\infty)$ model. The expression for X, on the other hand, is given by

$$X = \frac{100}{c} \sum_{n=0}^{c} (c - n)p_n$$

$$= 100\left(1 - \frac{\rho}{c}\right).$$

The solution of the problem can be recognized more conveniently by plotting W_s and X against c as shown in Figure 14–9. It is noticed that by locating α and β on the graph, one can immediately determine the acceptable range of c which satisfies both restrictions. Naturally, if these two conditions are not satisfied simultaneously, it would be necessary to relax one or both restrictions before a decision can be made.

---

[14] The material in this section is drawn from H. A. Taha, "A Case Study Comparison of Independent Channels Versus a Combined Pool," *The Journal of Industrial Engineering*, Vol. XIX, No. 3, 137–142 (1968).

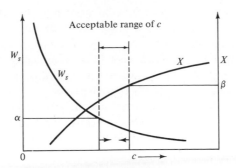

Figure 14–9

It is possible to compute the equivalent cost of waiting per customer per unit time, C_2, which is implied by the selection of c for the given aspiration levels. From the cost model of Section 14·9·1·2, the optimum c satisfies,

$$L_s(c) - L_s(c + 1) \le \frac{C_1}{C_2} \le L_s(c - 1) - L_s(c)$$

or

$$\frac{C_1}{L_s(c - 1) - L_s(c)} \le C_2 \le \frac{C_1}{L_s(c) - L_s(c + 1)}.$$

This determines the equivalent range of C_2 on the assumption that C_1, the cost per additional server per unit time, can be estimated. The given range of C_2 should give the equivalent monetary values as a result of selecting c according to the specified levels of aspiration, α and β.

§ 14·10
Case Study[15]

This section presents a case study of a certain type of service comparing the use of independent channels versus a combined pool. The study was initiated in a manufacturing company as a result of a common practice which called for allocating one typist to each department or section. It was noticed that the various work periods found some typists busy while others were relatively idle. Also, some typists complained of a heavy workload while others did not seem to have such a problem. This intuitively led to the conclusion that such irregularities in workloads could be smoothed through the establishment of typing pools. Such viewpoint seemed feasible since the concerned departments are located close to one another making it convenient to pool such services.

---

[15] Taha, *Ibid.*

Although the advantages of using the pool may be intuitively clear, the idea was received with considerable resentment, mainly because each department head preferred the independent typing service. Most superiors went further to claim that their typists were fully occupied and consequently the establishment of a pool would lead to little, if any, improvement. Others resented the change on the grounds that the typists would not report directly to them and this might create administrative problems. It then became evident that an effective quantitative measure justifying the use of the pool was necessary before any changes could be effected. This study was carried out as a result.

The purpose of the study is

1. To devise a quantitative measure expressing the effectiveness of using the pool.
2. To give a method for determining the number of servers (typists) in the pool.

This situation may be investigated quantitatively by queueing theory. Here, the material to be typed (usually in the form of written drafts) represents the customers arriving for service, while the typists represent the servers. The time required to complete each of the arriving items represents the service time. The present situation of one typist per department or section represents a queueing situation with a single server and unlimited source, while the proposed situation of a pool service represents a queueing situation with a multiple number of servers and unlimited source. This will be the basis of comparison in this case study.

The first step was to obtain the data on the situation. These data include

1. The distribution of the arrival times.
2. The distribution of the service times.

A sample of six departments were selected for this purpose. The conditions governing the selection of this sample were

1. The departments are located close to one another.
2. The departments carry out typing work of a homogeneous nature.

These two conditions are necessary for establishing a service pool since the location of the pool should be convenient to all concerned departments; also the servers must be able to handle work from all of the departments.

Two forms were designed for the collection of the data. The first form chronologically records the times at which the material arrives at the typists' desks. The second form is a log sheet recording the start and finish times for typing each item, as well as the times for the typists' other activities during work hours. The typists were instructed as to how these forms should be filled in and the recorded information was checked to avoid excessive bias in the data. The collection of data continued for six days (one work week).

From these data, distribution curves for arrival and service times were made up for the six departments. Chi-square tests of goodness of fit were employed to check the statistical conformity of the actual probability distributions of arrivals and services to the assumed theoretical Poisson and exponential probability distributions, respectively.[16] For all the six departments the test indicated a good fit at a 0.05 significance level. To illustrate, Figures 14–10 and 14–11 give the corresponding curves for Department 1. The results from the data for the six departments are summarized in Table 14–3.

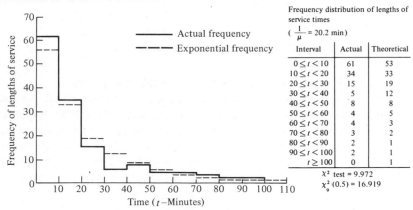

Frequency distribution of lengths of service times

$(\frac{1}{\mu} = 20.2 \text{ min})$

Interval	Actual	Theoretical
$0 \le t < 10$	61	53
$10 \le t < 20$	34	33
$20 \le t < 30$	15	19
$30 \le t < 40$	5	12
$40 \le t < 50$	8	8
$50 \le t < 60$	4	5
$60 \le t < 70$	4	3
$70 \le t < 80$	3	2
$80 \le t < 90$	2	1
$90 \le t < 100$	2	1
$t \ge 100$	0	1

$\chi^2 \text{ test} = 9.972$
$\chi^2_9 (0.5) = 16.919$

Figure 14–10

Distribution of Service Times

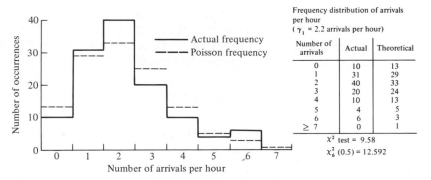

Frequency distribution of arrivals per hour

$(\gamma_1 = 2.2 \text{ arrivals per hour})$

Number of arrivals	Actual	Theoretical
0	10	13
1	31	29
2	40	33
3	20	24
4	10	13
5	4	5
6	6	3
≥ 7	0	1

$\chi^2 \text{ test} = 9.58$
$\chi^2_6 (0.5) = 12.592$

Figure 14–11

Distribution of Arrivals

---

[16] For a complete description of the Chi-square test, see B. Lindgren, *Statistical Theory*, Macmillan, New York, 1968, 325–329.

Table 14–3

Department i	Arrival rate per hour λ_i (Poisson)	Service rate per hour μ_i (Exponential)	Utilization factor ρ_i $= (\lambda_i/\mu_i)$
1	2.2	2.97	0.740
2	1.4	2.69	0.521
3	1.9	2.78	0.686
4	2.5	2.89	0.865
5	2.0	2.93	0.682
6	4.7	3.11	1.520

Investigation of such preliminary results reveals two points.

1. The service rates in the six departments are statistically equal. An analysis of variance table (one-way layout) was computed to test the hypothesis that the service rates in the six departments were equal.[17] The hypothesis was accepted at a 0.05 significance level. Consequently, for the purpose of this study, one service rate, μ, will be utilized. The best estimate (in statistical sense) for such service rates would then be the weighted average of the respective means, μ_i. This gives μ equal to 2.88 items per hour.

2. Department 6 has a utilization factor ρ_6 greater than 1. This indicates unstable conditions since a queue with such characteristics is said to explode (theoretically, such a queueing system cannot reach a steady state and the queue length could build up to infinity). The utilization factors of the other departments are less than 1.0 indicating that the servers in these departments may have some "slack" time. By pooling the six departments, such free time could be utilized to relieve the heavy load on Department 6. In fact, if all six typists were pooled, the pool utilization factor will be

$$\frac{14.7}{6 \times 2.88} = 0.85$$

which is less than 1. This preliminary investigation already reveals one of the advantages of pooling in this case.

Description of the Problem

In the present situation, each department, $i\,(i = 1, 2, 3, \ldots, N)$, has its own typist and the corresponding arrival rates are given by λ_i. As shown above, the same service rate, μ, will be used for all the departments. Each department will

---

[17] For a description of this test, see A. Bowker and G. Lieberman, *Engineering Statistics*, Prentice-Hall, Englewood Cliffs, N.J., 1959, Chapter X.

thus represent a queueing situation with a single server and an unlimited source. The measures for this situation are given in Section 14·4·1. It is only assumed that

$$\rho_i = \frac{\lambda_i}{\mu}$$

is the utilization factor for the ith department. Consequently, L_{qi} and W_{qi} will represent the expected number in the queue and the waiting time in the queue of the ith department, respectively.

In the case of using the pool service, the material to be typed is assumed to arrive from the different departments in one stream. Since the arrival distributions for each department, i, is Poisson with mean λ_i, the arrival distribution for the pool (which is the convolution of these Poisson distributions) is also Poisson with mean arrival rate

$$\sigma = \sum_{i=1}^{N} \lambda_i .$$

The pool situation represents a queueing system with N parallel servers and unlimited source. The measures of this situation are given in Section 14·4·4. The expected number in the queue and the expected waiting time in the queue are represented by L_q and W_q, respectively.

Independent Channels Versus Pool Service

Having justified the choice of the preceding queueing models, the operating characteristics of the pool may now be expressed in terms of the queueing theory results. Since the main concern here is connected with the relative waiting time in the two situations, a good measure may be defined as the ratio of the expected waiting time per customer in a pool to its equivalence in the corresponding independent channels. Using E to represent this measure, and defining $\overline{W}$ as the weighted mean of the expected waiting times in the different channels, then

$$E = \frac{\overline{W}}{W_q},$$

where

$$\overline{W} = \sum_{i=1}^{N} \frac{\lambda_i}{\sigma} W_{qi},$$

$$= \frac{1}{\sigma} \sum_{i=1}^{N} L_{qi} .$$

The definition of $\overline{W}$ follows from the fact that, under steady state conditions, the ratio of the customers served in channel i and the corresponding expected waiting time per customer in this channel are given by λ_i/σ and W_{qi} respectively.

Using the measure E, the question of whether the pooling of fully occupied channels (that is, $\rho_i \to 1$) would lead to significant reduction in waiting time can now be investigated. Consider the extreme situation where each of the N independent channels operates with a utilization factor very close to 1. Assume, for simplicity, that all the channels have the same utilization factor (that is, $\rho_i = \lambda/\mu$).

Employing Morse's approximate formula introduced at the end of Section 14·4·4 where it is shown that W_q approaches $1/(N\mu - \sigma)$ as $\sigma/N\mu$, the utilization factor of the pool, approaches 1, it follows under these conditions that

$$W_q = \frac{1}{N(\mu - \lambda)}$$

and

$$\overline{W} = \frac{\lambda}{\mu(\mu - \lambda)}.$$

Consequently,

$$E = \frac{W_q}{\overline{W}} = \frac{1}{N(\lambda/\mu)}.$$

Clearly,

$$\lim_{\lambda/\mu \to 1} E = \frac{1}{N}.$$

Since in a pool, $N \geq 2$, it follows that as the utilization factor per channel approaches 1, the *upper bound* on E will approach $\frac{1}{2}$. This shows that even under these extreme conditions, the use of the pool will still result in at least a 50 per cent reduction in the expected waiting time. This reduction becomes more acute as N increases.

Applying the measure E to the six-department sample, the necessary results for the independent channels are given in Table 14–4. It is noted that Department 6 is excluded from the present comparison since the available formulas do not apply to this unstable condition ($\rho_6 > 1$). Department 6, however, will be considered later in the discussion. It is shown in Table 14–4 that $\overline{W}$ is about 1.15 hours. Using the given formulas, the waiting time, W_q, for the corresponding pool ($N = 5$, $\sigma = 10.0$, and $\mu = 2.88$) is found equal to 0.075 hours. Thus, E is computed equal to 0.066. Consequently, in this case, if a customer is served in the pool, his expected waiting time will be less than 10 per cent of his counterpart's in the equivalent independent channels.

The above information provided a good basis for justifying the use of the pool. The final decision, however, was made in view of the administrative

Table 14–4

Department i	λ_i	L_{qi}	W_{qi}
1	2.2	2.456	1.120
2	1.4	0.461	0.328
3	1.9	1.273	0.675
4	2.5	5.700	2.280
5	2.0	1.573	0.787

$$\sum_i L_{qi} = 11.463, \qquad \overline{W} = 1.1463 \text{ hours}$$

problems that might accompany the new changes. These problems (which were mainly of an intangible nature) were studied in detail. It was finally decided that the tremendous reduction in the waiting time would still warrant the use of the pool.

Design of the Service Pool

The preceding discussion shows the advantages of using pools in place of an equivalent number of independent channels. The next question is: How many servers should be in a pool? An unnecessary increase in the number of servers involves high costs due to the large amount of idle time of the servers. On the other hand, not providing enough service gives rise to high costs due to long waiting lines. Both situations are undesirable. Thus, the chosen number of servers should balance the two extremes.

Such practice, however, is difficult to apply to the case reported here since there is no basis or clue as to how the cost per unit of waiting time can be estimated. It is impossible to assign a fixed monetary value to the delay in the typing of a letter. Here the "cost" associated with the delay in typing the material may vary from one item to another. In fact, for this situation, such "costs" could be a function of the time at which they take place so that the delay of the same item may involve different costs at different times. This indicates that the use of the cost model is inappropriate in this case. In addition, it seems difficult to define correctly the delay-cost function as the assumption of a direct proportionality between delay and cost seems erroneous.

An alternative method for the determination of the number of servers is the "level of aspiration" method discussed in Section 14·9·2. Here a compromise is made between the two conflicting measures: the expected waiting time, W_q, and the percentage of the pool's idle time, X. Such a compromise is effected by specifying the upper limits α and β on the values of W_q and X, respectively, and then determining the number of servers which satisfies these two conditions.

Applying this method to the case reported here, Table 14–5 gives the values of W_q and X for different values of N. Two cases are considered. First, Departments 1 through 5 are pooled, which yields $\sigma = 10$. Second, Department 6 is added to the pool and this increases σ to 14.7. (Notice that $\rho_6 > 1$.) The results of Table 14–5 are shown graphically in Figure 14–12. These graphs will be referred to as the "design curves" since they will be used for the purpose of designing the pool.

Table 14–5

	W_q (minutes)		$X\,(\%)$	
N	$\sigma = 10.0$	$\sigma = 14.7$	$\sigma = 10.0$	$\sigma = 14.7$
4	27.40	—	13	—
5	4.50	—	31	—
6	1.40	14.40	42	15
7	0.43	3.80	50	27
8	0.13	1.30	57	36
9	0.04	0.47	61	43
10	0.01	0.07	65	49
11	0.00	0.06	69	54

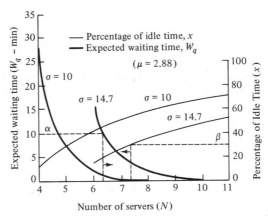

Figure 14–12

For $\sigma = 10$, by pooling the five typists ($N = 5$), the expected waiting time is reduced to about 5 minutes as compared to about 70 minutes in the case of independent channels. The percentage of idle time in this case is about 30 per cent. It is possible, however, to reduce the number of servers in the pool serving Department 1 through 5 by 1 ($N = 4$), and this will reduce the percentage of idle time to 13 per cent. In the meantime, the expected waiting time would be increased to about half an hour; that is, less than one half of the corresponding waiting time in the case of independent channels.

It is shown in Figure 14–12 that by adding Department 6 to the pool ($\sigma = 14.7$), no less than six typists could be employed. The expected waiting time would be as low as 15 minutes while the percentage of the pool idle time would be 15 per cent. Notice that because Department 6 is overworked ($\rho_6 > 1$), this department would eventually have employed one extra typist. In effect, then, the establishment of the pool saves one typist, besides it improves the efficiency of service substantially.

In generalizing this procedure to all the potential pools in the company, some departments were found to differ from the sample departments in service rates as their typing work is of a different nature. It was then necessary to construct new design curves which will account for the different values of service rates. It is seen that the formulas for L_q and X depend on the intensity factor, ρ, and not on the absolute values of σ and μ. Consequently, by replacing W_q in the design curves by L_q, the new design curves could be generalized to any multiple server queue having the indicated ρ. This does not change the above procedure since, knowing the value of σ, the formula for W_q can be used to change the L_q-scale to the appropriate W_q-scale. Figure 14–13 gives the new design curves which could be applied generally to determine the number of servers in a new pool. In addition, changes in the existing pools caused by variations in arrival rates and/or service rates could also be studied.

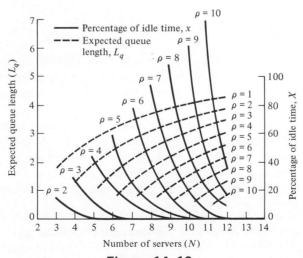

Figure 14–13

Conclusions

The theory of queues has proved useful in giving a quantitative measure for expressing the effectiveness of utilizing service pools in place of independent channels. It is found that, by using a pool, the efficiency of the system is increased through better utilization of the work time. Also, even though the independent channels may be fully utilized (that is, utilization factor very close to 1), the establishment of a pool could well lead to substantial improvement in the efficiency of the system.

In determining the "optimal" number of servers in the typing pool, the traditional cost models are shown to be inappropriate, as it is impractical to estimate the cost parameter per unit of waiting time. Also the waiting time-cost relationship is not definitely known. These difficulties may be common in many queueing situations. The proposed method selects the value of N which gives a compromise between the values of the two conflicting measures of the expected waiting time per customer and the percentage of the pool's idle time. This method is found to be both simple and significant.

SELECTED REFERENCES

1. Cox, D. R. and W. L. Smith, *Queues*, London: Methuen and Co., 1961.
2. Elmaghraby, S. E., *The Design of Production Systems*, New York: Reinhold, 1966, Chapter 5.
3. Lee, A., *Applied Queueing Theory*, Toronto: Macmillan, 1966.
4. Morse, P., *Queues, Inventories and Maintenance*, New York: Wiley, 1958.
5. Saaty, T., *Elements of Queueing Theory*, New York: McGraw-Hill, 1961.

PROBLEMS[18]

□ **14-1** Study the following system and then identify all the associated queueing situations. For each situation, define the customers, the server(s), the service discipline, the service time, the maximum queue length, and the calling source.

Orders for jobs are received at a workshop for processing. Upon receipt, the foreman decides whether it is a rush job or a regular job. Some of these orders require the use of one type of machine of which several are available. The remaining orders are processed in a two-stage production line of which two only are available. In each of the two groups, one facility is especially assigned

---

[18] Note: In the following exercises the reader will find it helpful to use the general computer subroutine in Appendix C for working the numerical problems (especially those of the $M/M/c$ models). Problems marked with (*) are designed primarily for the readers interested in the theoretical development of queueing models.

to handle rush jobs. Jobs arriving at any facility are processed in the order of their arrival. Completed orders are shipped upon arrival from a terminal shipping zone. This shipping zone is assumed to have a limited capacity.

Sharpened tools for the different machines are being supplied from a central tool crib where the operators exchange their old tools for new ones. When a machine breaks down, a repairman is called from the service pool to attend it. Machines working on rush orders always receive priorities both in acquiring new tools from the crib and in receiving repair service.

☐ **14-2** Customers arrive at a service facility according to a Poisson distribution. If the arrival rate is 20 per unit time and assuming that the system is empty at $t = 0$, find the following.

(a) The probability of having 20 in the system at $t = 30$ given there are 10 in the system at $t = 15$.
(b) The average number in the system at $t = 10$ and at $t = 20$.

☐ **14-3** Assume a Poisson arrival process with mean 2 per unit time. Suppose an arrival occurred at $t = 30$. What is the probability that an arrival will occur by $t = 40$? What is the probability that an arrival will occur before $t = 40$ and after $t = 35$?

☐ ***14-4** Solve the difference equations of the model in Section 14·3·2 using induction.

☐ ***14-5** Consider the pure birth process (Section 14·3·2) where the system starts with k customers at $t = 0$. Derive the system of equations describing the system and then show that

$$P_n(t) = \frac{e^{-\lambda t}(\lambda t)^{n-k}}{(n-k)!}, \qquad n = k, k+1, \ldots,$$

using (a) induction, and (b) z-transform.

☐ **14-6** Inventory is withdrawn from a stock of 80 items according to a Poisson distribution with mean 5 per day. What is the probability that after a period of 10 days at least 30 items are left? No items are left?

☐ **14-7** The probability of completing service during a small interval of time h is assumed directly proportional to h with the proportionality constant $C = 10$. During h, the service is either completed or not completed. Find the probability that the service is completed by $t = 50$ given it began at $t = 40$.

☐ **14-8** Cars arrive at a toll gate on a freeway according to a Poisson distribution with mean 90 per hour. The average time for passing through the gate is 38 seconds. Drivers complain of their long waiting time. The authorities are willing to decrease the passing time through the gate to 30 seconds by introducing new automatic devices. This can be justified only if under the old system the number of waiting cars exceeds 5. In addition the percentage of idle time of the gate under the new system should not exceed 10%. Can the new device be justified?

☐ **14-9** Customers arrive at a one-window drive-in bank according to a Poisson distribution with mean 10 per hour. Service time per customer is exponential with mean 5 minutes. The space in front of the window, including that for the serviced car, can accommodate a maximum of three cars. Other cars can wait outside this space.

(a) What is the probability that an arriving customer can drive directly to the space in front of the window?
(b) What is the probability that an arriving customer will have to wait outside the indicated space?
(c) How long an arriving customer is expected to wait before starting service?
(d) How many spaces should be provided in front of the window so that all the arriving cusomers can wait in front of the window at least 20 per cent of the time?

☐ *14-10 Show that for the $(M/M/1):(FCFS/\infty/\infty)$ model, the distribution of the waiting time in the queue is

$$w_q(T) = \begin{cases} 1 - \rho, & T = 0 \\ \mu\rho(1 - \rho)\lambda e^{-(\mu - \lambda)T}, & T > 0, \end{cases}$$

where $\rho = \lambda/\mu$. Then find W_q using the expression for $w_q(T)$.

☐ *14-11 For the $(M/M/1):(GD/\infty/\infty)$ model, show that,

(a) The expected number in the queue given the queue is not empty =
$$\frac{1}{1 - \rho}.$$
(b) The expected waiting time in queue for those who have to wait =
$$\frac{1}{\mu - \lambda}.$$

☐ *14-12 For the $(M/M/1):(GD/\infty/\infty)$ model, suppose that the model is generalized such that when n persons are in the system, a new arrival occurs according to a Poisson distribution with parameter λ_n and that service is performed according to an exponential distribution with mean $1/\mu_n$. Assuming that steady state probabilities exist, find the steady state difference equations describing the system. Then show that the steady state probabilities p_n are given by

$$p_n = p_0 \prod_{i=1}^{n} \frac{\lambda_{i-1}}{\mu_i}, \qquad n = 1, 2, \ldots .$$

☐ *14-13   For the model in Problem 14-12 suppose that

$$\lambda_n = \lambda,$$

$$\mu_n = n^\alpha \mu,$$

where λ, μ, and α are given positive constants. This model represents the case where the server regulates his output according to the number of customers, n, in the system. The constant α is known as the "pressure" coefficient.

Find the steady state difference equations describing the system and then solve showing that

$$p_0 = \frac{1}{Q}$$

$$p_n = \frac{(\lambda/\mu)^n}{(n!)^\alpha Q}, \qquad n = 1, 2, \ldots,$$

where

$$Q = \sum_{n=0}^{\infty} \frac{(\lambda/\mu)^n}{(n!)^\alpha}.$$

☐ 14-14   For the $(M/M/1):(GD/N/\infty)$ model (Section 14·4·3), show that the two expressions for λ_{eff} are equivalent, namely

$$\lambda_{\text{eff}} = \lambda(1 - p_N) = \mu(L_s - L_q).$$

☐ *14-15   For the $(M/M/1):(GD/N/\infty)$ model (Section 14·4·3), find the expression for L_s using the properties of the z-transform.

☐ 14-16   Patients arrive at a clinic according to a Poisson distribution at the rate of 30 patients per hour. The waiting room does not accommodate more than 14 patients. Examination time per patient is exponential with mean rate 20 per hour.

(a) Find the effective arrival rate at the clinic.
(b) What is the probability that an arriving patient will not wait? Will find a vacant seat in the room?
(c) What is the expected waiting time until a patient is discharged from the clinic?

☐ *14-17   Solve the steady state difference equations of the $(M/M/c)$: $(GD/\infty/\infty)$ model using the z-transform.

☐ 14-18   In an $(M/M/2):(GD/\infty/\infty)$ system, the mean service time is 5 minutes and the mean interarrival time is 8 minutes.

(a) What is the probability of a delay?
(b) What is the probability of at least one of the servers being idle?
(c) What is the probability that both servers are idle?

☐ **14-19** A computer center is equipped with three digital computers, all of the same type and capability. The number of users in the center at any time is equal to 10. For *each* user, the time for writing (and key punching) a program is exponential with mean rate 0.5 per hour. Once a program is completed, it is sent directly to the center for execution. The computer time per program is exponentially distributed with mean rate 2 per hour. Assuming the center is in operation on full-time basis, and neglecting the effect of computer down time, find the following.

(a) The probability that a program is not executed immediately upon receipt at the center.

(b) The average time until a program is released from the center.

(c) The average number of programs awaiting execution.

(d) The expected number of idle computers.

(e) The percentage of time the computer center is idle.

(f) The average percentage of idle time *per computer*.

☐ **14-20** An airport terminal services three types of customers; those arriving from rural areas, those arriving from suburban areas, and the transit customers who are changing planes at the airport. The arrival distribution for each of the three groups is assumed Poisson with mean arrival rates 10, 5, and 7 per hour, respectively. Assuming that all the customers require the same time of service at the terminal and that the service time is exponential with mean rate 10 per hour, how many counters should be provided at the terminal under each of the following conditions?

(a) The expected waiting time in the system per customer does not exceed 15 minutes.

(b) The expected number of customers in the system is at most 10.

(c) The probability that all counters are idle does not exceed .11.

☐ *__**14-21**__ For the $(M/M/c):(FCFS/\infty/\infty)$ model, show that the p.d.f. of the waiting time in the queue is given by

$$w_q(T) = \begin{cases} 1 - \dfrac{\rho^c p_0}{(c-1)!(c-\rho)}, & T = 0, \\[2mm] \dfrac{\mu\rho^c e^{-\mu(c-\rho)T}}{(c-1)!}\, p_0, & T > 0. \end{cases}$$

☐ *__**14-22**__ In Problem 14-21, show that

$$P\{T > y\} = P\{T > 0\}e^{-(c\mu-\lambda)y},$$

where $P\{T > 0\}$ is the probability that an arriving customer must wait.

☐ *__**14-23**__ For the $(M/M/c):(FCFS/\infty/\infty)$ model, show that the p.d.f. of the waiting time in the system is given by

$$w(\tau) = \mu e^{-\mu\tau} + \frac{\rho^c \mu e^{-\mu\tau} p_0}{(c-1)!(c-1-\rho)}\left\{\frac{1}{c-\rho} - e^{-\mu(c-1-\rho)\tau}\right\},$$

for $\tau \geq 0$. (Hint: τ is the convolution of the waiting in queue, T, (Problem 14-21) and the service time distribution.)

☐ *14-24 (a) In a service facility with c parallel servers, assume that customers arrive according to a Poisson distribution with mean rate λ. Rather than assuming that any customer can join any free server, customers will be assigned to the different servers on a rotational basis so that the first arriving customer is assigned to Server 1, the second customer to Server 2, and so on. After the cycle is completed for all c servers, the assignment starts again by considering Server 1. Find the p.d.f. of the interarrival time at each server.

(b) Suppose in (a) above the customers are assigned randomly to the different servers according to the probabilities α_i, where $\alpha_i \geq 0$, and $\alpha_1 + \alpha_2 + \cdots + \alpha_c = 1$. Find the p.d.f. of the interarrival time at each server.

☐ *14-25 For the $(M/M/c):(GD/\infty/\infty)$ model, show that

(a) The probability that someone is waiting $= \dfrac{\rho}{c - \rho} p_c$.

(b) The expected number in the queue given it is not empty $= \dfrac{c}{c - \rho}$.

(c) The expected waiting time in queue for customers that have to wait $=$
$\dfrac{1}{\mu(c - \rho)}$.

☐ 14-26 In a bank customers arrive in a Poisson stream with mean 36 per hour. The service time per customer is negative exponential with mean .035 hour. Assuming that the system can accommodate at most 30 customers at a time, how many tellers should be provided under each of the following two conditions?

(a) The probability of having more than $c + 3$ waiting is less than 0.20, where c is the number of tellers.

(b) The expected number in the system does not exceed 3.

☐ *14-27 For the $(M/M/c):(GD/N/\infty)$, derive the steady state equations describing the situation for $N = c$, then show that the expression for p_n is given by

$$p_n = \begin{cases} \dfrac{\rho^n}{n!} p_0, & n = 0, 1, 2, \ldots, c, \\ 0, & \text{otherwise,} \end{cases}$$

where

$$p_0 = \left(\sum_{n=0}^{c} \frac{\rho^n}{n!} \right)^{-1}.$$

□ **14-28** In a parking lot there are 10 parking spaces only. Cars arrive according to a Poisson distribution with mean 10 per hour. The parking time is exponentially distributed with mean 10 minutes. Using the results of Problem 14-27, find the following.

(a) The expected number of empty parking spaces.
(b) The probability that an arriving car will not find a parking space.
(c) The effective arrival rate of the system.

□ **14-29** For the $(M/M/5):(GD/20/\infty)$ model, the following probabilities are computed based on $\lambda = \frac{1}{3}$ and $\mu = \frac{1}{12}$.

n	0	1	2	3	4	5	6	7	8	9	10
p_n	.013	.053	.105	.141	.141	.112	.090	.072	.058	.046	.037

n	11	12	13	14	15	16	17	18	19	20	
p_n	.029	.024	.019	.015	.012	.010	.008	.006	.005	.004	

(a) Compute L_s and L_q and then show that $\lambda_{\text{eff}} = \mu(L_s - L_q) = \mu(c - \bar{c}) = \lambda(1 - p_{20})$ where $c = 5$ and $\bar{c}$ is the expected number of idle channels.
(b) Compute W_s and W_q.

□ **14-30** In a self-service facility arrivals occur according to a Poisson distribution with mean 50 per hour. Service times per customer is exponentially distributed with mean 5 minutes.

(a) Find the expected number of customers in service.
(b) What is the percentage of time the facility is idle?

□ **14-31** Ten machines are being attended by a single overhead crane. When a machine finishes its load, the overhead crane is called to unload the machine and to provide it with a new load from an adjacent storage area. The machining time per load is assumed exponential with mean 30 minutes. The time from the moment the crane moves to service a machine until a new load is installed is also exponential with mean 10 minutes.

(a) Find the percentage of time the crane is idle.
(b) What is the expected number of machines waiting for crane service?

□ **14-32** Two repairmen are attending five machines in a workshop. Each machine breaks down according to a Poisson distribution with mean 3 per hour. The repair time per machine is exponential with mean 15 minutes.

(a) Find the probability that the two repairmen are idle. That one repairman is idle.
(b) What is the expected number of idle machines not being serviced?

☐ **14-33** Consider the machine servicing models, $(M/M/1):(GD/6/6)$ and $(M/M/3):(GD/20/20)$. The rate of breakdown per machine is one per hour while the service rate is 10 per hour. The probabilities p_n are computed for the $(M/M/1):(GD/6/6)$ model as,

n	0	1	2	3	4	5	6
p_n	.4845	.2907	.1454	.0582	.0175	.0035	.0003

and for the $(M/M/3):(GD/20/20)$ model as,

n	0	1	2	3	4	5	6	7
p_n	.13625	.27250	.25890	.15533	.08802	.04694	.02347	.01095

n	8	9	10	11	12	13 to 20		
p_n	.00475	.00190	.00070	.00023	.00007	.0000		

Show that although in the first model one repairman is assigned to 6 machines while in the second model each repairman is responsible for $6\frac{2}{3}$ machines, the second model yields a smaller expected waiting time per machine. Justify this conclusion.

☐ **14-34** In the $(M/M/3):(GD/20/20)$ model given in Problem 14-33 above, show that

$$\lambda_{\text{eff}} = \mu(L_s - L_q) = \mu(R - \bar{R}) = \lambda(K - L_s),$$

where $R = 3$ and $K = 20$. The remaining symbols are as defined in the chapter.

☐ **14-35** Customers arrive at a service facility according to a Poisson distribution with mean 5 per hour. Service time per customer is constant and equal to 10 minutes. Find L_s, L_q, W_s, and W_q.

☐ **14-36** Show that for the exponential service time with mean $1/\mu$ the (P-K) formula for L_s (Section 14·5·1) reduces to the corresponding formula for the $(M/M/1):(GD/\infty/\infty)$ model.

☐ ***14-37** Service is performed in a service facility in three consecutive stages with the service time at each stage being described by an exponential distribution with mean $1/\mu$. A new customer cannot be admitted until the customer already in service is finished with all the three stages. Assuming that customers arrive according to a Poisson distribution with mean λ, find the expected number in the system. Generalize the problem to the case where there are *m* consecutive stages in the facility. (Hint: the convolution of *m*-fold exponential distributions is a gamma distribution. See Section 12·9.)

☐ **14-38**   Job orders arriving at a production facility are divided into three groups. Group 1 will take the highest priority for processing while Group 3 will be processed only if there are no waiting orders from Groups 1 and 2. It is assumed that a job once admitted to the facility must be completed before any new job is taken in. Orders from Groups 1, 2, and 3 occur according to Poisson distributions with means 4, 3, and 2 per day, respectively. The service times for the three groups are *constant* with rates 10, 9 and 10 per day, respectively. Find the following.

(a) The expected number of waiting jobs in each of the three groups.
(b) The expected waiting time in the system for each of the three queues.
(c) The expected waiting time in the system for *any* customer.
(d) The expected number waiting in the system.

☐ **14-39**   Repeat Problem 14-38 given that the service time distributions are *exponential* with service rates 10, 9, and 10 per day, respectively.

☐ **14-40**   Suppose in Problem 14-38 above, there are three production facilities in parallel. The service time distribution for each facility is negative exponential with mean 5 minutes. Find the expected number of waiting jobs in each group. What is the total number of waiting jobs?

☐ **14-41**   Repeat Problem 14-40 assuming there are five production facilities in parallel and compare the results.

☐ ***14-42**   Rework the model in Section 14·7 assuming three tandem stations. Assume all the remaining conditions to be the same as in the two stations model.

☐ **14-43**   In a production line suppose there are *k* stations in series. (See the figure below.) Assume that jobs arrive at Station 1 from an infinite source

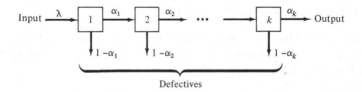

Defectives

according to a Poisson distribution with mean rate λ per unit time. The output from station *i* is used as input to station *i* + 1. Because there are defective items at each station, it is assumed that the percentage of good items from station *i* is equal to $100\alpha_i$, $0 \le \alpha_i \le 1$. The remaining percentage, $100(1 - \alpha_i)$, represents the defectives at station *i*. Assume that the service time distribution at station *i* is negative exponential with mean rate μ_i per unit time.

(a) Derive a general expression for determining the storage space associated with each station *i* such that all the arriving (good) items can be accommodated β per cent of the time.
(b) Let $\lambda = 20$ items per hour and $\mu_i = 30$ items per hour for all the stations. The percentage of defectives at each station can be assumed constant and equal to 10 per cent. Give a numerical answer for Part (a) given $k = 5$ and $\beta = 95\%$.
(c) Using the data in (b) above, what is the expected number of defective items from all the stations during a period of *T* hours?

☐ **14-44** Suppose in Problem 14-43 there is one rework station associated with each station in the production line. (See the figure below.) Defective

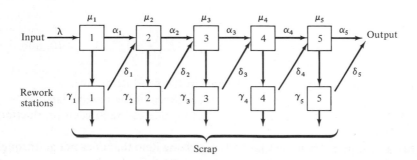

items are reworked in these "rework" stations and are sent to the station succeeding the one from which they arrive. Assume that for the *i*th rework station the service time distribution is exponential with mean rate γ_i per unit time and that the percentage of items that can be reworked successfully is equal to $\delta_i\%$.

(a) Answer Part (b) in Problem 13-43 if in addition $\gamma_i = 4$ items per hour for all *i* and $\delta_i = 1/(i + 1)$, $i = 1, 2, \ldots, 5$.
(b) How much space must be provided for each rework station in order to accommodate all the incoming defectives 90% of the time?
(c) What is the average number of defective items in each rework station (queue + in service)?
(d) What is the expected waiting time until an arriving item at Station 1 is released from Station $k = 5$?
(e) Answer Parts (a), (b), (c), and (d) assuming $\delta_i = 1$ for all *i*.

☐ **14-45** In Problem 14-44 suppose all the rework stations are pooled into parallel channels. The service time distribution for each channel is exponential with the same rate γ per unit time. Assume that the percentage of reworked items at each channel is equal to δ and that the output from the pooled facility is distributed back to the respective production stations according to the same input ratios to the facility.

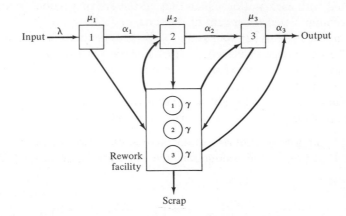

Let $k = 3$, $\lambda = 10$, $\mu_i = 15$ for all i, $\alpha_i = 1/2i$, $i = 1, 2, 3$, $\gamma = 10$, and $\delta = 90\%$. Find the following.

(a) The probability of having 3 items in the production line.
(b) The probability of having 2 or more items in the rework facility.
(c) The average number of items awaiting processing at each production-line station.
(d) The expected waiting time for an arriving item that does not go through the rework facility until it is released from Station k.
(e) The expected number in the entire system comprising both the production line and the rework facility.

□ **14-46** Show how the random deviates can be generated for each of the following p.d.f.'s.

(a) Binomial with parameters $n = 5$ and $p = .6$.
(b) Uniform continuous distribution on the interval (a, b), $a < b$.
(c) Negative binomial distribution with parameters $c = 3$ and $p = .3$.
(d) The distribution given by the p.d.f.

$$f(x) = \begin{cases} .08x, & 0 \le x \le 5, \\ 0, & \text{otherwise.} \end{cases}$$

□ **14-47** Simulate the $(M/M/1):(FCFS/\infty/\infty)$ queueing system using the variable time method. Assume $\lambda = 10$ per hour and $\mu = 15$ per hour. Compute L_s and L_q and compare with the steady state results given in Section 14·4·1.

□ **14-48** In Problem 14-47, compute W_q under *FCFS* and *LCFS* service disciplines using simulation. Sample from the simulation to determine the waiting time distribution in both cases and then compare the results.

☐ **14-49** Suppose in Problem 14-47 the service time distribution is described by the following discrete p.d.f.

t (minutes)	1	2	3	4	5
$p(t)$	.1	.3	.25	.25	.1

Simulate the resulting queueing system and compare the average waiting time in the queue with the steady state results given in Section 14·5·1.

☐ **14-50** An inventory stock is depleted and replenished according to Poisson distributions. Mean times between depletions and replenishments are equal to $1/\mu$ and $1/\lambda$, respectively. This process may be viewed as an $(M/M/1):(GD/\infty/\infty)$ queueing model.

Suppose every unit of time inventory is out of stock, a penalty cost C_2 is incurred. Also every unit of time n items of inventory are on hand, a holding cost $C_1 n$ is incurred, where $C_2 > C_1$.

(a) Find the expression for the *expected* total cost per unit time.
(b) What is the optimal value of $\rho = \lambda/\mu$?

☐ **14-51** For an $(M/M/1):(GD/\infty/\infty)$ model, find the optimal service rate μ given that the cost per unit increase in μ per unit time is \$10 while the cost of waiting per unit waiting per customer is \$1. The arrival rate is 20 per unit time.

☐ *****14-52** Verify the result

$$L_s(c) - L_s(c + 1) \le \frac{C_1}{C_2} \le L_s(c - 1) - L_s(c)$$

given in Section 14·9·1·2 for the optimal number of servers c.

☐ **14-53** In Section 14·9·1·2, suppose for the $(M/M/c):(GD/\infty/\infty)$ model $\lambda = 10$ and $\mu = 3$. The costs are $C_1 = 5$ and $C_2 = 25$. Find the number of servers that must be used in order to minimize the total expected costs.

☐ **14-54** Two repairmen are being considered for attending 10 machines in a workshop. The first repairman will be paid at the rate of \$3 per hour. He can repair machines at the rate of 5 per hour. The second repairman will be paid \$5 per hour but he can repair machines at the rate of 8 per hour. It is estimated that machine down time cost \$8 per hour.

Assuming that machines break down according to a Poisson distribution with mean 4 per hour and that the repair time is exponentially distributed, which repairman should be hired?

☐ **14-55** In an $(M/M/c):(GD/\infty/\infty)$ model with $\lambda = 17.5$ per hour and $\mu = 10$ per hour, it is desired to select the number of servers c such that the percentage of idle time does not exceed 15% and such that the time a customer spends in the system does not exceed 30 minutes. If the cost per additional server per unit time is $10, what is the implied cost of waiting (per customer per unit time) as dictated by the above decision criterion?

CHAPTER 15

Queueing Theory and Imbedded Markov Chains

§ 15·1
Introduction[1]

In the preceding chapter, it was shown that for the non-Poisson queues, the analysis using elementary probability theory is inconvenient mainly because the process becomes non-Markovian (see, for example, the derivation of the (P-K) formula, Section 14·5·1). In this chapter, a different type of analysis will be presented using the theory of imbedded Markov chains. Two general non-Poisson models will be investigated; $(M/G/1):(GD/\infty/\infty)$ and $(GI/M/1):(FCFS/\infty/\infty)$. Models such as $(E_m/M/1)$, $(D/M/1)$, $(M/E_m/1)$, and $(M/D/1)$ can then be treated as special cases of the above two models.

The concept of imbedded Markov chains was introduced by D. Kendall (1948). This concept implies that the $(M/G/1)$ model may be studied by observing the state of the system (number in the system) at the epochs of departure. The transition matrix is determined by the probabilities that certain numbers of arrivals will occur during a service time. Similarly, the $(GI/M/1)$ model can be studied by observing the epochs of arrival with the transition matrix being defined by the probabilities of certain numbers of departures occurring during an interarrival time. The indicated epochs of arrival and departure are also known as "regeneration points."

The basic advantage of using the above analysis is that the problem has reduced to a discrete time Markov chain even though the original system is non-Markovian. It should be noted, however, that the steady state results

---

[1] The reader should review Section 12·10 before proceeding with the material in this chapter.

obtained for this analysis are slightly different from those obtained by continuous time analysis. This follows since in the present analysis the averages are taken over discrete points in time (regeneration points). It suffices to say that for the $(GI/M/1)$ model, if L_s and L_s^d are respectively the continuous and discrete time averages of the number in the system, then

$$L_s^d \le L_s \le L_s^d + 1.$$

In the following models, this point should be kept in mind. No attempt will be made here, however, to introduce a new symbolism which will reflect the new definitions.

§ 15·2
$(M/G/1):(GD/\infty/\infty)$

This model derives the same result as the (P-K) formula of Section 14·5·1. Let $b(t)$ be the p.d.f. of service time. The system is observed only right after a service departure has been completed. Such instants in time define the *regeneration points*. If i customers are in the *system* at observation time, then at the next observation time, the number in the system, j, is given by

$$j = \begin{cases} k, & \text{if } i = 0, \\ i - 1 + k, & \text{if } i > 0, \end{cases}$$

where $k \, (= 0, 1, 2, \ldots)$ is the number of arrivals during a service time (cf. Figure 14–3).

Let q_k be the probability that k persons arrive during a service time. Since arrivals occur according to a Poisson distribution with mean arrival rate λ, then

$$q_k = \int_0^\infty \frac{e^{-\lambda t}(\lambda t)^k}{k!} \, b(t) \, dt, \qquad k = 0, 1, 2, \ldots.$$

The transition matrix between the beginning and the end of a service is given by

$$\mathbf{A} = \begin{array}{c|cccccc} {}_{i}\diagdown^{\,j} & 0 & 1 & 2 & 3 & 4 & \cdots \\ \hline 0 & q_0 & q_1 & q_2 & q_3 & q_4 & \cdots \\ 1 & q_0 & q_1 & q_2 & q_3 & q_4 & \cdots \\ 2 & 0 & q_0 & q_1 & q_2 & q_3 & \cdots \\ 3 & 0 & 0 & q_0 & q_1 & q_2 & \cdots \\ 4 & 0 & 0 & 0 & q_0 & q_1 & \cdots \\ \vdots & \vdots & \vdots & \vdots & \vdots & \vdots & \end{array}$$

Let $p_n \, (n = 0, 1, 2, \ldots)$ be the steady state probabilities that there are n in the system. It can be shown that the states of the matrix $\mathbf{A}$ are ergodic for

$\rho = \lambda E\{t\} < 1$. This means that under the same condition the corresponding Markov chain is ergodic. Thus the steady state probabilities are given by

$$(p_0, p_1, p_2, \ldots)A = (p_0, p_1, p_2, \ldots).$$

Or, for $n = 0, 1, 2, \ldots$,

$$p_0 q_n + p_1 q_n + p_2 q_{n-1} + p_3 q_{n-2} + \cdots + p_{n+1} q_0 = p_n.$$

These equations can now be put in the general form

$$p_n = p_0 q_n + \sum_{j=1}^{n+1} p_j q_{n+1-j}, \qquad n = 0, 1, 2, \ldots.$$

Now applying the z-transform to this last set of equations, then

$$\sum_{n=0}^{\infty} z^n p_n = \sum_{n=0}^{\infty} z^n p_0 q_n + \sum_{n=0}^{\infty} z^n \left(\sum_{j=1}^{n+1} p_j q_{n+1-j} \right)$$

$$= p_0 \sum_{n=0}^{\infty} z^n q_n + \frac{1}{z} \sum_{m=1}^{\infty} z^m \left\{ \sum_{j=0}^{m} p_j q_{m-j} - p_0 q_m \right\}.$$

To simplify this expression, consider,

$$r_m = \sum_{j=0}^{m} p_j q_{m-j}.$$

Clearly r_m is the convolution of p_m and q_m, and consequently (see Section 12·11·2),

$$Z(r_m) = Z(q_m)Z(p_m)$$

or,

$$R(z) = Q(z)P(z).$$

Thus, from the transformed equation given above,

$$P(z) = p_0 Q(z) + \frac{1}{z}\{R(z) - r_0\} - \frac{p_0}{z}\{Q(z) - q_0\}.$$

Since, $r_0 = p_0 q_0$ and $R(z) = Q(z)P(z)$, then

$$P(z) = p_0 \left(\frac{Q(z)}{1 + \dfrac{1 - Q(z)}{z - 1}} \right).$$

To determine p_0, it is noticed that

$$P(1) = 1 = \lim_{z \to 1} p_0 \left(\frac{Q(z)}{1 + \dfrac{1 - Q(z)}{z - 1}} \right).$$

$$= \lim_{z \to 1} p_0 \left\{ \frac{Q(z)(z - 1)}{z - Q(z)} \right\}.$$

Applying L'Hospital's rule, one gets finally,

$$p_0\left\{\frac{Q(1)}{1 - Q'(1)}\right\} = 1.$$

Since $Q(1) = 1$, then

$$p_0 = 1 - Q'(1).$$

To compute $Q'(1)$, one needs first to determine the expression for $Q(z)$.

$$Q(z) = \sum_{n=0}^{\infty} q_n z^n$$

$$= \sum_{n=0}^{\infty} z^n \int_0^\infty \frac{(\lambda t)^n e^{-\lambda t}}{n!} b(t)\, dt$$

$$= \int_0^\infty e^{\lambda t(z-1)} b(t)\, dt$$

$$= E\{e^{\lambda(z-1)t}\}.$$

Thus

$$Q'(1) = \int_0^\infty (\lambda t) e^{\lambda t(z-1)} b(t)\, dt \bigg|_{z=1} = \lambda E\{t\},$$

and it follows that

$$p_0 = 1 - \lambda E\{t\}$$

(Notice that $\rho = \lambda E\{t\}$ must be less than one as dictated by the ergodicity of the Markov chain.) The expression for $P(z)$ thus becomes,

$$P(z) = \frac{(1 - \lambda E\{t\})(z - 1)Q(z)}{(z - Q(z))}.$$

To obtain p_n, it is noticed that a general expression is not easily secured in this case because of the complexity of $P(z)$. Any individual probability can be obtained, however, using the formula

$$P^{(n)}(0) = n!\, p_n.$$

The expected number in the system can be obtained from $P(z)$ using the condition

$$P^{(1)}(1) = E\{n\} = L_s.$$

Thus, carrying out the differentiation and taking the limit as $z \to 1$, then

$$L_s = \lambda E\{t\} + \frac{Q''(1)}{2(1 - \lambda E\{t\})}.$$

But

$$Q''(1) = \lambda^2 \int_0^\infty t^2 e^{\lambda t(z-1)} b(t)\, dt \Big|_{z=1}$$

$$= \lambda^2 E\{t^2\}$$

$$= \lambda^2 (\text{Var}\{t\} + E^2\{t\}).$$

Thus

$$L_s = \lambda E\{t\} + \frac{\lambda^2 (\text{Var}\{t\} + E^2\{t\})}{2(1 - \lambda E(t)\})}.$$

This is the same as the (P-K) formula obtained in Section 14·5·1.

§ 15·2·1
(M/Em/1) : (GD/∞/∞)

This model will be treated as a special case of the above general model. Let the gamma service distribution be given by

$$b(t) = \frac{m\alpha (m\alpha t)^{m-1} e^{-m\alpha t}}{(m-1)!}, \qquad t > 0.$$

It is noticed that

$$E\{t\} = \frac{1}{\alpha} \quad \text{and} \quad \text{Var}\{t\} = \frac{1}{m\alpha^2}.$$

Now, to compute $P(z)$, it is necessary first to compute $Q(z)$. Thus, as shown previously,

$$Q(z) = \int_0^\infty e^{\lambda t(z-1)} b(t)\, dt$$

$$= \int_0^\infty e^{\lambda t(z-1)} \frac{m\alpha (m\alpha t)^{m-1} e^{-m\alpha t}}{(m-1)!}\, dt$$

$$= \frac{(m\alpha)^m}{(\lambda(1-z) + m\alpha)^m}$$

$$= \left(\frac{1-\beta}{1-\beta z} \right)^m,$$

where

$$\beta = \frac{\lambda}{\lambda + m\alpha}.$$

Hence, letting $\rho = \lambda E\{t\} = \lambda/\alpha$, then

$$P(z) = \frac{(1 - \rho)(1 - z)(1 - \beta)^m}{(1 - \beta)^m - z(1 - \beta z)^m}.$$

The general *inverse* of $P(z)$ ($= p_n$) is still difficult to obtain in this case. However, using the formula,

$$P^{(n)}(0) = n! p_n,$$

any particular p_n can be computed.

For the special case where $m = 1$, this model reduces to the $(M/M/1)$: $(GD/\infty/\infty)$ case. Another result can also be derived as a special case of the $(M/E_m/1)$ model. Since

$$E\{t\} = \frac{1}{\alpha} \quad \text{and} \quad \text{Var}\{t\} = \frac{1}{m\alpha^2},$$

it is noticed that as $m \to \infty$, Var $\{t\} = 0$. This is the characteristic of constant service time. Thus for the $(M/D/1)$ model, it can be shown that

$$P(z) = \frac{(1 - \rho)(1 - z)e^{\rho(z-1)}}{e^{\rho(z-1)} - z}$$

where $\rho = \lambda/\alpha$.

§ 15·3
$(GI/M/1):(FCFS/\infty/\infty)$

Let $a(v)$ be the density function of interarrival time and let μ be the service rate. The system is observed only right after an arrival occurs. Thus if i customers are in the system at observation time, then at the next observation time, the number in system j is given by

$$j = i + 1 - k, \qquad 0 \le k \le i$$

where k is the number of persons serviced between two successive arrivals.

Let d_k be the probability that k persons are serviced during time v. Since services (departures) occur according to a Poisson distribution with departure rate μ, then

$$d_k = \int_0^\infty \frac{(\mu v)^k e^{-\mu v}}{k!} a(v) \, dv.$$

The elements of the transition matrix $\mathbf{E} = \|e_{ij}\|$ are given by

$$e_{ij} = d_{i+1-j}, \qquad 1 \le j \le i + 1, \quad i \ge 0,$$

$$e_{i0} = 1 - \sum_{j=1}^{i+1} d_{i+1-j}$$

$$= 1 - \sum_{j=0}^{i} d_{i-j}$$

$$= 1 - \sum_{j=0}^{i} d_j = h_i.$$

Thus,

j i	0	1	2	3	4	$\cdots$
0	h_0	d_0	0	0	0	$\cdots$
1	h_1	d_1	d_0	0	0	$\cdots$
2	h_2	d_2	d_1	d_0	0	$\cdots$
3	h_3	d_3	d_2	d_1	d_0	$\cdots$
$\vdots$	$\vdots$	$\vdots$	$\vdots$	$\vdots$	$\vdots$	

$\mathbf{E} =$ (to the left of the table)

It can be proved that all the states of $\mathbf{E}$ are ergodic for $(1/\mu E\{v\}) < 1$. This means that the corresponding Markov chain is ergodic under the same condition. Thus, the steady state probabilities p_n are given by

$$(p_0, p_1, p_2, \ldots)\mathbf{E} = (p_0, p_1, p_2, \ldots).$$

Then from the arrangement of the positive elements e_{ij} of $\mathbf{E}$, it is obvious that for $j \geq 1$,

$$p_j = \sum_{i=j-1}^{\infty} p_i e_{ij}$$

$$= \sum_{k=0}^{\infty} p_{k+j-1} d_k, \qquad j \geq 1.$$

Since in computing the steady state probabilities of a Markov chain, one of the equations is redundant (see Section 12·10·2·3), it follows that the above set of equations holds also for p_0.

Now, to solve for p_n, consider the trial solution.

$$p_n = Bx^n, \qquad n \geq 0,$$

where B is a constant $(\neq 0)$ to be determined shortly and x is a parameter. This equation holds only for $(0 < x < 1)$ since for $x = 0$, $p_n = 0$, and for $x \geq 1$, the above trial solution cannot define a probability distribution $(\sum_{n=0}^{\infty} p_n > 1)$. Thus substituting the trial solution in the steady state equations above, then

$$Bx^n = \sum_{k=0}^{\infty} Bx^{k+n-1} d_k, \qquad n = 0, 1, 2, \ldots,$$

or,

$$x = \sum_{k=0}^{\infty} x^k d_k \equiv D(x).$$

In order to solve the equation,

$$x = D(x),$$

it is first noticed that $D(x)$ is a convex function in x. Also $D(0) = d_0 > 0$ and $D(1) = 1$. Thus, plotting $x = D(x)$ as shown in Figure 15–1, it follows that

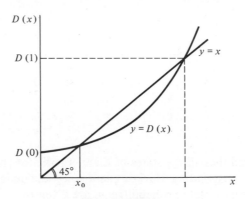

Figure 15–1

$x = D(x)$ will have a solution in the range $0 < x < 1$ if

$$\frac{dD(x)}{dx} > 1$$

at $x = 1$, that is, if $D'(1) > 1$. Since,

$$D(x) = \sum_{j=0}^{\infty} \int_0^{\infty} \frac{e^{-\mu v}(\mu x v)^j}{j!} \, a(v) \, dv,$$

then

$$D'(x) = \int_0^{\infty} e^{-\mu(1-x)v} \mu v a(v) \, dv$$

and

$$D'(1) = \mu \int_0^{\infty} v a(v) \, dv = \mu E\{v\}.$$

Thus $D'(1) > 1$ implies that $(1/\mu E\{v\}) < 1$ which ascertains the ergodicity condition of the Markov chain given above.

Under the given condition, let $x = x_0$ $(0 < x_0 < 1)$ be the solution of $x = D(x)$. Now, to determine the constant B, it is noticed that

$$\sum_{i=0}^{\infty} p_i = B \sum_{i=0}^{\infty} x_0^i$$

$$= \frac{B}{1 - x_0}, \qquad 0 < x_0 < 1.$$

Hence

$$B = (1 - x_0)$$

and,

$$p_n = (1 - x_0)x_0^n, \qquad n = 0, 1, 2, \ldots$$

It follows that p_n has a geometric distribution which is independent of the arrival distribution except naturally as it pertains to the determination of x_0. From this, it follows that

$$L_s = E\{n\} = \frac{x_0}{1 - x_0}.$$

§ 15·3·1
Distribution of the Waiting Time Based on *FCFS* Discipline

Since the service time distribution is exponential, the waiting time in the *system* of an arriving person given there are n persons ahead of him is gamma-distributed with parameters $(n + 1)$ and μ. Thus, the C.D.F. of the waiting time distribution is given by

$$W(\tau) = \sum_{n=0}^{\infty} W(\tau \,|\, n + 1)p_n$$

$$= \sum_{n=0}^{\infty} (1 - x_0)x_0^n \int_0^\tau \frac{\mu(\mu t)^n e^{-\mu t}}{n!} \, dt,$$

and the p.d.f. is then given by

$$w(\tau) = \frac{dW(\tau)}{d\tau}$$

$$= \sum_{n=0}^{\infty} \frac{\mu(\mu\tau)^n e^{-\mu\tau}(1 - x_0)\, x_0^n}{n!}$$

$$= \mu(1 - x_0)e^{-\mu(1-x_0)\tau}, \qquad \tau > 0,$$

which is negative exponential with mean

$$E\{\tau\} = \frac{1}{\mu(1 - x_0)} = W_s.$$

The results for the $(E_m/M/1)$ and $(D/M/1)$ models can also be derived as special cases of the above model using a procedure similar to the one followed in Section 15·2.

SELECTED REFERENCES

1. PARZEN, E., *Stochastic Processes*, San Francisco: Holden-Day, 1962.
2. PRABHU, N., *Queues and Inventories*, New York: Wiley, 1965.

PROBLEMS

☐ **15-1** Show that for the special case of exponential service time with mean $1/\mu$ the results of the $(M/G/1)$ model reduce to those of the $(M/M/1)$ model (Section 14·4·1).

☐ **15-2** Arrivals at a single-server queueing system occur according to a Poisson distribution with mean arrival rate of five per hour. If the service time (in minutes) follows the uniform distribution

$$f(x) = \begin{cases} 1/10, & 5 \le x \le 15, \\ 0, & \text{otherwise,} \end{cases}$$

find the following.

(a) The probability that the system is busy.
(b) The expected number of customers in the system.
(c) The expected waiting time in the queue.

☐ **15-3** Consider the single-server queueing system where the server upon commencing on a new customer will decide whether he needs to be serviced or not. The probability that a customer will not need any service is 0.3. The service time per serviced customer is 10 minutes. If customers arrive according to a Poisson distribution with mean five per hour, find the following.

(a) The probability that there are 10 persons in the system after a service is completed, given there were four persons in the system at the start of this service.
(b) The probability that there is no one in the system.
(c) The expected waiting time in the system.

☐ **15-4** In the $(GI/M/1)$ model, let the interarrival time be described by the gamma distribution.

$$a(v) = \frac{m\lambda(m\lambda v)^{m-1}e^{-m\lambda v}}{(m-1)!}, \qquad v > 0,$$

with $E\{v\} = 1/\lambda$ and $\text{Var}\{v\} = 1/m\lambda^2$. Show that

$$D(x_0) = \left(\frac{1-\sigma}{1-\sigma x_0}\right)^m,$$

where,

$$\sigma = \frac{\mu}{\mu + m\lambda}$$

and $D(x_0)$ is as defined in the chapter. Derive $D(x_0)$ for the constant inter-arrival case as a special case of the results for the gamma distribution.

☐ **15-5** Show that for exponential interarrival time with mean $1/\lambda$, the results of the $(GI/M/1)$ model reduce to those of the $(M/M/1)$ model (Section 14·4·1).

☐ **15-6** Consider a single server queueing system with constant interarrival time equal to 10 minutes. Departures occur in the system according to a Poisson distribution with mean 10 per hour. Find the following.

(a) The probability that there are two in the system when an arrival occurs given there were exactly four in the system when the immediately preceding arrival occurred.

(b) The probability that the system will have 2 or 3 customers when an arrival occurs given the system had exactly three customers when the immediately preceding arrival occurred.

(c) The expected number in the system.

(d) The expected waiting time in the system.

(e) The probability that there is no one in the system. At least two in the system.

☐ **15-7** The proof of the queueing formula $L_s = \lambda W_s$ (Section 14·2·5) requires that L_s be computed as a steady state average over all instants of time while only W_s can be calculated at regeneration points. This r.eans that the said formula does not apply in general to the results of the $(GI/M/1)$ model since L_s is computed by averaging over regeneration (imbedded) points. Verify this result by showing that for the *FCFS* service discipline and gamma distributed or constant interarrival time, the values of W_s obtained from the said formula and from the waiting time distribution (Section 15·3·1) are not consistent.

☐ **15-8** In Problem 15-7, regardless of the given restriction on the derivation of the formula $L_s = \lambda W_s$, show that for exponential interarrival time the two methods for computing W_s will yield the same result. Why is this true only for the case of Poisson arrivals?

Part 3

Nonlinear Programming

CHAPTER 16

Classical
Optimization Theory[1]

§ 16·1
Introduction

Classical optimization theory deals with the use of differential calculus to determine the points of *maxima* and *minima* (extrema) for both unconstrained and constrained continuous functions. Although, in general, the developed techniques are hardly suitable for efficient numerical computations, the underlying theory gives the basis for devising most of the nonlinear programming algorithms. (See Chapter 17.)

The topics introduced in this chapter include the development of the necessary and sufficient conditions for determining the extreme points for the unconstrained problem, the treatment of the constrained problem using the *Jacobian* and the *Lagrangian* methods, and the development of the *Kuhn-Tucker conditions* for the general problem with inequality constraints.

§ 16·2
Unconstrained Extremal Problems

In this section the problem of determining the extreme points of an unconstrained continuous function is considered. Mathematically, a point x_0 represents a maximum if for $|h|$ sufficiently small,

$$f(x_0 + h) - f(x_0) < 0.$$

Similarly, x_0 represents a minimum point if

$$f(x_0 + h) - f(x_0) > 0.$$

Figure 16–1 illustrates a continuous function $f(x)$ defined on the interval

---

[1] This chapter assumes familiarity with the material in Appendixes A and B.

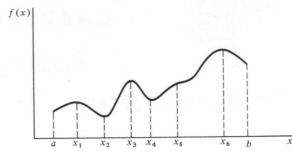

Figure 16–1

(a, b). The points x_1, x_2, x_3, x_4, and x_6 represent all the extreme points of $f(x)$. These include x_1, x_3, and x_6 as the points of maxima, and x_2 and x_4 as the points of minima. Since

$$f(x_6) = \max\{f(x_1), f(x_3), f(x_6)\},$$

$f(x_6)$ is called *global* or *absolute* maximum while $f(x_1)$ and $f(x_3)$ are called *local* or *relative* maxima. Similarly, $f(x_4)$ is a local minimum while $f(x_2)$ is a global minimum.

It will be shown now how extreme points can be identified for the general case of an *n*-variable function $f(\mathbf{X})$, $\mathbf{X} = \{x_1, x_2, \ldots, x_n\}$. Theorem 16·2-1 gives the necessary conditions for the occurrence of an extreme point and Theorem 16·2-2 establishes the sufficiency conditions. It will be assumed throughout this section that both the first and the second partial derivatives of $f(\mathbf{X})$ are continuous.

Theorem 16·2-1: *A necessary condition for $\mathbf{X}_0$ to be an extreme point of the continuous function $f(\mathbf{X})$ is that*

$$\nabla f(\mathbf{X}_0) = \mathbf{0}.$$

PROOF: By Taylor's theorem (Section B·5·1), for $0 < \theta < 1$,

$$f(\mathbf{X}_0 + \mathbf{h}) - f(\mathbf{X}_0) = \nabla f(\mathbf{X}_0)\mathbf{h} + \tfrac{1}{2}\mathbf{h}^T \mathbf{Hh} \Big|_{\mathbf{X}_0 + \theta\mathbf{h}}$$

where

$$\mathbf{h} = (h_1, \ldots, h_j, \ldots, h_n)^T,$$

and $|h_j|$ is sufficiently small for all $j = 1, 2, \ldots, n$.

For small $|h_j|$, the remainder term $\tfrac{1}{2}(\mathbf{h}^T \mathbf{Hh})$ is of the order h_j^2 and hence it will tend to zero as $h_j \to 0$. Thus,

$$f(\mathbf{X}_0 + \mathbf{h}) - f(\mathbf{X}_0) = \nabla f(\mathbf{X}_0)\mathbf{h} + 0(h_j^2)$$

$$\cong \nabla f(\mathbf{X}_0)\mathbf{h}.$$

Suppose now that $\mathbf{X}_0$ is a minimum point. It will be shown by contradiction that $\nabla f(\mathbf{X}_0)$ must vanish. For suppose it does not. Then for a specific j, either

$$\frac{\partial f(\mathbf{X}_0)}{\partial x_j} < 0 \quad \text{or} \quad \frac{\partial f(\mathbf{X}_0)}{\partial x_j} > 0.$$

Thus, by selecting h_j with the appropriate sign it is always possible to have

$$h_j \frac{\partial f(\mathbf{X}_0)}{\partial x_j} < 0.$$

Now, setting all other h_j equal to zero, then Taylor's expansion yields

$$f(\mathbf{X}_0 + h) - f(\mathbf{X}_0) < 0,$$

or

$$f(\mathbf{X}_0 + h) < f(\mathbf{X}_0).$$

This contradicts the assumption that $\mathbf{X}_0$ is a minimum point. Consequently, $\nabla f(\mathbf{X}_0)$ must vanish. This completes the proof of the theorem. ◄

A similar proof can be established for the maximization case. It thus follows that for $\mathbf{X}_0$ to be an extreme point, it is necessary that

$$\nabla f(\mathbf{X}_0) = \mathbf{0}.$$

This says that the partial derivatives of $f(\mathbf{X})$ with respect to x_j, $(j = 1, 2, \ldots, n)$ must vanish at the extreme point $\mathbf{X}_0$.

For the functions with one variable only (say, y), the above condition reduces to

$$f'(y_0) = 0.$$

It is noted that the above conditions are satisfied also for cases other than extreme points. These include, for example, inflection and saddle points. Consequently, the given conditions are necessary but not sufficient for identifying extreme points. It is thus more acceptable to refer to the points obtained from the solution of

$$\nabla f(\mathbf{X}_0) = \mathbf{0}$$

as *stationary* points. The next theorem establishes the sufficiency conditions for $\mathbf{X}_0$ to be an extreme point.

Theorem 16·2-2: *A sufficient condition for a stationary point* X_0 *to be an extreme point is that the Hessian matrix* H *evaluated at* X_0 *is*

(i) *positive-definite when* X_0 *is a minimum point, and*
(ii) *negative-definite when* X_0 *is a maximum point.*

PROOF: By Taylor's theorem, for $0 < \theta < 1$

$$f(X_0 + h) - f(X_0) = \nabla f(X_0)h + \tfrac{1}{2}h^T H h \Big|_{X_0 + \theta h} .$$

Since X_0 is a stationary point, then by Theorem 16·2-1, $\nabla f(X_0) = 0$. Thus,

$$f(X_0 + h) - f(X_0) = \tfrac{1}{2}h^T H h \Big|_{X_0 + \theta h} .$$

Let X_0 be a minimum point, then by definition,

$$f(X_0 + h) > f(X_0)$$

for all nonnull h. This means that for X_0 to be a minimum,

$$\tfrac{1}{2}h^T H h \Big|_{X_0 + \theta h} > 0.$$

However, by the continuity of the second partial derivative, the expression $\tfrac{1}{2}h^T H h$ must yield the same sign when evaluated at both X_0 and $X_0 + \theta h$. Since $h^T H h|_{X_0}$ defines a quadratic form (See Section A·3), this expression (and hence $h^T H h|_{X_0 + \theta h}$) is positive if, and only if, $H|_{X_0}$ is positive-definite. This means that a sufficient condition for the stationary point X_0 to be a minimum is that the Hessian matrix evaluated at the same point is positive-definite. This completes the proof for the minimization case. A similar proof can be established for the maximization case to show that the corresponding Hessian matrix is negative-definite. ◄

▶ **Example 16·2-1**
Consider the function

$$f(x_1, x_2, x_3) = x_1 + 2x_3 + x_2 x_3 - x_1^2 - x_2^2 - x_3^2.$$

Applying the necessary condition,

$$\nabla f(X_0) = 0,$$

this gives

$$\frac{\partial f}{\partial x_1} = 1 - 2x_1 = 0,$$

$$\frac{\partial f}{\partial x_2} = x_3 - 2x_2 = 0,$$

$$\frac{\partial f}{\partial x_3} = 2 + x_2 - 2x_3 = 0.$$

The solution of these simultaneous equations is given by

$$\mathbf{X}_0 = (\tfrac{1}{2}, \tfrac{2}{3}, \tfrac{4}{3}).$$

The sufficiency condition is checked now.

$$\mathbf{H}\bigg|_{\mathbf{X}_0} = \begin{bmatrix} \dfrac{\partial^2 f}{\partial x_1^2} & \dfrac{\partial^2 f}{\partial x_1\,\partial x_2} & \dfrac{\partial^2 f}{\partial x_1\,\partial x_3} \\[2ex] \dfrac{\partial^2 f}{\partial x_2\,\partial x_1} & \dfrac{\partial^2 f}{\partial x_2^2} & \dfrac{\partial^2 f}{\partial x_2\,\partial x_3} \\[2ex] \dfrac{\partial^2 f}{\partial x_3\,\partial x_1} & \dfrac{\partial^2 f}{\partial x_3\,\partial x_2} & \dfrac{\partial^2 f}{\partial x_3^2} \end{bmatrix}_{\mathbf{X}_0}$$

$$= \begin{bmatrix} -2 & 0 & 0 \\ 0 & -2 & 1 \\ 0 & 1 & -2 \end{bmatrix}.$$

The principal minor determinants of $\mathbf{H}|_{\mathbf{X}_0}$ have the values $-2, 4$, and -6, respectively. Thus, as indicated in Section A·3, $\mathbf{H}|_{\mathbf{X}_0}$ is negative-definite and $\mathbf{X}_0 = (\tfrac{1}{2}, \tfrac{2}{3}, \tfrac{4}{3})$ represents a maximum point. ◄

It should be noted that, in general, if $\mathbf{H}|_{\mathbf{X}_0}$ is indefinite, then $\mathbf{X}_0$ is not an extreme point. For the case where the Hessian matrix is semi-definite, the proof of sufficiency becomes rather involved.

The sufficiency condition established by Theorem 16·2-2 reduces readily for single variable functions to the following cases. Given y_0 is a stationary point, then

(i) $f''(y_0) < 0$ is a sufficient condition for y_0 to be a maximum extreme point.

(ii) $f''(y_0) > 0$ is a sufficient condition for y_0 to be a minimum extreme point.

These conditions are directly determined by considering the Hessian matrix with one element.

It must be noted that in the single variable function, if $f''(y_0)$ vanishes, the higher order derivatives must be investigated. This leads to the following theorem.

Theorem 16·2-3: *Given a function $f(y)$, if at a stationary point y_0 the first $(n - 1)$ derivatives vanish and $f^{(n)}(y) \neq 0$, then at $y = y_0$, $f(y)$ has*

(i) *an inflection point if n is odd, and*

(ii) *an extreme point if n is even. This extreme point will be a maximum if $f^{(n)}(y_0) < 0$ and a minimum if $f^{(n)}(y_0) > 0$.*

The proof of this theorem is left as an exercise for the reader.

▶ **Example 16·2-2**

Consider the two functions

(i) $f(y) = y^4$,

(ii) $g(y) = y^3$.

For $f(y) = y^4$,

$$f'(y) = 4y_3 = 0,$$

which yields $y_0 = 0$ as a stationary point. Now

$$f'(0) = f''(0) = f^{(3)}(0) = 0.$$

But $f^{(4)}(0) = 24 > 0$, hence $y_0 = 0$ is a minimum point. (See Figure 16-2.)

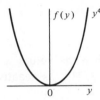

Figure 16–2

For $g(y) = y^3$,

$$g'(y) = 3y^2 = 0.$$

This yields $y_0 = 0$ as a stationary point. Since $g^{(n)}(0)$ is different from zero at $n = 3$, $y_0 = 0$ is an inflection point. ◀

§ 16·3
Constrained Extremal Problems

This section deals with the optimization of continuous functions subject to side conditions or constraints. Such constraints may be in the form of equation or inequation. Section 16·3·1 introduces the case with equality constraints while Section 16·3·2 introduces the other case with inequality constraints. The presentation in Section 16·3·1 is covered for the most part in Wilde and Beightler [4], pp. 31–41.

§ 16·3·1
Equality Constraints

§ 16·3·1·1
Constrained Derivatives (Jacobian) Method

Consider the problem:

$$\text{minimize} \quad x_0 = f(\mathbf{X}),$$

subject to

$$\mathbf{g}(\mathbf{X}) = 0,$$

where

$$\mathbf{X} = (x_1, x_2, \ldots, x_n),$$

$$\mathbf{g} = (g_1, g_2, \ldots, g_m)^T.$$

The functions $f(\mathbf{X})$ and $g_i(\mathbf{X})$, $i = 1, 2, \ldots, m$, are assumed twice continuously differentiable.

The idea of using constrained derivatives for solving the above problem is to find a closed form expression for the first partial derivatives of $f(\mathbf{X})$ at all the points which satisfy the constraints $\mathbf{g}(\mathbf{X}) = 0$. The corresponding stationary points are thus identified as the points at which these partial derivatives vanish. The sufficiency conditions introduced in Section 16·2 can be used then to check the identity of the stationary points.

To clarify this concept consider the function $f(x_1, x_2)$ illustrated in Figure 16–3. This function is to be minimized subject to the constraint.

$$g_1(x_1, x_2) = x_2 - b = 0,$$

where b is a constant. From Figure 16–3, the curve designated by the three

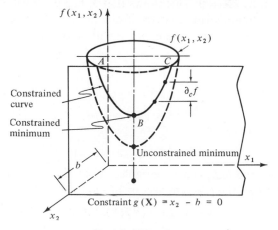

Figure 16–3

points A, B, and C represents the values of $f(x_1, x_2)$ for which the given constraint is always satisfied. The constrained derivatives method then defines the gradient of $f(x_1, x_2)$ at any point on the curve ABC. It then follows that the point at which the constrained derivatives vanish represents a stationary point for the constrained problem. In Figure 16–3, this is given by Point B. The figure also shows an example of the incremental *constrained* value of f, $\partial_c f$.

The method will be developed now mathematically. By Taylor's theorem, for the points $\mathbf{X} + \Delta\mathbf{X}$ in the feasible neighborhood of $\mathbf{X}$, it follows that

$$f(\mathbf{X}+\Delta\mathbf{X}) - f(\mathbf{X}) = \nabla f(\mathbf{X})\Delta\mathbf{X} + 0(\Delta x_j^2)$$

and

$$g(\mathbf{X}+\Delta\mathbf{X}) - g(\mathbf{X}) = \nabla g(\mathbf{X})\Delta\mathbf{X} + 0(\Delta x_j^2).$$

Since $0(\Delta x_j^2) \to 0$ as $\Delta x_j \to 0$, the above equations become

$$\partial f(\mathbf{X}) \simeq \nabla f(\mathbf{X})\, \partial\mathbf{X}$$

and

$$\partial g(\mathbf{X}) \simeq \nabla g(\mathbf{X})\, \partial\mathbf{X}.$$

Since $g(\mathbf{X}) = 0$, then $\partial g(\mathbf{X}) = 0$ and it follows that,

$$\partial f(\mathbf{X}) - \nabla f(\mathbf{X})\, \partial\mathbf{X} = 0,$$

$$\nabla g(\mathbf{X})\, \partial\mathbf{X} = 0.$$

This reduces to $(m + 1)$ equations in $(n + 1)$ unknowns; the unknowns being given by $\partial f(\mathbf{X})$ and $\partial\mathbf{X}$. The unknown $\partial f(\mathbf{X})$ is determined, however, as soon as $\partial\mathbf{X}$ is known. This means that there are in effect m equations in n unknowns.

If $m > n$, this implies that at least $(n - m)$ equations are redundant. After eliminating this redundancy, the system reduces to an effective number of independent equations such that $m \leq n$. Now, for the case where $m = n$ the solution is given by $\partial\mathbf{X} = 0$. This shows that $\mathbf{X}$ has no feasible neighborhood and hence the solution space consists of one point only. Such a case is of no interest. The remaining case where $m < n$ will be considered in detail.

Let

$$\mathbf{X} = (\mathbf{Y}, \mathbf{Z}).$$

Define

$$\mathbf{Y} = (y_1, y_2, \ldots, y_m)$$

and

$$\mathbf{Z} = (z_1, z_2, \ldots, z_{n-m}).$$

as the *dependent* and *independent* variables, respectively, corresponding to the vector $\mathbf{X}$. Rewriting the gradient vectors of f and g in terms of $\mathbf{Y}$ and $\mathbf{Z}$, then

$$\nabla f(\mathbf{Y}, \mathbf{Z}) = (\nabla f(\mathbf{Y}), \nabla f(\mathbf{Z})),$$

$$\nabla g(\mathbf{Y}, \mathbf{Z}) = (\nabla g(\mathbf{Y}), \nabla g(\mathbf{Z})).$$

Define

$$J = \mathbf{V}\mathbf{g}(\mathbf{Y}) = \begin{bmatrix} \nabla g_1(\mathbf{Y}) \\ \vdots \\ \nabla g_m(\mathbf{Y}) \end{bmatrix}$$

$$C = \mathbf{V}\mathbf{g}(\mathbf{Z}) = \begin{bmatrix} \nabla g_1(\mathbf{Z}) \\ \vdots \\ \nabla g_m(\mathbf{Z}) \end{bmatrix}.$$

The matrix $\mathbf{J}_{m \times m}$ is called the *Jacobian* matrix while $\mathbf{C}_{m \times n-m}$ is called the *control* matrix. The Jacobian $\mathbf{J}$ is assumed nonsingular. This is always possible since the given m equations are independent by definition. The components of the vector $\mathbf{Y}$ thus can be selected from those of $\mathbf{X}$ such that $\mathbf{J}$ is nonsingular.

Using the above definitions, the original set of equations in $\partial f(\mathbf{X})$ and $\partial \mathbf{X}$ may be written as

$$\partial f(\mathbf{Y}, \mathbf{Z}) = \nabla f(\mathbf{Y}) \, \partial \mathbf{Y} + \nabla f(\mathbf{Z}) \, \partial \mathbf{Z},$$

and

$$\mathbf{J} \, \partial \mathbf{Y} = -\mathbf{C} \, \partial \mathbf{Z}.$$

Since $\mathbf{J}$ is nonsingular, it inverses $\mathbf{J}^{-1}$ exists. Hence

$$\partial \mathbf{Y} = -\mathbf{J}^{-1}\mathbf{C} \, \partial \mathbf{Z}.$$

This set of equations relates the effect of variation in $\partial \mathbf{Z}$ ($\mathbf{Z}$ being the independent vector) on $\partial \mathbf{Y}$. Thus by substituting for $\partial \mathbf{Y}$ in the equation for $\partial f(\mathbf{Y}, \mathbf{Z})$, this should give ∂f as a function of $\partial \mathbf{Z}$. That is,

$$\partial f(\mathbf{Y}, \mathbf{Z}) = (\nabla f(\mathbf{Z}) - \nabla f(\mathbf{Y})\mathbf{J}^{-1}\mathbf{C}) \, \partial \mathbf{Z}.$$

From this equation, the constrained derivative with respect to the independent vector $\mathbf{Z}$ is given by

$$\mathbf{V}_c f = \frac{\partial_c f(\mathbf{Y}, \mathbf{Z})}{\partial_c \mathbf{Z}} = (\nabla f(\mathbf{Z}) - \nabla f(\mathbf{Y})\mathbf{J}^{-1}\mathbf{C}),$$

where $\mathbf{V}_c f$ represents the *constrained* gradient vector of f with respect to $\mathbf{Z}$. Thus, $\nabla f(\mathbf{Y}, \mathbf{Z})$ must be null at the stationary points.

The sufficiency conditions are similar to those developed in Section 16·2. In this case, however, the Hessian matrix will correspond to the elements of the independent vector $\mathbf{Z}$. In the mean time, the elements of the Hessian matrix must be the *constrained* second derivatives. To show how this is obtained, let

$$\mathbf{V}_c f = \nabla f(\mathbf{Z}) - \mathbf{W}\mathbf{C},$$

where $\mathbf{W} \equiv \nabla f(\mathbf{Y}) \mathbf{J}^{-1}$ is a row-vector which is a function of $\mathbf{Y}$. It thus follows that the ith row of the Hessian matrix is given by

$$\frac{\partial_c}{\partial_c z_i}\left(\nabla_c f(\mathbf{Z})\right) = \frac{\partial}{\partial z_i}\left(\nabla f(\mathbf{Z})\right) + \left(\frac{\partial \mathbf{g}(\mathbf{Z})}{\partial z_i}\right)^T (\nabla_y \mathbf{W}^T) \mathbf{J}^{-1}\mathbf{C} - \mathbf{W}\left(\frac{\partial^2 \mathbf{g}(\mathbf{Z})}{\partial z_i^2}\right).$$

This expression is derived from the expression for $\nabla_c f$ in a straightforward manner. The derivation is facilitated by converting the right-hand side into summation form rather than matrix form. Notice that $\nabla_y \mathbf{W}^T$ is an $(m \times m)$-matrix with its ith row being equal to the gradient vector of the ith element of $\mathbf{W}$ with respect to $\mathbf{Y}$. Notice that also $(\partial \mathbf{Y}/\partial \mathbf{Z}) = -\mathbf{J}^{-1}\mathbf{C}$ as given by the previous derivations. By using this substitution, the effect of the constraints is included in the above expression so that the second derivatives are automatically computed in the feasible region only.

▶ **Example 16·3-1**

In this example it will be shown how ∂f can be estimated at a given point using the formulas given above. Example 16·3-2 will then illustrate the application of the constrained derivative.

Consider the problem in which

$$f(\mathbf{X}) = x_1^2 + 3x_2^2 + 5x_1 x_3^2,$$

$$g_1(\mathbf{X}) = x_1 x_3 + 2x_2 + x_2^2 - 11 = 0,$$

and

$$g_2(\mathbf{X}) = x_1^2 + 2x_1 x_2 + x_3^2 - 14 = 0.$$

Given the feasible point $\mathbf{X}^0 = (1, 2, 3)$ it is required to study the variation in $f (= \partial_c f)$ in the feasible neighborhood of $\mathbf{X}^0$.

Let

$$\mathbf{Y} = (x_1, x_3),$$

and

$$\mathbf{Z} = x_2.$$

Thus

$$\nabla f(\mathbf{Y}) = \left(\frac{\partial f}{\partial x_1}, \frac{\partial f}{\partial x_3}\right) = (2x_1 + 5x_3^2, 10x_1 x_3),$$

$$\nabla f(\mathbf{Z}) = \frac{\partial f}{\partial x_2} = 6x_2,$$

$$\mathbf{J} = \begin{pmatrix} \dfrac{\partial g_1}{\partial x_1} & \dfrac{\partial g_1}{\partial x_3} \\ \dfrac{\partial g_2}{\partial x_1} & \dfrac{\partial g_2}{\partial x_3} \end{pmatrix} = \begin{pmatrix} x_3 & x_1 \\ 2x_1 + 2x_2 & 2x_3 \end{pmatrix},$$

$$\mathbf{C} = \begin{pmatrix} \dfrac{\partial g_1}{\partial x_2} \\[2mm] \dfrac{\partial g_2}{\partial x_2} \end{pmatrix} = \begin{pmatrix} 2x_2 + 2 \\[2mm] 2x_1 \end{pmatrix}.$$

Suppose now it is required to estimate $\partial_c f$ in the feasible neighborhood of the given feasible point $\mathbf{X}^0 = (1, 2, 3)$ as a result of a small change $\partial x_2 = .01$. Then, at $\mathbf{X}^0$,

$$\mathbf{J}^{-1}\mathbf{C} = \begin{pmatrix} 3 & 1 \\ 6 & 6 \end{pmatrix}^{-1} \begin{pmatrix} 6 \\ 2 \end{pmatrix}$$

$$= \begin{pmatrix} 6/12 & -1/12 \\ -6/12 & 3/12 \end{pmatrix} \begin{pmatrix} 6 \\ 2 \end{pmatrix} \cong \begin{pmatrix} 2.83 \\ -2.50 \end{pmatrix}.$$

Hence

$$\partial_c f = (\nabla f(\mathbf{Z}) - \nabla f(\mathbf{Y})\mathbf{J}^{-1}\mathbf{C}) \, \partial \mathbf{Z}$$

$$= \left(6(2) - (47, 30) \begin{bmatrix} 2.83 \\ -2.5 \end{bmatrix} \right) \partial x_2$$

$$\cong -46 \, \partial x_2$$

$$= -0.46.$$

Notice that by specifying the value of ∂x_2 for the *independent* variable x_2, the feasible values of ∂x_1 and ∂x_2 are automatically determined for the *dependent* variables x_1 and x_3 using the formula,

$$\partial \mathbf{Y} = -\mathbf{J}^{-1}\mathbf{C} \, \partial \mathbf{Z}.$$

Or for $\partial x_2 = .01$, this gives,

$$\begin{pmatrix} \partial x_1 \\ \partial x_3 \end{pmatrix} = -\mathbf{J}^{-1}\mathbf{C} \, \partial x_2 = \begin{pmatrix} -0.0283 \\ 0.0250 \end{pmatrix}.$$

To check the value of $\partial_c f$ obtained above, one can compute the value of f at $\mathbf{X}^0$ and $\mathbf{X}^0 + \partial \mathbf{X}$. Thus,

$$\mathbf{X}^0 + \partial \mathbf{X} = (1 - 0.0283, 2 + 0.01, 3 + 0.025)$$

$$= (.9717, 2.01, 3.025).$$

This yields

$$f(\mathbf{X}^0) = 58$$

and

$$f(\mathbf{X}^0 + \partial \mathbf{X}) = 57.523$$

or

$$\partial_c f = f(\mathbf{X}^0 + \partial \mathbf{X}) - f(\mathbf{X}^0) = -0.477.$$

This indicates a decrease in the value of f as obtained by the formula for $\partial_c f$. The difference between the two answers $(-.477$ and $-.46)$ is the result of the linear approximation at $\mathbf{X}^0$. This indicates that the given formula is good only for very small variations around $\mathbf{X}^0$. ◀

▶ **Example 16·3-2**
This example will now illustrate the use of constrained derivatives. Consider the problem:

$$\text{minimize}\quad f(\mathbf{X}) = x_1^2 + x_2^2 + x_3^2,$$

subject to

$$g_1(\mathbf{X}) = x_1 + x_2 + 3x_3 - 2 = 0,$$

$$g_2(\mathbf{X}) = 5x_1 + 2x_2 + x_3 - 5 = 0.$$

It is required to determine the extreme points of this problem.
Let

$$\mathbf{Y} = (x_1, x_2),$$

$$\mathbf{Z} = x_3.$$

Thus

$$\nabla f(\mathbf{Y}) = \left(\frac{\partial f}{\partial x_1}, \frac{\partial f}{\partial x_2}\right) = (2x_1, 2x_2),$$

$$\nabla f(\mathbf{Z}) = \frac{\partial f}{\partial x_3} = 2x_3,$$

$$\mathbf{J} = \begin{pmatrix} 1 & 1 \\ 5 & 2 \end{pmatrix},$$

$$\mathbf{J}^{-1} = \begin{pmatrix} -2/3 & 1/3 \\ 5/3 & -1/3 \end{pmatrix},$$

$$\mathbf{C} = \begin{pmatrix} 3 \\ 1 \end{pmatrix}.$$

Hence

$$\nabla_c f = \frac{\partial_c f}{\partial_c x_3} = 2x_3 - (2x_1, 2x_2)\begin{pmatrix} -2/3 & 1/3 \\ 5/3 & -1/3 \end{pmatrix}\begin{pmatrix} 3 \\ 1 \end{pmatrix}$$

$$= \frac{10}{3}x_1 - \frac{28}{3}x_2 + 2x_3.$$

At a stationary point, $\nabla_c f = \mathbf{0}$. These equations together with $g_1(\mathbf{X}) = 0$ and

$g_2(\mathbf{X}) = 0$ should give the required stationary point(s). That is, the equations,

$$\begin{pmatrix} 10 & -28 & 6 \\ 1 & 1 & 3 \\ 5 & 2 & 1 \end{pmatrix}\begin{pmatrix} x_1 \\ x_2 \\ x_3 \end{pmatrix} = \begin{pmatrix} 0 \\ 2 \\ 5 \end{pmatrix},$$

give the solution,

$$\mathbf{X} \simeq (0.81, 0.35, 0.28).$$

The identity of this stationary point is now checked by considering the sufficiency condition for the Jacobian method. Using the notation given, previously, then,

$$\mathbf{W} \equiv \nabla f(\mathbf{Y})\mathbf{J}^{-1} = (2x_1, 2x_2)\begin{pmatrix} -2/3 & 1/3 \\ 5/3 & -1/3 \end{pmatrix}$$

$$= \left(-\frac{4}{3}x_1 + \frac{10}{3}x_2, \frac{2}{3}x_1 - \frac{2}{3}x_2 \right) \equiv (w_1, w_2),$$

$$\frac{\partial}{\partial z_i}(\nabla f(\mathbf{Z})) \equiv \frac{\partial}{\partial x_3}(2x_3) = 2,$$

$$\left(\frac{\partial \mathbf{g}(\mathbf{Z})}{\partial z_i} \right)^T \equiv \left(\frac{\partial g_1}{\partial x_3}, \frac{\partial g_2}{\partial x_3} \right) = (3, 1),$$

$$\nabla_y \mathbf{W}^T \equiv \begin{pmatrix} \dfrac{\partial w_1}{\partial x_1} & \dfrac{\partial w_1}{\partial x_2} \\ \dfrac{\partial w_2}{\partial x_1} & \dfrac{\partial w_2}{\partial x_2} \end{pmatrix} = \begin{pmatrix} -4/3 & 10/3 \\ 2/3 & -2/3 \end{pmatrix}.$$

Also

$$\mathbf{J}^{-1}\mathbf{C} = \begin{pmatrix} -2/3 & 1/3 \\ 5/3 & -1/3 \end{pmatrix}\begin{pmatrix} 3 \\ 1 \end{pmatrix} = \begin{pmatrix} -5/3 \\ 14/3 \end{pmatrix},$$

and

$$\frac{\partial^2 \mathbf{g}(\mathbf{Z})}{\partial z_i^2} \equiv \begin{pmatrix} \dfrac{\partial^2 g_1}{\partial x_3^2} \\ \dfrac{\partial^2 g_1}{\partial x_3^2} \end{pmatrix} = \begin{pmatrix} 0 \\ 0 \end{pmatrix}.$$

Thus, since there is only one independent variable, x_3, the Hessian matrix consists of one element only. Namely, substitution of the above expressions in the sufficiency condition yields,

$$\frac{\partial_c^2 f}{\partial_c x_3^2} = 2 + (3, 1) \begin{pmatrix} -4/3 & 10/3 \\ 3/2 & -2/3 \end{pmatrix} \begin{pmatrix} -5/3 \\ 14/3 \end{pmatrix}$$

$$- \left(-\frac{4}{3} x_1 + \frac{10}{3} x_2, \frac{2}{3} x_1 - \frac{2}{3} x_2 \right) \begin{pmatrix} 0 \\ 0 \end{pmatrix},$$

$$= \frac{460}{9} > 0.$$

Hence X^0 is the minimum point.

It is important to notice that the above result can be computed directly from $\nabla_c f$ of the problem. That is, since

$$\nabla_c f = \frac{\partial_c f}{\partial_c x_3} = \frac{10}{3} x_1 - \frac{28}{3} x_2 + 2x_3,$$

then

$$\frac{\partial_c^2 f}{\partial_c x_3^2} = \frac{10}{3} \left(\frac{dx_1}{dx_3} \right) - \frac{28}{3} \left(\frac{dx_2}{dx_3} \right) + 2,$$

$$= \left(\frac{10}{3}, -\frac{28}{3} \right) \begin{pmatrix} \dfrac{dx_1}{dx_3} \\ \dfrac{dx_2}{dx_3} \end{pmatrix} + 2.$$

From the development of the Jacobian method,

$$\begin{pmatrix} \dfrac{dx_1}{dx_3} \\ \dfrac{dx_2}{dx_3} \end{pmatrix} = -J^{-1}C = \begin{pmatrix} 5/3 \\ -14/3 \end{pmatrix}.$$

Substitution gives the above result directly. ◄

The application of the Jacobian method as presented above is hindered, in general, by the difficulty of obtaining J^{-1} for a large number of constraints. This difficulty is overcome, however, by applying Cramer's rule to solve for ∂f in terms of ∂Z using the constraint equations. Thus, if z_j represents the jth element of Z and y_i represents the ith element of Y, then it can be shown that

$$\frac{\partial_c f}{\partial_c z_j} = \frac{\partial(f, g_1, \ldots, g_m)/\partial(z_j, y_1 \ldots, y_m)}{\partial(g_1, \ldots, g_m)/\partial(y_1, \ldots, y_m)},$$

where

$$\frac{\partial(f, g_1 \ldots, g_m)}{\partial(z_j, y_1 \ldots, y_m)} \equiv \begin{vmatrix} \dfrac{\partial f}{\partial z_j} & \dfrac{\partial f}{\partial y_1} & \cdots & \dfrac{\partial f}{\partial y_m} \\[2mm] \dfrac{\partial g_1}{\partial z_j} & \dfrac{\partial g_1}{\partial y_1} & \cdots & \dfrac{\partial g_1}{\partial y_m} \\[1mm] \vdots & \vdots & & \vdots \\[1mm] \dfrac{\partial g_m}{\partial z_j} & \dfrac{\partial g_m}{\partial y_1} & \cdots & \dfrac{\partial g_m}{\partial y_m} \end{vmatrix},$$

and

$$\frac{\partial(g_1, \ldots, g_m)}{\partial(y_1, \ldots, y_m)} \equiv \begin{vmatrix} \dfrac{\partial g_1}{\partial y_1} & \cdots & \dfrac{\partial g_1}{\partial y_m} \\[2mm] \vdots & & \vdots \\[1mm] \dfrac{\partial g_m}{\partial y_1} & \cdots & \dfrac{\partial g_m}{\partial y_m} \end{vmatrix} = |\mathbf{J}|.$$

Thus, the necessary conditions become

$$\frac{\partial_c f}{\partial_c z_j} = 0, \quad j = 1, 2, \ldots, n - m.$$

Similarly, in the matrix expression

$$\frac{\partial \mathbf{Y}}{\partial \mathbf{Z}} = -\mathbf{J}^{-1}\mathbf{C},$$

the (i, j)th element is given by,

$$\frac{\partial y_i}{\partial z_j} = -\frac{\partial(g_1, \ldots, g_m)/\partial(y_1, \ldots, y_{i-1}, z_j, y_{i+1}, \ldots, y_m)}{\partial(g_1, \ldots, g_m)/\partial(y_1, \ldots, y_m)}$$

which represent the rate of variation of the dependent variable y_i with respect to the independent variable z_j.

Finally in order to obtain the sufficiency condition given previously, determinant expressions for the elements of $\mathbf{W} \equiv \nabla f(\mathbf{Y})\mathbf{J}^{-1}$ must be given. Thus, the ith element of $\mathbf{W}$ is given by

$$w_i = \frac{\partial(g_1, \ldots, g_{i-1}, f, g_{i+1}, \cdots g_m)/\partial(y_1, \ldots, y_m)}{\partial(g_1, \ldots, g_m)/\partial(y_1, \ldots, y_m)}$$

To illustrate the application of the above method consider the determination of the necessary condition for Example 16·3-2. Thus,

$$\frac{\partial_c f}{\partial_c x_3} = \frac{\begin{vmatrix} 2x_3 & 2x_1 & 2x_2 \\ 3 & 1 & 1 \\ 1 & 5 & 2 \end{vmatrix}}{\begin{vmatrix} 1 & 1 \\ 5 & 2 \end{vmatrix}}$$

$$= \frac{10}{3} x_1 - \frac{28}{3} x_2 + 2x_3.$$

This is the same as given previously.

§ 16·3·1·1·1
Sensitivity Analysis in the Jacobian Method

The above Jacobian method can be used to study the sensitivity of the optimal value of f due to small changes in the right-hand sides of the constraints. For example, suppose that the right-hand side of the ith constraint $g_i(\mathbf{X}) = 0$ is changed to ∂g_i instead of zero, what effect will this have on the optimum value of f? This type of investigation is called sensitivity analysis and, in some sense, is similar to the one carried out for the linear programming problem (see Chapter 4). The analysis in this case is carried out only in the small neighborhood of the extreme point due to the absence of linearity. The development will be helpful, however, in the study of the Lagrangian method for solving constrained problems. (See next section.)

It is shown above that

$$\partial f(\mathbf{Y}, \mathbf{Z}) = \nabla f(\mathbf{Y}) \, \partial \mathbf{Y} + \nabla f(\mathbf{Z}) \, \partial \mathbf{Z},$$

$$\partial \mathbf{g} = \mathbf{J} \, \partial \mathbf{Y} + \mathbf{C} \, \partial \mathbf{Z}.$$

Suppose that $\partial \mathbf{g} \neq \mathbf{0}$, then

$$\partial \mathbf{Y} = \mathbf{J}^{-1} \, \partial \mathbf{g} - \mathbf{J}^{-1} \mathbf{C} \, \partial \mathbf{Z}.$$

Substituting in the equation for $\partial f(\mathbf{Y}, \mathbf{Z})$, this gives,

$$\partial f(\mathbf{Y}, \mathbf{Z}) = \nabla f(\mathbf{Y}) \mathbf{J}^{-1} \, \partial \mathbf{g} + \nabla_c f(\mathbf{Y}, \mathbf{Z}) \, \partial \mathbf{Z},$$

where

$$\nabla_c f(\mathbf{Y}, \mathbf{Z}) = (\nabla f(\mathbf{Z}) - \nabla f(\mathbf{Y}) \mathbf{J}^{-1} \mathbf{C}),$$

as defined previously. The expression for $\partial f(\mathbf{Y}, \mathbf{Z})$ can be used to study the variation in f in the feasible neighborhood of a feasible point $\mathbf{X}^0$ due to small changes $\partial \mathbf{g}$ and $\partial \mathbf{Z}$.

Now, at the extreme (optimum) point $\mathbf{X}_0 = (\mathbf{Y}_0, \mathbf{Z}_0)$, the constrained gradient $\nabla_c f$ must vanish. Thus,

$$\partial f(\mathbf{Y}_0, \mathbf{Z}_0) = \nabla f(\mathbf{Y}_0) \mathbf{J}^{-1} \, \partial \mathbf{g}(\mathbf{Y}_0, \mathbf{Z}_0)$$

or

$$\frac{\partial f}{\partial \mathbf{g}} = \nabla f(\mathbf{Y}_0)\mathbf{J}^{-1},$$

evaluated at $\mathbf{X}_0$. Consequently, the effect of small variations in $\mathbf{g}$ ($= \partial \mathbf{g}$) on the *optimum* value of f can be studied by evaluating the rate of change of f with respect to $\mathbf{g}$. These rates are usually referred to as *sensitivity coefficients*.

It should be noted that, in general, at the optimum point, $\partial f/\partial \mathbf{g}$ is independent of the specific choice of the variables in the vector $\mathbf{Y}$. This follows from the fact that the expression for the sensitivity coefficients does not include $\mathbf{Z}$. Hence, the partitioning of $\mathbf{X}$ between $\mathbf{Y}$ and $\mathbf{Z}$ is not an effective factor in this case. The given coefficients are thus constant regardless of the specific choice of $\mathbf{Y}$.

Notice that the expression for the sensitivity coefficients is the same as that for $\mathbf{W}$ as given in the derivation of the sufficiency conditions for the Jacobian method. Consequently the same determinant expression for the elements of $\mathbf{W}$ can be used to obtain the sensitivity coefficients.

▶ **Example 16·3-3**

Consider the same problem of Example 16·3-2. The optimum point is given by $\mathbf{X}_0 = (x_1^0, x_2^0, x_3^0) = (0.81, 0.35, 0.28)$. Since $\mathbf{Y}_0 = (x_1^0, x_2^0)$, then

$$\nabla f(\mathbf{Y}_0) = \left(\frac{\partial f}{\partial x_1}, \frac{\partial f}{\partial x_2}\right) = (2x_1^0, 2x_2^0)$$

$$= (1.62, 0.70).$$

Consequently,

$$\left(\frac{\partial f}{\partial g_1}, \frac{\partial f}{\partial g_2}\right) = \nabla f(\mathbf{Y}_0)\mathbf{J}^{-1} = (1.62, 0.7)\begin{pmatrix} -2/3 & 1/3 \\ 5/3 & -1/3 \end{pmatrix}$$

$$= (0.0876, 0.3067).$$

This implies that if $\partial g_1 = 1$, f will increase *approximately* by 0.0867. Similarly, if $\partial g_2 = 1$, f will increase *approximately* by 0.3067. ◀

§ 16·3·1·1·2
Example of the Application of the Jacobian Method to a Linear Programming Problem

Consider the linear programming problem:

$$\text{maximize} \quad x_0 = 2x_1 + 3x_2,$$

subject to

$$x_1 + x_2 + x_3 \qquad = 5,$$
$$x_1 - x_2 \qquad + x_4 = 3,$$
$$x_1 \geq 0, \quad x_2 \geq 0, \quad x_3 \geq 0, \quad x_4 \geq 0.$$

The direct application of the Jacobian method to the above problem will yield no useful information since the resulting $\mathbf{V}_c f$ will be equal to a constant and thus, the required necessary conditions may not be satisfied. The following transformation can be used, however, to overcome this difficulty.

Consider the nonnegativity constraints $x_j \geq 0$. Let w_j^2 be the corresponding (nonnegative) slack variable. Thus, $x_j - w_j^2 = 0$, or $x_j = w_j^2$. Using this substitution, the original problem becomes

$$\text{maximize} \quad x_0 = 2w_1^2 + 3w_2^2,$$

subject to

$$w_1^2 + w_2^2 + w_3^2 = 5,$$

$$w_1^2 - w_2^2 + w_4^2 = 3.$$

In order to apply the Jacobian method, let

$$\mathbf{Y} = (w_1, w_2),$$

$$\mathbf{Z} = (w_3, w_4).$$

(Notice that in the terminology of linear programming, $\mathbf{Y}$ and $\mathbf{Z}$ correspond to the basic and nonbasic variables, respectively.) Thus,

$$\mathbf{J} = \begin{pmatrix} 2w_1 & 2w_2 \\ 2w_1 & -2w_2 \end{pmatrix}, \quad \mathbf{J}^{-1} = \begin{pmatrix} \dfrac{1}{4w_1} & \dfrac{1}{4w_1} \\ \dfrac{1}{4w_2} & \dfrac{-1}{4w_2} \end{pmatrix}; \quad w_1 \text{ and } w_2 \neq 0,$$

$$\mathbf{C} = \begin{pmatrix} 2w_3 & 0 \\ 0 & 2w_4 \end{pmatrix}, \quad \mathbf{V}f(\mathbf{Y}) = (4w_1, 6w_2), \quad \mathbf{V}f(\mathbf{Z}) = (0, 0).$$

So that

$$\mathbf{V}_c f = (0, 0) - (4w_1, 6w_2) \begin{pmatrix} \dfrac{1}{4w_1} & \dfrac{1}{4w_1} \\ \dfrac{1}{4w_2} & \dfrac{-1}{4w_2} \end{pmatrix} \begin{pmatrix} 2w_3 & 0 \\ 0 & 2w_4 \end{pmatrix}$$

$$= (-5w_3, w_4).$$

Now, solving $\mathbf{V}_c f = \mathbf{0}$ together with the constraints of the problem, it follows that $(w_1 = 2, w_2 = 1, w_3 = 0, w_4 = 0)$ represents a stationary point. The sufficiency condition is given by

$$\mathbf{H}_c = \begin{pmatrix} \dfrac{\partial_c^2 f}{\partial_c w_3^2} & \dfrac{\partial_c^2 f}{\partial_c w_3 \, \partial_c w_4} \\ \dfrac{\partial_c^2 f}{\partial_c w_3 \, \partial_c w_4} & \dfrac{\partial_c^2 f}{\partial_c w_4^2} \end{pmatrix} = \begin{pmatrix} -5 & 0 \\ 0 & 1 \end{pmatrix}.$$

Since $\mathbf{H}_c$ is indefinite, the given stationary point does not yield a maximum.

The above result is not surprising actually. Notice in the above solution that the (nonbasic) variables w_3 and w_4 (and hence x_3 and x_4) are equal to zero as is contemplated by the theory of linear programming. This means that depending on the specific choice of $\mathbf{Y}$ and $\mathbf{Z}$, the Jacobian method solution determines the corresponding extreme point of the solution space. This may or may not be the optimal solution. The Jacobian method has the power, however, to identify the optimum point through the use of the sufficiency conditions.

The preceding discussion suggests that one has to keep on altering the specific choices of $\mathbf{Y}$ and $\mathbf{Z}$ until the sufficiency condition is satisfied. Thus, for the above example, let $\mathbf{Y} = (w_2, w_4)$, $\mathbf{Z} = (w_1, w_3)$. Then, following the same procedure given above, the corresponding constrained gradient vector becomes,

$$\nabla_c f = (4w_1, 0) - (6w_2, 0)\begin{pmatrix} \dfrac{1}{2w_2} & 0 \\ \dfrac{1}{2w_4} & \dfrac{1}{2w_4} \end{pmatrix}\begin{pmatrix} 2w_1 & 2w_3 \\ 2w_1 & 0 \end{pmatrix}$$

$$= (-2w_1, -6w_3).$$

The corresponding stationary point is given by $w_1 = 0$, $w_2 = \sqrt{5}$, $w_3 = 0$, $w_4 = \sqrt{8}$. Now,

$$\mathbf{H}_c = \begin{pmatrix} -2 & 0 \\ 0 & -6 \end{pmatrix},$$

which is negative-definite. This means that the given solution corresponds to a maximum point.

The above result is verified graphically in Figure 16–4. Notice that the first solution obtained above ($x_1 = 4$, $x_2 = 1$) is not optimal while the second solution ($x_1 = 0$, $x_2 = 5$) gives the optimal solution. The reader can verify

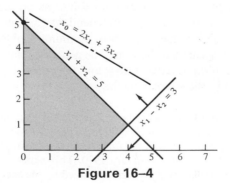

Figure 16–4

that the remaining two extreme points of the solution space in Figure 16–4 do not yield maximum points. In fact, the extreme point $(x_1 = 0, x_2 = 0)$ can be shown by the sufficiency condition to yield a minimum point.

It is interesting to note that the sensitivity coefficients, $\nabla f(\mathbf{Y}_0)\mathbf{J}^{-1}$, introduced in Section 16·3·1·1·1, when applied to the linear programming problem will actually yield the values of its dual variables. To illustrate this point for the given numerical example, let u_1 and u_2 be the corresponding dual variables. At the optimum point $(w_1 = 0, w_2 = \sqrt{5}, w_3 = 0, w_4 = \sqrt{8})$, these dual variables are given by,

$$(u_1, u_2) = \nabla f(\mathbf{Y}_0)\mathbf{J}^{-1}$$

$$= (6w_2, 0)\begin{pmatrix} \dfrac{1}{2w_2} & 0 \\ \dfrac{1}{2w_4} & \dfrac{1}{2w_4} \end{pmatrix}$$

$$= (3, 0).$$

The corresponding dual objective value is equal to $5u_1 + 3u_2 = 15$ which is the same as the optimal primal objective value. The given solution also satisfies the dual constraints and hence it is optimal and feasible. This shows that the sensitivity coefficients are the same as the dual variables. In fact, one will notice that they both have the same interpretation.

It is now possible to draw some general conclusions from the application of the Jacobian method to the linear programming problem. It is noticed from the numerical example that the necessary condition requires that the independent variables be equal to zero. Also the sufficiency condition indicates that the Hessian matrix is a diagonal matrix. Thus, all its diagonal elements must be positive for a minimum point and negative for a maximum point.

The above observations suggest that the necessary condition is equivalent to specifying that only " basic" (feasible) solutions are needed to locate the optimum solution. In this case, the independent variables are equivalent to the nonbasic variables in the linear programming problem. Also, the sufficiency condition suggests that there may be a strong relationship between the diagonal elements of the Hessian matrix and the optimality indicator, $z_j - c_j$, (see Section 8·5·2) in the simplex method.[2]

---

[2] For a formal proof of the validity of these results for the general linear programming problem, see, H. Taha and G. Curry, "Classical Derivation of the Necessary and Sufficient Conditions for Optimal Linear Programs," Research Report, University of Arkansas, January 1970. This paper actually shows that all the key ideas of the simplex method can be derived by the Jacobian method.

§ 16·3·1·2
Lagrange's Multipliers Method

In the above section it is shown that the sensitivity coefficients,

$$\frac{\partial f}{\partial \mathbf{g}} = \nabla f(\mathbf{Y}_0)\mathbf{J}^{-1},$$

can be used to study the effect of small variations in the constraints on the *optimum* value of f. It has also been indicated that these coefficients are constant. It will be shown now how these properties can be used to solve the constrained problems with equality constraints.

Let

$$\lambda = \nabla f(\mathbf{Y}_0)\mathbf{J}^{-1}$$

$$= \frac{\partial f}{\partial \mathbf{g}}.$$

Thus

$$\partial f - \lambda\, \partial \mathbf{g} = 0.$$

This equation satisfies the *necessary* conditions for stationary points since, as shown in Section 16·3·1·1·1, the expression for $\partial f/\partial \mathbf{g}$ is computed such that $\nabla_c f = \mathbf{0}$. A more convenient form for presenting these same equations, however, is obtained by taking their partial derivatives with respect to all x_j. This yields

$$\frac{\partial}{\partial x_j}(f - \lambda \mathbf{g}) = 0, \qquad j = 1, 2, \ldots, n.$$

The resulting equations together with the constraint equations,

$$\mathbf{g} = \mathbf{0},$$

must yield the feasible values of $\mathbf{X}$ and λ which satisfy the *necessary* conditions for stationary points.

The above procedure defines the so-called *Lagrangian method* for identifying the stationary points for optimization problems with equality constraints. This procedure can be developed formally as follows. Let

$$L(\mathbf{X}, \lambda) = f(\mathbf{X}) - \lambda \mathbf{g}(\mathbf{X}).$$

The function L is called the Lagrangian function while the parameters λ are called the *Lagrange multipliers*. By definition, these multipliers have the same interpretation as the sensitivity coefficients introduced in Section 16·3·1·1·1.

Now, the equations

$$\frac{\partial L}{\partial \lambda} = \mathbf{0} \quad \text{and} \quad \frac{\partial L}{\partial \mathbf{X}} = \mathbf{0}$$

yield the same necessary conditions given above and hence the Lagrangian function can be used directly to generate these conditions. This means that the optimization of the function $f(\mathbf{X})$ subject to $\mathbf{g}(\mathbf{X}) = \mathbf{0}$ is equivalent to the optimization of the Lagrangian function $L(\mathbf{X}, \lambda)$. This has the advantage of determining directly the sensitivity coefficients ($= \lambda$) as a by-product of the calculations.

The sufficiency conditions for the Lagrangian method will be stated without proof. Define

$$\mathbf{H}^B = \left(\begin{array}{c|c} \mathbf{0} & \mathbf{P} \\ \hline \mathbf{P}^T & \mathbf{Q} \end{array} \right)_{(m+n) \times (m+n)},$$

where

$$\mathbf{P} = \left(\begin{array}{c} \nabla g_1(\mathbf{X}) \\ \vdots \\ \nabla g_m(\mathbf{X}) \end{array} \right)_{m \times n},$$

$$\mathbf{Q} = \left\| \frac{\partial^2 L(\mathbf{X}, \lambda)}{\partial x_i \, \partial x_j} \right\|_{n \times n}, \qquad \text{for all } i \text{ and } j.$$

The matrix $\mathbf{H}^B$ is called the *bordered Hessian matrix*.

Given the stationary point $(\mathbf{X}_0, \lambda_0)$ for the Lagrangian function $L(\mathbf{X}, \lambda)$ and the bordered Hessian matrix $\mathbf{H}^B$ evaluated at $(\mathbf{X}_0, \lambda_0)$, then $\mathbf{X}_0$ is

(1) a maximum point if, starting with the principal minor determinant of order $(2m + 1)$, the *last* $(n - m)$ principal minor determinant of $\mathbf{H}^B$ form an alternating sign pattern starting with $(-1)^{m+1}$; and

(2) a minimum point if, starting with the principal minor determinant of order $(2m + 1)$, the *last* $(n - m)$ principal minor determinants of $\mathbf{H}^B$ have the sign of $(-1)^m$.

It must be noted that the above conditions are sufficient for identifying an extreme point, but not necessary. In other words, a stationary point may be an extreme point without satisfying the above conditions.

Other conditions exist which are both necessary and sufficient for identifying extreme points. The disadvantage here is that this procedure is computationally infeasible for most practical purposes. Define the matrix

$$\Delta = \left(\begin{array}{c|c} \mathbf{0} & \mathbf{P} \\ \hline \mathbf{P}^T & \mathbf{Q} - \mu \mathbf{I} \end{array} \right),$$

evaluated at the stationary point $(\mathbf{X}_0, \lambda_0)$; where $\mathbf{P}$ and $\mathbf{Q}$ are as defined above and μ is an unknown parameter. Consider the determinant $|\Delta|$, then each of the real $(n - m)$ roots, μ_i, of the polynomial,

$$|\Delta| = 0,$$

must be, (1) negative if $\mathbf{X}_0$ is a maximum point, and (2) positive if $\mathbf{X}_0$ is a minimum point.

▶ **Example 16·3-4**

Consider the same problem of Example 16·3-2. The Lagrangian function is given by

$$L(\mathbf{X}, \lambda) = x_1^2 + x_2^2 + x_3^2 - \lambda_1(x_1 + x_2 + 3x_3 - 2) - \lambda_2(5x_1 + 2x_2 + x_3 - 5).$$

This yields the following necessary conditions,

$$\frac{\partial L}{\partial x_1} = 2x_1 - \lambda_1 \quad 5\lambda_2 = 0,$$

$$\frac{\partial L}{\partial x_2} = 2x_2 - \lambda_1 - 2\lambda_2 = 0,$$

$$\frac{\partial L}{\partial x_3} = 2x_3 - 3\lambda_1 - \lambda_2 = 0,$$

$$\frac{\partial L}{\partial \lambda_1} = -(x_1 + x_2 + 3x_3 - 2) = 0,$$

$$\frac{\partial L}{\partial \lambda_2} = -(5x_1 + 2x_2 + x_3 - 5) = 0.$$

The solution to these simultaneous equations yields

$$\mathbf{X}_0 = (x_1, x_2, x_3) = (0.81, 0.35, 0.28),$$

$$\lambda = (\lambda_1, \lambda_2) = (0.0867, 0.3067).$$

This solution combines the results of Examples 16·3-2 and 16·3-3. The values of the Lagrange multipliers, λ, are the same as the sensitivity coefficients obtained in Example 16·3-3. This ascertains the point that these coefficients are independent of the choice of the dependent vector **Y** in the Jacobian method.

To show that the given point corresponds to a minimum, consider

$$\mathbf{H}^B = \begin{bmatrix} 0 & 0 & 1 & 1 & 3 \\ 0 & 0 & 5 & 2 & 1 \\ \hline 1 & 5 & 2 & 0 & 0 \\ 1 & 2 & 0 & 2 & 0 \\ 3 & 1 & 0 & 0 & 2 \end{bmatrix}.$$

Since $n = 3$, $m = 2$, then $n - m = 1$. This means that one needs to check the determinant of $\mathbf{H}^B$ only and it must have the sign of $(-1)^2$. Now, since det $\mathbf{H}^B = 460 > 0$, $\mathbf{X}_0$ is a minimum point. ◄

In some cases it is not generally possible to solve the equations resulting from the necessary conditions explicitly for the values of **X** and λ. A convenient method of solution in this case is to select successive numerical values of λ and then solve the given equations for **X**. This is repeated until for some values of λ, the resulting **X** satisfies all the active constraints in equation form. This method was illustrated in Chapter 13 as an application to a single constraint inventory problem. (See Example 13·3-1.) Consequently, no similar example is presented here. It must be noted that this procedure becomes very tedious computationally as the number of constraints increases. In this case one may resort to an appropriate numerical technique to solve the resulting equations.

▶ **Example 16·3-5**

Consider the problem

$$\text{minimize} \quad x_0 = x_1^2 + x_2^2 + x_3^2,$$

subject to

$$4x_1 + x_2^2 + 2x_3 - 14 = 0.$$

Now, the corresponding Lagrangian function is

$$L(\mathbf{X}, \lambda) = x_1^2 + x_2^2 + x_3^2 - \lambda(4x_1 + x_2^2 + 2x_3 - 14).$$

This yields the following necessary conditions,

$$\frac{\partial L}{\partial x_1} = 2x_1 - 4\lambda = 0,$$

$$\frac{\partial L}{\partial x_2} = 2x_2 - 2\lambda x_2 = 0,$$

$$\frac{\partial L}{\partial x_3} = 2x_3 - 2\lambda = 0,$$

$$\frac{\partial L}{\partial \lambda} = -(4x_1 + x_2^2 + 2x_3 - 14) = 0.$$

The solution of the above equations give,

$$(\mathbf{X}_0, \lambda_0)_1 = (2, 2, 1, 1),$$

$$(\mathbf{X}_0, \lambda_0)_2 = (2, -2, 1, 1),$$

$$(\mathbf{X}_0, \lambda_0)_3 = (2.8, 0, 1.4, 1.4).$$

Applying the sufficiency conditions, then

$$\mathbf{H}_4 = \left[\begin{array}{c|ccc} 0 & 4 & 2x_2 & 2 \\ \hline 4 & 2 & 0 & 0 \\ 2x_2 & 0 & 2 - 2\lambda & 0 \\ 2 & 0 & 0 & 2 \end{array}\right]$$

Since $m = 1$ and $n = 3$, then the sign of the last $(3 - 1) = 2$ principal minor determinants must be that of $(-1)^m = -1$ in order for a stationary point to be a minimum.

Thus, for $(\mathbf{X}_0, \lambda_0)_1 = (2, 2, 1, 1)$,

$$\begin{vmatrix} 0 & 4 & 4 \\ 4 & 2 & 0 \\ 4 & 0 & 0 \end{vmatrix} = -32 < 0, \qquad \begin{vmatrix} 0 & 4 & 4 & 2 \\ 4 & 2 & 0 & 0 \\ 2 & 0 & 0 & 0 \\ 2 & 0 & 0 & 2 \end{vmatrix} = -64 < 0,$$

and for $(\mathbf{X}_0, \lambda_0)_2 = (2, -2, 1, 1)$,

$$\begin{vmatrix} 0 & 4 & -4 \\ 4 & 2 & 0 \\ -4 & 0 & 0 \end{vmatrix} = -32 < 0, \qquad \begin{vmatrix} 0 & 4 & -4 & 2 \\ 4 & 2 & 0 & 0 \\ -4 & 0 & 0 & 0 \\ 2 & 0 & 0 & 2 \end{vmatrix} = -64 < 0,$$

and finally for $(\mathbf{X}_0, \lambda_0)_3 = (2.8, 0, 1.4, 1.4)$,

$$\begin{vmatrix} 0 & 4 & 0 \\ 4 & 2 & 0 \\ 0 & 0 & -.8 \end{vmatrix} = 12.8 > 0, \qquad \begin{vmatrix} 0 & 4 & 0 & 2 \\ 4 & 2 & 0 & 0 \\ 0 & 0 & -.8 & 0 \\ 2 & 0 & 0 & 2 \end{vmatrix} = 32 > 0.$$

It thus follows that $(\mathbf{X}_0)_1$ and $(\mathbf{X}_0)_2$ are minimum points. The fact that $(\mathbf{X}_0)_3$ does not satisfy the sufficiency conditions of either a maximum or a minimum does not necessarily mean that it is not an extreme point. This, as explained earlier, follows from the fact that the given conditions although sufficient may not be satisfied for every extreme point. In such a case, one may have to have the other sufficiency condition.

To illustrate the use of the other sufficiency condition which employs the roots of the polynomial, consider

$$\Delta = \left[\begin{array}{c|ccc} 0 & 4 & 2x_2 & 2 \\ \hline 4 & 2 - \mu & 0 & 0 \\ 2x_2 & 0 & 2 - 2\lambda - \mu & 0 \\ 2 & 0 & 0 & 2 - \mu \end{array} \right].$$

Now, for $(\mathbf{X}_0, \lambda_0)_1 = (2, 2, 1, 1)$.

$$|\Delta| = 9\mu^2 - 26\mu + 16 = 0.$$

This gives $\mu = 2$ or $\frac{8}{9}$. Since all $\mu > 0$, then $(\mathbf{X}_0)_1 = (2, 2, 1)$ is a minimum point. Again, for $(\mathbf{X}_0, \lambda_0)_2 = (2, -2, 1, 1)$,

$$|\Delta| = 9\mu^2 - 26\mu + 16 = 0,$$

which is the same as in the previous case. Hence $(X_0)_2 = (2, -2, 1)$ is a minimum point. Finally, for $(X_0, \lambda_0)_3 = (2.8, 0, 1.4, 1.4)$,

$$|\Delta| = 5\mu^2 - 6\mu - 8 = 0.$$

This gives $\mu = 2$ and -0.8. This means that $(X_0)_3 = (2.8, 0, 1.4)$ is not an extreme point. ◄

§ 16·3·2
Inequality Constraints

§ 16·3·2·1
The Kuhn-Tucker Conditions

This section develops the Kuhn-Tucker *necessary* conditions for identifying the stationary points of the general constrained problem subject to inequality constraints. The development is based mainly on the Lagrangian method. These conditions are also sufficient under certain limitations which will be stated later.

Consider the problem:

$$\text{maximize} \quad x_0 = f(X),$$

subject to

$$g(X) \leq 0.$$

It is assumed that the set of constraints $g(X) \leq 0$ may include the nonnegativity constraints $X \geq 0$. In this case, these constraints are written as $-X \leq 0$ to agree with the above notation.

In the above problem each of the inequality constraints may be converted into equations by adding the appropriate *nonnegative* slack variables. Thus to satisfy the nonnegativity condition, let S_i^2 (≥ 0) be the slack quantity added to the ith constraint $g_i(X) \leq 0$. Define,

$$S = (S_1, S_2, \ldots, S_m)^T,$$

and

$$S^2 = (S_1^2, S_2^2, \ldots, S_m^2)^T,$$

where m is the total number of inequality constraints. The Lagrangian function is thus given by

$$L(X, S, \lambda) = f(X) - \lambda G(X),$$

where

$$G(X) = g(X) + S^2.$$

It is noted in this case that given the constraints

$$g(X) \le 0,$$

a necessary condition for optimality is that λ be nonnegative for maximization problems and nonpositive for minimization problems. This is justified as follows. Since λ measures the rate of variation of f with respect to g; that is,

$$\lambda = \frac{\partial f}{\partial g},$$

then for the maximization case, as the right-hand side of the constraint $g \le 0$ increases above zero, the solution space becomes less constrained and hence f cannot decrease. This means that $\lambda \ge 0$. Similarly, for the minimization case, as the resource increases, f cannot increase which implies that $\lambda \le 0$. It must be noted that if the constraints are equalities; that is, $g(X) = 0$, then λ becomes unrestricted in sign.

The restrictions on λ given above must hold as part of the Kuhn-Tucker necessary conditions. The remaining conditions will now be derived.

Taking the partial derivatives of L with respect to X, S, and λ, then

$$\frac{\partial L}{\partial X} = \nabla f(X) - \lambda \nabla G(X)$$

$$= \nabla f(X) - \lambda \nabla g(X) = 0,$$

$$\frac{\partial L}{\partial S_i} = -2\lambda_i S_i = 0, \qquad i = 1, 2, \ldots, m,$$

$$\frac{\partial L}{\partial \lambda} = -G(X)$$

$$= -(g(X) + S^2) = 0.$$

The second set of equations reveals the following interesting results.

(i) If λ_i is greater than zero, then $S_i^2 = 0$. This means that the corresponding resource is scarce and consequently this resource is exhausted completely (equality constraint).

(ii) If $S_i^2 > 0$ then $\lambda_i = 0$. This means that the ith resource is not scarce and consequently, it does not affect the value of f, $\left(\lambda_i = \frac{\partial f}{\partial g_i} = 0 \right)$.

From the second and third sets of equations it follows that

$$\lambda_i\, g_i(X) = 0, \qquad i = 1, 2, \ldots, m.$$

This new condition essentially repeats the above argument since if $\lambda_i > 0$, $g_i(X) = 0$, or $S_i^2 = 0$. Similarly, if $g_i(X) < 0$; that is, $S_i^2 > 0$, then $\lambda_i = 0$.

The Kuhn-Tucker conditions necessary for $\mathbf{X}$ and λ to be a stationary point of the above maximization problem can be summarized now as follows.

(i) $$\lambda \geq 0,$$

(ii) $$\nabla f(\mathbf{X}) - \lambda \nabla g(\mathbf{X}) = 0,$$

(iii) $$\lambda_i\, g_i(\mathbf{X}) = 0, \qquad i = 1, 2, \ldots, m,$$

(iv) $$g(\mathbf{X}) \leq 0.$$

The reader can verify that these conditions apply to the minimization case with the exception that λ must be nonpositive. (See Problem 16-14.) It must be noted in both the maximization and the minimization cases, that the Lagrange multipliers corresponding to *equality* constraints must be unrestricted in sign. (See Problem 16-15.)

The above necessary conditions are also sufficient if $f(\mathbf{X})$ is concave and the feasible space is convex; that is, if $f(\mathbf{X})$ is concave and $g_i(\mathbf{X})$, $(i = 1, 2, \ldots, m)$ is convex. This is proved by showing that $L(\mathbf{X}, \mathbf{S}, \lambda)$ is concave in $\mathbf{X}$ under these conditions. In this case the stationary point obtained from the Kuhn-Tucker conditions must be the global maximum point. Thus,

$$L(\mathbf{X}, \mathbf{S}, \lambda) = f(\mathbf{X}) - \lambda \mathbf{G}(\mathbf{X}).$$

Now,

$$\lambda \mathbf{G}(\mathbf{X}) = \lambda \mathbf{g}(\mathbf{X}) + \lambda \mathbf{S}^2.$$

By the necessary conditions, $\lambda \mathbf{S}^2 = 0$. Since $\mathbf{g}(\mathbf{X})$ is convex and $\lambda \geq 0$, hence $\lambda \mathbf{g}(\mathbf{X})$ is also convex and $-\lambda \mathbf{g}(\mathbf{X})$ is concave. It follows that $f(\mathbf{X}) - \lambda \mathbf{g}(\mathbf{X})$ or $L(\mathbf{X}, \mathbf{S}, \lambda)$ concave in $\mathbf{X}$. By a similar argument, it can be proved that for the minimization problem, the Kuhn-Tucker conditions are sufficient provided $f(\mathbf{X})$ and $\mathbf{g}_i(\mathbf{X})$ for all i are convex.

▶ **Example 16·3-6**
Consider the following *minimization* problem:

$$\text{minimize} \quad f(\mathbf{X}) = x_1^2 + x_2^2 + x_3^2,$$

subject to

$$g_1(\mathbf{X}) = 2x_1 + x_2 - 5 \leq 0,$$

$$g_2(\mathbf{X}) = x_1 + x_3 - 2 \ \leq 0,$$

$$g_3(\mathbf{X}) = 1 - x_1 \qquad \leq 0,$$

$$g_4(\mathbf{X}) = 2 - x_2 \qquad \leq 0,$$

$$g_5(\mathbf{X}) = \ \ - x_3 \qquad \leq 0.$$

Since this is a minimization problem, then $\lambda \le 0$. The Kuhn-Tucker conditions are thus given as follows.

(i) $(\lambda_1, \lambda_2, \lambda_3, \lambda_4, \lambda_5) \le 0$,

(ii) $(2x_1, 2x_2, 2x_3) - (\lambda_1, \lambda_2, \lambda_3, \lambda_4, \lambda_5) \begin{bmatrix} 2 & 1 & 0 \\ 1 & 0 & 1 \\ -1 & 0 & 0 \\ 0 & -1 & 0 \\ 0 & 0 & -1 \end{bmatrix} = 0$,

(iii) $\lambda_1 g_1 = \lambda_2 g_2 = \cdots = \lambda_5 g_5 = 0$,

(iv) $g(X) \le 0$.

These conditions simplify to the following.

$$\lambda_1, \lambda_2, \lambda_3, \lambda_4, \lambda_5 \quad \le 0$$

$$2x_1 - 2\lambda_1 - \lambda_2 + \lambda_3 = 0$$

$$2x_2 - \lambda_1 + \lambda_4 \quad = 0$$

$$2x_3 - \lambda_2 + \lambda_5 \quad = 0$$

$$\lambda_1(2x_1 + x_2 - 5) \quad = 0$$

$$\lambda_2(x_1 + x_3 - 2) \quad = 0$$

$$\lambda_3(1 - x_1) \quad = 0$$

$$\lambda_4(2 - x_2) \quad = 0$$

$$\lambda_5 x_3 \quad = 0$$

$$2x_1 + x_2 \quad \le 5$$

$$x_1 + x_3 \quad \le 2$$

$$x_1 \ge 1, \quad x_2 \ge 2, \quad x_3 \ge 0$$

This yields the solution $x_1 = 1$, $x_2 = 2$, $x_3 = 0$; $\lambda_1 = \lambda_2 = \lambda_5 = 0$, $\lambda_3 = -2$, $\lambda_4 = -4$. Since the function $f(X)$ is convex and the solution space $g(X) \le 0$ is also convex then $L(X, S, \lambda)$ must be convex and the resulting stationary point will give the global constrained minimum. The given example shows, however, that it is difficult in general to solve the resulting conditions explicitly. Consequently, this procedure is not suitable for numerical computations. The importance of the Kuhn-Tucker conditions will come in developing the nonlinear programming algorithms as shown in Chapter 17. ◄

SELECTED REFERENCES

1. COURANT, R., *Differential and Integral Calculus*, New York: Wiley-Interscience, 1936, Vol. II.
2. COURANT, R. and D. HILBERT, *Methods of Mathematical Physics*, New York: Wiley-Interscience, 1937, Vol. I.
3. HADLEY, G., *Nonlinear and Dynamic Programming*, Reading, Massachusetts: Addison-Wesley, 1964.
4. WILDE, D. and C. BEIGHTLER, *Foundations of Optimization*, Englewood Cliffs, N.J.: Prentice-Hall, 1967.

PROBLEMS

☐ **16-1**   Examine the following functions for extreme points.

(i) $f(x) = x^3 + x$

(ii) $f(x) = x^4 + x^2$

(iii) $f(x) = 4x^4 - x^2 + 5$

(iv) $f(x) = (3x - 2)^2(2x - 3)^2$

(v) $f(x) = 6x^5 - 4x^3 + 10$

☐ **16-2**   Examine the following functions for extreme points.

(i) $f(\mathbf{X}) = x_1^3 + x_2^3 - 3x_1x_2$

(ii) $f(\mathbf{X}) = 2x_1^2 + x_2^2 + x_3^2 + 6(x_1 + x_2 + x_3) + 2x_1x_2x_3$

☐ **16-3**   Verify that the function,

$$f(x_1, x_2, x_3) = 2x_1x_2x_3 - 4x_1x_3 - 2x_2x_3 + x_1^2 + x_2^2 + x_3^2$$
$$- 2x_1 - 4x_2 + 4x_3,$$

has the stationary points $(0, 3, 1)$, $(0, 1, -1)$, $(1, 2, 0)$, $(2, 1, 1)$ and $(2, 3, -1)$. Use the sufficiency condition to check for the extreme points.

☐ **16-4**   Prove Theorem 16·2-3.

☐ **16-5**   Apply the Jacobian method to Example 16·3-1 by selecting $\mathbf{Y} = (x_2, x_3)$ and $\mathbf{Z} = (x_1)$.

☐ **16-6**   Solve by the Jacobian method.

$$\text{Minimize} \quad f(\mathbf{X}) = \sum_{i=1}^{n} x_i^2,$$

subject to

$$\prod_{i=1}^{n} x_i = C,$$

where C is a positive constant. Suppose that the right-hand side of the constraint is changed to $C + \delta$ where δ is a small quantity, find the corresponding change in the optimal value of f.

☐ **16-7** Solve by the Jacobian method.

$$\text{Minimize} \quad f(X) = 5x_1^2 + x_2^2 + 2x_1 x_2,$$

subject to

$$g(X) = x_1 x_2 - 10 = 0.$$

(a) Find the change in the optimal value of $f(X)$ if the constraint is replaced by $x_1 x_2 - 9.99 = 0$.

(b) Find the change in the value of $f(X)$ in the neighborhood of the feasible point $(2, 5)$ given $x_1 x_2 = 9.99$ and $\partial x_1 = .01$.

☐ **16-8** Consider the problem:

$$\text{maximize} \quad f(X) = x_1^2 + 2x_2^2 + 10x_3^2 + 5x_1 x_2,$$

subject to

$$g_1(X) = x_1 + x_2^2 + 3x_2 x_3 - 5 = 0,$$
$$g_2(X) = x_1^2 + 5x_1 x_2 + x_3^2 - 7 = 0.$$

Apply the Jacobian method to find $\partial f(X)$ in the feasible neighborhood of the feasible point $(1, 1, 1)$. Assume that this feasible neighborhood is specified by $\partial g_1 = .01$, $\partial g_2 = .02$, and $\partial x_1 = .01$.

☐ **16-9** Consider the problem:

$$\text{minimize} \quad f(X) = x_1^2 + x_2^2 + x_3^2 + x_4^2,$$

subject to

$$g_1(X) = x_1 + 2x_2 + 3x_3 + 5x_4 - 10 = 0,$$
$$g_2(X) = x_1 + 2x_2 + 5x_3 + 6x_4 - 15 = 0.$$

Show that by selecting x_3 and x_4 as the independent variables, the Jacobian method fails to give the solution. Then solve the problem using x_1 and x_3 as the independent variables and apply the sufficiency condition to examine the resulting stationary point. Find the sensitivity coefficients of the problem.

☐ **16-10** Consider the linear programming problem:

$$\text{maximize} \quad f(X) = \sum_{j=1}^{n} c_j x_j,$$

subject to

$$g_i(\mathbf{X}) = \sum_{j=1}^{n} a_{ij} x_j - b_i = 0, \qquad i = 1, 2, \ldots, m,$$

$$x_j \geq 0, \qquad j = 1, 2, \ldots, n.$$

Neglecting the nonnegativity constraint, show that the constrained derivatives, $\mathbf{V}_c f(\mathbf{X})$, for this problem yield the same expression for $\{z_j - c_j\}$ defined by the optimality condition of the linear programming problem. (Section 8·5·2.) That is,

$$\{z_j - c_j\} = \{\mathbf{C}_B \mathbf{B}^{-1} \mathbf{P}_j - c_j\}, \qquad \text{for all } j.$$

Can the constrained-derivative method be applied directly to the linear programming problem? Why or why not?

☐ **16-11** Solve the following linear programming problem by both the Jacobian and the Lagrangian methods.

$$\text{Maximize} \quad f(\mathbf{X}) = 5x_1 + 3x_2,$$

subject to

$$g_1(\mathbf{X}) = x_1 + 2x_2 + x_3 - 6 = 0,$$

$$g_2(\mathbf{X}) = 3x_1 + x_2 + x_4 - 9 = 0,$$

$$x_1 \geq 0, \quad x_2 \geq 0, \quad x_3 \geq 0, \quad x_4 \geq 0.$$

☐ **16-12** Find the optimal solution to the following problem.

$$\text{Minimize} \quad f(\mathbf{X}) = x_1^2 + 2x_2^2 + 10x_3^2,$$

subject to

$$g_1(\mathbf{X}) = x_1 + x_2^2 + x_3 - 5 = 0,$$

$$g_2(\mathbf{X}) = x_1 + 5x_2 + x_3 - 7 = 0.$$

Suppose $g_1(\mathbf{X}) = .01$ and $g_2(\mathbf{X}) = .02$. Find the corresponding change in the optimal value of $f(\mathbf{X})$.

☐ **16-13** Solve Problem 16-9 by the Lagrangian method and verify that the value of the Lagrange multipliers are the same as the sensitivity coefficients obtained in Problem 16-9.

☐ **16-14** Show that the Kuhn-Tucker conditions for the problem,

$$\text{maximize} \quad f(\mathbf{X})$$

subject to

$$g(\mathbf{X}) \geq 0,$$

are the same as in Section 16·3·2·1 except that the Lagrange multipliers, λ, are nonpositive.

☐ **16-15** Show that the Kuhn-Tucker conditions for the problem,

$$\text{maximize} \quad f(\mathbf{X}),$$

subject to

$$g(\mathbf{X}) = 0,$$

are

(i) $\quad\quad\quad\quad\quad\quad\quad$ λ unrestricted in sign,

(ii) $\quad\quad\quad\quad\quad\quad$ $\nabla f(\mathbf{X}) - \lambda \nabla g(\mathbf{X}) - 0,$

(iii) $\quad\quad\quad\quad\quad\quad\quad$ $g(\mathbf{X}) = 0,$

where λ are the Lagrangian multipliers.

☐ **16-16** Write the Kuhn-Tucker necessary conditions for the following problems.

(i) Maximize $f(\mathbf{X}) = x_1^3 - x_2^2 + x_1 x_3^2,$

subject to

$$x_1 + x_2^2 + x_3 = 5.$$
$$5x_1^2 - x_2^2 - x_3 \geq 2,$$
$$x_1, x_2, x_3 \geq 0.$$

(ii) Minimize $f(\mathbf{X}) = x_1^4 + x_2^2 + 5x_1 x_2 x_3,$

subject to

$$x_1^2 - x_2^2 + x_3^3 \leq 10,$$
$$x_1^3 + x_2^2 + 4x_3^2 \geq 20.$$

☐ **16-17** Consider the problem:

$$\text{maximize} \quad f(\mathbf{X}),$$

subject to

$$g(\mathbf{X}) = 0.$$

Given $f(\mathbf{X})$ is concave and $g_i(\mathbf{X})$, $i = 1, 2, \ldots, m$, is a *linear* function, show that the Kuhn-Tucker necessary conditions are also sufficient. Is this result true if $g_i(\mathbf{X})$ is a convex *non*linear function for all i? Why?

CHAPTER 17

Nonlinear Programming Algorithms

§ 17·1
Introduction

The general nonlinear programming problem may be defined as:

$$\text{maximize (or minimize)} \quad x_0 = f(\mathbf{X}),$$

subject to

$$\mathbf{g}(\mathbf{X}) \leq \mathbf{0}.$$

The nonnegativity conditions $\mathbf{X} \geq \mathbf{0}$ are assumed to be part of the given set of constraints. It is further assumed that at least one of the functions $f(\mathbf{X})$ and $\mathbf{g}(\mathbf{X})$ is nonlinear. For the purpose of this presentation, these functions are supposed to be continuously differentiable.

Unlike the linear programming case, there exists no general algorithm for handling nonlinear models. This is attributed mainly to the irregular behavior of the nonlinear functions. Perhaps the most general result applicable to the above problem is that given by the Kuhn-Tucker conditions. It was shown in Section 16·3·2·1 that unless $f(\mathbf{X})$ and $\mathbf{g}(\mathbf{X})$ are well-behaved functions (convexity and concavity conditions), the Kuhn-Tucker theory will yield only the necessary conditions for an optimum point. This sets a big limitation on the application of the said conditions to the general problem.

This chapter presents a number of algorithms which treat special cases of the nonlinear programming problem. Section 17·2 introduces the approximating method called *separable programming*. In this case, all the nonlinear functions must satisfy the so-called separability condition. Section 17·3 presents the most well-behaved nonlinear algorithm called *quadratic programming*. In this algorithm the objective function is convex (minimization) or concave (maximization) and all the constraints are linear. Section 17·4 discusses the new technique called *geometric programming*. This technique will yield excellent results if certain conditions are satisfied. *Stochastic programming* is presented in Section 17·5. In this case it is assumed that some of the parameters of the problem are *probabilistic* rather than deterministic. The objective here is to show how the problem can be converted into an equivalent *deterministic* case. Finally, Section 17·6 presents the so-called *gradient methods*.

§ 17·2
Separable Programming

A function $f(x_1, x_2, \ldots, x_n)$ is said to be separable if it can be expressed as the sum of n single-variable functions $f_1(x_1), f_2(x_2), \ldots, f_n(x_n)$; that is,

$$f(x_1, x_2, \ldots, x_n) = f_1(x_1) + f_2(x_2) + \cdots + f_n(x_n).$$

For example, the linear function

$$h(x_1, x_2, \ldots, x_n) = a_1 x_1 + a_2 x_2 + \cdots + a_n x_n$$

(where the a's are constants) is a separable function. On the other hand, the function,

$$h(x_1, x_2, x_3) = x_1^2 + x_1 \sin(x_2 + x_3) + x_2 e^{x_3},$$

is not a separable function.

It must be noted that there are some functions which are not directly separable but which can be made so using simple substitutions. Consider, for example, the case of maximizing $x_0 = x_1 x_2$. Letting $y = x_1 x_2$, then $\ln y = \ln x_1 + \ln x_2$. Hence, the problem becomes:

$$\text{maximize} \quad x_0 = y,$$

subject to

$$\ln y = \ln x_1 + \ln x_2$$

which is separable now. Notice that the above substitution assumes that x_1 and x_4 are *positive* variables; otherwise, if these variables assume nonpositive values, the logarithmic function is undefined.

The case where x_1 and x_2 assume zero values (that is, $x_1, x_2 \geq 0$) may be handled as follows. Let

$$w_1 = x_1 + \delta_1,$$
$$w_2 = x_2 + \delta_2.$$

where δ_1 and δ_2 are positive constants. This means that w_1 and w_2 are strictly positive. Now,

$$x_1 = w_1 - \delta_1,$$
$$x_2 = w_2 - \delta_2.$$

Hence

$$x_1 x_2 = w_1 w_2 - \delta_2 w_1 - \delta_1 w_2 + \delta_1 \delta_2.$$

Let $y = w_1 w_2$, then the problem becomes equivalent to:

$$\text{maximize} \quad x_0 = y - \delta_2 w_1 - \delta_1 w_2 + \delta_1 \delta_2,$$

subject to

$$\ln y = \ln w_1 + \ln w_2$$

which is properly separable.

Other functions that can be made readily separable (using substitution) are exemplified by $e^{x_1 + x_2}$ and $x_1^{x_2}$. A variant of the above procedure can be applied to such cases to effect the required separability.

Separable programming deals with nonlinear problems in which the objective function and all the constraints are separable. In this section, it is shown how an approximate solution can be obtained for any separable problem using linear approximation and the simplex method of linear programming.

It was shown in Section 10·5·4 how a nonlinear single-variable function $f(x)$ can be approximated by a piecewise linear function using mixed integer linear programming. Let a_k, $k = 1, 2, \ldots, K$, be the kth breaking points on the x-axis of the function $f(x)$. Then

$$f(x) = \sum_{k=1}^{K} f(a_k) t_k,$$

$$x = \sum_{k=1}^{K} a_k t_k,$$

where t_k is a nonnegative weight associated with the kth breaking point such that

$$\sum_{k=1}^{K} t_k = 1.$$

Mixed integer programming is then introduced to ensure that the given approximation is valid. Specifically, the approximation is valid if (1) at most two t_k are positive, and (2) if t_{k^*} is a positive then only an adjacent t_k (t_{k^*+1} or t_{k^*-1}) is allowed to take a positive value. The additional constraints given in Section 10·5·4 will ensure that these conditions are satisfied.

Consider now the separable problem:

$$\text{maximize (or minimize)} \quad x_0 = \sum_{i=1}^{n} f_i(x_i),$$

subject to

$$\sum_{i=1}^{n} g_i^j(x_i) \le b_j, \qquad j = 1, 2, \ldots, m.$$

This problem can be approximated as a mixed integer programming problem as follows. Let the number of breaking points for the ith variable, x_i, be equal to K_i and let a_i^k be its kth breaking value. Let t_i^k be the weight associated with the kth breaking point of the ith variable. Then the equivalent mixed problem is:

$$\text{maximize (or minimize)} \quad x_0 = \sum_{i=1}^{n} \sum_{k=1}^{K_i} f_i(a_i^k) t_i^k,$$

subject to

$$\sum_{i=1}^{n} \sum_{k=1}^{K_i} g_i^j(a_i^k) t_i^k \le b_j, \qquad j = 1, 2, \ldots, m,$$

$$0 \le t_i^1 \le y_i^1,$$

$$0 \le t_i^k \le y_i^{k-1} + y_i^k, \qquad k = 2, 3, \ldots, K_i - 1,$$

$$0 \le t_i^{K_i} \le y_i^{K_i-1},$$

$$\sum_{k=1}^{K_i-1} y_i^k = 1,$$

$$\sum_{k=1}^{K_i} t_i^k = 1,$$

$$y_i^k = 0 \text{ or } 1, \quad k = 1, 2, \ldots, K_i, \quad i = 1, 2, \ldots, n.$$

It is noticed that the variables for the approximating problem are given by t_i^k and y_i^k.

The above formulation shows how any separable problem can be solved, at least in principle, using mixed integer programming. The problem here, however, is that the number of constraints increases rather rapidly with the number of breaking points. In particular, the computational feasibility of the procedure is highly questionable since there are no efficient computer programs for handling large mixed integer programming problems.

Another method for solving the approximating problem is to use the regular simplex method (Chapter 3) under the condition of *restricted basis*. In this case, the additional constraints involving y_i^k are disregarded. The restricted basis condition specifies that *no more* that two t_i^k can appear in the basis. Moreover, two t_i^k can be positive only if they are adjacent. Thus, the strict optimality condition of the simplex method is used to select the entering variable t_i^k *only if* it satisfies the above conditions. Otherwise, the variable t_i^k having the next best optimality indicator ($z_i^k - c_i^k$) is considered for entering the solution. The process is repeated until the optimality condition is satisfied or until it is impossible to introduce new t_i^k without violating the restricted basis condition, whichever occurs first. At this point, the last tableau gives the approximate optimum solution to the problem.

It should be noted that while the mixed integer programming method yields the global optimum to the approximate problem, the restricted basis method can only guarantee a local optimum. Also, in the two methods, the approximate solution may not be a feasible solution to the original problem. In fact the approximating problem may give rise to additional extreme points which do not exist in the original problem. This depends mainly on the degree of refinement of the linear approximation used. These inherent risks thus must be taken into consideration when using the indicated methods.

▶ **Example 17·2-1**
Consider the problem:

$$\text{maximize} \quad x_0 = x_1 + x_2^4,$$

subject to

$$3x_1 + 2x_2^2 \leq 9,$$

$$x_1 \geq 0, \quad x_2 \geq 0.$$

This example will illustrate the application of the restricted basis method.

The exact optimum solution to this problem can be obtained by inspection and it is given by $x_1^* = 0$, $x_2^* = \sqrt{\frac{9}{2}} = 2.13$, and $x_0^* = 20.25$. To show how the approximating method is used, consider the separable functions,

$$f_1(x_1) = x_1,$$

$$f_2(x_2) = x_2^4,$$

$$g_1^1(x_1) = 3x_1,$$

$$g_1^2(x_2) = 2x_2^2.$$

Because $f_1(x_1)$ and $g_1^1(x_1)$ are already linear, they are left in their present form. In this case x_1 is treated as a regular variable. Now considering $f_2(x_2)$ and $g_1^2(x_2)$, it is assumed that there are four breaking points ($K_2 = 4$). Since the value of x_2 cannot exceed 3, then

k	a_2^k	$f_2(a_2^k)$	$g_1^2(a_2^k)$
1	0	0	0
2	1	1	2
3	2	16	8
4	3	81	18

This yields

$$f_2(x_2) \cong t_2^1 f_2(a_2^1) + t_2^2 f_2(a_2^2) + t_2^3 f_2(a_2^3) + t_2^4 f_2(a_2^4),$$

$$\cong 0(t_2^1) + 1(t_2^2) + 16(t_2^3) + 81(t_2^4),$$

$$\cong t_2^2 + 16t_2^3 + 81t_2^4.$$

Similarly

$$g_1^2(x_2) \cong 2t_2^2 + 8t_2^3 + 18t_2^4.$$

The approximating problem thus becomes:

$$\text{maximize } x_0 = x_1 + t_2^2 + 16t_2^3 + 81t_2^4,$$

subject to

$$3x_1 + 2t_2^2 + 8t_2^3 + 18t_2^4 \le 9,$$

$$t_2^1 + t_2^2 + t_2^3 + t_2^4 = 1,$$

$$t_2^k \ge 0, \qquad k = 1, 2, 3, 4,$$

together with the restricted basis condition.

The initial simplex tableau (with rearranged columns to give a starting solution) is given by

Basic	x_0	x_1	t_2^2	t_2^3	t_2^4	S_1	t_2^1	Solution
x_0	①	-1	-1	-16	-81	0	0	0
S_1	0	3	2	8	18	①	0	9
t_2^1	0	0	1	1	1	0	①	1

where $S_1 (\ge 0)$ is a slack variable. (Notice that this problem happened to have an obvious starting solution. In general, one may have to use the artificial variables techniques, Sections 3·5 and 3·6·4·1.)

From the x_0-row coefficients, the optimality indicator shows that t_2^4 is the entering variable. Since t_2^1 is basic, it must be dropped first before t_2^4 can enter the solution (restricted basis condition). From the feasibility condition it is noticed that S_1 must be the leaving variable. This means that t_2^4 cannot enter the solution. Next consider t_2^3 (next best entering variable). Again t_2^1 must be dropped first. From the feasibility condition it follows that t_2^1 is the leaving variable as desired. The new tableau becomes

Basic	x_0	x_1	t_2^2	t_2^3	t_2^4	S_1	t_2^1	Solution
x_0	①	-1	15	0	-65	0	16	16
S_1	0	3	-6	0	10	①	-8	1
t_2^3	0	0	1	①	1	0	1	1

Clearly t_2^4 is the entering variable. Since t_2^3 is in the basis, t_2^4 is an admissible entering variable. The simplex method shows that S_1 will be dropped. Thus,

Basic	x_0	x_1	t_2^2	t_2^3	t_2^4	S_1	t_2^1	Solution
x_0	①	$18\frac{1}{2}$	-24	0	0	$6\frac{1}{2}$	-36	$22\frac{1}{2}$
t_2^4	0	$3/10$	$-6/10$	0	①	$1/10$	$-8/10$	$1/10$
t_2^3	0	$-3/10$	$16/10$	①	0	$-1/10$	$18/10$	$9/10$

This tableau shows that t_2^1 and t_2^2 are candidates for the entering variable. Since t_2^1 is not an adjacent point to the basic t_2^3 and t_2^4, it cannot be admitted. Again, t_2^2 also cannot be admitted since t_2^4 cannot be dropped. Consequently, the process ends at this point and the given solution is the best feasible solution for the approximating problem.

In order to find the solution in terms of x_1 and x_2, one considers

$$t_2^3 = \frac{9}{10}, \quad t_2^4 = \frac{1}{10}.$$

Thus

$$x_2 \cong 2t_2^3 + 3t_2^4 = 2\left(\frac{9}{10}\right) + 3\left(\frac{1}{10}\right) = 2.1,$$

$$x_1 = 0,$$

and

$$x_0 = 22.5.$$

It is noted that the approximate optimum value of $x_2 (= 2.1)$ is very close to the true optimum value $(= 2.13)$. The value of x_0 differs by about 10% error, however. The approximation may be improved in this case by using finer breaking points. ◄

§ 17·2·1
Separable Convex Programming

A special case of separable programming occurs when the functions $g_i^j(x_i)$ are convex so that the solution space of the problem is a convex set. In addition, the function $f_i(x_i)$ is convex in case of minimization and concave in case of maximization. Under such conditions, the following simplified approximation can be used.

Consider a minimization problem and let $f_i(x_i)$ be as shown in Figure 17–1. The kth breaking point of the function $f_i(x_i)$ is determined by $x_i = a_{ki}$, $k = 0, 1, \ldots, K_i$. Let x_{ki} define the increment of the variable x_i in the range $(a_{k-1,\,i},\, a_{ki})$, $k = 1, 2, \ldots, K_i$, and let ρ_{ki} be the corresponding slope of the

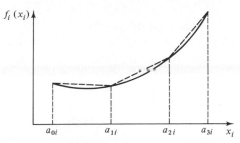

Figure 17–1

line segment in the same range. Then

$$f_i(x_i) \cong \sum_{k=1}^{K_i} (\rho_{ki} x_{ki}) + f_i(a_{0i}),$$

$$x_i = \sum_{k=1}^{K_i} x_{ki},$$

provided that

$$0 \le x_{ki} \le a_{ki} - a_{k-1,i}, \qquad k = 1, 2, \ldots, K_i.$$

The fact that $f_i(x_i)$ is convex insures that $\rho_{1i} < \rho_{2i} < \cdots < \rho_{K_i i}$. This means that in the minimization problem for $p < q$, the variable x_{pi} is more attractive that x_{qi}. Consequently, x_{pi} will always enter the solution before x_{qi}. The only limitation here is that every x_{ki} must be restricted by its upper bound $(a_{ki} - a_{k-1,i})$.

The convex constraint functions $g_i^j(x_i)$ are approximated in essentially the same way. Let ρ_{ki}^j be the slope of the kth line segment corresponding to $g_i^j(x_i)$, then

$$g_i^j(x_i) = \sum_{k=1}^{K_i} \rho_{ki}^j x_{ki} + g_i^j(a_{0i}).$$

The complete problem is thus given by:

$$\text{minimize} \quad x_0 = \sum_{i=1}^{n} \left(\sum_{k=1}^{K_i} \rho_{ki} x_{ki} + f_i(a_{0i}) \right),$$

subject to

$$\sum_{i=1}^{n} \left(\sum_{k=1}^{K_i} \rho_{ki}^j x_{ki} + g_i^j(a_{0i}) \right) \le b_j, \qquad j = 1, 2, \ldots, m,$$

$$0 \le x_{ki} \le a_{ki} - a_{k-1,i}; \qquad k = 1, 2, \ldots, K_i, \qquad i = 1, 2, \ldots, n,$$

where

$$\rho_{ki} = \frac{f_i(a_{ki}) - f_i(a_{k-1,i})}{a_{ki} - a_{k-1,i}},$$

$$\rho_{ki}^j = \frac{g_i^j(a_{ki}) - g_i^j(a_{k-1,i})}{a_{ki} - a_{k-1,i}}.$$

It is clear that the maximization problem is treated in essentially the same way. In this case $\rho_{1i} > \rho_{2i} > \cdots > \rho_{K_i i}$, which shows that, for $p < q$, the variable x_{pi} will always enter the solution before x_{qi}. (See Problem 17-7 for the proof.)

The new problem can be solved now using the simplex method with upper bounded variables (Section 8·7·3). The restricted basis concept is not necessary here since the convexity (concavity) of the functions ascertain the proper selections of the variables.

▶　**Example 17·2-2**

Consider the problem:

$$\text{minimize} \quad x_0 = x_1^2 + x_2^2 + 5,$$

subject to

$$3x_1^4 + x_2 \le 243,$$
$$x_1 + 2x_2^2 \le 32,$$
$$x_1 \ge 0, \quad x_2 \ge 0.$$

The separable functions of this problem are

$$f_1(x_1) = x_1^2, \quad f_2(x_2) = x_2^2 + 5,$$
$$g_1^1(x_1) = 3x_1^4, \quad g_1^2(x_2) = x_2,$$
$$g_2^1(x_1) = x_1, \quad g_2^2(x_2) = 2x_2^2.$$

These functions satisfy the convexity condition required for the minimization problems.

The range of the variables x_1 and x_2 are calculated from the constraints and are given by $0 \le x_1 \le 3$ and $0 \le x_2 \le 4$. Thus x_1 and x_2 are partitioned in these ranges. Let $K_1 = 3$ and $K_2 = 4$ with a $a_{01} = a_{02} = 0$. The slopes corresponding to the above separable functions are:

for $i = 1$

k	a_{k1}	ρ_{k2}	ρ_{k1}^1	ρ_{k1}^2	x_{k1}
1	1	1	3	1	x_{11}
2	2	3	45	1	x_{21}
3	3	5	195	1	x_{31}

for i = 2

k	a_{k2}	ρ_{k2}	ρ_{k2}^1	ρ_{k2}^2	x_{k2}
1	1	1	1	2	x_{12}
2	2	3	1	6	x_{22}
3	3	5	1	10	x_{23}
4	4	7	1	14	x_{42}

The complete problem then becomes:

minimize $x_0 \cong x_{11} + 3x_{21} + 5x_{31} + x_{12} + 3x_{22} + 5x_{32} + 7x_{42} + 5,$

subject to

$$3x_{11} + 45x_{21} + 195x_{31} + x_{12} + x_{22} + x_{32} + x_{42} \leq 243,$$

$$x_{11} + x_{21} + x_{31} + 2x_{12} + 6x_{22} + 10x_{32} + 14x_{42} \leq 32,$$

$$0 \leq x_{k1} \leq 1, \quad k = 1, 2, 3,$$

$$0 \leq x_{k2} \leq 1, \quad k = 1, 2, 3, 4.$$

After solving this problem using upper bounding technique, let x_{k1}^* and x_{k2}^* be the corresponding optimal values. Thus, the optimal value of x_1 and x_2 are given by,

$$x_1^* = \sum_{k=1}^{3} x_{k1}^*,$$

$$x_2^* = \sum_{k=1}^{4} x_{k2}^*. \quad \blacktriangleleft$$

§ 17·3
Quadratic Programming

A quadratic programming model is defined as follows.

$$\text{Maximize (or minimize)} \quad x_0 = \mathbf{CX} + \mathbf{X}^T\mathbf{DX},$$

subject to

$$\mathbf{AX} \leq \mathbf{P}_0,$$

$$\mathbf{X} \geq \mathbf{0},$$

where

$$X = (x_1, x_2, \ldots, x_n)^T,$$

$$C = (c_1, c_2, \ldots, c_n),$$

$$P_0 = (b_1, b_2, \ldots, b_m),$$

$$A = \begin{bmatrix} a_{11} & \cdots & a_{1n} \\ \vdots & & \vdots \\ a_{m1} & \cdots & a_{mn} \end{bmatrix},$$

$$D = \begin{bmatrix} d_{11} & \cdots & d_{1n} \\ \vdots & & \vdots \\ d_{n1} & \cdots & d_{nn} \end{bmatrix}.$$

The function $X^T DX$ defines a quadratic form (Section A·3) with D being a symmetric matrix. The matrix D is assumed negative-definite if the problem is of the maximization type and positive-definite if the problem is of the minimization type. This means that x_0 is strictly convex in X for the minimization case and strictly concave for the maximization case. The constraints are assumed linear in this case which guarantees a convex solution space.

The solution to this problem is secured by the direct application of the Kuhn-Tucker necessary conditions (Section 16·3·2·1). Since x_0 is strictly convex (concave) and since the solution space is a convex set, these necessary conditions (as proved in Section 16·3·2·1) are also sufficient for a global optimum.

The quadratic programming problem will be treated now for the maximization case. It is a trivial task to change the formulation to the minimization case. Thus the problem may be written as:

$$\text{maximize} \quad x_0 = CX + X^T DX,$$

subject to

$$G(X) = \begin{pmatrix} A \\ -I \end{pmatrix} X - \begin{pmatrix} P_0 \\ 0 \end{pmatrix} \leq 0.$$

Let,

$$\lambda = (\lambda_1, \lambda_2, \ldots, \lambda_m)^T$$

$$U = (\mu_1, \mu_2, \ldots, \mu_n)^T$$

be the Lagrange multipliers corresponding to the two sets of constraints $AX - P_0 \leq 0$ and $-X \leq 0$, respectively. Thus, the application of the Kuhn-Tucker conditions immediately yields

$$\lambda \geq 0,$$

$$U \geq 0,$$

$$\nabla x_0 - (\lambda^T, U^T) \nabla G(X) = 0,$$

$$\lambda_i(b_i - \sum_{j=i}^{n} a_{ij} x_j) = 0, \qquad i = 1, 2, \ldots, m,$$

$$\mu_j x_j = 0, \qquad j = 1, 2, \ldots, n,$$

$$AX \le P_0,$$

$$-X \le 0.$$

Now

$$\nabla x_0 = C + 2X^T D,$$

$$\nabla G(X) = \begin{pmatrix} A \\ -I \end{pmatrix}.$$

Let $S = P_0 - AX \ge 0$ be the slack variables of the constraints. The above conditions reduce to

$$-2X^T D + \lambda^T A - U^T = C,$$

$$AX + S = P_0,$$

$$\mu_j x_j = 0 = \lambda_i S_i, \qquad \text{for all } i \text{ and } j,$$

$$\lambda \ge 0, \quad U \ge 0, \quad X \ge 0, \quad S \ge 0.$$

Observing that $D^T = D$, the transpose of the first set of equations is

$$-2DX + A^T \lambda - U = C^T.$$

Hence the above necessary conditions may be combined as,

$$\left(\begin{array}{c|c|c|c} -2D & A^T & -I & 0 \\ \hline A & 0 & 0 & I \end{array} \right) \begin{pmatrix} X \\ \lambda \\ U \\ S \end{pmatrix} = \begin{pmatrix} C^T \\ P_0 \end{pmatrix},$$

$$\mu_j x_j = 0 = \lambda_i S_i, \qquad \text{for all } i \text{ and } j,$$

$$\lambda \ge 0, \quad U \ge 0, \quad X \ge 0, \quad S \ge 0.$$

Except for the conditions $\mu_j x_j = 0 = \lambda_i S_i$, the remaining equations are linear functions in X, λ, U, and S. The problem is thus equivalent to finding the solution to a set of linear equations which also satisfies the additional conditions $\mu_j x_j = 0 = \lambda_i S_i$. Because x_0 is strictly concave and the solution space is convex, the *feasible* solution satisfying all these conditions must give the optimum solution directly. It is noted from the conditions imposed on x_0 and the solution space (that is, x_0 is strictly concave and the solution space is convex) that the solution to the above set of equations (when it exists) must be unique. Otherwise the Lagrangian function will not be strictly concave in X as proved in Section 16·3·2·1.

The solution of the above system is obtained using Phase I of the two-phase method (section 3·6·4·1). The objective here, of course, is to find a feasible solution and hence the problem does not require a consideration of Phase II. The only restriction here is that the condition $\lambda_i S_i = 0 = \mu_j x_j$ should be maintained all the time. This means that if λ_i is in the basic solution at a *positive level*, then S_i cannot be basic at a positive level. Similarly, μ_j and x_j cannot be positive simultaneously. This is actually the same idea of the *restricted basis* used in Section 17·2. It is noted that Phase I will end in the usual manner with the sum of the artificial variables equal to zero only if the problem has a feasible space. The feasibility of the solution space can be easily checked however by checking whether the system $\mathbf{AX} \leq \mathbf{P}_0$ encloses a feasible space.

▶ **Example 17·3-1**
Consider the problem:

$$\text{maximize} \quad x_0 = 4x_1 + 6x_2 - 2x_1^2 - 2x_1x_2 - 2x_2^2,$$

subject to

$$x_1 + 2x_2 \leq 2,$$

$$x_1 \geq 0, \quad x_2 \geq 0.$$

This problem can be put in matrix form as follows.

$$\text{Maximize} \quad x_0 = (4, 6)\begin{pmatrix} x_1 \\ x_2 \end{pmatrix} + (x_1, x_2)\begin{pmatrix} -2 & -1 \\ -1 & -2 \end{pmatrix}\begin{pmatrix} x_1 \\ x_2 \end{pmatrix},$$

subject to

$$(1, 2)\begin{pmatrix} x_1 \\ x_2 \end{pmatrix} \geq 2,$$

$$x_1 \geq 0, \quad x_2 \geq 0.$$

This automatically defines all the information required for constructing the Kuhn-Tucker conditions.

Thus, the Kuhn-Tucker conditions corresponding to the above problem are given by,

$$\left(\begin{array}{cc|c|cc|c} 4 & 2 & 1 & -1 & 0 & 0 \\ 2 & 4 & 2 & 0 & -1 & 0 \\ \hline 1 & 2 & 0 & 0 & 0 & 1 \end{array}\right)\begin{pmatrix} x_1 \\ x_2 \\ \lambda_1 \\ \mu_1 \\ \mu_2 \\ S_1 \end{pmatrix} = \begin{pmatrix} 4 \\ 6 \\ 2 \end{pmatrix}.$$

The initial tableau for Phase I is obtained by introducing the artificial variables R_1 and R_2. Thus,

Basic	r_0	x_1	x_2	λ_1	μ_1	μ_2	R_1	R_2	S_1	Solution
r_0	①	6	6	3	-1	-1	0	0	0	10
R_1	0	4	2	1	-1	0	①	0	0	4
R_2	0	2	4	2	0	-1	0	①	0	6
S_1	0	1	2	0	0	0	0	0	①	2

First iteration: Since $\mu_1 = 0$; x_1 the most promising entering variable (minimization problem) can be made basic with R_1 as the leaving variable. This yields the tableau

Basic	r_0	x_1	x_2	λ_1	μ_1	μ_2	R_1	R_2	S_1	Solution
r_0	①	0	3	$3/2$	$1/2$	-1	$-3/2$	0	0	4
x_1	0	①	$1/2$	$1/4$	$-1/4$	0	$1/4$	0	0	1
R_2	0	0	3	$3/2$	$1/2$	-1	$-1/2$	①	0	4
S_1	0	0	$3/2$	$-1/4$	$1/4$	0	$-1/4$	0	①	1

Second iteration: The most promising variable x_2 can be made basic since $\mu_2 = 0$. This gives,

Basic	r_0	x_1	x_2	λ_1	μ_1	μ_2	R_1	R_2	S_1	Solution
r_0	①	0	0	2	0	-1	-1	0	-2	2
x_1	0	①	0	$1/3$	$-1/3$	0	$1/3$	0	$-1/3$	$2/3$
R_1	0	0	0	2	0	-1	0	①	-2	2
x_2	0	0	①	$-1/6$	$1/6$	0	$-1/6$	0	$2/3$	$2/3$

Third iteration: Since $S_1 = 0$, hence λ_1 can be introduced into the solution. This yields,

Basic	r_0	x_1	x_2	λ_1	μ_1	μ_2	R_1	R_2	S_1	Solution
r_0	①	0	0	0	0	0	-1	-1	0	0
x_1	0	①	0	0	$-1/3$	$1/6$	$1/3$	$-1/6$	0	$1/3$
λ_1	0	0	0	①	0	$-1/2$	0	$1/2$	-1	1
x_2	0	0	①	0	$1/6$	$-1/12$	$-1/6$	$1/12$	$1/2$	$5/6$

The last tableau gives the optimal solution for Phase I. Since $r_0 = 0$, the given solution is feasible. Thus, $x_1^* = \frac{1}{3}$, $x_2^* = \frac{5}{6}$. The optimal value of x_0 can be computed from the original problem and is equal to 4.16. ◀

§ 17·4
Geometric Programming

A rather interesting technique for solving a special case of nonlinear problems is the so-called *geometric* programming. This technique, developed by R. Duffin and C. Zener (1964), finds the solution to the problem by considering an associated dual problem (to be defined later). The advantage here is that it is usually much simpler to work with the dual problem than with the primal.

Geometric programming deals with problems in which the objective and the constraint functions are of the following type.

$$x_0 = f(\mathbf{X}) = \sum_{j=1}^{N} U_j,$$

where

$$U_j = c_j \prod_{i=1}^{n} x_i^{a_{ij}}, \qquad j = 1, 2, \ldots, N.$$

It is assumed that all $c_j > 0$ and that N is finite. The exponents a_{ij} are unrestricted in sign. The function $f(\mathbf{X})$ takes the form of a polynomial except that the exponents a_{ij} may be negative. For this reason, and because all $c_j > 0$, Duffin and Zener have given $f(\mathbf{X})$ the name *posynomial*.

This section will present the unconstrained case of geometric programming. The objective here is only to familiarize the reader with this type of analysis. The treatment of the constrained problem is beyond the scope of this chapter. The interested reader may refer to the excellent presentation by Wilde and Beightler ([7], Chapter 4) for a more detailed treatment of the subject. The complete theory of geometric programming is given in Duffin, Peterson, and Zener [2].

Consider the *minimization* of the function $f(\mathbf{X})$ as defined in the posynomial form given above. This problem will be referred to as the *primal* problem. The variables x_i are assumed to be *strictly positive* so that the region $x_i \leq 0$ represents an infeasible space. It will be shown later that the requirement $x_i \neq 0$ plays an essential part in the derivation of the results.

Using the regular differential approach, the first partial derivative of x_0 must vanish at the minimum point. Thus,

$$\frac{\partial x_0}{\partial x_k} = \sum_{j=1}^{N} \frac{\partial U_j}{\partial x_k}$$

$$= \sum_{j=1}^{N} c_j a_{kj}(x_k)^{a_{kj}-1} \prod_{i \neq k}(x_i)^{a_{ij}} = 0, \qquad k = 1, 2, \ldots, n.$$

Now, since each $x_k > 0$ by assumption, then

$$\frac{\partial x_0}{\partial x_k} = 0 = \frac{1}{x_k} \sum_{j=1}^{N} a_{kj} U_j, \qquad k = 1, 2, \ldots, n.$$

Let x_0^* be the minimum value of x_0. It follows from the definition of x_0 as a posynomial and from the fact that each $x_k^* > 0$, that $x_0^* > 0$. Thus, define

$$y_j = \frac{U_j^*}{x_0^*}.$$

This shows that $y_j > 0$ and $\sum_{j=1}^{N} y_j = 1$. The value of y_j thus represents the relative contribution of the jth term, U_j, to the optimal value of the objective function, x_0^*.

The above *necessary* conditions can be written now as

$$\sum_{j=1}^{N} a_{kj} y_j = 0, \qquad k = 1, 2, \ldots, n,$$

$$\sum_{j=1}^{N} y_j = 1,$$

$$y_j > 0.$$

These are known as the *orthogonality* and *normality* conditions and will yield a unique solution for y_j if $(n + 1) = N$ and all the equations are independent. The problem becomes more complex when $N > (n + 1)$ since the values of y_j are no longer unique. It is shown later, however, that it is possible to determine y_j uniquely for the purpose of minimizing x_0.

Suppose now that y_j^* are the unique values which are determined from the above equations. These values are used to determine x_0^* and x_i^*, $i = 1, 2, \ldots, n$ as follows. Consider

$$x_0^* = (x_0^*)^{\sum\limits_{j=1}^{N} y_j^*}$$

Since by definition $x_0^* = U_j^*/y_j^*$, then

$$x_0^* = \left(\frac{U_1^*}{y_1^*}\right)^{y_1^*}\left(\frac{U_2^*}{y_2^*}\right)^{y_2^*}\cdots\left(\frac{U_N^*}{y_N^*}\right)^{y_N^*},$$

$$= \left\{\prod_{j=1}^{N}\left(\frac{c_j}{y_j^*}\right)^{y_j^*}\right\}\left\{\prod_{j=1}^{N}\left(\prod_{i=1}^{n}x_i^{*a_{ij}}\right)^{y_j^*}\right\},$$

$$= \left\{\prod_{j=1}^{N}\left(\frac{c_j}{y_j^*}\right)^{y_j^*}\right\}\left\{\prod_{i=1}^{N}(x_i^*)^{\sum_{i=1}^{N}a_{ij}y_j^*}\right\},$$

$$= \prod_{j=1}^{N}\left(\frac{c_j}{y_j^*}\right)^{y_j^*}.$$

The last step is justified since $\sum_{j=1}^{N}a_{ij}y_j = 0$. The value of x_0^* is thus determined as soon as y_j^* are determined. Now, given y_j^* and x_0^*, $U_j^* = y_j^*x_0^*$ can be determined. Since

$$U_j^* = c_j\prod_{i=1}^{n}(x_i^*)^{a_{ij}}, \qquad j = 1, 2, \ldots, n;$$

simultaneous solution of these equations should yield x_i^*.

The above procedure shows that the solution to the original posynomial x_0 can be transformed into the solution of a set of linear equations in y_j. Observe that y_j^* are determined from the necessary conditions for a minimum. It can be shown, however, that these conditions are also sufficient. The proof (under the given restrictions on x_0) may be found in Wilde and Beightler ([7], p. 104) and consequently, it is not reproduced here.

The y_j-variables actually define the dual variables associated with the above x_0-primal problem. In order to show this relationship, consider the primal problem in the form

$$x_0 = \sum_{j=1}^{N}y_j\left(\frac{U_j}{y_j}\right).$$

Now define the function

$$y_0 = \prod_{j=1}^{N}\left(\frac{U_j}{y_j}\right)^{y_j}.$$

Since $\sum_{j=1}^{N}y_j = 1$ and $y_j > 0$, then by Cauchy's inequality[1], one has

$$y_0 \leq x_0.$$

---

[1] The Cauchy's inequality states that for $z_j > 0$,

$$\sum_{j=1}^{N}w_j z_j \geq \prod_{j=1}^{N}(z_j)^{w_j}, \quad \text{where } w_j > 0 \quad \text{and} \quad \sum_{j=1}^{N}w_j = 1.$$

This also is called the arithmetic-geometric mean inequality. (For a proof of this inequality see the note following the solution to Example 7·3-4.)

The function y_0 with its variables $y_1, y_2, \ldots, y_N$ defines the dual problem to the above primal. Since y_0 represents the lower bound on x_0 and since x_0 is associated with the minimization problem it follows that by maximizing y_0,

$$y_0^* = \max_{y_j} y_0 = \min_{x_i} x_0 = x_0^*.$$

(Compare with the equivalent case in linear programming.) This means that the maximum value of y_0 ($= y_0^*$) over the values of y_j is equal to the minimum value of x_0 ($= x_0^*$) over the values of x_i.

▶ **Example 17·4-1**

In this example a problem is considered in which $N = (n + 1)$ so that the solution to the orthogonality and normality conditions yields unique values of y_j. The next example will illustrate the other case where $N > (n + 1)$.

Consider the problem:

$$\text{minimize} \quad x_0 = 7x_1x_2^{-1} + 3x_2 x_3^{-2} + 5x_1^{-3}x_2 x_3 + x_1 x_2 x_3.$$

This function may be written as

$$x_0 = 7x_1^1 x_2^{-1} x_3^0 + 3x_1^0 x_2^1 x_3^{-2} + 5x_1^{-3} x_2^1 x_3^1 + x_1^1 x_2^1 x_3^1,$$

so that

$$(c_1, c_2, c_3, c_4) = (7, 3, 5, 1).$$

$$\begin{pmatrix} a_{11} & a_{12} & a_{13} & a_{14} \\ a_{21} & a_{22} & a_{23} & a_{24} \\ a_{31} & a_{32} & a_{33} & a_{34} \end{pmatrix} = \begin{pmatrix} 1 & 0 & -3 & 1 \\ -1 & 1 & 1 & 1 \\ 0 & -2 & 1 & 1 \end{pmatrix}.$$

The orthogonality and normality conditions are thus given by,

$$\begin{pmatrix} 1 & 0 & -3 & 1 \\ -1 & 1 & 1 & 1 \\ 0 & -2 & 1 & 1 \\ 1 & 1 & 1 & 1 \end{pmatrix} \begin{pmatrix} y_1 \\ y_2 \\ y_3 \\ y_4 \end{pmatrix} = \begin{pmatrix} 0 \\ 0 \\ 0 \\ 1 \end{pmatrix}.$$

This yields the unique solution

$$y_1^* = \frac{12}{24}, \quad y_2^* = \frac{4}{24}, \quad y_3^* = \frac{4}{24}, \quad y_4^* = \frac{3}{24}.$$

Thus

$$x_0^* = \left(\frac{7}{12/24}\right)^{12/24} \left(\frac{3}{4/24}\right)^{4/24} \left(\frac{5}{5/24}\right)^{5/24} \left(\frac{1}{3/24}\right)^{3/24}$$

$$= 15.22.$$

Since

$$U_j^* = y_j^* x_0^*,$$

then

$$7x_1 x_2^{-1} = U_1 = \frac{1}{2}(15.22) = 7.61,$$

$$3x_2 x_3^{-2} = U_2 = \frac{1}{6}(15.22) = 2.54,$$

$$5x_1^{-3} x_2 x_3 = U_3 = \frac{5}{24}(15.22) = 3.17,$$

$$x_1 x_2 x_3 = U_4 = \frac{1}{8}(15.22) = 1.90.$$

The solution of these equations is given by

$$x_1^* = 1.315, \quad x_2^* = 1.21, \quad x_3^* = 1.2,$$

which yields the optimal solution to the primal problem. ◄

▶ **Example 17·4-2**

Consider the problem:

$$\text{minimize} \quad x_0 = 5x_1 x_2^{-1} + 2x_1^{-1} x_2 + 5x_1 + x_2^{-1}$$

The orthogonality and normality conditions are given by

$$\begin{pmatrix} 1 & -1 & 1 & 0 \\ -1 & 1 & 0 & -1 \\ 1 & 1 & 1 & 1 \end{pmatrix} \begin{pmatrix} y_1 \\ y_2 \\ y_3 \\ y_4 \end{pmatrix} = \begin{pmatrix} 0 \\ 0 \\ 1 \end{pmatrix}.$$

Since $N > (n + 1)$, these equations do not yield the required y_j directly. Thus solving for y_1, y_2, and y_3 in terms of y_4, this gives

$$\begin{pmatrix} 1 & -1 & 1 \\ -1 & 1 & 0 \\ 1 & 1 & 1 \end{pmatrix} \begin{pmatrix} y_1 \\ y_2 \\ y_3 \end{pmatrix} = \begin{pmatrix} 0 \\ y_4 \\ 1 - y_4 \end{pmatrix},$$

or

$$y_1 = \tfrac{1}{2}(1 - 3y_4),$$

$$y_2 = \tfrac{1}{2}(1 - y_4),$$

$$y_3 = y_4.$$

The dual problem may now be written as:

$$\text{maximize} \quad y_0 = \left(\frac{5}{\tfrac{1}{2}(1 - 3y_4)} \right)^{\frac{1 - 3y_4}{2}} \left(\frac{2}{\tfrac{1}{2}(1 - y_4)} \right)^{\frac{1 - y_4}{2}} \left(\frac{5}{y_4} \right)^{y_4} \left(\frac{1}{y_4} \right)^{y_4}.$$

The maximization of y_0 is equivalent to the maximization of $\ln y_0$. The latter is a more convenient form, however. Thus,

$$\ln y_0 = \frac{1 - 3y_4}{2}\{\ln 10 - \ln(1 - 3y_4)\} + \frac{1 - y_4}{2}\{\ln 4 - \ln(1 - y_4)\}$$

$$+ y_4\{\ln 5 - \ln y_4 + (\ln 1 - \ln y_4)\}.$$

The value of y_4 maximizing $\ln y_0$ must be unique (since the primal problem has a unique minimum). Hence

$$\frac{\partial \ln y_0}{\partial y_4} = -\tfrac{3}{2}\ln 10 - \{(-\tfrac{3}{2}) + (-\tfrac{3}{2})\ln(1 - 3y_4)\}$$

$$+ (-\tfrac{1}{2})\ln 4 - \{(-\tfrac{1}{2}) + (-\tfrac{1}{2})\ln(1 - y_4)\}$$

$$+ \ln 5 - \{1 + \ln y_4\}$$

$$+ \ln 1 - \{1 + \ln y_4\} = 0.$$

This gives after simplification

$$-\ln\left(\frac{2 \times 10^{3/2}}{5}\right) + \ln \frac{(1 - 3y_4)^{3/2}(1 - y_4)^{1/2}}{y_4^2} = 0,$$

or

$$\frac{\sqrt{(1 - 3y_4)^3(1 - y_4)}}{y_4^2} = 12.6,$$

which yields $y_4^* \simeq 0.16$. Hence $y_3^* = 0.16$, $y_2^* = 0.42$ and $y_1^* = 0.26$.
The value of x_0^* is obtained from

$$x_0^* = y_0^* = \left(\frac{5}{.26}\right)^{.26}\left(\frac{2}{.42}\right)^{.42}\left(\frac{5}{.16}\right)^{.16}\left(\frac{1}{.16}\right)^{.16} \simeq 9.506.$$

Hence

$$U_3 = .16(9.506) = 1.52 = 5x_1,$$

$$U_4 = .16(9.506) = 1.52 = x_2^{-1}.$$

The solution here yields $x_1^* = .304$ and $x_2^* = .66$. ◄

§ 17·5
Stochastic Programming

Stochastic programming deals with situations where some or all the parameters of the problem are described by random variables rather than by deterministic quantities. Such cases seem typical of real-life problems where it is difficult to determine the values of the required parameters exactly. It was shown in Chapter 4 that, in case of linear programming, sensitivity analysis can be used to study the effect of changes in the problems parameters on the optimal solution. This, however, represents a partial answer to the problem especially when the parameters are actually random variables. The objective of stochastic programming is to consider these random effects explicitly in the solution of the model.

The basic idea of all stochastic programming models is to convert the probabilistic nature of the problem into an equivalent deterministic model. Several models have been developed to handle special cases of the general problem described above. In this section, the idea of employing deterministic equivalence will be illustrated by introducing the interesting technique of *chance-constrained programming* due to Charnes and Cooper.[2]

A chance-constrained model is defined generally as:

$$\text{maximize} \quad x_0 = \sum_{j=1}^{n} c_j x_j,$$

subject to

$$P\left\{\sum_{j=1}^{n} a_{ij} x_j \leq b_i\right\} \geq 1 - \alpha_i, \qquad i = 1, 2, \ldots, m, \qquad x_j \geq 0.$$

The name "chance-constrained" follows from the fact that each constraint,

$$\sum_{j=1}^{n} a_{ij} x_j \leq b_i,$$

is realized with a minimum probability of $1 - \alpha_i$, $0 < \alpha_i < 1$.

In the general case, it is assumed that c_j, a_{ij}, and b_i are all random variables. The fact that c_j is a random variable can always be treated by replacing it by its expected value. The solution of the case in which both a_{ij} and b_j are simultaneously treated as random variables in the same constraint will not be presented. In what follows, only two special cases are considered. These correspond to the separate considerations of a_{ij} and b_i as random variables. In both cases it will be further assumed that the parameters are normally distributed with known means and variances.

Case 1:

In this case it is assumed that each a_{ij} is normally distributed with mean $E\{a_{ij}\}$ and variances $\text{Var}\{a_{ij}\}$. It is further assumed that the covariances between a_{ij} and $a_{i'j'}$ is given by $\text{Cov}\{a_{ij}, a_{i'j'}\}$.

Consider the ith constraint,

$$P\left\{\sum_{j=1}^{n} a_{ij} x_j \leq b_i\right\} \geq 1 - \alpha_i,$$

---

[2] A. Charnes and W. Cooper, "Chance-Constrained Programming," *Management Science*, Vol. 6, 1959, pp. 73–79.

and define

$$h_i = \sum_{j=1}^{n} a_{ij} x_j.$$

Then h_i is normally distributed with mean

$$E\{h_i\} = \sum_{j=1}^{n} E\{a_{ij}\} x_j$$

and variance

$$\text{Var}\{h_i\} = \mathbf{X}^T \mathbf{D}_i \mathbf{X}$$

where

$$\mathbf{X} = (x_1, \ldots, x_n)^T,$$

$$\mathbf{D}_i = i\text{th covariance matrix}$$

$$= \begin{pmatrix} \text{Var}\{a_{i1}\} & \cdots & \text{Cov}\{a_{i1}, a_{in}\} \\ \vdots & & \vdots \\ \text{Cov}\{a_{in}, a_{i1}\} & \cdots & \text{Var}\{a_{in}\} \end{pmatrix}.$$

Now,

$$P\{h_i \le b_i\} = P\left\{\frac{h_i - E\{h_i\}}{\sqrt{\text{Var}\{h_i\}}} \le \frac{b_i - E\{h_i\}}{\sqrt{\text{Var}\{h_i\}}}\right\} \ge 1 - \alpha_i,$$

where $\left(\dfrac{h_i - E\{h_i\}}{\sqrt{\text{Var}\{h_i\}}}\right)$ is normally distributed with mean zero and variance one.
This means that

$$P\{h_i \le b_i\} = \Phi\left(\frac{b_i - E\{h_i\}}{\sqrt{\text{Var}\{h_i\}}}\right)$$

where Φ represents the C.D.F. of standard normal distribution.
Let K_{α_i} be the standard normal value such that

$$\Phi(K_{\alpha_i}) = 1 - \alpha_i.$$

Then the statement, $P\{h_i \le b_i\} \ge 1 - \alpha_i$, is realized if and only if

$$\frac{b_i - E\{h_i\}}{\sqrt{\text{Var}\{h_i\}}} \ge K_{\alpha_i}.$$

This yields the following nonlinear constraint

$$\left(\sum_{j=1}^{n} E\{a_{ij}\} x_j + K_{\alpha_i}\sqrt{\mathbf{X}^T \mathbf{D}_i \mathbf{X}}\right) \le b_i,$$

which is equivalent to the original stochastic constraint.

For the special case where the normal distributions are independent, then $\text{Cov}\{a_{ij}, a_{i'j'}\} = 0$ and the last constraint reduces to

$$\left(\sum_{j=1}^{n} E\{a_{ij}\}x_j + K_{\alpha_i} \sqrt{\sum_{j=1}^{n} \text{Var}\{a_{ij}\}x_j^2} \right) \leq b_i.$$

This constraint can now be put into the separable programming form (Section 17·2) using the substitution

$$y_i = \sqrt{\sum_{j=1}^{n} \text{Var}\{a_{ij}\}x_j^2}, \qquad \text{for all } i.$$

Thus the original constraint is equivalent to

$$\left(\sum_{j=1}^{n} E\{a_{ij}\}x_j + K_{\alpha_i} y_i \right) \leq b_i$$

and

$$\left(\sum_{j=1}^{n} \text{Var}\{a_{ij}\}x_j^2 - y_i^2 \right) = 0,$$

where $y_i \geq 0$. The constraint is now properly separable.

Case 2:

In this case it is assumed that only b_i is a normal random variable with mean $E\{b_i\}$ and variance $\text{Var}\{b_i\}$. The analysis in this case is very similar to that of Case 1 above. Consider the stochastic constraint.

$$P\left\{ b_i \geq \sum_{j=1}^{n} a_{ij}x_j \right\} \geq \alpha_i.$$

Thus, as in Case 1,

$$P\left\{ \frac{b_i - E\{b_i\}}{\sqrt{\text{Var}\{b_i\}}} \geq \frac{\sum_{j=1}^{n} a_{ij}x_j - E\{b_i\}}{\sqrt{\text{Var}\{b_i\}}} \right\} \geq \alpha_i.$$

This can only hold if,

$$\left(\frac{\sum_{j=1}^{n} a_{ij}x_j - E\{b_i\}}{\sqrt{\text{Var}\{b_i\}}} \right) \leq K_{\alpha_i}.$$

This means that the stochastic constraint is equivalent to the deterministic linear constraint,

$$\sum_{j=1}^{n} a_{ij}x_j \leq (E\{b_i\} + K_{\alpha_i}\sqrt{\text{Var}\{b_i\}}).$$

This shows that in Case 2 the chance-constrained model can be converted into an equivalent linear programming problem.

▶ **Example 17·5-1**

Consider the chance-constrained problem:

$$\text{maximize} \quad x_0 = 5x_1 + 6x_2 + 3x_3,$$

subject to

$$P\{a_{11}x_1 + a_{12}x_2 + a_{13}x_3 \le 8\} \ge .95,$$

$$P\{5x_1 + x_2 + 6x_3 \le b_2\} \ge 0.10,$$

with all $x_j \ge 0$. Suppose the a_{1j}'s are *independent* normally distributed random variables with the following means and variances.

$$E\{a_{11}\} = 1, \quad E\{a_{12}\} = 3, \quad E\{a_{13}\} = 9$$

$$\text{Var}\{a_{11}\} = 25, \quad \text{Var}\{a_{12}\} = 16, \quad \text{Var}\{a_{13}\} = 4$$

The parameter b_2 is normally distributed with mean 7 and variance 9.

From the standard normal tables

$$K_{\alpha_1} = K_{.05} \simeq 1.645,$$

$$K_{\alpha_2} = K_{.10} \simeq 1.285.$$

Now, for the first constraint, the equivalent deterministic constraint is given by

$$(x_1 + 3x_2 + 9x_3 + 1.645\sqrt{25x_1^2 + 16x_2^2 + 4x_3^2}) \le 8,$$

and for the second constraint

$$[5x_1 + x_2 + 6x_3] \le [7 + 1.285(3)] = 10.855.$$

Letting

$$y = 25x_1^2 + 16x_2^2 + 4x_3^2,$$

the complete problem then becomes:

$$\text{maximize} \quad x_0 = 5x_1 + 6x_4 + 3x_3,$$

subject to

$$x_1 + 3x_2 + 9x_3 + 1.645y \le 8,$$

$$25x_1^2 + 16x_2^2 + 4x_3^2 - y^2 = 0,$$

$$5x_1 + x_2 + 6x_3 \le 10.855,$$

$$x_1, x_2, x_3, y \ge 0,$$

which can now be solved by separable programming. ◀

§ 17·6
Gradient Methods

In the preceding sections, the nonlinear problem is solved by actually dealing with an associated problem. Thus, all the previous algorithms basically convert the nonlinear problem into an equivalent linear one. In this sense, these algorithms are of the *indirect* type. This section will be concerned with the development of *direct* methods for solving the nonlinear problem. By this it is meant that a search technique will be applied directly to the original problem. Specifically, the procedure starts with an initial feasible point from which a new point is generated and in such a way that the new value of the objective function is improved. The procedure is repeated always generating an improved solution and is terminated when no further improvements are possible. A typical illustration of this procedure which the reader is already familiar with is the simplex method of linear programming.

Although the proposed procedure is direct in the sense that it searches "directly" among the feasible solutions, other optimization aids (such as classical and linear programming techniques) are used to explore the best direction in which the next move is to be made. In fact, as will be shown later, it might be necessary first to convert the original problem to a modified version which will facilitate direct searching.

The key point in the above technique lies in the generation of successive solution points. Logically, the next solution point should be selected in the direction of the fastest rate of improvement in the objective value. In general, this direction is determined by using the information provided by the *gradient* of the objective function at the current trial point. (This should explain the reason these methods are called "gradient" algorithms.) Because of this fact, the nonlinear problem must satisfy certain regularization conditions before the proposed method can be used. These conditions generally stipulate that the objective and constraint functions must be continuously differentiable and that the objective function must possess a finite optimum over its feasible range.

There is a variety of gradient techniques which have been developed to exploit the special structures of certain nonlinear problems. These methods differ basically in the procedures for generating the successive solution points. In this section, only three methods will be presented. The *steepest ascent* (*descent*) method deals with the unconstrained problem. The solution of problems having *linear* and nonnegativity constraints is investigated using the *convex combinations* method. Finally, a method called *SUMT* is presented in which both the objective and constraint functions are nonlinear but must satisfy certain convexity and concavity conditions.

In order to standardize the discussion, consider the general nonlinear problem:

$$\text{maximize} \quad x = f(\mathbf{X}),$$

subject to

$$g_i(\mathbf{X}) \leq 0, \qquad i = 1, 2, \ldots, m,$$

$$\mathbf{X} \geq \mathbf{0},$$

where $\mathbf{X} = (x_1, x_2, \ldots, x_n)$ represent the variables vector. As mentioned above, the functions of f and g are continuously differentiable. Further, f possesses a finite maximum in the feasible region. The specific conditions that may pertain to the different solution methods will be given separately.

§ 17·6·1
Steepest Ascent Method

This method deals with the unconstrained problem only. Although this may appear impractical, Section 17·6·3 will present an approach for the constrained problem which is based on this method.

The method is initialized by selecting any point $\mathbf{X}^0$. Let $\mathbf{X}^k$ be the solution point at the kth iteration. The objective now is to show how $\mathbf{X}^{k+1}$ is generated. Define

$$\mathbf{X}^{k+1} = \mathbf{X}^k + r^k \nabla f(\mathbf{X}^k),$$

where r^k is a parameter. Since $\mathbf{X}^k$ is known, the determination of $\mathbf{X}^{k+1}$ is achieved by selecting the parameter r^k in some optimal way. In this case, r^k is known as the optimal *step size*.

The motivation behind the above formula is that the gradient represents the direction of the fastest rate of increase in f in the neighborhood of $\mathbf{X}^k$. Consequently, this seems to be the most promising direction in which $\mathbf{X}^{k+1}$ should be defined.

The determination of r^k is achieved as follows. Since the objective is to determine $\mathbf{X}^{k+1}$ which gives the largest improvement in the value of f, r^k is determined as the optimal value of r such that

$$h(r) = f(\mathbf{X}^k + r \nabla f(\mathbf{X}^k))$$

is maximized over r. This is achieved by using the classical technique in Section 16·2.

The iterative process will terminate when two successive trial points $\mathbf{X}^k$ and $\mathbf{X}^{k+1}$ are approximately the same. In this case

$$r^k \nabla f(\mathbf{X}^k) \simeq \mathbf{0},$$

which can occur if the gradient vector, $\nabla f(\mathbf{X}^k)$, is null. This actually is the necessary condition for an extreme point. (Notice that these conditions are only *necessary*.) Consequently, the termination of the method can at best lead to a local optimum. There is a possibility also that the procedure may be trapped at a stationary point which is not extremum. The convergence of the algorithm is assured by the fact that each new point must necessarily be an improved point. In general, however, the convergence may be infinite. In this case, the procedure can be terminated when every element of the gradient vector is *approximately* equal to zero.

▶ **Example 17·6-1**

Consider the maximization of the function

$$f(x_1, x_2) = 4x_1 + 6x_2 - 2x_1^2 - 2x_1x_2 - 2x_2^2.$$

Although this problem can be solved easily by classical techniques, it serves as a good illustration of the steepest ascent method.

Let the initial point be given by $\mathbf{X}^0 = (1, 1)$. Now,

$$\nabla f(\mathbf{X}) = (4 - 4x_1 - 2x_2, 6 - 2x_1 - 4x_2).$$

First Iteration:

$$\nabla f(\mathbf{X}^0) = (-2, 0).$$

The next point $\mathbf{X}^1$ is obtained by considering

$$\mathbf{X} = (1, 1) + r(-2, 0) = (1 - 2r, 1).$$

Thus,

$$h(r) = f(1 - 2r, 1),$$
$$= -2(1 - 2r)^2 + 2(1 - 2r) + 4.$$

The optimal step size yielding the maximum value of $h(r)$ is $r^1 = \frac{1}{4}$. This gives $\mathbf{X}^1 = (\frac{1}{2}, 1)$.

Second Iteration:

$$\nabla f(\mathbf{X}^1) = (0, 1).$$

Consider

$$\mathbf{X} = (\tfrac{1}{2}, 1) + r(0, 1) = (\tfrac{1}{2}, 1 + r).$$

Thus,

$$h(r) = -2(1 + r)^2 + 5(1 + r) + \tfrac{3}{2}.$$

This gives $r^2 = \frac{1}{4}$, or $\mathbf{X}^2 = (\frac{1}{2}, \frac{5}{4})$.

Third Iteration:

$$\nabla f(\mathbf{X}^2) = (-\tfrac{1}{2}, 0).$$

Consider

$$\mathbf{X} = \left(\frac{1}{2}, \frac{5}{4}\right) + r\left(-\frac{1}{2}, 0\right) = \left(\frac{1 - r}{2}, \frac{5}{4}\right).$$

Thus,

$$h(r) = -\frac{1}{2}(1-r)^2 + \frac{3}{4}(1-r) + \frac{35}{8}.$$

This gives $r^3 = \frac{1}{4}$, or $\mathbf{X}^3 = (\frac{3}{8}, \frac{5}{4})$.

Fourth Iteration:

$$\nabla f(\mathbf{X}^3) = (0, \tfrac{1}{4}).$$

Consider

$$\mathbf{X} = \left(\frac{3}{8}, \frac{5}{4}\right) + r\left(0, \frac{1}{4}\right) = \left(\frac{3}{8}, \frac{5+r}{4}\right).$$

Thus,

$$h(r) = -\frac{1}{8}(5+r)^2 + \frac{21}{16}(5+r) + \frac{39}{32}.$$

This gives $r^4 = \frac{1}{4}$, or $\mathbf{X}^4 = (\frac{3}{8}, \frac{21}{16})$.

Fifth Iteration:

$$\nabla f(\mathbf{X}^4) = (-\tfrac{1}{8}, 0).$$

Consider

$$\mathbf{X} = \left(\frac{3}{8}, \frac{21}{16}\right) + r\left(-\frac{1}{8}, 0\right) = \left(\frac{3-r}{8}, \frac{21}{16}\right).$$

Thus

$$h(r) = -\frac{1}{32}(3-r)^2 + \frac{11}{64}(3-r) + \frac{567}{128}.$$

This gives $r^5 = \frac{1}{4}$, or $\mathbf{X}^5 = (\frac{11}{32}, \frac{21}{16})$.

Sixth Iteration:

$$\nabla f(\mathbf{X}^5) = (0, \tfrac{1}{16}).$$

Since $\nabla f(\mathbf{X}^5) \simeq \mathbf{0}$, the process can be terminated at this point. The *approximate* maximum point is given by $\mathbf{X}^5 = (.3437, 1.3125)$. Notice that the exact optimum is $\mathbf{X}^* = (.3333, 1.3333)$. ◄

§ 17·6·2
Convex Combinations Method

This method deals with the constrained problem in which all the constraints are linear. Specifically, the problem is given as

$$\text{maximize} \quad z = f(\mathbf{X}),$$

subject to

$$AX \leq b,$$

$$X \geq 0,$$

where A is a matrix of constant elements and b is a constant vector.

The procedure used in the steepest ascent method cannot be implemented successfully for the *constrained* problem since the direction specified by the gradient vector may not yield feasible points. Moreover, the gradient vector will not necessarily be null at the optimum (constrained) point. A different procedure must thus be developed.

Let X^k be the *feasible* trial point at the kth iteration. The objective function $f(X)$ can be expanded in the neighborhood of X^k using Taylor's series. This gives

$$f(X) \simeq f(X^k) + \nabla f(X^k)(X - X^k),$$

$$\simeq (f(X^k) - \nabla f(X^k)X^k) + \nabla f(X^k)X.$$

The procedure then calls for determining a feasible point $X = X^*$ such that $f(X)$ is maximized subject to the regular linear constraints of the problem. Since $(f(X^k) - \nabla f(X^k)X^k)$ is a constant, the problem of determining X^* becomes

$$\text{maximize} \quad w_k(X) = \nabla f(X^k)X,$$

subject to

$$AX \leq b,$$

$$X \geq 0.$$

This is a linear programming problem in X which can now be used to determine X^*.

Since w_k is constructed from the gradient of $f(X)$ at X^k, an improved solution point can be secured if, and only if, $w_k(X^*) > w_k(X^k)$. From Taylor's expansion, this does not guarantee that $f(X^*) > f(X^k)$ unless X^* is in the neighborhood of X^k. However, given $w_k(X^*) > w_k(X^k)$, there must exist a point, X^{k+1}, on the line segment $(X^k; X^*)$ such that $f(X^{k+1}) > f(X^k)$. The objective now is to determine X^{k+1}.

Define

$$X^{k+1} = (1 - r)X^k + rX^*$$

$$= X^k + r(X^* - X^k), \quad 0 < r \leq 1.$$

This means that X^{k+1} is a *convex combination* of X^k and X^*. Since X^k and X^* are two feasible points in a *convex* solution space, the point X^{k+1} is also feasible. Notice that by comparison with the steepest ascent method (Section 17·6·1), the parameter r can be regarded as a step size.

The point X^{k+1} is determined such that $f(X)$ is maximized. Since X^{k+1} is a function of r only, the determination of X^{k+1} is secured by maximizing

$$h(r) = f(X^k + r(X^* - X^k))$$

in terms of r.

The above procedure is repeated as necessary until at the kth iteration the condition $w_k(X^*) \le w_k(X^k)$ is satisfied. At this point, no further improvements are possible. The process is then terminated with X^k as the best solution point.

Notice that the linear programming problems generated at the successive iterations differ only in the coefficients of the objective function. The sensitivity analysis procedure presented in Section 4·6 thus may be used to carry out the calculations efficiently.

▶ **Example 17·6-2**

Consider the quadratic programming of Example 17·3-1. This is given by

$$\text{maximize} \quad f(X) = 4x_1 + 6x_2 - 2x_1^2 - 2x_1x_2 - 2x_2^2,$$

subject to

$$x_1 + 2x_2 \le 2,$$

where x_1 and x_2 are nonnegative.

Let the initial trial point be $X^0 = (\frac{1}{2}, \frac{1}{2})$ which is feasible. Now,

$$\nabla f(X) = (4 - 4x_1 - 2x_2, 6 - 2x_1 - 4x_2).$$

First Iteration:

$$\nabla f(X^0) = (1, 3).$$

The associated linear programming is to maximize $w_1 = x_1 + 3x_2$ subject to the same constraints in the original problem. This gives the optimal solution $X^* = (0, 1)$. The values of w_1 at X^0 and X^* are equal to 2 and 3, respectively. Hence a new trial point must be determined. Thus,

$$X^1 = \left(\frac{1}{2}, \frac{1}{2}\right) + r\left[(0, 1) - \left(\frac{1}{2}, \frac{1}{2}\right)\right] = \left(\frac{1-r}{2}, \frac{1+r}{2}\right).$$

Now, the maximization of

$$h(r) = f\left(\frac{1-r}{2}, \frac{1+r}{2}\right)$$

yields, $r^1 = 1$. Thus, $X^1 = (0, 1)$ with $f(X^1) = 4$.

Second Iteration:

$$\nabla f(X^1) = (2, 2).$$

The objective function of the new linear programming problem is $w_2 = 2x_1 + 2x_2$. The optimum solution to this problem yields $X^* = (2, 0)$. Since the values of w_2 at $\mathbf{X}^1$ and $\mathbf{X}^*$ are 2 and 4, respectively, a new trial point must be determined. Thus,

$$\mathbf{X}^2 = (0, 1) + r[(2, 0) - (0, 1)] = (2r, 1 - r).$$

The maximization of

$$h(r) = f(2r, 1 - r)$$

yields $r^2 = \frac{1}{6}$. Thus, $\mathbf{X}^2 = (\frac{1}{3}, \frac{5}{6})$ with $f(\mathbf{X})^2 \cong 4.16$.

Third Iteration:

$$\nabla f(\mathbf{X}^2) = (1, 2).$$

The corresponding objective linear function is $w_3 = x_1 + 2x_2$. The optimum solution of this problem yields the alternative solutions $\mathbf{X}^* = (0, 1)$ and $\mathbf{X}^* = (2, 0)$. The value of w_3 at both values of $\mathbf{X}^*$ is equal to its value at $\mathbf{X}^2$. Consequently, no further improvements are possible. The "approximate" optimum solution is $\mathbf{X}^2 = (\frac{1}{3}, \frac{5}{6})$ with $f(\mathbf{X}^2) \cong 4.16$. This happens to be the exact optimum. ◀

§ 17·6·3
SUMT Algorithm

In this section, a more general gradient method will be presented. It is assumed that the objective function $f(\mathbf{X})$ is concave and that each constraint function $g_i(\mathbf{X})$ is convex. Moreover, the solution space is assumed to have an interior. This rules out both implicit and explicit use of *equality* constraints.

The concept of SUMT (*Sequential Unconstrained Maximization Technique*) algorithm is based on transforming the constrained problem into an equivalent *un*constrained problem. The procedure is more or less similar to the use of the Lagrange multipliers method. The transformed problem can then be solved using the steepest ascent method (Section 17·6·1).

To clarify the above concept, consider the new function

$$p(\mathbf{X}, t) = f(\mathbf{X}) + t\left[\sum_{i=1}^{m} \frac{1}{g_i(\mathbf{X})} - \sum_{j=1}^{n} \frac{1}{x_j}\right],$$

where t is a nonnegative parameter. The second summation sign is based on the nonnegativity constraints which must be put in the form $-x_j \leq 0$ in order to conform with the original constraints $g_i(\mathbf{X}) \leq 0$. Since $g_i(\mathbf{X})$ is convex, it follows that $1/g_i(\mathbf{X})$ is concave. This means that $p(\mathbf{X}, t)$ is concave in $\mathbf{X}$. Consequently, $p(\mathbf{X}, t)$ possesses a unique maximum. It is now shown that the optimization of the original constrained problem is equivalent to the optimization of $p(\mathbf{X}, t)$.

The algorithm is initiated by arbitrarily selecting an initial *nonnegative* value for t. An initial point $\mathbf{X}^0$ is selected as the first trial solution. This point must be an interior point; that is, it must not lie on the boundaries of the solution space. Given the value of t, the steepest ascent method is used to determine the corresponding optimal solution (maximum) of $p(\mathbf{X}, t)$.

It is noticed that the new solution point will always be an interior point since if the solution point is close to the boundaries, at least one of the functions $1/g_i(\mathbf{X})$ or $(-1/x_i)$ will acquire a very large negative value. Since the objective is to maximize $p(\mathbf{X}, t)$, such solution points are automatically excluded. The main result here is that the successive solution points will always be interior points. Consequently, the problem can always be treated as an unconstrained case.

Once the optimum solution corresponding to a given value of t is reached, a new value of t is generated and the optimization process (using the steepest ascent method) is repeated. Thus, if t' is the current value of t, the next value, t'', must be selected such that $0 < t'' < t'$.

The SUMT procedure is terminated if for two successive values of t, the corresponding *optimum* values of $\mathbf{X}$ obtained by maximizing $p(\mathbf{X}, t)$ are nearly the same. At this point, further trials will produce little improvements.

The actual implementation of SUMT involves more details than have been presented here. Specifically, the selection of the initial value of t is a very important factor which affects the speed of convergence. Further, the determination of an initial interior point may require special techniques. These details can be found in Reference [3] at the end of this chapter.

§ 17·7
Concluding Remarks

This chapter has presented a number of nonlinear programming algorithms. The objective here is to familiarize the reader with some of these techniques. There are several important topics which are beyond the scope of this short presentation. The reader interested in more details may consult specialized books in this area. References [4], [5], [7], and [8] should prove useful in this respect.

SELECTED REFERENCES

1. BRACKEN, J., and G. MCCORMICK, *Selected Applications of Nonlinear Programming*, New York: Wiley, 1968.
2. DUFFIN, R., E. PETERSON, and C. ZENER, *Geometric Programming*, New York: Wiley, 1967.
3. FIACCO, A., and G. MCCORMICK, *Nonlinear Programming, Sequential Unconstrained Minimization Techniques*, New York: Wiley, 1968.
4. HADLEY, G., *Nonlinear and Dynamic Programming*, Reading, Massachusetts: Addison-Wesley, 1964.

5. MANGASARIAN, O., *Nonlinear Programming*, New York: McGraw-Hill, 1969.
6. SPANG, H., III, "A Review of Minimization Techniques for Nonlinear Functions," *SIAM Review*, 4, 343–365 (1962).
7. WILDE, D. and C. BEIGHTLER, *Foundations of Optimization*, Englewood Cliffs, N.J.: Prentice-Hall, 1967.
8. ZANGWILL, W., *Nonlinear Programming—A Unified Approach*, Englewood Cliffs, N.J.: Prentice-Hall, 1969.

PROBLEMS

☐ **17-1** Formulate the following problem using the approximating mixed integer programming method.

$$\text{Maximize} \quad x_0 = e^{-x_1} + x_1 + (x_2 + 1)^2,$$

subject to

$$x_1^2 + x_2 \le 3,$$

$$x_1, x_2 \ge 0.$$

☐ **17-2** Repeat Problem 17-1 using the restricted basis method. Then find the optimal solution.

☐ **17-3** Consider the problem:

$$\text{maximize} \quad x_0 = x_1 x_2 x_3,$$

subject to

$$x_1^2 + x_2 + x_3 \le 4,$$

$$x_1, x_2, x_3 \ge 0.$$

Approximate the problem as a linear programming model for use with the restricted basis method.

☐ **17-4** Show how the following problem can be made separable.

$$\text{Maximize} \quad x_0 = x_1 x_2 + x_3 + x_1 x_3,$$

subject to

$$x_1 x_2 + x_2 + x_1 x_3 \le 10,$$

$$x_1, x_2, x_3 \ge 0.$$

☐ **17-5** Show how the following problem can be made separable.

$$\text{Minimize} \quad x_0 = e^{2x_1 + x_2^2} + (x_3 - 2)^2,$$

subject to

$$x_1 + x_2 + x_3 \le 6,$$

$$x_1, x_2, x_3 \ge 0.$$

☐ **17-6** Show how the following problem can be made separable.

$$\text{Maximize} \quad x_0 = e^{x_1 x_2} + x_2^2 x_3 + x_4,$$

subject to

$$x_1 + x_2 x_3 + x_3 \le 10,$$

$$x_1, x_2, x_3 \ge 0,$$

x_4 unrestricted in sign.

☐ **17-7** Show that in separable convex programming (Section 17·2·1), it is never optimal to have $x_{ki} > 0$ when $x_{k-1, i}$ is not at its upper bound.

☐ **17-8** Solve as a separable convex programming problem.

$$\text{Minimize} \quad x_0 = x_1^4 + 2x_2 + x_3^2$$

subject to

$$x_1^2 + x_4 + x_3^2 \le 4,$$

$$|x_1 + x_2| \le 3,$$

$$x_1, x_3 \ge 0,$$

x_2 unrestricted in sign.

☐ **17-9** Solve the following as a separable convex programming problem.

$$\text{Minimize} \quad x_0 = (x_1 - 2)^2 + 4(x_2 - 6)^2,$$

subject to

$$6x_1 + 3(x_2 + 1)^2 \le 12,$$

$$x_1, x_2 \ge 0.$$

☐ **17-10** Consider the problem:

$$\text{maximize} \quad x_0 = 6x_1 + 3x_2 - 4x_1 x_2 - 2x_1^2 - 3x_2^2,$$

subject to

$$x_1 + x_2 \le 1,$$

$$2x_1 + 3x_2 \le 4,$$

$$x_1, x_2 \ge 0.$$

Show that x_0 is strictly concave and then solve the problem using the quadratic programming algorithm.

☐ **17-11** Consider the problem:

$$\text{minimize} \quad x_0 = 2x_1^2 + 2x_2^2 + 3x_3^2 + 2x_1x_2$$
$$+ 2x_2x_3 + x_1 - 3x_2 - 5x_3,$$

subject to

$$x_1 + x_2 + x_3 \geq 1,$$
$$3x_1 + 2x_2 + x_3 \leq 6,$$
$$x_1, x_2, x_3 \geq 0.$$

Show that x_0 is strictly convex and then solve by the quadratic programming technique.

☐ **17-12** Solve by geometric programming:

$$\text{minimize} \quad x_0 = 2x_1^{-1}x_2^2 + x_1^4x_2^{-2} + 4x_1^2$$
$$x_1, x_2 > 0.$$

☐ **17-13** Solve by geometric programming:

$$\text{minimize} \quad x_0 = 5x_1x_2^{-1}x_3^2 + x_1^{-2}x_3^{-1} + 10x_2^3$$
$$+ 2x_1^{-1}x_2 x_3^{-3},$$
$$x_1, x_2, x_3 > 0.$$

☐ **17-14** Solve by geometric programming:

$$\text{minimize} \quad x_0 = 2x_1^2x_2^{-3} + 8x_1^{-3}x_2 + 3x_1x_2,$$
$$x_1, x_2 > 0.$$

☐ **17-15** Solve by geometric programming:

$$\text{minimize} \quad x_0 = 2x_1^3x_2^{-3} + 4x_1^{-2}x_2 + x_1x_2$$
$$+ 8x_1x_2^{-1},$$
$$x_1, x_2 > 0.$$

☐ **17-16** Convert the following stochastic problem into an equivalent deterministic model.

$$\text{Maximize} \quad x_0 = x_1 + 2x_2 + 5x_3,$$

subject to

$$P\{a_1x_1 + 3x_2 + a_3 x_3 \leq 10\} \geq 0.9,$$
$$P\{7x_1 + 5x_2 + x_3 \leq b_2\} \geq 0.1,$$
$$x_1, x_2, x_3 \geq 0.$$

Assume a_1 and a_3 are independent and normally distributed random variables with means, $E\{a_1\} = 2$ and $E\{a_3\} = 5$, and variances, $\text{Var}\{a_1\} = 9$ and $\text{Var}\{a_3\} = 16$. Assume further that b_2 is normally distributed with mean 15 and variance 25.

☐ **17-17** Consider the following stochastic programming model:

$$\text{maximize} \quad x_0 = x_1 + x_2^2 + x_3,$$

subject to

$$P\{x_1^2 + a_2 x_2^3 + a_3\sqrt{x_3} \le 10\} \ge 0.9$$

$$x_1, x_2, x_3 \ge 0$$

where a_2 and a_3 are independent and normally distributed random variables with means 5 and 2, and variance 16 and 25, respectively. Convert the problem into the (deterministic) separable programming form.

☐ **17-18** Find the maximum point(s) of the functions in Problem 16-2 (Chapter 16) using the steepest ascent method.

☐ **17-19** Solve the following problem by the convex combination method.

$$\text{Minimize} \quad f(\mathbf{X}) = x_1^3 + x_2^3 - 3x_1x_2,$$

subject to

$$3x_1 + x_2 \le 3,$$

$$5x_1 - 3x_2 \le 5,$$

with x_1 and x_2 being nonnegative.

Review of Vectors and Matrices

§ A·1
Vectors

§ A·1·1
Definition of a Vector

Let $p_1, p_2, \ldots, p_n$ be any n real numbers and let **P** be an ordered set of these real numbers; that is,

$$\mathbf{P} = (p_1, p_2, \ldots, p_n),$$

then **P** is called an n-vector (or simply a vector). The ith component of **P** is given by p_i. For example, $\mathbf{P} = (1, 2)$ is a two-dimensional vector which joins the origin and the point $(1, 2)$.

§ A·1·2
Addition (Subtraction) of Vectors

Let

$$\mathbf{P} = (p_1, p_2, \ldots, p_n)$$

and

$$\mathbf{Q} = (q_1, q_2, \ldots, q_n),$$

be two vectors in the n-dimensional space, then the components of the vector $\mathbf{R} = (r_1, r_2, \ldots, r_n)$ such that $\mathbf{R} = \mathbf{P} \pm \mathbf{Q}$ are given by

$$r_i = p_i \pm q_i.$$

In general, given the vectors $\mathbf{P}$, $\mathbf{Q}$, and $\mathbf{S}$, then,

$$\mathbf{P} \pm \mathbf{Q} = \mathbf{Q} \pm \mathbf{P} \qquad \text{(commutative law)},$$

$$(\mathbf{P} + \mathbf{Q}) + \mathbf{S} = \mathbf{P} + (\mathbf{Q} + \mathbf{S}) \qquad \text{(associative law)},$$

$$\mathbf{P} + (-\mathbf{P}) = \mathbf{0}, \text{ a zero vector.}$$

§ A·1·3
Multiplication of Vectors by Scalars

Given a vector $\mathbf{P}$ and a scalar (constant) quantity θ, there exists a new vector $\mathbf{Q}$ such that

$$\mathbf{Q} = \theta \mathbf{P} = (\theta p_1, \theta p_2, \ldots, \theta p_n),$$

where $\mathbf{Q}$ is called a *scalar product* of $\mathbf{P}$ and θ.

In general, given the vectors $\mathbf{P}$ and $\mathbf{S}$ and the scalars θ and γ,

$$\theta(\mathbf{P} + \mathbf{S}) = \theta \mathbf{P} + \theta \mathbf{S} \qquad \text{(distributive law)},$$

$$\theta(\gamma \mathbf{P}) = (\theta \gamma) \mathbf{P} \qquad \text{(associative law)}.$$

§ A·1·4
Linearly Independent Vectors

A set of vectors $\mathbf{P}_1, \mathbf{P}_2, \ldots, \mathbf{P}_n$ are said to be *linearly independent* if, and only if, for all real θ_j,

$$\sum_{j=1}^{n} \theta_j \mathbf{P}_j = \mathbf{0}$$

implies that all $\theta_j = 0$, where θ_j are scalar quantities. If

$$\sum_{j=1}^{n} \theta_j \mathbf{P}_j = \mathbf{0}$$

for some $\theta_j \neq 0$, the vectors are said to be *linearly dependent*. For example, the vectors

$$\mathbf{P}_1 = (1, 2),$$

$$\mathbf{P}_2 = (2, 4),$$

are linearly dependent since there exist $\theta_1 = 2$ and $\theta_2 = -1$ for which

$$\theta_1 \mathbf{P}_1 + \theta_2 \mathbf{P}_2 = \mathbf{0}.$$

§ A·2
Matrices

§ A·2·1
Definition of a Matrix

A matrix is a rectangular array of elements. The element a_{ij} is said to be the (i, j)th element of the matrix **A** if it stands in the ith row and jth column of the array. The order (size) of a matrix is said to be $(m \times n)$ if the matrix includes m rows and n columns. For example,

$$A = \begin{pmatrix} a_{11} & a_{12} & a_{13} \\ a_{21} & a_{22} & a_{23} \\ a_{31} & a_{32} & a_{33} \\ a_{41} & a_{42} & a_{43} \end{pmatrix} = \|a_{ij}\|_{4 \times 3}$$

is a (4×3)-matrix.

§ A·2·2
Types of Matrices

1. A *square* matrix is a matrix in which $m = n$.

2. An *identity* matrix is a square matrix in which all the diagonal elements are "one" and all the off-diagonal elements are "zero"; that is,

$$a_{ij} = 1, \qquad \text{for } i = j,$$

$$a_{ij} = 0, \qquad \text{for } i \neq j.$$

For example, a (3×3) identity matrix is given by

$$\mathbf{I}_3 = \begin{pmatrix} 1 & 0 & 0 \\ 0 & 1 & 0 \\ 0 & 0 & 1 \end{pmatrix}.$$

3. A *row vector* is a matrix with one row and n columns.

4. A *column vector* is a matrix with m rows and one column.

5. The matrix $\mathbf{A}^T$ is called the *transpose* of **A** if the element a_{ij} in **A** is equal to element a_{ji} in A^T for all i and j. For example, if

$$\mathbf{A} = \begin{pmatrix} 1 & 4 \\ 2 & 5 \\ 3 & 6 \end{pmatrix},$$

then

$$A^T = \begin{pmatrix} 1 & 2 & 3 \\ 4 & 5 & 6 \end{pmatrix}.$$

In general A^T is obtained by interchanging the rows and the columns of A. Consequently if A is of the order $(m \times n)$, A^T is of the order $(n \times m)$.

6. A matrix $B = 0$ is called a *zero matrix* if every element of B is equal to zero.

7. Two matrices $A = \|a_{ij}\|$ and $B = \|b_{ij}\|$ are said to be *equal matrices* if, and only if, they have the same order and if each element a_{ij} is equal to the corresponding b_{ij} for all i and j.

§ A·2·3
Matrix Arithmetic Operations

In matrices only addition (subtraction) and multiplication are defined. The division although not defined is replaced by the concept of inversion which will be introduced in Section A·2·6.

§ A·2·3·1
Addition (Subtraction) of Matrices

Two matrices $A = \|a_{ij}\|$ and $B = \|b_{ij}\|$ can be added together if they are of the same order $(m \times n)$. The sum $D = A + B$ is obtained by adding the corresponding elements. Thus

$$\|d_{ij}\|_{m \times n} = \|a_{ij} + b_{ij}\|_{m \times n}.$$

Assuming that the matrices A, B and C have the same order, then

$$A \pm B = B \pm A \qquad \text{(commutative law)},$$

$$A \pm (B \pm C) = (A \pm B) \pm C \qquad \text{(associative law)},$$

$$(A \pm B)^T = A^T \pm B^T.$$

§ A·2·3·2
Product of Matrices

Two matrices $A = \|a_{ij}\|$ and $B = \|b_{ij}\|$ can be multiplied in the order AB if, and only if, the number of columns of A is equal to the number of rows of B. That is, if A is of the order $(m \times r)$, then B is of the order $(r \times n)$, where m and n are arbitrary sizes.

Let $\mathbf{D} = \mathbf{AB}$, then $\mathbf{D}$ is of the order $(m \times n)$ and its elements d_{ij} are given by

$$d_{ij} = \sum_{k=1}^{r} a_{ik} b_{kj}, \quad \text{for all } i \text{ and } j.$$

For example, if

$$\mathbf{A} = \begin{pmatrix} 1 & 3 \\ 2 & 4 \end{pmatrix}, \quad \text{and} \quad \mathbf{B} = \begin{pmatrix} 5 & 7 & 9 \\ 6 & 8 & 0 \end{pmatrix},$$

then

$$\mathbf{D} = \begin{pmatrix} 1 & 3 \\ 2 & 4 \end{pmatrix} \begin{pmatrix} 5 & 7 & 9 \\ 6 & 8 & 0 \end{pmatrix} = \begin{pmatrix} (1 \times 5 + 3 \times 6) & (1 \times 7 + 3 \times 8) & (1 \times 9 + 3 \times 0) \\ (2 \times 5 + 4 \times 6) & (2 \times 7 + 4 \times 8) & (2 \times 9 + 4 \times 0) \end{pmatrix}$$

$$= \begin{pmatrix} 23 & 31 & 9 \\ 34 & 46 & 18 \end{pmatrix}.$$

Notice that, in general, $\mathbf{AB} \neq \mathbf{BA}$ even if $\mathbf{BA}$ is defined.

Matrix multiplication follows the following general properties.

$$\mathbf{I}_m \mathbf{A} = \mathbf{AI}_n = \mathbf{A}, \quad \text{where } \mathbf{I} \text{ is an identity matrix,}$$

$$(\mathbf{AB})\mathbf{C} = \mathbf{A}(\mathbf{BC}),$$

$$\mathbf{C}(\mathbf{A} + \mathbf{B}) = \mathbf{CA} + \mathbf{CB},$$

$$(\mathbf{A} + \mathbf{B})\mathbf{C} = \mathbf{AC} + \mathbf{BC},$$

$$\alpha(\mathbf{AB}) = (\alpha\mathbf{A})\mathbf{B} = \mathbf{A}(\alpha\mathbf{B}), \quad \alpha \text{ is a scalar.}$$

§ A·2·3·3
Multiplication of Partitioned Matrices

Let $\mathbf{A}$ be an $(m \times r)$-matrix and $\mathbf{B}$ an $(r \times n)$-matrix. If $\mathbf{A}$ and $\mathbf{B}$ are partitioned into submatrices as follows,

$$\mathbf{A} = \left(\begin{array}{c|c|c} \mathbf{A}_{11} & \mathbf{A}_{12} & \mathbf{A}_{13} \\ \hline \mathbf{A}_{21} & \mathbf{A}_{22} & \mathbf{A}_{23} \end{array} \right), \quad \mathbf{B} = \left(\begin{array}{c|c} \mathbf{B}_{11} & \mathbf{B}_{12} \\ \hline \mathbf{B}_{21} & \mathbf{B}_{22} \\ \hline \mathbf{B}_{31} & \mathbf{B}_{32} \end{array} \right),$$

such that the number of columns of $\mathbf{A}_{ij}$ is equal to the number of rows of $\mathbf{B}_{ji}$ and such that the number of columns of $\mathbf{A}_{ij}$ and $\mathbf{A}_{i+1,j}$ are equal, for all i and j, then

$$\mathbf{A} \cdot \mathbf{B} = \left(\begin{array}{c|c} \mathbf{A}_{11}\mathbf{B}_{11} + \mathbf{A}_{12}\mathbf{B}_{21} + \mathbf{A}_{13}\mathbf{B}_{31} & \mathbf{A}_{11}\mathbf{B}_{12} + \mathbf{A}_{12}\mathbf{B}_{22} + \mathbf{A}_{13}\mathbf{B}_{32} \\ \hline \mathbf{A}_{21}\mathbf{B}_{11} + \mathbf{A}_{22}\mathbf{B}_{21} + \mathbf{A}_{23}\mathbf{B}_{31} & \mathbf{A}_{21}\mathbf{B}_{12} + \mathbf{A}_{22}\mathbf{B}_{22} + \mathbf{A}_{23}\mathbf{B}_{32} \end{array} \right).$$

For example,

$$\begin{pmatrix} \left. \begin{matrix} 1 & 2 & 3 \end{matrix} \right. \\ \hline \begin{matrix} 1 & 0 & 5 \\ 2 & 5 & 6 \end{matrix} \end{pmatrix} \begin{pmatrix} 4 \\ - \\ 1 \\ 8 \end{pmatrix} = \begin{pmatrix} (1)(4) + (2 \quad 3)\begin{pmatrix} 1 \\ 8 \end{pmatrix} \\ \hline \begin{pmatrix} 1 \\ 2 \end{pmatrix}(4) + \begin{pmatrix} 0 & 5 \\ 5 & 6 \end{pmatrix}\begin{pmatrix} 1 \\ 8 \end{pmatrix} \end{pmatrix} = \begin{pmatrix} 4 + 2 + 24 \\ \hline \begin{pmatrix} 4 \\ 8 \end{pmatrix} + \begin{pmatrix} 40 \\ 53 \end{pmatrix} \end{pmatrix}$$

$$= \begin{pmatrix} 30 \\ 11 \\ 61 \end{pmatrix}.$$

The usefulness of partitioned matrices will come later in considering the inversion of matrices.

§ A·2·4
The Determinant of a Square Matrix

Given the n-square matrix

$$\mathbf{A} = \begin{pmatrix} a_{11} & a_{12} & \cdots & a_{1n} \\ a_{21} & a_{22} & \cdots & a_{2n} \\ \vdots & \vdots & & \vdots \\ a_{n1} & a_{n2} & \cdots & a_{nn} \end{pmatrix},$$

consider the product,

$$P_{j_1 j_2 \cdots j_n} = a_{1 j_1} a_{2 j_2} \cdots a_{n j_n},$$

the elements of which are selected such that each column and each row of $\mathbf{A}$ is represented exactly once among the subscripts of $P_{j_1 j_2 \cdots j_n}$. Next define $\varepsilon_{j_1 j_2 \cdots j_n}$ equal to $+1$ if $j_1 j_2 \cdots j_n$ is an even permutation and -1 if $j_1 j_2 \cdots j_n$ is an odd permutation. Thus the scalar

$$\sum_\rho \varepsilon_{j_1 j_2 \cdots j_n} P_{j_1 j_2 \cdots j_n}$$

is called the *determinant* of $\mathbf{A}$ where ρ represents the summation over all $n!$ permutations. The notation $\det \mathbf{A}$ or $|\mathbf{A}|$ is usually used to represent the determinant of $\mathbf{A}$.

To illustrate, consider

$$\mathbf{A} = \begin{pmatrix} a_{11} & a_{12} & a_{13} \\ a_{21} & a_{22} & a_{23} \\ a_{31} & a_{32} & a_{33} \end{pmatrix},$$

then

$$|\mathbf{A}| = a_{11}(a_{22} a_{33} - a_{23} a_{32}) - a_{12}(a_{21} a_{33} - a_{31} a_{23})$$
$$+ a_{13}(a_{21} a_{32} - a_{22} a_{31}).$$

The major properties of determinants can be summarized as follows:

1. If every element of a column or a row is zero, then the value of the determinant is zero.
2. The value of the determinant is not changed if its rows and columns are interchanged.
3. If $\mathbf{B}$ is obtained from $\mathbf{A}$ by interchanging any two of its rows (or columns) then $|\mathbf{B}| = -|\mathbf{A}|$.
4. If two rows (or columns) of $\mathbf{A}$ are identical, then $|\mathbf{A}| = 0$.
5. The value of $|\mathbf{A}|$ remains the same if a scalar α times a column (row) vector of $\mathbf{A}$ is added to another column (row) vector of $\mathbf{A}$.
6. If every element of a column (or a row) of a determinant is multiplied by a scalar α, the value of the determinant is multiplied by α.
7. If $\mathbf{A}$ and $\mathbf{B}$ are two n-square matrices, then

$$|\mathbf{AB}| = |\mathbf{A}|\,|\mathbf{B}|.$$

Definition of the Minor of a Determinant
The minor M_{ij} of the element a_{ij} in the determinant $|\mathbf{A}|$ is obtained from the matrix $\mathbf{A}$ by striking out the ith row and jth column of $\mathbf{A}$. For example, for

$$\mathbf{A} = \begin{pmatrix} a_{11} & a_{12} & a_{13} \\ a_{21} & a_{22} & a_{23} \\ a_{31} & a_{32} & a_{33} \end{pmatrix},$$

$$M_{11} = \begin{vmatrix} a_{22} & a_{23} \\ a_{32} & a_{33} \end{vmatrix}, \quad M_{22} = \begin{vmatrix} a_{11} & a_{13} \\ a_{31} & a_{33} \end{vmatrix}, \quad \dots \quad \text{and so forth.}$$

Definition of the Adjoint Matrix
Let $A_{ij} = (-1)^{i+j} M_{ij}$ be defined as the cofactor of the element a_{ij} of the square matrix $\mathbf{A}$. Then, by definition, the adjoint matrix of $\mathbf{A}$ is given by

$$\text{adj } \mathbf{A} = \|A_{ij}\|^T = \begin{pmatrix} A_{11} & A_{21} & \cdots & A_{n1} \\ A_{12} & A_{22} & \cdots & A_{n2} \\ \vdots & \vdots & & \vdots \\ A_{1n} & A_{2n} & \cdots & A_{nn} \end{pmatrix}.$$

For example, if

$$\mathbf{A} = \begin{pmatrix} 1 & 2 & 3 \\ 2 & 3 & 2 \\ 3 & 3 & 4 \end{pmatrix},$$

then, $A_{11} = (-1)^2(3 \times 4 - 2 \times 3) = 6, \quad A_{12} = (-1)^3(2 \times 4 - 2 \times 3) = -2$
$\dots$, and so forth, or

$$\text{adj } \mathbf{A} = \begin{pmatrix} 6 & 1 & -5 \\ -2 & -5 & 4 \\ -3 & 3 & -1 \end{pmatrix}.$$

§ A·2·5
Nonsingular Matrix

A matrix is said to be of a rank r if the largest *square* array in the matrix whose determinant does not vanish is of order r. A *square* matrix whose determinant does not vanish is called a *full-rank* or a *nonsingular* matrix.

For example,

$$\mathbf{A} = \begin{pmatrix} 1 & 2 & 3 \\ 2 & 3 & 4 \\ 3 & 5 & 7 \end{pmatrix}$$

is a *singular* matrix since

$$|\mathbf{A}| = 1(21 - 20) - 2(14 - 12) + 3(10 - 9) = 0.$$

$\mathbf{A}$ has a rank $r = 2$ since

$$\begin{pmatrix} 1 & 2 \\ 2 & 3 \end{pmatrix} = -1 \neq 0.$$

§ A·2·6
The Inverse of a Matrix

If $\mathbf{B}$ and $\mathbf{C}$ are two n-square matrices such that $\mathbf{BC} = \mathbf{CB} = \mathbf{I}$, then $\mathbf{B}$ is called the inverse of $\mathbf{C}$ and $\mathbf{C}$ the inverse of $\mathbf{B}$. The common notation for the inverse is to write $\mathbf{B}^{-1}$ and $\mathbf{C}^{-1}$.

Theorem: *If* $\mathbf{BC} = \mathbf{I}$, *and* $\mathbf{B}$ *is* **nonsingular** *then* $\mathbf{C} = \mathbf{B}^{-1}$ *which means that the inverse is unique.*

PROOF: By assumption,

$$\mathbf{BC} = \mathbf{I},$$

then

$$\mathbf{B}^{-1}\mathbf{BC} = \mathbf{B}^{-1}\mathbf{I},$$

or

$$\mathbf{IC} = \mathbf{B}^{-1},$$

or

$$\mathbf{C} = \mathbf{B}^{-1}. \quad \blacktriangleleft$$

Two important results can be proved for nonsingular matrices.

(i) If $\mathbf{A}$ and $\mathbf{B}$ are nonsingular n-square matrices then $(\mathbf{AB})^{-1} = \mathbf{B}^{-1}\mathbf{A}^{-1}$.

(ii) If $\mathbf{A}$ is nonsingular, then $\mathbf{AB} = \mathbf{AC}$ implies that $\mathbf{B} = \mathbf{C}$.

The concept of matrix inversion is useful in solving n linearly independent equations. Consider

$$\begin{pmatrix} a_{11} & a_{12} & \cdots & a_{1n} \\ a_{21} & a_{22} & \cdots & a_{2n} \\ \vdots & \vdots & & \vdots \\ a_{n1} & a_{n2} & \cdots & a_{nn} \end{pmatrix} \begin{pmatrix} x_1 \\ x_2 \\ \vdots \\ x_n \end{pmatrix} = \begin{pmatrix} b_1 \\ b_2 \\ \vdots \\ b_n \end{pmatrix},$$

where x_i represent the unknowns and a_{ij} and b_i are constants. These n equations can be written in the form

$$\mathbf{AX} = \mathbf{b}.$$

Since the equations are independent, it follows that $\mathbf{A}$ is nonsingular. Thus

$$\mathbf{A}^{-1}\mathbf{AX} = \mathbf{A}^{-1}\mathbf{b}$$

or

$$\mathbf{X} = \mathbf{A}^{-1}\mathbf{b}$$

gives the solution of the n unknowns.

§ A·2·7
Methods of Computing the Inverse of a Matrix

(i) *Adjoint Matrix Method:* Given $\mathbf{A}$ a nonsingular matrix of size n, then

$$\mathbf{A}^{-1} = \frac{1}{|\mathbf{A}|} \text{ adj } \mathbf{A} = \frac{1}{|\mathbf{A}|} \begin{pmatrix} A_{11} & A_{21} & \cdots & A_{n1} \\ A_{12} & A_{22} & \cdots & A_{n2} \\ \vdots & \vdots & & \vdots \\ A_{1n} & A_{2n} & \cdots & A_{nn} \end{pmatrix}.$$

For example, for

$$\mathbf{A} = \begin{pmatrix} 1 & 2 & 3 \\ 2 & 3 & 2 \\ 3 & 3 & 4 \end{pmatrix}, \quad \text{adj } \mathbf{A} = \begin{pmatrix} 6 & 1 & -5 \\ -2 & -5 & 4 \\ -3 & 3 & -1 \end{pmatrix}, \quad \text{and} \quad |\mathbf{A}| = -7.$$

Hence

$$\mathbf{A}^{-1} = \frac{1}{-7}\begin{pmatrix} 6 & 1 & -5 \\ -2 & -5 & 4 \\ -3 & 2 & -1 \end{pmatrix} \begin{pmatrix} -6/7 & -1/7 & 5/7 \\ 2/7 & 5/7 & -4/7 \\ 3/7 & -3/7 & 1/7 \end{pmatrix}.$$

(ii) *Row Transformation Method:* Consider the partitioned matrix $(\mathbf{A}\,|\,\mathbf{I})$, where $\mathbf{A}$ is nonsingular. By premultiplying this matrix by $\mathbf{A}^{-1}$, then

$$(\mathbf{A}^{-1}\mathbf{A}\,|\,\mathbf{A}^{-1}\mathbf{I}) = (\mathbf{I}\,|\,\mathbf{A}^{-1}).$$

Thus by applying a sequence of row transformations only, the matrix A is changed to I and I is changed to A^{-1}.

For example, consider the system of equations of the form $AX = b$

$$\begin{pmatrix} 1 & 2 & 3 \\ 2 & 3 & 2 \\ 3 & 3 & 4 \end{pmatrix} \begin{pmatrix} x_1 \\ x_2 \\ x_3 \end{pmatrix} = \begin{pmatrix} 3 \\ 4 \\ 5 \end{pmatrix}$$

The solution of X and the inverse of basis matrix can be obtained directly by considering

$$A^{-1}(A|I|b) = (I|A^{-1}|A^{-1}b).$$

Thus, applying row transformation operation, one gets,

$$\begin{pmatrix} 1 & 2 & 3 & | & 1 & 0 & 0 & \| & 3 \\ 2 & 3 & 2 & | & 0 & 1 & 0 & \| & 4 \\ 3 & 3 & 4 & | & 0 & 0 & 1 & \| & 5 \end{pmatrix}.$$

Iteration 1:

$$\begin{pmatrix} 1 & 2 & 3 & | & 1 & 0 & 0 & \| & 3 \\ 0 & -1 & -4 & | & -2 & 1 & 0 & \| & -2 \\ 0 & -3 & -5 & | & -3 & 0 & 1 & \| & -4 \end{pmatrix}$$

Iteration 2:

$$\begin{pmatrix} 1 & 0 & -5 & | & -3 & 2 & 0 & \| & -1 \\ 0 & 1 & 4 & | & 2 & -1 & 0 & \| & 2 \\ 0 & 0 & 7 & | & 3 & -3 & 1 & \| & 2 \end{pmatrix}$$

Iteration 3:

$$\begin{pmatrix} 1 & 0 & 0 & | & -6/7 & -1/7 & 5/7 & \| & 3/7 \\ 0 & 1 & 0 & | & 2/7 & 5/7 & -4/7 & \| & 6/7 \\ 0 & 0 & 1 & | & 3/7 & -3/7 & 1/7 & \| & 2/7 \end{pmatrix}$$

This gives $x_1 = 3/7$, $x_2 = 6/7$, and $x_3 = 2/7$. The inverse of A is given by the right-hand side matrix. This is the same as the inverse obtained by the method of adjoint matrix.

(iii) *Partitioned Matrix Method:* Let the two nonsingular matrices A and B of size n be partitioned as shown below such that A_{11} is nonsingular.

$$A = \begin{pmatrix} \begin{array}{c} A_{11} \\ (p \times p) \end{array} & \begin{array}{c} A_{12} \\ (p \times q) \end{array} \\ \hline \begin{array}{c} A_{21} \\ (q \times p) \end{array} & \begin{array}{c} A_{22} \\ (q \times q) \end{array} \end{pmatrix} \quad \text{and} \quad B = \begin{pmatrix} \begin{array}{c} B_{11} \\ (p \times p) \end{array} & \begin{array}{c} B_{12} \\ (p \times q) \end{array} \\ \hline \begin{array}{c} B_{21} \\ (q \times p) \end{array} & \begin{array}{c} B_{22} \\ (q \times q) \end{array} \end{pmatrix}$$

If **B** is the inverse of **A**, then from $\mathbf{AB} = \mathbf{I}_n$,

$$\mathbf{A}_{11}\mathbf{B}_{11} + \mathbf{A}_{12}\mathbf{B}_{21} = \mathbf{I}_p$$
$$\mathbf{A}_{11}\mathbf{B}_{12} + \mathbf{A}_{12}\mathbf{B}_{22} = 0.$$

Also from $\mathbf{BA} = \mathbf{I}_n$,

$$\mathbf{B}_{21}\mathbf{A}_{11} + \mathbf{B}_{22}\mathbf{A}_{21} = 0,$$
$$\mathbf{B}_{21}\mathbf{A}_{12} + \mathbf{B}_{22}\mathbf{A}_{22} = \mathbf{I}_q.$$

Since $\mathbf{A}_{11}$ is nonsingular, that is $|\mathbf{A}_{11}| \neq 0$, then solving for $\mathbf{B}_{11}$, $\mathbf{B}_{12}$, $\mathbf{B}_{21}$, and $\mathbf{B}_{22}$ one gets,

$$\mathbf{B}_{11} = \mathbf{A}_{11}^{-1} + (\mathbf{A}_{11}^{-1}\mathbf{A}_{12})\mathbf{D}^{-1}(\mathbf{A}_{21}\mathbf{A}_{11}^{-1}),$$
$$\mathbf{B}_{12} = -(\mathbf{A}_{11}^{-1}\mathbf{A}_{12})\mathbf{D}^{-1},$$
$$\mathbf{B}_{21} = -\mathbf{D}^{-1}(\mathbf{A}_{21}\mathbf{A}_{11}^{-1}),$$
$$\mathbf{B}_{22} = \mathbf{D}^{-1},$$

where

$$\mathbf{D} = \mathbf{A}_{22} - \mathbf{A}_{21}(\mathbf{A}_{11}^{-1}\mathbf{A}_{12}).$$

To illustrate the use of these formulas, consider the same example given previously.

$$\mathbf{A} = \left(\begin{array}{c|cc} 1 & 2 & 3 \\ \hline 2 & 3 & 2 \\ 3 & 3 & 4 \end{array}\right),$$

where

$$\mathbf{A}_{11} = (1), \quad \mathbf{A}_{12} = (2, 3), \quad \mathbf{A}_{21} = \binom{2}{3}, \quad \text{and} \quad \mathbf{A}_{22} = \begin{pmatrix} 3 & 2 \\ 3 & 4 \end{pmatrix}.$$

It is obvious that $\mathbf{A}_{11}^{-1} = 1$, and

$$\mathbf{D} = \begin{pmatrix} 3 & 2 \\ 3 & 4 \end{pmatrix} - \binom{2}{3}(1)(2, 3) = \begin{pmatrix} -1 & -4 \\ -3 & -5 \end{pmatrix},$$
$$\mathbf{D}^{-1} = -1/7\begin{pmatrix} -5 & 4 \\ 3 & -1 \end{pmatrix} = \begin{pmatrix} 5/7 & -4/7 \\ -3/7 & 1/7 \end{pmatrix}.$$

Thus

$$\mathbf{B}_{11} = (-6/7), \quad \mathbf{B}_{12} = (-1/7 \quad 5/7)$$
$$\mathbf{B}_{21} = \binom{2/7}{3/7}, \quad \text{and} \quad \mathbf{B}_{22} = \begin{pmatrix} 5/7 & -4/7 \\ -3/7 & 1/7 \end{pmatrix},$$

which directly give $\mathbf{B} = \mathbf{A}^{-1}$.

§ A·3
Quadratic Forms

Given

$$\mathbf{X} = (x_1, x_2, \ldots, x_n)^T$$

and

$$\mathbf{A} = \begin{pmatrix} a_{11} & a_{12} & \cdots & a_{1n} \\ a_{21} & a_{22} & \cdots & a_{2n} \\ \vdots & \vdots & & \vdots \\ a_{n1} & a_{n2} & \cdots & a_{nn} \end{pmatrix},$$

the function,

$$Q(\mathbf{X}) = \mathbf{X}^T \mathbf{A} \mathbf{X} = \sum_{i=1}^{n} \sum_{j=1}^{n} a_{ij} x_i x_j,$$

is called a *quadratic form*. The matrix $\mathbf{A}$ can always be assumed symetric since each element of every pair of coefficients a_{ij} and a_{ji} $(i \neq j)$ can be replaced by $(a_{ij} + a_{ji})/2$ without changing the value of $Q(\mathbf{X})$. This assumption has several advantages and hence is taken as a restriction.

To illustrate, the quadratic form,

$$Q(\mathbf{X}) = (x_1, x_2, x_3) \begin{pmatrix} 1 & 0 & 1 \\ 2 & 7 & 6 \\ 3 & 0 & 2 \end{pmatrix} \begin{pmatrix} x_1 \\ x_2 \\ x_3 \end{pmatrix},$$

is the same as

$$Q(\mathbf{X}) = (x_1, x_2, x_3) \begin{pmatrix} 1 & 1 & 2 \\ 1 & 7 & 3 \\ 2 & 3 & 2 \end{pmatrix} \begin{pmatrix} x_1 \\ x_2 \\ x_3 \end{pmatrix}.$$

Notice that $\mathbf{A}$ is symmetrical in the second case.

The above quadratic form is said to be

(i) *Positive-definite* if $Q(\mathbf{X}) > 0$ for every $\mathbf{X} \neq \mathbf{0}$.
(ii) *Positive-semidefinite* if $Q(\mathbf{X}) \geq 0$ for every $\mathbf{X}$ and there exist $\mathbf{X} \neq \mathbf{0}$ such that $Q(\mathbf{X}) = \mathbf{0}$.
(iii) *Negative-definite if* $-Q(\mathbf{X})$ is positive-definite.
(iv) *Negative-semidefinite if* $-Q(\mathbf{X})$ is positive-semidefinite.
(v) *Indefinite* if it is none of the above cases.

It can be proved that the necessary and sufficient conditions for the realization of the above cases are given by

(i) $Q(\mathbf{X})$ is positive-definite (semidefinite) if the values of the principal minor determinants of $\mathbf{A}$ are positive (nonnegative).[1] In this case $\mathbf{A}$ is said to be positive-definite (semidefinite).

(ii) $Q(\mathbf{X})$ is negative-definite if the value of kth principal minor determinant of $\mathbf{A}$ has the sign of $(-1)^k$, $k = 1, 2, \ldots, n$. In this case, $\mathbf{A}$ is called negative-definite.

(iii) $Q(\mathbf{X})$ is negative-semidefinite if the kth principal minor determinant of $\mathbf{A}$ is either zero or has the sign of $(-1)^k$, $k = 1, 2, \ldots, n$.

SELECTED REFERENCES

1. HADLEY, G., *Matrix Algebra*, Reading, Massachusetts: Addison-Wesley, 1961.

2. HOHN, F., *Elementary Matrix Algebra*, New York: Macmillan, 1964, (second edition).

PROBLEMS

☐ **A-1** Show that the following vectors are linearly dependent.

(a) $\begin{pmatrix} 1 \\ -2 \\ 3 \end{pmatrix}$, $\begin{pmatrix} -2 \\ 4 \\ -2 \end{pmatrix}$, $\begin{pmatrix} 1 \\ -2 \\ -1 \end{pmatrix}$.

(b) $\begin{pmatrix} 2 \\ -3 \\ 4 \\ 5 \end{pmatrix}$, $\begin{pmatrix} 4 \\ -6 \\ 8 \\ 10 \end{pmatrix}$.

☐ **A-2** Given

$$\mathbf{A} = \begin{pmatrix} 1 & 4 & 9 \\ 2 & 5 & -8 \\ 3 & 7 & 2 \end{pmatrix}, \quad \mathbf{B} = \begin{pmatrix} 7 & -1 & 2 \\ 9 & 4 & 8 \\ 3 & 6 & 10 \end{pmatrix}$$

---

[1] The kth *principal minor* determinant of $\mathbf{A}_{n \times n}$ is defined by

$$\begin{vmatrix} a_{11} & a_{12} & \cdots & a_{1k} \\ a_{21} & a_{22} & \cdots & a_{2k} \\ \vdots & \vdots & & \vdots \\ a_{k1} & a_{k2} & & a_{kk} \end{vmatrix}, \quad k = 1, 2, \ldots, n.$$

Find

  (a) $\mathbf{A} + 7\mathbf{B}$

  (b) $2\mathbf{A} - 3\mathbf{B}$

  (c) $(\mathbf{A} + 7\mathbf{B})^T$

☐ **A-3** In Problem A-2 show that $\mathbf{AB} \neq \mathbf{BA}$.

☐ **A-4** Given the partitioned matrices,

$$\mathbf{A} = \left(\begin{array}{c|cc} 1 & 5 & 7 \\ 2 & -6 & 9 \\ \hline 3 & 7 & 2 \\ 4 & 9 & 1 \end{array}\right), \quad \mathbf{B} = \left(\begin{array}{cc|cc} 2 & 3 & -4 & 5 \\ \hline 1 & 2 & 6 & 7 \\ 3 & 1 & 0 & 9 \end{array}\right),$$

Find $\mathbf{AB}$ using partitioning.

☐ **A-5** In Problem A-2 find $\mathbf{A}^{-1}$ and $\mathbf{B}^{-1}$ using

  (a) Adjoint matrix method.

  (b) Row-transformation method.

  (c) Partitioned matrix method.

☐ **A-6** Verify the formulas given in Section A·2·7 for obtaining the inverse of a partitioned matrix.

☐ **A-7** Find the inverse of

$$\mathbf{A} = \begin{pmatrix} 1 & \mathbf{G} \\ \mathbf{H} & \mathbf{B} \end{pmatrix}$$

where $\mathbf{B}$ is a nonsingular matrix.

☐ **A-8** Show that the quadratic form,

$$Q(x_1, x_2) = 6x_1 + 3x_2 - 4x_1 x_2 - 2x_1^2 - 3x_2^2,$$

is negative-definite.

☐ **A-9** Show that the quadratic form,

$$Q(x_1, x_2, x_3) = 2x_1^2 + 2x_2^2 + 3x_3^2 + 2x_1 x_2 + 2x_2 x_3,$$

is positive-definite.

Review of
Basic Theorems in
Differential Calculus

§ B·1
Definitions

§ B·1·1
Continuous Function

A single-variable function $f(x)$ is said to be continuous at a point x_0 if for any $\varepsilon > 0$, however small, there exists δ such that for $|h| < \delta$, $\delta > 0$,

$$|f(x_0 + h) - f(x_0)| \leq \varepsilon.$$

Similarly, an n-variable function $f(\mathbf{X})$, $\mathbf{X} = (x_1, x_2, \ldots, x_n)$, is continuous at a point $\mathbf{X}_0$ if for any $\varepsilon > 0$, however small, there exists δ such that for $|\mathbf{h}| < \delta$,

$$|f(\mathbf{X}_0 + \mathbf{h}) - f(\mathbf{X}_0)| \leq \varepsilon,$$

where

$$\mathbf{h} = (h_1, h_2, \ldots, h_n),$$
$$\delta = (\delta_1, \delta_2, \ldots, \delta_n) > 0.$$

§ B·1·2
Partial Derivative

For a single variable function $f(x)$, the limit,

$$\lim_{h \to 0} \frac{f(x_0 + h) - f(x_0)}{h},$$

680

at the point x_0, when it exists, defines the derivative of the function at x_0. This is usually written as $f'(x_0)$ or $df(x_0)/dx$.

For an n-variable function, an equivalent definition of the first *partial derivative* of the function with respect to any one of its n variables at a point $\mathbf{X_0} = (x_1^0, x_2^0, \ldots, x_n^0)$ is given by

$$\frac{\partial f(\mathbf{X_0})}{\partial x_i} = \lim_{h_i \to 0} \frac{f(x_1^0, \ldots, x_{i-1}^0, x_i^0 + h_i, x_{i+1}^0, \ldots, x_n^0) - f(\mathbf{X_0})}{h_i},$$

provided that the limit exists.

The first partial derivatives of a function $f(\mathbf{X})$ at a certain point define the slopes of the tangent to the function with respect to the n coordinate axes. A useful notation for summarizing these first partial derivatives is to use the so-called *gradient vector* which is given by

$$\nabla f = \left(\frac{\partial f}{\partial x_1}, \ldots, \frac{\partial f}{\partial x_n} \right).$$

The second partial derivative is defined by taking the partial derivatives of the functions resulting from the first partial derivatives provided, of course, that they exist. This is written as

$$\frac{\partial^2 f}{\partial x_i \, \partial x_j}, \qquad \text{all } i, j.$$

A compact way for summarizing the second partial derivatives is to use the so-called *Hessian* matrix. This is defined for $f(\mathbf{X})$ by

$$\mathbf{H} = \begin{bmatrix} \dfrac{\partial^2 f}{\partial x_1^2} & \dfrac{\partial^2 f}{\partial x_1 \, \partial x_2} & \cdots & \dfrac{\partial^2 f}{\partial x_1 \, \partial x_n} \\[2mm] \vdots & \vdots & & \vdots \\[2mm] \dfrac{\partial^2 f}{\partial x_n \, \partial x_1} & \dfrac{\partial^2 f}{\partial x_n \, \partial x_2} & \cdots & \dfrac{\partial^2 f}{\partial x_n^2} \end{bmatrix}.$$

§ B·2
Rolle's Theorem

Given the function $f(x)$ which is continuous in the closed interval $[a, b]$ with $f(a) = f(b)$. There exists at least one point ξ such that $a < \xi < b$ at which the first derivative of f vanishes; that is, $f'(\xi) = 0$.

The proof of this theorem can be found in [1].

§ B·3
Mean Value Theorems

§ B·3·1
First Mean Value Theorem

Theorem: *Given a function $f(x)$ which is continuous in the closed interval $[a, b]$ and its first derivative exists at every interior point, there exists a point ξ in the open interval (a, b) which satisfies*

$$\frac{f(b) - f(a)}{b - a} = f'(\xi), \qquad a < \xi < b.$$

Or, if $b = a + h$, then

$$\frac{f(a + h) - f(a)}{h} = f'(a + \theta h), \qquad 0 < \theta < 1.$$

PROOF: Let $H(x) = f(x) - cx$, where c is determined such that $H(a) = H(b)$. This means that

$$c = \frac{f(b) - f(a)}{b - a}.$$

Since $H(x)$ satisfies Rolle's theorem (Section B·2), then for some ξ in the open interval (a, b),

$$H'(\xi) = f'(\xi) - c = 0$$

or

$$\frac{f(b) - f(a)}{b - a} = f'(\xi).$$

(See figure B–1). ◄

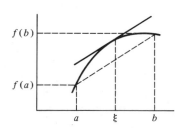

Figure B–1

§ B·3·2
Cauchy's Second Mean Value Theorem

Theorem: *Given the two functions $f(x)$ and $g(x)$ which are continuous at every point in the closed interval $[a, b]$ with $g(a) \neq g(b)$. Furthermore, their first derivatives exist at every interior point and do not vanish simultaneously at any interior point. There exists a point ξ, $a < \xi < b$, such that*

$$\frac{f(b) - f(a)}{g(b) - g(a)} = \frac{f'(\xi)}{g'(\xi)}, \qquad a < \xi < b.$$

Or, if $b = a + h$, then

$$\frac{f(a + h) - f(a)}{g(a + h) - g(a)} = \frac{f'(a + \theta h)}{g'(a + \theta h)}, \qquad 0 < \theta < 1.$$

PROOF: Let $H(x) = f(x) - cg(x)$ and determine c such that $H(a) = H(b)$. Thus

$$c = \frac{f(b) - f(a)}{g(b) - g(a)}.$$

By Rolle's theorem,

$$H'(\xi) = f'(\xi) - cg'(\xi) = 0$$

or

$$\frac{f(b) - f(a)}{g(b) - g(a)} = c = \frac{f'(\xi)}{g'(\xi)}, \qquad a < \xi < b. \quad \blacktriangleleft$$

§ B·4
L'Hospital's Rule

Theorem: *Given two functions $f(x)$ and $g(x)$ which both vanish $(= 0)$ at $x = a$. If $f(x)$ and $g(x)$ are continuous in the closed interval $[a, b]$ and are differentiable at every x, $a < x < b$ such that*

$$\lim_{x \to a} \frac{f'(x)}{g'(x)} = B,$$

then,

$$\lim_{x \to a} \frac{f(x)}{g(x)} = B.$$

PROOF: Since $f(a) = g(a) = 0$, then for some x, $a < x \le b$, by the second mean value theorem

$$\frac{f(x)}{g(x)} = \frac{f(x) - f(a)}{g(x) - g(a)} = \frac{f'(\xi)}{g'(\xi)}, \qquad a < \xi < x.$$

Since $a < \xi < x$, then as $x \to a$, $\xi \to a$. Hence

$$\lim_{x \to a} \frac{f(x)}{g(x)} = \lim_{\xi \to a} \frac{f'(\xi)}{g'(\xi)}. \quad \blacktriangleleft$$

L'Hospital's rule applies also to the undetermined forms of the type ∞/∞. The proof is not given here, however. Other forms including $0 \cdot \infty$, 0^0, ∞^0, 1^∞, and $\infty - \infty$ can be reduced to the form ∞/∞ or $0/0$ using simple transformations. For example, if $f - g = \infty$, then,

$$fg\left(\frac{1}{g} - \frac{1}{f}\right) \equiv \infty \cdot 0$$

or,

$$\frac{\left(\dfrac{1}{g} - \dfrac{1}{f}\right)}{\left(\dfrac{1}{fg}\right)} = \frac{0}{0},$$

for which the above L'Hospital rule is now applicable. The other undetermined forms including 0^0, ∞^0, and 1^∞ are transformed to the indicated forms by taking their logarithms.

§ B·5
Polynomial Approximation

Given a function $f(x)$ which together with its first n derivatives are defined at the point $x = a$, then $f(x)$ can be approximated by the nth order polynomial,

$$p_n(x) = \sum_{i=0}^{n} c_i(x - a)^i$$

where c_i are constants to be determined as follows.

$$p_n(a) = f(a)$$

and

$$p_n^{(i)}(a) = f^{(i)}(a), \qquad i = 1, 2, \ldots, n,$$

where the superscript (i) signifies the ith derivative. Thus

$$c_0 = p_n(a) = f(a)$$

and

$$c_i = \frac{f^{(i)}(a)}{i!}.$$

This yields,

$$p_n(x) = \sum_{i=1}^{n} \frac{f^{(i)}(a)}{i!}(x-a)^i.$$

To illustrate, consider

$$f(x) = 5x^3 + 6x^2 - 3x + 5.$$

For $a = 1$,

$$f(1) = 13, \quad f'(1) = 24, \quad f''(1) = 42, \quad f'''(1) = 30,$$

and

$$f^{(i)}(1) = 0, \quad i = 4, 5, \ldots.$$

Thus

$$f(x) = p_3(x) = 13 + 24(x-1) + 21(x-1)^2 + 5(x-1)^3.$$

Consider next $f(x) = \sin x$, for $a = 0$.

$$f(0) = 0$$

$$f^{(i)}(0) = \begin{cases} 1, & i = 1, 5, 9, \ldots \\ -1, & i = 3, 7, 11, \ldots \\ 0, & i = 2, 4, 6, \ldots \end{cases}$$

Thus

$$p_n(x) = x - \frac{x^3}{3!} + \frac{x^5}{5!} - \cdots + (-1)^{n+1}\frac{x^{2n-1}}{(2n-1)!}.$$

It is noticed in the first example that $f(x) = p_3(x)$ because $f(x)$ itself is polynomial with a vanishing fourth derivative. In the second example $f^{(i)}(0)$ exists for every $i \geq 1$ and hence $p_n(x)$ can only be used as an approximation to $f(x)$.

The next step now is to find an expression for $f(x) - p_n(x)$. This is called the *remainder* and may be written as

$$R_n(x) = f(x) - p_n(x).$$

By definition, since $f(a) = p_n(a)$ and $f^{(i)}(a) = p_n^{(i)}(a)$, for all i, then $R_n(a) = 0$ and $R_n^{(i)}(a) = 0$, for all i.

Assume that $f^{(n+1)}(x)$ exists at all points in the *closed interval* $[a, b]$. Thus $f^{(n)}(x)$ must exist also in the same interval and must be continuous. Consequently, $f^{(i)}(x)$, $i = 1, 2, \ldots, n - 1$ must also be continuous in $[a, b]$. Define,

$$Q_n(x) = (x - a)^{n+1}$$

which obviously possesses the first n derivatives at $x = a$. Also, $Q_n(a) = 0$ and $Q_n^{(i)}(a) = 0$, $i = 1, 2, \ldots, n$.

Now

$$\frac{R_n(x)}{Q_n(x)} = \frac{R_n(x) - R_n(a)}{Q_n(x) - Q_n(a)}.$$

By the second mean value theorem

$$\frac{R_n(x)}{Q_n(x)} = \frac{R_n'(\xi_1)}{Q_n'(\xi_1)}, \qquad a < \xi_1 < x < b.$$

Again, since

$$\frac{R_n'(\xi_1)}{Q_n'(\xi_1)} = \frac{R_n'(\xi_1) - R_n'(a)}{Q_n'(\xi_1) - Q_n'(a)},$$

then by the same theorem

$$\frac{R_n'(\xi_1)}{Q_n'(\xi_1)} = \frac{R_n''(\xi_2)}{Q_n''(\xi_2)}, \qquad a < \xi_2 < \xi_1 < x < b.$$

Carrying this out n times, it follows that

$$\frac{R_n(x)}{Q_n(x)} = \frac{R_n'(\xi_1)}{Q_n'(\xi_1)} = \cdots = \frac{R_n^{(n)}(\xi_n)}{Q_n^{(n)}(\xi_n)}, \qquad a < \xi_n < \cdots < \xi_1 < x < b.$$

But since

$$P_n^{(n)}(x) = n!\,\frac{f^{(n)}(a)}{n!} = f^{(n)}(a),$$

then, from the definition $R_n(x) = f(x) - p_n(x)$, one gets,

$$R_n^{(n)}(x) = f^{(n)}(x) - f^{(n)}(a)$$

So that

$$\frac{R_n(x)}{Q_n(x)} = \frac{1}{(n + 1)!}\,\frac{f^{(n)}(\xi_n) - f^{(n)}(a)}{(\xi_n - a)}$$

By the first mean value theorem (Section B·2·1)

$$\frac{f^{(n)}(\xi_n) - f^{(n)}(a)}{\xi_n - a} = f^{(n+1)}(\xi), \qquad a < \xi < \xi_n.$$

Thus

$$R_n(x) = \frac{f^{(n+1)}(\xi)}{(n+1)!}(x - a)^{n+1}, \qquad a < \xi < x$$

The above result leads to Taylor's theorem which is presented in the next section.

§ B·5·1
Taylor's Theorem

Given that the $(n + 1)$st derivative of $f(x)$ exists at every point of the closed interval $[a, b]$, then for $0 < h \leq b - a$,

$$f(a + h) = f(a) + \sum_{i=1}^{n} \frac{f^{(i)}(a)}{i!} h^i + R_n(a + \theta h)$$

$$= f(a) + \sum_{i=1}^{n} \frac{f^{(i)}(a)}{i!} h^i + \frac{f^{(n+1)}(a + \theta h)}{(n+1)!} h^{n+1}, \qquad 0 < \theta < 1.$$

This theorem follows directly from the development given above.

If $R_n(a + \theta h) \to 0$ as $n \to \infty$, then the theorem yields

$$f(a + h) = f(a) + \frac{f'(a)h}{1!} + \frac{f''(a)h^2}{2!} + \cdots.$$

For example, for $f(x) = e^x$, $f^{(n)}(x) = e^x$. Let $a = 0$, $f^{(n)}(0) = 1$. Consequently

$$f(0 + h) = f(0) + \frac{f'(0)}{1!} h + \frac{f''(0)h^2}{2!} + \cdots + \frac{f^{(n+1)}(0 + \theta h)}{(n+1)!} h^{n+1}$$

$$= 1 + h + \frac{h^2}{2!} + \cdots + \frac{h^n}{n!} + \frac{e^{\theta h}}{(n+1)!} h^{n+1}.$$

It can be shown that

$$\lim_{n \to \infty} \frac{h^{n+1}}{(n+1)!} = 0.$$

Hence

$$e^x = 1 + x + \frac{x^2}{2!} + \cdots.$$

Taylor's theorem may be extended to functions of n variables as follows. Assume that the second partial derivatives of $f(\mathbf{X})$ exist and are continuous. Let $\mathbf{h} = (h_1, h_2, \ldots, h_n)^T$, Taylor's expansion around $\mathbf{X}_0$ is given by

$$f(\mathbf{X}_0 + \mathbf{h}) = f(\mathbf{X}_0) + \nabla f(\mathbf{X}_0)\mathbf{h} + \tfrac{1}{2}\mathbf{h}^T \mathbf{H} \mathbf{h}\Big|_{\mathbf{X}_0 + \theta \mathbf{h}}$$

where $\nabla f(\mathbf{X}_0)$ is the gradient-vector evaluated at $\mathbf{X}_0$ and $\mathbf{H}$ is the Hessian matrix evaluated at $\mathbf{X}_0 + \theta\mathbf{h}$ (see Section B·1·2). The third term is the expression representing the remainder.

In the case where the nth partial derivative of f exists and is continuous, the Taylor's expansion can be generalized to $(n + 1)$ terms. This generalization is not needed in this presentation and hence it is not included.

To illustrate the expansion of an n-variable function, consider,

$$f(\mathbf{X}) = f(x_1, x_2) = x_1^2 + 3x_1 \exp(x_2).$$

It is required to expand $f(\mathbf{X})$ around $\mathbf{X}_0 = (1, 0)$. Thus,

$$\mathbf{h} = \begin{pmatrix} h_1 \\ h_2 \end{pmatrix} = \begin{pmatrix} x_1 \\ x_2 \end{pmatrix} - \begin{pmatrix} 1 \\ 0 \end{pmatrix} = \begin{pmatrix} x_1 - 1 \\ x_2 \end{pmatrix},$$

$$\mathbf{X}_0 + \theta\mathbf{h} = \begin{pmatrix} 1 \\ 0 \end{pmatrix} + \theta\begin{pmatrix} x_1 - 1 \\ x_2 \end{pmatrix} = \begin{pmatrix} 1 - \theta + \theta x_1 \\ \theta x_2 \end{pmatrix},$$

$$\nabla f(\mathbf{X}_0) = \left(\frac{\partial f}{\partial x_1}, \frac{\partial f}{\partial x_2} \right) = (2x_1 + 3e^{x_2}, 3x_1 e^{x_2})|_{\mathbf{X}_0}$$

$$= (5, 3),$$

$$\mathbf{H} = \begin{pmatrix} \dfrac{\partial^2 f}{\partial x_1^2} & \dfrac{\partial^2 f}{\partial x_1 \partial x_2} \\ \dfrac{\partial^2 f}{\partial x_2 \partial x_1} & \dfrac{\partial^2 f}{\partial x_2^2} \end{pmatrix}$$

$$= \begin{pmatrix} 2 & 3e^{x_2} \\ 3e^{x_2} & 3x_1 e^{x_2} \end{pmatrix}.$$

Hence,

$$f(\mathbf{X}) = f(1, 0) + \nabla f(1, 1)\mathbf{h} + \mathbf{h}^T\mathbf{H}\mathbf{h}\Big|_{\mathbf{X}_0 + \mathbf{h}}$$

$$= 4 + (5, 3)\begin{pmatrix} x_1 - 1 \\ x_2 \end{pmatrix}$$

$$+ \tfrac{1}{2}(x_1 - 1, x_2)\begin{pmatrix} 2 & 3e^{\theta x_2} \\ 3e^{\theta x_2} & 3(1 - \theta + \theta x_1)e^{\theta x_2} \end{pmatrix}\begin{pmatrix} x_1 - 1 \\ x_2 \end{pmatrix}.$$

Taylor's theorem will prove especially useful in developing the sufficiency conditions for identifying the maxima and minima of a differentiable function.

§ B·6
Convex and Concave Functions

A function $f(\mathbf{X})$ is said to be strictly convex if for any two other distinct points $\mathbf{X}_1$ and $\mathbf{X}_2$,

$$f(\lambda\mathbf{X}_1 + (1 - \lambda)\mathbf{X}_2) < \lambda f(\mathbf{X}_1) + (1 - \lambda)f(\mathbf{X}_2),$$

where $0 < \lambda < 1$. On the other hand, a function $f(\mathbf{X})$ is strictly concave if $-f(\mathbf{X})$ is strictly convex.

An important special case of the convex (concave) function is the quadratic form (see Section A·3),

$$f(\mathbf{X}) = \mathbf{CX} + \mathbf{X}^T\mathbf{AX},$$

where $\mathbf{C}$ is a constant vector and $\mathbf{A}$ is a symmetric matrix. It can be proved that $f(\mathbf{X})$ is strictly convex if $\mathbf{A}$ is positive-definite. Similarly, $f(\mathbf{X})$ is strictly concave if $\mathbf{A}$ is negative-definite.

SELECTED REFERENCES

1. BRAND, L., *Advanced Calculus*, New York: Wiley, 1955.
2. KAPLAN, W., *Advanced Calculus*, Reading, Massachusetts: Addison-Wesley, 1952.
3. RUDIN, W., *Principles of Mathematical Analysis*, New York: McGraw-Hill, 1964, (second edition).

PROBLEMS

☐ **B-1**   Given $f(x, y) = 0$, use Taylor's series to derive the expression for dy/dx in terms of the partial derivatives of $f(x, y)$.

☐ **B-2**   Expand the following function around $(1, 1, 0)$.

$$f(x, y, z) = 5x^2 \ln y + 3xye^z$$

☐ **B-3**   Using Taylor's series expand the function,

$$f(x) = \cos x,$$

around $x = 0$. Show that the remainder tends to zero as the number of terms n tends towards infinity.

☐ **B-4**   Show that the function $f(x) = e^x$ is strictly convex over all real values of x.

☐ **B-5**   Show that the quadratic function,

$$f(x_1, x_2, x_3) = 5x_1^2 + 5x_2^2 + 4x_3^2 + 4x_1x_2 + 2x_2x_3,$$

is strictly convex.

☐ **B-6**   In Problem B-5, show that $-f(x_1, x_2, x_3)$ is strictly concave.

General Program for Computing Poisson Queueing Formulas

The computer program in this appendix is written in FORTRAN IV. It computes the basic steady state results of any queueing model having the format $(M/M/c) : (GD/N/K)$. The use of the program is summarized below.

1. *Input*
Only five elements of information are needed for the input data of each model. These are

1. The arrival rate, λ.
2. The service rate, μ.
3. The number of parallel servers, c.
4. The maximum number allowed in the system, N.
5. The maximum limit on the source, K.

These data are taken in the same order in which they appear in the Kendall notation, $(M/M/c) : (GD/N/K)$, and are punched on one card according to the floating point format (5F10.0). If any of the elements, c, N, and K is equal to ∞ (that is, infinite number of servers, infinite system limit, or infinite source), this is entered in the input card as 9999. The program is coded such that any number of models can be computed in the same run.

2. *Output*
The output of the program summarizes the basic input data in addition to the values of λ_{eff} and ρ. The basic output information of the model includes W_s, W_q, L_s, and L_q. In addition, the values of p_n are computed for successive

value of n until $p_n < 10^{-5}$ or until p_{200} is computed, which ever occurs first. The limit $n = 200$ is specified by the DIMENSION statement, $P(200)$, of the program. This can be increased as necessary if the computations terminate before $p_n < 10^{-5}$. Notice that the value of "M" as indicated by the second statement in the program must always be the same as the dimension of P. (See the actual output listing given below for several illustrative examples.)

3. *Error Message*

The program checks automatically for invalid input data which include, (1) $\rho/c \geq 1$ for the $(M/M/c):(GD/\infty/\infty)$, and (2) $K > 200$ in a *finite* source model. In both cases, the message INVALID DATA will be printed out. The first case leads to a situation where no steady state results exist. The second case can be accounted for by increasing the dimension of P to at least K.

Program Listing

```
      DIMENSION P(200)
      M=200
800   FORMAT(5F10.0)
900   FORMAT(2H0*46X5H(M/M/I3,6H)-(GD/I3,1H/I3,1H))
901   FORMAT(1H030X7HLAMBDA=E12.5,5X11HLAMBDA EFF=E12.5,/
     131X3HMU=E12.5,9X4HRHO=E12.5)
902   FORMAT(1H030X3HWS=E12.5,6X3HWQ=E12.5,/31X3HLS=E12.5,6X3HLQ=E12.5)
903   FORMAT(1H030X25HVALUES OF P(N) FOR N=0 TOI4,12H, OTHERWISE
     117HP(N) .LT. 0.00001/(30X6F10.5))
904   FORMAT(1H1)
905   FORMAT(1H030X12HINVALID DATA)
      WRITE(6,904)
  5   READ(5,800) XLAM,XMU,C,XN,XK
      IT=1
      NC=C
      N=XN
      K=XK
      RHO=XLAM/XMU
      ELAM=XLAM
      WRITE(6,900) NC,N,K
      IF(K.LT.9999.AND.K.GT.M.AND.N.GT.M) GO TO 350
      NN=MINO(M,N,K)
      RC=RHO/C
      PZ=1.
      DO 10 I=1,NN
 10   P(I)=0.
      IF(NC.GT.1) GO TO 60
      IF(K.LT.9999) GO TO 30
      IF(RC.GE.1..AND.N.EQ.9999) GO TO 350
      PZ=PZ-RHO
      IF(N.LT.9999) PZ=PZ/(1.-RHO**(N+1))
      P(1)=PZ*RHO
      DO 20 I=2,NN
      P(I)=P(I-1)*RHO
      IF(P(I).LT.1.E-5) IF(IT) 20,150,20
      IT=0
```

```
 20 CONTINUE
    I=NN+1
    GO TO 150
 30 P(1)=XK*RHO
    PZ=PZ+P(1)
    DO 40 I=2,NN
    X=K-I+1
    P(I)=P(I-1)*X*RHO
 40 PZ=PZ+P(I)
 45 PZ=1./PZ
    DO 50 I=1,NN
    P(I)=PZ*P(I)
    IF(P(I).LT.1.E-5) IF(IT) 50,55,50
    IT=0
 50 CONTINUE
    I=NN+1
 55 LL=I-1
    QL=0.
    DO 56 J=NC,LL
    X=J-NC
 56 QL=QL+X*P(J)
    R=C*PZ
    DO 57 J=1,NC
    X=NC-J
 57 R=R+X*P(J)
    ELAM=XMU*(C-R)
    GO TO 160
 60 IF(NC.LT.9999) GO TO 80
    PZ=EXP(-RHO)
    P(1)=PZ*RHO
    DO 70 I=2,NN
    X=I
    P(I)=P(I-1)*RHO/X
    IF(P(I).LT.1.E-5) IF(IT) 70,75,70
    IT=0
 70 CONTINUE
    I=NN+1
 75 QL=0.
    GO TO 160
 80 IF(K.LT.9999) GO TO 120
    IF(RC.GE.1..AND.N.EQ.9999) GO TO 350
    P(1)=RHO
    DO 90 I=2,NC
    X=I
    P(I)=P(I-1)*RHO/X
 90 PZ=PZ+P(I-1)
    X=P(NC)/(1.-RC)
    IF(N.LT.9999) X=X*(1.-RC**(N-NC+1))
    PZ=PZ+X
    PZ=1./PZ
    DO 100 I=1,NC
100 P(I)=PZ*P(I)
    DO 110 I=NC,NN
    P(I)=P(I-1)*RC
```

```
      IF(P(I).LT.1.E-5) IF(IT) 110,150,110
      IT=0
110 CONTINUE
      I=NN+1
      GO TO 150
120 P(1)=XK*RHO
      DO 130 I=2,NC
      X=I
      Y=K-I+1
      P(I)=P(I-1)*RHO*Y/X
130 PZ=PZ+P(I-1)
      DO 140 I=NC,NN
      X=K-I+1
      P(I)=P(I-1)*RC*X
140 PZ=PZ+P(I)
      GO TO 45
150 QL=RC*P(NC)/(1.-RC)**2
      IF(N.LT.9999) QL=QL*(1.-RC**(N-NC)-(XN-C)*RC**(N-NC)*(1.-RC))
      ELAM=XLAM*(1.-P(NN))
160 SL=QL+ELAM/XMU
      WS=SL/ELAM
      WQ=QL/ELAM
200 MAX=I-1
      WRITE(6,901) XLAM,ELAM,XMU,RHO
      WRITE(6,902) WS,WQ,SL,QL
      WRITE(6,903) MAX,PZ,(P(I),I=1,MAX)
      GO TO 5
350 WRITE(6,901) XLAM,ELAM,XMU,RHO
      WRITE(6,905)
      GO TO 5
      END
```

Examples of Computer Output

```
                  (M/M/  2)-(GD/***/***)

LAMBDA= 0.75000E 01      LAMBDA EFF= 0.75000E 01
MU= 0.12000E 02          RHO= 0.62500E 00

WS= 0.92352E-01          WQ= 0.90188E-02
LS= 0.69264E 00          LQ= 0.67641E-01

VALUES OF P(N) FOR N=0 TO    9, OTHERWISE P(N) .LT. 0.00001
    0.52381    0.32738    0.10231    0.03197    0.00999    0.00312
    0.00098    0.00030    0.00010    0.00003

                  (M/M/  5)-(GD/ 20/***)

LAMBDA= 0.33333E 00      LAMBDA EFF= 0.33201E 00
MU= 0.83333E-01          RHO= 0.40000E 01

WS= 0.17827E 02          WQ= 0.58271E 01
LS= 0.59188E 01          LQ= 0.19347E 01
```

```
VALUES OF P(N) FOR N=0 TO  20, OTHERWISE P(N) .LT. 0.00001
   0.01319    0.05277    0.10554    0.14072    0.14072    0.11258
   0.09006    0.07205    0.05764    0.04611    0.03689    0.02951
   0.02361    0.01889    0.01511    0.01209    0.00967    0.00774
   0.00619    0.00495    0.00396
```

                    (M/M/***)-(GD/***/***)

```
LAMBDA= 0.50000E 02     LAMBDA EFF= 0.50000E 02
MU= 0.12000E 02         RHO= 0.41667E 01

WS= 0.83333E-01     WQ= 0.00000E-38
LS= 0.41667E 01     LQ= 0.00000E-38
```

```
VALUES OF P(N) FOR N=0 TO  15, OTHERWISE P(N) .LT. 0.00001
   0.01550    0.06460    0.13458    0.18692    0.19471    0.16226
   0.11268    0.06707    0.03493    0.01617    0.00674    0.00255
   0.00089    0.00028    0.00008    0.00002
```

                    (M/M/ 2)-(GD/ 5/ 5)

```
LAMBDA= 0.30000E 01     LAMBDA EFF= 0.70099E 01
MU= 0.40000E 01         RHO= 0.75000E 00

WS= 0.37995E 00     WQ= 0.12995E 00
LS= 0.26634E 01     LQ= 0.91092E 00
```

```
VALUES OF P(N) FOR N=0 TO   5, OTHERWISE P(N) .LT. 0.00001
   0.04305    0.16144    0.24215    0.27242    0.20432    0.07662
```

                    (M/M/ 1)-(GD/***/***)

```
LAMBDA= 0.30000E 01     LAMBDA EFF= 0.30000E 01
MU= 0.10000E 01         RHO= 0.30000E 01
```

INVALID DATA

Index

A